MECHANICAL OPERATIONS FOR CHEMICAL ENGINEERS

(Incorporating Computer-Aided Analysis)

OTHER RELATED BOOKS

Units Operation of Chemical Engineering Vol. I
By *P. Chattopadhyay*

CONTENTS :

Applied Hydraulics ; Compressible Flow ; Pumps, Compressors, Blowers and Fans ; Particulate Solids Flow and Hydro Mechanical Separations ; Classification ; Sedimentation ; Filtration ; Fluidization ; Molecular Diffusion in Fluids ; Mass- Transfer Coefficients ; Diffusion in Solids ; Interphase Mass Transfer ; Equipment for Gas-liquid Operations ; Heat transfer ; Flow Meters and Flow Measurement.

Units Operation of Chemical Engineering Vol. II
by *P. Chattopadhyay*

CONTENTS :

Mass Transfer Operations ; Simple Counter Current Processes ; Phase Equilibrium ; Vapour-Liquid Equilibrium Calculations ; Equipment for Gas-Liquid Operations ; Binary Distillation, Batch Distillation ; Steam Distillation ; Multicomponent Distillation ; Vacuum Distillation ; Revamping Trayed Columns with Packings ; Energy Conservation in Distillation ; Gamma Scanning ; Operational Problems in Distillation Columns.

Heat Transfer Through Problems
by P. Chattopadhyay

CONTENTS :

Fundamentals of Heat Transfer ; Steady-State Conduction ; Conduction from Extended Surfaces ; Steady-State Conduction — Multidimensional ; Unsteady-State Conduction ; Principles of Convection ; Free Convection ; Force Convection ; Forced Crossflow over Tubes ; Forced Flowing Tubes ; Boiling and Condensation Heat Transfer ; Radiation Heat Transfer ; Heat Exchangers.

MECHANICAL OPERATION FOR CHEMICAL ENGINEERS

[*Incorporating Computer-Aided Analysis*]

Dr. C.M. Narayanan
Department of Chemical Engineering
Regional Engineering College
Durgapur-713209

Dr. B.C. Bhattacharya
Department of Chemical Engineering
Indian Institute of Technology
Kharagpur-721302

KHANNA PUBLISHERS
Operational Office :
B-35/9, G.T. Karnal Road Industrial Area,
(Near Telephone Exchange), Delhi-110033
Phones : 011-27224179, 011-45033819 • *Mob.* 09811541460
email : contactus@khannapublishers.in

Published by :
Romesh Chander Khanna & Vineet Khanna
for **KHANNA PUBLISHERS**
2-B, Nath Market, Nai Sarak
Delhi- 110 006 (India)

Website : www.khannapublishers.in

Hologram & Description

To all readers of our books, to prevent yourself from being defrauded by piraters, please make sure that there is an Hologram on the cover of our books with the below specifications. If you find any book without Hologram and Description, please mail us at **contactus@khannapublishers.in**

Thanking you

ISBN No. 978-81-7409-036-3

First Edition : 1990
Third Edition :
Fourth Reprint : 2021

***Price :* ₹ 369.00**

PREFACE TO THE THIRD EDITION

We are glad to note that the earlier editions of this book were well-received by the members of Engineering Community. We are thankful to all those students, practising engineers and academicians who sent us critical comments regarding the future improvement of the book.

The revised edition is going to press with a few modifications. First of all, all the printing errors that inadvertently appeared in the earlier editions have been erased. Secondly, a new full-fledged chapter on Fluidisation has been included (Chapter – 8). This is as per recommendations from a large cross-section of students and teachers of various engineering disciplines. Further, an additional section on Continuous Countercurrent Decantation (C.C.D.) has been added to Chapter – 4.

To make the computer aided analysis more palpable, sample computer programs are given in most of the chapters, apart from computation flow graphs.

Our word of gratitude to Dr. K.J.R. Sharma (retired Professor of Chemical Engineering, Manipal Institute of Technology) and Prof. (Dr.) U.P. Ganguly (IIT, Kharagpur) for their valuable suggestions towards the new getup of the revised edition. We also extend our compliments to Mr. Vikas Narayan and Ms. Sandhya Narayan for their assistances during testing and verifying the computer programs and computation of flow charts.

We once again solicit suggestions and criticisms from our eminent readers which are the exclusive means of inspiration to us.

Dr. C.M. Narayanan
Dr. B.C. Bhattacharya

PREFACE TO THE THIRD EDITION

We are glad to note that the earlier editions of this book were well-received by the members of Engineering Community. We are thankful to all those students, practising engineers and academicians who sent us critical comments regarding the future improvement of the book.

The revised edition is going to press with a few modifications. First of all, all the printing errors that inadvertently appeared in the earlier editions have been erased. Secondly, a new full-fledged chapter on Fluidisation has been included (Chapter – 8). This is as per recommendations from a large cross-section of students and teachers of various engineering disciplines. Further, an additional section on Continuous Countercurrent Decantation (C.C.D.) has been added to Chapter – 4.

To make the computer aided analysis more palpable, sample computer programs are given in most of the chapters, apart from computation flow graphs.

Our word of gratitude to Dr. K.J.R. Sharma (retired Professor of Chemical Engineering, Manipal Institute of Technology) and Prof. (Dr.) U.P. Ganguly (IIT, Kharagpur) for their valuable suggestions towards the new getup of the revised edition. We also extend our compliments to Mr. Vikas Narayan and Ms. Sandhya Narayan for their assistances during testing and verifying the computer programs and computation of flow charts.

We once again solicit suggestions and criticisms from our eminent readers which are the exclusive means of inspiration to us.

Dr. C.M. Narayanan
Dr. B.C. Bhattacharya

industry.
and meta
deal in
date. Only
Unit Opera
as much a
to bear a
of this topi
maximum
simulations from
ment
industr

each pro
in Comp
have been

hope this
and pr
gineering
lated as
teachers
man
sisted
books
South A
ing Colle
for his
example
(Dept of
gapur)
on Mech
our con
through

welcome
of this

C.M. Na
B.C. B

PREFACE TO THE FIRST EDITION

Mechanical operations play a vital role in any Chemical process industry. They are also of primary importance in mineral processing and metallurigical industries. However, consolidated text books that deal in detail with all these operations are painfully scarce till this date. Only scattered information are available in some of the books on Unit Operations. The authors wish to fill this void through this book as much as possible. This book could, therefore, be the first of its kind to bear a title like this and also to give a fully comprehensive treatment of this topic under a separate and exclusive identity.

One of the special features of the book is that in each chapter, maximum emphasis has been given to fundamental analysis and simulation of each operation rather than lengthy description of equipment used. A large number of worked examples based on real- life industrial data are also included in each chapter.

Secondly, the book also incorporates computer-aided analysis of each process or operation. This is to keep in line with the present trend in Computer Aided Design and Simulation. Condensed CAD flow-sheets have been given in each chapter to elucidate the matter more vividly.

SI units have been followed throughout the text. We sincerely hope that this shall serve as a valuable text book for undergraduate and post-graduate students in chemical engineering, mineral engineering, metallurgical engineering, mechanical engineering and related areas. It is also expected to be an excellent reference book for teachers, practising engineers as well as research scientists.

We are thankful to our students and colleagues alike who assisted us in various capacities during the course of preparation of this book. The name of one of our students, Mr. Roshan Ali Ibabatali of South America (student of Dr. C.M. Narayanan at Regional Engineering College, Durgapur during 1984-1988) deserves particular mention for his assistance in workingout the numerical solutions to most of the examples treated in this book. We are also grateful to Prof. A.K. Sen (Dept. of Mechanical Engineering, Regional Engineering College, Durgapur) for his valuable help during the preparation of the last chapter on Mechanical Handling and Transport of Solids. Last, but not least, our compliments to Mrs. Valsala Narayanan for patiently passing through the typescripts and removing all obvious errors.

Suggestions are criticisms from our eminent readers are most welcome, which shall be highly useful to us for the future improvement of this book.

C.M. Narayanan
B.C. Bhattacharya

CONTENTS

1

Particle Technology

1.1. Particle Size and Shape

There is a reputed saying that a liquid is a hen-pecked husband whereas a solid particle is a male chauvinist pig. The hint behind this statement is obvious. A liquid does not have any definite shape, it takes the shape of its container; whereas every solid particle has a specific shape of its own. Thus, whenever we handle any system involving solid particles, which we encounter quite often in chemical process industries, for defining the system, first we have to specify the size and shape of the particles involved. The task however, is not an easy one.

If the particle conforms itself to any of the standard configurations we are familiar with such as spherical, cubical, cylindrical etc., then its size can be easily specified. For example, the size of a spherical particle is nothing but its diameter and that of a cubical particle the length of its side. However, many of the particles commonly encountered in industrial practices do not conform to any of these standard configurations. We can call them, in general, irregular particles. How to define the size of such an irregular particle is now the question before us.

During the early stages of development of particle technology, a number of authors proposed empirical definitions to particle size. For example Martin (1931) defined the size of an irregular particle as the length of the line bisecting the maximum cross-sectional area of the particle. Similarly, Feret (1929) defined particle size as the distance between the two most extreme points on the particle surface. The limitations of such definitions are obvious. For instance, if the distance between the farthest edges on the particle surface remains the same but the rest of its configuration changes, its Feret's diameter shall remain unaltered. Obviously, such a definition cannot describe the actual size or shape of an irregular particle.

It was in the later years, the latest system of defining particle size by comparison with a standard configuration (normally by comparing with a spherical particle) got developed. Thus, we utilise what is called the equivalent size or equivalent diameter of an irregular particle which can be broadly defined as *the size of a spherical particle having the same controlling characteristic as the particle under consideration.* Naturally, to apply this definition, we must first specify what this "controlling characteristic" is. This depends on the system and the process in which the particle is involved. For example, for catalyst particles, the surface area is the most controlling parameter. Therefore, for defining the size of a catalyst particle we can use the surface diameter (d_s) which will thus be defined as the diameter of a spherical particle having the same surface area as the particle. If S_p is the surface area of the particle, then

$$S_p = \pi d_s^2$$

or,

$$d_s = \sqrt{S_p/\pi} \qquad ...(1.1.1)$$

The gravitational free settling velocity of a particle in a liquid is very much controlled by the mass of the particle (or, for a given density, its volume). We can therefore define the particle size for such a case by the volumetric diameter (d_v) which is once again defined as the diameter of a spherical particle having the same volume as the particle under consideration. Thus, if V_p is the volume of the particle,

$$V_p = \pi d_v^3/6$$

or,

$$d_v = (6V_p/\pi)^{\frac{1}{3}} \qquad ...(1.1.2)$$

The dynamics of gas bubbles in a liquid or that of liquid drops in a liquid or gas depend not only on the bubble or drop volume but also on the interfacial tension at the gas-liquid or liquid-liquid interface. Thus, both the volume as well as the surface area of the bubble or drop are controlling parameters here. In such cases, the bubble size or drop size is defined using the volume-surface diameter or more commonly called the Sauter diameter (d_{vs}). This is accordingly defined as the diameter of a spherical particle having the same specific surface (surface area per unit volume) as the particle (bubble or drop) under consideration. Thus,

$$s_p = \frac{(\pi\, d_{vs}^2)}{(\pi\, d_{vs}^3/6)} = \left(\frac{6}{d_{vs}}\right)$$

or, $$d_{vs} = (6/s_p) \qquad \text{...(1.1.3)}$$

where s_p is the specific surface (surface area per unit volume) of the particle (bubble or drop).

Thus, once the controlling characteristic is specified, we can define the size of any irregular particle using the above methodology. Another popularly employed definition of particle size is the screen size or the screen average size, d_{avg}. This in fact is the aperture size of a standard screen through which the particle just passes or more correctly, the arithmetic average of the aperture sizes of two successive standard screens, one of which lets the particle pass through whereas the other retains it. We shall be discussing about screening and particle size analysis using screening in more detail in the subsequent sections.

Once we have defined the particle size, let us now discuss how the particle shape can be defined. Again, the exact shape of an irregular particle is difficult to specify. One of the methods of defining particle shape is by using the term *sphericity* (ψ_s). It is defined as the ratio of the surface area of a spherical particle having the same volume as the particle to the surface area of the particle. Since the diameter of a spherical particle having the same volume as the particle is d_v,

$$\psi_s = \frac{\pi\, d_v^2}{S_p} \qquad \text{...(1.1.4)}$$

It must be noted that since sphericity compares the surface area of the particle to that of the equivalent spherical particle, it defines only the particle shape and is independent of particle size. Sphericity of a spherical particle is obviously 1.0. The sphericity of a cubical particle of side a can be determined as follows :

From equation (1.1.2), the volumetric diameter of the cubical particle,

$$d_v = \left[\frac{6V_p}{\pi}\right]^{1/3} = \left(\frac{6a^3}{\pi}\right)^{1/3}$$

$$= (1.24)a \qquad \text{...(1.1.5)}$$

Now, from equation (1.1.4),

$$\psi_s = [\pi\,(1.24\,a)^2/6a^2] = 0.806 \qquad \text{...(1.1.6)}$$

Similarly, the value of sphericity for a cylindrical particle of length equal to its diameter will be 0.874. Typical values of sphericities for some common materials are given in Table (1.1). Every mineral has a given crystallographic structure, thus a given shape or configuration and therefore a specific sphericity.

The reciprocal of sphericity is commonly called the shape factor or more precisely, the *surface shape factor* (λ_s). Thus,

$$\lambda_s = (1/\psi_s) \qquad ...(1.1.7)$$

Table 1.1

Material	*Sphericity,* (ψ_s)
Sand (rounded)	0.83
Fused flue dust	0.89
Fused flue dust (aggregates)	0.55
Tungsten powder	0.89
Sand (angular)	0.73
Pulverised coal	0.73
Coal dust (upto 10 mm)	0.65
Flint sand (jagged flakes)	0.43
Mica flakes	0.28
Berl saddles	0.3 (average)
Raschig rings	0.3 (average)

Another popularly used parameter in this connection is the *specific surface ratio* (n). It is defined as the ratio of the specific surface (surface area per unit mass) of the particle to the specific surface of a spherical particle of the same diameter. Let the average size of the particle be d_{avg}. Then,

$$n = s_p/(6/\rho_s\, d_{avg}) \qquad ...(1.1.8)$$

where ρ_s is the density of the particle.

or

$$s_p = \frac{6n}{\rho_s\, d_{avg}} \qquad ...(1.1.9)$$

It will be interesting to find out how the specific surface ratio (n) and the sphericity (ψ_s) are inter-related. From equation (1.1.4),

Surface area of the particle,

$$S_p = \pi d_v^2/\psi_s \qquad ...(1.1.10)$$

Therefore, the specific surface (s_p) of the particle

$$= \frac{S_p}{(\pi d_v^3/6)\,\rho_s}$$

$$= (6\pi d_v^2)/\psi_s\,(\pi d_v^3)\,\rho_s$$

$$= \frac{6}{\rho_s \, d_v \, \psi_s} \qquad \text{...(1.1.11)}$$

Comparing equations (1.1.9) and (1.1.11), we get

$$\frac{(n)}{d_{avg}} = \frac{1}{\psi_s \, d_v}$$

or

$$n = \left(\frac{d_{avg}}{d_v}\right)\frac{1}{\psi_s} = \left(\frac{d_{avg}}{d_v}\right)\lambda_s \qquad \text{...(1.1.12)}$$

If the screen diameter of the particle is very nearly equal to its volumetric diameter, then,

$$(d_{avg}/d_v) \approx 1$$

and

$$n = \lambda_s \qquad \text{...(1.1.13)}$$

In the above case, n can be taken as a constant for a given material since it is now equal to its shape factor. However, this is true only for the specific case when $d_{avg} \approx d_v$. Otherwise, it must be noted that unlike sphericity, the specific surface ratio n is a function of the particle size (d_{avg}). Standard log-log plots of n versus d_{avg} for different materials are available in the literature[1,2]. One such set of plots is reproduced in Fig. (1.1).

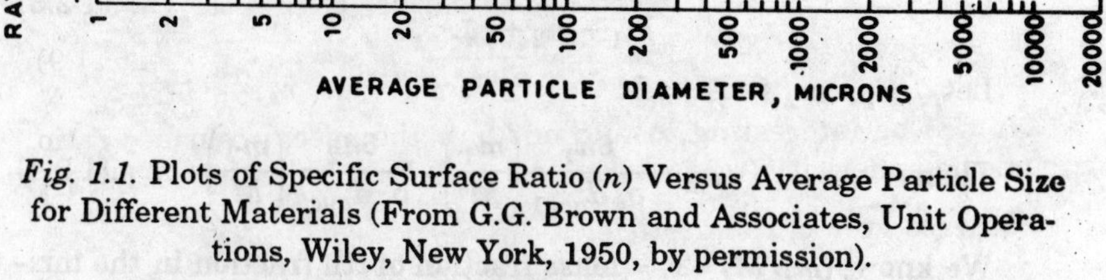

Fig. 1.1. Plots of Specific Surface Ratio (n) Versus Average Particle Size for Different Materials (From G.G. Brown and Associates, Unit Operations, Wiley, New York, 1950, by permission).

Another shape factor, designated as the *volume shape factor* (λ_v), is sometimes used for calculating the volume of an irregular particle. We know that the volume of a spherical particle is proportional to the cube of its diameter. If we assume the same is true for an irregular particle as well, then

$$V_p \, \alpha \, d_{avg}^3$$

or, $$V_p = \lambda_v \, d_{avg}^3 \qquad ...(1.1.14)$$

where λ_v is the constant of proportionality and is called the volume shape factor. Its value is ($\pi/6$) for spherical particles. In the strict sense, λ_v is not a constant (though designated as shape factor), but is a function of the particle size. However, for a number of cases, its variation with particle size is not very large and therefore an average value of λ_v could be used for a number of process calculations.

1.2. Mixture of Particles

In the earlier section, we have considered the case of a single particle only. However, in actual industrial practices, we normally come across mixtures of particles of different sizes. In such a case, the mixture can be separated into a number of fractions each fraction consisting of particles of a given size d_{avg_i}. Let m_i designate the total mass of the *i-th* fraction. Since each fraction contains particles of the same size, the specific surface of *i-th* fraction can be computed using equation (1.1.9). Thus,

$$s_i = \frac{6n_i}{\rho_s \, d_{avg_i}} \qquad ...(1.2.1)$$

and, surface area of *i*th fraction,

$$S_i = m_i \, s_i = (6 \, n_i \, m_i/\rho_s \, d_{avg_i}) \qquad ...(1.2.2)$$

Therefore, the specific surface of the mixture of particles will be,

$$s_m = \frac{\text{Total surface area of all fractions}}{\text{Total mass of mixture}}$$

$$= \frac{(6n_1 \, m_1/\rho_s \, d_{avg1}) + (6n_2 \, m_2/\rho_s \, d_{avg2}) + \ldots}{m_1 + m_2 + \ldots} \qquad ...(1.2.3)$$

Let, $m_1 + m_2 + \ldots = M$

Then, $$s_m = \frac{6n_1}{\rho_s \, d_{avg1}}\left(\frac{m_1}{M}\right) + \frac{6n_2}{\rho_s \, d_{avg2}}\left(\frac{m_2}{M}\right) + \ldots \qquad ...(1.2.4)$$

We know, $(m_i/M) = x_i$ = mass fraction of *i*th fraction in the mixture.

Thus, $(m_1/M) = x_1$, $(m_2/M) = x_2$ and so on. Equation (1.1.18) therefore becomes,

$$s_m = \frac{6n_1 \, x_1}{\rho_s \, d_{avg1}} + \frac{6n_2 \, x_2}{\rho_s \, d_{avg2}} + \ldots$$

$$= \frac{6}{\rho_s}\left[\frac{n_1 x_1}{d_{avg1}} + \frac{n_2 x_2}{d_{avg2}} + \ldots\right]$$

$$= (6/\rho_s)\sum_i \frac{n_i x_i}{d_{avg_i}} \qquad \ldots(1.2.5)$$

The total number of particles in the mixture can also be computed in a similar way. Thus, the number of particles in the *i*th fraction will be,

$$N_i = \frac{\text{Total mass of } i\text{th fraction}}{\text{Mass of each particle in the fraction}}$$

$$= \frac{m_i}{\rho_s \text{ (volume of each particle in the fraction)}}$$

Volume of each particle in the fraction can be computed using equation (1.1.14). Thus,

$$N_i = \frac{m_i}{\rho_s\,[\lambda_{vi}\, d_{avg_i}^3]} \qquad \ldots(1.2.6)$$

The total number of particles per unit mass of the mixture will be therefore,

$$\left(\frac{N}{M}\right) = \overline{N} = \frac{\dfrac{m_1}{\rho_s \lambda_{v1} d_{avg1}^3} + \dfrac{m_2}{\rho_s \lambda_v 2\, d_{avg2}^3} + \ldots}{M}$$

$$= \frac{x_1}{\rho_s \lambda_{v1} d_{avg1}^3} + \frac{x_2}{\rho_s \lambda_{v2} d_{avg2}^3} + \ldots$$

$$= \frac{1}{\rho_s}\sum_i \frac{x_i}{\lambda_{vi}\, d_{avg_i}^3} \qquad \ldots(1.2.7)$$

If we assume that the variation of λ_v within the size range under consideration is small and a constant average value of λ_v could be therefore assumed, then

$$\left(\frac{N}{M}\right) = \overline{N} = \frac{1}{\lambda_s\, \rho_s}\sum_i \frac{x_i}{d_{avg_i}^3} \qquad \ldots(1.2.8)$$

The specific surface and the number of particles per unit mass of a mixture of particles can be thus computed, once the size distribution is known.

1.3. Statistical Mean Diameters

While handling mixtures of particles, if it is desired to express the average size of the entire mixture, then we can do it using any of the statistical averages. However, if particles with a wide range of sizes are present in the mixture, a statistical mean of all the sizes may not give any realistic picture. Also, the statistical mean can be defined in a very large number of ways such as the length mean, surface mean, volume mean, square root mean, cube root mean, harmonic mean etc. It is therefore practically impossible to propose in advance which type of mean shall be best suitable for a given industrial application. The matter can be decided only from experience. Also, it is seen on many occasions that if the average size of a mixture is computed using all the above definitions, each yields an entirely different value of average size, clearly indicating that their applicabilities cannot be mutually compared with each other. Some of the popular methods of defining statistical average are given below.

(*a*) Arithmetic or number mean, D_A or $D_N = \dfrac{\Sigma N_i d_i}{\Sigma N_i}$

where N_i = number of particles of size d_i. If d_i is defined by the screen size d_{avg_i}, then N_i in the above equation can be re-expressed using equation (1.2.6). Thus,

$$D_A \text{ or } D_N = \frac{\dfrac{M}{\rho_s} \sum_i \left(\dfrac{x_i}{\lambda_{vi}\, d_{avg_i}^3} \right) d_{avg_i}}{\dfrac{M}{\rho_s} \sum_i \dfrac{x_i}{\lambda_{vi}\, d_{avg_i}^3}}$$

$$= \frac{\sum_i [x_i/\lambda_{vi}\, d_{avg_i}^2]}{\sum_i [x_i/\lambda_{vi}\, d_{avg_i}^3]} \qquad \text{...(1.3.1)}$$

(*b*) Length mean, $D_L = \dfrac{\Sigma N_i d_i^2}{\Sigma N_i d_i}$ ...(1.3.2)

(*c*) Surface mean, $D_s = \dfrac{\Sigma N_i d_i^3}{\Sigma N_i d_i^2}$ ...(1.3.3)

(*d*) Volume mean, $D_v = \dfrac{\Sigma N_i d_i^4}{\Sigma N_i d_i^3}$ ...(1.3.4) (*e*) Square root mean, $D_{SR} = \left[\frac{\Sigma N_i \, d_i^2}{\Sigma N_i} \right]^{1/2}$ ...(1.3.5)

This is designated as surface mean by Brown.[4]

(*f*) Cube root mean, $D_{CR} = \left[\frac{\Sigma N_i \, d_i^3}{\Sigma N_i} \right]^{1/3}$ ...(1.3.6)

This is designated as volume mean by Brown.[4]

(*g*) Harmonic mean, $D_H = \frac{\Sigma N_i}{\Sigma (N_i / d_i)}$ ...(1.3.7)

Let us now consider an illustrative example in which we shall compute the statistical average diameter of a mixture of particles using all of the above methods. Consider the following size distribution :

Number of particles, N_i	*Particle size, d_i (microns)*
155,000	2.0
25,600	5.0
6,200	10.0
1,750	20.0
660	30.0
156	40.0
100	50.0
87	60.0

The computed values of statistical average diameters are given below :

D_A or D_N = 3.0 microns (1 micron = 10^{-3} mm)

D_L = 7.0 microns

D_S = 21.0 microns

D_V = 36.4 microns

D_{SR} = 4.6 microns

D_{CR} = 7.6 microns

D_H = 2.3 microns

It can be easily noticed that the value of statistical average diameter computed using each method is significantly different from that computed by other methods.

1.4. Determination of Particle Size

The size of a particle or the size distribution of a mixture of particles can be determined using a number of methods such as screening (best applicable for particles of size above 40 microns), gravity sedimentation (for size 1—100 microns), centrifugal sedimentation (for sizes 0.005 to 3 microns) and elutriation under gravity (for sizes 5—100 microns) and under centrifugal field (for sizes 1—60 microns). More sophisticated techniques such as ultra microscopy (for sizes 0.005 to 0.2 microns), electron microscopy (for sizes 0.0005 to 5.0 microns), light scattering (for sizes 0.1 to 10 microns) and X-ray scattering (for sizes 0.005 to 0.05 microns) are used when high precision is desired in the particle size determination. In this section, we shall confine our discussion to screening which is one of the cheapest and easiest methods of particle size analysis. Sedimentation and Elutriation have been discussed in subsequent chapters.

The importance of particle size analysis in industrial practices need not have to be over-emphasized. Particles must be separated according to their size before using them for any industrial operation since the process efficiency very much depends on the particle size employed. As for example, the effectiveness of catalyst particles is dependent on their surface area which in turn depends on their size. The hiding power of a paint pigment is controlled by the projected area of the pigment particles which once again is a function of their size. The setting rate of Portland cement and the final strength of concrete depend substantially on the uniform size of cement dust and the size of sand and gravel used to prepare the concrete mix. In the combustion of solid fuels like coal, uniformity of the fuel bed is a very crucial parameter. Even in practices like carbonisation and gasification, it is absolutely necessary that the coal bed is composed of particles of uniform size to ascertain satisfactory yields and quality of products. As stated earlier, screening offers to be one of the easiest and most rapid method of particle size analysis and separation.

1.4.1. Screening

What is a screen ?

A screen can be called an open container usually cylindrical with uniformly spaced openings at the base. It is normally made of wire mesh cloth, the wire diameter and the interspacing between wires being accurately specified. The openings are commonly square though rectangular openings are not unusual. The size of the square opening (the length of clear space between individual wires) is called the *aper-*

Table 1.2. Indian Standard Test Sieves

Sieve Designation Number	Sieve Opening or Width of Aperture		Permissible Variation in Width of Aperture				Wire Diameter			Equivalent Mesh Number of Other Standard Screens		
			Average opening		Maximum opening							
	mm	inch	Microns	Percent	Microns	Percent	mm	inch	SWG	ASTM	BSS	Tyler
(1)	(2)	(3)	(4)	(5)	(6)	(7)	(8)	(9)	(10)	(11)	(12)	(13)
570	5.660	0.2230	± 170	± 3.0	+ 566	+ 10	2.184	0.086	13.5	3.5	—	3.5
480	4.760	0.1870	± 143	± 3.0	+ 476	+ 10	2.032	0.080	14	4	3/16"	4
400	4.000	0.1570	± 120	± 3.0	+ 400	+ 10	1.829	0.072	15	5	—	5
340	3.353	0.1320	± 108	± 3.2	+ 370	+ 11	1.727	0.068	15.5	6	5	6
320	3.180	0.1252	± 102	± 3.2	+ 350	+ 11	1.829	0.072	15	—	1/8"	—
280	2.818	0.1109	± 97	± 3.4	+ 309	+ 11	1.422	0.056	17	7	6	7
240	2.399	0.0945	± 91	± 3.8	+ 263	+ 11	1.219	0.048	18	8	7	8
200	2.032	0.0800	± 93	± 4.6	+ 244	+ 12	1.118	0.044	18.5	10	8	9
170	1.676	0.0659	± 55	± 3.3	+ 201	+ 12	0.864	0.034	20.5	12	10	—
160	1.600	0.0630	± 54	± 3.4	+ 192	+ 12	0.965	0.038	19.5	—	1/16"	10
140	1.405	0.0553	± 48	± 3.4	+ 168	+ 12	0.711	0.028	22	14	12	12
120	1.201	0.0473	± 46	± 3.8	+ 156	+ 13	0.610	0.024	23	16	14	14
100	1.000	0.0394	± 50	± 5.0	+ 150	+ 15	0.584	0.023	23.5	18	16	16
85	0.842	0.0332	± 44	± 5.2	+ 126	+ 15	0.559	0.022	24	20	18	20
80	0.790	0.0311	± 38	± 4.8	+ 111	+ 14	0.533	0.021	24.5	—	1/32"	—
70	0.708	0.0279	± 38	± 5.4	+ 106	+ 15	0.457	0.018	26	25	22	24

Sieve Designation Number	Sieve Opening or Width of Aperture		Permissible Variation in Width of Aperture				Wire Diameter			Equivalent Mesh Number of Other Standard Screens		
			Average opening		Maximum opening							
	mm	inch	Microns	Percent	Microns	Percent	mm	inch	SWG	ASTM	BSS	Tyler
(1)	(2)	(3)	(4)	(5)	(6)	(7)	(8)	(9)	(10)	(11)	(12)	(13)
60	0.592	0.0233	± 33	± 5.6	+ 95	+ 16	0.417	0.0164	27	30	25	28
50	0.500	0.0197	± 25	± 5.0	+ 85	+ 17	0.345	0.0136	29	35	30	32
40	0.420	0.0165	± 21	± 5.0	+ 106	+ 25	0.284	0.0112	31.5	40	36	35
35	0.351	0.0138	± 19	± 5.4	+ 88	+ 25	0.224	0.0088	34.5	45	44	42
30	0.296	0.0117	± 16	± 5.4	+ 74	+ 25	0.193	0.0076	36	50	52	48
25	0.251	0.0099	± 13	± 5.2	+ 63	+ 25	0.173	0.0068	37	60	60	60
20	0.211	0.0083	± 12	± 5.5	+ 53	+ 25	0.142	0.0056	38.5	70	72	65
18	0.177	0.0070	± 11	± 6.2	+ 71	+ 40	0.122	0.0048	40	80	85	80
15	0.151	0.0060	± 11	± 7.3	+ 61	+ 40	0.102	0.0040	42	100	100	100
12	0.124	0.0049	± 8	± 6.5	+ 50	+ 40	0.086	0.0034	43.5	120	120	115
10	0.104	0.0041	± 7	± 7.1	+ 43	+ 41	0.066	0.0026	45.5	140	150	150
9	0.089	0.0035	± 7	± 7.4	+ 44	+ 49	0.061	0.0024	46	170	170	170
8	0.075	0.0030	± 7	± 9.3	+ 46	+ 60	0.051	0.0020	47	200	200	200
6	0.064	0.0025	± 8	± 12.0	+ 58	+ 90	0.041	0.0016	48	230	240	230
5	0.053	0.0021	± 5	± 9.0	+ 48	+ 90	0.030	0.0012	49	270	300	270
4	0.044	0.0017	± 3	± 7.0	+ 40	+ 90	0.030	0.0012	49	325	—	325

ture size of the screen. Screens are usually designated by their mesh number. The mesh number indicates the number of apertures per linear length. For example, a screen having 10 square openings per cm may be called a 10 mesh screen and in that case, the aperture size of the screen will be 0.1 cm minus the wire diameter. Clearly, higher the mesh number, smaller will be the aperture size of the screen. For instance, a 200 mesh screen will have a very small aperture width, whereas a 20 mesh screen will have a large aperture size. This is the practice followed in British standard screens (BSS), American standard screens (ASTM and Tyler standard screens), German standard screens (DIN 1171) etc.

The Indian standard screens (ISS) however follow a different type of designation. For an IS screen, the mesh number is equal to its aperture size expressed to the nearest deca-micron (0.01 mm). Thus, an IS screen of mesh number 50 will have an aperture width of approximately 500 microns. Such a method of designation has the simplicity that the aperture width is readily indicated from the mesh number. The specification of Indian standard test screens and the equivalent specifications of other standard screens (such as ASTM, BS and Tyler) are given in Table (1.2).

Standard test screens are usually made of phosphor bronze wires. Brass or mild steel wires are also sometimes used. It is always preferable to maintain a *standard screen interval* between successive test screens. The screen interval is the factor by which the aperture size of a test screen is to be divided to get the aperture size of the next successive test screen. An internationally accepted standard screen interval is $(2)^{1/4}$, that is 1.189.

In a standard sieve shaker, test screens are stacked one above the other in the ascending order of their aperture size. That is, the top-most screen will have the largest aperture size and the bottom-most screen the smallest. A weighed amount of the feed material is fed to the top-most screen and the whole assembly is shaken continuously either manually or more preferably mechanically. A bottom pan is kept below the bottom-most screen to collect the fines and the top-most screen is provided with a cover to prevent loss of fines. After a period of time when no more fines are being collected in the bottom pan, the vibration is stopped and the screens are desembled. The material retained on each screen (including the material in the bottom pan) is weighed. The data collected is as given below :

Material retained on	*Mass (gm)*
ISS No. 480	0.0
400	m_1
340	m_2
320	m_3
280	m_4
240	m_5
200	m_6
—	—
—	—
—	—
—	—
8	m_{27}
Bottom pan	m_b

The material that passes through the screen is called the minus (–) material or the undersize and the material that is retained on the screen is called the plus (+) material or the oversize. It can be seen that m_1 is the mass of the material that has passed through the 480 mesh screen but retained by the 400 mesh screen. It is therefore designated as the (– 480 + 400) fraction. The average size of the particles in this fraction will be therefore the arithmetic average of the aperture sizes of these two screens. Thus, from table (1.2), the d_{avg} of this fraction will be $\frac{4.76 + 4.00}{2} = 4.38$ mm.

If M is the total mass of the feed material, then the mass fraction of material having average size 4.38 mm will be (m_1/M), say x_1. Similarly, m_2 is the mass of (– 400 + 340) fraction and its average size (d_{avg2}) will be 3.6765 mm and its mass fraction in the mixture is $x_2 = (m_2/M)$.

Thus, the above data can be reported in a better way as follows :

Table 1.3

ISS mesh	*Average size, mm*	*Mass fraction*
+ 480	> 4.760	0.0
– 480 + 400	d_{avg1} (= 4.380)	x_1
– 400 + 340	d_{avg2} (= 3.6765)	x_2

ISS mesh	*Average size, mm*	*Mass fraction*
– 340 + 320	d_{avg3}	x_3
– 320 + 280	d_{avg4}	x_4
– 280 + 240	d_{avg5}	x_5
– 240 + 200	d_{avg6}	x_6
—	—	—
—	—	—
—	—	—
– 9 + 8	d_{avg27}	x_{27}
– 8	< 0.075	x_b

The above method of representing size distribution of a mixture is called the differential size analysis. The data may also be represented graphically by plotting x versus d_{avg} on rectangular co-ordinates or on a semi-log graph paper with d_{avg} on the log scale. Representation on log-log graph paper is most recommended since this avoids crowding of points particularly in the small size range.

It may be noted that the size distribution given above is in fact incomplete since the size distribution of the material collected in the bottom pan is not known. All that we know is that all particles in this fraction will have a size less than the aperture size of the 8 mesh screen, that is, less than 0.075 mm. For estimating the size distribution of a fraction that contains such fine particles only, we can make use of the Gaudin-Schumann size distribution law. This distribution is precisely applicable in the case of well-ground products from a fine grinding unit. According to this law, for particles of very fine sizes, a log-log plot of mass fraction x versus average size d_{avg} shall give a straight line. Mathematically,

$$ln\,(x) = m\; ln\,(d_{avg}) + ln\,B \qquad ...(1.4.1)$$

where m and B are constants.

Thus, once the mass fraction x has been plotted against d_{avg} on a log-log graph paper, the graph can be extrapolated back to the y-axis and the slope of the extrapolated portion will be equal to m and its y-intercept will give the value of B. Once the constants m and B are evaluated, the size distribution of -8 fraction can be determined using equation (1.4.1).

It must be noted that in equation (1.4.1), d_{avg} is the screen size of the particles. It is therefore essential that while applying the above equation, the values of d_{avg} must conform to the standard screen interval employed for the test screens. Also, Gaudin-Schumann distribution is valid for products from a fine grinder, but it's applicability for a classified product cannot be guaranteed. We shall now illustrate a numerical example.

Example 1.1. *Estimate the specific surface and sauter diameter of a sample of galena (specific gravity = 7.43) having the screen analysis below :*

Mesh	*Mass fraction*
– 570 + 480	0.01
– 480 + 340	0.04
– 340 + 240	0.081
– 240 + 160	0.115
– 160 + 120	0.160
– 120 + 85	0.148
– 85 + 60	0.132
– 60 + 40	0.081
– 40 + 30	0.062
– 30 + 20	0.041
– 20 + 15	0.036
– 15 + 10	0.022
– 10 + 8	0.019
– 8	0.053

Assume Gaudin-Schumann distribution is valid for sizes below 8 mesh.

Solution. The Specific surface of the sample can be computed from equation (1.2.5)

$$s_m = \frac{6}{\rho_s} \sum_i \frac{n_i \, x_i}{d_{avg_i}} \quad \text{where } \rho_s = 7.43 \text{ gm/cc.}$$

If D_{vs} is the volume surface diameter (sauter diameter) of the sample, then by definition,

$$s_m = 6/(\rho \, D_{vs})$$

or

$$D_{vs} = 1/\sum_i \frac{n_i \, x_i}{d_{avg_i}}$$

The values of specific surface ratio n can be obtained from the standard plot given in Fig. (1.1). The average size d_{avg} of each fraction is computed from the aperture sizes of screens given in Table (1.2). The results are given below :

Mesh	*Average size, d_{avg}* (cm)	*Specific surface ratio, n*	*Mass fraction, x*
– 570 + 480	$\frac{0.566 + 0.476}{2} = 0.521$	4.0	0.01
– 480 + 340	0.4056	3.8	0.04
– 340 + 240	0.2876	3.55	0.081
– 240 + 160	0.19995	3.2	0.115
– 160 + 120	0.14005	2.8	0.160

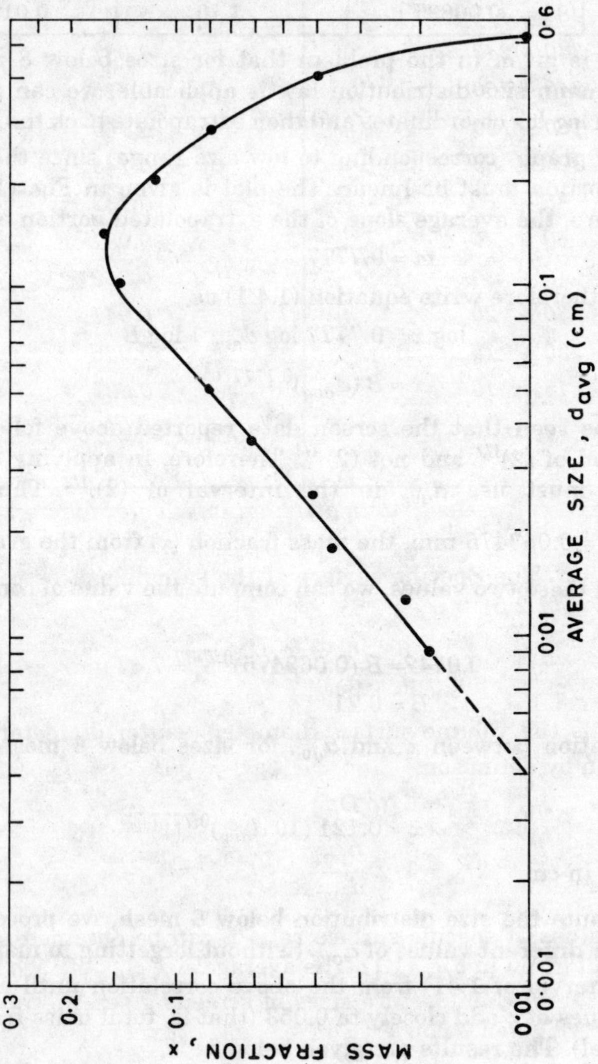

Fig. 1.1.1. Log-Log Plot of Mass Fraction Versus Average Particle Size.

Mesh	*Average size, d_{avg} (cm)*	*Specific surface ratio, n*	*Mass fraction, x*
– 120 + 85	0.10215	2.7	0.148
– 85 + 60	0.0717	2.5	0.132
– 60 + 40	0.0506	2.3	0.081
– 40 + 30	0.0358	2.1	0.062
– 30 + 20	0.02535	2.0	0.041
– 20 + 15	0.0181	1.85	0.036
– 15 + 10	0.01275	1.75	0.022
– 10 + 8	0.00895	1.70	0.019

Since it is given in the problem that for sizes below 8 mesh, Gaudin-Schumann size distribution law is applicable, we can plot x versus d_{avg} on log-log co-ordinates and then extrapolate back the lower portion of the graph (corresponding to low size range) since the plot within this portion must be linear. The plot is given in Fig. (1.1.1). From the figure, the average slope of the extrapolated portion is,

$$m = 0.7777$$

We can therefore write equation (1.4.1) as,

$$\log x = 0.7777 \log d_{avg} + \log B$$

or

$$x = B\,(d_{avg})^{0.7777}$$

It can be seen that the screen data reported above follows a screen interval of $(2)^{1/2}$ and not (2).$^{1/4}$ Therefore, in applying above relation, we must use d_{avg} in the interval of (2).$^{1/2}$ Thus, at $d_{avg} = \dfrac{0.0895}{1.41} = 0.063475$ mm, the mass fraction (x) from the graph is 0.0142. Using these two values, we can compute the value of constant B as,

$$0.0142 = B\,(0.063475)^{0.7777}$$

or

$$B = 0.21$$

The relation between x and d_{avg} for sizes below 8 mesh thus becomes,

$$x = 0.121\,(10\,d_{avg})^{0.7777}$$

where d_{avg} is in cm.

To compute the size distribution below 8 mesh, we proceed to calculate x for different values of d_{avg} (without forgetting to maintain the screen interval of 1.41) from the above correlation until all the computed values of x add closely to 0.053 (that is, total mass fraction ...aterial). The results are given below :

d_{avg}, cm	x	*Specific Surface ratio (n)*
0.0063475	0.0142	1.65
0.0045	0.0108	1.60
0.00319275	0.0083	1.5
0.002264	0.00636	1.5
0.001606	0.00486	1.45
0.0011389	0.003725	1.40
0.000810	0.002852	1.35
0.000573	0.002183	1.30
	Total = 0.05328	

Having thus made the size distribution complete, let us now compute (mx/d_{avg}) for all the fractions :

Mass Fraction (x)	(nx/d_{avg})
0.01	0.07677
0.04	0.37475
0.081	0.9998
0.115	1.84046
0.160	3.1988
0.148	3.9120
0.132	4.6025
0.081	3.6818
0.062	3.6368
0.041	3.2347
0.036	3.6795
0.022	3.0196
0.019	3.6089
0.0142	3.6912
0.0108	3.84
0.0083	3.8995
0.00636	4.2138
0.00486	4.3879
0.003725	4.579
0.002852	4.75[illegible]
0.002183	4.9527
	$\Sigma \dfrac{n_i x_i}{d_{avg_i}} = 70.18378 \text{ cm}^{-1}$

Specific surface of sample,

$$s_m = \frac{6}{7.43}[70.18378] = 56.676 \text{ cm}^2/\text{gm} = 5.667 \text{ m}^2/\text{kg}$$

Sauter diameter,

$$D_{vs} = 1/\Sigma \frac{n_i\, x_i}{d_{avg_i}} = 1/[70.18378] = 0.14248 \text{ mm.}$$

Example 1.2. *In the above example, estimate the total number of particles per kg of the sample, if the volume shape factor (λ_v) of the material is 2.0 and may be assumed to be essentially constant within the size range under consideration.*

Solution. The number of particles per unit mass of the sample can be computed from equation (1.2.8) :

$$(N/M) = \frac{1}{\lambda_v\, \rho_s} \sum_i \frac{x_i}{d^3_{avg_i}}$$

where $\lambda_v = 2.0$ and $\rho_s = 7.43$ gm/cc. Let us therefore compute the value of (x/d^3_{avg}) for all the fractions.

x	d_{avg}, cm	$[x/d^3_{avg}]$, cm^{-3}
0.01	0.521	0.0707
0.04	0.4056	0.5995
0.081	0.2876	3.405
0.115	0.19995	14,386
0.16	0.14005	58.247
0.148	0.10215	138.850
0.132	0.0717	358.110
0.081	0.0506	625.221
0.062	0.0358	1351.27
0.041	0.02535	2516.807
0.036	0.0181	6071.09
0.022	0.01275	10,614.318
0.019	0.00895	26,502.352
0.0142	0.0063475	55,523.928
0.0108	0.0045	118,518.50
0.0083	0.00319275	255,037.29
0.00636	0.002264	548,059.50

x	d_{avg} cm	$[x/d_{avg}^3]$, cm^{-3}
0.00486	0.001606	1,173,274.50
0.003725	0.0011389	2,521,560.20
0.002852	0.00081	5,366,540.30
0.002183	0.000573	11,603,524.0
		$\Sigma \dfrac{x_i}{d_{avg_i}^3} = 21,690,292.0$

Therefore,

$$(N/M) = \frac{1}{(2.0)\,(7.43)} [21,690,292.0] = 14,59,643 \text{ per gm.}$$

Number of particles per kg = **1459.643 × 10⁶**

Another popular method of reporting screen data is on the cumulative basis. In *cumulative analysis*, our interest will be to estimate the total mass of that fraction in which all particles have sizes below (or sometimes above) a particular value.

For example, cumulative mass fraction X_i corresponds to mass fraction of the material having size less than d_i, or all particles in that fraction pass through a screen of aperture d_i mm. Consider the differential analysis reported in Table (1.3).

Since there is no + 480 material, it is evident that all material fed have passed through the 480 mesh screen, or all material in the feed have sizes below the aperture size of 480 mesh screen. In other words, the cumulative mass fraction for 480 mesh is 1.0. The mass fraction of material retained by 400 mesh screen is x_1 and therefore cumulative mass fraction for 400 mesh will be $(1 - x_1)$. Similarly we can compute cumulative mass fraction corresponding to each screen and the data can be tabulated as shown in Table (1.4).

Let $X_1 = 0.8$, $X_2 = 0.6$ and $X_3 = 0.4$. This means 80% of particles in the mixture have size less than 4 mm, 60% have size less than 3.353 mm and 40% less than 3.18 mm. The data of cumulative analysis can also be represented graphically by plotting X versus the aperture size (d_p) either on rectangular co-ordinates or on a semi-log graph paper (with aperture size on the log scale). One of the applications of cumulative size analysis we shall be discussing in the next section. Incidentally, if the cumulative analysis is available, then equation (1.2.8) that determines the number of particles in unit mass of a mixture can be rewritten as,

Table 1.4

Screen Mesh	*Aperture Size, mm*	*Cumulative Mass Fraction, X*
480	4.760	1.00
400	4.000	$(1-x_1)=X_1$
340	3.353	$(1-x_1-x_2)=X_2$
320	3.180	$(1-x_1-x_2-x_3)=X_3$
280	2.818	$(1-x_1-x_2-x_3-x_4)=X_4$
240	2.399	$(1-x_1-x_2-x_3-x_4-x_5)=X_5$
200	2.032	$(1-x_1-x_2-x_3-x_4-x_5-x_6)=X_6$
—	—	—
—	—	—
—	—	—
8	0.075	$x_b=X_b$

$$(N/M)=\frac{1}{\lambda_v\,\rho_s}\int_0^1\frac{dX}{d_p^3} \quad ...(1.4.2)$$

where d_p is the aperture size. The integral on the right hand side of the above equation can be evaluated either numerically or graphically.

1.4.2. Screening errors and Screen Effectiveness

Screening is undoubtedly one of the easiest and most rapid methods of particle size analysis and separation. However, it cannot be called a very accurate method. It must be remembered that the probability of a particle passing through a screen depends very much also on the direction or configuration in which the particle approaches the screen. This is because for an irregular particle, its surface area exposed to the screen opening is different in different directions. As a result, it is very possible that when fed in one particular direction or configuration, the particle may pass through the screen but when fed in another direction the same particle may be retained by the screen. This therefore induces uncertainties in size analysis, since in screening the particle size is determined based on whether the particle passes through the screen or is retained by it. It is therefore absolutely necessary that while performing standard screen test on a mixture of particles, the test is repeated three to four times until consistent results are obtained. Also, the screens must be subjected to a type of vibratory, oscillatory, gyratory or rotary motion so that each particle gets chances of approaching the screen in almost all directions or configurations possible.

The presence of the so called "near mesh particles" always causes hindrances in screening operation. Near mesh particles to a screen are those particles having size very close to the aperture size of the screen. As a result, it is very possible that in one particular configuration, one of such particles passes only partly through the screen. It thus sits on the screen thereby causing clogging or blinding of the screen. Other disturbing factors are cohesion of particles to each other due to electrostatic forces or if the particles are moist, they tend to stick to the surface of the screen and also to each other causing difficulties in screening. If the particles are dry (very low moisture content) or if they are fed in a stream of water (wet screening), then the screening process will be faster and more efficient.

The effectiveness of a classifying screen is a parameter that has been defined in different ways by different authors[2,3,4]. In general, the efficiency of an industrial screen depends on two aspects : firstly, it must separate almost all particles of the desired size from the feed (recovery of desired material) and secondly, the classified product must contain very little number of particles having sizes other than the desired size (rejection of undesired material). Therefore, one of the most general methods of defining classifying screen effectiveness (E_c) is,

$$E_c = \text{(Recovery) (Rejection)} \qquad \text{...(1.4.3)}$$

Let y_F be the mass fraction of the desired material (particles of desired size) in the feed, y_P that in the product and y_R that in the reject stream. It must be kept in mind that either the undersize (material that has passed through the screen) or the oversize (material that has been retained by the screen) can be our final product. If excess fines are not permissible in the product, then the oversize is collected as the product and if it is desired that the product must contain particles of below a particular size only, then the undersize stream shall constitute the final product. Now we can define rejection and recovery as,

$$\text{Recovery} = \frac{\text{Desired material in the product}}{\text{desired material in the feed.}}$$

$$= \frac{Py_P}{Fy_F} \qquad \text{...(1.4.4)}$$

where F is the feed rate (kg/s) and P is the product rate.

$$\text{Recovery} = \frac{\text{Undesired material in the reject}}{\text{Undesired material in the feed}}$$

$$= \frac{R(1-y_R)}{F(1-y_F)} = \frac{F(1-y_F) - P(1-y_P)}{F(1-y_F)}$$

$$= 1 - \frac{P\,(1 - y_P)}{F\,(1 - y_F)} \qquad ...(1.4.5)$$

Thus,
$$E_c = \frac{P y_P}{F y_F}\left[1 - \left(\frac{P}{F}\right)\frac{(1 - y_P)}{(1 - y_F)}\right] \qquad ...(1.4.6)$$

The (P/F) ratio in the above equation can be expressed in terms of mass fractions by making a material balance around the screen :

$$F = P + R \qquad ...(1.4.7)$$

Also, desired material in the feed

= (desired material in the product) + (desired material in reject)

That is,
$$F y_F = P y_P + R y_R \qquad ...(1.4.8)$$

Combining above two equations, we get

$$F y_F = P y_P + (F - P)\, y_R$$

or,
$$F\,(y_F - y_R) = P\,(y_P - y_R)$$

$$(P/F) = (y_F - y_R)/(y_P - y_R) \qquad ...(1.4.9)$$

Substituting (1.4.9) in equation (1.4.6), we get

$$E_c = \frac{(y_F - y_R)\, y_P}{(y_P - y_R)\, y_F}\left[1 - \frac{(y_F - y_R)\,(1 - y_p)}{(y_p - y_R)\,(1 - y_F)}\right] \qquad ...(1.4.10)$$

Let us consider a few numerical examples :

Example 1.3. *Anthracite coal from a pulverization unit has been found to contain an excess of fine material (75% by weight). In order to remove these fines, it is screened using a 1.5 mm screen. Estimate the effectiveness of the screen from the following data :*

	Mass fraction	
Particle size, mm	*Oversize from Screen*	*Undersize from Screen*
– 3.33 + 2.36	*0.143*	*0.00*
– 2.36 + 1.65	*0.211*	*0.098*
– 1.65 + 1.17	*0.230*	*0.234*
– 1.17 + 0.83	*0.186*	*0.277*
– 0.83 + 0.59	*0.196*	*0.149*
– 0.59 + 0.42	*0.034*	*0.101*
– 0.42 + 0.29	*0.00*	*0.141*

Solution. Since the objective of screening is to remove the fine material, undersize from screen which will contain most of the fine material is the reject and the oversize material from the screen is the product. The aperture size of classifying screen is 1.5 mm. It is obviously not a standard screen, but is an industrial screen constructed specifically for the purpose. Our desired material is therefore the + 1.5 material. Let X_P' and X_R' be cumulative mass fraction corresponding to the particle size of 1.5 mm in case of product (oversize from screen) and reject (undersize from screen) respectively. Therefore, by definition, X_P' is the total mass fraction of material having size less than 1.5 mm in the product. The mass fraction of + 1.5 material (the desired material) in the product will be then $(1 - X_P')$. Thus, $y_P = [1 - X_P']$.

Similarly, $y_R = [1 - X_R']$

Since the feed contains 75% fine material,

$$y_F = 0.25$$

To find the values X_P' and X_R', let us construct a cumulative mass fraction table from the data given :

Particle size, mm	X_P	X_R
3.33	1.0	1.0
2.36	0.857	1.0
1.65	0.646	0.902
1.17	0.416	0.668
0.83	0.230	0.391
0.59	0.034	0.242
0.42	0.0	0.141

We now plot both X_P and X_R against particle size on a semi-log graph paper. The plot is given in Fig. (1.3.1). From the Fig., the cumulative mass fractions corresponding to a particle size of 1.5 mm are obtained as,

$$X'_P = 0.57$$

$$X'_R = 0.85$$

Therefore, $y_P = (1 - X_P') = 0.43$

$$y_R = (1 - X_R') = 0.15$$

Substituting the values of y_P, y_F, and y_R in equation (1.4.10), we can estimate the screen effectiveness :

$$E_c = \frac{(0.43)\,(0.1)}{(0.25)\,(0.28)}\left[1 - \frac{(0.1)\,(0.57)}{(0.28)\,(0.75)}\right](100)$$

$$= 44.755\%$$

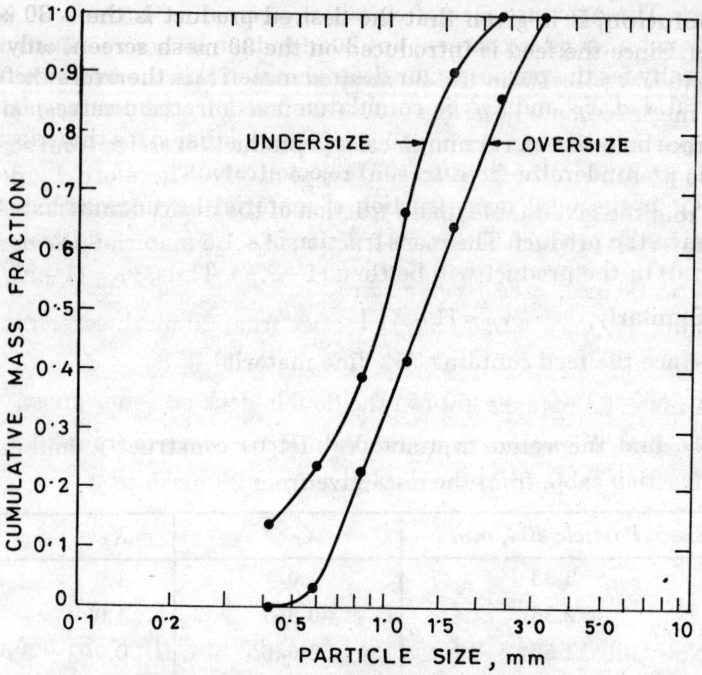

Fig. 1.3.1. Plots of Cumulative Mass Fraction Versus Particle Size on Semi-log Coordinates.

Example 1.4. *Table salt is being fed to a vibrating screen at the rate of 150 kg/hr. The desired product is – 30 + 20 mesh fraction. A 30 mesh and a 20 mesh screen are therefore used (double deck), the feed being introduced on the 30 mesh screen. During the operation, it was observed that the average proportion of oversize (from 30 mesh screen) : oversize (from 20 mesh screen) : undersize (from 20 mesh screen) is 2 : 1.5 : 1. Calculate the effectiveness of the screener from the following data :*

Mesh	*Mass fraction*			
	Feed	*Oversize from 30 Mesh Screen*	*Oversize from 20 Mesh Screen*	*Undersize from 20 Mesh Screen*
– 85 + 60	*0.097*	*0.197*	*0.026*	*0.0005*
– 60 + 40	*0.186*	*0.389*	*0.039*	*0.0009*
– 40 + 30	*0.258*	*0.337*	*0.322*	*0.0036*
– 30 + 20	*0.281*	*0.066*	*0.526*	*0.3490*
– 20 + 15	*0.091*	*0.005*	*0.061*	*0.2990*
– 15 + 10	*0.087*	*0.006*	*0.026*	*0.3470*

Solution. It is given that the desired product is the – 30 + 20 fraction. Since the feed is introduced on the 30 mesh screen, only the – 30 material will fall on the 20 mesh screen. Thus the oversize from the 20 mesh screen will be the – 30 + 20 fraction (the product). However, since both screens are not 100% efficient, other sizes than desired are also present in the product and reject streams.

From the given table, mass fraction of the desired material (– 30 + 20 material) in the feed is 0.281. Thus,

$$y_F = 0.281$$

Similarly, y_P = 0.526 (since oversize from 20 mesh screen is the product stream).

A material balance around the double-deck screener gives,

Feed (F) = oversize from 30 mesh (R_1) + oversize from 20 mesh (P) + undersize from 20 mesh (R_2)

Since it is given that $R_1 : P : R_2 = 2 : 1.5 : 1$,

$$\left(\frac{P}{F}\right) = \frac{P}{P + R_1 + R_2} = \frac{1.5}{4.5} = \frac{1}{3}$$

Now substituting the values of y_F, y_P, and (P/F) in equation (1.4.6), we can compute the effectiveness of the screener :

$$E_c = \frac{(0.526)}{3\,(0.281)}\left[1 - \frac{(1 - 0.526)}{(1 - 0.281)\,(3.0)}\right]$$

$$= 0.486 = 48.6\%.$$

1.4.3. Industrial Screening Equipment

Grizzlies are the most rugged types of industrial screens. They are used for screening large sizes of rocks of 25 mm and above, as for example, for sizing the feed to a primary crushing unit. They consist of a set of parallel bars usually made of manganese steel and of trapezoidal in cross-section. Stationary grizzlies are the simplest, requiring no external power supply and needs little maintenance. They are used to handle dry materials of sizes 50 mm and above, but are not suitable for moist or sticky materials. Vibrating grizzlies use a cam arrangement or an eccentric to impart lengthwise reciprocal movement to alternate bars which permit easy flow of material and prevent clogging. Flat grizzlies are used above feed bins of coal and ores or below the unloading trestles to retain huge lumps. Inclined grizzlies maintain a slope of $20^0 - 50^0$ with the horizontal. Chain grizzlies in which the bars are replaced by endless chains passing over sheaves are used for handling sticky or clay-like material.

Vibrating screens are one of the most popular ones used in chemical industry. They can handle large tonnages of material, possess high efficiency, provide good accuracy of sizing, require less maintenance per ton of material handled and also provide a saving in weight and installation space. They can be mechanically vibrated using an eccentric or unbalanced flywheel which will constitute a circular motion in the vertical plane, or electrically vibrated using an electromagnet. The frequency or speed of vibration varies from 1500 to 7200 per minute. They can handle a wide variety of materials starting from 480 mesh to 4 mesh.

Oscillating screens are characterised by relatively low speed oscillations (300 to 400 per minute) in a plane parallel to the screen cloth. They are one of the cheapest types of industrial screens and are widely used for batch screening of coarse material of 5 to 15 mm and fine, light, free-flowing materials of 4 to 8 mesh.

Reciprocating screens are popularly used in the chemical industry for handling materials down upto 4 mesh. They are driven by an eccentric under the screen at the feed end. The motion varies from gyratory at the feed end to reciprocating motion at the discharge end. The speed varies from 500 to 600 per minute. They are usually kept inclined at around 5° with the horizontal. They are widely used for handling dry chemicals, light metal powders, powdered food and granular materials, but are not suitable for handling heavy tonnages of rock or gravel.

Gyratory screens are box-like machines either square or round with series of screen cloths nested one upon the other. Eccentrics impart oscillations in circular or near-circular orbits. Examples are the vibro-energy separators and the gyratory riddles (widely used in batch screening).

Trommels are revolving screens usually cylindrical or conical in shape, open at both ends and are normally inclined at 5 – 10° with the horizontal. They are rotated about their axis at around 15 – 20 rpm. Trommels have relatively low capacity and low efficiency. They are however quite efficient for coarse sizes. Conical trommels which have the shape of a truncated cone are normally mounted horizontal. Compound trommels can be constructed using a number of screens of gradually increasing aperture size along the length of the cylinder, the feed being introduced at the finest screen. Thus, a number of products of different sizes can be collected from a single trommel. However, it will be more efficient to use a number of simple trommels in series, with the undersize from one trommel passing to the next. In concentric trommels, a number of trommels are mounted one inside the other on a common shaft. The innermost screen will be the coarsest and the outermost the finest, the feed being introduced into the innermost screen. Provisions are also made for separate removal of oversize from each screening surface. The capacity of a trommel increases with increase in speed of rotation upto a stage when blinding occurs due to overcrowding of particles at the screen surface. If the speed is further increased to the so-called "critical speed," then the material will no longer cascade over the screen surface but will be carried around by centrifugal force. Thus, there will be no size separation and the trommel becomes inoperative. Since the critical speed of rotation of a trommel is thus the speed at which the force of gravity on the particle just becomes equal to the centrifugal force acting on it, we can write,

$$mg = m\,\omega_c^2\,r \qquad ...(1.4.11)$$

where m = mass of particle

g = acceleration due to gravity

ω_c = critical angular velocity of particle (equal to that of trommel)

$= \dfrac{2\,\pi\,N_c}{60}$

N_c = critical speed of rotation of trommel, rpm

r = radius of rotation of particle.

Since the maximum radius of rotation of particle (at critical speed) is the radius of the trommel, we can put $r = D/2$, where D is the diameter of the trommel. Thus, equation (1.4.11) becomes,

$$\left[\frac{4\pi^2 N_c^2}{3600}\right]\left(\frac{D}{2}\right) = g$$

or,

$$N_c = \frac{60}{2\pi}\sqrt{2g/D} \qquad ...(1.4.12)$$

Thus, the critical speed is governed by the diameter of the trommel (for concentric trommels, diameter of the outermost screen). Obviously, the operating speed of trommel must be below its critical speed. Usually, 33 to 45% of N_c is preferred.

1.5. Computer-aided Analysis

Today's era is commonly called the "computer era." The computations discussed above involving specific surface of particle mixtures, screen effectiveness etc. can be made faster and more accurate if the help of high speed computers is sought.

The primary step in computer-aided analysis is the preparation of the computation flow graph. It is nothing but a flow sheet illustrating all the steps of the computation process and the detailed procedure followed in each step. The initial specifications of the problem (that are available at the outset) are kept stored in one of the memory files of the computer, commonly called the "father file." On-the-spot specifications to be supplied at different stages of the computation are supplied from the "*son files*". Data bases are used for storing standard tables, charts or graphs from which the value of any particular parameter can be retrieved whenever necessary. These are particularly useful when the value of a parameter cannot be computed using any specific correlation, but is available from standard tables, charts or graphs.

We shall present here the computation flow graph corresponding to examples (1.1) and (1.2) discussed in the earlier sections. The flow sheet is given in Fig. (1.2).

In the flow sheet, M_j (j = 1, 2, . . ., 14) are the mesh numbers of the screens. Thus, in example (1.1), $M_1 = 570$, $M_2 = 480$ and so on. Finally, $M_{14} = 8$. Data base – 1 stores the specifications of Indian standard screens (given in table 1.2). Thus, once the mesh number M_j is specified, its aperture size a_j can be retrieved from this data base. S_{int} is the screen interval followed and in the present problem, S_{int} = 1.41. The total mass fraction of – 8 material is denoted as x_{fine}. Thus, in the present case, $x_{fine} = 0.053$. Data base – 2 stores the standard plot of specific surface ratio (n) versus average size (d_{avg}), given in figure (1.1.).

Once the computation flow graph has been prepared, it can be easily translated into any of the popular computer languages such as FORTRAN or PASCAL and then executed on any of the available high speed computers. The computer program for fitting straight line using the method of least squares (used in the above computation flow graph under 'EXTRAPOLATION') is given in the appendix. Under 'NUMPART' the alternate method of computing number of particles per unit mass of the sample ($\overline{N}$) based on cumulative analysis, that is, using equation (1.4.2), is given.

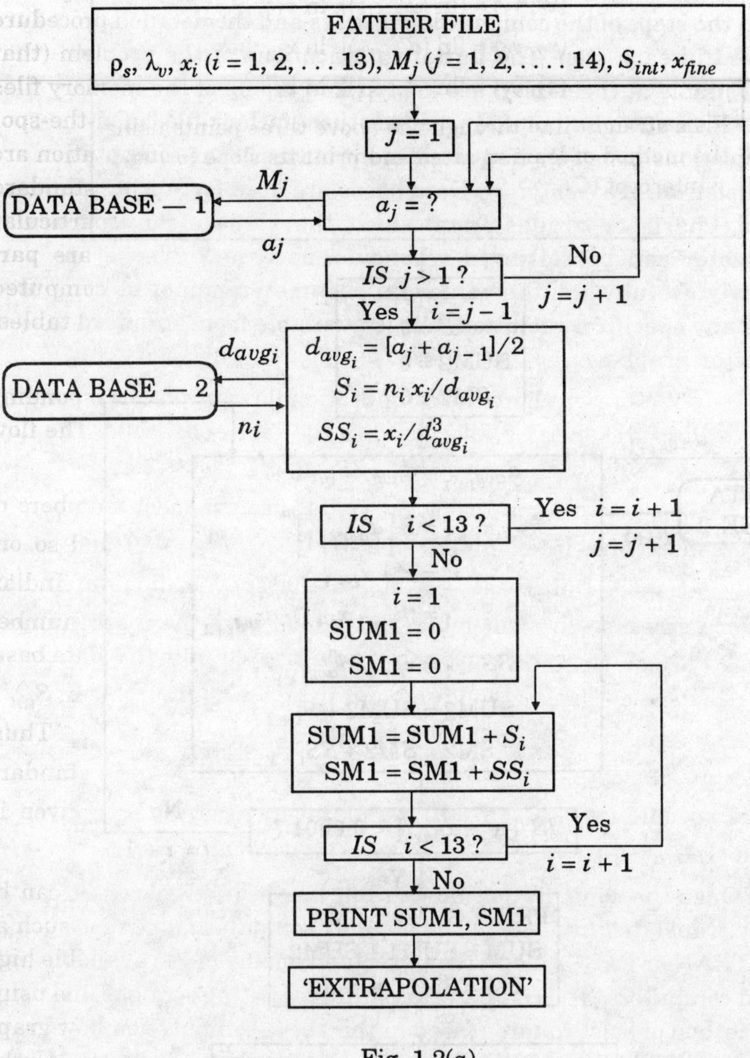
FATHER FILE
ρs, λv, xi (i = 1, 2, . . . 13), Mj (j = 1, 2, ... 14), Sint, xfine
j = 1
Mj
DATA BASE — 1
aj = ?
aj
IS j > 1 ?
No
j = j + 1
Yes
i = j – 1
davgi
davgi = [aj + aj – 1]/2
Si = ni xi/davgi
SSi = xi/d3avgi
DATA BASE — 2
ni
IS i < 13 ?
Yes
i = i + 1
j = j + 1
No
i = 1
SUM1 = 0
SM1 = 0
SUM1 = SUM1 + Si
SM1 = SM1 + SSi
IS i < 13 ?
Yes
i = i + 1
No
PRINT SUM1, SM1
'EXTRAPOLATION'

Fig. 1.2(*a*)

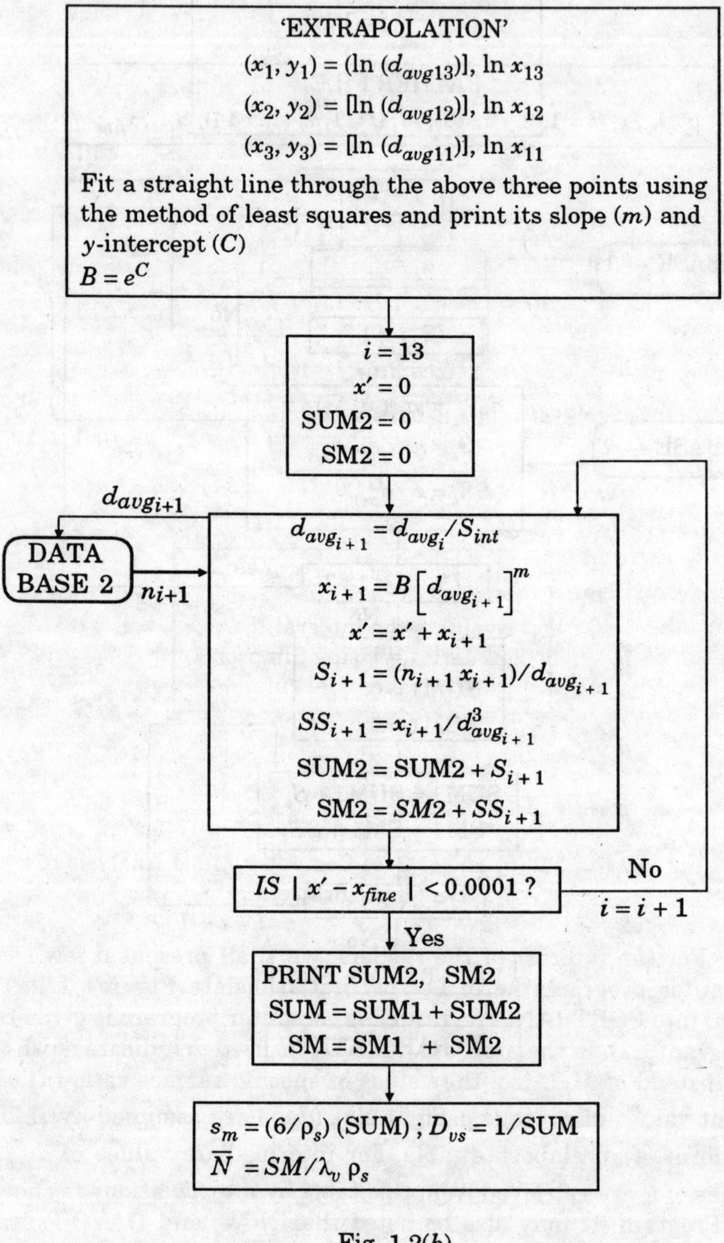
'EXTRAPOLATION'
$(x_1, y_1) = (\ln (d_{avg13})], \ln x_{13}$
$(x_2, y_2) = [\ln (d_{avg12})], \ln x_{12}$
$(x_3, y_3) = [\ln (d_{avg11})], \ln x_{11}$
Fit a straight line through the above three points using the method of least squares and print its slope (m) and y-intercept (C)
$B = e^C$
$i = 13$
$x' = 0$
SUM2 = 0
SM2 = 0
$d_{avg_{i+1}}$
DATA BASE 2
n_{i+1}
$d_{avg_{i+1}} = d_{avg_i}/S_{int}$
$x_{i+1} = B\left[d_{avg_{i+1}}\right]^m$
$x' = x' + x_{i+1}$
$S_{i+1} = (n_{i+1}\, x_{i+1})/d_{avg_{i+1}}$
$SS_{i+1} = x_{i+1}/d^3_{avg_{i+1}}$
$\text{SUM2} = \text{SUM2} + S_{i+1}$
$\text{SM2} = SM2 + SS_{i+1}$
$IS \mid x' - x_{fine} \mid < 0.0001$?
No
$i = i + 1$
Yes
PRINT SUM2, SM2
SUM = SUM1 + SUM2
SM = SM1 + SM2
$s_m = (6/\rho_s)\,(\text{SUM})\,;\ D_{vs} = 1/\text{SUM}$
$\overline{N} = SM/\lambda_v\, \rho_s$

Fig. 1.2(*b*)

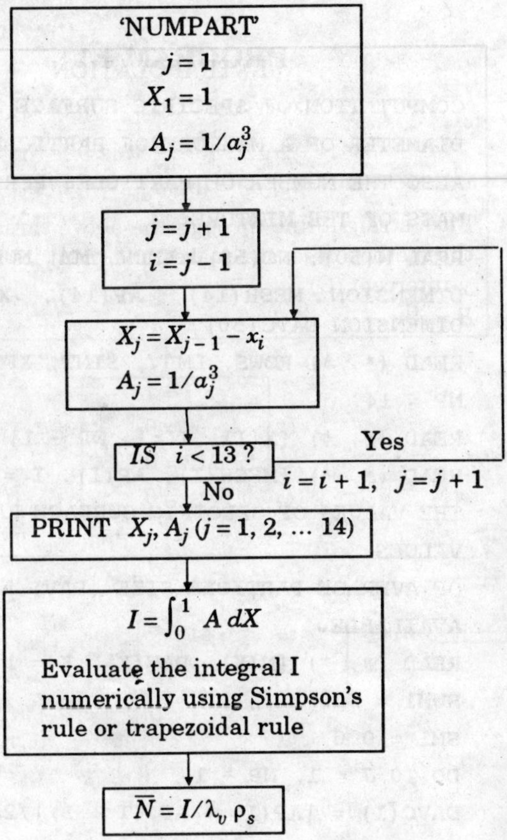

Fig. 1.2 (*c*)

Fig. 1.2 (*a*), 1.2 (*b*) and (1.2 (*c*) Computer Aided Analysis of a Screening Problem

For the interest of the readers, we shall present a few sample computer programs here. Let us first translate Figures 1.2(*a*) and 1.2(*b*) into FORTRAN. The resulting computer program is given below (Program 1.1). In the program, MESH(I) is used to indicate mesh number instead of M_j. Also, the values of specific surface ratio (n) at different values of average particle size (d_{avg}) are assumed available in the form of an elaborate table. For intermediate values of d_{avg}, the values of n are retrieved from this table by interpolation, as shown in the Program. It may also be noted that NC(I) and DAVC(I) are the calculated values of specific surface ratio and average particle size respectively.

PROGRAM 1.1

```
C**   COMPUTATION OF SPECIFIC SURFACE AND SAUTER
C**   DIAMETER OF A MIXTURE OF PARTICLES AND
C**   ALSO THE NUMBER OF PARTICLES PER UNIT
C**   MASS OF THE MIXTURE.
      REAL N(50), NC(50), LMDV, MM, NUMR, NUMP
      DIMENSION  MESH(14),  AP(14),  X(50),  DAV  (50)
      DIMENSION DAVC(50)
      READ (*, *) ROWS, LMDV, SINT, XFINE
      NP = 14
      READ (*, *) [X(I), I =1, NP - 1]
      READ (*, *) [MESH(I), AP(I), I = 1, NP]
C**   THE VALUES OF SPECIFIC SURFACE RATIO AT DIFFERENT
C**   VALUES
C**   OF AVERAGE PARTICLE SIZE (DAV) ARE ASSUMED
C**   AVAILABLE.
      READ (*, *) [N(K), DAV(K), K = 1,50]
      SUM1 = 0.0
      SM1 = 0.0
      DO 10 J = 1, NP - 1
      DAVC(I) = [AP(I) + AP (I + 1)]/2.0
      DO 15 K = 1,50
      IF [DAV(K). GE. DAVC(I)] GO TO 20
 15   CONTINUE
 20   NC(I) = N (K - 1) + [N(K) - N (K - 1)] * [DAVC(I)
      - DAV (K - 1)]/[DAV(K) - DAV (K - 1)]
      SUM1 = SUM1 + NC(I) * X(I)/DAVC(I)
      SM1 = SM1 + X(I)/DAVC(I) * * 3
 10   CONTINUE
C**   GAUDIN-SCHUMANN DISTRIBUTION LAW IS ASSU-
C**   MED APPLICABLE FOR FINE SIZES BELOW DAVC (NP-4)
C**   THE CONSTANTS B AND MM OF G-S DISTRIBUTION
C**   LAW ARE EVALUATED BY FITTING A STRAIGHT
C**   LINE THROUGH THE POINTS {ALOG [DAVC(I)],
C**   ALOG[X(I)]}, I = NP-3, NP-2, NP-1 USING
C**   THE METHOD OF LEAST SQUARES.
```

```
      SUMX = 0.0
      SUMY = 0.0
      SUMXY = 0.0
      SUMXX = 0.0
      DO 25 I = NP-3, NP-1
      SUMX = SUMX + ALOG [DAVC(I)]
      SUMY = SUMY + ALOG[X(I)]
      SUMXY = SUMXY + ALOG [DAVC(I)] * ALOG[X(I)]
      SUMXX = SUMXX + ALOG [DAVC(I)] * * 2
      AN = 3.0
      NUMR = AN * SUMXY - SUMX * SUMY
      DENR = AN * SUMXX - SUMX * * 2
      MM = NUMR/DENR
      C = (SUMY - MM * SUMX)/AN
      B = EXP(C)
      I = NP - 1
      SX = 0.0
      SUM2 = 0.0
      SM2 = 0.0
30    DAVC (I + 1) = DAVC(I)/SINT
      X (I + 1) = B * DAVC (I + 1) * * MM
      DO 35 K = 1,50
      IF [DAV(K). GE. DAVC(I + 1)] GO TO 40
35    CONTINUE
40    NC (I + 1) = N (K - 1) + [N(K).- N(K - 1)] * [DAVC
      (I + 1) - DAV (K - 1)]/[DAV(K) - DAV (K - 1)]
      SUM2 = SUM2 + NC (I + 1) * X(I + 1)/DAVC (I + 1)
      SM2 = SM2 + X (I + 1)/DAVC (I + 1) * * 3
      SX = SX + X (I + 1)
      DIF = ABS (SX - XFINE)
      IF (DIF. LT. 0.0001) GO TO 45
      I = I + 1
      GO TO 30
45    SUM = SUM1 + SUM2
      SM = SM1 + SM2
      SS = (6.0/ROWS) * SUM
```

```
      DVS = 1.0/SUM
      NUMP = SM/(LMDV * ROWS)
      WRITE (*, *) SS, DVS, NUMP
      STOP
      END
```

Let us now consider computation of the number of particles in a mixture using cumulative size analysis (as illustrated in Figure 1.2*c*). The computer program is given below (Program 1.2). The size distribution table is first made complete by extrapolation and making use of Gaudin-Schumann size distribution law. The values of cumulative mass fraction, represented as CX(I) in the program, are now computed and the integral of equation (1.4.2) evaluated using trapezoidal rule (Simpson's rule cannot be used here since CX(I) values are not at equal intervals). The rule is given below :

$$\int_{x_0}^{x_n} f(x)\,dx = (1/2) \sum_{i=1}^{n} h_i\,[f(x_{i-1}) + f(x_i)] \qquad ...(1.5.1)$$

where $$h_i = [x_i - x_{i-1}] \qquad ...(1.5.2)$$

PROGRAM 1.2

```
C**   COMPUTATION OF NUMBER OF PARTICLES IN A
C**   MIXTURE USING CUMULATIVE SIZE ANALYSIS
C**   (USING EQUATION 1.4.2)
      REAL LMDV, MM, NUMR, NUMP
      DIMENSION MESH(14), AP(50), X(50), DAV(3)
      READ (*, *) ROWS, LMDV, SINT, XFINE
      NP = 14
      READ (*, *) [X(I), I = 1, NP - 1]
      READ (*, *) [MESH(I), AP(I), I = 1, NP]
C**   DETERMINE SIZE DISTRIBUTION BELOW AP(NP)
C**   BY EXTRAPOLATION.
C**   GAUDIN-SCHUMANN DISTRIBUTION LAW IS
C**   ASSUMED VALID FOR FINE SIZES BELOW AP (NP - 3).
      DAV (NP - 3) = [AP (NP - 4) + AP (NP - 3)]/2.0
      DAV (NP - 2) = [AP (NP - 3 ) + AP (NP - 2)]/2.0
      DAV (NP - 1) = [AP (NP - 2) + AP (NP - 1)]/2.0
C**   FIND THE CONSTANTS B AND MM OF G-S
C**   DISTRIBUTION LAW BY FITTING A STRAIGHT
```

```
C**     LINE THROUGH THE ABOVE THREE VALUES
C**     OF DAV AND CORRESPONDING VALUES OF X
C**     ON LOG-LOG COORDINATES.
        SUMX = 0.0
        SUMY = 0.0
        SUMXX = 0.0
        SUMXY = 0.0
        DO 10 I = NP - 3, NP - 1
        SUMX = SUMX + ALOG [DAV(I)]
        SUMY = SUMY + ALOG [X(I)]
        SUMXY = SUMXY + ALOG [DAV(I)] * ALOG [X(I)]
  10    SUMXX = SUMXX + ALOG [DAV(I)] * * 2
        AN = 3.0
        NUMR = AN * SUMXY - SUMX * SUMY
        DENR = AN * SUMXX - SUMX * * 2
        MM = NUMR/DENR
        C = (SUMY - MM * SUMX)/AN
        B = EXP (C)
        I = NP
        SX = 0.0
  15    AP (I + 1) = AP (I) /SINT
        DAV(I) = [AP(I) + AP (I + 1)]/2.0
        X(I) = B * DAV(I) * * MM
        SX = SX + X(I)
        DIF = ABS (SX - XFINE)
        IF (DIF. LT. 0.0001) GO TO 20
        I = I + 1
        GO TO 15
  20    MP = I
C**     COMPUTE THE VALUES OF CUMULATIVE MASS
C**     FRACTIONS, CX(I).
        CX(1) = 1.0
        DO 25 I = 1, MP - 2
        CX (I + 1) = CX(I) - X(I)
  25    CONTINUE
        CX (MP) = X (MP)
```

```
      CX (MP + 1) = 0.0
C**   EVALUATE INTEGRAL OF EQUATION (1.4.2)
C**   USING TRAPEZOIDAL RULE.
      SUM = 0.0
      F(1) = 1.0/AP(1) * * 3
      DO 30 I = 1, MP
      H(I) = CX (I) - CX (I + 1)
      F (I + 1) = 1.0/AP (I + 1) * * 3
 30   SUM = SUM + [H(I)/2.0] * [F(I) + F (I + 1)]
      NUMP = SUM/(LMDV * ROWS)
      WRITE (*, *) NUMP
      STOP
      END
```

NOMENCLATURE

a_j	**aperture size of *j*-th screen, corresponding to mesh number M_j (used in CAD flowsheet), *m***
d_{avg}	**average screen size of a particle, *m*.**
d_{avg_i}	**average screen size of the *i*th fraction of a mixture of particles, *m*.**
d_p	**particle size/aperture size, *m*.**
d_s	**surface diameter of an irregular (non-spherical) particle, *m*.**
d_v	**volumetric diameter of an irregular particle, *m*.**
d_{vs}	**volume-surface diameter (sauter diameter) of an irregular particle, *m*.**
D	**diameter of trommel, *m*.**
D_A (or D_N)	**arithmetic mean (or, number mean) size of a mixture of particles, *m*.**
D_{CR}	**cube-root mean size of a mixture of particles, *m*.**
D_H	**harmonic mean size of a mixture of particles, *m*.**
D_L	**length mean size of a mixture of particles, *m*.**
D_S	**surface mean size of a mixture of particles, *m*.**
D_{SR}	**square-root mean size of a mixture of particles, *m*.**
D_v	**volume mean size of a mixture of particles, *m*.**
D_{vs}	**volume-surface diameter (sauter diameter) of a mixture of particles, *m*.**

E_c screen effectiveness, dimensionless

F feed rate, kg/s.

g gravitational acceleration, m/s^2

m, B constants in Gaudin-Schumann size distribution law (see eq. 1.4.1).

m_i mass of the ith fraction of a mixture of particles, kg.

M total mass of a particle mixture, kg.

M_j mesh number of j-th test screen (see the CAD flowsheet) corresponding to aperture size a_j.

n specific surface ratio, dimensionless.

n_i specific surface ratio of ith fraction of a mixture of particles, dimensionless

$N, \overline{N}$ total number of particles and numper of particles per unit mass respectively, in a mixture of particles.

N_i number of particles of size d_i (or d_{avg_i})

N_c critical speed of rotation of trommel, rpm.

P product discharge rate, kg/s.

R reject (or recycle) rate, kg/s.

s_i specific surface of ith fraction, m^2/kg.

s_p specific surface of particle, m^2/m^3 or m^2/kg.

s_m specific surface of a mixture of particles, m^2/kg.

S_i surface area of ith fraction, m^2.

S_{int} standard screen interval (see the CAD flowsheet), dimensionless.

S_p surface area of a particle, m^2

V_p volume of a particle, m^3

x_i mass fraction of particles of size d_{avg_i} in a mixture.

X cumulative mass fraction

y_F mass fraction of desired material (material of desired size) in the feed to the screen.

y_P mass fraction of desired material in the product from the screen.

y_R mass fraction of desired material in the reject stream from the screen.

λ_s shape factor (or, surface shape factor), dimensionless

λ_v volume shape factor, dimensionless

ψ_s sphericity, dimensionless

ρ_s solid density, kg/m^3

Computer Notations

AP(I) aperture size of i-th standard screen (a_i)

B constant in Gaudin-Schumann law (eq. 1.4.1)

CX(I) cumulative mass fraction corresponding to aperture size a_i

DAV(I) average screen size of i-th fraction (d_{avg_i})

DAVC(I) calculated value of DAV(I)

DVS volume-surface diameter of a mixture of particles (D_{vs})

LMDV volume shape factor (λ_v)

MM constant in Gaudin-Schumann size distribution law (m)

MESH(I) mesh number of i-th standard screen (M_i)

N(I) specific surface ratio (n_i) of particles of size d_{avg_i}

NC(I) calculated value of N(I)

NUMP number of particles per unit mass ($\overline{N}$)

ROWS solid density (ρ_s)

SINT screen interval (S_{int})

SS specific surface of a mixture of particles (s_m)

X(I) mass fraction of particles of size d_{avg_i} (x_i)

XFINE total mass fraction of fine material whose size distribution is not known (x_{fine}).

REFERENCES

1. Foust, A.S. and Associates, Principles of Unit Operations, Wiley, New York, 1960.
2. Perry, R.H., Chemical Engineer's Handbook, 6th edition, McGraw- Hill, New York, 1984.
3. Taggart, A.F., Handbook of Mineral Dressing, Wiley, New York, 1945.
4. Brown, G.G. and Associates, Unit Operations, Wiley, New York, 1950.

2

Comminution

Comminution is the generic term for size reduction. The objectives of comminution are two fold : firstly, to produce solids of desired sizes (or size ranges) or specific surfaces and secondly, to break apart materials that are intimately in contact with each other. Solid particles can be reduced in size by compression, shear, impact, attrition (rubbing) or by cutting or tearing action. Compressive, impact or shearing loads are used for breaking brittle materials like coal and minerals whereas fibrous materials like wood and asbestos are disintegrated by exerting tearing loads.

Comminution is an operation that is almost omnipresent in process industries. Whether in mineral dressing or chemical processing, whether it is the raw material or the finished product, we require solid rocks to be reduced to a given size distribution. However, until recently, comminution was being considered an art more than science. It is only in the recent years, attempts are being made to analyse the mechanism of comminution more deeply and construction of comminution equipment being done more scientifically. It must be noted that in many manufacturing processes such as in the manufacture of cement, paint and pigments etc., a major percentage of the total power consumption of the plant is in the operation of comminution equipment. The economy of many process industries thus depends very much on efficient construction and operation of comminution equipment.

In a comminution process, the feed rock is crushed into pieces by colliding against the grinding media (such as steel balls, rods etc.) or by mutual collision between particles or by direct collision against the moving parts of the machine. As the size reduction proceeds, the number of particles increases thus requiring more number of collisions per unit mass. The capacity of a comminution equipment (kg of material handled per unit time) of fixed dimensions will be therefore much less for smaller sizes of particles since they have to remain in the crusher for longer time to receive the required number of collisions and thus to achieve the desired degree of size reduction. There is hardly any equipment that is capable of automatically adjusting itself to the varying requirements of contact or collision. In commercial operations therefore, it is desirable to conduct the size reduction process at least in three different stages such as coarse size reduction if the feed rock is of size 50 to 250 mm or more, intermediate size reduction for feeds of 25 to 75 mm in size and fine size reduction when the feed size is 5 to 15 mm.

2.1. Factors Affecting Comminution

The primary factor affecting a comminution process is the properties of the feed rock handled. The grindability of the feed depends on the hardness, toughness, crystallinity and cleavage. Hardness of a mineral, measured by the so called Moh scale, denotes its resistance to scratching and is thus a good indication of the abrasive character of the mineral and its resistance to crushing. It also tells about the extent of wear that will be caused on the grinding media. Based on the Moh scale, materials may be classified into three broad categories such as the soft materials (Moh hardness = 1 – 3) like talc, gypsum etc., materials of intermediate hardness (Moh hardness = 4 – 6) like limestone, magnesite, felspar, ilmenite etc. and hard materials with Moh hardness 7 and above such as diamond, saphire, quartz.

Toughness indicates the impact resistance of the material. It is the inverse to friability or brittleness. It is to be noted that the hardness of a mineral is not a sure criterion of its brittleness. For example, gypsum, horn and some plastics are soft and tough and are not easily broken by impact, whereas coal is both soft and friable.

Every true solid material has a specific crystalline structure. That is, the atoms in the crystal are arranged in a definite, repeating geometric pattern and there are certain planes in the crystal called cleavage planes along which breakage occurs when sufficient pressure is applied on the rock. When the material is broken into segments during comminution, the shape of the segments formed depends on its crystalline structure. For example, galena breaks into cubes, mica into flat scales and magnetite into rounded grains. Fibrous materials like wood and asbestos do not possess cleavage planes and therefore are not readily crushed and they are to be torn or shredded. The *grindability index* of a mineral can be determined by the drop weight method (which we shall be discussing later) or by the Hardgrove method.[1]

The *moisture content* of the feed rock is another influencing parameter in comminution. If the moisture content of the rock is more than 3 – 4% (by weight), it forms sticky or pasty mass and tends to clog the machine. Moisture content below 3 – 4% is considered desirable since it acts as a binding agent and thus helps in preventing loss of fines. When comminution is conducted in presence of a large excess of water (50% or more) with or without dispersion agents, it is called *wet grinding*. This is done when the product is desired in the form of a suspension or slurry.

The *reduction ratio* is defined as the ratio of the average size of feed to the average size of product. Thus,

$$RR = (D_F/D_P) \qquad ...(2.1.1)$$

The value of (RR) for coarse crushers is 3 to 7, whereas fine grinders have reduction ratio as high as 100.

If the comminution process is carried out in such a way that the product material is continuously discharged almost as soon as it is produced, then it is called "free crushing." The product may be removed either by flow under gravity or by injecting compressed air (pneumatic discharge) or water (hydraulic discharge) or by centrifugal means. Such units will have large capacity and they prevent formation of excess of fines. Conversely, the crusher may be equipped with a feed hopper and kept filled (or choked) so that it does not freely discharge the crushed product. This is called "choke feeding." This lowers the capacity of the machine but is employed when large quantity of fines is desired in the final product.

No industrial comminution equipment can produce a product that conforms exactly to the size range desired. It is therefore preferable to send the product from a size reduction unit to a size separation unit (which may be a screen or a classifier) operating in conjunction so that the oversize material from the size separation unit can be recycled back to the crusher or grinder for further processing. This is called *closed circuit operation* which produces a product of more uniform size, permits smaller units for the same capacity and

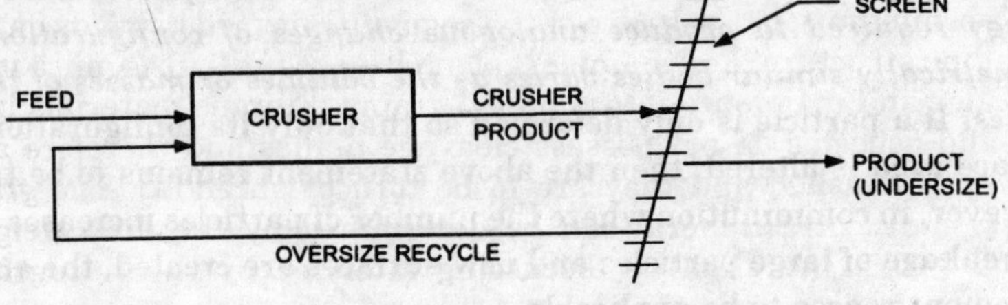

Fig 2.1. Closed Circuit Grinding Unit

economises the power consumption. If there is no such provision for recycling the oversize material, it is called *open circuit operation.* A crusher operating in closed circuit with a classifying screen is shown schematically in Figure (2.1).

The last and most important parameter in comminution is the *power consumption* which decides the energy efficiency of the comminution equipment. When a particle is reduced in size, we know its specific surface (surface area per unit mass) increases. It can be said therefore that comminution causes creation of new surface. However, out of the total energy supplied to a comminution equipment, only a small portion is consumed for the creation of new surface. The rest is spent or lost to overcome friction (in the bearings and other moving parts of the machine) and inertia and also in what are called *inefficient blows.* A good amount of energy is also converted to heat and wasted. The so called inefficient blows are those blows delivered by the crusher on the feed rock but do not rupture the rock, they may at best deform the rock. The energy expended in such blows are thus virtually wasted. Whether a blow delivered by the crusher ultimately causes rupture of the particle or not depends not only on the nature of the particle but also on the direction in which the blow has been delivered. Thus, in an industrial comminution equipment handling a large number of particles, a good proportion of the blows delivered could be inefficient that do not result in creation of new surface. The energy efficiency (defined as the fraction of energy used for creating new surface to the total energy supplied) of many of the comminution equipment in the market remaining apallingly low is due to this.

The laws of comminution proposed by different authors help us determine the energy consumed in comminution, that is, for the creation of new surface. Many of them do not take care of the mechanical losses in the crusher and none of them can account for the energy expended in inefficient blows. The most popular comminution laws are those proposed by Kick[2], Rittinger[3] and Bond.[4]

Kick's law in its original form which, in fact, is not applicable to comminution but only to plastic deformation of solids, states that the *energy required to produce analogous changes of configuration of geometrically similar bodies varies as the volumes or masses of these bodies.* If a particle is only deformed so that only its configuration or surface area is altered, then the above statement remains to be true. However, in comminution where the number of particles increases due to breakage of large particles and new surfaces are created, the above statement ceases to be applicable.

The modified Kick's law that can be applied to crushing states that *the work required for crushing a given quantity of material is constant for a given reduction ratio irrespective of original size.* Mathematically, this law can be expressed as,

$$(E/M) = K_k \log (D_F/D_P) \qquad \text{...(2.1.2)}$$

where, E = energy required for crushing M kg. of material

K_k = Kick's constant

$(D_F/D_P) = RR$ (reduction ratio)

Thus, according to this law, comminution energy depends only on the reduction ratio and is independent of the original size of the feed. This itself speaks for its limitation. It is obviously ridiculous to say that the energy required for reducing a 100 mm particle to 50 mm size will be the same as that for reducing a 1 mm particle to 0.5 mm. In fact, higher amount of energy is required for reducing fine particles to still finer size than for breaking down large pieces of rock. Kick's law can be applied without much serious error to coarse crushing where the feed size is quite large and the reduction ratio is quite low.

A more accurate law of comminution has been proposed by Rittinger.[3] According to Rittinger's law, *the work required for size reduction is directly proportional to the new surface created.* Mathematically this can be expressed as,

$$(E/M) = K_R\,(s_P - s_F) \qquad \text{...(2.1.3)}$$

where, s_P, s_F = specific surfaces of product and feed respectively

K_R = Rittinger's constant

The reciprocal of K_R is called the *Rittinger's number*. Thus, equation (2.1.3) can be rewritten as,

$$(E/M) = \frac{s_P - s_F}{\text{(Rittinger's Number)}} \qquad \text{...(2.1.4)}$$

Rittinger's number thus designates the new surface created per unit mechanical energy absorbed by the material being crushed. Its value is usually determined by the drop weight test. In this test, a standard weight, *m* (normally 3.5 kg) is allowed to fall freely on a given mass of the feed rock from a given height *h* (usually 0.787 m or 31 inches). The specific surface of the crushed product and that of the feed are determined by screen analysis as discussed in Chapter 1. Since the energy input is (mgh) multiplied by the number of falls of the weight, the value of Rittinger's number can be now computed from equation (2.1.4). In practice, the increase in surface area of 100 gm of material after 5, 10, 15 and 20 drops are determined and the increase in surface is plotted against the number of drops or directly against the energy input. The slope of the curve will give the value of Rittinger's number. A few values of Rittinger's number as determined by a drop weighι crusher are given below :

Table 2.1

Material	*Rittinger's Number* (m^2/J)
Galena	0.0957
Sphalerite	0.0573
Pyrite	0.02303
Quartz	0.0179
Calcite	0.07745

It is clear that the larger the Rittinger's number of a material, the larger will be its grindability. If $D_{VS,P}$ and $D_{VS,F}$ are the sauter diameter (volume—surface diameter) of the product and the feed respectively, then equation (2.1.3) can be rewritten as,

$$(E/M) = \frac{6K_R}{\rho_s}\left[\frac{1}{D_{VS,P}} - \frac{1}{D_{VS,F}}\right]$$

$$= K_R'\left[\frac{1}{D_{VS,P}} - \frac{1}{D_{VS,F}}\right] \quad ...(2.1.5)$$

where $K_R' = (6\,K_R/\rho_s)$.

It is to be noted that Rittinger's law does not account for the mechanical losses (due to friction and inertia) in the comminution equipment. These mechanical losses however can be determined by running the crusher empty without any charge. The energy efficiency of a crushing equipment can be thus defined in two ways, such as the overall energy efficiency and the theoretical energy effectiveness :

Overall energy efficiency = (Energy required to create new surface)/(Total energy supplied)

Theoretical effectiveness = (Energy required to create new surface)/(Energy supplied minus that required for running empty mill)

Rittinger's law is best applicable to coarse and intermediate size reduction.

Bond and his coworkers[4] have proposed a number of laws for estimating the comminution energy. However, it is Bond's third law, sometimes called "Universal law," that has received wide acceptance. It states that *the total work useful in breakage that has been applied to a given weight of homogeneous broken material is inversely proportional to the square root of the average size of product particles, directly proportional to the length of crack tips formed and directly proportional to the square root of new surface created.* Mathematically, Bond's law may be expressed as,

$$(E/M) = K_b \left[\frac{1}{\sqrt{D_P}} - \frac{1}{\sqrt{D_F}} \right] \quad ...(2.1.6)$$

where K_b = Bond's constant.

To apply Bond's law therefore, we have to evaluate the Bond's constant K_b. K_b is evaluated by defining what is called the *work index*, W_i. It is defined as the gross energy (in kWh/tonne of feed) necessary to reduce a very large feed to such a size that 80% of product particles will pass through a 0.1 mm screen. Therefore, based on this definition we can write that,

if $D_F = \infty$ and $D_P = 0.1$ mm, $(E/M) = W_i$ kWh/tonne.

Substituting these in equation (2.1.6), we get,

$$W_i = K_b/\sqrt{0.1}$$

or

$$K_b = \sqrt{0.1}\, W_i = 0.3162\, W_i \quad ...(2.1.7)$$

Thus, if 80% of feed particles pass through a D_{Fb} mm screen and 80% of product passes through a D_{Pb} mm screen, then

$$(E/M) = 0.3162\, W_i \left[\frac{1}{D_{Pb}^{1/2}} - \frac{1}{D_{Fb}^{1/2}} \right] \quad ...(2.1.8)$$

Typical values of work index for some of the common materials are given in the following table (2.2). These values are for wet grinding and do not change materially from one equipment to another. For dry grinding however, these values must be multiplied by 1.34.

Table 2.2

Material	*Specific Gravity*	*Work index (kWh / tonne)*
Limestone	2.66	12.74
Gypsum rock	2.69	6.73
Quartz	2.65	13.57
Cement clinker	3.15	13.45
Coal	1.40	13.00
Bauxite	2.20	8.78

It may be noted that if the value of work index has been determined for closed circuit grinding, then it must be multiplied by 1.34 to obtain its value for open circuit operation. Also, if the product size is extrapolated below 70 microns, an additional correction factor, given by $(10.3 + D_P)/(1.145\ D_P)$, is also required to be incorporated (where D_P is the product size in microns).

Since work index has been defined with respect to gross energy, it includes the mechanical losses as well. Bond's law therefore predicts the gross power consumption in comminution. Its applicability has been found to be best for fine grinders.

Walker, Lewis, McAdams and Gilliland[5] have combined the above three laws into the form of a differential equation :

$$dE = C\frac{dD}{D^n} \quad \text{...(2.1.9)}$$

where C is a constant.

Putting $n = 1$ and integrating from D_F to D_P, we get,

$$E = C \log (D_F/D_P) \quad \text{...(2.1.10)}$$

This is nothing but Kick's law.

Putting $n = 2$ and integrating we get,

$$E = C\left[\frac{1}{D_P} - \frac{1}{D_F}\right] \quad \text{...(2.1.11)}$$

This represents Rittinger's Law.

For all values of n greater than 1, we can integrate equation (2.1.9) from D_F to D_P to get,

$$E = \frac{C}{(n-1)}\left[\frac{1}{D_P^{n-1}} - \frac{1}{D_F^{n-1}}\right] \quad \text{...(2.1.12)}$$

Now, if we put $n = 3/2$ in the above equation, we get,

$$E = 2C\left[\frac{1}{D_P^{1/2}} - \frac{1}{D_F^{1/2}}\right] \quad \text{...(2.1.13)}$$

This represents Bond's third law.

Many other authors have proposed a large number of empirical correlations for estimating power consumption in comminution for a given feed rock, for a specific crusher and within a specific size range. For example, one such correlation has been given by Taggart[6] for intermediate size reduction in a hammer mill :

$$P = C\,(RR)\,Q \quad \text{...(2.1.14)}$$

where, P = Power consumption, kWs

RR = Reduction ratio

Q = Capacity of the mill, tonnes/hr.

C is an empirical constant and its value varies from 0.1 to 0.15.

Such correlations are however highly empirical in nature and they can be applied with confidence only to those specific cases for which they have been derived.

Example 2.1. *A grinder is to be used (which is 8% efficient) to handle 10 tonnes per hour of a siliceous ore (specific gravity = 2.65). The feed and product analysis are given below :*

Screen Size, mm	*Feed Mass Fraction*	*Product Mass Fraction*
– 3.327 + 2.362	0.143	0.0
– 2.362 + 1.651	0.211	0.0
– 1.651 + 1.168	0.230	0.0
– 1.168 + 0.833	0.186	0.098
– 0.833 + 0.589	0.120	0.234
– 0.589 + 0.417	0.076	0.277
– 0.417 + 0.295	0.03·	0.149
– 0.295 + 0.208	0.0	0.101
– 0.208 + 0.147	0.0	0.068
– 0.147 + 0.104	0.0	0.044
– 0.104	0.0	0.029

The grinder costs Rs. 40,000. It operates on a 24 hour basis for 300 days per year and the maintenance, overhead and replacement costs amount to 50% of the power cost. Electricity costs 70p. per kWh. If the machine depreciates on a straight line basis for 10 years, estimate the annual processing cost of the ore if the work index of the ore is 13.57 kWh/tonne.

Solution. Since the work index of the ore is given, we can use Bond's third law for estimating the power consumption in comminution. Thus, from equation (2.1.8),

$$(E/M) = 0.3162\, W_i \left[\frac{1}{D_{Pb}^{1/2}} - \frac{1}{D_{Fb}^{1/2}} \right]$$

where $\quad W_i = 13.57$ kWh/tonne

$M = 10$ tonnes/hr.

D_{Pb} and D_{Fb} are the aperture sizes (in mm) of screens through which 80% of the material (product and feed material) passes through. In other words, 80% of product particles are of size less than D_{Pb} mm and 80% of feed particles are of size less than D_{Fb} mm. From the definition of cumulative analysis discussed in Chapter 1, D_{Pb} and D_{Fb} are therefore the aperture sizes (in mm) corresponding to a cumulative mass fraction of 0.8 for the product stream and feed stream respectively. Let us therefore construct the cumulative mass fraction table for both feed and product :

Aperture size, mm	*Cumulative Mass Fraction*	
	Feed (X_F)	*Product* (X_P)
3.327	1.0	1.0
2.362	0.857	1.0
1.651	0.646	1.0
1.168	0.416	1.0
0.833	0.230	0.902
0.589	0.110	0.668
0.417	0.034	0.391
0.295	0.0	0.242
0.208	0.0	0.141
0.147	0.0	0.073
0.104	0.0	0.029

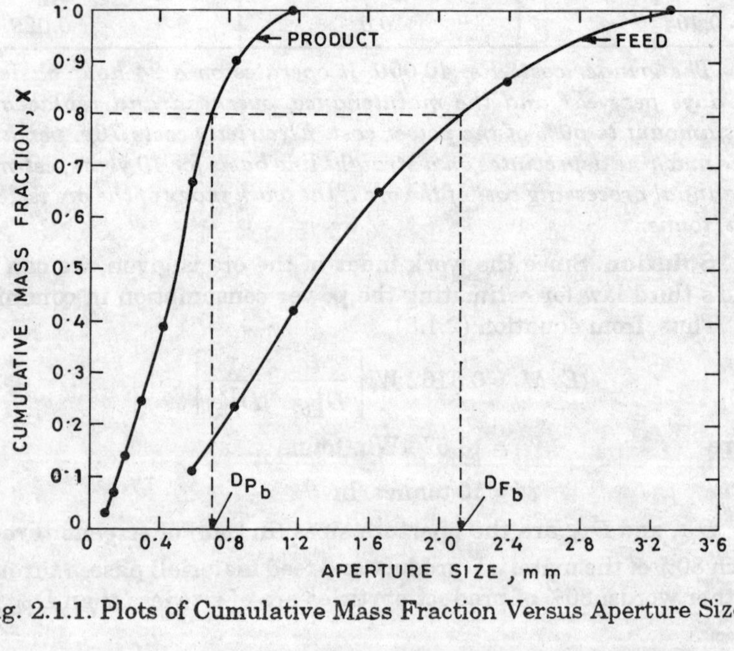

Fig. 2.1.1. Plots of Cumulative Mass Fraction Versus Aperture Size.

Now, we plot X_F and X_P versus aperture size on a rectangular graph paper. The plots are given in Figure (2.1.1). From the Figure, the aperture size corresponding to $X_F = 0.8$ is 2.12 mm and that corresponding to $X_P = 0.8$ is 0.7 mm.

Thus, $D_{Fb} = 2.12$ mm

$D_{Pb} = 0.7$ mm

Substituting these values in the expression for E, we get,

$$E = 0.3162\ (13.57)\ 10\left[\frac{1}{(0.7)^{1/2}} - \frac{1}{(2.12)^{1/2}}\right]$$

$$= 21.816 \text{ kW}.$$

Since the efficiency of the grinder is 8 per cent,

Total power consumption = 21.816/0.08 = 272.696 kW

Annual power consumption = (272.696) (24) (300)

= 19,63,413.6 kWh.

No doubt, this is a substantially large power load.

Annual power cost = (19,63,413.6) 0.70

= Rs. 13, 74, 389.50 = Rs. 13.744 lakh

Maintenance, overload and replacement cost

= (13.744) (0.5) = Rs. 6.872 lakh

Assuming the scrap value of the machine after its useful life of 10 years to be negligible,

Annual depreciation cost = 40,000/10 = Rs. 4,000

Therefore, annual processing cost of the ore

= (13.744 + 6.872 + 0.04) lakh

= Rs. 20.656 lakh.

Example 2.2. *A hard rock (specific gravity = 3.8) is fed at 5,000 kg per hour to a cone crusher operating in closed circuit with a 30 mesh screen. Regular checks on the possibility of oversize particles passing through the screen show that all materials in the undersize stream from the screen will pass through a 60 mesh screen. Drop weight laboratory tests upon the material being crushed indicate that absorption of 0.98 joules of energy will result in the creation of 175 cm^2 of new surface. These tests also indicate that the specific surface ratios for the material are identical with those of sphalerite. The crusher consumes 4 kW when running empty and 7.5 kW when delivering 5000 kg per hour of the rock. Estimate the overall and theoretical energy effectiveness of the* *crusher and the classifying screen effectiveness if the known streams have the analyses given below :*

Screen Size, mm	*Mass Fraction*		
	Raw feed to crusher	*Discharge from crusher*	*Oversize from screen*
– 6.680 + 4.699	0.10	0.0	0.0
– 4.699 + 3.327	0.20	0.0	0.0
– 3.327 + 2.362	0.40	0.0	0.0
– 2.362 + 1.651	0.20	0.0	0.0
– 1.651 + 1.168	0.10	0.02	0.3
– 1.168 + 0.833	0.0	0.04	0.06
– 0.833 + 0.592	0.0	0.06	0.09
– 0.592 + 0.417	0.0	0.25	0.05
– 0.417 + 0.296	0.0	0.30	0.30
– 0.296 + 0.208	0.0	0.20	0.08
– 0.208 + 0.147	0.0	0.06	0.05
– 0.147 + 0.104	0.0	0.04	0.04
– 0.104 + 0.074	0.0	0.03	0.0

Solution. The sketch of the process is given below :

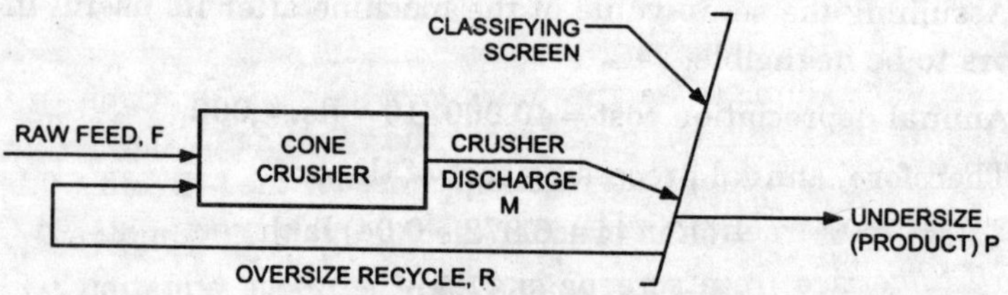

Fig. 2.1.2.

According to Rittinger's law,

$$(E/M) = (s_P - s_F)/(\text{Rittinger's Number})$$

Given that the feed rate (M in above equation) is 5000 kg per hour. Since it is stated that based on drop weight tests, 0.98 joules of energy is required to create 175 cm^2 of new surface, Rittinger's Number for the material (which is defined as the new surface created per unit mechanical energy absorbed) will be 178.57 cm^2/joule. The specific surfaces of feed and product can be computed from the following expressions :

$$s_P = \frac{6}{\rho_s} \sum_i \frac{n_i \, x_{Pi}}{D_{avg_i}}$$

$$s_F = \frac{6}{\rho_s} \sum_i \frac{x_i \, x_{Fi}}{D_{avg_i}}$$

where $\rho_s = 3.8$ gm/cm^3 or 3800 kg/m^3. The values of specific surface ratio n are obtained from the standard plot of n versus d_{avg} (given in Figure (1.1) of Chapter 1). The curve for sphalerite is to be chosen since it is given that specific surface ratios for the rock are identical with those for sphalerite.

The size distribution of the product (undersize from screen) is not given. This can be computed by making a material balance around the classifying screen :

$$M = P + R$$

A partial material balance gives,

$$Mx_M = Px_P + Rx_R$$

Combining the two equations, we get,

$$(M/P)\, x_M = x_P + (R/P)\, x_R$$

$$= x_P + [M/P - 1]\, x_R \qquad \text{...}(i)$$

It is given that all materials in the undersize stream from the screen (product stream) pass through a 60 mesh (0.592 mm) screen. That means, in the product stream there are no particles having size more than 0.592 mm. If we therefore consider any fraction in the size distribution table having size more than 0.592 mm (say, – 1.168 + 0.833 fraction), $x_P = 0$ for that fraction. Since for the (– 1.168 + 0.833) fraction, x_M (mass fraction in crusher discharge) is 0.04 and x_R (mass fraction in oversize from screen) is 0.06, the above equation (*i*) becomes,

$$(M/P)\, 0.04 = 0.0 + [M/P - 1]\, 0.06$$

or,

$$(M/P) = 3.0 \qquad \text{...}(ii)$$

Substituting in equation (*i*) we get,

$$x_P = 3\, x_M - 2x_R \qquad \text{...}(iii)$$

From this expression, the values of x_P for all fractions (– 0.592 + 0.417) and below can be computed. For all the coarser fractions, x_P will be zero. The results are given below :

Screen size, mm	Average size, D_{avg}	Specific surface ratio, n	Mass Fraction: Raw feed to crusher, x_F	Mass Fraction: Underize from screen, x_P	$\frac{nx_F}{D_{avg}}$ (cm^{-1})	$\frac{nx_P}{D_{avg}}$ (cm^{-1})
– 6.680 + 4.699	0.569	5.0	0.10	0.0	0.88	0.0
– 4.699 + 3.327	0.4013	4.6	0.20	0.0	2.30	0.0
– 3.327 + 2.362	0.2845	4.2	0.40	0.0	5.91	0.0
– 2.362 + 1.651	0.2007	3.8	0.20	0.0	3.79	0.0
– 1.651 + 1.168	0.141	3.4	0.10	0.0	2.41	0.0
– 1.168 + 0.833	0.1001	3.3	0.0	0.0	0.0	0.0
– 0.833 + 0.592	0.0712	2.7	0.0	0.0	0.0	0.0
– 0.592 + 0.417	0.0506	2.5	0.0	0.05	0.0	2.49
– 0.417 + 0.296	0.0356	2.4	0.0	0.30	0.0	20.23
– 0.296 + 0.208	0.0252	2.2	0.0	0.44	0.0	38.41
– 0.208 + 0.147	0.0178	2.0	0.0	0.08	0.0	8.99
– 0.147 + 0.104	0.0126	1.8	0.0	0.04	0.0	5.71
– 0.104 + 0.074	0.0089	1.6	0.0	0.09	0.0	16.18
				Total =	15.29	92.01

Therefore, $s_P - s_F = \frac{6}{\rho_s}[92.01 - 15.29] = \frac{6}{3.8}(76.72)$

$$= 121.137 \text{ cm}^2/\text{gm}$$

$$= 1{,}21{,}137 \text{ cm}^2/\text{kg}$$

Thus, $E = \frac{(1{,}21{,}137)}{(178.57)}\frac{(5000)}{(3600)} = 942.184 \text{ watts}$

Overall energy efficiency of the crusher

$$= \frac{(942.184)}{(7.5)(1000)}(100) = 12.56\%$$

Theoretical effectiveness

$$= \frac{(942.184)}{(7.5-4)(1000)}(100) = 26.92\%$$

The effectiveness of classifying screen can be computed from equation (1.4.10) given in Chapter 1 :

$$E_c = \frac{(y_F - y_R)\, y_P}{(y_P - y_R)\, y_F}\left[1 - \frac{(y_F - y_R)\,(1 - y_P)}{(y_P - y_R)\,(1 - y_F)}\right]$$

where y_F, y_P, y_R = mass fraction of desired material in feed, product and reject stream respectively.

It must be noted that in the present case, the feed to the screen is the product from the crusher, M. Thus, in the above equation y_F is actually y_M. Since a 30 mesh screen has been used as the classifying screen and the undersize from screen is collected as the final product, our desired material is the – 30 material (that is, particles having size less than 0.296 mm. By definition, the total mass fraction of particles having size less than 0.296 mm in any stream is nothing but the cumulative mass fraction corresponding to 0.296 mm. Thus, y_F (here, y_M), y_P and y_R are cumulative mass fraction corresponding to the aperture size of 0.296 mm in streams M, P and R respectively. Since the aperture size of 0.296 mm is available in the table, we can compute the values of y_M, y_P and y_R directly from the table itself. Thus,

$$y_M = (1 - 0.02 - 0.04 - 0.06 - 0.25 - 0.30) = 0.33$$

It can also be computed as,

$$y_M = (0.20 + 0.06 + 0.04 + 0.03) = 0.33$$

Similarly,

$$y_R = (0.08 + 0.05 + 0.04) = 0.17$$

$$y_P = (0.44 + 0.08 + 0.04 + 0.09) = 0.65$$

Substituting the above values in the expression for E_c, we get,

$$E_c = \frac{(0.33 - 0.17)\, 0.65}{(0.65 - 0.17)\, 0.33}\left[1 - \frac{(1 - 0.65)\,(0.33 - 0.17)}{(1 - 0.33)\,(0.65 - 0.17)}\right]$$

$$= 0.5422 \text{ or } 54.22\%$$

We would like to caution the readers here that in case the size distribution given in above example is incomplete, a log-log plot of x_P versus D_{avg} should not be extrapolated for determining the size distribution in the fine size range. This is because x_P represents the mass fraction of various sizes in the classified product and as stated in Chapter 1, Gaudin-Schumann distribution is valid for the product from a grinder but is not certain to be applicable to a classified product. A log-log plot of x_M versus D_{avg} therefore must be constructed. Since x_M represents mass fraction of various sizes in the mill product, this plot can be extrapolated back and the size distribution of finer mesh particles be determined using Gaudin-Schumann size distribution law (a numerical example illustrating application of this law has already been discussed in Chapter 1). From the values of x_M in the extrapolated portion, corresponding values of x_P can be then computed from the relation,

$$(M/P)\, x_M = x_P + [(M/P) - 1]\, x_R$$

Since there are no finer sizes in the recycle, $x_R = 0.0$ and the value of (M/P) has already been determined to be 3.0 in the above example. Thus, for finer sizes in the extrapolated portion, $x_P = 3\, x_M$.

2.2. Industrial Comminution Equipment

We shall briefly describe here some of the popular comminution equipment used in process industries. For more detailed coverage of comminution equipment, references (1), (6) or (7) may be consulted.

Among the coarse crushers, jaw and gyratory crushers are most popular. The *jaw crusher* is a reciprocating crusher consisting of two crushing surfaces called jaws, one fixed and the other movable. In the Blake jaw crusher, the movable jaws is pivoted at the top and the bottom end is free to execute a reciprocating motion, alternately approaching and receding from the fixed jaw, by means of an eccentric-pitman-toggle arrangement. The pitman is made to execute a vertical motion by the eccentric which is communicated horizontally to the movable jaw by the toggles, thus moving the jaw back and forth. A tension spring is incorporated to control the reciprocating movements of the jaw. Considering Figure (2.2), let F_1 be the force on the pitman and θ be the angle between pitman and toggle (assumed to be the same for both toggles). Then, by a simple force balance,

$$F_1 = 2F_2 \cos \theta$$

or,

$$F_2 = F_1/(2 \cos \theta) \qquad \text{...(2.2.1)}$$

The horizontal thrust F_z on particles at the toggle block will obviously be the horizontal component of F_2. Thus,

$$F_z = F_2 \sin \theta = (F_1/2) \tan \theta \qquad \text{...(2.2.1)}$$

If F_x is the horizontal thrust at any distance x from the pivot, then,

$$F_x\,(x) = F_z\,(L)$$

or,

$$F_x = F_z\, L/x = (F_1\, L \tan \theta)/2x \qquad \text{...(2.2.3)}$$

Since θ is nearly equal to 90°, the value of tan θ is very large. Thus, a small force F_1 exerted on the pitman is communicated to the movable jaw as a very large force by the toggle. Since in the Blake jaw crusher the pivot is at the top, maximum thrust will be on the large feed particles introduced from the top. Also, since the maximum movement of the jaw is at the bottom, there is no tendency for the crusher to clog, though this may permit some uncrushed rock also to pass through. It is to be noted that crushing is accomplished only in one stroke, that is when the movable jaw moves towards the fixed jaw when the particles get compressed against the fixed jaw and thus get crushed. The crushing process is therefore intermittent leading to intermittent power requirement and thus uneven loading on the machine. Heavy flywheels are therefore incorporated to take care of this.

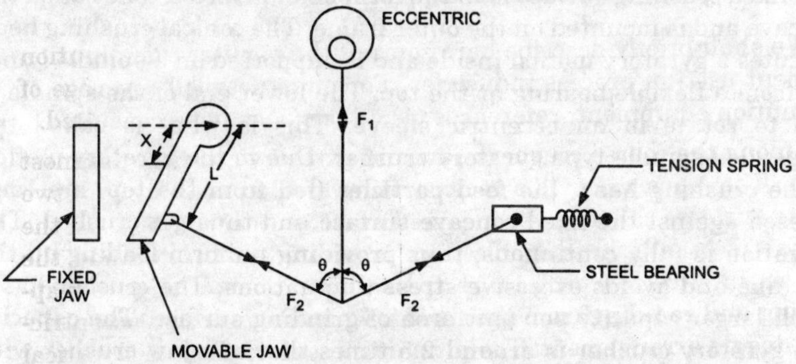

Fig. 2.2. Force Balance on the Movable Jaw of a Blake Jaw Crusher.

In the Dodge jaw crusher, the movable jaw is pivoted at the bottom and the top end executes the reciprocating motion. Since the width of discharge opening is practically constant, a more uniform and closely sized product can be obtained. The jaw is operated through the pitman by the eccentric. No toggles are required. The large feed opening at the top also permits larger feed and provides larger size reduction. However, the constant opening at the discharge end gives the crusher an annoying tendency to clog. As a result, enormous stresses are developed in the machine, often leading to failure. Dodge jaw crushers are therefore constructed only in small sizes and are used only for small capacity installations. The Universal jaw crusher combines the principles of both Blake and Dodge jaw crushers. Here the pivot is slightly above the bottom end of the movable jaw and therefore it provides two strokes per revolution.

The jaws are usually made of a brittle material like chilled cast iron and are also lined with manganese steel to provide good abrasion resistance. The speed of operation varies from 100 to 400 strokes per minute. The *angle of nip*, defined as the maximum permissible angle between the convergent faces of the reciprocating crusher at the point of contact with the feed rock, is normally around 30°. The maximum distance between the crushing surfaces is called the *gape*. The feed opening at the top is called the mouth and the discharge opening at the bottom the throat. The distance between jaws measured at the throat is called the *set*. It is called closed set when the jaws are closest to each other and open set when the jaws are maximum apart. The length of travel of movable jaw measured at the throat is called the *throw* of the crusher.

The *gyratory crusher* is similar to jaw crusher in operation. It also consists of two crushing surfaces, one fixed and the other moving. The fixed crushing surface is in the form of an inverted cone called the concave and is mounted on the outer frame. The conical crushing head executes a gyratory motion inside and is supported on a spindle hanging from a flexible bearing at the top. The lower end of the spindle is free to rotate in an eccentric sleeve. This is what is called the suspended-spindle type gyratory crusher. Due to the gyratory motion of the crushing head, the feed particles (fed from the top) are compressed against the fixed concave surface and thus get crushed. The operation is fully continuous, thus providing uniform loading on the machine and avoids excessive stress fluctuations. The crusher has a much larger capacity per unit area of grinding surface. The capacity of a gyratory crusher is around 2.5 times that of a jaw crusher with the same gape, handling the same feed stock and for the same product size range. Due to the symmetry of the machine, there is also a marked reduction in machine weight per unit capacity.

The power requirements being essentially the same, the choice between a jaw crusher and a gyratory crusher is usually made based on capacity. Due to its low initial cost, jaw crusher is preferred for small capacity installations. According to Taggart[6], if (T/G^2), where T is the capacity in tonnes per hour and G the gape in inches, is less than 0.115, a jaw crusher is to be used and if more than 0.115, a gyratory is to be preferred. Taggart has also proposed an empirical formula for determining the capacity of jaw and gyratory crushers :

$$T = 93.0\,(LS) \qquad \text{...(2.2.4)}$$

where T = capacity, kg/hr.

L = length of feed opening, cm

S = maximum width of discharge opening, cm

The above equation is valid for gapes of 10 to 60 cm. For jaw crushers, L is to be measured normal to the gape and for gyratory crushers, L is taken to be the perimeter of the circle with diameter equal to the arithmetic average of the diameters of the two cones.

For crushing relatively soft materials like coal, gypsum, ice etc., such heavy and expensive equipment like jaw and gyratory crushers are not required. Comparatively lighter and cheaper machines can be employed here. One such example is the *Bradford breaker* used widely for the primary crushing of run-of-mine coal. It consists of a slightly inclined cylindrical chamber with a perforated surface that acts as a reinforced screen. It is rotated about its axis at a low rpm. The coal particles are lifted on the interior shelves and broken by falling and striking the coal below as the cylinder is rotated. When the particles are sufficiently reduced in size, they pass through the perforations and are collected. Bradford breaker may be called an *autogeneous crusher* since this does not use any external grinding media and the particles are crushed due to mutual collision or impact. It is less expensive and has a higher throughput than jaw or gyratory crushers.

The *toothed roll crusher* is another simple device that is extensively used for crushing coal, ice, gypsum etc. It consists of the toothed or knobbed crushing roll which rotates close to a breaker plate. The feed rock collides against the teeth or knobs and gets crushed by compression and shearing between the teeth and the breaker plate.

The *squirrel-cage disintegrator* used widely for tearing apart fibrous materials such as wood and asbestos, consists of two or more concentric cages (resembling the squirrel cages) rotated in opposite directions. The feed is introduced into the inner cage. Centrifugal forces drive the material into the space between the rotating cages where it is torn apart and then discharged.

The *hammer mill* is one of the most versatile type of comminution equipment available. This may be used for brittle materials like coal or fibrous materials like bark and leather. It can handle both hard and soft materials. It consists of heavy blocks of steel (in the form of hammers) that are hinged or pinned along the periphery of a rotating disk called the rotor that rotates at a high rpm inside a sturdy housing. These hammers deliver heavy blows to the feed rock driving it against a breaker plate until it is fine enough to pass through the openings between the cage bars at the bottom of the mill constituting the screen. The hammer mill can be used as a fine pulveriser as well, the size of the product being controlled by the size of the discharge screen. The individual hammers could weigh as much as 100-150 kg. As a result, very sturdy housings are required to be provided for such hammer mills built in such large sizes. When handling wet materials, the cages or screens are replaced by corrugated grinding plates. The capacity of a hammer mill can be computed using one of the correlations proposed by Taggart[6] :

$$T = \frac{KD^2 \, L \, N^2}{3.543 \, (RR - 1)} \qquad ...(2.2.5)$$

where T = capacity, kg/hr.

D = diameter of rotor, m

L = length of rotor, m

N = rpm of rotor

RR = reduction ratio

K is an empirical constant and its value varies from 4.0 to 6.2.

For intermediate size reduction, the most commonly used crushers are cone crushers and crushing rolls. *Cone crushers* provide much higher reduction ratio, around 2-3 times that of crushing rolls and they require less maintenance. Their operation is quite similar to that of gyratory crushers except that in this case the outer stationary crushing plate flares outward providing an increase in discharge area. Also, this stationary plate is held in position by a nest of helical tension springs so that when any uncrushable material like tramp iron enters the crushing zone, the plate is lifted due to compression of springs, thus preventing fracture of the plate and injury to the machine. Cone crushers are usually available in two sizes, one for coarser feed and

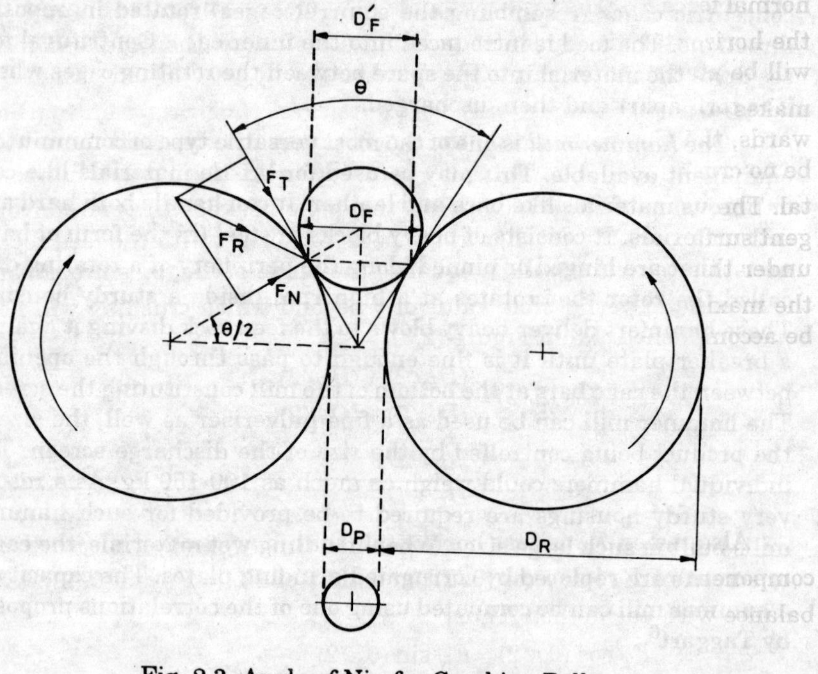

Fig. 2.3. Angle of Nip for Crushing Rolls.

the other for finer feed ("short head"). These crushers handle essentially dry feed and give best results when operating in closed circuit with screens.

The *crushing rolls* consist of two smooth heavy cylinders revolving towards each other (usually at the same speed) and the feed rock is nipped between the rolls and pulled downward through the rolls by friction. The size reduction is relatively small, the average size of product being about 1/4th of that of feed. However, the diameter of rolls and the interspacing between rolls (which is equal to the maximum size of product) can be varied over wide ranges, thus permitting considerable variations in feed and product sizes. It is this flexibility combined with the low initial cost that have made crushing rolls still popular in spite of their low reduction ratio.

It will be interesting to derive an expression for the angle of nip which shall depend on the diameter of rolls and the product and feed sizes. Consider a spherical particle of diameter D_F fed to a pair of crushing rolls each of diameter D_R and let D_P be the interspacing between rolls (see Figure 2.3). Assuming a spherical product of maximum size, its diameter will also be D_P. The two forces acting on the feed rock (neglecting gravity force) are the tangential force F_T and the normal force F_N. The resultant force F_R if makes a negative angle with the horizontal and thus acts pointing downwards, then the feed rock will be pushed through the rolls and thus will get crushed. But if F_R makes a positive angle with horizontal and thus acts pointing upwards, the feed rock will be thrown out from the rolls and there will be no crushing. The limiting case is therefore when F_R is just horizontal. The value of angle θ (which is the angle between the two convergent surfaces of the crusher at the point of contact with the feed rock) under this condition will be equal to the angle of nip, θ_n since this is the maximum permissible value of θ beyond which crushing will not be accomplished. From Figure (2.3),

$$\cos(\theta/2) = \frac{(D_R/2) + (D_P/2)}{(D_R/2) + (D_F/2)}$$

$$= \frac{D_R + D_P}{D_R + D_F} \qquad \text{...(2.2.6)}$$

Also, when F_R is just horizontal (that is, at $\theta = \theta_n$), the vertical component of F_T [$= F_T \cos(\theta/2)$] and that of F_N [$= F_N \sin(\theta/2)$] will balance with each other. Thus,

$$F_T \cos(\theta_n/2) = F_N \sin(\theta_n/2)$$

or $$F_T/F_N = \mu' = \tan(\theta_n/2) \quad \text{...(2.2.7)}$$

where μ' is the coefficient of friction.

Thus, angle of nip, $$\theta_n = 2\tan^{-1}\mu' \quad \text{...(2.2.8)}$$

If the feed is an endless rectangular ribbon of width D_F' and is reduced to a ribbon product of width D_P (shown in dotted lines in Fig. 2.3), then,

$$\cos(\theta/2) = 1 - \left[\frac{D_F' - D_P}{D_R}\right] \quad \text{...(2.2.9)}$$

Gravity stamps, the oldest conventional devices, are still used (especially for crushing gold ores) due to their ease of construction and high reduction ratio (as much as 150) in spite of their low capacity and relatively high cost.

Tumbling mills are most extensively used as fine grinders. Here, grinding is accomplished due to the tumbling action of the grinding media (steel balls, rods, ceramic pebbles etc.) over the feed rock. *Ball mills* consist of horizontal rotating cylindrical or conical chambers made of steel or rubber-lined steel with approximately half full of steel balls. The length to diameter ratio (L/D ratio) of the chamber is close to 1.0. Size reduction is achieved by the impact of balls on the feed particles as they fall back after being lifted by the rotating chamber. They accept coarser feed than rod mills and give a product of 60 mesh or finer. Most ball mills are continuous in operation, the feed entering at one end through a hollow trunnion and leaving at the other end either through another trunnion or through peripheral openings in the shell. Ball mills can be operated either wet or dry. The tube mills on the other hand use a steel shell of (L/D) ratio more than 2.0, employ smaller balls and give finer size reduction. If the product is discharged through openings in a vertical grate or diaphragm, then the mill is termed as a grate mill. In grate mills, the pulp level or the quantity of material being ground in the mill can be independently controlled at any desired level and therefore they are more efficient than the simple overflow types. The product is of more uniform and accurate size. Moreover, the low pulp level and decreased time in the mill assist in minimising overgrinding of particles. In a compartment mill or compound ball mill, grinding is performed in stages. This consists of two to four cylindrical compartments separated by grates or perforated partitions. Each successive compartment is of smaller diameter than the previous one and contains balls of smaller diameter. In such a series-operation, heavy balls break the large particles and smaller and lighter balls break the small particles. The comminution efficiency is thus very much improved. This idea of increasing the efficiency by segregation of different sizes of balls in a grinding unit is also utilised in cylindroconical ball mills. In such a mill, the larger balls and larger particles segregate to good extent in the cylindrical portion where the diameter of the mill is maximum. Since the lifting effect on the balls is maximum at the largest diameter, larger balls (which meet larger particles) are lifted maximum, providing greater impact on the larger particles of the rock. This evidently enhances the efficiency of size reduction.

In *rod mills*, steel rods of around 2-12 cm. in diameter and that extend approximately over the full length of the mill are used as grinding media. The (L/D) ratio of the steel shell is normally 1.5 to 3.0. They produce more uniform and granular product but are relatively more expensive to operate. They are particularly useful for handling sticky materials which would hold the balls together in aggregates since in rod mills the greater weight of rods will cause them to pull apart again.

Pebble mills are used when iron contamination in the product is highly objectionable such as in the manufacture of paints and pigments, cosmetics industry etc. They use ceramic-pebbles made of flint or porcelain as the grinding media inside a cylindrical chamber also made of a ceramic material. Tumbling mills may be operated as autogeneous mills, that is without using any separate grinding media, comminution being achieved exclusively through interparticle collisions. These can be employed when the feed rock to be handled is of high specific gravity and where contamination with grinding media cannot be tolerated.

The speed of rotation is evidently a crucial parameter for tumbling mills. At low speeds of operation, the grinding media (say, balls) are lifted and they roll back over the feed rock. Comminution takes place by attrition and the mill is said to be *cascading*. At higher rpm, the balls are lifted and they fall back by gravity on the feed particles below. Grinding takes place by impact and the mill is said to be *cataracting*. If the speed of rotation is still further increased, a stage will be reached when the balls remain sticking to the wall of the mill due to centrifugal forces and there will be practically no crushing taking place. The mill is then said to be *centrifuging*. The speed at which centrifuging just starts is called the *critical speed* N_c of the mill.

Since at the critical speed, the centrifugal force and the gravity force on the ball will be just equal to each other, we can write,

$$mg = m\,\omega_c^2\,(D - d)/2$$

or, $$\omega_c^2 = \left[\frac{2\pi N_c}{60}\right]^2 = \frac{2g}{(D - d)} \qquad \text{...(2.2.10)}$$

where D = diameter of mill

d = diameter of ball

Therefore,
$$N_c = \frac{60}{\pi}\left[\frac{g}{2(D-d)}\right]^{1/2} \quad ...(2.2.11)$$

The optimum speed of operation depends on many parameters such as the shape of the tumbling body, volume of charge and type of grinding action desired (cascading or cataracting). Normally, an operating speed of 50-90% of N_c is used. Incidentally, even at super-critical speed, some grinding has been found to be taking place. This might be due to inter-particle and particle to ball attrition and also due to the fact that since the critical speed for balls in the inner zone of the mill will be higher, they could still be operating below their critical speed. Since the magnitude of N_c for dry grinding is less than that for wet grinding, the peripheral speed of dry mills is normally kept at around 90% of that of wet mills. If power consumption per kg of tumbling charge is compared, the rod mills consume relatively higher power than ball mills and ball mills consume more than pebble mills. Similarly, the specific power consumption is more for cylindrical mills than for conical mills. When the volume of charge is increased, power consumption also increases. However, the net power consumption increases upto a charge of 50% of mill volume and then decreases. This is because at high volumes of charge, interparticle collisions facilitate size reduction more significantly.

The recent advent among comminution equipment are the *fluid energy mills* which are used as ultrafine grinders. In one category of fluid energy mills, high velocity fluid streams are injected at an angle around a portion or whole of the periphery of the grinding and classifying chamber and in another category, high velocity fluid streams convey the particles into a chamber where the streams impact on each other. The Microniser and the Jet-o-Mizer belong to the first category of fluid energy mills whereas the Majac jet pulveriser is of the second category. In both cases, there is a high order of turbulence and an enormous energy release in the grinding chamber and as a result, the particles are ground to micron or submicron sizes. The fluid used is usually either superheated steam or compressed air. Due to absence of mechanical moving parts, there is little wear and tear on the machine and these mills produce an essentially uncontaminated product. Therefore, they are of great use in industries like manufacture of paints, insecticides, cosmetics, drugs and pharmaceuticals etc. Fluid energy mills can handle safely heat sensitive and explosive materials and if compressed air is used as the motive fluid, simultaneous drying and grinding can be achieved.

The *vibratory mills* like the Podmore-Boulton mills and the Vibratom use high speed three dimensional vibrations to affect comminution. Vibrational modes at around 20 hertz are introduced by means of off-centre weighting of a base-mounted motor or through an eccentrically rotating horizontal shaft. The grinding media are balls made of alumina, zirconia or silicon carbide of diameter 10-100 times that of feed, kept in spring-supported grinding chamber. Product sizes of one micron and less can be obtained from these mills.

2.3. Computer Simulation of Comminution Process

Computer simulation of the comminution process that enables one to predict the size distribution of the product material from any comminution equipment has always been an attractive proposal. However, insufficient information and too much subjective nature of the controlling parameters have been the chief obstacles. For the purpose of simulation, we define two parameters such as the grinding rate function G_i (or G_u) and the breakage function $b_{i,u}$. The suffix i denotes any particular screen in the standard test series starting from the coarsest (top most) screen and the screens above or coarser than i are designated by the suffix u. The grinding rate function G_u denotes the fraction of a material coarser than $D_{avg,i}$ that is broken in a given time whereas the breakage function $b_{i,u}$ gives the size distribution resulting from the breakage of the coarser material. Thus,

$$\frac{dx_u}{dt} = -G_u x_u \qquad \text{...(2.3.1)}$$

Obviously, $b_{i,u}$ will depend on i and u. It also varies with the composition of the material in the mill, since coarse particles break differently in presence of large amounts of fines than they do in the absence of fines. In a batch mill therefore, both G_u and $b_{i,u}$ could vary with time as well as with all other comminution variables.

Defining G_u and $b_{i,u}$ as functions of time and the various comminution variables is the primary step in computer simulation, which, as can be seen, by itself is a highly difficult task. The rate and breakage functions must generally be determined by tracer experiments. They may also be determined by grinding each size of feed separately in the mill, but this ignores the interaction of various sizes. Back calculation of grinding rate function from mill performance data often involves computational difficulties.

Once these two functions G_u and $b_{i,u}$ have been defined, than the rate at which the mass fraction x_i of the material of size D_{avg_i} varies with time can be determined as,

$$\frac{dx_i}{dt} = -G_i x_i + \sum_{u=1}^{i-1} x_i G_u b_{i,u} \qquad ...(2.3.2)$$

As for an example, the simulation package for crushing of coal is shown in figures 2.4(*a*) and 2.4(*b*). In crushing coal, for particles larger than 60 mesh (0.592 mm) it has been reported[8] that

$$G_i \propto D^3_{avg_i} \qquad ...(2.3.3)$$

and
$$B_{i,u} = \left[\frac{D_{avg_i}}{D_{avg_u}}\right]^{\beta} \qquad ...(2.3.4)$$

where β may be taken as a constant. The function $B_{i,u}$ is different from the previously defined breakage function $b_{i,u}$ and the distinction between the two should be properly understood. $B_{i,u}$ denotes the total mass fraction of material having size less than D_{avg_i} (thus, the cumulative mass fraction) resulting from breakage of particles of size D_{avg_u} whereas $b_{i,u}$ represents the mass fraction of size D_{avg_i} resulting from breakage of D_{avg_u}. For $i > u$,

$$b_{i,u} = B_{i-1,u} - B_{i,u} \qquad ...(2.3.5)$$

For $i \le u$, $\quad b_{i,u} = 0$

The values of G_i and $b_{i,u}$ are thus evaluated under 'GRINDRAT' and 'BREKFUN' using equations (2.3.3), (2.3.4) and (2.3.5). Equation (2.3.2) is then solved to get the size distribution of the material after any given interval of time Δt using Euler's approximation, given by,

$$\frac{dx_i}{dt} \cong \frac{\Delta x_i}{\Delta t} = \frac{(x_{i,t+1} - x_{i,t})}{\Delta t} \qquad ...(2.3.6)$$

Equation (2.3.2) therefore becomes,

$$x_{i,t+1} = x_{i,t}(1 - G_i \Delta t) + \Delta t\, x_{i,t} \sum_{u=1}^{i-1} G_u b_{i,u} \qquad ...(2.3.7)$$

Thus, starting from the feed size distribution $x_{i,o}$ the values of $x_{i,t}$ for different increments of Δt can be computed from equation (2.3.7) as shown under 'SIZDISBUT'. This is continued until the ultimate size distribution after time t_T (total crushing time) is obtained. For example, let $\Delta t = 10$ seconds. Thus, the size distribution after 10 seconds of comminution will be,

D_{avg_1} $\quad$ D_{avg_2} .... D_{avg_k}

$x_{1,\,1}$ $\quad$ $x_{2,\,1}$ .... $x_{k,\,1}$

After another 10 seconds, the size distribution will be

D_{avg_1} $\quad$ D_{avg_2} .... D_{avg_k}

$x_{1,\,2}$ $\quad$ $x_{2,\,2}$ .... $x_{k,\,2}$

and so on. After time t_T, the size distribution is,

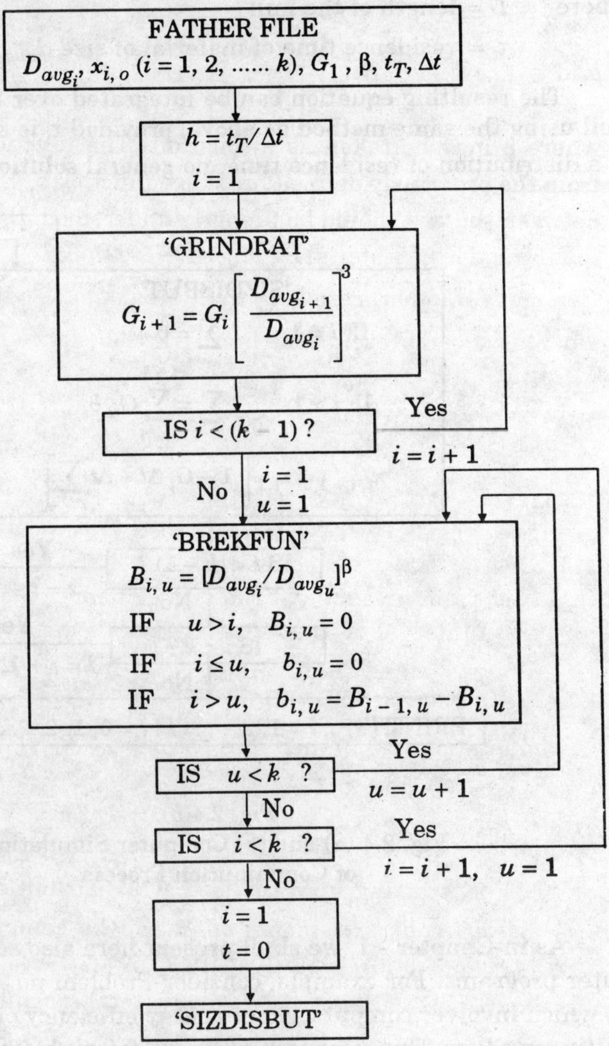

Fig. 2.4(*a*)

D_{avg_1} D_{avg_2} .... D_{avg_k}

$x_{1,h}$ $x_{2,h}$ .... $x_{k,h}$

The equation for continuous mill can be obtained from batch mill equation by noting that

$$\frac{dx_i}{dt} = (L/\tau_i)\,\frac{d\,(d_{avg_i})}{dL} \qquad \text{...(2.3.8)}$$

where L = length of the mill

τ_i = residence time of material of size d_{avg_i} in the mill.

The resulting equation can be integrated over the length of the mill using the same method as above, provided τ_i is specified. If there is a distribution of residence time, no general solution is possible.

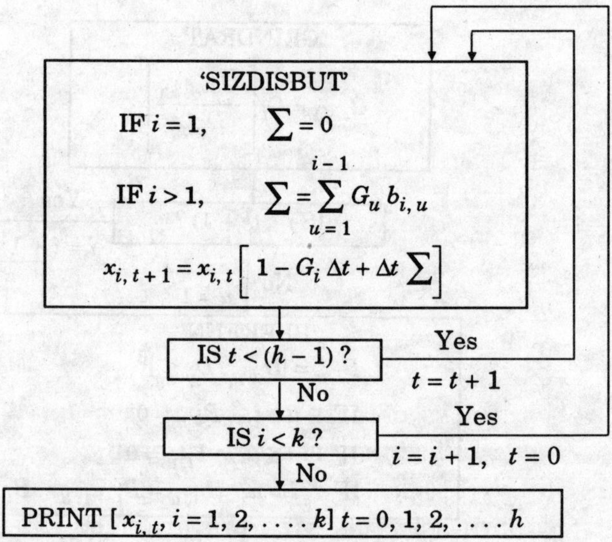

Fig. 2.4(*b*).

Fig. 2.4 (*a*) and (*b*) Computer Simulation of Comminution Process.

As in Chapter - 1, we shall present here also some sample computer programs. For example, consider Problem no. 14 of Appendix - B, which involves computation of energy efficiency of a crusher using Rittinger's law. The computer program for problems of this kind is given below (Program 2.1).

PROGRAM 2.1

```
C**     COMPUTATION OF ENERGY EFFICIENCY OF
C**     A CRUSHER USING RITTINGER'S LAW
        REAL N(50), NC(50)
        REAL M, MM, NUMR
        DIMENSION  MESH(13),  AP(13),  XF(12),  XR(12)
        DIMENSION XM(50), XP(50), DAV(50), DAVC(50)
        READ (*, *) F, R, W, ROWS, RN, SINT, XPFIN
        NP = 13
        READ (*, *) [XF(I), XP(I), XR(I), I = 1, NP-1]
        READ (*, *) [MESH(I), AP(I), I = 1, NP]
        SUMF = 0.0
        SUMP1 = 0.0
        DO 10 I = 1, NP-1
        DAVC(I) = [AP(I) + AP(I + 1)]/2.0
        DO 15 K = 1, 50
        IF [DAV(K). GE. DAVC(I)] GO TO 20
 15     CONTINUE
 20     NC(I) = N (K - 1) + [N(K) - N (K - 1)] * [DAVC (I)
        - DAV (K - 1)]/[DAV (K) - DAV (K - 1)]
        SUMF = SUMF + NC(I) * XF(I)/DAVC(I)
        SUMP1 = SUMP1 + NC(I) * XP(I)/DAVC(I)
 10     CONTINUE
C**     PARTICLES OF SIZE LESS THAN DAVC (NP - 1)
C**     ARE ASSUMED NOT PRESENT IN FEED.
        SF = (6.0/ROWS) * SUMF
C**     GAUDIN-SCHUMANN SIZE DISTRIBUTION LAW
C**     IS ASSUMED APPLICABLE FOR FINE SIZES
C**     BELOW DAVC (NP-4).
C**     COMPUTE THE VALUES OF XM(I) SINCE G-S DISTRI-
C**     BUTION LAW IS VALID FOR THE PRODUCT FROM
C**     A GRINDER ONLY AND NOT NECESSARILY FOR A
C**     CLASSIFIED PRODUCT.
        P = F
        M = P + R
        DO 25 I = 1, NP-1
```

```
25    XM(I) = [P * XP(I) + R * XR(I)]/M
C**   THE CONSTANTS B AND MM OF G-S DISTRIBUTION
C**   LAW ARE EVALUATED BY FITTING A STRAIGHT
C**   LINE THROUGH THE POINTS {ALOG [DAVC(I)], ALOG
C**   [XM(I)]}, I = NP-3, NP-2, NP-1, BY THE
C**   METHOD OF LEAST SQUARES.
      SUMX = 0.0
      SUMY = 0.0
      SUMXX = 0.0
      SUMXY = 0.0
      DO 30 I = NP-3, NP-1
      SUMX = SUMX + ALOG [DAVC(I)]
      SUMY = SUMY + ALOG [XM(I)]
      SUMXY = SUMXY + ALOG [DAVC(I)] * ALOG [XM(I)]
30    SUMXX = SUMXX + ALOG [DAVC(I)] * * 2
      AN = 3.0
      NUMR = AN * SUMXY - SUMX * SUMY
      DENR = AN * SUMXX - SUMX * * 2
      MM = NUMR/DENR
      C = (SUMY - MM * SUMX)/AN
      B = EXP(C)
C**   PARTICLES OF SIZE LESS THAN DAVC (NP-1) ARE
C**   ASSUMED NOT PRESENT IN THE RECYCLE STREAM.
      XMFIN = XPFIN * P/M
      I = NP-1
      SX = 0.0
      SUMP2 = 0.0
35    DAVC (I + 1) = DAVC (I)/SINT
      XM (I + 1) = B * DAVC (I + 1) * * MM
      XP (I + 1) = XM (I + 1) * M/P
      DO 40 K = 1, 50
      IF [DAV(K) . GE . DAVC (I + 1)] GO TO 45
40    CONTINUE
45    NC (I + 1) = N (K - 1) + [N (K) - N (K - 1)] * [DAVC
      (I + 1) - DAV (K - 1)]/[DAV (K) - DAV (K - 1)]
      SUMP2 = SUMP2 + NC (I + 1) * XP (I + 1)/ DAVC (I + 1)
```

```
      SX = SX + XM (I + 1)
      DIF = ABS (SX - XMFIN)
      IF (DIF. LT. 0.0001) GO TO 50
      I = I + 1
      GO TO 35
50    SUMP = SUMP1 + SUMP2
      SP = (6.0/ROWS) * SUMP
C**   COMPUTE THE ENERGY CONSUMPTION FROM RITTINGER'S
C**   LAW.
      ER = [(SP - SF)/RN] * F
      EFF = (ER/W) * 100.0
      WRITE (*, *) SF, SP, ER, EFF
      STOP
      END
```

The computation flow graph given in figures 2.4(*a*) and 2.4(*b*) may also be conveniently translated into FORTRAN for easy execution on a Personal Computer. The program is given below (Program 2.2).

PROGRAM 2.2

```
C**   COMPUTER SIMULATION OF A BATCH COMMINUTION
C**   PROCESS
C**   FEED TO GRINDER CONSISTS OF COAL PARTICLES
C**   LARGER THAN 600 MESH (0.592 MM) IN SIZE.
C**   INITIAL SIZE DISTRIBUTION OF FEED IS SPECIFIED.
      DIMENSION DAV(50), X(50, 101), G(50), B(50, 50)
      DIMENSION SB(50, 50)
      READ (*, *) NP
      READ (*, *) [DAV(I), X(I, 1), I = 1, NP]
      READ (*, *) G(1),BETA, TT
      H = 100.0
      DT = TT/H
C**   SIZE DISTRIBUTION OF PARTICLES IN THE GRINDER
C**   AFTER A TIME TT IS TO BE DETERMINED
      DO 10 I = 1, NP-1
      G (I + 1) = G(I) * [DAV (I + 1)/DAV(I)] * * 3
10    CONTINUE
      DO 15 I = 1, NP
```

```
      DO 20 J = 1, NP
      B(I, J) = [DAV(I)/DAV(J)] * * BETA
      IF (J. GT. I) B (I, J) = 0.0
      IF (I. LE. J) SB (I, J) = 0.0
      IF (I. GT. J) SB (I, J) = B (I-1, J) - B (I, J)
20    CONTINUE
15    CONTINUE
      DO 25 I = 1, NP
      T = 0.0
      K = 1
      SUM = 0.0
      IF (I. EQ. 1) GO TO 35
      DO 30 J = 1, I - 1
30    SUM = SUM + G(J) * SB (I, J)
35    X(I, K + 1) = X(I, K) *[1.0 - G(I) * DT + SUM * DT]
      IF (T. EQ. TT) GO TO 25
      T = T + DT
      K = K + 1
      GO TO 35
25    CONTINUE
      WRITE (*, *) [(X (I, K), I = 1, NP), K = 1, H + 1]
      STOP
      END
```

NOMENCLATURE

- $b_{i,u}$ breakage function, dimensionless.
- $B_{i,u}$ function in equations (2.3.4) and (2.3.5), dimensionless.
- D diameter of tumbling mill, *m*, diameter of the rotor of hammer mill, *m*
- d ball diameter, *m*
- D_{avg_i} average screen size of *i*-th fraction, *m*.
- D_{Fb}, D_{Pb} aperture size of screen through which 80 per cent of feed particles and 80 per cent of product particles respectively pass through, *mm*.
- D_R diameter of crushing roll, *m*.
- $D_{VS,P}, D_{VS,F}$ volume-surface diameter (sauter diameter) of feed and product particles respectively, *m*.

E	energy consumed for the comminution of M kg of material, J.
E_c	effectiveness of classifying screen, dimensionless.
g	gravitational acceleration, m/s^2
G_i (or G_u)	grinding rate function, s^{-1}
K_b	Bond's constant (see equation 2.1.6)
K_k	Kick's constant, J/kg (see equation 2.1.2)
K_R	Rittinger's constant, J/m^2 (see equation 2.1.3)
n_i	specific surface ratio of particles of size D_{avg_i}, dimensionless.
N_c	critical speed of a tumbling mill, rpm.
Q	capacity of mill, tonnes/hr.
RR	reduction ratio, dimensionless.
s_F	specific surface of feed particles, m^2/kg.
s_P	specific surface of product particles, m^2/kg.
T	capacity of crusher or grinder, kg/hr.
t_T	total crushing time, s.
x_{Fi}, x_{Pi}	mass fraction of particles of size $D_{avg\,i}$ in the feed stream and product stream respectively.
X	cumulative mass fraction.
y_F, y_P, y_R	mass fraction of desired material (material of desired size) in the feed to the screen, product from the screen and reject from the screen respectively.
W_i	work index, kWh/tonne.

Greek Letters

β	exponent used in equation (2.3.4)
θ_n	angle of nip, degrees
μ'	coefficient of friction, dimensionless
ρ_s	solid density, kg/m^3
τ	residence time, s.

Computer Notations

AP(I)	aperture size of i-th standard screen (a_i), m
B	constant in Gaudin-Schumann size distribution law (equation 1.4.1)

B(I, J)	function in equations (2.3.4) and (2.3.5), dimensionless ($B_{i,u}$)
BETA	exponent used in equation - 2.3.4 (β)
DAV(I)	average screen size of i-th fraction (D_{avg_i})
DAVC(I)	calculated value of DAV(I), m
DT	time interval (ΔT), s
EFF	overall energy efficiency of comminution process
ER	energy consumption per unit mass (E), J/kg
F	feed rate (F), kg/s
G(I)	grinding rate function (G_i or G_u), s^{-1}
M	rate of discharge from crusher (M), kg/s
MM	constant in Gaudin-Schumann size distribution law (m), dimensionless
MESH(I)	mesh number of i-th standard screen (M_i)
N(I)	specific surface ratio (n_i) of particles of size D_{avg_i}
NC(I)	calculated value of N(I)
P	product rate (P) kg/s
R	recycle rate (R), kg/s
RN	Rittinger's number, m^2/J
ROWS	solid density (ρ_s), kg/m^3
SB(I, J)	breakage function ($b_{i,u}$), dimensionless
SF	specific surface of feed particles (s_F), m^2/kg
SINT	screen interval (S_{int}), dimensionless
SP	specific surface of product particles (s_P), m^2/kg
TT	total crushing time (t_T), s
W	total energy supplied to the crusher, W
X(I, K)	mass fraction of particles of size D_{avg_i} at k-th interval of time ($x_{i,t}$)
XF(I)	mass fraction of particles of size D_{avg_i} in feed (x_{Fi})
XM(I)	mass fraction of particles of size D_{avg_i} in the mill product (x_{Mi})
XMFIN	total mass fraction of fines (whose size distribution is not given) in mill product

XP(I) mass fraction of particles of size D_{avg_i} in classified product (x_{Pi})

XPFIN total mass fraction of fines (whose size distribution is not given) in classified product

XR(I) mass fraction of particles of size D_{avg_i} in recycle (or reject) stream (x_{Ri}).

REFERENCES

1. Perry J.H. (ed.), Chemical Engineer's Handbook, 5th edition, McGraw-Hill, New York, 1973.
2. Stadler, W., Trans. Inst. Mining Met. (London), **20**, 420, 1911.
3. Von Rittinger, P.R., Lehrbuch der Aufbereitungskunde, Berlin, 1867.
4. Bond, F.C., Trans. Am. Inst. Mining Met. Engrs, **193**, 484, 1952.
5. Walker, W.H., Lewis, W.K., McAdams, W.H. and Gilliland, E.R., Principles of Chemical Engineering, 3rd ed., McGraw-Hill, New York, 1937.
6. Taggart, A.F., Handbook of Mineral Dressing, Wiley, New York, 1945.
7. Brown, G.G. and Associates, Unit Operations, Wiley, New York, 1950.
8. Arbiter, N. and Harris, C.C., Br. Chem. Eng., **10**, 240, 1965.

3

Particle Dynamics

3.1. Motion of Particles in a Fluid

There is a well-known riddle which is a favourite question of many quiz masters while conducting quiz programmes among school students, which states that a canoe containing a number of heavy steel articles is floating on water in a pond and if all these steel articles are dumped into the water from the canoe, will the water level in the pond change ? It must be remembered that whether a solid particle will float in a liquid or not depends not only on the particle size and its density relative to that of the liquid, but also on the surface characteristics of the solid or its wettability by the liquid. We know that by carefully placing a dry steel needle on the surface of water it can be made to float, but if the needle is melted to form a steel shot and then placed on water, it will sink down. The dynamics of a solid particle in a fluid thus depends on many parameters and the inter-relation among these parameters is pretty complex. Let us therefore start with a simplified analysis of the phenomenon making the following assumptions :

(*i*) The shape and size of the particle are defined. For the simplest case, let us assume that the particle is spherical of diameter d_p.

(*ii*) The particle is non-porous and incompressible (that is, its density remains constant). The particle is thus insoluble in the fluid and does not react chemically with it.

(*iii*) The density and viscosity of the fluid are constant.

(*iv*) The effect of surface characteristics or interfacial conditions between the solid and the fluid on the dynamics of the particle is neglected.

(*v*) The particle is freely settling (under gravity). This means, other particles are either absent or even if present, do not interfere with the motion of the particle under consideration.

(*vi*) The fluid forms an infinite medium. In other words, the particle under consideration is at an infinite (very large) distance from the fluid boundaries and therefore, the boundary effect or commonly called the wall effects on the dynamics of the particle can be neglected.

(*vii*) The fluid can be considered to be a continuous medium, or the particle size is much larger than the mean free path of the fluid molecules. Thus, the effect of slip between the particles and the fluid molecules can be neglected.

We are thus in a comfortable position to estimate mathematically the settling velocity of a particle in a fluid (say, liquid). When a particle falls in a liquid, the forces acting on it are, (*i*) the force of gravity acting downwards and is equal to the weight of the particle, (*ii*) as the particle moves down, it displaces a volume of liquid equal to its own volume and this displaced liquid moves up exerting an upward force on the particle called the buoyancy force, which is thus equal to the weight of the displaced liquid, (*iii*) the frictional resistance offered by the liquid on the particle due to the relative motion between the particle and the liquid. If m is the mass of the particle and ρ_s its density, then a force balance on the particle yields,

$$ma_e = mg - (m/\rho_s)\,\rho_f g - F_R \qquad \text{...(3.1.1)}$$

where (ma_e) is the net force acting on the particle and a_e is its net or effective acceleration. The frictional drag F_R increases with increase in the velocity of particle and is often called the kinematic force. At the initial stages of settling when the particle velocity is small, F_R will also be negligibly small. As a result, the magnitude of (a_e) will be quite large. Thus the particle will have a high acceleration and its velocity will start increasing rapidly. But, as the velocity of the particle increases, the kinematic force F_R (which is resisting its motion) also increases and the rate of change of velocity diminishes. Ultimately, a stage is reached when the total downward force acting on the particle (the force of gravity) becomes just equal to the total upward force acting on it (the sum of buoyancy force and kinematic force). Consequently, there will be no net force acting on the particle and the particle will then move with a constant velocity or zero acceleration. This ultimate settling velocity of the particle is called the terminal settling velocity, V_t. Therefore, once the particle has attained its terminal settling velocity, equation (3.1.1) can be written as,

$$mg\left[1-\frac{\rho_f}{\rho_s}\right]=F_R \qquad ...(3.1.2)$$

Since we have assumed the particle to be spherical,

$$\left(\frac{\pi\, d_p^3}{6}\right)\rho_s\, g\left[1-\frac{\rho_f}{\rho_s}\right]=F_R \qquad ...(3.1.3)$$

The kinematic force F_R can be expressed in general as,

$$F_R = A\,K f \qquad ...(3.1.4)$$

where A = characteristic area of the system

K = characteristic kinetic energy per unit volume

f = a dimensionless parameter

The terms A and K are to be defined depending on the situation, the system and the process under consideration. For the free fall of a spherical particle in a fluid, Newton (1724) proposed that,

A = projected area of the particle, measured in a plane perpendicular to the direction of motion of the particle

$$= \pi\, d_p^2/4$$

$$K = (1/2)\,\rho_f\, V^2$$

where V is the relative velocity between the particle and the liquid. Assuming the liquid to be stationary, V will be the free settling velocity of the particle. Since in this case F_R is the frictional drag on the particle,

$$f = f_D = \text{drag coefficient}$$

Thus, equation (3.1.3) can be rewritten as,

$$(\pi\, d_p^3/6)\, g\, (\rho_s - \rho_f) = (\pi\, d_p^2/4)\,(\rho_f\, V_t^2/2)\, f_D$$

or

$$f_D = (4/3)\left(\frac{\rho_s-\rho_f}{\rho_f}\right)\frac{g d_p}{V_t^2} \qquad ...(3.1.5)$$

Alternately,

$$V_t = \left[\frac{4}{3}\left(\frac{\rho_s-\rho_f}{\rho_f}\right)\frac{g d_p}{f_D}\right]^{1/2} \qquad ...(3.1.6)$$

If the particle velocity is quite low so that it can be assumed to be settling in the "laminar zone," then F_R can be estimated using a simpler expression proposed by Stokes (1851) :

$$F_R = 3\,\pi\,\mu_f\, d_p\, V \qquad ...(3.1.7)$$

If we substitute the above expression for F_R in equation (3.1.3), we get,

$$(\pi\, d_p^3/6)\, g\, (\rho_s - \rho_f) = 3\, \pi\, \mu_f\, d_p\, V_t$$

or
$$V_t = \frac{(\rho_s - \rho_f)\, g d_p^2}{18\, \mu_f} \qquad \text{...(3.1.8)}$$

Since Stokes' law has been developed for the specific case of laminar free settling of particles, its range of validity can be analysed by substituting equation (3.1.8) in Newton's equation (3.1.5). Thus,

$$f_D = \frac{4}{3}\left[\frac{\rho_s - \rho_f}{\rho_f}\right] \frac{g d_p\, (18\, \mu_f)}{V_t\, (\rho_s - \rho_f)\, g d_p^2}$$

$$= \frac{24\, \mu_f}{d_p\, V_t\, \rho_f} = 24/\left(\frac{d_p\, V_t\, \rho_f}{\mu_f}\right)$$

$$= 24/Re_P \qquad \text{...(3.1.9)}$$

where $Re_P = d_p\, V_t\, \rho_f/\mu_f$ and is called the particle Reynolds number. Taking logarithm on both sides of equation (3.1.9), we get,

$$\log f_D = -\log Re_p + \log (24) \qquad \text{...(3.1.10)}$$

Thus, a log-log plot of f_D versus Re_p will be a straight line within the laminar settling zone. The standard plot of drag coefficient (f_D) versus particle Reynolds number (Re_p) on log-log co-ordinates is given in Figure (3.1). It can be seen that the plot is linear for Re_p less than 0.1 which demarks the laminar settling zone within which the Stokes' law is applicable. For large values of particle Reynolds number ($Re_p > 1{,}000$), the plot is essentially flat indicating that the drag coefficient is constant and practically independent of the Reynolds number, Re_p. This is called the turbulent settling zone. For the transition zone ($0.1 < Re_p < 1{,}000$) it is difficult to propose a hard and fast correlation between f_D and Re_p. Approximately,

$$f_D = b_1/Re_p^n \qquad \text{...(3.1.11)}$$

where b_1 is a constant and n is the absolute slope of the tangent drawn to the curve that represents the dependence of f_D on Re_p (on log-log co-ordinates) at the point corresponding to the particular value of Re_p under consideration. A large number of empirical correlations based on experimental data have been proposed in the literature[1] for estimating the drag coefficient in the transition zone. Two such correlations such as those proposed by Schiller and Naumann (1933) and by Langmuir and Blodgett (1946) are given below :

According to Schiller and Naumann,

$$f_D = (24/Re_p)\,(1 + 0.15\,Re_p^{0.687}) \qquad ...(3.1.12)$$

The above relation is applicable for $0.5 < Re_p < 800$. According to Langmuir and Blodgett

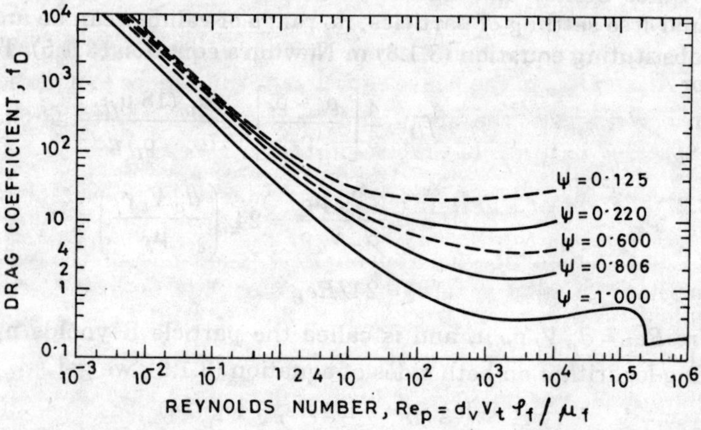

Fig. 3.1. Drag Coefficient as a Function of particle Reynolds number (from G.G. Brown and Associates, Unit Operations, Wiley, New York, 1950, with Permission).

$$f_D = (24/Re_p)\,[1 + 0.197\,Re_p^{0.63} + 0.0026\,Re_p^{1.38}] \qquad ...(3.1.13)$$

This relation is valid for $1.0 < Re_p < 100$.

It is to be noted that when the value of Particle Reynolds Number Re_p becomes too large (beyond 200,000), the drag coefficient decreases sharply. This is due to the formation of an eddy in the fluid behind the particle which travels with particle, resulting in sharp decrease in the drag on the particle.

In a more compact form, Newton's law of settling may be expressed in terms of another dimensionless parameter called Archimedes number (Ar), which is defined as

$$Ar = [\rho_s - \rho_f]\,\rho_f\,g\,d_p^3/\mu_f^2 \qquad ...(3.1.14)$$

Equation (3.1.6) can be, therefore, rewritten as

$$f_D = (4/3)\,[Ar/Re_p^2] \qquad ...(3.1.15)$$

If the relationship between f_D and Re_p is predicted by equation (3.1.11), then

$$Ar/Re_p^{2-n} = 3b_1/4 \qquad ...(3.1.16)$$

If settling zone is laminar, $n = 1.0$.

Accordingly,

$$Ar/Re_p = 3b_1/4 \quad \text{...(3.1.17)}$$

For spherical particles, $b_1 = 24.0$ and the above equation further reduces to

$$Ar/Re_p = 18.0 \quad \text{...(3.1.18)}$$

Readers can easily notice that if we substitute the expressions for Ar and Re_p in the above equation, it will reduce to equation (3.1.8). In other words, the above equation is nothing but the Stokes' law expressed in terms of the Archimedes number.

3.2. Effect of Particle Shape

If the particle is nonspherical, then one of the widely used methods to take care of its irregularity is to use the volumetric diameter d_v of the particle in place of d_p in all the above relations and also to incorporate the sphericity ψ_s of the particle as an additional parameter. The particle Reynolds number Re_p is then defined accordingly as,

$$Re_P = d_v\, V_t\, \rho_f/\mu_f \quad \text{...(3.2.1)}$$

Figure (3.1) gives the plots of drag coefficient (f_D) versus Re_p (defined as above) for different values of sphericity (ψ_s). For spherical particles, $\psi_s = 1.0$.

A number of authors[1, 2] have proposed empirical correlations (based on experimental results) to take care of the particle shape. Pettyjohn and Christiansen[3] proposed that for $Re_p < 0.05$,

$$V_t = \left[\frac{(\rho_s - \rho_f)\, g d_v^2}{18\, \mu_f}\right] K_1 \quad \text{...(3.2.2)}$$

where $K_1 = 0.843 \log_{10} [\psi_s/0.065]$

They have also proposed that for turbulent settling zone at $Re_p > 2000$,

$$f_D = K_2 = 5.31 - 4.88\, \psi_s \quad \text{...(3.2.3)}$$

Therefore,

$$V_t = \left[\frac{4}{3}\left(\frac{\rho_s - \rho_f}{\rho_f}\right)\frac{g d_v}{K_2}\right]^{1/2} \quad \text{...(3.2.4)}$$

The above relations are valid for isometric particles like cubes, octahedra, tetrahedra etc. for which the value of sphericity varies from 0.67 to 0.906. Equation (3.2.2) has been extended to non-isometric particles by Heiss and Coull[4]. They have given the values of the correction factor K_1 for non-isometric particles like cylinders, spheroids and rectangular parallelopipeds graphically as a function of particle sphericity and the ratio of volumetric diameter to projected area diameter of the particle.

3.3. Wall Effects

If the fluid does not form an infinite medium but is bounded within a confined space (say, a cylindrical container), the upward velocity of the displaced liquid will be higher which increases the resistance to the fall of the particle and thereby decreases its settling velocity. The projected area of the particle reduces the effective cross-sectional area of the container, reducing the effective flow area of the displaced liquid and as a result, its velocity increases. The effect of fluid boundaries or container walls on the dynamics of the particle thus depends on the geometry of the vessel and therefore a generalised correlation is difficult to propose to take care of this effect. We have to therefore depend on experimental correlations. For the laminar settling of a spherical particle in a cylindrical vessel, Francis[5] has proposed a correction factor as,

$$C_f = [1 - (d_p/D_c)]^{2.25} \qquad \text{...(3.3.1)}$$

If the settling zone is turbulent, Monroe's[6] correction factor could be employed :

$$C_f = 1 - (d_p/D_c)^{1.5} \qquad \text{...(3.3.2)}$$

where D_c = diameter of the container.

The settling velocity computed must be multiplied by C_f to incorporate the wall effects. For irregular particles, the above correlations (3.3.1) and (3.3.2) may still be used without serious error after replacing d_p by the volumetric diameter d_v of the particle.

3.4. Hindered Settling

When there is a mixture of particles or when it is a concentrated suspension, the individual particles tend to interfere with each other's dynamics and therefore the velocity of motion or rate of settling of each individual particle will be considerably less than that for the free settling conditions. While the motion of large particles gets hindered, the small particles tend to get dragged downwards by the large ones and thus get accelerated. It must be noted that each particle is in fact settling through a suspension of other particles in the liquid rather than through the simple liquid itself. The effective density and viscosity of a concentrated suspension (ρ_b and μ_b, commonly called the bulk density and bulk viscosity) are much larger than those of the clear liquid. The settling medium therefore offers higher resistance to the motion of the particle and thus the particle gets retarded. The upward velocity of the displaced liquid in a concentrated suspension will be appreciably large and also the velocity gradients in the liquid close to the particles are increased as a result of decrease in area and change in shape of the flow spaces. Also, since the particles are closer together, flocculation of particles takes place much more easily. Flocculation means mutual adherence of particles forming large aggregates or flocs. Each floc behaves like a single particle of coarser size and different shape than the individual particles and settles at a much larger velocity. Since the ultimate size and shape of a floc are uncertain, it is more difficult to analyse its dynamics.

Because of these additional complicacies as discussed above, the hindered settling velocity of a particle is difficult to predict accurately. It can be approximately estimated from Newton's law (equation 3.1.6) or Stokes' law (equation 3.1.8) after replacing ρ_f and μ_f by ρ_b and μ_b. The bulk density ρ_b of a suspension can be computed as,

$$\rho_b = \rho_s (1 - \varepsilon) + \rho_f \varepsilon \qquad \text{...(3.4.1)}$$

where ε = volume fraction of liquid in the suspension. To be precise, suspensions are non-Newtonian fluids. The apparent viscosity of a suspension therefore depends on its rheological characteristics. Suspensions are also two-phase systems and this two-phase character cannot also be neglected. The bulk viscosity of suspensions containing spherical particles can be however estimated empirically[7] as,

$$(\mu_b/\mu_f) = \frac{10^{1.82(1-\varepsilon)}}{\varepsilon} \qquad \text{...(3.4.2)}$$

If we substitute ρ_b and μ_b in Stokes' law, we get,

$$V_H \text{ (hindered settling velocity)} = \frac{(\rho_s - \rho_b) g d_p^2}{18 \mu_b}$$

$$= \frac{(\rho_s - \rho_f) g d_p^2}{18 \mu_f} \left[\frac{\varepsilon^2}{10^{1.82(1-\varepsilon)}} \right]$$

$$= V_t F_s \qquad \text{...(3.4.3)}$$

where V_t is the free settling velocity and $F_s = \varepsilon^2/10^{1.82(1-\varepsilon)}$. F_s is therefore the ratio of hindered settling velocity (V_H) of the particle to its free settling velocity (V_t) and its magnitude will evidently be less than

1.0. Standard plots of F_s versus ε and the viscosity ratio (μ_b/μ_f) versus ε are available in the literature.[7]

Angular particles (or even spheres once they form flocs which are often angular) tend to carry with them a volume of liquid that remains essentially immobilised within the angularities of the particle. This liquid is not adsorbed on the solid surface and the volume fraction of this stagnant liquid depends on the particle shape, size and degree of flocculation. Since this effect is more pronounced in flocculated suspensions, flocculation decreases the rate in hindered settling though it increases the free settling velocity of the particle.

3.5. Submicron Particles Settling in a Gas

The classical theories of Stokes and Newton, discussed in earlier sections, assume that the medium in which the particle settles is a continuous medium. However, if the settling medium is a gas and the particle size is so small that it is close to the mean free path of gas molecules, then there will be slip between the particle and the gas molecules which cannot be neglected. As a result, the settling velocity of the particle will be more than that computed from Stokes' law or Newton's law. Cunningham[1] has proposed a correction factor to be applied to Stokes' law to account for this effect :

$$K_m = 1 + (J\lambda/d_P) \qquad \text{...(3.5.1)}$$

where K_m = Stokes-Cunningham correction factor

$$J = 2.514 + 0.8 \exp(-0.55\, d_P/\lambda)$$

λ = mean free path of gas molecules.

The mean free path can be computed using Chapman-Enskog equation

$$\lambda = \mu_g/0.499\, \rho_g\, \bar{u} \qquad \text{...(3.5.2)}$$

where μ_g, ρ_g = viscosity and density of gas in kg/(m.s) and kg/m^3 respectively.

$\bar{u}$ = average velocity of gas molecules, m/s

$$= (8RT/\pi M)^{1/2}$$

T = absolute temperature, °K

R = universal gas constant

M = molecular weight of gas

It has been reported that this slip correction is as much as 300 per cent for 0.1 micron particles settling in ambient air.

Example 3.1. *Square mica plates 0.8 mm thick and 6.5 mm² in area (specific gravity = 3.0) are falling randomly through oil of viscosity 0.15 poise and specific gravity 0.9. Estimate terminal setting velocity of the particle assuming free settling prevails.*

Solution. To estimate the terminal free settling velocity, we can use Newton's law (equation 3.1.6) :

$$V_t = \left[\frac{4}{3} \left(\frac{\rho_s - \rho_f}{\rho_f} \right) \frac{g d_v}{f_D} \right]^{1/2} \quad ...(i)$$

where the value of drag coefficient f_D is to be obtained from the standard plot of f_D versus particle Reynolds number Re_p, corresponding to the sphericity of the particle.

Volume of each mica plate = $(6.5 \times 10^{-6})\ (8 \times 10^{-4})$

$= 5.2 \times 10^{-9}\ m^3$

Volumetric diameter (d_v) of the particle = $\left[\left(\frac{6}{\pi} \right) 5.2 \times 10^{-9} \right]^{1/3}$

$= 2.15 \times 10^{-3}\ m = 2.15\ mm$

Surface area of mica plate = $(6.5 \times 2) + [\sqrt{6.5}\ (0.8)\ 4]$

$= 21.2\ mm^2$

$= 21.2 \times 10^{-6}\ m^2$

Sphericity of the particle = $\left(\frac{\pi d_v^2}{S_P} \right) = \frac{\pi\ (2.15)^2}{21.2}$

$= 0.69 \cong 0.7$

Since the settling velocity V_t is unknown, we cannot compute Re_p and therefore the value of f_D cannot be obtained. The solution thus requires a trial and error procedure. However, the trial and error computation which could often be tedious can be avoided by using a graphical procedure as given below :

From equation (*i*), $f_D = \frac{4}{3} \left(\frac{\rho_s - \rho_f}{\rho_f} \right) \frac{g d_v}{V_t^2}$

Substituting for V_t in terms of Re_p we get,

$$f_D = \frac{4}{3} \left(\frac{\rho_s - \rho_f}{\rho_f} \right) \frac{g d_v}{[Re_P\ \mu_f / d_v\ \rho_f]^2} = \left[\frac{4\ (\rho_s - \rho_f)\ \rho_f\, g\ d_v^3}{3\ \mu_f^2} \right] \frac{1}{Re_p^2}$$

$$= K_v / Re_p^2 \quad ...(ii)$$

where $K_v = 4\,(\rho_s - \rho_f)\,\rho_f g\, d_v^3/3\,\mu_f^2$

Since, $\rho_s = 3 \times 10^3$ kg/m^3, $\rho_f = 0.9 \times 10^3$ kg/m^3,

$\mu_f = 0.015$ kg/(m.s), $d_v = 2.15 \times 10^{-3}$ m,

$$K_v = \frac{4\,(3.0 - 0.9)\,0.9 \times 10^6 \times 9.81 \times (0.00215)^3}{3\,(0.015)^2}$$

$$= 1090.84$$

Thus, $f_D = 1090.84/Re_p^2$

or $\ln(f_D) = \ln(1090.84) - 2\ln(Re_P)$ ...(*iii*)

When $Re_p = 1.0$, $f_D = 1090.84$ and when $f_D = 1.0$, $Re_p = (1090.84)^{1/2} = 33.03$. Thus, from equation (*iii*), a log-log plot of f_D versus Re_p will yield a straight line of slope $= -2$ and this straight line will pass through the points (1,1090.84) and (33.03,1). This straight line cuts the standard plot of f_D versus Re_p (on log-log co-ordinates) corresponding to particle sphericity of 0.7 at *M* as shown in Figure (3.1.1). The value of Re_p corresponding to this point of intersection is 8.0. Thus

$$Re_p = 8.0 = d_v V_t \rho_f/\mu_f$$

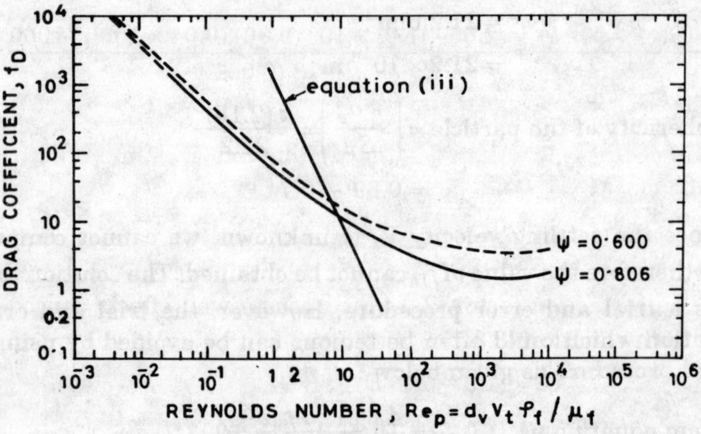

Fig. 3.1.1.

or, $$V_t = \frac{8.0\,\mu_f}{d_v\,\rho_f} = \frac{8.0\,(0.015)}{(2.15 \times 10^{-3})\,(0.9 \times 10^3)}$$

$$= 0.06 \text{ m/s.}$$

Example 3.2. *Compute the maximum velocity at which particles of silica 0.04 mm in diameter (specific gravity = 2.65) will fall through quiet water that fills a 50 mm ID glass cylinder, if*

(a) the slurry is so dilute that free settling prevails.

(b) the mass ratio of water to silica is 2.0.

Assume the particles to be essentially spherical.

Solution. Since the particle size is quite small and the liquid is water, there is every possibility that the settling zone is laminar. However, we have to first verify this. For settling zone to be laminar,

$$Re_p < 0.1$$

or,
$$\left(\frac{d_P V_t \rho_f}{\mu_f}\right) < 0.1 \quad ...(i)$$

For laminar settling of spherical particles, from Stokes' law,

$$V_t = (\rho_s - \rho_f)\, g d_p^2 / 18\, \mu_f$$

Substituting this in equation (*i*),

$$\frac{(\rho_s - \rho_f)\, g d_P^3\, \rho_f}{18\, \mu_f^2} < 0.1$$

The left hand side of above equation can be now computed by sub-stituting $\rho_s = 2.65 \times 10^{-3}$ kg/m^3, $\rho_f = 1000$ kg/m^3, $d_p = 0.04 \times 10^{-3}$ m and $\mu_f = 0.001$ kg/(m.s.). Thus,

$$\frac{(\rho_s - \rho_f)\, g d_P^3\, \rho_f}{18\, \mu_f^2} = \frac{(2.65 - 1.0) \times 10^3\, (9.80)\, (0.04 \times 10^{-3})^3\, 1000}{18\, (0.001)^2}$$

$$= 0.05749$$

Since this is less than 0.1, the settling zone is laminar. Therefore, the terminal free settling velocity is given by,

$$V_t = \frac{(0.05749)\, \mu_f}{d_P\, \rho_f} C_f \quad ...(ii)$$

The correction factor C_f to incorporate wall effects can be computed from equation (3.3.1) :

$$C_f = [1.0 - (d_P/D_c)]^{2.25}$$

$$= [1.0 - (0.04/50)]^{2.25} = 0.998$$

It can be seen that the correction factor is very close to unity since the particle size is much smaller than the vessel diameter. Substituting in equation (*ii*),

$$V_t = \frac{(0.05749)\,(0.001)}{(0.04 \times 10^{-3})\, 1000} (0.998) = 0.14343 \times 10^{-2} \text{ m/s}$$

(*b*) If hindered settling prevails, since particles are essentially spherical we can still use Stokes' law after replacing ρ_f by ρ_b and μ_f

by μ_b (equation 3.4.3). Since mass ratio of water to silica is given to be 2.0,

ε = volume fraction of liquid in the slurry

$$= \frac{(2/\rho_f)}{(2/\rho_f) + (1/\rho_s)} = \frac{(2/1000)}{(2/1000) + (1/2650)}$$

$$= 0.84$$

$$F_s = \varepsilon^2 / 10^{1.82\,(1-\varepsilon)}$$

$$= (0.84)^2 / 10^{1.82\,(1-0.84)} = 0.36$$

Hindered settling velocity, $V_H = V_t\, F_s$

$$= (0.14343 \times 10^{-2})\,(0.36) = 0.0516 \times 10^{-2} \text{ m/s.}$$

3.6. Bubble and Drop Dynamics

It is much more complex to analyse the dynamics of gas bubbles rising in a quiescent liquid or liquid drops falling in a liquid or gas. Till today, no generalised correlations are available that can predict the bubble or drop velocity accurately. The literature is flooded with a large number of experimental correlations that are highly empirical in nature and possess only restricted applicability. An elaborate coverage of all these correlations is beyond the scope of this book. We shall however discuss here the additional parameters that have to be taken into account while analysing the dynamics of bubbles and drops :

First of all, as we have already stated in Chapter 1, the velocity of a bubble or drop depends not only on its volume but also on the interfacial tension σ_i at the gas-liquid or liquid-liquid interface. Since this interfacial tension is dependent on the surface area of the bubble or drop, the bubble or drop size must be expressed as the volume-surface diameter, d_{vs}. The effect of interfacial tension is further taken care of by introducing an additional dimensionless group called Weber number, We which is defined as,

$$We = d_{vs}\, V_t^2\, \rho/\sigma_i \qquad \text{...(3.6.1)}$$

ρ being the density of the continuous phase. The dynamics of bubbles and drops therefore depend not only on the Reynolds number but also on the Weber number. Graphical plot of drag coefficient versus Reynolds number for air bubbles rising in water has been given by Haberman and Morton[2]. For the rise or fall of liquid drops in liquid media, Hu and Kinter[8] have graphically correlated the dimensionless group $(Re/p^{0.15})$ against $(f_D\, We\, p^{0.15})$ where p is a dimensionless parameter defined as $[3\, Re^4/4\, f_D\, We^3]$ and f_D is the drag coefficient. Their data are applicable to systems characterised by low liquid viscosities (close to that of water).

Unlike solid particles, drops and bubbles are compressible media. It has been shown that liquid drops rising or falling in another immiscible liquid can be considered as solid spheres if the Reynolds number is less than 10. Similarly, liquid drops falling in gases can be treated as solid spheres if the Reynolds number is within 100. However, at larger Reynolds numbers, the bubbles and drops tend to deform. At the point of discharge from the distributor nozzle, bubbles may be considered spherical, but as they move up through a column of liquid they get flattened and deformed. Also, the discrete phase, being compressible, has a tendency to shatter and shred into smaller bubbles and drops.

Coalescence of bubbles and drops is another phenomenon that is required to be considered. Gas bubbles can coalesce both in vertical and horizontal directions though vertical coalescence is more predominant than that in the horizontal direction. The effective size of the bubble or drop increases due to coalescence and suitable correction factors are required to be incorporated to take care of this effect.

Since gases possess much lower viscosity than liquids, there will be internal circulation of gas within the bubble and this in fact enhances the momentum of the bubble. For small droplets or bubbles, this effect is however not significant since the surface tensional forces resist the circulation of the fluid within the drop or bubble. One of the correction factors available in the literature[9], with which the terminal velocity of a drop or bubble within the Stokes' region must be multiplied to account for the internal circulation is given below :

$$C_F = \frac{3\mu_c + 3\mu_d}{2\mu_c + 3\mu_d}$$

$$= \frac{1 + (\mu_d/\mu_c)}{(2/3) + (\mu_d/\mu_c)} \qquad \text{...(3.6.2)}$$

where μ_c is the viscosity of the continuous phase (liquid or gas) and μ_d that of the discrete phase (fluid forming drop or bubble). It can be seen that in case of gas bubbles rising in a liquid μ_d is much smaller than μ_c and therefore (μ_d/μ_c) is too small so that the value of C_F will be approximately 1.5. But, for liquid drops falling in a gas, (μ_d/μ_c) is large and therefore C_F approaches unity. Thus, the phenomenon of internal circulation is more pronounced for gas bubbles rising in a liquid rather than for liquid drops falling in a gas. This is understandable because if the fluid inside the drop is very viscous, then the amount of energy required to induce internal circulation of the fluid will be large and consequently, the circulation effects will be small.

3.7. Classification

The term "classification" is used to designate separation of solid particles based on the difference in their terminal settling velocities in a fluid. Since the terminal settling velocity of a particle in a fluid depends both on its size as well as density, separation is affected based on both size and density. If particles of same density are separated according to their sizes, the operation is often termed as sizing. Sizing is thus a possible alternative to screening. If materials of same equivalent size are separated according to their densities, the operation is called sorting.

The basic criterion therefore required for separating two materials by classification is that their terminal settling velocities in a given fluid must not be equal. Particles (say, A and B) having the same terminal settling velocity in a fluid are called "equally falling" particles. The ratio of sizes of A and B when they are equally falling is called the *settling ratio.* If the particles are spherical, the expression for settling ratio can be derived as follows :

Since, the particles are equally falling,

$$V_{tA} = V_{tB}$$

or, from equation (3.1.6),

$$\left(\frac{4}{3}\right)\left[\frac{\rho_A - \rho_f}{\rho_f}\right]\frac{gd_A}{f_{DA}} = \left(\frac{4}{3}\right)\left[\frac{\rho_B - \rho_f}{\rho_f}\right]\frac{gd_B}{f_{DB}}$$

or, $$(d_A/d_B) = [(\rho_B - \rho_f)/(\rho_A - \rho_f)]\ [f_{DA}/f_{DB}] \qquad ...(3.7.1)$$

If the settling zone is laminar, we know that $f_D = 24/Re_p$. Therefore,

$$(f_{DA}/f_{DB}) = (Re_P)_B/(Re_P)_A = (d_B/d_A) \qquad ...(3.7.2)$$

Substituting in equation (3.7.1), we get,

$$(d_A/d_B)^2 = (\rho_B - \rho_f)/(\rho_A - \rho_f) \qquad ...(3.7.3)$$

Similarly, in the turbulent zone ($1000 < Re_p < 200{,}000$), f_D is essentially constant and independent of Re_p. Therefore, $f_{DA} = f_{DB}$.

Equation (3.7.1) then becomes,

$$(d_A/d_B) = (\rho_B - \rho_f)/(\rho_A - \rho_f) \qquad ...(3.7.4)$$

If the settling ratio of two particles is equal to that computed from equation (3.7.1), then these particles cannot be separated by classification using that particular fluid in question. A large settling ratio is therefore desirable to permit separation of material having wide size ranges. One way of accomplishing this is to use a fluid of high density as the settling medium. Density of water can be increased by adding salts to it, but this could increase corrosion problems. Use of suspensions such as magnetite suspensions in water or suspension of galena fines in water as the settling media helps in increasing the settling ratio (since the bulk density ρ_b of a suspension is much larger than that of a pure liquid) and thereby in achieving sharper separation of materials. It can be seen from equation (3.7.1) that when the density of fluid approaches that of one of the solid materials, the settling ratio approaches infinity and therefore it will be possible to sort particles of any size range. The ratio of the average size of the largest particle in the mixture to that of the smallest particle is termed as the *size ratio* and if the settling ratio is equal to the *size ratio*, complete separation is possible.

A large number of classification equipment are available in the market. The operating principle of all of them is basically the same. One of the simplest type of classifiers is the *surface velocity classifier* which basically consists of an empty tank into which the feed, consisting of the solid particles suspended in water, is admitted horizontally at a high velocity. As the suspension enters the enlarged cross-section of the tank, its horizontal velocity is decreased and as a result, the particles tend to settle to the bottom of the tank. This is because the gravity force acting on the particle now exceeds the horizontal force exerted by the fluid by virtue of its surface velocity in the horizontal direction. The tank can be divided into a number of compartments in the order of increasing area using vertical baffles. Particles of different sizes (and densities) will settle in different compartments and thus the feed mixture can be separated into a number of fractions. The fastest settling particles (coarsest and heaviest) will settle in the first compartment while the slow-settling particles (fine and light) will be carried over in the overflow from the last compartment. The same principle of operation is used in what is called the *Spitzkasten* in which the classifying chambers are conical in shape and they are arranged in series in the order of increasing cross-sectional area. The feed enters the smallest cone in which the coarsest and heaviest fraction is collected while the fines are collected in the overflow from the last and largest cone. Surface velocity classifiers though simplest in construction, have poor separation efficiency and cannot be employed for affecting sharp separations.

Elutriators use the velocity of an ascending stream of fluid to affect separation. The feed mixture containing solid particles of different sizes and density is fed from the top and the fluid (normally water or air) is sent up from the bottom. Particles whose free settling velocity is more than the upward velocity of fluid settle down and are collected as the underflow from the bottom of the chamber, whereas particles whose free settling velocity is less than the upward velocity of fluid are carried over by the ascending fluid and are collected in the overflow from the top of the column. By using a number of elutriation columns of increasing cross-sectional area in series, several fractions of solids can be sorted. The coarsest fraction is collected from the first elutriator in which the fluid velocity is maximum and the finest fraction is collected from the last column in which the fluid velocity will be the least.

The *rake classifier* consists of a settling tank with a sloping bottom and in which movable rakes (railings with fixed vertical plates) are suspended. These are often built with two or more rakes side by side. The lower end of the tank is provided with an overflow lip over which the fine particles which hardly settle and are thrown above the rakes flow out in a continuous stream. The coarser and heavier particles settle to the bottom where the rakes carry them gently upwards to the upper end the tank (which is open) and are discharged. A closer sizing of the fines can be obtained by admitting a spray of water at the discharge end of fines (lower end of tank) which will dilute the pulp and thus permit the operation to approach free settling. The Akins classifier operates in a similar manner but utilises a rotating shaft that carries a helix whereas the bowl classifier is used for classifying fine material. The power and operating costs of rake classifiers are relatively low and they are best suitable for operating in closed circuit with crushing or grinding equipment.

The *double cone classifier* is in principle an elutriator. It uses two cones, the outer one fixed whereas the inner truncated cone is supported in such a way that its height relative to the outer cone can be adjusted using a handwheel. The feed is introduced from the top into the inner cone and the hydraulic water is injected from the bottom. The feed particles move down the inner cone and as they move out the bottom opening (against a baffle), they meet the upcoming stream of water and are carried up through the space between the two cones which thus functions as the analysing column. The fines are carried over by water into the overflow, while the coarse material sinks down and is collected through the bottom-most outlet. Elutriators can also be operated with air if dry fractions of solids are desired. However, particle settling velocity will be much larger (around a hundred times larger) in air due to the low density and viscosity of air.

Example 3.3. *A mixture of an ore (specific gravity = 2.0) and the gangue (specific gravity = 7.0) has to be separated in a hydraulic free settling elutriator. If the mixture has the following size distribution (valid for both ore and the gangue) and the relation $f_D = 18.5/Re_p^{0.6}$ is valid for the flow zone under consideration, estimate the upward velocity of hydraulic water to be used in the elutriator so that the entire ore is collected in the overflow. Will the overflow be gangue-free ?*

Particle size (mm)	*Mass fraction*
– 0.58 + 0.49	0.62
– 0.49 + 0.40	0.21
– 0.40 + 0.36	0.17

Solution. If the upward velocity of the hydraulic water is more than the terminal free settling velocity of the largest ore particle, we can be certain that the entire ore will be carried over and collected in the overflow. Since from the size distribution table the largest possible size is 0.58 mm, let us estimate the terminal free settling velocity V_{tA} of 0.58 mm ore particle. Neglecting wall effects, V_{tA} can be computed from equation (3.1.6) :

$$V_{tA} = \left[\frac{4}{3}\left(\frac{\rho_A - \rho_f}{\rho_f}\right)\frac{gd_A}{f_{DA}}\right]^{1/2} \quad ...(i)$$

It is given that, $f_{DA} = 18.5/Re_P^{0.6}$

$$= \frac{18.5\,(\mu_f)^{0.6}}{(d_A\, V_{tA}\, \rho_f)^{0.6}} \quad ...(ii)$$

Substituting for f_{DA} in equation (*i*) and solving for V_{tA}, we get,

$$V_{tA}^{1.4} = \frac{4}{3}\left[\frac{\rho_A - \rho_f}{\rho_f^{0.4}}\right]\frac{gd_A^{1.6}}{18.5\,\mu_f^{0.6}} \quad ...(iii)$$

where ρ_A = density of ore = 2000 kg/m^3

ρ_f = density of water = 1000 kg/m^3

d_A = 0.58 mm = 5.8×10^{-4}m

μ_f = viscosity of water = 0.001 kg/(m.s)

Substituting these values in equation (*iii*), we get,

$$V_{tA} = 0.058 \text{ m/s}$$

Thus, upward velocity of hydraulic water must be equal to (or more than) 0.058 m/s to yield all the ore particles in the overflow.

To find out whether the overflow will be gangue-free, let us determine the terminal settling velocity V_{tB} of the smallest gangue particle.

Thus,

$$d_B = 0.36 \text{ mm} = 3.6 \times 10^{-4} \text{ m}$$

$$\rho_B = 7000 \text{ kg/m}^3$$

Equation (*iii*) can be rewritten as,

$$V_{tB}^{1.4} = \left(\frac{4}{3}\right)\left(\frac{\rho_B - \rho_f}{\rho_f^{0.4}}\right)\frac{g d_B^{1.6}}{18.5\ \mu_f^{0.6}} \quad \ldots(iv)$$

Substituting numerical values of ρ_B, ρ_f, d_B and μ_f we get,

$$V_{tB} = 0.121 \text{ m/s}$$

Since the settling velocity of even the smallest gangue particle is much more than 0.058 m/s, no gangue particles will be carried over into the overflow and thus the overflow will be gangue-free.

Example 3.4. *A mixture containing 30% (by weight) of galena (specific gravity = 7.5) and balance silica (specific gravity = 2.65) is to be elutriated with water flowing at 0.006 m/s. If the size distribution of the mixture (valid for both components) is as given below and the flow zone is essentially laminar, what fraction of galena fed will be in the overhead and bottom products and what will be the mass fraction of galena (on dry basis) in these products ?*

Particle size (microns) :	*20*	*30*	*40*	*50*	*60*	*70*	*80*	*90*	*100*
Mass fraction (cumulative) :	*0.33*	*0.53*	*0.67*	*0.77*	*0.83*	*0.88*	*0.91*	*0.93*	*0.95*

Solution. Let us first find out the size of galena particles whose terminal free settling velocity is equal to the upward velocity of water. Since the flow zone is given to be laminar, we can apply Stokes' Law. Thus, neglecting wall effects,

$$V_t = \frac{(\rho_s - \rho_f)\, g d_P^2}{18\ \mu_f} \quad \text{or,} \quad d_P = \left[\frac{18\ \mu_f V_t}{(\rho_s - \rho_f)\, g}\right]^{1/2}$$

Given that, $\rho_s = 7.5 \times 10^3 \text{ kg/m}^3$

$$\rho_f = 1000 \text{ kg/m}^3$$

$$\mu_f = 0.001 \text{ kg/m.s}$$

$$V_t = 0.006 \text{ m/s}$$

Therefore, $d_P = d_{P1} = 4.12 \times 10^{-5} \text{ m} = 41.2 \text{ microns}$

We now plot a graph of cumulative mass fraction versus particle size (on rectangular co-ordinates). The plot is given in Figure (3.4.1). From the figure, the cumulative mass fraction corresponding to a particle size of 41.2 microns is 0.685. This means, 68.5% of galena particles have a size less than 41.2 microns. Since all galena particles having size less than 41.2 microns will have a settling velocity less

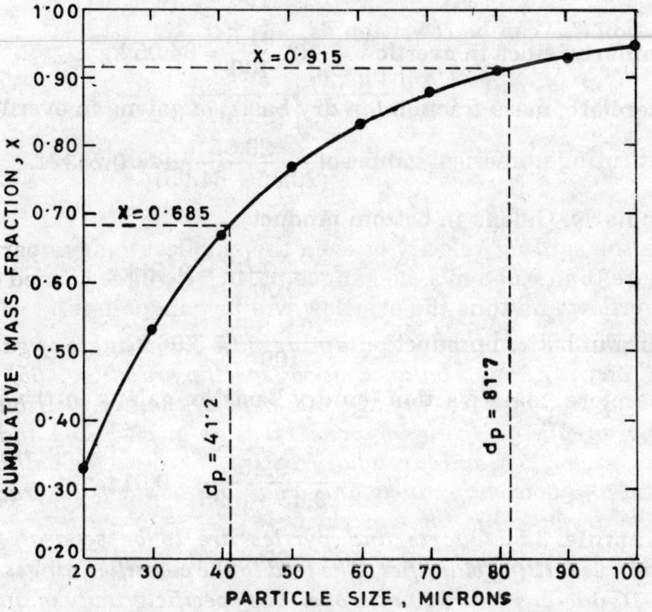

Fig. 3.4.1. Plot of Cumulative Mass Fraction Versus Particle Size.

than 0.006 m/s (upward velocity of water), we can conclude that 68.5% of galena fed will be in the overflow. Obviously, the remaining 31.5% will be in the bottom product.

To find out the mass fraction (on dry basis) of galena in the overhead and bottom products, we require to know the amount of silica in these products. Therefore, following a similar procedure, the diameter of silica particles having terminal free settling velocity equal to upward velocity of water (0.006 m/s) will be,

$$d_{p2} = \left[\frac{18 \times 0.001 \times 0.006}{(2.65 - 1.0) \times 10^3 \times 9.8} \right]^{1/2}$$

$$= 8.17 \times 10^{-5} \text{ m} = 81.7 \text{ microns}$$

From Figure (3.4.1), corresponding to a particle size of 81.7 microns, the cumulative mass fraction = 0.915. Therefore, 91.5% of silica fed will be in the overhead and the rest in the bottom product.

Let the total feed be 100 kg.

Mass of galena fed = 30 kg

Since 68.5% of galena fed has been found to be present in the overflow,

$$\text{galena in overflow} = (30)\frac{68.5}{100} = 20.55 \text{ kg}$$

$$\text{Similarly, silica in overflow} = (70)\frac{91.5}{100} = 64.05 \text{ kg}$$

Therefore, mass fraction (on dry basis) of galena in overflow

$$= \frac{20.55}{(20.55 + 64.05)} = 0.243$$

Similarly, Galena in bottom product

$$= \frac{30 \times 31.5}{100} = 9.45 \text{ kg}$$

$$\text{Silica in bottom product} = \frac{70 \times 8.5}{100} = 5.95 \text{ kg}$$

Therefore, mass fraction (on dry basis) of galena in the bottom product

$$= \frac{9.45}{9.45 + 5.95} = 0.614.$$

Example 3.5. *Quartz and pyrites are to be separated in a hydraulic free settling classifier. The feed to the classifier ranges in size between 10 microns and 300 microns. The specific gravity of quartz is 2.65 and that of pyrites 5.1. If the mixture is best separated into three fractions such as one containing only quartz, another containing only pyrites and the third a mixture of quartz and pyrites, estimate the size ranges of the two materials in these fractions. Assume the flow zone to be essentially laminar.*

Solution. Let us first find out the size of the quartz particle that is equally falling with the smallest pyrites particle. Since the flow zone is laminar and assuming the particles to be essentially spherical, from equation (3.7.3),

$$\left[\frac{d_A}{d_B}\right]^2 = \frac{(\rho_B - \rho_f)}{(\rho_A - \rho_f)} \qquad ...(i)$$

where A and B denote pyrites and quartz respectively.

Now, $\rho_A = 5.1 \text{ gm/cm}^3$

$\rho_B = 2.65 \text{ gm/cm}^3$

$\rho_f = 1.0 \text{ gm/cm}^3$

Since we are considering the smallest pyrites particle,

$$d_A = 10 \text{ microns}$$

Thus,
$$\left[\frac{10}{d_B}\right]^2 = \frac{(2.65 - 1.0)}{(5.1 - 1.0)} = \frac{(1.65)}{(4.1)}$$

or
$$d_B = 15.76 \text{ microns.}$$

This is the size of quartz particles that settle with the same velocity as the smallest pyrites particles. Evidently, quartz particles smaller than 15.76 microns will settle only after even the smallest particle of pyrite has already settled. Thus, these quartz particles ranging in size from 10 microns to 15.76 microns will constitute an overhead fraction containing only quartz.

Let us now find out the size of pyrites particles that are equally falling with the largest quartz particles. Thus, $d_B = 300$ microns and corresponding value of d_A can be computed from (*i*) :

$$\left[\frac{d_A}{300}\right]^2 = \left[\frac{2.65 - 1.0}{5.1 - 1.0}\right] = \left[\frac{1.65}{4.1}\right]$$

or
$$d_A = 190.314 \text{ microns}$$

This is thus the size of pyrites particles having settling velocity equal to that of the largest quartz particles. Evidently, pyrites particles having size larger than 190.314 microns would settle down even before the largest quartz particle has started to settle. In other words, all pyrites particles having size 190.314 to 300 microns would have settled down even before the quartz particles have started settling and thus will constitute a bottom product containing only pyrites.

The middle fraction will therefore contain the remaining pyrites particles (having size from 10 to 190.314 microns) and the remaining quartz particles having size from 15.75 to 300 microns. Summarising, the three fractions obtained shall have following size ranges :

(*i*)	Overhead fraction (only quartz)	10 to 15.76 microns
(*ii*)	Bottom product (only pyrites)	190.314 to 300 microns
(*iii*)	Middle fraction	Pyrites (10.0 to 190.314 microns) and quartz (15.76 to 300 microns)

This middle fraction may be further elutriated with water to separate the pyrites and quartz particles.

3.8. Jigging

It has been stated in the earlier section that the process of classification is possible only if the particles have different terminal settling velocities in a given fluid. Equal falling particles cannot be separated by classification. However, even if the terminal settling velocities of two particles (say, A and B) in a fluid are the same, their initial settling velocities could be different. In such cases, these particles can be separated by making use of the difference in their initial settling velocities or initial acceleration. The process of jigging is based on this principle.

In jigging, the settling of particles is confined to a very short duration and thus sufficient time is not given to the particles to attain their terminal settling velocities. The particles will be then moving with their initial velocities. We have stated at the beginning of this chapter that during the initial stages of settling when the particle velocity is quite low, the frictional drag F_R on the particle will also be negligibly small. Thus, the two principal forces acting on the particle will be then the gravitational force and the buoyancy force. The force balance equation therefore reduces to,

$$ma_i = mg - \left(\frac{m}{\rho_s}\right)\rho_f g$$

or,
$$a_i = [1 - (\rho_f/\rho_s)]\, g \qquad \text{...(3.8.1)}$$

Thus, the initial acceleration which is the jigging acceleration depends on the density of the particle and that of the fluid, but is independent of the size or shape of the particle. Therefore, jigging can be used to separate two materials according to their densities irrespective of their sizes or size distribution. The process of jigging may be thus defined as a special form of hindered settling in which stratification of particles into layers of different densities is achieved by repeatedly allowing a thick suspension to settle for a given short duration of time.

Industrial jigs are usually rectangular tanks fitted with a screen at a short distance below the rim in horizontal or slightly inclined position. Hydraulic jigs use water as the fluid medium whereas pneumatic jigs use air. Pneumatic jigs are used when dry product is desired, but due to the low density of air they do not provide sharp separation (from equation 3.8.1, it is clear that when ρ_f is very small a_i will be approximately equal to g and therefore all particles will have essentially the same initial acceleration and consequently they cannot be separated). The screen or water is given a pulsating or "jigging" motion which causes alternate upward and downward surges of liquid through the screen so that the particles are lifted off the screen over a short height and then allowed to settle down within that height. Since the height over which they are allowed to settle is very small, their settling time will also be very short and therefore, they will **settle** with their initial settling velocities. As a result, the particles will reach the screen at different intervals of time and thereby collect in different layers on the screen. The coarse and heavy particles reach the screen first and therefore form a layer just above the screen. The coarse and light particles reach the screen later and thus form a different layer above that of the coarse, heavy ones. Fine and light particles hardly settle and therefore are collected in the pulp overflow. Fine, heavy particles settle slowly and reach the bed of coarse particles already formed on the screen. Since they are fine, they pass through the interstices between the coarse particles, reach the screen, pass through the screen and are ultimately collected from the bottom chamber as the *hutch product.* Thus, we see that the fine particles settle down whereas the coarse particles remain stationary on the screen. This thus appears like the inverse of classification process in which the fines hardly settle while the coarser ones sink down to the bottom and is often termed as *reverse classification*. It is also called *consolidation trickling.*

Jigs differ among each other mainly over the method that is employed for imparting the jigging motion. In Harz jigs, the reciprocating movements of a plunger (operated by an eccentric) are used to pulsate water. The Denver mineral jig uses a rubber diaphragm to seal the plunger to the frame so that leakage of water around the plunger is avoided and this also helps in producing more positive pulsion and suction. In the Hancock jig, the screen itself is moved up and down as well as fore and aft to produce the jigging action. In Baum jigs, popularly used in coal washeries, compressed air is injected alternately to impart the jigging action.

Jigs find large scale application in coal washeries. Since small particles of slate and larger particles of coal can form equally falling particles in water, jigging is recommended for separating slate from coal.

3.9. Heavy Medium Separation

If the densities of two materials are wide apart and if they are fed into a fluid medium having density in between those of the two solid materials, then one of them will float on the fluid while the other sinks down. Thus, if $\rho_A << \rho_B$ and if the density of the fluid ρ_m is such that $\rho_A < \rho_m < \rho_B$, then A will float on the surface of the fluid whereas B will sink down to the bottom and in this way they can be separated. This is the principle behind heavy medium (or dense medium) separation.

The crucial factor in heavy medium separation is therefore to select a fluid medium that has the appropriate specific gravity to affect a sharp separation. In commercial practices, a sample of the feed is first tested in the laboratory using what is called the *float and sink experiment.* This is a simple experiment, the set-up for which consists of a number of graduated cylinders each containing a liquid of known density (see Figure 3.2). Also, each cylinder contains a liquid having density higher than that in the previous cylinder. Thus, the first cylinder contains the lightest liquid of density ρ_1 whereas the last cylinder contains the heaviest liquid of density, say ρ_4. A known weight of the feed sample (say, coal) crushed to a specific size is fed to the first cylinder. Part of the material floats and the rest sinks down. The heavy material that has sunk down to the bottom of the first cylinder is now fed to the second cylinder and the sink from the second cylinder to the third and so on. In laboratories when the test is done on coal, usually organic liquids like bromoform and carbon tetrachloride are mixed at different proportions and are used as media of different densities. It is important that the media chosen should neither dissolve nor chemically react with the solid particles.

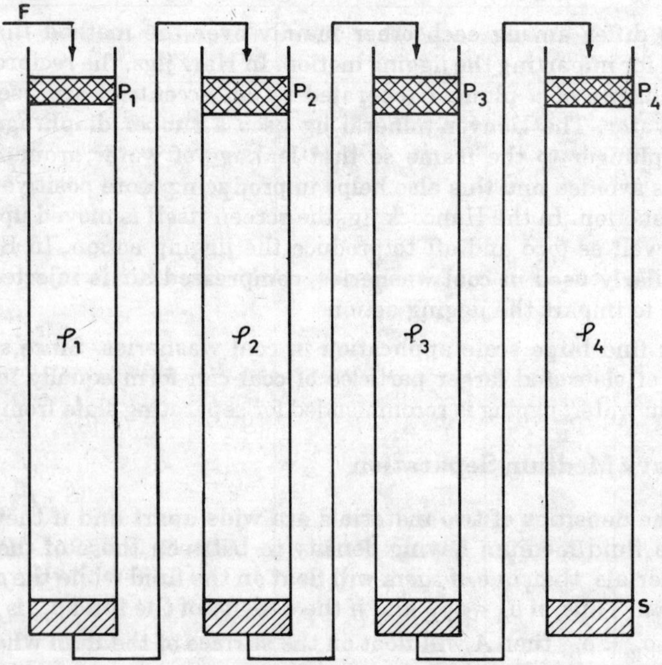

Fig. 3.2. Float and Sink Test.

The floated fractions from each cylinder and the sink from the last cylinder are now collected, dried and weighed. The fractions are then analysed. In case of coal, since the purpose of coal cleaning is to remove the mineral matter and thus to reduce its ash content, the fractions are analysed to determine the ash content of each (proximate analysis). The data can be tabulated as follows :

Specific gravity		*Yield, %*	*Ash, %*
Sink	*Float*		
—	ρ_1	P_1	A_1
ρ_1	ρ_2	P_2	A_2
ρ_2	ρ_3	P_3	A_3
ρ_3	ρ_4	P_4	A_4
ρ_4	—	S	A_s

A differential analysis of the kind given above does not enable us to directly determine the specific gravity of the medium to be employed for cleaning coal to the desired ash content. A cumulative analysis table is therefore prepared as given below :

Specific gravity		*Cumulative analysis of Float*		*Cumulative analysis of Sink*	
Sink	*Float*	*Yield, %*	*Ash, %*	*Yield, %*	*Ash, %*
—	ρ_1	P_1	$[P_1 A_1/P_1]$	$(S + P_4 + P_3 + P_2 + P_1) = 100$	A_F
ρ_1	ρ_2	$(P_1 + P_2)$	$[P_1 A_1 + P_2 A_2]/[P_1 + P_2]$	$(S + P_4 + P_3 + P_2)$	$[SA_s + P_4 A_4 + P_3 A_3 + P_2 A_2]/[S + P_4 + P_3 + P_2]$
ρ_2	ρ_3	$(P_1 + P_2 + P_3)$	$[P_1 A_1 + P_2 A_2 + P_3 A_3]/[P_1 + P_2 + P_3]$	$(S + P_4 + P_3)$	$[SA_s + P_4 A_4 + P_3 A_3] / [S + P_4 + P_3]$
ρ_3	ρ_4	$(P_1 + P_2 + P_3 + P_4)$	$[P_1 A_1 + P_2 A_2 + P_3 A_3 + P_4 A_4]/[P_1 + P_2 + P_3 + P_4]$	$(P_4 + S)$	$[SA_s + P_4 A_4]/[S + P_4]$
ρ_4	—	$(P_1 + P_2 + P_3 + P_4 + S) = 100$	$[P_1 A_1 + P_2 A_2 + P_3 A_3 + P_4 A_4 + SA_s]/100 = A_F$	S	$[SA_s/S]$

We know that by definition, cumulative yield of float means the total amount of material (expressed as the percentage of total feed) that would have floated if the entire coal had been fed to the liquid of that given specific gravity. Thus, the cumulative yield of float in ρ_1 will be P_1 itself since all the coal has been fed to ρ_1. If the entire coal is fed to ρ_2, what would have floated is $(P_1 + P_2)$, because since ρ_2 is larger than ρ_1, whichever will float in ρ_1 will also float in ρ_2. The cumulative yield of float corresponding to ρ_2 is therefore $(P_1 + P_2)$ and its ash content is,

$$= \frac{(\text{ash in } P_1) + (\text{ash in } P_2)}{(P_1 + P_2)}$$

$$= (P_1 A_1 + P_2 A_2)/(P_1 + P_2) \qquad \text{...(3.9.1)}$$

Similarly for all other specific gravities. As for sink, we prepare the table from bottom to the top in a similar way. If the entire coal is fed to ρ_4, what would have sunk is S only since ρ_4 represents the density of the densest liquid used. If the entire coal had been fed to ρ_3, what would have sunk is $[100 - (P_1 + P_2 + P_3)] = (S + P_4)$. Alternately, what is sunk in ρ_3 is what is fed to ρ_4, which is equal to the sum of float from ρ_4 and sink from ρ_4, that is $(S + P_4)$. Proceeding similarly, the table can be completed upwards. It can be seen that the first row (top-most row) in the table is in fact fictitious for sink fraction and the bottom-most row is fictitious for the float. These have been included to make the tabulation complete and also to compute the ash content of the feed coal, A_F. If the computed values of A_F from the float column and the sink column do not agree, some error in computation must be suspected.

The above data can be more conveniently represented graphically. From the plots, we can easily find out the specific gravity of medium required for affecting a given separation. We shall illustrate this with a numerical example.

Example 3.6. *A coal washery cleans the coal stock by dense medium separation using a magnetite-water suspension as the medium. A sample of coal was tested using the float and sink experiment and the data obtained are given below. If the ultimate ash content of clean coal should not exceed 6%, determine the specific gravity of the medium to be used and the percentage recovery.*

	FLOAT						*SINK*
Specific gravity	*1.287*	*1.314*	*1.341*	*1.377*	*1.423*	*1.461*	*1.461*
Weight of coal, %	*5.52*	*19.16*	*16.22*	*20.58*	*19.12*	*9.97*	*9.43*
Ash, %	*0.91*	*3.17*	*8.39*	*12.75*	*14.67*	*21.44*	*27.73*

Solution. Let us first prepare the cumulative analysis table from the differential analysis provided, as follows :

Specific gravity		*Differential analysis*		*Cumulative analysis of Float*		*Cumulative analysis of Sink*	
Sink	*Float*	*Weight of coal, %*	*Ash, %*	*Yield, %*	*Ash, %*	*Yield, %*	*Ash, %*
—	1.287	5.52	0.91	5.52	0.91	100.0	12.18
1.287	1.314	19.16	3.17	24.68	2.67	94.48	12.83
1.314	1.341	16.22	8.39	40.90	4.93	75.32	15.34
1.341	1.377	20.58	12.75	61.48	7.55	59.10	17.20
1.377	1.423	19.12	14.67	80.60	9.26	38.52	19.60
1.423	1.461	9.97	21.44	90.57	10.53	19.40	24.30
1.461	—	9.43	27.73	100.0	12.18	9.43	27.73

Now, we prepare three plots such as (cumulative yield of float) versus ash content (on cumulative basis), (cumulative yield of sink)

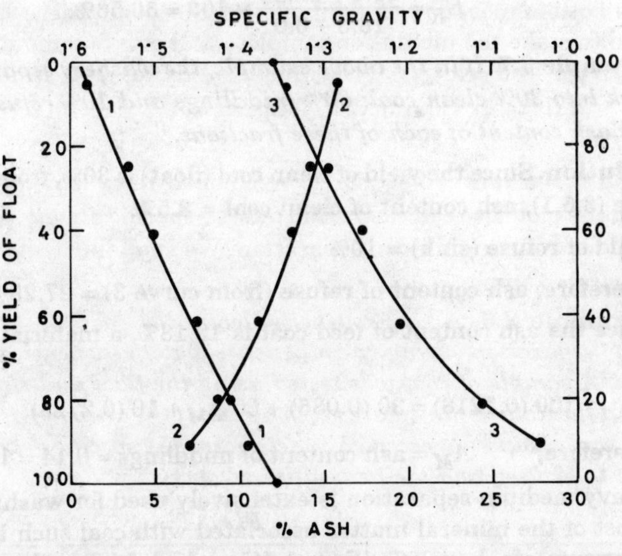

Fig. 3.6.1. Plots of (1) Percentage Yield of Float Versus Ash Content (Cumulative), (2) Specific Gravity of Medium Versus Percentage Yield of Float, (3) Percentage Yield of Sink Versus Ash Content (cumulative).

versus (ash content) and (specific gravity of medium) versus (cumulative yield of float). The plots are given in Figure (3.6.1).

From the figure, the cumulative yield of float corresponding to an ash content of 6% is (from curve-1) 53%. Corresponding to this yield, the specific gravity of medium (from curve-2) = 1.355. Thus, if the concentration of magnetite in water is so adjusted that the medium density is 1.355, then 53% of clean coal with 6% ash content will be floated off.

The percentage recovery E_R can be computed from the relation,

$$E_R = \frac{\%\text{ ash in refuse} - \%\text{ ash in feed coal}}{\%\text{ ash in refuse} - \%\text{ ash in clean coal}} \times 100 \quad ...(i)$$

From the table of cumulative analysis,

A_F = % ash in feed coal = 12.18%

Percent ash in clean coal = 6%

The ash content of refuse can be obtained from curve-3 of Figure (3.6.1). Since the yield of float is 53%, the yield of sink (assuming no middlings are collected) will be 47%. Corresponding to this yield, the ash content of sink (from curve-3) = 18.5%. Substituting in equation (*i*),

$$E_R = \frac{18.5 - 12.18}{18.5 - 6.0} \times 100 = 50.56\%.$$

Example 3.7. *If in the above example, the washery separates the coal stock into 30% clean coal, 60% middlings and 10% refuse, determine the ash content of each of these fractions.*

Solution. Since the yield of clean coal (float) is 30%, from curve-1 of Figure (3.5.1), ash content of clean coal = 3.5%.

Yield of refuse (sink) = 10%

Therefore, ash content of refuse (from curve-3) = 27.25%

Since the ash content of feed coal is 12.18%, a material balance yields,

$$100\ (0.1218) = 30\ (0.035) + 60\ A_M + 10\ (0.2725)$$

Therefore, $\quad A_M$ = ash content of middlings = 0.14 = 14%.

Heavy medium separation is extensively used for washing coal. Since most of the mineral matter associated with coal such as shale, pyrite, gypsum etc. have specific gravities much higher than that of clean coal, they can be conveniently separated by heavy medium separation. As stated in the above example, suspensions of finely ground magnetite in water are used as the dense media. However, it should be noted that the actual separation achieved in a commercial practice will not be exactly equal to that predicted from float and sink tests. This is because in actual practice additional disturbances like agitation of medium, inlet and exit turbulences during introduction of feed and removal of float and sink fractions etc. come into play. Also, with systems of high throughput, it will not be practically possible always to provide sufficiently large retention time for perfect separation.

The economic suitability of a heavy medium separation process depends chiefly on the availability of a low cost medium that can be easily recovered and reused. The recovery of the medium is particularly important when magnetite-water suspensions are used as the media since magnetite is relatively expensive and losses could significantly affect the economy of the process. The medium recovery system consists of drainage and washing screens, thickeners (sedimentation tanks) and magnetic separators. A magnetiser is also sometimes used to flocculate the magnetite particles so that the rate of sedimentation in the thickener will be larger. The particles are however demagnetised back before returning to the bath.

3.10. Falling Film Concentration

The principle of falling film concentrators or concentrating tables has been well-known for years. Tabling involves separation of solid particles according to their densities by feeding them into a shaking table or deck kept inclined at around 2 – 5° with the horizontal and a stream of water is allowed to flow down the table in the form of a thin film. The table is given a reciprocating motion or shake at the rate of 200-300 strokes per minute. The table has a roughened surface and is provided with grooves or cleats to form riffles that are usually parallel to the direction of motion of the table. The feed and water are supplied at the right upper side of the deck. Since the deck or table is tilted, the light particles are washed down by the flowing film of water whereas the dense particles settle into the grooves or riffles and due to the jerking motion of the table they are impelled forward towards the left and thus are discharged over the left edge or lower left corner of the table. The light material that is carried by water in suspension downstream overflows along the lower margin of the table and is discharged into suitable launders. The downstream movement of the particles depends apart from the density and size of the particle, on the angle of tilt of the table, the flow rate of water and the thickness of water film on the table. Provisions are therefore made to alter the degree of tilt of the table. The frequency and amplitude of the jerking strokes can also be varied within a specific range.

Tables are capable of making good separations at satisfactorily high efficiency provided the feed does not contain large percentages of middlings. They are widely used in mineral beneficiation like for the concentration of tin, gold, tungsten and some iron ores and also for the cleaning of fine coal. Dry tables or pneumatic tables use instead of water a dry blast of air. They provide dry product and are therefore suitable for application where wetting of particles is objectionable or the cost of subsequent drying operations is prohibitive.

3.11. Magnetic and Electrostatic Separations

Solid particles can be separated based on the difference in their magnetic properties by subjecting a continuously moving stream of particles to a powerful magnetic field. The response of the particles to the action of the magnetic field will depend on their magnetic susceptibility as well as the velocity of motion.

In the Davies magnetic separator, the material is fed over a magnetic feed plate when the magnetic constituents of the feed are picked up and retained by rotating electromagnets. The non- magnetic constituents pass over the feed plate into a collecting hopper. As the electromagnets pass over a collecting bin, the current is automatically switched off so that the magnetic materials adhering to them fall into the bin and thus get discharged. The Ball-Norton magnetic separator employs two horizontally staggered belt conveyors running parallel, one above the other. The material is fed to the lower belt and is conveyed under the top belt when it is subjected to a strong magnetic field. As a result, the magnetic material adheres to the lower side of the top belt, while the non-magnetic material is conveyed forward along the bottom belt. The retention time of the particles within the magnetic field can be adjusted by modifying the speed of the belts. For removing small quantities of magnetic impurities like scrap iron from a feed stock, a magnetic pulley is frequently incorporated in the belt conveyor on which the stock is being conveyed. The non-magnetic material is carried along and discharged at the far end whereas the magnetic material adheres to the belt and falls off from the underside.

Utilisation of difference in electrostatic properties to affect separation between different solid particles though known long back, is being practised today on large scale mainly for classifying fine material. If one or more materials in a granular mixture are subjected to a surface electrical charge on or before entering an electrostatic field, the particles of that material will be repelled from one of the electrodes and attracted towards the opposite electrode depending on the sign of charge on the particles. By using one or more splitters, such particles can be made to fall into separate chutes and thus a separation can be affected.

Commercial electrostatic separators consist of a grounded rotor revolving at around 200-400 rpm in an electric field. The electric field is controlled by the voltage applied to one or more electrodes (in the form of rods or more preferably as fine wires) in the vicinity of the rotor but not in contact with it. Particles fed onto the surface of the rotor either receive the charge or are grounded to the rotor and are separated accordingly. The conductive particles assume the potential of the rotor which is opposite to that of the active electrode and therefore are attracted towards the active electrode. The non-conductive particles get polarised and by virtue of their polar orientation cling to the rotor or get repelled by the active electrode. A properly placed splitter can therefore help them be collected in separate fractions. By using a pinpoint electrode, additional charging by ion bombardment can be obtained which will cause the nonconductive particles to adhere more firmly to the rolls and thus a much sharper separation can be achieved.

Electrostatic separators have become an integral part of treatment of beach sands all over the world.

3.12. Computer-aided Analysis

In the earlier sections we have discussed determination of terminal settling velocity of particles in a fluid. However, on many occasions it may be desired to determine the settling velocity of a particle at any instant or the time required for attaining a given velocity or the distance travelled by the particle within a given period of time. A generalised treatment will be required in such cases. Also, we have considered only unidimensional motion of particles (under gravity) in the earlier sections and we have assumed that the forces acting on the particle are collinear. The motion of the particle could be often two-directional (both in the horizontal as well as vertical directions) and such systems can be studied only through a more rigorous analysis with the aid of high speed computers.

Let us first consider one-directional motion of the particle under gravity, but the particle may or may not have attained its terminal velocity. We can therefore use equation (3.1.1) as,

$$ma_e = m\frac{dV_v}{dt} = mg\left[1 - \frac{\rho_f}{\rho_s}\right] - F_R \qquad \text{...(3.12.1)}$$

F_R can be substituted from equation (3.1.4) as,

$$F_R = AKf$$

$$= A\ [(1/2)\ \rho_f V_v^2]\ f_D$$

where A = characteristic area of the particle. It can be taken to be the projected area of the particle perpendicular to the direction of its motion, which however will depend on the orientation of particle in the fluid.

Thus, equation (3.12.1) reduces to,

$$\frac{dV_v}{dt} = g\,[1-(\rho_f/\rho_s)] - \frac{A\,\rho_f\,V_v^2\,f_D}{2m} \qquad ...(3.12.2)$$

Replacing V_v in terms of Reynolds number Re_p (since $V_v = Re_p\,\mu_f/d_p\,\rho_f$) we get,

$$\left(\frac{\mu_f}{d_p\,\rho_f}\right)\frac{d\,Re_p}{dt} = g\left[\frac{\rho_s-\rho_f}{\rho_f}\right] - \frac{A\,f_D\,Re_p^2\,\mu_f^2}{2m\,d_p^2\,\rho_f} \qquad ...(3.12.3)$$

Dividing throughout by $(\mu_f/d_p\,\rho_f)$ and rearranging we get,

$$\frac{d\,Re_p}{dt} = \frac{\mu_f A}{2d_p\,m}\left[\frac{2g\,\rho_f\,m d_p^2\,(\rho_s-\rho_f)}{A\,\rho_s\,\mu_f^2} - f_D\,Re_p^2\right]$$

$$= \frac{\mu_f A}{2d_p\,m}\,[\phi - f_D\,Re_p^2] \qquad ...(3.12.4)$$

where $\phi = [2g\,\rho_f\,m\,d_p^2\,(\rho_s-\rho_f)/A\,\rho_s\,\mu_f^2]$ which in fact is the maximum value of $(f_D\,Re_p^2)$ for the particle under consideration.

The above equation (3.12.4) can be now integrated between the limits $t = 0$ (when $V_v = v_o$ and $Re_p = Re_o$) and $t = t$. Thus,

$$\int_{Re_o}^{Re_p} \frac{d\,Re_p}{[\phi - f_D\,Re_p^2]} = \frac{\mu_f A}{2d_p\,m}\int_0^t dt = \frac{\mu_f A t}{2d_p\,m}$$

or,

$$t = \frac{2d_p\,m}{\mu_f A}\int_{Re_o}^{Re_p} \frac{d\,Re_p}{[\phi - f_D\,Re_p^2]} \qquad ...(3.12.5)$$

The integral on the right hand side can be evaluated either graphically or numerically with the help of the standard plot (Fig. 3.1) that gives the dependence of f_D on Re_p. From the solution of equation (3.12.5), we can thus estimate the time required for attaining a given velocity or the velocity of the particle after a given elapse of time. The distance travelled by the particle S_v within a given interval of time is given by,

$$S_v = \int_0^t V_v\,dt = \frac{\mu_f}{d_p\,\rho_f}\int_0^t Re_p\,dt \qquad ...(3.12.6)$$

The integral on the right hand side of the above equation can also be evaluated graphically or numerically once the values of Re_p at different values of t have already been computed from equation (3.12.5).

The computation flow graph for the above procedure is given in Figure (3.3). In the figure, it has been assumed that at $t = 0$, $V_v = v_o$ and at $t = t$, $V_v = (V_v)_f$ (correspondingly, $Re_p = (Re_p)_f$). We thus compute the time t required for attaining a velocity $(V_v)_f$ and the displacement of the particle S_v within that time. It can be seen that the values of f_D corresponding to different values of Re_p, obtained from the standard plot, are kept stored in Database-1. Preparation of such a database will not be very difficult since we know that within the laminar zone ($Re_p < 0.1$), $f_D = C_1/Re_p$ where C_1 is a constant and is equal to 24.0 for spherical particles. Similarly, in the turbulent zone ($1000 < Re_p < 200{,}000$), f_D is essentially constant and is equal to about 0.44 for spherical particles. In the intermediate or transition zone, values of f_D are to be taken from the plot at different values of Re_p. To sophisticated computers possessing excellent graphic facility, a few sample points could be supplied and the computer may be asked to fit a smooth curve through them keeping the truncation error the minimum. Once this plot is stored in the computer memory, the value of f_D at any particular value of Re_p (within the transition zone) can be retrieved from it. Empirical correlations (like equations 3.1.12 and 3.1.13) could also be used for computing the values of f_D in the transition zone, provided their limitations and specific range of applicability are not overlooked. Confusion may arise in defining A and d_p in equation (3.12.5). If the plot of f_D versus Re_p corresponding to a specific particle sphericity is used in Database-1, then d_p can be taken as d_v and A as $(\pi d_v^2/4)$.

We shall now discuss some of the simplified cases of equation (3.12.5). If the motion of the particle is in laminar zone, we can write $f_D = C_1/Re_p$. Substituting this in equaiton (3.12.5) and integrating we get,

$$t = \frac{2\, d_p\, m}{\mu_f A C_1} \ln\left[\frac{\phi - C_1\, Re_o}{\phi - C_1\, Re_p}\right] \qquad ...(3.12.7)$$

Substituting for ϕ and Re_p, the above equation can be rewritten as

$$t = K_L \ln\left[\frac{V_t - v_o}{V_t - V_v}\right] \qquad ...(3.12.8)$$

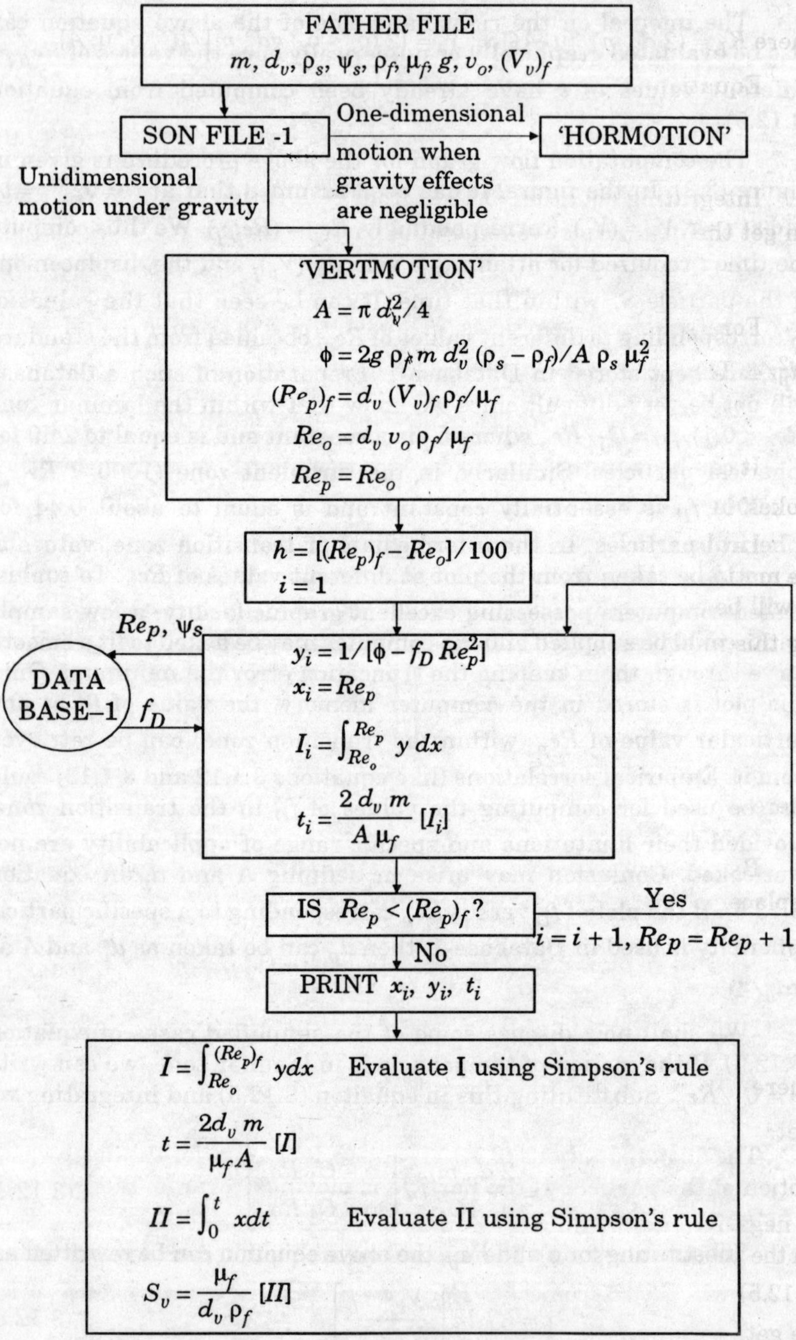

Fig. 3.3. Computer-aided Analysis of Particle Dynamics.

where $K_L = (2\, d_p\, m)/(\mu_f A C_1)$; $V_t = [2\, (\rho_s - \rho_f)\, g d_p\, m]/[C_1\, \rho_s\, \mu_f A]$

Equation (3.12.8) may be rearranged as,

$$V_v = V_t - (V_t - v_o)\, e^{-t/K_L} = \frac{dS}{dt} \qquad \text{...(3.12.9)}$$

Integrating equation (3.12.9) from $t = 0$ (when $S = 0$) to $t = t$, we can get the distance travelled by the particle in time t :

$$S_v = K_L\, (V_t - v_o)\, [e^{-t/K_L} - 1] + V_t\, t \qquad \text{...(3.12.10)}$$

For spherical particles, $C_1 = 24.0$, $m = (\pi\, d_p^3/6)\, \rho_s$ and $A = \pi\, d_p^2/4$. Thus, the expressions for K_L and V_t reduce to,

$$K_L = \rho_s\, d_p^2/18\mu_f\, ;\ V_t = (\rho_s - \rho_f)\, g d_p^2/18\, \mu_f$$

It can be seen that the above expression for V_t is nothing but the Stokes' law given in equation (3.1.8).

Let us now consider another specific case of equation (3.12.5). If the motion of the particle is in the fully developed turbulent zone, then f_D will be essentially constant so that we can write $f_D = K_t$. Substituting this in equation (3.12.5) and integrating we get,

$$t = \frac{d_p\, m}{\mu_f A\, \sqrt{K_t\, \phi}}\, ln \left[\left(\frac{V_t + V_v}{V_t + v_o} \right) \left(\frac{V_t - v_o}{V_t - V_v} \right) \right] \qquad \text{...(3.12.11)}$$

where $$V_t = \left[\frac{2g\, (\rho_s - \rho_f)\, m}{\rho_s\, \rho_f A K_t} \right]^{1/2}$$

By rearranging equation (3.12.11) and integrating we can get the displacement S_v of the particle in time t :

$$S_v = 2K_1\, V_t\, ln \left\{ \frac{1}{2V_t}\, [V_t + v_o + (V_t - v_o)\, e^{-t/K_1} \right\} + V_t\, t \qquad \text{...(3.12.12)}$$

where $$K_1 = \left[\frac{d_p\, m}{\mu_f A\, \sqrt{K_t\, \phi}} \right]$$

The above equations (3.12.11) and (3.12.12) are for the downward motion of the particle. If the particle is moving upwards, then V_v will be negative and the fluid drag on the particle will be acting downwards (in the positive direction). The integral on the right hand side of equation (3.12.5) will then become $\int (d\, Re_p)/(\phi + f_D\, Re_p^2)$. Integrating for $f_D = K_t$ we get,

$$t = 2K_1 \tan^{-1}\left[\frac{(v_o - V_v)\,V_t}{v_o V_v + V_t^2}\right] \quad ...(3.12.13)$$

Solving for V_v and then integrating, we get the displacement S_v as,

$$S_v = -\,2\,K_1\,V_t\,ln\left[\cos(t/2K_1) - \frac{v_o}{V_t}\sin(t/2K_1)\right] \quad ...(3.12.14)$$

If the particle is spherical, then $K_t = 0.44$, $A = \pi\,d_p^2/4$ and $m = \pi\,d_p^3\,\rho_s/6$. Thus, the expressions for K_1 and V_t will become,

$$K_1 = \frac{d_p\,\rho_s}{0.66\,V_t\,\rho_f}\,;\; V_t = \left[\frac{4\,(\rho_s - \rho_f)\,g d_p}{3\,\rho_f\,(0.44)}\right]^{1/2}$$

It can be seen that the above expression for V_t is nothing but the Newton's law given in equation (3.1.6).

Let us now consider the unidimensional motion of the particle when the effect of gravity is negligible as compared to the frictional resistance offered by the fluid. The particle will then move with a horizontal velocity, V_h. Though such a case is relatively unlikely (except in situations like where the particle density is very close to that of the fluid), its analysis is of academic importance for use in the analysis of two-directional motion of the particle. Equation (3.12.2) can be thus rewritten for the present case as,

$$\frac{dV_h}{dt} = -\,\frac{\rho_f A f_D\,V_h^2}{2m} \quad ...(3.12.15)$$

Substituting for V_h in terms of Re_p and rearranging we get,

$$\int_0^t dt = t = -\,\frac{2d_p\,m}{\mu_f A}\int_{Re_o}^{Re_p}\frac{dRe_p}{f_D\,Re_p^2} \quad ...(3.12.16)$$

As before, the integral on the right hand side is to be evaluated either graphically or numerically. The displacement of the particle S_h is then obtained as,

$$S_h = \int_0^t V_h\,dt = \frac{\mu_f}{d_p\,\rho_f}\int_0^t Re_p\,dt \quad ...(3.12.17)$$

The computation flow graph for this case is given in Figure (3.4). In the figure, it is taken that at $t = 0$, $V_h = v_o'$ and at $t = t$, $V_h = (V_h)_f$.

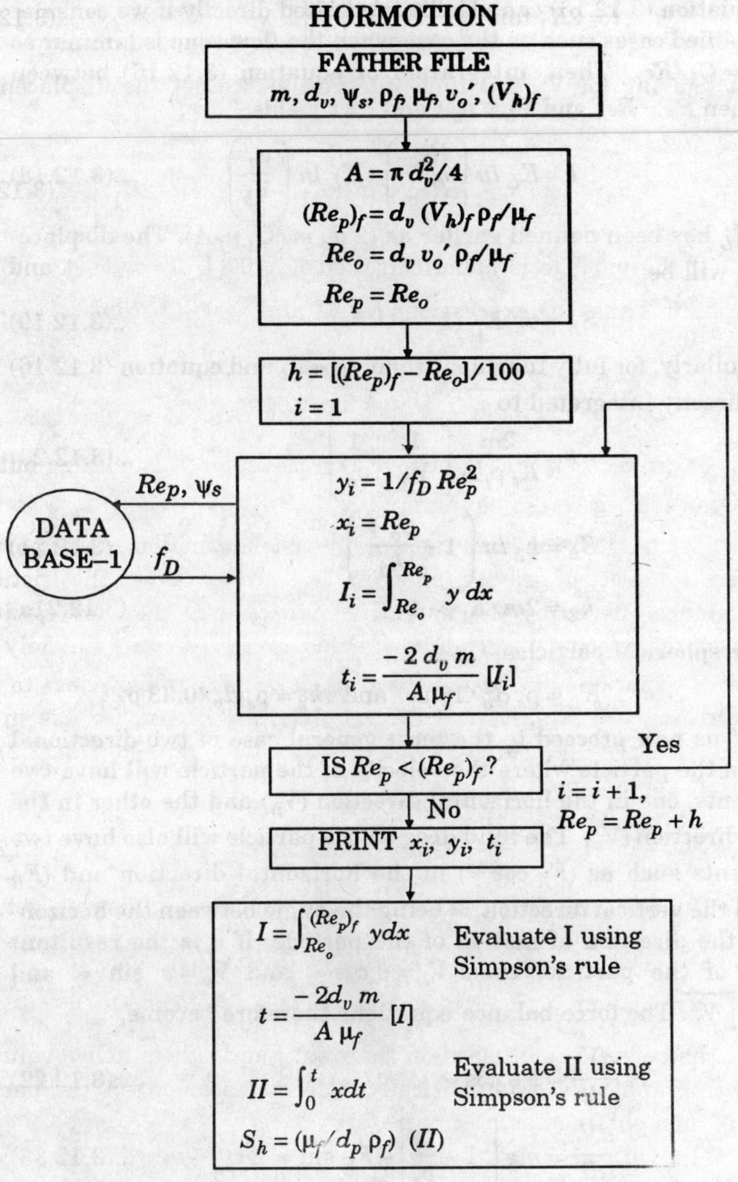

Fig. 3.4.

The time t required to attain a velocity $(V_h)_f$ and the displacement of the particle within that time (S_h) are thus computed.

Equation (3.12.16) can also be integrated directly if we consider the simplified cases such as the case when the flow zone is laminar so that $f_D = C_1/Re_p$. Then, integration of equation (3.12.16) between $t = 0$ (when $Re = Re_o$ and $V_h = v_o'$) and $t = t$ yields,

$$t = K_L \ ln \left(\frac{Re_o}{Re_p} \right) = K_L \ ln \left(\frac{v_o'}{V_h} \right) \qquad ...(3.12.18)$$

where K_L has been defined earlier as $(2 \, d_p \, m/C_1 \, \mu_f A)$. The displacement S_h will be,

$$S_h = v_o' \, K_L \, (1 - e^{-t/K_L}) \qquad ...(3.12.19)$$

Similarly, for fully turbulent zone, $f_D = K_t$ and equation (3.12.16) can be directly integrated to

$$t = \frac{2m}{K_t \, \rho_f A} \left[\frac{1}{V_h} - \frac{1}{v_o'} \right] \qquad ...(3.12.20)$$

and,
$$S_h = k_2 \ ln \left(1 + \frac{v_o' \, t}{k_2} \right) \qquad ...(3.12.21)$$

where
$$k_2 = 2m/K_t \, \rho_f A \qquad ...(3.12.21a)$$

For spherical particles,

$$K_L = \rho_s \, d_p^2/18 \, \mu_f \quad \text{and} \quad k_2 = \rho_s \, d_p/0.33 \, \rho_f$$

Let us now proceed to the most general case of two-directional motion of the particle where the velocity of the particle will have two components, one in the horizontal direction (V_h) and the other in the vertical direction (V_v). The fluid drag on the particle will also have two components such as ($F_R \cos \propto$) in the horizontal direction and ($F_R \sin \propto$) in the vertical direction, $\propto$ being the angle between the horizontal and the direction of motion of the particle. If v is the resultant velocity of the particle, then $V_h = v \cos \propto$ and $V_v = v \sin \propto$ and $v = \sqrt{V_h^2 + V_v^2}$. The force balance equations therefore become,

$$m \frac{dV_h}{dt} = F_R \cos \propto \qquad ...(3.12.22)$$

$$m \frac{dV_v}{dt} = mg \left[1 - \frac{\rho_f}{\rho_s} \right] - F_R \sin \propto \qquad ...(3.12.33)$$

Substituting for F_R we can rewrite the above equations as,

$$\frac{dV_h}{dt} = -\frac{A \, \rho_f v^2}{2m} f_D \cos \propto = -\frac{A \, \rho_f}{2m} f_D \, V_h \sqrt{V_h^2 + V_v^2} \qquad ...(3.12.24)$$

$$\frac{dV_v}{dt} = g\left(\frac{\rho_s - \rho_f}{\rho_f}\right) - \frac{A\rho_f}{2m} f_D\, V_v \sqrt{V_h^2 + V_v^2} \qquad \text{...(3.12.25)}$$

The above two equations are to be solved simultaneously. Due to the complex nature of the equations and since for a general case the dependence of f_D on Re_p (and thereby on v) can only be known numerically from the standard plot, only numerical solution of the equations is possible using the calculus of finite differences and following an iterative procedure with the help of a high speed computer.[10, 11]

However, if we consider the flow zone to be laminar, then we can write

$$f_D = C_1/Re_p$$

and, $$v f_D = \sqrt{V_h^2 + V_v^2}\, f_D = V_h\,(f_D)_h = V_v\,(f_D)_v \qquad \text{...(3.12.26)}$$

where $$(f_D)_v = C_1/(Re_p)_v = C_1\,\mu_f/d_p\,V_v\,\rho_f$$

$$(f_d)_h = C_1/(Re_p)_h = C_1\,\mu_f/d_p\,V_h\,\rho_f$$

Equations (3.12.24) and (3.12.25) will therefore simplify as,

$$\frac{dV_h}{dt} = -\rho_f A\,(f_D)_h\,V_h^2/2m \qquad \text{...(3.12.27)}$$

$$\frac{dV_v}{dt} = g\,[1 - (\rho_f/\rho_s)] - \frac{A\,\rho_f\,V_v^2\,(f_D)_v}{2m} \qquad \text{...(3.12.28)}$$

The above two equations are mutually independent and therefore can be solved separately. The values of $(f_D)_v$ and $(f_D)_h$ can be obtained from the same standard plot of f_D versus Re_p except that $(f_D)_v$ will depend on $(Re_p)_v$ whereas $(f_D)_h$ on $(Re_p)_h$. It can be seen that the above equations (3.12.27) and (3.12.28) are identical with equation (3.12.15) [for unidimensional motion of the particle when gravity effects are negligible] and with equation (3.12.2) (for unidimensional motion of the particle under gravity) respectively, the solutions to which have already been given before. Thus,

$$V_h = v_o'\,e^{-t/K_L} \qquad \text{...(3.12.27-a)}$$

$$S_h = v_o'\,K_L\,[1 - e^{-t/K_L}] \qquad \text{...(3.12.27-b)}$$

and, $$V_v = V_t - (V_t - v_o)\,e^{-t/K_L} \qquad \text{...(3.12.28-a)}$$

$$S_v = K_L\,(V_t - v_o)\,[e^{-t/K_L} - 1] + V_t\,t \qquad \text{...(3.12.28-b)}$$

If we eliminate t between equations (3.12.27-*b*) and (3.12.28-*b*), then we can get a relation between the y-displacement S_v and the x-displacement S_h of the particle. Thus, from equation (3.12.27- *b*),

$$t = K_L \, ln \left[\frac{v_o' K_L}{v_o' K_L - S_h} \right] \qquad ...(3.12.29)$$

Substituting for t in equation (3.12.28-b) and replacing S_h by x and S_v by y, we get,

$$y = [(v_o - V_t)/v_o'] \, x - V_t K_L \, ln \, [1 - (x/v_o' K_L)] \qquad ...(3.12.30)$$

where $V_t = \dfrac{2\,(\rho_s - \rho_f)\, g\, d_p\, m}{C_1\, \rho_s\, A\, \mu_f}$ and $K_L = 2d_p\, m/A\, C_1\, \mu_f$

The above equation helps us in determining the trajectory of the particle in the fluid.

To make the computer-aided analysis more handy, we shall present here a few sample computer programs as well. Let us first consider the most generalised case of computing the terminal free settling velocity of an irregular particle in a Newtonian fluid. This involves a trial and error procedure since the settling zone is not known in advance. The plots given in Figure (3.1) are to be used as a database. It shall be more convenient if this graphical database is transformed into a numerical database by converting these plots into numerical tables. Accordingly, tables (3.1) and (3.2) are prepared.

We know that in laminar zone, $f_D = C_1/Re_p$ where C_1 is a constant, the value of which depends on the sphericity of the particle (ψ_s). Similarly, if the particle is settling in the fully developed turbulent zone, then $f_D = K_t$ = constant, the value of K_t being once again dependent on the particle sphericity. The values of K_t and C_1 at different values of ψ_s are listed in Table (3.1). For the transition zone, f_D may be computed from equation (3.1.12) if particles are spherical in shape. For nonspherical particles, the values of f_D at different Re_p are listed in Table (3.2). The data of this table may be interpolated with allowable error.

Table 3.1

Particle Sphericity (ψ_s)	*Laminar constant,* C_1	*Turbulent constant,* K_t
0.125	72.0	20.0
0.22	60.0	8.0
0.600	56.67	3.60
0.806	42.0	1.60
1.00	24.0	0.44

Table 3.2

Reynolds number, Re_p	*Drag coefficient,* f_D				
	$\psi_s = 0.125$	$\psi_s = 0.22$	$\psi_s = 0.6$	$\psi_s = 0.806$	$\psi_s = 1.0$
0.1	720.0	600.0	566.67	420	240.0
0.2	395.0	340.0	320.0	220	125.96
0.4	220.0	180.0	170.0	120	64.80
0.6	170.0	140.0	110.0	80.0	44.22
0.8	140.0	100.0	85.0	65.0	33.86
1.0	120.0	90.0	75.0	53.3	27.60
2.0	75.0	56.67	45.0	42.2	14.898
4.0	50.0	36.0	30.0	20.0	8.33
6.0	40.0	30.0	20.0	17.0	6.055
8.0	37.0	26.0	18.0	14.0	4.877
10.0	34.0	21.5	16.0	11.0	4.151
20.0	28.0	16.0	10.0	7.2	2.6095
40.0	24.0	13.0	8.0	5.0	1.7346
60.0	22.0	12.0	7.2	4.0	1.40
80.0	21.0	10.0	6.0	3.7	1.2133
100.0	20.0	9.5	5.67	3.4	1.0917
200.0	20.0	8.5	5.0	2.6	0.8056
400.0	20.0	8.0	4.25	1.95	0.612
600.0	20.0	8.0	4.0	1.85	0.5261
800.0	20.0	8.0	3.8	1.75	0.474
1000.0	20.0	8.0	3.6	1.60	0.44

In the computer program (Program 3.1) given below, the drag coefficient is computed based on the above two tables.

PROGRAM 3.1

```
C**     COMPUTATION OF TERMINAL SETTLING VELOCITY
C**     OF A SOLID PARTICLE IN A NEWTONIAN FLUID.
        REAL KT(5)
        REAL MP, MEUF, KTC
        DIMENSION PSI(5), C1(5), REP(13), FD(13, 5)
```

```
      READ (*, *) MP, ROWS, PSIS, ROWF, MEUF
C**   SINCE THE SETTLING ZONE IS NOT
C**   KNOWN, A TRIAL AND ERROR PROCEDURE IS
C**   ADOPTED. ASSUME A VALUE OF VT. TO START
C**   WITH, ASSUME THAT VT IS EQUAL TO THAT
C**   OBTAINED FROM STOKES' LAW.
      PI = 3.14
      VP = MP/ROWS
      DV = (6.0 * VP/PI) * * 0.3333
      G = 9.8
      VT = [(ROWS - ROWF) * G * DV * * 2]/(18.0 * MEUF)
 10   X = VT
      REPC = DV * VT * ROWF/MEUF
C**   COMPUTE THE DRAG COEFFICIENT AT REP = REPC
      IF (REPC. LE. 0.1) GO TO 15
      IF (REPC. GE. 1000.0) GO TO 20
      IF (PSIS. EQ. 1.0) THEN
      FDC = (24.0/REPC) * [1.0 + 0.15 * REPC * * 0.687]
      GO TO 65
      ELSE
      READ (*, *) (PSI(J), J = 1, 5)
      READ (*, *) (REP(I), I = 1, 21)
      READ (*, *) [(FD(I, J), I = 1, 21), J = 1, 5]
      END IF
      DO 25 I = 1, 13
      IF [REPC. LE. REP(I)] GO TO 30
 25   CONTINUE
 30   DO 35 J = 1, 5
      IF [PSIS. LE. PSI(J)] GO TO 40
 35   CONTINUE
 40   FD1 = FD (I - 1, J) + [FD (I, J) - FD (I - 1, J)]*
      [REPC - REP (I - 1)]/[REP (I) - REP (I - 1)]
      FD2 = FD (I - 1, J - 1) + [FD (I, J - 1) - FD (I -
      1, J - 1)] * [REPC - REP (I - 1)]/[REP (I) - REP
      (I - 1)]
      FDC = FD2 + (FD1 - FD2) * [PSIS - PSI (J - 1)]/[PSI
      (J) - PSI (J - 1)]
```

```
      GO TO 65
15    READ (*, *) (PSI(J), C1(J), J = 1, 5)
      DO 45 J = 1, 5
      IF [PSIS. LE. PSI(J)] GO TO 50
45    CONTINUE
50    C1C = C1 (J - 1) + [C1 (J) - C1 (J - 1)] * [PSIS -
      PSI (J - 1)]/[PSI (J) - PSI (J - 1)]
      FDC = C1C/REPC
      GO TO 65
20    READ (*, *) [PSI (J), KT (J), J = 1, 5]
      DO 55 J = 1, 5
      IF [PSIS. LE. PSI(J)] GO TO 60
55    CONTINUE
60    KTC = KT (J - 1) + [KT (J) - KT (J - 1)] * [PSIS -
      PSI (J - 1)]/[PSI(J) - PSI (J - 1)]
      FDC = KTC
C**   COMPUTE THE TERMINAL FREE SETTLING VELOCITY
65    VT = [(4.0/3.0) * (ROWS - ROWF) * G * DV/(ROWF *
      FDC)] * * 0.5
C**   CHECK FOR CONVERGENCE
      DIF = ABS (VT - X)/X
      IF (DIF. LT. 0.001) GO TO 70
      VT = (VT + X)/2.0
      GO TO 10
70    WRITE (*, *) VT
      STOP
      END
```

Let us now translate the computation flow graph given in Figure (3.3) into FORTRAN. We shall consider unidirectional motion of solid particle under gravity. The program is presented below (Program 3.2). In the program, Simpson's rule has been used to evaluate the integral of equation (3.12.5) while for evaluating the integral of equation (3.12.6), trapezoidal rule has been employed. (Numerical integration by trapezoidal rule is discussed in the last section of Chapter – 1).

PROGRAM 3.2

```
C**   COMPUTATION OF TIME OF SETTLING AND
C**   DISPLACEMENT OF A SOLID PARTICLE
```

```
C**     THAT EXECUTES UNIDIRECTIONAL MOTION
C**     UNDER GRAVITY IN A NEWTONIAN FLUID.
        REAL KT (5)
        REAL MP, MEUF, KTC
        DIMENSION REP(13), FD(13, 5), PSI(5), C1(5),
        DIMENSION REPC (100), Y(100), T(100), H2(100)
        READ (*, *) MP, ROWS, PSIS, ROWF, MEUF, VO, VVF
        G = 9.8
        VP = MP/ROWS
        PI = 3.14
        DV = (6.0 * VP/PI) * * 0.3333
        A = PI * DV * DV/4.0
        PHIL = 2.0 * G * ROWF * MP * DV * DV * (ROWS -
        ROWF)/(A * ROWS * MEUF * * 2)
        REPF = DV * VVF * ROWF/MEUF
        REO = DV * VO * ROWF/MEUF
        N = 100
        H = (REPF - REO)/N
        M = 1
        REPC(M) = REO + H
C**     COMPUTE T(M) BY NUMERICALLY INTEGRATING
C**     EQUATION (3.12.5) USING SIMPSON'S RULE.
 10     N = 100
        H1 = (REPC (M) - REO)/N
        DO 11 K = 1, N + 1
        REPI = (K - 1) * H1 + REO
C**     COMPUTE DRAG COEFFICIENT AT REP = REPI
        IF (REPI. LE. 0.1) GO TO 15
        IF (REPI. GE. 1000.0) GO TO 20
        IF (PSIS. EQ. 1.0) THEN
        FDC = (24.0/REPC) * (1.0 + 0.15 * REPC * * 0.687)
        GO TO 65
        ELSE
        READ (*, *) (PSI(J), J = 1, 5)
        READ (*, *) (REP(I), I = 1, 13)
        READ (*, *) [(FD (I, J), I = 1, 13), J = 1, 5]
```

```
      END IF
      DO 25 I = 1, 13
      IF [REPI. LE. REP(I)] GO TO 30
 25   CONTINUE
 30   DO 35 J = 1, 5
      IF [PSIS. LE. PSI(J)] GO TO 40
 35   CONTINUE
 40   FD1 = FD (I - 1, J) + [FD (I, J) - FD (I - 1, J)]
      * [REPI - REP (I - 1)]/[REP(I) - REP (I - 1)]
      FD2 = FD (I - 1, J - 1) + [FD (I, J - 1) - FD
      (I - 1, J - 1)] * [REPI - REP (I - 1)]/[REP (I) -
      REP (I - 1)]
      FDC = FD2 + (FD1 - FD2) * [PSIS - PSI (J - 1)]/[PSI
      (J) - PSI (J - 1)]
      GO TO 65
 15   READ (*, *) (PSI (J)  C1 (J), J = 1, 5)
      DO 45 J = 1, 5
      IF [PSIS. LE. PSI(J)] GO TO 50
 45   CONTINUE
 50   C1C = C1 (J - 1) + [C1(J) - C1 (J - 1)] * [PSIS -
      PSI (J - 1)]/[PSI (J) - PSI (J - 1)]
      FDC = C1C/REPC
      GO TO 65
 20   READ (*, *) (PSI(J), KT(J), J = 1, 5)
      DO 55 J = 1, 5
      IF [PSIS. LE. PSI(J)] GO TO 60
 55   CONTINUE
 60   KTC = KT (J - 1) + [KT(J) - KT (J - 1)] * [PSIS -
      PSI (J - 1)]/[PSI (J) - PSI (J - 1)]
      FDC = KTC
 65   Y(K) = 1.0/(PHIL - FDC * REPI * * 2)
 11   CONTINUE
      SUM = Y(1) + Y (N + 1)
      KK = 4
      DO 70 L = 2, N
      SUM = SUM + KK * Y (L)
      KK = 6 - KK
```

```
 70     CONTINUE
        SUM = (H1/3.0) * SUM
        T(M) = [2.0 * DV * MP/(A * MEUF)] * SUM
        IF [REPC(M). LT. REPF] THEN
        M = M + 1
        REPĊ (M) = REPC (M - 1) + H
        GO TO 10
        ELSE
        TT = T (M)
        END IF
C**     COMPUTE THE DISPLACEMENT OF THE PARTICLE
C**     BY NUMERICAL INTEGRATION OF EQUATION (3.12.6)
        USING TRAPEZOIDAL RULE.
        N = 100
        SUM = 0.0
        DO 75 I = 1,N
        IF (I. EQ. 1) THEN
        H2(I) = T(I)
        SUM = SUM + 0.5 * H2(I) * (REPC(I) + REO)
        ELSE
        H2(I) = T(I) - T (I - 1)
        SUM = SUM + 0.5 * H2(I) * [REPC (I - 1) + REPC (I)]
        END IF
 75     CONTINUE
        SV = [MEUF/(DV * ROWF)] * SUM
        WRITE (*, *) TT, SV
        STOP
        END
```

As we have stated earlier, a rigorous analysis of two-dimensional motion of solid particles is pretty complex. However, if the settling zone is known to be laminar, then the velocity and displacement of the particles can be evaluated from equations (3.12.27*a*) to (3.12.28*b*). The computer program for such a situation is given below (Program 3.3).

PROGRAM 3.3

```
C**     COMPUTATION OF VELOCITY AND DISPLACEMENT
C**     OF A SOLID PARTICLE THAT EXECUTES TWO-
C**     DIMENSIONAL MOTION IN LAMINAR ZONE
```

```
C**      IN A NEWTONIAN FLUID
C**      VELOCITY AND DISPLACEMENT OF PARTICLE
C**      AT ANY TIME T ARE COMPUTED.
         REAL MP, KL, MEUF
         DIMENSION PSI(5), C1(5)
         READ (*, *) MP, ROWS, PSIS, ROWF, MEUF, VO, VOP, T
         READ (*, *) [PSI(I), C1(I), I = 1, 5]
         DO 10 I = 1, 5
         IF [PSIS. LE. PSI(I)] GO TO 15
  10     CONTINUE
  15     C1C = C1 (I - 1) + [C1 (I) - C1 (I - 1)] * [PSIS -
         PSI (I - 1)]/[PSI (I) - PSI (I - 1)]
         VP = MP/ROWS
         PI = 3.14
         DV = (6.0 * VP/PI) * * 0.3333
         A = PI * DV * DV/4.0
         KL = 2.0 * DV * MP/(A * C1C * MEUF)
         G = 9.8
         VT = 2.0 * (ROWS - ROWF) * G * DV * MP/(C1C * A *
         ROWS * MEUF)
         VH = VOP * EXP (- T/KL)
         VV = VT - (VT - VO) * EXP ( - T/KL)
         V = SQRT (VV * * 2 + VH * * 2)
         SH = VOP * KL * [1.0 - EXP ( - T/KL)]
         SV = KL * (VT - VO) * [EXP (- T/KL) - 1.0] + (VT * T)
         WRITE (*, *) V, VH, VV, SH, SV
         STOP
         END
```

NOMENCLATURE

- A characteristic area of the system (see equation 3.1.4), m^2 ; ash content of coal sample (see under heavy medium separation)
- A_F ash content of feed coal.
- A_M ash content of middlings.
- a_e effective (or, net) acceleration of a particle settling in a fluid, m/s^2.

a_i initial acceleration of a particle settling in a fluid, m/s^2.

C_f correction factor to account for wall effects (see equations 3.3.1 and 3.3.2), dimensionless.

C_F Correction factor to account for internal circulation (see equation 3.6.2), dimensionless

d_p particle size (diameter), m.

d_v volumetric diameter of particle, m.

d_{vs} volume-surface diameter (Sauter diameter) of particle, bubble or drop, m.

D_c diameter of container, m.

E_R percentage recovery in heavy medium separation.

F_R kinematic force, N.

F_s ratio of hindered settling velocity of a particle to its free settling velocity, dimensionless.

f_D drag coefficient, dimensionless.

g gravitational acceleration, m/s^2.

J coefficient used in equation (3.5.1).

K characteristic kinetic energy per unit volume (see equation 3.1.4), N/m^2.

K_m Stokes-Cunningham correction factor, dimensionless.

m mass of the particle, kg.

Re_p particle Reynolds number, dimensionless.

Re_o value of Re_p at $t = 0$, dimensionless.

S_h horizontal displacement (x-displacement) of the particle, m.

S_v vertical displacement (y-displacement) of the particle, m.

$\overline{u}$ average velocity of gas molecules, m/s.

V relative velocity between the particle and the fluid, m/s.

V_h horizontal velocity of the particle, m/s.

V_H hindered settling velocity of the particle, m/s.

v_o vertical velocity of the particle at $t = 0$, m/s.

v_o' horizontal velocity of the particle at $t = 0$, m/s.

V_t terminal settling velocity of the particle in the fluid, m/s.

V_v vertical velocity of the particle, m/s.

$(V_h)_f$, $(V_v)_f$ horizontal velocity and vertical velocity respectively of theparticle after a time t, m/s.

We Weber number, dimensionless.

X cumulative mass fraction.

Greek Letters

λ mean free path of gas molecules, m.

ε volume fraction of liquid in a suspension

ψ_s sphericity, dimensionless

ρ density of continuous phase, kg/m^3

ρ_b bulk density of suspension, kg/m^3

ρ_f fluid density, kg/m^3

ρ_g density of gas, kg/m^3

ρ_m density of medium used in heavy medium separation, kg/m^3.

ρ_s solid density, kg/m^3.

μ_b bulk viscosity of suspension, kg/(ms).

μ_c viscosity of continuous phase, kg/(ms).

μ_d viscosity of discrete phase, kg/(ms).

μ_f fluid viscosity, kg/(ms).

μ_g viscosity of gas, kg/(ms).

σ_i interfacial tension, N/m.

Computer Notations

A characteristic area of the particle, m^2

C1(I) values of empirical constant (see Table 3.1)

C1C calculated value of C1

DV volumetric diameter of particle (d_v), m

FD(I, J) drag coefficient at any specified values of Re_p and ψ_s (see Table 3.2)

FDC calculated value of drag coefficient

KL parameter (K_L) defined in equation (3.12.8)

KT(I) values of drag coefficient in fully developed turbulent zone (K_t, see Table 3.1)

KTC calculated value of KT

MP	mass of particle (m), kg
MEUF	viscosity of fluid (μ_f), kg/(m.s)
PHIL	parameter (ϕ) defined in equation (3.12.4)
PSIS	sphericity (ψ_s) of particle under consideration
PSI(J)	values of particle sphericity (see Table 3.1)
REP(I)	values of particle Reynolds number (see Table 3.2)
REPC	calculated value of particle Reynolds number
REPC(I)	value of Re_p at time T(I)
REPF	value of Re_p at the end of the specified settling time [$(Re_p)_f$]
REPO	value of Re_p at $t = 0$ (Re_o)
ROWF	fluid density (ρ_f), kg/m^3
ROWS	solid density (ρ_s), kg/m^3
SH	horizontal displacement of particle (S_h), m/s
SV	vertical displacement of particle (S_v), m/s
T(I)	time, s
TT	stipulated settling time, s
V	resultant velocity of particle executing two-directional motion, m/s
VH	horizontal velocity of particle (V_h), m/s
VO	vertical velocity of particle at $t = 0$ (v_o), m/s
VOP	horizontal velocity of particle at $t = 0$ (v_o'), m/s
VP	volume of particle, m^3
VT	terminal free settling velocity of particle in the fluid (V_t), m/s
VV	vertical velocity of particle (V_v), m/s
VVF	vertical velocity of particle at the end of the specified settling time [$(V_v)_f$], m/s

REFERENCES

1. Strauss, W., Industrial Gas Cleaning, Pergamon Press, Oxford, 1966.
2. Perry, J.H. (ed.), Chemical Engineers' Handbook, 5th edition, McGraw-Hill, New York, 1973.
3. Pettyjohn, E.S. and Christiansen, E.B., Chem. Eng. Prog., **44**, 157, 1948.
4. Heiss, J.F. and Coull, J., Chem. Eng. Prog., **48**, 133, 1952.

5. Francis, A.W., Physics, **4**, 403, 1933.
6. Munroe, H.S., Trans. Am. Inst. Mining Met. Engrs., **17**, 637, 1889.
7. Brown, G.G. and Associates, Unit Operations, Wiley, New York, 1950.
8. Hu and Kinter, AIChE J., **1**, 42, 1955.
9. Coulson, J.M. and Richardson, J.F., Chemical Engineering, Vol. 2, Pergamon Press, Oxford, 1962.
10. Hildebrand, F.B., Introduction to Numerical Analysis, 2nd edition, McGraw-Hill, New York, 1974.
11. Krishnamurthy, E.V. and Sen, S.K., Computer Based Numerical Algorithms, East-West Press, New Delhi, 1976.

4

Sedimentation

Sedimentation involves separation of a suspension or a slurry into a supernatant clear liquid that is essentially free from particles and a thick sludge containing a high concentration of solids. It is thus a process of phase separation. The sedimentor is called thickener if the concentrated sludge is our primary desired product and it is called clarifier if the objective is to recover the clear liquid from the suspension.

Industrial sedimentation is conducted as a continuous process in thickeners or gravity sedimentation tanks that are usually shallow tanks several meters in diameter that receive the slurry at the centre or side, permit the overflow of the supernatant liquid (over weirs) and produce a thick sludge from the bottom. The tank bottom is often made conical to facilitate the discharge of the underflow sludge. The tanks are also fitted with rakes (which are rotating railings with fixed vertical plates) positioned slightly above the tank bottom. These rakes scrap or sweep the tank floor, thereby directing the sludge towards the central discharge. When a suspension containing very fine particles is being handled, the rate of sedimentation will be extremely low. The rate can be artificially increased by adding an electrolyte which causes precipitation of colloidal particles and the formation of flocs. The suspension may also be heated to lower the viscosity of the liquid. Slow agitation of the slurry can also help in reducing the apparent viscosity of the suspension as well as assist in the consolidation of the sediment.

A sedimentor has a two-fold function. Firstly, it must produce a clarified liquid that is as free from particles as possible. This is called the clarifying capacity of the sedimentor. If the overflow liquid must be free from particles, then the upward velocity of the liquid must be always less than the settling velocity of the particles. Thus, for a given throughput, the clarifying capacity depends on the diameter or cross-sectional area of the tank. Secondly, it must produce a thick sludge that is as concentrated with solids as possible. The degree of thickening of the sludge is controlled by the time of residence of the particles in the tank and hence by the depth of the tank below the feed inlet. Since industrial thickeners are constructed in large sizes, even a minor over-design of the tank could fetch significant financial loss to the concern.

4.1. Design of Gravity Sedimentation Tanks

Though apparently appears to be a simple process, sedimentation in fact is a complex phenomenon to analyse and its rate is difficult to predict as a large number of factors are involved. As the process of sedimentation proceeds, the slurry becomes more and more concentrated and as a result, the rate of settling of particles decreases. Sedimentation is thus a time-dependent phenomenon, its rate decreasing with time and therefore a transient analysis of the phenomena becomes imperative. As the slurry gets concentrated, the tendency of the particles to interact with each other's dynamics becomes more predominant and since the particles get closer together, they tend to form flocs. Since the ultimate size and shape of a floc is difficult to predict, its dynamics is more complex to analyse as its trajectory becomes uncertain with respect to the flow parameters. As we have discussed in Chapter 2, the apparent viscosity of the suspension is normally empirically computed. Its accurate determination requires accurate knowledge of the rheological properties of the suspension. We know that the upward velocity of the displaced liquid in a concentrated suspension is appreciable that decreases the apparent settling velocity of the particles relative to the liquid. Also, the velocity gradients in the fluid close to the particles are increased as a result of the change in area and shape of the flow spaces. Because of these many-sided complicacies involved, a preliminary study of the phenomenon is usually performed in the laboratory on a sample of the slurry in what is called the *batch sedimentation test*.

The procedure of the batch sedimentation test is quite simple. A sample of the slurry is taken in a graduated cylinder and is kept under observation. The height of the free surface from the bottom of the cylinder Z_o at $t = 0$ is first noted down. The test is to be conducted under isothermal conditions since temperature variations can cause free convection currents in the medium. At the outset, the particles settle at their maximum hindered settling velocity and the rate of sedimentation will be essentially constant. Soon a zone of clear liquid (CL) develops at the top, below it appears the thickening zone (TH) of essentially uniform concentration of solids and the heavy sludge or sediment that accumulates at the bottom constitutes the compression zone (CMP). A transition zone (TS) may also appear between the thickening zone and the compression zone, however this will fast disappear (see Figure 4.1).

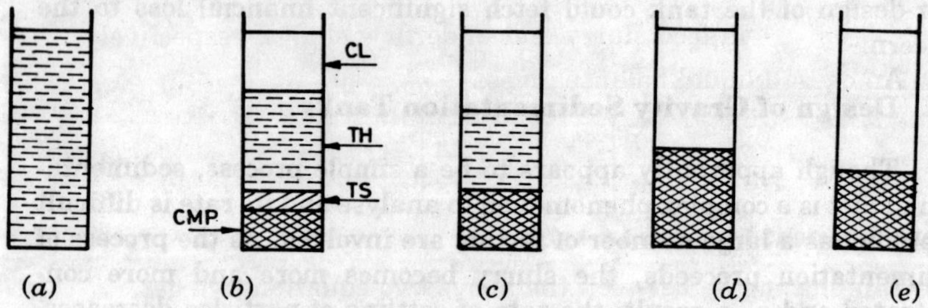

Fig. 4.1. Batch Sedimentation Test.

As settling proceeds, the interface between the thickening zone and the clear liquid zone descends down, decreasing the height of the thickening zone and increasing that of the clear liquid and compression zones. The height of this interface (measured from the bottom of the cylinder) is thus measured at different intervals of time t and the data are recorded. As the process is in progress, the density and viscosity of the suspension increase and the sedimentation rate gradually decreases. Ultimately a stage is reached when the thickening zone disappears and the two interfaces (the interface between the thickening zone and clear liquid zone and that between thickening zone and compression zone) merge with each other leaving behind only two zones such as the clear liquid zone and the compression zone. The time at which this occurs is called the *critical sedimentation time* t_c. *The process of sedimentation in fact is not complete at this stage and further sedimentation results in compaction or consolidation of the bottom sediment (compression zone) with liquid being squeezed out through the bed of particles until the ultimate height* (Z_∞) *of the compression zone is reached.* The batch sedimentation test data can be thus reported as given below :

Time :	0	t_1	t_2	t_3	.....	∞
Height of interface :	Z_0	Z_1	Z_2	Z_3	.....	Z_∞

This data is now translated to a continuous process to scale up the design of industrial sedimentors.

Let us first consider determination of thickener area. Let F be the volumetric feed rate (m^3/s) of the slurry into the sedimentor, L_u

the rate of discharge of underflow sludge (m^3/s) and V_o the overflow rate (m^3/s) of clear liquid. Assuming that the overflow liquid contains no solid particles, a material balance for solids yields,

$$FC_F = L_u C_u \quad \text{...(4.1.1)}$$

where C_F, C_u = concentration of solids (kg. of solids per m^3 of slurry) in feed slurry and underflow sludge, respectively.

An overall liquid balance gives,

$$F\left[1-\frac{C_F}{\rho_s}\right]-L_u\left[1-\frac{C_u}{\rho_s}\right]=V_o \quad \text{...(4.1.2)}$$

where ρ_s = density of solids, kg/m^3.

Eliminating L_u between the above two equations we get,

$$F\left[1-\frac{C_F}{\rho_s}\right]-\frac{FC_F}{C_u}\left[1-\frac{C_u}{\rho_s}\right]=V_o$$

or,

$$FC_F\left[\frac{1}{C_F}-\frac{1}{C_u}\right]=V_o \quad \text{...(4.1.3)}$$

Dividing both sides by the cross-sectional area A of the tank, we get

$$\frac{FC_F}{A}=\frac{Q}{A}=\frac{(V_o/A)}{[(1/C_F)-(1/C_u)]}=\frac{v}{(1/C_F)-(1/C_u)} \quad \text{...(4.1.4)}$$

where $Q = FC_F$ = feed rate of slurry on dry basis (kg/s).

As stated earlier, in order that the overflow liquid does not contain any solid particles, the upward velocity of liquid must be less than or equal to the settling velocity of particles (or, rate of sedimentation), v. Therefore, (V_o/A) has been replaced by v in the above equation.

Equations of the kind (4.1.1) are strictly valid only for the perfectly mixed vessels in which the concentration inside the vessel can be taken to be equal to that in the outlet stream. However, this is not precisely true for sedimentors since sedimentation is a slow and time-dependent process. It is however possible to rewrite equation (4.1.4) considering a capacity-limiting layer[1,2] (which is the concentration layer requiring maximum area to pass a unit quantity of solids). If such a layer exists and if C_L is the concentration of solids in that layer, then equation (4.1.4) is rewritten in terms of C_L and the corresponding downflow rate L as,

$$\left(\frac{LC_L}{A}\right) = \frac{v}{(1/C_L) - (1/C_u)} \qquad \text{...(4.1.5)}$$

Since we do not know which particular value of C_L represents the true limit, values of (LC_L/A) are required to be computed at different values of v and C_L and the minimum value of (LC_L/A) will determine the maximum value of A, which is the thickener cross-sectional area to be used for final design.

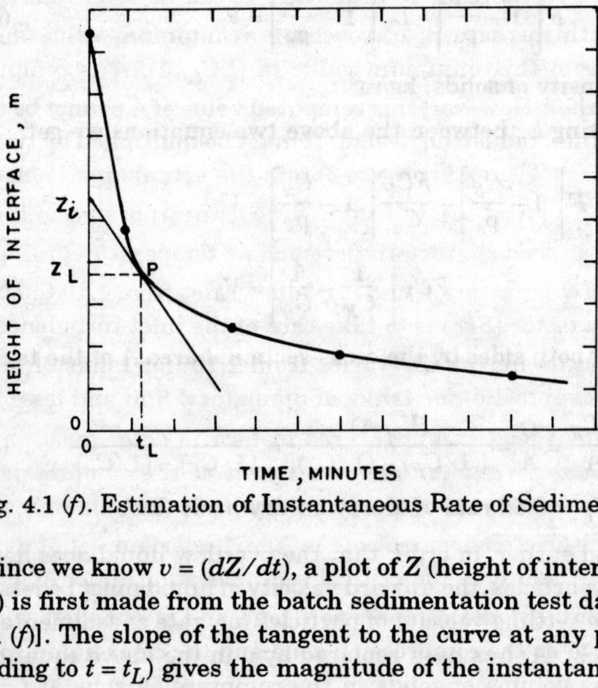

Fig. 4.1 (*f*). Estimation of Instantaneous Rate of Sedimentation.

Since we know $v = (dZ/dt)$, a plot of Z (height of interface) versus time (t) is first made from the batch sedimentation test data [see Figure 4.1 (*f*)]. The slope of the tangent to the curve at any point P (corresponding to $t = t_L$) gives the magnitude of the instantaneous rate of sedimentation, v_L. Thus, the values of v at different values of t can be computed. To determine the instantaneous concentration C_L, Kynch[3,1] has shown that

$$Z_i \, C_L = C_F \, Z_o \qquad \text{...(4.1.6)}$$

where C_F is the initial concentration (concentration of feed slurry) at $t = 0$ and $Z = Z_0$. In other words, Z_i will be the height of interface if all the solids present were at a concentration C_L. From figure (4.1*f*),

$$Z_i = Z_L + \left(\frac{dZ}{dt}\right)_{t = t_L} t_L \qquad \text{...(4.1.7)}$$

From equations (4.1.6) and (4.1.7), since (dZ/dt) at $t = t_L$ is v_L,

$$C_L = \frac{C_F Z_o}{Z_L + v_L t_L} \qquad ...(4.1.18)$$

From the above equation, the values of C_L at different values of t can be computed.

Once the instantaneous values of v and C_L are known, we can compute (LC_L/A) from equation (4.1.5). A plot of (LC_L/A) versus v is then made on rectangular co-ordinates. It can be seen that (LC_L/A) decreases with increase in v, reaching a minimum value and then increases. From this minimum value of (LC_L/A), A is computed as discussed earlier. However, this computed value of A cannot be directly used for the final industrial design. It must be multiplied by two safety factors such as $(SF)_1$ and $(SF)_2$ to obtain the actual area to be used in final design. The first safety factor $(SF)_1$ is incorporated to take care of variations in feed characteristics such as temperature, p_H, particle size and solid concentration and its value varies from 1.10 to 1.25. The second safety factor $(SF)_2$ is to take care of the inlet turbulence at the feed inlet and its magnitude varies from 1.10 (for tanks of diameter 35 m and above) to 1.5 (for tanks of diameter 4.5 m and less).

The height or depth of the sedimentor is determined in an indirect way. First we determine the depth of the compression zone within the retention time $(t_u - t_c)$, where t_u is the time required to attain the desired concentration in the underflow (that is, when $C_L = C_u, t = t_u$) and t_c is the critical sedimentation time. At $t = t_c$, all solids have entered the compression zone and we are left with only two zones such as the compression zone and the clear liquid zone and therefore, the volume of solids in the compression zone at $t = t_c$ and after will be equal to the total volume of solids fed. Thus, the volume of compression zone V_c within the retention time can be written as,

$$V_c = \text{(Volume of solids)} + \text{(Volume of liquid)}$$

$$= \frac{Q}{\rho_s}(t_u - t_c) + \frac{Q}{\rho_f}\int_{t_c}^{t_u} (L/S)\, dt \qquad ...(4.1.9)$$

where (L/S) is the mass ratio of liquid to solid, commonly called the *consistency* of the slurry. The instantaneous values of (L/S) can be computed from those of C_L using the following relationship :

$$(L/S) = \left[\frac{1}{C_L} - \frac{1}{\rho_s}\right]\rho_f \qquad \text{...(4.1.10)}$$

Equation (4.1.9) can also be rewritten in terms of C_L as,

$$V_c = \int_{t_c}^{t_u} \left[\frac{Q}{\rho_s} + \frac{Q}{\rho_f}\left(\frac{L}{S}\right)\right] dt$$

$$= Q \int_{t_c}^{t_u} \left[\frac{1}{\rho_s} + \frac{1}{C_L} - \frac{1}{\rho_s}\right] dt$$

$$\left[\text{since } \frac{1}{\rho_f}(L/S) = \frac{1}{C_L} - \frac{1}{\rho_s}\right]$$

$$= Q \int_{t_c}^{t_u} (1/C_L)\, dt \qquad \text{...(4.1.11)}$$

Since the values of C_L at different t have already been computed, the integral on the right hand side of equation (4.1.9) or (4.1.11) can be easily evaluated either graphically or numerically, once the critical sedimentation time t_c is known.

The value of critical sedimentation time t_c can be determined by using either the method of Coe and Clevenger[4] or that proposed by Roberts[5]. According to Roberts, the rate of settling in the compression zone is essentially linear with respect to time so that,

$$\frac{dZ}{dt} = -k\,(Z - Z_\infty) \qquad \text{...(4.1.12)}$$

where Z, Z_α = height of compression zone at any time t and at infinite time, respectively

k = constant for a particular system

Roberts therefore suggests that a plot of $y = (Z - Z_\infty)/(Z_0 - Z_\infty)$ against time (t) be made on semi-log co-ordinates (with y on log scale and t on rectangular scale) and the bottom portion of the curve (that is, the compression curve) is extrapolated back to zero time to cut the y-axis at say, $y = y'$. Then the time corresponding to $y = (1 + y')/2$ gives the critical sedimentation time, t_c. This graphical method is fairly accurate and well-accepted. Incidentally, if the value of Z_∞ is not known from the experiment, then its value is to be determined by trial and error. First a value of Z_∞ is assumed and the plot of $ln\,(Z - Z_\infty)/(Z_0 - Z_\infty)$ versus t is constructed. If the bottom portion of the curve is not essentially linear, then another value of Z_∞ is assumed and the procedure repeated, until the compression curve satisfies the equation (4.1.12).

Once the volume of compression zone V_c has been computed, the height of compression zone can be obtained as,

$$H_c = V_c/A \qquad ...(4.1.13)$$

The computed height H_c is multiplied by a safety factor of 1.75 to ensure maximum sludge concentration and permit a limited amount of sludge storage. The total depth of the thickener is then obtained by adding to the estimated height of the compression zone the following allowances :

For clear liquid zone	= 0.3 – 1.5 m
For feed zone	= 0.6 m
For transition zone	= 0.6 m
For the pitch of the bottom	= 0.3 – 0.6 m
For storage capacity to cover interruptions or irregularities in discharge	= 0.3 – 0.6 m.

Example 4.1. *An aqueous slurry containing 1.2 per cent by weight of solids (specific gravity = 2.0) is to be clarified by continuous sedimentation. Feed to the thickener is 3600 m³ per day and the underflow from the unit analyses 8 per cent solids. Specify the depth and diameter of the thickener. A batch sedimentation test on the feed material gave the following information :*

Time (min) :	*0*	*5*	*10*	*20*	*40*	*60*	*180*	*240*	∞
Height of interface (cm) :	*31*	*21*	*10*	*3.2*	*2.2*	*2.1*	*2.0*	*1.96*	*1.94*

Solution. We can use equation (4.1.5) for computing the cross-sectional area of the sedimentor :

$$\left(\frac{LC_L}{A}\right) = \frac{v}{(1/C_L) - (1/C_u)} \qquad ...(i)$$

Since the underflow contains 8% by weight of solids,

$$C_u = \frac{8}{(8/\rho_s) + (92/\rho_f)} = \frac{8}{(8/2) + 92} \text{ gm/cm}^3$$

$$= 0.0833 \text{ gm/cm}^3$$

To find the values of instantaneous rate of sedimentation v, we plot a graph between the height of interface (Z) and the time (t) as shown in Figure (4.1.1). The slope of the tangent to the curve at any point (corresponding to a given value of t) gives the magnitude of v at that time. For example, at $t = 15$ min, the tangent to the curve has a slope of 0.4 and it cuts the *y*-axis at $Z = 11$ cm. Therefore, v (at $t = 15$ min) = 0.4 cm/min and $Z_i = 11$ cm. Thus, from equation (4.1.6), the value of C_L at this time will be,

$$C_L = C_F Z_o / Z_i = \frac{C_F (31)}{11}$$

Since feed contains 1.2% by weight of solids

$$C_F = \frac{1.2}{(1.2/2) + 98.8} = 0.01207 \text{ gm/cm}^3$$

Therefore, C_L (at $t = 15$ min) = (0.01207) (31/11)

$$= 0.034 \text{ gm/cm}^3$$

Similarly, the values of v and C_L at different values of t can be obtained. The results are given in table 4.1.1.

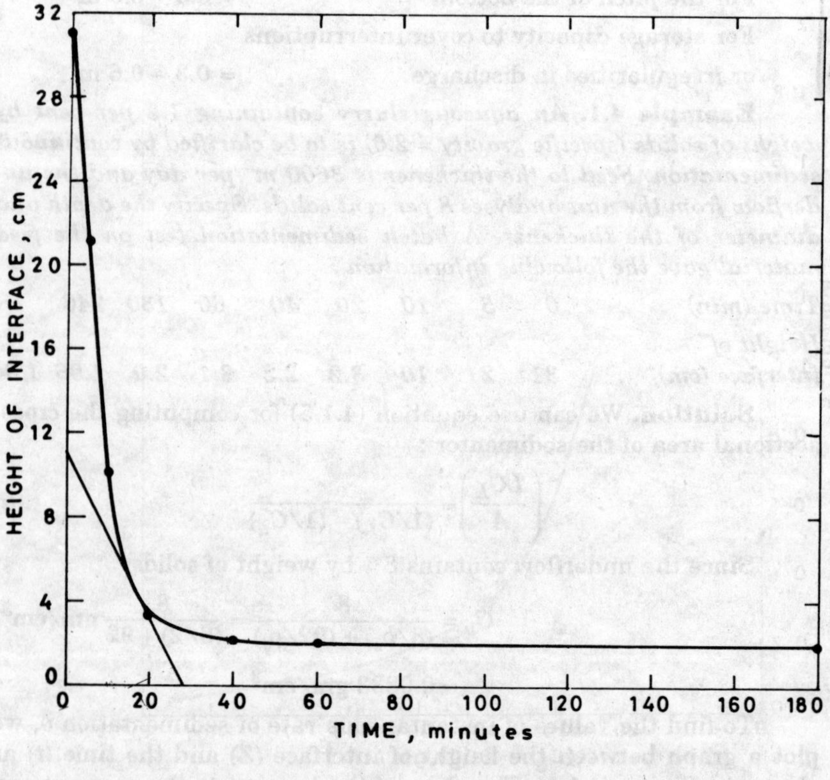

Fig. 4.1.1. Plot of Height of Interface (Z) Versus Time (t) for Determining dZ/dt and C_L.

Table 4.1.1

t (min)	$v = dZ/dt$, *cm/min*	Z_i, *cm*	C_L *gm/cm*^{3}
5	2.143	31.0	0.01207
15	0.4	11.0	0.034
20	0.222	8.0	0.04677
25	0.1077	5.4	0.06929
30	0.0667	4.4	0.085

Since the above table is not sufficiently elaborate, it will be better to plot a graph of v versus C_L. This plot is given in Figure (4.1.2). From the figure, we can get different values of v and C_L and correspondingly

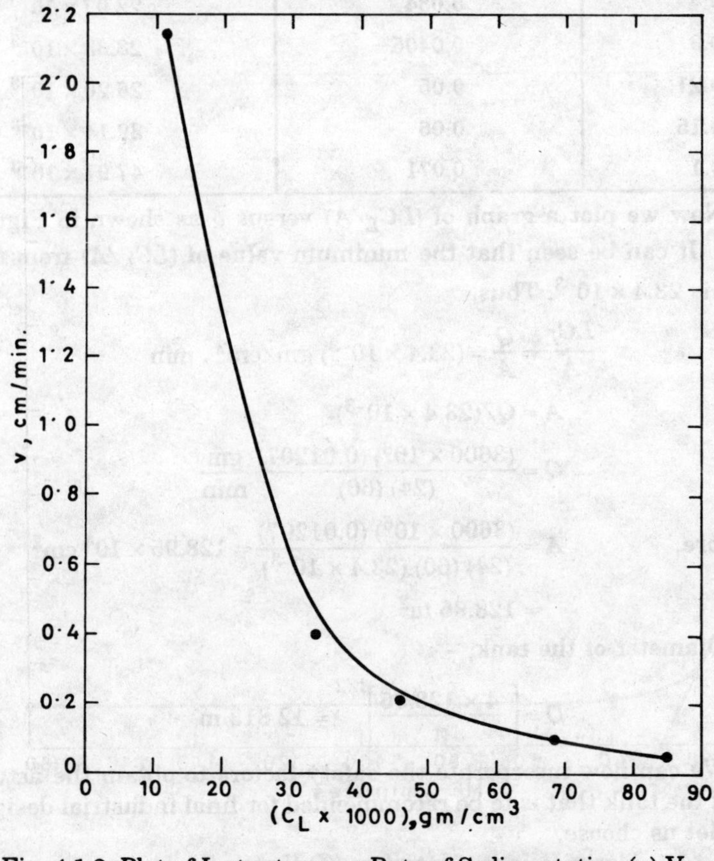

Fig. 4.1.2. Plot of Instantaneous Rate of Sedimentation (v) Versus Instantaneous Concentration (C_L).

we can compute (LC_L/A) using equation (*i*). The results are given in the table 4.1.2.

Table 4.1.2

v, *cm/min*	C_L, *gm/cm*^{3}	$\frac{LC_L}{A} = \frac{v}{(1/C_L)-(1/C_u)}$ (*gm/cm*^{2} *min*)
1.0	0.0245	34.7×10^{-3}
0.8	0.027	31.95×10^{-3}
0.6	0.0305	28.86×10^{-3}
0.5	0.0325	26.639×10^{-3}
0.4	0.034	22.97×10^{-3}
0.3	0.0405	23.63×10^{-3}
0.21	0.05	26.20×10^{-3}
0.15	0.06	32.14×10^{-3}
0.1	0.071	47.97×10^{-3}

Now we plot a graph of (LC_L/A) versus v as shown in Figure (4.1.3). It can be seen that the minimum value of (LC_L/A) from the figure is 23.4×10^{-3}. Thus,

$$\frac{LC_L}{A} = \frac{Q}{A} = (23.4 \times 10^{-3})\ \text{gm/cm}^2 \,.\, \text{min}$$

or,
$$A = Q/(23.4 \times 10^{-3})$$

where
$$Q = \frac{(3600 \times 10^6)\ (0.01207)}{(24)\ (60)}\ \frac{\text{gm}}{\text{min}}$$

therefore,
$$A = \frac{(3600 \times 10^6)\ (0.01207)}{(24)\ (60)\ (23.4 \times 10^{-3})} = 128.95 \times 10^4\ \text{cm}^2$$

$$= 128.95\ \text{m}^2$$

Diameter of the tank,

$$D = \left[\frac{4 \times 128.95}{\pi}\right]^{1/2} = 12.813\ \text{m.}$$

We can now incorporate the safety factors to obtain the actual area of the tank that is to be recommended for final industrial design. Thus, let us choose,

$$(SF)_1 = 1.10$$

$(SF)_2 = 1.30$ (since the computed tank diameter is less than 35 m. but more than 4.5 m)

Therefore, $A_{ctual} = (128.95)\,(1.10)\,(1.3) = 184.4\ m^2$

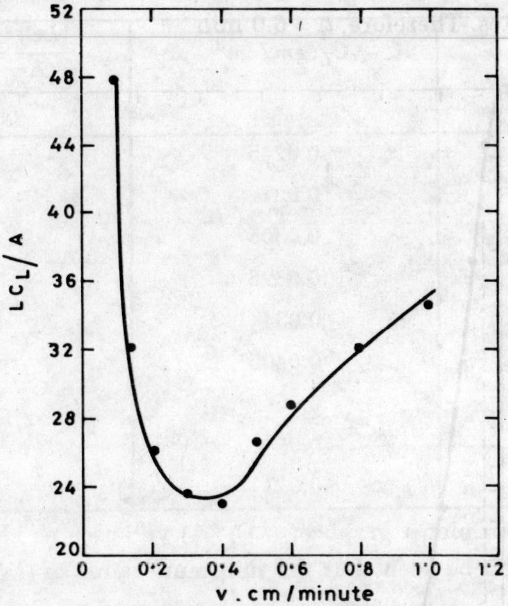

Fig. 4.1.3. Determination of Thickener Area.

Let us now proceed to determine the height or depth of the sedimentor. First let us determine the critical sedimentation time t_c using the method suggested by Roberts. Since, $Z_o = 31$ cm and Z_∞ = 1.94 cm, we can compute the values of $(Z - Z_\infty)/(Z_0 - Z_\infty)$ as given below :

t, min.	$(Z - Z_\infty)/(Z_0 - Z_\infty)$
0.0	1.0
5.0	0.6559
10.0	0.27735
20.0	0.0433
40.0	0.008947
60.0	0.00550
180.0	0.00206
240.0	6.88×10^{-4}
∞	0.0

The plot of $(Z - Z_\infty)/(Z_0 - Z_\infty)$ versus time (t) on a semi-log graph paper is given in Figure (4.1.4). The bottom portion of the curve when extrapolated back to zero time cuts the log-axis at 0.0082. Thus, the time at which $(Z - Z_\infty)/(Z_0 - Z_\infty) = [(1 + 0.0082)/2] = 0.5041$ is seen to be 6.0 minutes. Therefore, $t_c = 6.0$ min.

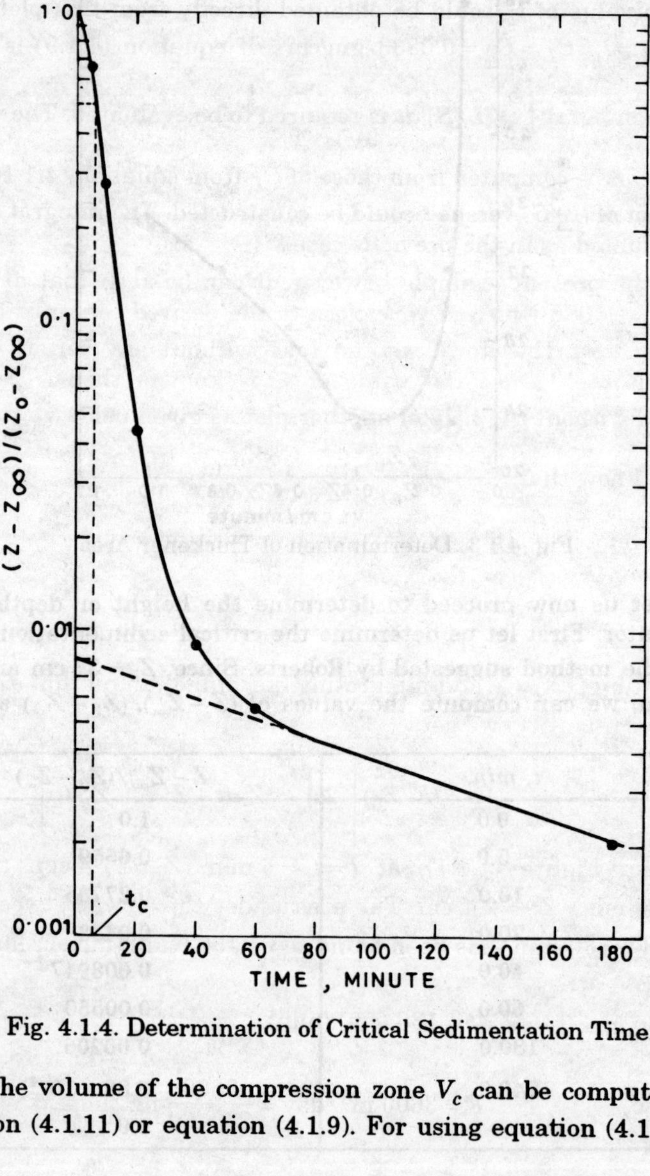

Fig. 4.1.4. Determination of Critical Sedimentation Time.

The volume of the compression zone V_c can be computed from equation (4.1.11) or equation (4.1.9). For using equation (4.1.11), we require to compute the value of the integral $\int_{t_c}^{t_u} (1/C_L)\, dt$. Since the values of C_L at different t are given in table (4.1.1), a plot of $(1/C_L)$ versus t can be easily made and the area under the curve between the ordinates $t = t_u$ and $t = t_c$ gives the value of the above integral. Incidentally, the value of t_u could be obtained directly from this plot itself since at $t = t_u$, $C_L = C_u = 0.0833$ gm/cm^3. If equation (4.1.9) is being used, the integral $\int_{t_c}^{t_u} (L/S)\, dt$ is required to be evaluated. The values of (L/S) can be computed from those of C_L from equation (4.1.10) and then a plot of (L/S) versus t could be constructed. The integral can be then evaluated as in the previous case.

In the present example however, it can be seen that at $t = 30$ min., $C_L = 0.085$ which is very close to the desired concentration in the underflow. Therefore, we can take without any serious error, $t_u = 30$ minutes. Once the value of t_u is known, then V_c can be evaluated without the help of another plot as given below :

We know that, $C_L = \dfrac{C_F Z_0}{Z_i} = \dfrac{C_F Z_0}{Z + (dZ/dt)\, t}$

Therefore equation (4.1.11) can be rewritten as,

$$V_c = \frac{Q}{C_F Z_0} \int_{t_c}^{t_u} [Z + (dZ/dt)\, t]\, dt$$

Putting $Q = FC_F$ and integrating (keeping in mind that dZ/dt is a negative quantity) we get,

$$V_c = (F/Z_0) \left[2 \int_{t_c}^{t_u} Z\, dt + Z_c\, t_c - Z_u\, t_u \right] \qquad \text{...(ii)}$$

From Figure (4.1.1), at $t = t_c = 6$ min, $Z_c = 17.4$ cm. and at $t = t_u = 30$ min., $Z_u = 2.4$ cm. The area under the curve between $t = 6$ min. and $t = 30$ min. has been found to be 136 (cm.) (min.) Thus,

$$\int_{t_c}^{t_u} Z\, dt = 136 \text{ (cm) (min)}$$

Also, $\qquad F = 3600 \text{ m}^3/\text{day} = \dfrac{3600}{24 \times 60} \text{ m}^3/\text{min.}$

$$Z_0 = 31 \text{ cm.}$$

Substituting in equation (*ii*), we get,

$$V_c = 24.548 \text{ m}^3$$

Now, height of compression zone,

$$H_c = \frac{V_c}{A} = \frac{24.548}{184.4}$$

$$= 0.133 \text{ m.}$$

Therefore, total depth of the tank will be,

$$H = (1.75)\, H_c + \text{allowances}$$

Let us choose the allowances from the prescribed ranges as given below

For clear liquid zone = 0.5 m

For feed zone = 0.6 m

For transition zone = 0.6 m

For the pitch of the bottom = 0.3 m

For irregularities in discharge = 0.3 m

Thus, $$H = (1.75)\,(0.133) + 2.3 = 2.532 \text{ m.}$$

4.2. Centrifugal Sedimentation

When centrifugal forces are incorporated in the processes of separation, they overwhelm the weak gravitational forces and as a result, the separation efficiency gets very much enhanced. We know that when a particle of mass m rotates along a curved trajectory of radius r, it experiences a centripetal force of magnitude $(m\,\omega^2\,r)$, ω being its angular velocity in radians per second, acting towards the center of the path. The centrifugal force is equal to centripetal force in magnitude but acts in the opposite direction. It must not be forgotten that though the particle may be rotating at a constant linear velocity, equal to $(\omega\, r)$, it is executing an accelerated motion since the direction of its motion is changing continuously. The ratio of centrifugal force to gravitational force $(\omega^2\, r/g)$, commonly called the acceleration in "*gees*", is often of the order of several thousands and is a measure of the separating power of the machine incorporating centrifugal force. Separations can be therefore carried out much more rapidly in a centrifuge than under the action of gravity. The degree of separation will be much larger since the forces available are of much higher magnitude.

Centrifugal sedimentors or classifiers are commonly called centrifuges. The so-called centrifugals are centrifugal filters and we shall be dealing about them in the subsequent chapter. Centrifuges are widely used for separating or classifying fine solids in suspension (as the particles are very fine, gravity sedimentation will be ineffective or laboriously lengthy) and also to separate liquids of different densities. They consist of imperforate baskets (baskets with solid wall) that are rotated at a high speed. Solids are deposited at the walls and the clarified liquid is removed through a skimming tube or over an overflow weir. When a mixture of two liquids is to be separated, the denser liquid collects near the walls and the lighter liquid forms an inner layer. Overflow weirs are arranged for the continuous removal of the two constituents.

Centrifuges that are commonly used for industrial applications are essentially of two types such as the tubular bowl and the disk bowl. The *tubular bowl centrifuges* employ bowls of 8 to 15 cm. in diameter and upto 1.5 m in length rotated at 5,000 to 15,000 rpm. The feed enters the bottom of the bowl through a feed nozzle. When used for separating fine suspended solids from a liquid, the bowl contains only one discharge port at the top centre for removing the clarified liquid, but when used for separating two liquids it employs two discharge ports, the inner annular port for the lighter liquid and the outer one for the denser liquid. When large quantities of solids are deposited on the walls of the bowl, they tend to plug the machine and therefore the bowl is required to be cleaned occasionally. This often limits the operation of the machine to suspensions containing only few per cent of suspended solids. In some practices however, like in dewaxing of lubricating oils, the solid wax separated is continuously removed by injecting hot water. The chilled wax is thus melted and discharged while afloat on water. Tubular bowls can also be operated under pressure, vacuum or in presence of an inert gas.

Disk bowl centrifuges operate at lower speeds and use bowls of larger diameter. They consist of stacks of conical disks spaced at a distance equal to or more than twice the size of the largest particle in suspension inside a short, wide bowl rotating about a vertical axis. The feed enters at the top and flows down the central tube set into the neck of the bowl, passes out through feed ports at the bottom and then flows up through a series of holes in the conical disks. As the feed moves upward, the centrifugal forces throw the solids or the heavier liquid outwards along the underside of the disks. When the centrifuge is used for separating two liquids, the lighter liquid flows towards the centre along the upper surfaces of the disks and is discharged at the top from the inner annular port while the denser liquid flows downward and outward, discharging from the outer port. When the centrifuge is used as a clarifier or sedimentor, only the inner discharge port is provided to remove the clarified liquid while the solids are thrown outward and collect in the bowl. The separated solids can be continuously discharged alongwith a small amount of liquid through radial nozzles in the periphery of the bowl. Valves which open automatically after a certain amount of solids have collected in the bowl may also be used in place of nozzles. The concentration of the discharged sludge can be adjusted by recirculating part of the sludge into the centrifuge. The separated solids can also be removed continuously with the help of a helical conveyor turning slightly slower than the bowl as in the case of helical conveyor centrifuge. Since the solids are given a chance to drain while still under centrifugal action, the sludge discharged will be much thicker in this case. *Ultracentrifuges* are equipment of small diameter operated at very large speeds, as much as 100,000 rpm, and are used for difficult separations such as the separation of isotopes based on their slight difference in density or molecular weight. They are also used in the laboratory for determining particle size or molecular weight by recording the rate of separation of suspended particles. Disk centrifuges find maximum application in the separation of cream from milk and in the concentration of rubber latex.

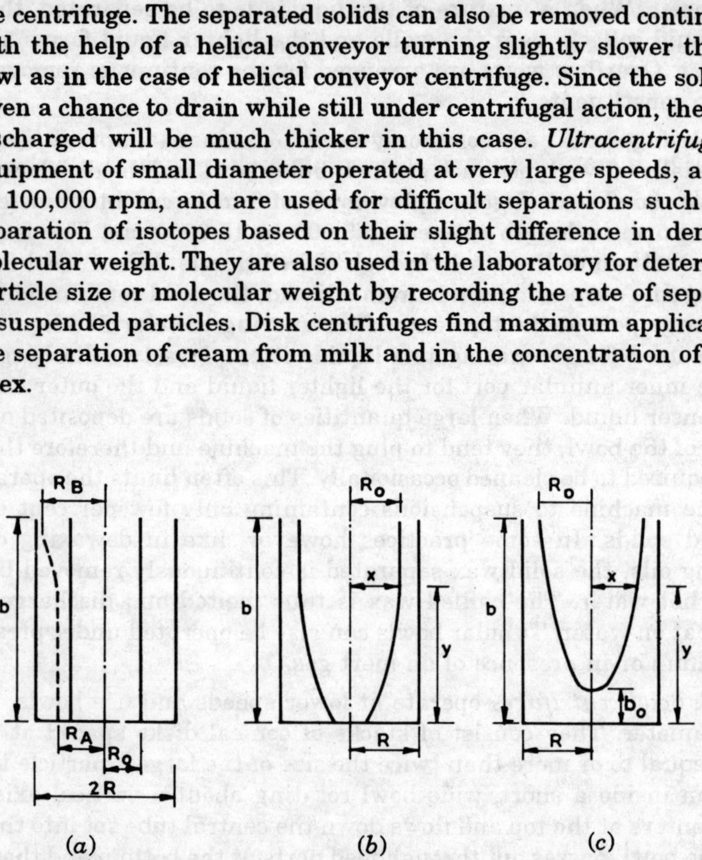

Fig. 4.2.

Let us now proceed to analyse the performance of a centrifuge. When a centrifuge basket of radius R and height b is rotated, the liquid inside it forms a vortex. The shape of the vortex depends very much on the volume of liquid in the bowl or basket and the speed of rotation. At high speeds of rotation, the centrifugal force will be so large compared with the gravitational force that the liquid surface will be almost vertical or the vortex formed will be parallel to the walls of the bowl as shown in Figure 4.2(*a*). However, at lower speeds of operation, the vortex could be parabolic as shown in figures 4.2(*b*) and (*c*). In such cases, the shape of the liquid surface can be determined as follows :

Since a liquid element at a distance y from the bottom of the bowl and at a distance x from the axis of rotation will experience a centrifugal force ($\omega^2 x$) per unit mass acting in the radial direction and a gravitational force (g) per unit mass acting in the downward direction, the slope of liquid surface at a point (x, y) will be,

$$\frac{dy}{dx} = \frac{\omega^2 x}{g} \qquad \text{...(4.2.1)}$$

On integration using the condition that at $y = b$, $x = R_o$, where R_o is the radius of the inner surface of the liquid at the top of the bowl, we get,

$$y = \frac{\omega^2}{2g}(x^2 - R_o^2) + b \qquad \text{...(4.2.2)}$$

The volume of the liquid in the bowl V_L can also be estimated as,

$$V_L = \int_o^b \pi (R^2 - x^2)\, dy \qquad \text{...(4.2.3)}$$

[for the case as in Figure 4.2(*b*)]

Substituting for x from equation (4.2.2) and integrating, we get,

$$V_L = \pi b\, [b\, (g/\omega^2) + (R^2 - R_o^2)] \qquad \text{...(4.2.4)}$$

For the case as in Figure 4.2 (*c*),

$$V_L = \pi R^2\, b_o + \int_{b_o}^b (R^2 - x^2)\, dy$$

$$= \pi\, [R^2 b - (g/\omega^2)\, (b - b_o)^2] \qquad \text{...(4.2.5)}$$

where b_o is the height of the liquid surface at the centre of the basket, as shown in the figure. Since $y = b_o$, at $x = 0$, from equation (4.2.2) we get,

$$b_o = b - \left(\frac{\omega^2}{2g}\right) R_o^2 \qquad \text{...(4.2.6)}$$

Substituting for b_o in equation (4.2.5),

$$V_L = \pi\left[R^2 b - \frac{\omega^2 R_o^4}{4g}\right] \qquad \text{...(4.2.7)}$$

Equation (4.2.2) can be therefore re-expressed by replacing R_o in terms of V_L.

As the feed is introduced to the centrifuge from the bottom, each solid particle tends to get dragged upwards by the liquid and at the same time it also moves radially under the action of the centrifugal force. The effective trajectory of the particle will be therefore as shown in Figure 4.2(a). However, since the centrifugal action is much more pronounced in magnitude, let us make a simplified assumption that the particle settles essentially in the radial direction. Thus, let initially at $t = 0$, the particle be in the liquid at a radial distance $(x + h_1)$ from the vessel axis and it moves to a point that is at $(x + h_2)$ from the vessel axis during its residence time t_T in the vessel. We can therefore write the force balance on the particle, as we have done in Chapter 3, as

$$ma_e = \frac{m}{\rho_s}(\rho_s - \rho_f)\,\omega^2\,(x+h) - F_R \qquad \text{...(4.2.8)}$$

Since the centrifuges are usually used for the separation of very fine particles, let us assume that the particle is settling in the laminar zone. We can therefore use the expression proposed by Stokes (given in Chapter 3) for estimating the fluid resistance F_R. Thus, for a spherical particle,

$$F_R = 3\pi\,\mu_f\,d_p\,v = 3\pi\,\mu_f\,d_p\,\frac{d\,(x+h)}{dt} \qquad \text{...(4.2.9)}$$

Equation (4.2.8) can be therefore rewritten as,

$$\left(\frac{\pi d_p^3}{6}\right)\rho_s\left[\frac{d^2\,(x+h)}{dt^2}\right] - \left(\frac{\pi\,d_p^3}{6}\right)(\rho_s - \rho_f)\,\omega^2\,(x+h) + 3\pi\,\mu_f\,d_p\,\frac{d\,(x+h)}{dt} = 0 \qquad \text{...(4.2.10)}$$

For a given x, the above differential equation can be solved using the method of characteristics[6] since it is of the form,

$$\frac{d^2 Z}{dt^2} + A_1\frac{dZ}{dt} + B_1 Z = 0$$

where $\qquad A_1 = 18\,\mu_f/d_p^2\,\rho_s$

$\qquad B_1 = -(\rho_s - \rho_f)\,\omega^2/\rho_s$

and $\qquad Z = (x + h)$

The integration constants can be evaluated using the conditions that at $t = 0$, $Z = (x + h_1)$ and at $t = t_T$, $Z = (x + h_2)$.

Equation (4.2.10) can be further simplified if we assume that the particle is moving at its terminal velocity. Strictly speaking, such an assumption is not precisely valid since the accelerating force in fact increases as the particle approaches the wall of the centrifuge basket. If the particle acceleration is neglected, then equation (4.2.10) becomes,

$$\frac{d\,(x+h)}{dt} = \frac{(\rho_s - \rho_f)\, d_p^2}{18\, \mu_f}\, \omega^2\, (x+h) \qquad \text{...(4.2.11)}$$

The above equation can be directly integrated between the limits $t = 0$ and $t = t_T$ as,

$$t_T = \frac{18\, \mu_f}{(\rho_s - \rho_f)\, d_p^2\, \omega^2} \ln \left[\frac{x + h_2}{x + h_1} \right] \qquad \text{...(4.2.12)}$$

where t_T is the residence time of the particle in the centrifuge basket.

If the particles are large, turbulent motion is to be expected. Thus, if the particle is moving in fully developed turbulent zone so that the drag coefficient f_D can be assumed to be essentially constant ($f_D = K_t$), then we can rewrite the expression for F_R as,

$$F_R = \left(\frac{\pi\, d_p^2}{4} \right) \frac{1}{2}\, \rho_f \left[\frac{d\,(x+h)}{dt} \right]^2 K_t \qquad \text{...(4.2.13)}$$

Substituting this in equation (4.2.8) and neglecting particle acceleration we get,

$$\left[\frac{d\,(x+h)}{dt} \right]^2 = \left(\frac{4}{3\, K_t} \right) \omega^2\, d_p \left[\frac{\rho_s - \rho_f}{\rho_f} \right] (x+h)$$

$$= K_c^2\, (x+h) \qquad \text{...(4.2.14)}$$

where $$K_c^2 = \left(\frac{4}{3K_t} \right) \omega^2\, d_p \left(\frac{\rho_s - \rho_f}{\rho_f} \right)$$

Integrating between $t = 0$ and $t = t_T$,

$$t_T = (2/K_c)\, [\sqrt{x + h_2} - \sqrt{x + h_1}] \qquad \text{...(4.2.15)}$$

If the speed of rotation of the centrifuge is large, which is so in the case of most of the industrial centrifuges, then the liquid surface will be vertical as shown in Figure 4.2(*a*) and in such case we can rewrite equation (4.2.12) as,

$$t_T = \frac{18\,\mu_f}{(\rho_s - \rho_f)\,\omega^2\,d_p^2}\ln(r_B/r_A) \qquad \text{...(4.2.16)}$$

Similarly, equation (4.2.15) becomes,

$$t_T = (2/K_c)\,[\sqrt{r_B} - \sqrt{r_A}] \qquad \text{...(4.2.17)}$$

The above equations (4.2.12) and (4.2.15) or (4.2.16) and (4.2.17) cannot be used directly for the design of industrial centrifuges since we do not know at what x the particle is settling or at what position in the liquid (r_A or h_1) the particle originally was at $t = 0$. However, it is clear that during its residence time t_T in the centrifuge bowl, if the particle reaches the wall of the bowl it will be separated from the liquid. In other words, if $r_B = R$, the particle is separated, but if $r_B < R$, it will be carried off by the liquid. In fact, the velocity of the fluid relative to the rotating bowl varies with the distance from the surface of the rotating bowl or disks. But, if an average linear velocity is assumed for the fluid relative to the disk or bowl, the approximate time during which the fluid remains in the centrifugal field (equal to the residence time t_T of the particle) can be obtained by dividing the volume of liquid in the bowl by the rate of flow of liquid through the bowl. Thus,

$$t_T = \frac{[\pi R^2 - \pi R_o^2]\,b}{Q} \qquad \text{...(4.2.18)}$$

Further, we define a "cut size" of the particle d_{pc} such that the particle of size d_{pc} will settle through a distance equal to half the thickness of the liquid layer inside the bowl during its residence time in the bowl. Thus, the cut size particle settles through a distance $(R - R_o)/2$ within the residence time t_T. Therefore, if this particle is to be separated from the liquid, then

$$r_A = R - \left(\frac{R - R_o}{2}\right) = (R + R_o)/2 \qquad \text{...(4.2.19)}$$

Substituting equations (4.2.19) and (4.2.18) is equation (4.2.16), we get for the particle of cut size,

$$Q_c = \frac{\pi\,b\,(\rho_s - \rho_f)\,\omega^2\,d_{pc}^2}{18\,\mu_f}\;\frac{(R^2 - R_o^2)}{\ln(2R/R + R_o)} \qquad \text{...(4.2.20)}$$

Similarly, equation (4.2.17) becomes,

$$Q_c = \frac{\pi\,b\,(R^2 - R_o^2)\,K_c'}{2\,[\sqrt{R} - \sqrt{(R + R_o)/2}]} \qquad \text{...(4.2.21)}$$

where $$K_c' = \left[\frac{4\,\omega^2\, d_{pc}\,(\rho_s - \rho_f)}{3\,K_t\,\rho_f}\right]^{1/2}$$

Thus, if Q_c is the volumetric flow rate of the fluid through the centrifuge basket, then all particles of diameter equal to or more than d_{pc} will be separated from the fluid stream. Equations (4.2.20) and (4.2.21) therefore help us in determining the separation efficiency of a centrifuge.

It can be seen that if the thickness of liquid layer inside the basket is very small so that $R_o \approx R$, the above two equations become indeterminate. However, in such case, we can assume that the particle is settling with a constant velocity equal to

$$V_r = \frac{(\rho_s - \rho_f)\, d_p^2}{18\,\mu_f}\,(\omega^2 R) \qquad \text{...(4.2.22)}$$

(for fine particles settling in laminar zone)

For the cut size particle, since the distance traversed by it is $(R - R_o)/2$,

$$t_T = \frac{(R - R_o)/2}{V_r} = \frac{9\,\mu_f\,(R - R_o)}{(\rho_s - \rho_f)\, d_{pc}^2\,(\omega^2 R)} \qquad \text{...(4.2.23)}$$

Since the liquid layer thickness is very small, the volume of liquid inside the bowl will be $(2\pi R)\, b\, (R - R_o)$. Therefore,

$$t_T = \frac{(2\pi R)\, b\, (R - R_o)}{Q_c}$$

or $$Q_c = \frac{2\pi b\,(\rho_s - \rho_f)\, d_{pc}^2\, \omega^2 R^2}{9\,\mu_f} \qquad \text{...(4.2.24)}$$

It is possible to rewrite the above equation as,

$$Q_c = 2\,\frac{(\rho_s - \rho_f)\, g\, d_{pc}^2}{18\,\mu_f}\left(\frac{2\pi b\,\omega^2 R^2}{g}\right)$$

$$= 2\, V_t\, \Sigma \qquad \text{...(4.2.25)}$$

where $\Sigma = 2\pi b\,\omega^2 R^2/g$.

It can be seen that this factor Σ depends only on the geometrical dimensions of the centrifuge and its operating speed. Physically, this factor represents the area of a gravity sedimentation tank that has the same clarification capacity or sedimentation characteristics as the centrifuge. Based on the value of Σ-factor, the performance of a centrifuge can be compared with that of a gravity sedimentation tank.

It can also be used for comparing the performances of different centrifuges among each other. From equation (4.2.20), the expression for Σ will be,

$$\Sigma = \frac{\pi\, b\, \omega^2 (R^2 - R_o^2)}{2g \ln (2R/R + R_o)} \quad ...(4.2.26)$$

Ambler[7] reports that for a disk bowl centrifuge, the expression for Σ will be,

$$\Sigma = \frac{2\pi (N-1)(R_b^3 - R_a^3)\,\omega^2}{3g \tan \theta} \quad ...(4.2.27)$$

where N = number of disks in the stack

R_a, R_b = inner and outer radii of the disk stack

θ = conical half angle

Accurate determination of the value of Σ-factor often requires laboratory experimental data on centrifuge performance while handling ideal systems and subsequent extrapolation to commercial systems. Some typical values of Σ-factor for three different types of centrifuges are given below :

Table 4.1

Type of Centrifuge	*Specification*	*Speed (rpm)*	Σ, m^2
Tubular bowl	10.5 cm in diameter and 0.75 m long	15,000	2,710
Disk bowl	$R_a = 7.5$ cm $R_b = 14.5$ cm $\theta = 45°$ $N = 50$	6,000	13,300
Helical conveyor centrifuge	D = 35 cm L = 0.575 m	3,250	890

Thus, if the same separation achieved in a 10.5 cm diameter tubular bowl centrifuge operating at 15,000 rpm is to be obtained in a gravity sedimentation tank, its area must be 2,710 m^2. This clearly illustrates the enhanced separation efficiency of centrifuges.

The minimum required wall thickness of the centrifuge basket can be computed by estimating the total stress on the wall. If ρ_m is the density of the material of construction of the basket and δ its wall thickness, then the centrifugal pressure resulting from the rotation of the empty basket will be ($\rho_m \, \delta R \, \omega^2$). The centrifugal pressure on the wall due to the fluid contents of the basket will be $(1/2) \, \rho_b \, \omega^2 \, (R^2 - x^2)$ or $(1/2) \, \rho_b \, \omega^2 \, (R^2 - R_o^2)$, where ρ_b is the density of the fluid inside the bowl. The total centrifugal pressure on the wall of the basket will be therefore,

$$P_c = (1/2) \, \rho_b \, \omega^2 \, (R^2 - R_o^2) + \rho_m \, \delta \, \omega^2 R \qquad \text{...(4.2.28)}$$

This load must be balanced by the radial component of the tension in the material. Consider the differential element of thickness dy as shown in Figure 4.2(*d*). The total radial component of the tensile force is $2(dT) \sin (d\theta/2)$. Thus,

$$P_c \, (Rd \, \theta) \, dy = 2 \, (dT) \sin (d \, \theta/2)$$

$$= 2 \, (dT) \, (d \, \theta/2)$$

(since $d\theta$ is very small, $\sin (d\theta/2) \approx d\theta/2$)

$$= (dT) \, (d\theta) \qquad \text{...(4.2.29)}$$

The tensile stress on the walls (σ_t) is therefore,

$$\sigma_t = \frac{dT}{\delta \, dy} = \frac{P_c \, Rdy}{\delta \, dy} = (P_c \, R/\delta) \qquad \text{...(4.2.30)}$$

where $P_c = (1/2) \, \rho_b \, \omega^2 \, (R^2 - R_o^2) + \rho_m \, \delta \, \omega^2 R$

For safe design, σ_t must not exceed the maximum permissible stress of the material of construction of the centrifuge basket, *f*. Thus, by putting $\sigma_t = f$ in the above equation, we can estimate the minimum required wall thickness of the centrifuge basket.

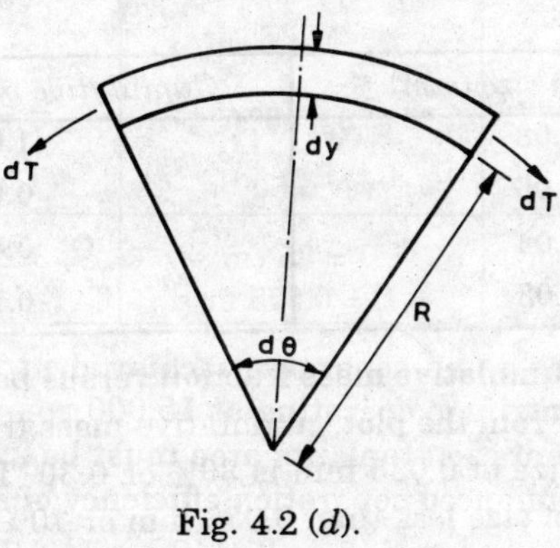

Fig. 4.2 (*d*).

Example 4.2. *A tubular bowl centrifuge 0.60 cm in diameter and 0.40 m in height operating at 1000 rpm is used to clarify a suspension* *containing solid particles (specific gravity = 1.6) in a liquid of specific gravity 1.3 and viscosity 3.0 centipoises at the rate of 100 m^3/hr. If a 7.5 cm thick liquid layer is formed inside the bowl and the particles have the following size distribution, estimate what per cent of particles shall be separated.*

Particle size (mm)	*Mass fraction*
– 0.08 + 0.06	0.18
– 0.06 + 0.04	0.35
– 0.04 + 0.03	0.28
– 0.03 + 0.02	0.19

Solution. Since particles are of fine sizes, let us assume that they settle in the laminar zone. Therefore, we can apply equation (4.2.20) :

$$Q_c = \frac{\pi b (\rho_s - \rho_f) \omega^2 d_{pc}^2}{18 \mu_f} \frac{(R^2 - R_o^2)}{\ln (2R/R + R_o)} \quad ...(4.2.20)$$

Substituting $Q_c = (100 \times 10^6/3600)$ cm^3/s, $b = 40$ cm, $R = 30$ cm

$\rho_s = 1.6$ gm/cm^3, $\rho_f = 1.3$ gm/cm^3, $\mu_f = 0.03$ gm/cm.s,

$R_o = (30 - 7.5) = 22.5$ cm, and $\omega = [2\pi\ (1000)/60]$ rps,

we get, $d_{pc} = 3.5 \times 10^{-3}$ cm $= 0.035$ mm.

Thus, all particles having size more than 0.035 mm will be separated from the liquid. To find out how much per cent of particles are of size more than 0.035 mm, let us look at the size distribution on cumulative basis :

Particle size (mm)	*Cumulative mass fraction*
0.08	1.0
0.06	0.82
0.04	0.47
0.03	0.19

The plot of cumulative mass fraction versus particle size is given in Figure (4.2.1). From the plot, cumulative mass fraction corresponding to a particle size of 0.035 mm is 30% or 0.30. This means 30% of the particles are of size less than 0.035 mm or 70% of particles are of size more than 0.035 mm. Therefore, 70% of particles will be separated from the liquid.

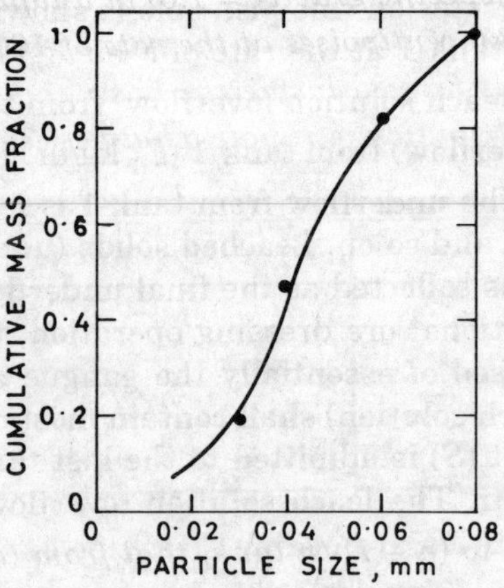

Fig. 4.2.1. Cumulative mass fraction versus particle size plot.

4.3. Continuous Countercurrent Decantation (C.C.D.)

Thickeners are widely used as leaching equipment. Leaching or solid-liquid extraction is an operation that is extensively employed in mineral processing (ore dressing). The process involves agitating the impure ore with a solvent in which the ore is soluble while the gangue is insoluble (it may also be vice versa). Consequently, the solvent selectively dissolves off the ore and this solution overflows from the top of the thickener. The gangue particles, being insoluble, settle down and are collected from the bottom of the tank as the underflow. The underflow thus contains the leached solids and the overflow forms the leach solution. Apart from mineral beneficiation, leaching is also widely used for the extraction of oil from vegetable seeds and animal livers, extraction of sugar from beets, washing of chemical precipitates (for example, washing off caustic soda from precipitated calcium carbonate in lime-soda process) etc. In general, this process can be used for the separation/purification of any solid mixture, provided a solvent that is selective to one of the components is available.

When the solvent is valuable, it is continuously recovered from the leach solution (usually, by distillation) and recycled back to the unit. This recovery and reuse of the solvent enhances the overall economy of the process.

In large capacity installations, a number of thickeners are used in series. Countercurrent operation (in which the leach solution and the leached solids move in opposite directions) is most popularly employed since this provides higher separation with a limited amount of solvent. The schematic of a continuous countercurrent decantation

(C.C.D.) unit that operates on this principle is shown in Figure (4.3). The feed solids enter tank-1 at the rate of F (or R_o) kg/hr where they are leached with the leach solution (overflow) from tank-2 (E_2 kg/hr). The leach solution (overflow) from tank-1 (E_1 kg/hr) is collected as the final leach solution. The underflow from tank-1 is fed to tank-2, that from tank-2 to tank-3 and so on. Leached solids (underflow) from the last tank (n-th tank) is collected as the final underflow (final leached solids). In the conventional ore dressing operation, the final leached solids shall be composed of essentially the gangue and the overflow from tank-1 (final leach solution) shall contain most of the ore in solution. The fresh solvent (S) is admitted to the last tank (n-th tank) at the rate of E_{n+1} kg/hr. The leach solution (overflow) from the n-th tank (E_n kg/hr) is fed to $(n - 1)$*-th tank, that from* $(n - 1)$-th tank to $(n - 2)$-th tank and so on. The final leach solution (product solution) is the overflow from tank-1 (E_1 kg/hr).

CCD units are widely used for washing chemical precipitates and the solvent used is usually water. The tanks may be arranged at different elevations (as shown in Figure 4.3) so that the leach solution could flow by gravity from one tank to another.

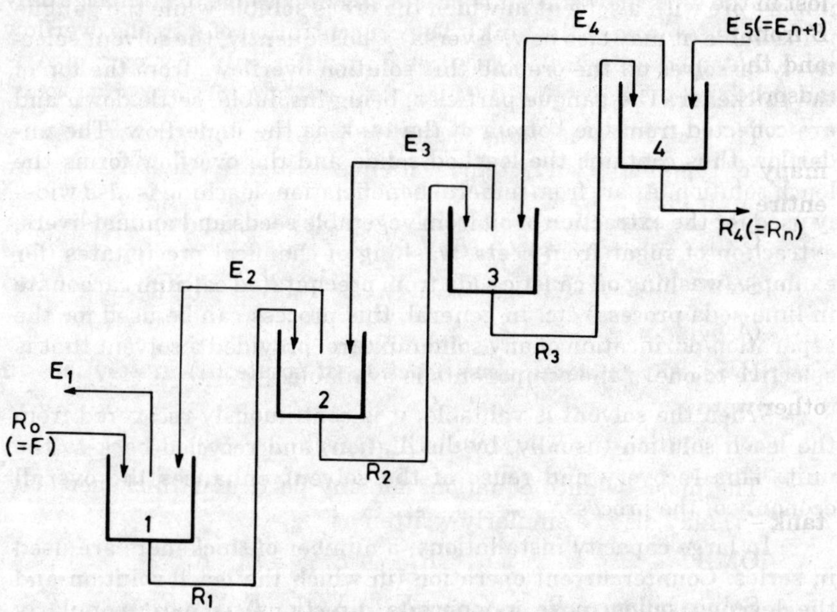

Fig. 4.3. Schematic of C.C.D. Unit showing four thickeners (n = 4).

Analysis of a C.C.D. unit involves writing down the material balance equations (overall material balance and partial material balance equations) for each thickener/stage and then solving them simultaneously. The following assumptions are usually made :

1. The feed consists of only one solute component (A) and all the remaining components of the feed are collectively referred to as non-solute (B). The solute (A) is fully soluble in the solvent (S), while B is fully insoluble.

2. The overflow from each thickener/stage (E_i kg/hr) is a clear solution of A in S. It does not contain any suspended particles of B.

3. The underflow sludge from each thickener consists of particles of B suspended in a solution of A in S. The amount of this solution is represented as R_i (in kg/hr). The total amount of underflow sludge discharged will be, therefore, $(G_B + R_i)$, where G_B is the mass of B in the underflow (in kg/hr). To note that since no B is lost in the overflow, (mass of B in underflow) = (mass of B in feed).

4. The concentration of A in the overflow solution (E_i) and that in the solution leaving with the underflow (R_i) is the same. (This is equivalent to saying that A dissolves in S forming a solution which overflows from the top of the tank; a part of this solution however gets lost in the underflow since it is practically impossible to discharge only B from the bottom of the tank). The concentration of A in the overflow and that in the underflow solution can differ only if a part of A is adsorbed by the nonsolute B (this occurs only on rare occasions).

The above assumptions are fairly realistic and are satisfied by many of the industrial systems. The mass balance equations for the entire unit are

OMB : $$R_o + E_{n+1} = R_n + E_1 \qquad \text{...(4.3.1)}$$

Solute balance: $$R_o X_o + E_{n+1} X_{n+1} = R_n X_n + E_1 X_1 \qquad \text{...(4.3.2)}$$

(A-balance)

Here, X represents mass fraction of solute (A) in solution. In other words,

$$X = (\text{Mass of } A)/(\text{Mass of } A + S) \qquad \text{...(4.3.3)}$$

The mass balance equations for any particular thickener (say, tank – i) may also be similarly written as

OMB : $$R_{i-1} + E_{i+1} = E_i + R_i \qquad \text{...(4.3.4)}$$

Solute balance : $$R_{i-1} X_{i-1} + E_{i+1} X_{i+1} = E_i X_i + R_i X_i$$
$$= (E_i + R_i) X_i \qquad \text{...(4.3.5)}$$

If N represents the solid to liquid ratio in the underflow, then

$$N = \frac{(\text{Mass of } B)}{\text{Mass of solution } (A + S)} \qquad \text{...(4.3.6)}$$

Since no B is lost in the overflow, the mass flow rate of B (namely, G_B) from each thickener shall be the same and will be equal to that in the fresh feed. In other words,

$$G_B = R_0 N_0 = R_1 N_1 = \ldots\ldots = R_n N_n \qquad \text{...(4.3.7)}$$

or

$$R_i = G_B / N_i \qquad \text{...(4.3.8)}$$

The mass balance equations, namely equations (4.3.4) and (4.3.5), alongwith equation (4.3.8) are to be solved simultaneously for each tank/thickener.

Let us consider some of the specific cases. For example, let the consistency (liquid to solid ratio, L/S) of underflow from each thickener is the same. This is called the *constant underflow* system. This means that N (which is the reciprocal of consistency) is a constant and its value does not vary from tank to tank (that is, $N_1 = N_2 = \ldots\ldots = N_n = N$). It, therefore, follows from equation (4.3.8) that $R_i = G_B/N$ = constant. In other words, $R_1 = R_2 = \ldots\ldots = R_n = R$. Accordingly, it can be seen from equation (4.3.4) that $E_2 = E_3 = \ldots\ldots = E_{n+1} = E$. To note that E_1 need not be equal to E, since R_o (or F), that is the fresh feed rate, need not be equal to R. In other words, for all tanks except tank-1, $(R_i/E_i) = (R/E)$ = constant.

Equation (4.3.5) therefore gets reduced to

$$RX_{i-1} + EX_{i+1} = (R + E)\, X_i$$

or

$$X_{i+1} = X_i\,(1 + R/E) - (R/E)\, X_{i-1} \qquad \text{...(4.3.9)}$$

The above equation is valid for $i > 1$ (but not necessarily for $i = 1$). Now, for $i = 2$,

$$X_3 = X_2\,(1 + R/E) - (R/E)\, X_1 \qquad \text{...(4.3.10)}$$

On rearrangement,

$$\frac{(X_1 - X_2)}{(X_1 - X_3)} = \frac{1}{1 + (R/E)}$$

$$= \frac{(E/R)}{(E/R) + 1} \qquad \text{...(4.3.11)}$$

If we multiply both the numerator and the denominator of RHS by $(E/R) - 1$, we get

$$\frac{(X_1 - X_2)}{(X_1 - X_3)} = \frac{(E/R)^2 - (E/R)}{(E/R)^2 - 1} \qquad \text{...(4.3.12)}$$

Similarly, for $i = 3$, equation (4.3.9) becomes

$$X_4 = X_3 (1 + R/E) - (R/E) X_2$$

Substituting for X_2 from equation (4.3.10) and on similar rearrangement, we get

$$\frac{(X_1 - X_3)}{(X_1 - X_4)} = \frac{(E/R)^3 - (E/R)}{(E/R)^3 - 1} \quad \text{...(4.3.13)}$$

It, therefore, follows that if there are n tanks in the unit, then

$$\frac{(X_1 - X_n)}{(X_1 - X_{n+1})} = \frac{(E/R)^n - (E/R)}{(E/R)^n - 1} \quad \text{...(4.3.14)}$$

or

$$n = \frac{\log \left[1 + \dfrac{(E/R - 1.0)(X_1 - X_{n+1})}{(X_n - X_{n+1})} \right]}{\log (E/R)} \quad \text{...(4.3.15)}$$

The above relation is often called *Kremser-Brown-Souders correlation*. It permits direct computation of the number of thickeners (or equilibrium stages) required for affecting a given separation. Equation (4.3.15) may be rewritten in terms of only mass fractions as,

$$n - 1 = \frac{\log [(X_{n+1} - X_n)/(X_2 - X_1)]}{\log [(X_{n+1} - X_2)/(X_n - X_1)]} \quad \text{...(4.3.16)}$$

It may be noted that for the present case of constant underflow, equations (4.3.1) and (4.3.2) reduce to

$$R_o + E = R + E_1 \quad \text{...(4.3.17)}$$

$$R_o X_o + E X_{n+1} = R X_n + E_1 X_1 \quad \text{...(4.3.18)}$$

The quantities usually known at the outset are the mass flow rate and composition of feed solids (R_o, X_o, N_o), the mass flow rate and composition of fresh solvent fed to system (E_{n+1}, X_{n+1}) and the concentration of A desired in the final leach solution (namely, X_1). For the present case, $E_{n+1} = E$. Also, if the feed does not contain any solvent, then

$$X_o = 1.0$$

$$N_o = (\text{mass of } B)/(\text{mass of } A) \quad \text{...(4.3.19)}$$

Since N is a constant, $R = G_B/N = (R_o N_o)/N$. Equations (4.3.17) and (4.3.18) can be thus solved simultaneously for the only two unknowns, such as E_1 and X_n. Once X_n is known, the number of thickeners required (n) can be computed from equation (4.3.15) or (4.3.16).

Let us now consider another specific case. For example, let the mass ratio of nonsolute (B) to solvent (S) in the underflow from each thickener is the same. In other words,

$$N/(1 - X) = (\text{Mass of } B)/(\text{Mass of } S)$$

$$= \alpha = \text{constant}$$

or

$$N = \alpha - \alpha X \qquad \text{...(4.3.20)}$$

Thus, N is not a constant but a linear function in X. Readers could easily verify that in a situation like this also, the number of thickeners required could be computed from equation (4.3.16) itself, provided all the mass fractions are expressed on solute-free basis. Thus,

$$n - 1 = \frac{\log [(X'_{n+1} - X'_n)/(X'_2 - X'_1)]}{\log [(X'_{n+1} - X'_2)/(X'_n - X'_1)]} \qquad \text{...(4.3.21)}$$

where

$$X' = X/(1 - X) \qquad \text{...(4.3.22)}$$

We have thus considered two important cases of operation of C.C.D. units :

Case-I : N = constant, for all underflow streams (constant underflow)

Case-II : N is not a constant but a linear function in X. That is, $N/(1 - X) = \alpha$, or $N = \alpha\,(1 - X)$, where α is a constant. This occurs when the mass ratio of nonsolute (B) to solvent (S) is the same in all underflow streams.

A still more generalised (the most generalised, in fact) situation is when N is a nonlinear function in X. Thus, N versus X plot is not a straight line but a curve. In such cases, a stage to stage (tank to tank) computation is to be performed based on equations (4.3.4) and (4.3.5). Analysis using graphical construction is also possible. For details, references (10) and (11) may be consulted.

It must be kept in mind that in the process analysis described above, we have assumed that equilibrium has been established in each thickener and consequently, each thickener acts as an equilibrium stage.

Example 4.3. *Copper is extracted from malachite ore by agitating the well-ground ore with dilute sulfuric acid, followed by multistage countercurrent washing with neutral water to wash the gangue free of the copper-bearing solution. The washing system consists of a series of Dorr thickeners. The slurry from the agitation tanks containing 6.1 per cent $CuSO_4$, 14.92 per cent gangue and rest water, is fed to the thickeners at the rate of 300 tonnes/hour. The rich solution from the washing system is to contain 6.69 per cent copper sulphate. This solution is* *treated for the removal of dissolved aluminium and iron and then sent to electrolytic cells for the precipitation of copper. It is desired that 98 per cent of copper sulfate initially loaded to the system be recovered. Determine the number of thickeners and the quantity of wash water required, if*

(a) each tonne of gangue retains 1.22 tonnes of solution,

(b) each tonne of gangue retains 1.22 tonnes of water.

The overflow from each thickener is clear (contains no gangue) and equilibrium is attained in each thickener such that the overflow solution and the solution in the underflow have the same composition.

Solution. Since the feed to system contains 6.1 per cent copper sulfate, 14.92 per cent gangue and rest (= 78.98 per cent) water,

$$X_o = (6.1)/(6.1 + 78.98)$$

$$= 0.0717$$

$$N_o = (14.92)/(6.1 + 78.98)$$

$$= 0.17536$$

Given that, $R_o = 300$ tonnes/hr

$$X_1 = 0.0669$$

$X_{n+1} = 0.0$ (since pure water is used as solvent)

$$G_B = R_o N_o$$

$= (300)(0.17536) = 52.6093$ tonnes/hr

Since 98 per cent of copper sulfate is to be recovered,

$$E_1 X_1 = (0.98) R_o X_o$$

or $E_1 = (0.98)(300)(0.0717)/(0.0669)$

$= 315.082$ tonnes/hr

Also, from equation (4.3.2), since $X_{n+1} = 0.0$,

$$R_n X_n = R_o X_o - E_1 X_1$$

$$= R_o X_o - (0.98) R_o X_o$$

$$= (0.02) R_o X_o$$

$$= (0.02)(300)(0.0717)$$

$= 0.43$ tonnes/hr

(*a*) Since each tonne of gangue retains 1.22 tonnes of solution,

$N = 1/1.22 =$ constant.

This is thus the case of constant underflow. Therefore,

$$R = G_B/N$$

$$= (52.6093)\ (1.22)$$

$$= 64.1833 \text{ tonnes/hr}$$

Since $R_n = R$ and $R_n X_n = 0.43$ (computed earlier),

$$X_n = (0.43)/(64.1833)$$

$$= 0.0067$$

Also, from equation (4.3.1),

$$E_{n+1} = E = R + E_1 - R_o$$

$$= (64.1833) + (315.082) - (300.0)$$

$$= 79.265 \text{ tonnes/hr}$$

$$(E/R) = (79.265)/(64.1833)$$

$$= 1.235$$

Substituting these values in equation (4.3.15), we get

$$n = 5.723 \simeq \mathbf{6.0}$$

Thus, six thickeners are required to affect the given separation. The amount of wash water required is,

$$E_{n+1} = E = \mathbf{79.265 \text{ tonnes/hr}}$$

(*b*) If each tonne of gangue retains 1.22 tonnes of water, then

$$N/(1 - X) = 1/(1.22)$$

or $$N = (1 - X)/1.22 \qquad \ldots(i)$$

Since $R_n X_n = 0.43$, $R_n = 0.43/X_n$. Also, $R_n = G_B/N_n = G_B\,(1.22)/(1 - X_n)$. Therefore,

$$(0.43/X_n) = (1.22)\ (52.6093)/(1 - X_n)$$

or $$X_n = 0.006655$$

$$R_n = (0.43)/(0.006655)$$

$$= 64.613 \text{ tonnes/hr}$$

$$X'_n = (0.006655)/(1 - 0.006655)$$

$$= 0.0067$$

$$X'_1 = (0.0669)/(1 - 0.0669)$$

$$= 0.071696$$

To obtain the value of X_2, let us solve the mass balance equations for the first stage ($i = 1$). Thus, equation (4.3.4) becomes (for $i = 1$),

$$R_o + E_2 = E_1 + R_1$$

$$(300.0) + E_2 = (315.082) + R_1$$

Since from equation (*i*), $N_1 = (1 - X_1)/(1.22) = (1 - 0.0669)/(1.22) = 0.7648$,

$$R_1 = G_B/N_1$$

$$= (52.6093)/(0.7648)$$

$$= 68.785 \text{ tonnes/hr}$$

Therefore, $E_2 = (315.082) + (68.785) - (300.0)$

$$= 83.867 \text{ tonnes/hr}$$

Equation (4.3.5) becomes (for $i = 1$),

$$R_o X_o + E_2 X_2 = (E_1 + R_1) X_1$$

$$(300)(0.0717) + (83.867) X_2 = (315.082 + 68.785)(0.0669)$$

or $X_2 = 0.04973$

$$X_2' = (0.04973)/(1.0 - 0.04973)$$

$$= 0.05233$$

Substituting these values in equation (4.3.21), we get

$$n - 1 = 4.8969$$

or $n = 5.8969 \cong$ **6.0**

The number of thickeners required is essentially the same as in part (*a*). This is due to the fact that since the values of X are fairly small, the magnitudes of X and X' do not differ significantly from each other. Now, from equation (4.3.1),

$$E_{n+1} = R_n + E_1 - R_o$$

$$= (64.613) + (315.082) - (300.0)$$

$$= \mathbf{79.695} \text{ tonnes/hr}$$

Thus, the solvent (wash water) requirement is slightly larger than that in part (*a*).

4.4. Computer-aided Determination of Thickener Dimensions

As we have discussed in the earlier chapters, if the aid of a high speed computer is sought, the computation procedure (for the determination of thickener dimensions) can be made faster and more precise. A fairly elaborate and accurate batch sedimentation test data is the primary pre-requisite for this, which we shall keep stored in the "Father file" of the computer. A consolidated software package can be then prepared[8] that helps us determine the sedimentor dimensions based on this batch test data.

Since the batch test enlists the values of Z (height of interface) against time (t), the primary step in developing the package will be to fit a correlation between Z and t. However, it may not be always possible to correlate Z with t through a single correlation. As discussed in section (4.1), during the early stages, the particles settle with their maximum hindered settling velocity and the rate of sedimentation (dZ/dt) remains essentially constant. Thereafter, the rate falls sharply with time and after a sufficient lapse of time the rate becomes very small and henceforth decreases only sluggishly with time. The entire process can be thus divided into three zones such as the zone-1 ($0 < t \leq t_N$) in which the rate of sedimentation is essentially constant, zone-2 ($t_N < t \leq t_M$) where the rate decreases significantly with time and zone-3 ($t > t_M$) in which the rate is very low and decreases very slightly with time.

A hard and fast demarcation of these three zones is usually difficult. One of the most straight-forward procedures for curve fitting will therefore be to consider the first three values of t and Z and fit them into a correlation for zone-1. Though a linear relationship of the form $Z = A_1 + B_1 t$ could be often satisfactory for this zone, an exponential correlation of the type $Z = A_1 + B_1 e^{-C_1 t}$ has been found to fit the data more accurately.[8] The values of A_1, B_1 and C_1 are evaluated using the method of least squares[9] (see Appendix). The truncation error q in the least square fit is defined as,

$$q = \sum_{i=1}^{n} [Z_i - f(t_i)]^2 \qquad \text{...(4.4.1)}$$

where n is the number of points and $f(t)$ is the function of t to which Z has been correlated. For example, for the present case, $f(t) = A_1 + B_1 e^{-C_1 t}$.

If the magnitude of q is found to be reasonably low, one more pair of values of t and Z is included into zone-1 and the procedure is repeated. When the magnitude of q is found to exceed the minimum acceptable limit, it is marked as the end of zone-1 ($t = t_N$). The rest of the points are now considered for zone-2.

A similar procedure is now followed for zone-2. For this zone, Z can be correlated with t according as $Z = A_2 + B_2 e^{-C_2 t}$. A polynomial fit of mth degree (normally m = 5 will be satisfactory) can also be used to describe the relationship. The least square fit is now made in the same way as before starting from three points such as t_{N+1}, t_{N+2} and

t_{N+3} (correspondingly, $Z = Z_{N+1}, Z_{N+2}, Z_{N+3}$) and the number of points are increased step by step until the truncation error q exceeds the minimum acceptable limit ($t = t_M$). For $t > t_M$ (zone-3), Z correlates easily with t according to the relation, $Z = A_3 + B_3\, e^{-C_3 t}$.

Once we have successfully correlated Z with t, the instantaneous rate of sedimentation $v = dZ/dt$ *and concentration* C_L *can be computed as follows :*

For $t \le t_N$, $\quad v = (dZ/dt) = -\,C_1\, B_1\, e^{-C_1 t}$ ...(4.4.2)

For $t_N < t \le t_M$, $\quad v = -\,C_2\, B_2\, e^{-C_2 t}$ ...(4.4.3)

For $t > t_M$, $\quad v = -\,C_3\, B_3\, e^{-C_3 t}$ ...(4.4.4)

In all the above three cases,

$$C_L = \frac{(C_F Z_o)}{Z + vt} \quad \text{...(4.4.5)}$$

Thus, we can prepare an elaborate table enlisting Z, v and C_L at different values of t. Let us say, at different t_i, $i = 1, 2 \,....k$. It is always preferable to maintain a constant interval of t (say h) in the table. Normally, $h = 5$ minutes will be satisfactory for most of the situations since gravity sedimentation is basically a slow process.

We can now proceed to compute the cross-sectional area of the tank. For this, we can use equation (4.1.5) :

$$\left(\frac{LC_L}{A}\right) = \left(\frac{Q}{A}\right) = \frac{v}{(1/C_L) - (1/C_u)} \quad \text{...(4.4.6)}$$

However, the above equation can be rewritten by substituting for C_L from equation (4.4.5) as,

$$A = \frac{Q}{C_F Z_o}\left[\left(\frac{Z}{v}\right) + t\right] - \left(\frac{Q}{C_u v}\right) \quad \text{...(4.4.7)}$$

The values of A_i are thus to be computed at different values of t_i ($i = 1, 2, ...k$) and the maximum value of A_i computed is to be selected for final design.

The critical sedimentation time can be now determined using the procedure proposed by Roberts (discussed in section 4.1). Let us consider the last three points such as (t_i, Z_i), $i = k, k-1, k-2$, which shall definitely be within the compression curve. Now, assume a value Z_∞ (if not already given in the batch test data).

Let $\quad y_i = \ln\,[(Z_i - Z_\infty)/(Z_o - Z_\infty)]$ ...(4.4.8)

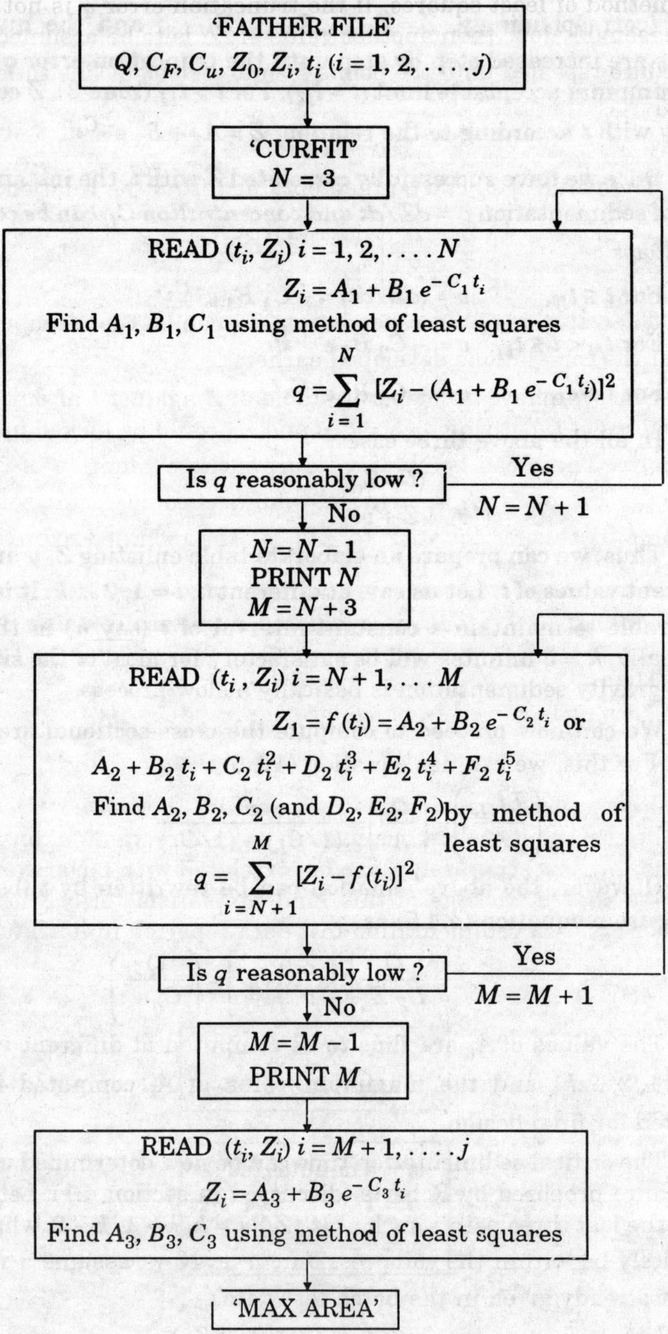
'FATHER FILE'
$Q, C_F, C_u, Z_0, Z_i, t_i \; (i = 1, 2, \ldots j)$
'CURFIT'
$N = 3$
READ (t_i, Z_i) $i = 1, 2, \ldots N$
$Z_i = A_1 + B_1 e^{-C_1 t_i}$
Find A_1, B_1, C_1 using method of least squares
$q = \sum_{i=1}^{N} [Z_i - (A_1 + B_1 e^{-C_1 t_i})]^2$
Is q reasonably low ?
Yes
$N = N + 1$
No
$N = N - 1$
PRINT N
$M = N + 3$
READ (t_i, Z_i) $i = N + 1, \ldots M$
$Z_1 = f(t_i) = A_2 + B_2 e^{-C_2 t_i}$ or
$A_2 + B_2 t_i + C_2 t_i^2 + D_2 t_i^3 + E_2 t_i^4 + F_2 t_i^5$
Find A_2, B_2, C_2 (and D_2, E_2, F_2) by method of least squares
$q = \sum_{i=N+1}^{M} [Z_i - f(t_i)]^2$
Is q reasonably low ?
Yes
$M = M + 1$
No
$M = M - 1$
PRINT M
READ (t_i, Z_i) $i = M + 1, \ldots j$
$Z_i = A_3 + B_3 e^{-C_3 t_i}$
Find A_3, B_3, C_3 using method of least squares
'MAX AREA'

Fig. 4.4.(*a*)

Now we fit a straight line through (t_i, y_i), $i = k, k-1, k-2$, using the method of least squares. If the truncation error q is not found to be reasonably low, then another value of Z_∞ is to be assumed and the procedure repeated until the points fit into a straight line satisfactorily. Thus,

$$y_i = A_4 - B_4\, t_i \qquad \text{...(4.4.9)}$$

The value of Z_c can be then obtained from the relation,

$$\left[\frac{Z_c - Z_\infty}{Z_o - Z_\infty}\right] = \frac{1 + \exp{(A_4)}}{2} \qquad \text{...(4.4.10)}$$

The value of t_c, corresponding to Z_c, can be then computed from any of the correlations developed earlier.

Since we have an elaborate table of Z against t at our disposal, the values of t_u (at which $C_L = C_u$) and Z_u could be picked up without difficulty. These can be obtained during the evaluation of C_{Li} itself. Once the value of t_u is known, the volume of compression zone V_c can be computed using equation (4.1.11) or the modified expression discussed in example (4.1.1). In either case, the integral, either $\int_{t_c}^{t_u} (1/C_L)\, dt$ or $\int_{t_c}^{t_u} Z\, dt$, is evaluated numerically using Simpson's rule. Then,

$$H_c = V_c/A$$

and

$$H = (1.75)\, H_c + \text{allowances.}$$

The software package is illustrated in Figure (4.4). Needless to say, the success of such a computation procedure, though consolidated, depends on how accurately Z can be correlated with t. Narayanan[8] has reported that a package of this kind fits satisfactorily with a large number of batch sedimentation test data reported in literature.

'MAXAREA'

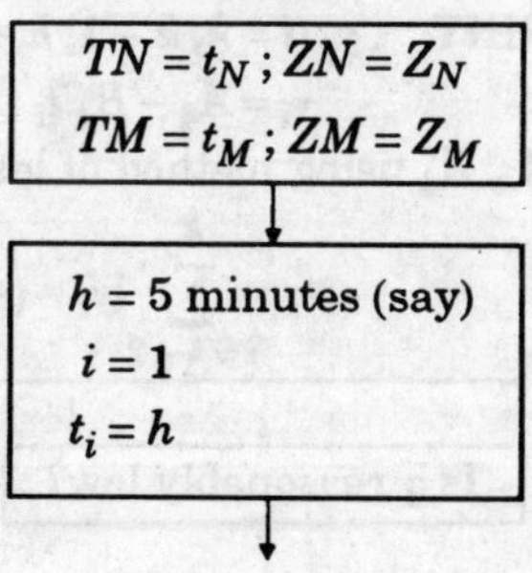

Contd...

IF $t_i \le TN, Z_i = A_1 + B_1\, e^{-C_1 t_i}$

$$v_i = -B_1\, C_1\, e^{-C_1 t_i}$$

IF $TN < t_i \le TM, Z_i = A_2 + B_2\, e^{-C_2 t_i}$

$$v_i = -B_2\, C_2\, e^{-C_2 t_i}$$

IF $t_i > TM, Z_i = A_3 + B_3\, e^{-C_3 t_i}$

$$v_i = -B_3\, C_3\, e^{-C_3 t_i}$$

$$C_{Li} = (C_F Z_o)/(Z_i + v_i\, t_i)$$

IF $\dfrac{|C_{Li} - C_u|}{C_u} \le 0.01,\ t_u = t_i \text{ and } Z_u = Z_i$

IF $(C_u - C_{Li}) \le 0.0$, GO TO 'AREA'

$$A_i = \frac{Q}{C_F Z_o}\,[(Z_i/v_i) + t_i] - \frac{Q}{C_u}\,[1/v_i]$$

'TRIAL'

IS $i < k$?

Yes: $i = i + 1,\ t_i = t_{i-1} + h$

'AREA'

A' = Maximum among A_i

$A_{\text{actual}} = A = A'\,(SF)_1\,(SF)_2$

'CRI TIME'

Fig. 4.4.(*b*)

'CRI TIME'

Let $Z_\infty = Z_k - 1$ mm

READ (t_i, Z_i) $i = k, k-1, k-2$

$$y_i = ln\,[(Z_i - Z_\infty)/(Z_o - Z_\infty)]$$

PRINT $y_i\ (i = k, k-1, k-2)$

$$y_i = A_4 - B_4\, t_i$$

Find A_4, B_4 using method of least squares

$$q = \sum_{i=k-2}^{k} [y_i - (A_4 - B_4\, t_i)]^2$$

Is q reasonably low?

No: $Z_\infty = Z_{\infty-1}$ mm

$$Z_c = Z_\infty + \left[\frac{1 + e^{A_4}}{2}\right](Z_o - Z_\infty)$$

$$\text{IF } Z_c \le ZN,\ t_c = \frac{1}{C_1}\ln\left[\frac{B_1}{Z_c - A_1}\right]$$

$$\text{IF } ZN < Z_c \le ZM,\ t_c = \frac{1}{C_2}\ln\left[\frac{B_2}{Z_c - A_2}\right]$$

'SEDHITE'

$$I = \int_{t_c}^{t_u} Z\,dt$$

Evaluate I using Simpson's rule

$$V_c = \frac{Q}{C_F Z_o}\,[2I + Z_c\,t_c - Z_u\,t_u]$$

$$H_c = V_c/A$$

$$H = (1.75)\,H_c + \text{Allowances}$$

Fig. 4.4.(*c*)

NOMENCLATURE

- A cross-sectional area of thickener, m^2
- a_e effective acceleration of particle, m/s^2
- b height of centrifuge basket, m.
- C_F concentration of solids in the feed slurry, kg/m^3
- C_L instantaneous concentration, kg/m^3
- C_u concentration of solids desired in the underflow, kg/m^3
- D diameter of sedimentor, m.
- d_p particle size, m.
- D_{pc} cut-size of particle, m.
- E_i mass flow rate of leach solution (overflow) from *i*-th tank, kg/s.
- F volumetric feed rate of slurry to the thickener, m^3/s.
- F_R kinematic force (drag force), *N*.
- f maximum permissible stress of the material of construction of centrifuge basket, N/m^2.

f_D drag coefficient, dimensionless.

G_B mass flow rate of nonsolute, kg/s.

g gravitational acceleration, m/s^2.

H height (depth) of sedimentation tank, m.

H_c height of compression zone, m.

L_u volumetric rate of discharge of underflow sludge, m^3/s.

(L/S) mass ratio of liquid to solid in the suspension (consistency of suspension).

N number of disks in the stack of disk bowl centrifuge; mass ratio solids to liquid in underflow, dimensionless.

P_c total centrifugal pressure on the wall of the centrifuge basket, N/m^2.

Q feed rate of slurry to thickener on dry basis, kg/s, volumetric flow rate of liquid through the centrifuge bowl, m^3/s.

R radius of centrifuge basket, m.

R_a, R_b inner and outer radius respectively of the disk stack of disk bowl centrifuge, m.

R_o radius of inner surface of liquid layer at the top of centrifuge basket, m.

r_A, r_B initial (at $t = 0$) and final (at $t = t_T$) radial position of the particle respectively measured from the vessel axis, m.

t_c critical sedimentation time, s.

t_T residence time of particle in the centrifuge basket, s.

t_u time required to attain the desired concentration in the underflow, s.

V_c volume of compression zone, m^3.

V_L volume of liquid in the centrifuge bowl, m^3.

V_o overflow rate of clear liquid from the thickener, m^3/s.

V_t gravitational free settling velocity of the particle, m/s.

v rate of sedimentation, m/s.

v_L rate of sedimentation at $t = t_L$, m/s.

X cumulative mass fraction ; mass fraction of solute in solution.

Z height of interface at any time t between clear liquid zone and thickening zone measured from the vessel bottom in the batch sedimentation test, m.

Z_c height of interface at critical sedimentation time (at $t = t_c$), m.

Z_i height of interface if all the solids present were at uniform concentration C_L (see equation 4.1.7), m.

Z_o, Z_∞ height of interface at $t = 0$ and at infinite time ($t = \infty$) respectively, m.

Greek Letters

δ wall thickness of centrifuge basket, m

θ conical half angle (see under disk bowl centrifuge), degrees

μ_f fluid viscosity, kg/(ms)

ρ_b bulk density, kg/m^3

ρ_f fluid density, kg/m^3

ρ_m density of material of construction of centrifuge basket, kg/m^3

ρ_s density of solid particle, kg/m^3

Σ Stigma factor, m^2

σ_t tensile stress on the walls of centrifuge basket, N/m^2

ω angular velocity of centrifuge, radians/s.

REFERENCES

1. Foust, A.S., Wenzel, L.A., Clump, C.W., Maus, L. and Andersen, L.B., Principles of Unit Operations, Wiley, New York, 1960.
2. Talmadge, W.L. and Fitch, E.B., Ind. Eng. Chem. **47,** 38, 1955.
3. Kynch, G.J., Trans. Faraday Soc., **48**, 166, 1952.
4. Coe, H.S. and Clevenger, G.H., Trans. Am. Inst. Mining Met. Engrs., **55**, 356, 1916.
5. Roberts, E.J., Trans. Am. Inst. Mining Met. Engrs., **184**, 61, 1949.
6. Kreyszig, E., Advanced Engineering Mathematics, 3rd edition, Wiley, New Delhi., 1980, p. 53.
7. Ambler, C.M., Chem. Eng. Progr., **48**, 150, 1952.
8. Narayanan, C.M., A Software Package for Computer Aided Determination of Thickener Dimensions, Proc., National

Seminar on Transfer Processes in Multiphase Systems, Banaras Hindu University, India, 1987.

9. Guest, P.G., Numerical Methods of Curve Fitting, Cambridge University Press, New York, 1961.

10. Treybal, R.E., Mass Transfer Operations, McGraw Hill, New York, 1981.

5

Filtration

Filtration is the process in which solids are separated from a fluid by passing the suspension through a porous medium (commonly called the filter medium) that is permeable only to the fluid. Though filtration can be employed for gas-solid separations and also for the separation of liquid mist from gases, we shall confine our discussion here to liquid-solid separations only. Gas-solid separation has been dealt in the subsequent chapter.

Since the filter medium is permeable only to the fluid, it retains the solid particles and permits only the fluid to pass through which is collected as the filtrate. The volume of filtrate collected per unit time (dV/dt) is termed as the rate of filtration. As the filtration process proceeds, solid particles accumulate on the filter medium forming a packed bed of solids, called filter cake. The thickness of the cake thus increases as filtration continues and it offers more and more resistance to the flow of filtrate and consequently the rate of filtration gradually decreases. If the rate is to be maintained constant, then the pressure of filtration, more precisely the pressure difference driving force ($-\Delta P$), will have to be increased gradually to overcome the increased resistance offered by the cake as it accumulates. A batch filter can be thus operated either at constant pressure (where the rate of filtration decreases with time) or at constant rate where ($-\Delta P$) will have to be gradually increased as filtration proceeds. It is preferable to operate the batch filter first at constant rate and then at constant pressure so that the overall output of filtrate will be large. The constant rate filtration is continued until ($-\Delta P$) becomes substantially high (beyond which the operation could be uneconomical) and then the filter is operated at constant pressure until the rate of filtration has fallen to unacceptably low value or until the required amount of filtrate has been delivered. The cake is then washed with wash water and drained. The filter is then opened, cake disposed off, cleaned and reassembled.

Fresh slurry is now fed and filtration restarted. A batch filtration cycle therefore involves the following steps :

Filtration

Draining the liquor

Filling with wash water

Washing

Draining the wash water

Opening, dumping and reassembling

Filling with slurry

If some means of continuous removal of deposited cake can be incorporated, then the process can be made continuous. This we shall discuss later.

5.1. Filtration Equations for Batch Filtration

Since the cake forms a porous bed over the filter medium, the flow of filtrate through the accumulated cake is analogous to fluid flow through a packed bed of granular solids. Since the particles forming the filter cake are normally small and the rate of flow of filtrate low, we can safely assume that the flow of filtrate through the cake is laminar. Let us also make another simplifying assumption that all the particles in the cake are uniformly wet by the filtrate. This is to assume that there is no channeling of the liquid through the cake. In such a case, we can use Kozeny's equation[1] for determining the pressure drop across the cake. Kozeny's equation has been developed based on the "capillary bundle theory". That is, we assume that the total void space of the packed bed (interstitial space between particles) is equivalent to a bundle of capillary tubes and therefore Hagen - Poiseiulleu's equation for laminar flow through straight conduits can be used here after replacing the radius of the tube by the hydraulic radius R_H of the system. Thus, the velocity of fluid U' through the bed can be written as,

$$U' = \frac{(-\Delta P)}{K\,\mu_f L} R_H^2 \qquad \text{...(5.1.1)}$$

where K = Kozeny's constant

= 25/6, for random packed particles of definite size and shape

$(-\Delta P)$ = pressure drop across the bed

L = height (or thickness) of the bed

R_H = hydraulic radius

= (flow area/wetted perimeter)

Since we have assumed that all the voids are completely filled with the liquid and all particles have been uniformly wet with the liquid,

$$R_H = \frac{\text{Void volume}}{\text{Total surface area of particles}}$$

$$= \frac{\varepsilon}{s_p\,(1-\varepsilon)} \qquad \text{...(5.1.2)}$$

where ε = Void fraction (sometimes called porosity) of the bed = (Void volume/total volume)

s_p = Specific surface (surface area per unit volume) of the particles.

Therefore, equation (5.1.1) becomes,

$$U' = \frac{(-\Delta P)}{K\,\mu_f\,L}\,\frac{\varepsilon^2}{s_p^2\,(1-\varepsilon)^2} \qquad \text{...(5.1.3)}$$

The superficial velocity of the liquid U_{sup} is defined as the volumetric flow rate of the liquid divided by the total (or empty) cross-sectional area and can be related U' as,

$$\frac{U_{sup}}{U'} = \frac{\text{Void area}}{\text{Total area}} = \frac{\text{Void volume}}{\text{Total volume}} = \varepsilon \qquad \text{...(5.1.4)}$$

Therefore from equation (5.1.3),

$$U_{sup} = \frac{(-\Delta P)}{K\,\mu_f\,L}\,\frac{\varepsilon^3}{s_p^2\,(1-\varepsilon)^2} \qquad \text{...(5.1.5)}$$

Since the volumetric flow rate of filtrate is (dV/dt) and if A is the area of filtration (flow area perpendicular to the direction of flow of filtrate), then we can write for filtrate,

$$U_{sup} = \frac{1}{A}\,(dV/dt) = \frac{(-\Delta P_c)}{K\,\mu_f\,L_c}\,\frac{\varepsilon^3}{s_p^2\,(1-\varepsilon)^2} \qquad \text{...(5.1.6)}$$

where

$(-\Delta P_c)$ = pressure drop across the cake

L_c = thickness of the cake

Since the cake is deposited parallel to the filter medium, the cross-sectional area of the cake and that of filter medium can be taken to be the same and equal to the filtration area A. Equation (5.1.6) is usually written as,

$$\frac{1}{A}\,\frac{dV}{dt} = \frac{(-\Delta P_c)}{\alpha\,\mu_f\,L_c} \qquad \text{...(5.1.7)}$$

where $$\alpha = \frac{K s_p^2 (1-\varepsilon)^2}{\varepsilon^3}$$

The factor α is called the *specific cake resistance* and is a measure of the resistance offered by the cake to the flow of filtrate. It can be seen that the dimension of α is m^{-2}. From equation (5.1.7),

$$(-\Delta P_c) = \frac{\alpha \mu_f L_c}{A} (dV/dt) \qquad \text{...(5.1.8)}$$

The average value of α is determined experimentally for each sludge.

Filter cakes can be classified as incompressible cakes and compressible cakes. The voidage ε of incompressible cakes remains essentially constant and thus the cake resistance is not significantly affected by the pressure drop across the cake or by the rate of deposition of material. Thus, for incompressible cakes, α can be assumed to be a constant. If the cake is compressible, then increase in pressure drop or rate of flow of filtrate can cause formation of a denser cake that offers higher resistance. Thus, it is possible that on certain occasions if the cake is highly compressible, increase of pressure difference could actually decrease the rate filtration. An empirical correlation between α and $(-\Delta P)$ has been proposed by Sperry[2] :

$$\alpha = \alpha_o (-\Delta P)^s \qquad \text{...(5.1.9)}$$

where α_o and s are empirical constants. The factor s is called the *compressibility coefficient* of the cake. It is zero for incompressible cakes and normally varies between 0.2 and 0.8 for compressible sludges. Equation (5.1.9) being empirical should not be used in a range of $(-\Delta P)$ much different from that used for experimental evaluation of α_o and s. For certain highly compressible hydroxide sludges, s could be as high as 0.9. For such materials, very little increase is obtained in the rate of filtration by increasing the pressure difference. Equation (5.1.9) has the inherent limitation that it predicts zero resistance when the pressure drop is zero. A more realistic correlation has been proposed by Ruth[3] that contains three empirical constants :

$$\alpha = \alpha_o [1 + m (-\Delta P)^s] \qquad \text{...(5.1.10)}$$

where α_o, m and s are empirical constants. Equations (5.1.9) and (5.1.10) assume that the specific cake resistance α of compressible cakes is a function of the filtration pressure $(-\Delta P)$ only. Therefore, for compressible sludges also, α may be assumed to be a constant if the filtration is being conducted at constant pressure. However, it has been reported by Donald and Hunneman[4] that the velocity of flow of filtrate can influence the specific resistance of a compressible filter cake since the orientation of the particles and their compactness will be affected by the velocity with which they are deposited. Also, at higher velocities, the smaller particles will have a higher tendency to be drawn forward in the cake. Donald and Hunneman therefore proposed that,

$$\alpha = (\text{constant}) \left[\frac{1}{A} \frac{dV}{dt} \right]^n \quad ...(5.1.11)$$

n being another empirical constant. Its value is zero for incompressible cakes and can be as large as 20 for highly compressible sludges. If we combine equations (5.1.10) and (5.1.11), we get a generalized correlation of the form,

$$\alpha = \alpha_o \, [1 + m \, (-\Delta P)^s] \left[\frac{1}{A} \frac{dV}{dt} \right]^n \quad ...(5.1.12)$$

For applying equation (5.1.8) to industrial problems, it will be convenient to express the thickness of the cake L_c in terms of the volume of filtrate V, cake voidage ε and the concentration of feed slurry. If we assume that the filtrate is a solid-free liquid, then we can write

Mass of solids in the cake = Mass of solids in the feed slurry

If x is the mass fraction of solids in the feed slurry, then,

Mass of solids in the feed slurry

$$= \frac{x}{1-x} \, [(\text{ Volume of filterate}) + (\text{Volume of liquid in the voids of the cake})] \, \rho_f$$

$$= \frac{x}{1-x} \, [V + \varepsilon \, (AL_c)] \, \rho_f \quad ...(5.1.13)$$

Mass of solids in the cake

$$= (1 - \varepsilon) \, (AL_c) \, \rho_s \quad ...(5.1.14)$$

Thus, we can write

$$(1 - \varepsilon) \, (AL_c) \, \rho_s = \left[\frac{x}{1-x} \right] [V + \varepsilon AL_c] \, \rho_f$$

or,

$$L_c = \frac{V}{A} \left[\frac{(\rho_f x)}{\rho_s \, (1-\varepsilon) \, (1-x) - \rho_f x \, \varepsilon} \right]$$

$$= V \upsilon / A \quad ...(5.1.15)$$

where $\upsilon = \rho_f x / [\rho_s \, (1 - \varepsilon) \, (1 - x) - \rho_f x \, \varepsilon]$. The significance of υ can be easily understood since from the above equation, $\upsilon = (AL_c/V)$ or it is nothing but the volume of cake deposited by passage of unit volume of filtrate. For small values of ε (as is so for many of the filter cakes), v can be approximated as,

$$v \cong \frac{x}{(1-x)} \frac{\rho_f}{\rho_s} \qquad ...(5.1.16)$$

Equation (5.1.8) can be thus rewritten as,

$$(-\Delta P_c) = \frac{(\alpha\, v)\, \mu_f\, V}{A^2} \left(\frac{dV}{dt}\right) \qquad ...(5.1.17)$$

Let us now consider the resistance offered by the filter medium. Woven materials made of cotton, wool, silk, nylon, teflon, polyester and glass fibres and metal wires are most commonly used as filter media. Beds of granular solids such as sand, gravel are also sometimes used as media particularly for handling highly corrosive sludges. The essential characteristics of the filter medium are, it must be mechanically strong, inexpensive, resistant to the corrosive action of the fluid and offer as little resistance as possible to the flow of filtrate. It is important to note that the function of the filter cloth is basically to act as a support to the filter cake while the first layer of deposited solids acts as the true medium. Commencement of the operation should be therefore carried out with great care. Initially, the filtrate delivered could be cloudy, but it gradually grows clear. The cloudy filtrate is recycled back for refiltration.

The resistance of the filter cloth therefore cannot be considered separately from that of the initial layer of the cake. But at the same time, it has been observed that the combined resistance of the two is considerably greater than the resistance of the clean cloth plus that of the initial layer of the cake. This is because solid particles have a tendency to get embedded within the pores of the cloth and thus increase the cloth resistance several fold. As a result, if the cloth gets considerably clogged with particles, it requires to be discarded. The flow of filtrate through the filter medium is therefore complicated for an accurate theoretical treatment. In many practices however, it is usual to regard the cloth plus the initial layer of the cake as equivalent to a cake of a given thickness. Therefore, an equation similar to (5.1.8) can be used to describe the filter medium resistance :

$$(-\Delta P_m) = \frac{R_m\, \mu_f}{A} \left(\frac{dV}{dt}\right) \qquad ...(5.1.18)$$

where R_m = filter medium resistance constant. It can be seen that the dimension of R_m is m^{-1}. The value of R_m is to be determined empirically using experimental results. As stated earlier, R_m strictly is not a constant. Its value is affected by changes in pressure drop, filtrate flow rate and also due to plugging of pores with solid particles. However, since the filter medium resistance usually is important only during the early stages of filtration, the assumption that R_m is a constant does not cause any serious error in many of the computations. When treated as an empirical constant, it also includes any resistance to flow that may exist in the flow passages to and from the filter.

The total resistance to filtration is thus the sum of the resistance offered by the filter cake and that of the filter medium. The total pressure differential $(-\Delta P)$ therefore is equal to the sum of $(-\Delta P_c)$ and $(-\Delta P_m)$. Thus,

$$(-\Delta P) = \frac{(\alpha v)\,\mu_f\,V}{A^2}\left(\frac{dV}{dt}\right) + \frac{R_m\,\mu_f}{A}\left(\frac{dV}{dt}\right)$$

$$= \frac{\mu_f}{A}\left[\frac{(\alpha v)}{A}V + R_m\right]\frac{dV}{dt} \qquad \text{...(5.1.19)}$$

The above equation forms the ultimate *filtration equation.* It can also be written as,

$$\frac{dt}{dV} = \frac{\mu_f}{A\,(-\Delta P)}\left[\frac{(\alpha v)}{A}V + R_m\right] \qquad \text{...(5.1.20)}$$

Let us now consider some of the specific cases. Let filtration be conducted at constant pressure on an incompressible sludge. Since the sludge is incompressible, α = constant and so is v. Equation (5.1.20) can be therefore re-expressed as,

$$\frac{dt}{dV} = K_P\,V + B \qquad \text{...(5.1.21)}$$

where $$K_P = \frac{\mu_f\,(\alpha v)}{A^2\,(-\Delta P)} = \text{constant}$$

$$B = \frac{\mu_f R_m}{A\,(-\Delta P)} = \text{constant}$$

For practical purposes, equation (5.1.21) can be approximated as,

$$\left(\frac{\Delta t}{\Delta V}\right) = K_P\,V_{avg} + B \qquad \text{...(5.1.22)}$$

where $$V_{avg} = \frac{V + (V + \Delta V)}{2} = V + (\Delta V/2)$$

From experimental results, a plot of $(\Delta t/\Delta V)$ *versus* V_{avg} can be made which will be thus a straight line. The slope of the line gives K_p from which the value of α can be deduced and its y-intercept is equal to B from which R_m can be evaluated. Once he filtration constants

α and R_m are known, any information such as the time required for collecting a given volume of filtrate or the volume of filtrate collected within a given interval of time, the rate of filtration at any instant etc. can be computed from equation (5.1.21). Incidentally, equation (5.1.21) can be integrated from $t = 0$ to $t = t$ (correspondingly from $V = 0$ to $V = V$) as,

$$t = K_P \frac{V^2}{2} + BV \qquad ...(5.1.23)$$

Now, let us consider filtration being conducted at constant rate. That is,

$$\left(\frac{dV}{dt}\right) = \text{constant} = (V/t) \qquad ...(5.1.24)$$

Equation (5.1.19) therefore takes the form,

$$(-\Delta P) = K_r V + B_r \qquad ...(5.1.25)$$

where
$$K_r = \frac{\mu_f (\alpha v)}{A^2}\left(\frac{dV}{dt}\right) = \text{constant}$$

$$B_r = \frac{\mu_f R_m}{A}\left(\frac{dV}{dt}\right) = \text{constant}$$

Equation (5.1.25) can also be written as,

$$(-\Delta P) = K_r\left(\frac{V}{t}\right)t + B_r$$

$$= K_r' t + B_r \qquad ...(5.1.26)$$

where
$$K_r' = K_r\left(\frac{V}{t}\right) = \text{constant}$$

Thus, a plot of $(-\Delta P)$ *versus* V or t yields a straight line the slope of which will be K_r or K_r' from which the value of α can be obtained and from its y-intercept B_r, R_m can be computed.

Let us now consider compressible sludges. Let a constant pressure filtration be conducted on a compressible sludge. If the specific resistance of the compressible cake be expressed as per equation (5.1.9), then equation (5.1.20) can be rewritten for the present case as,

$$\frac{dt}{dV} = \frac{\mu_f}{A(-\Delta P)}\left[\frac{(\alpha_o v)(-\Delta P)^s}{A} V + R_m\right]$$

$$= \left[\frac{\mu_f (\alpha_o v)}{A^2 (-\Delta P)^{1-s}}\right] V + \left[\frac{R_m \mu_f}{A(-\Delta P)}\right] \qquad ...(5.1.27)$$

Assuming v to be constant (v is constant for small values of ε and for most of filter cakes particularly compressible cakes, ε is small)

$$\frac{dt}{dV} = K_P' V + B$$

or,
$$\left(\frac{\Delta t}{\Delta V}\right) = K_P' V_{avg} + B \qquad ...(5.1.28)$$

where
$$K_P' = \frac{\mu_f (\alpha_o v)}{A^2 (-\Delta P)^{1-s}} = \text{constant}$$

$$B = \frac{R_m \mu_f}{A(-\Delta P)} = \text{constant}$$

Since there are three empirical constants such as α_o, s and R_m, a number of straight line plots of $(\Delta t/\Delta V)$ *versus* V_{avg} at different values of $(-\Delta P)$ are required to be made. From the y-intercept of each, the average value of R_m can be computed. Since,

$$K_P' = \frac{\mu_f (\alpha_o v)}{A^2 (-\Delta P)^{1-s}}$$

$$\ln K_P' = \ln\left(\frac{\mu_f (\alpha_o v)}{A^2}\right) - (1-s) \ln (-\Delta P) \qquad ...(5.1.29)$$

Thus, if a plot of K_P' (slopes of straight line plots already prepared) *versus* $(-\Delta P)$ is made on log-log co-ordinates, it will yield a straight line having a negative slope of magnitude $(1-s)$ and a y-intercept of $(\mu_f \alpha_o v/A^2)$. The constant s and α_0 can be thus evaluated.

Let the filtration be now at constant rate. Equation (5.1.19) therefore becomes,

$$(-\Delta P) = \frac{\mu_f}{A}\left[\frac{(\alpha_o v)(-\Delta P)^s}{A} V + R_m\right]\frac{dV}{dt} \qquad ...(5.1.30)$$

The values of the three empirical constants α, s and R_m cannot be determined directly from the above equation. However, Hughes *et.al.*[5] have proposed that at least for large values of pressure drop, equation (5.1.9) can be approximated as,

$$\alpha = \alpha_o (-\Delta P_c)^s \qquad ...(5.1.31)$$

Then, we can write equation (5.1.30) as,

$$(-\Delta P) = \frac{\mu_f}{A}\left[\frac{(\alpha_o v)(-\Delta P_c)^s}{A} V + R_m\right]\frac{dV}{dt} \qquad ...(5.1.30)$$

or, $$[(-\Delta P)-(-\Delta P_m)] = \frac{\mu_f (\alpha_o v)}{A^2}(-\Delta P_c)^s \left(\frac{dV}{dt}\right) V \quad ...(5.1.32)$$

$$\left[\text{since, } \left(\frac{R_m \mu_f}{A}\frac{dV}{dt}\right) = (-\Delta P_m)\right].$$

Since we know that

$$[(-\Delta P)-(-\Delta P_m)] = (-\Delta P_c),$$

the above equation reduces to,

$$(-\Delta P_c)^{1-s} = \frac{(\alpha_o v)\mu_f}{A^2}\left(\frac{dV}{dt}\right) V$$

$$= (\alpha_o v)\mu_f \left(\frac{1}{A}\frac{dV}{dt}\right)^2 t \quad ...(5.1.33)$$

$$\left[\text{since } \frac{dV}{dt} = \frac{V}{t}, \left(\frac{1}{A^2}\frac{dV}{dt}V\right) = \frac{1}{A^2}\left(\frac{V}{t}\right)\left(\frac{V}{t}\right)t = \left(\frac{V}{At}\right)^2 t = \left(\frac{1}{A}\frac{dV}{dt}\right)^2 t\right]$$

Since we have assumed R_m to be a constant, $(-\Delta P_m)$ is also a constant. To evaluate $(-\Delta P_m)$ as a first approximation, we plot a graph of $(-\Delta P)$ *versus* time (t). A smooth curve is drawn through the points and the curve is then extrapolated back to $t = 0$. The value of $(-\Delta P)$ at $t = 0$ is taken as $(-\Delta P_m)$. Once the value of $(-\Delta P_m)$ is known (which is a constant), the values of $(-\Delta P_c)$ can be computed and from equation (5.1.33),

$$(-\Delta P_c)^{1-s} = K_r' \, t$$

or, $$\ln t = (1-s)\ln(-\Delta P_c) - \ln K_r' \quad ...(5.1.34)$$

where, $$K_r' = (\alpha_o v)\mu_f \left(\frac{1}{A}\frac{dV}{dt}\right)^2 = \text{constant}$$

Thus, a plot of t *versus* $(-\Delta P_c)$ on log-log co-ordinates must yield a straight line of slope $(1-s)$. If the plot is not linear, the value of $(-\Delta P_m)$ computed initially must be manipulated, until a straight line plot is obtained. The factor K_r' is then computed using equation (5.1.34) from the co-ordinates of any convenient point on the line.

The specific resistance of compressible filter cakes can be expressed using equations (5.1.10) and (5.1.12) as well. However, though these expressions are more accurate, the number of empirical constants involved are more and their evaluation will necessitate lengthy trial and error procedures starting from elaborate experimental data.

Example 5.1. *A leaf filter with 1.0 m^2 of filtering surface operated at a constant pressure of 1.8 bar (gage) gave the following results :*

Filtrate volume (m^3)	*3.99*	*6.09*	*7.65*	*9.63*	*11.33*
Time (min)	*10*	*20*	*30*	*45*	*60*

The original slurry contained 10% by weight of solid calcium carbonate (specific gravity = 2.72) in water and the cake formed is essentially incompressible.

(a) Determine the time required to wash the cake formed at the end of 70 minutes of filtering at the same pressure using 3.0 m^3 of wash water.

(b) If the time for dumping the cake and reassembling the press is 60 minutes, what is the optimum cycle time and what is the volume of filtrate collected per cycle ? Assume wash water is used in the same proportion to the final filtrate as in (a).

Solution. Since the filtration is conducted at constant pressure on an incompressible sludge, we can use equation (5.1.22) :

$$\frac{\Delta t}{\Delta V} = K_P V_{avg} + B \qquad ...(i)$$

where
$$K_P = \frac{(\alpha v)\mu_f}{A^2(-\Delta P)}, \; B = \frac{R_m \mu_f}{A(-\Delta P)}$$

$$V_{avg} = V + \left(\frac{\Delta V}{2}\right)$$

Let us therefore compute $(\Delta t/\Delta V)$ and V_{avg} from the given data :

Time, t (sec)	*Filtrate Volume, V (m^3)*	*Δt (sec)*	*ΔV (m^3)*	*($\Delta t/\Delta V$)*	*V_{avg}*
600	3.99	600	2.10	285.71	5.04
1200	6.09	600	1.56	384.62	6.87
1800	7.65	900	1.98	454.55	8.64
2700	9.63	900	1.70	529.41	10.48
3600	11.33				

Now, we plot a graph of $(\Delta t/\Delta V)$ *versus* V_{avg} as shown in Figure (5.1.1). From the figure, slope of the straight line $= K_p = 44.8 \text{ s m}^{-6}$, *y*-intercept $= B = 70 \text{ s m}^{-3}$.

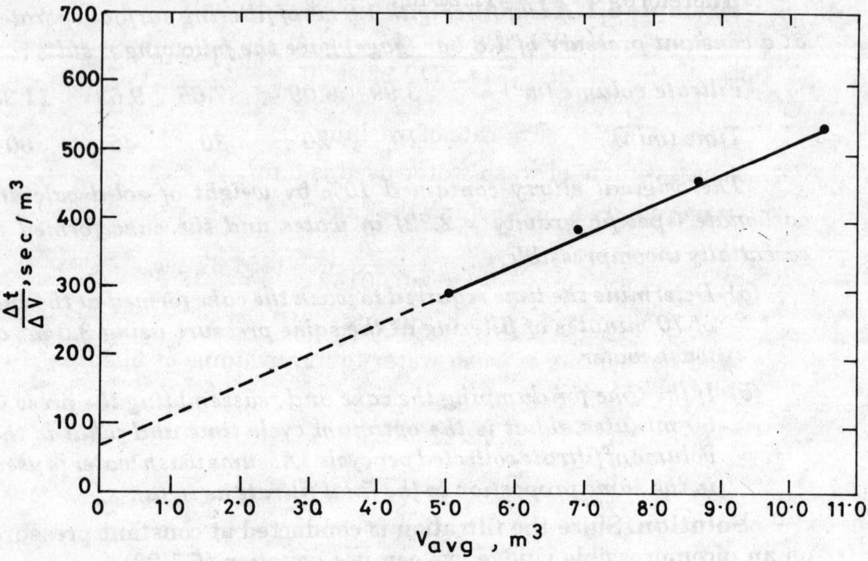

Fig. 5.1.1. $(\Delta t/\Delta V)$ versus V_{avg} plot.

Equation (*i*) can be therefore written as.

$$\frac{dt}{dV} = (44.8)\, V + 70 \qquad \text{...}(ii)$$

(*a*) We have to determine the time of washing at the end of 70 minutes (4200 seconds) of filtering at the same pressure. Since the same liquid as the filtrate is used for washing the cake (or, the liquid used for washing has the same physical and transport properties as the filtrate and is miscible with the filtrate) and since washing is done at the same pressure as filtration, the rate of washing will be equal to the final rate of filtration, $(dV/dt)_f$. From equation (*ii*),

$$\left(\frac{dV}{dt}\right)_f = \frac{1}{(44.8)\, V_f + 70} \qquad \text{...}(iii)$$

where V_f = final volume of filtrate collected.

Integration of equation (*ii*) gives,

$$t = (22.4)\, V^2 + 70V \qquad \text{...}(iv)$$

Therefore, V_f can be computed by putting t = 4200 seconds in the above equation :

$$4200 = (22.4)\, V_f^2 + 70\, V_f$$

or,

$$22.4\, V_f^2 + 70\, V_f - 4200 = 0$$

Therefore, $V_f = 12.22 \text{ m}^3$

$$\left(\frac{dV}{dt}\right)_f = \frac{1}{44.8\,(12.22) + 70} = 0.00162 \text{ m}^3/\text{s}$$

$$= \text{rate of washing}$$

Since volume of wash water used is 3 m^3,

time required for washing the cake

$$= t_{wash} = \frac{3}{0.00162} = 1852.37 \text{ sec.}$$

$$= 30.87 \text{ minutes}$$

Ratio of volume of wash water to final volume of filtrate

$$\frac{V_{wash}}{V_f} = \frac{3}{12.22} = 0.25$$

(*b*) The total cycle time is given by,

$$t_{cycle} = t_f + t_{wash} + t_{etc}$$

where t_f = time of filtration = $22.4\,V_f^2 + 70\,V_f$

t_{etc} = time for draining, filling, opening, dumping the cake and reassembling = 60 minutes = 3600 seconds

t_{wash} = time of washing the cake

$$= \frac{\text{Volume of wash water}}{\text{rate of washing}}$$

As in (*a*), we assume that the rate of washing is equal to the final rate of filtration $(dV/dt)_f$. Also, since it is given that wash water is used in the same proportion to the final filtrate as in (*a*), $V_{wash} = 0.25\,V_f$.

Therefore, $$t_{wash} = \frac{0.25\,V_f}{1/(44.8\,V_f + 70)} = (11.2\,V_f^2 + 17.5\,V_f)$$

Thus the expression for t_{cycle} becomes,

$$t_{cycle} = (22.4\,V_f^2 + 70\,V_f) + (11.2\,V_f^2 + 17.5\,V_f) + 3600$$

$$= 33.6\,V_f^2 + 87.5\,V_f + 3600$$

The cycle time is optimised on the basis of maximising the daily output of filtrate. Thus,

$$\text{Number of cycles per day} = \frac{24 \times 3600}{t_{cycle}}$$

Daily output of filtrate $= V_{day} = \dfrac{24(3600)}{t_{cycle}} V_f$

$$= \frac{86{,}400\ V_f}{33.6\ V_f^2 + 87.5\ V_f + 3600}$$

For maximum V_{day}, $\dfrac{dV_{day}}{dV_f} = 0$

That is, $86{,}400\ (3600) - 86{,}400\ (33.6)\ V_f^2 = 0$

or, $$(V_f)_{opt} = 10.35 \text{ m}^3$$

Therefore, optimum cycle time will be,

$$(t_c)_{opt} = 33.6\ (10.35)^2 + 87.5\ (10.35) + 3600$$

$$= 8105.71 \text{ seconds} = \mathbf{2.25\ hours}$$

It will be of interest to deduce a relation between the time for filtration and washing and the time for which the filter is out of use for a batch filtration cycle under optimum conditions. Let us consider a constant pressure filtration conducted on an incompressible sludge and let the filter medium resistance be negligible. Then, we can write equation (5.1.21) as,

$$\frac{dt}{dV} = K_p\ V \qquad \text{...(5.1.35)}$$

where $$K_P = \frac{(\alpha\ v)\ \mu_f}{A^2\ (-\Delta P)} = \text{constant}$$

On integration, $$t = K_P\ V^2/2 \qquad \text{...(5.1.36)}$$

Since at $t = 0$, $V = 0$, the constant of integration = 0. Let x be the ratio of volume of wash water used to the final volume of filtrate collected and let y be the ratio of the rate of washing to the final rate of filtration. Then,

Time for washing the cake

$$= t_{wash} = \frac{x\ V_f}{y\ [1/K_P\ V_f]}$$

$$= \left(\frac{x}{y}\right) K_P\ V_f^2 \qquad \text{...(5.1.37)}$$

where V_f = final volume of filtrate collected. If t_{etc} denotes the time for draining, opening, dumping and reassembling (that is, the time for which the filter is out of use), then the total cycle time will be

$$t_{cycle} = t_f + t_{wash} + t_{etc}$$

$$= (K_P\ V_f^2/2) + (x/y)\ K_P\ V_f^2 + t_{etc} \qquad \text{...(5.1.38)}$$

As stated in Example (5.1), the cycle time is optimised on the basis of maximising the daily output of filtrate. Thus,

$$\text{Number of cycles per day} = \frac{24}{t_{cycle}}$$

$$\text{Daily output of filtrate}, V_{day} = \frac{24\ V_f}{t_{cycle}}$$

$$= \frac{24\ V_f}{(K_P\ V_f^2/2) + (x/y)\ K_P\ V_f^2 + t_{etc}}$$

Differentiating V_{day} with respect to V_f and putting equal to zero, we get

$$\left(\frac{K_P}{2}\right) V_f^2 + \left(\frac{x}{y}\right) K_P\ V_f^2 - t_{etc} = 0 \quad \text{...(5.1.39)}$$

or
$$(V_f)_{opt} = \left[\frac{t_{etc}}{(K_P/2) + (xK_P/y)}\right]^{1/2}$$

$$= \left[\frac{2y\ t_{etc}}{K_P\ (2x + y)}\right]^{1/2} \quad \text{...(5.1.40)}$$

Also, from equation (5.1.39), $(K_P\ V_f^2/2) + (x/y)\ K_p\ V_f^2 = t_{etc}$

or,
$$(t_f + t_{wash}) = t_{etc} \quad \text{...(5.1.41)}$$

Thus, at optimum cycle time, the time for filtration and washing will be equal to the time for which the filter is out of use.

$$(t_{cycle})_{opt} = t_f + t_{wash} + t_{etc} = 2t_{etc} \quad \text{...(5.1.42)}$$

Example 5.2. *A plate and frame filter press handles a compressible sludge containing 80 kg of dry solids per m³ of solid-free liquid (viscosity = 1.0 centipoise). The filter must deliver 12.0 m³ of solid-free filtrate over an operating time of 2.0 hours when the pressure difference driving force over the filter unit is constant at 171.5 kN/m². On the basis of the following data obtained on a small experimental filter press with a filtering area of 0.75 m² operating on the same sludge, estimate the total area of filtering surface required.*

Volume of filtrate, m³	*Time (hours)*		
	(– ΔP) = 138.2 kN/m²	*(– ΔP) = 206.8 kN/m²*	*(– ΔP) = 275.4 kN/m²*
0.142	*0.34*	*0.25*	*0.21*
0.227	*0.85*	*0.64*	*0.52*
0.283	*1.32*	*1.00*	*0.81*
0.340	*1.90*	*1.43*	*1.17*

Assume that the filter medium resistance is constant and is the same for both the experimental filter as well as the filter press.

Solution. Since filtration is at constant pressure but on a compressible sludge, we have to use equation (5.1.28) :

$$\left(\frac{\Delta t}{\Delta V}\right) = K_P' \, V_{avg} + B \qquad ...(i)$$

where
$$K_P' = \frac{(\alpha_o \, v)\, \mu_f}{A^2 \, (-\Delta P)^{1-s}}$$

$$B = \frac{R_m \, \mu_f}{A \, (-\Delta P)}$$

$$V_{avg} = V + (\Delta V/2)$$

We have assumed that the relation $\alpha = \alpha_o \, (-\Delta P)^s$ describes the specific resistance of the compressible cake and the cake porosity is fairly small so that v can be assumed to be a constant. Let us therefore compute the value of $\Delta t/\Delta V$ and V_{avg} for each value of $(-\Delta P)$ under consideration. The results are given below :

Table 5.2.1

(ΔV), m^3	Δt *(seconds)*			$(\Delta t/\Delta V)$, sm^{-3}			V_{avg}, m^3
	$(-\Delta P_1)$ =138.2 kN/m^2	$(-\Delta P_2)$ =206.8 kN/m^2	$(-\Delta P_3)$ =275.4 kN/m^2	$(-\Delta P_1)$	$(-\Delta P_2)$	$(-\Delta P_3)$	
0.085	1836	1404	1116	21,600	16,517.65	13,129.41	0.185
0.056	1692	1296	1044	30,214.29	23,142.86	18,642.86	0.255
0.057	2088	1548	1296	36,631.58	27,157.9	22,736.84	0.312

Now we plot $(-\Delta t/\Delta V)$ *versus* V_{avg} for each value of $(-\Delta P)$ as shown in Figure (5.2.1). The magnitudes of slope (K_P') and y-intercept (B) of each straight line are given below in Table 5.2.2. Since $B = R_m \, \mu_f / A \, (-\Delta P)$, R_m can be computed as,

$$R_m = \frac{A\,(-\Delta P)}{\mu_f}\,(B) = \frac{0.75}{0.001}\,(-\Delta P)\,(B)$$

$$= 750\,(-\Delta P)\,(B), \text{ m}^{-1}$$

Table 5.2.2

$(-\Delta P), N/m^2$	K_P', sm^{-6}	B, sm^{-3}	R_m, m^{-1}
13.82×10^4	1,12,584.04	1800.0	1.87×10^{11}
20.68×10^4	83,781.50	1200.0	1.86×10^{11}
27.54×10^4	71,824.21	1000.0	2.07×10^{11}

Let us therefore choose an average value of R_m as 1.86×10^{11} m^{-1}. To evaluate the other two constants α_o and s, we make use of equation (5.1.29) :

$$\ln K_P' = \ln\left[\frac{\mu_f(\alpha_0 v)}{A^2}\right] - (1-s)\ln(-\Delta P) \qquad ...(ii)$$

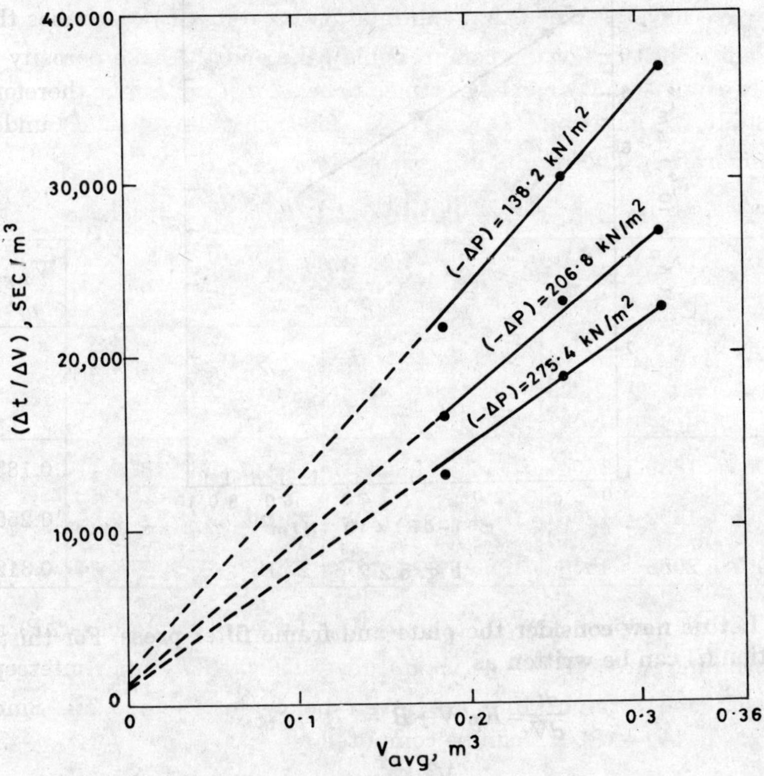

Fig. 5.2.1

Thus we make a plot of K_P' *versus* $(-\Delta P)$ as shown in Figure (5.2.2). From the figure,

Slope of the straight line = $(1 - s) = 0.62$

or $s = 0.38$

Let us now consider a convenient point on the straight line. For example, when $(-\Delta P) = 24 \times 10^4$ N/m², $K_P' = 80{,}000.0$

Therefore,

$$80{,}000 = \frac{(\alpha_o\, v)\, \mu_f}{A^2\, (24 \times 10^4)^{0.62}} = \frac{(\alpha_o\, v)\, (0.001)}{(0.75)^2\, (24 \times 10^4)^{0.62}}$$

or, $$(\alpha_o\, v) = 9748.63 \times 10^7 \text{ m}^{-2}/(\text{N m}^{-2})^{0.38}$$

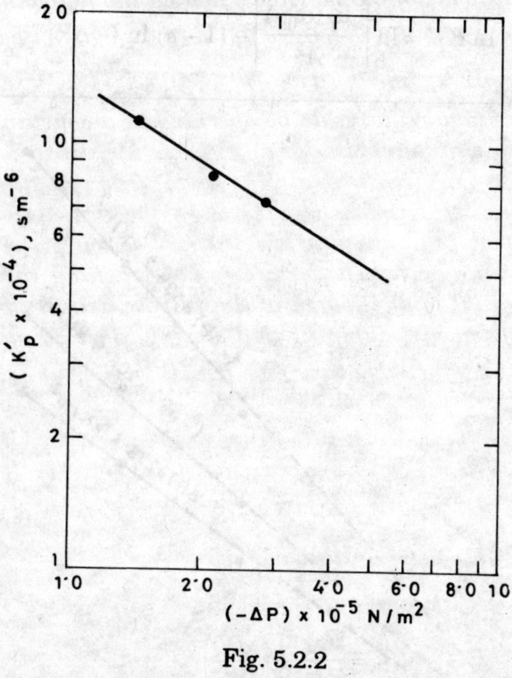

Fig. 5.2.2

Let us now consider the plate and frame filter press. For this, equation (*i*) can be written as,

$$\frac{dt}{dV} = K_P'\, V + B$$

On integration, $$t = K_P' \frac{V^2}{2} + BV$$

$$= \frac{(\alpha_o\, v)\, \mu_f}{A^2\, (-\Delta P)^{1-s}} \left(\frac{V^2}{2}\right) + \frac{R_m\, \mu_f}{A\, (-\Delta P)}\, V \qquad ...(iii)$$

We are to find the area of the filtering surface (A), if 12.0 m^3 of filtrate is being delivered in 2 hours (7600 seconds). That is, $t = 7200$ s, $V = 12.0\ m^3$, $(-\Delta P) = 17.15 \times 10^4\ N/m^2$. Substituting these values and also the values of R_m, s and $(\alpha_o\ v)$ already determined in equation (*iii*), we get a quadratic equation in A as,

$$0.72\,A^2 - (1.3)\,A - 399.05 = 0$$

or,
$$A = \mathbf{24.46\ m^2}.$$

Example 5.3. *A certain filter press when tested on a homogeneous slurry containing 10% by weight of solids (specific gravity = 2.33) in water at a constant rate of 0.3 m^3/hour yielded the following data :*

Time (minutes) :	*1.0*	*3.0*	*5.0*	*6.0*	*10.0*	*20.0*	*30.0*
$(-\Delta P)$, kN/m^2 :	*42*	*56*	*70*	*77*	*105*	*175*	*245*

This press is now required to be operated at a constant pressure drop of 70 kN/m^2 on the same sludge until 1.0 m^3 of filtrate is collected. Fifteen minutes are required to drain the liquor from the filter and ten minutes to fill the filter with wash water. The cake formed in each cycle is to be washed with an amount of water equal to one-sixteenth times the volume of filtrate delivered per cycle. The washing rate remains constant and is equal to one-fourth of the filtrate delivery rate at the end of filtration. Opening, dumping and closing takes 30 minutes.

Determine the total cycle time. What will be the cake thickness ? Assume the cake formed is incompressible.

Solution. For constant rate filtration on an incompressible sludge, equation (5.1.26) can be used :

$$(-\Delta P) = K_r'\, t + B_r \qquad \ldots(i)$$

where
$$K_r' = \frac{(\alpha v)\,\mu_f}{A^2}\left(\frac{dV}{dt}\right)^2$$

$$B_r = \frac{R_m\,\mu_f}{A}\left(\frac{dV}{dt}\right)$$

A plot of $(-\Delta P)$ *versus* time (t) is thus made as shown in Fig. (5.3.1). From the figure,

$$\text{Slope} = K_P' = 7.0\ \text{kN}/(\text{m}^2\ \text{hr})$$

$$y\text{-intercept} = B_r = 35\ \text{kN/m}^2$$

Therefore,
$$\frac{(\alpha v)\,\mu_f}{A^2} = K_r'/(dV/dt)^2$$

$$= \frac{(7.0)}{(0.3)^2}\,(3600)\,(1000)\ \text{N . sm}^{-8}$$

$$= 28 \times 10^7 \text{ N sm}^{-8}$$

$$\left(\frac{R_m \mu_f}{A}\right) = B_r/(dV/dt) = \frac{(35)}{0.3}(3600)\,(1000) \text{ N sm}^{-5}$$

$$= 42 \times 10^7 \text{ N sm}^{-5}$$

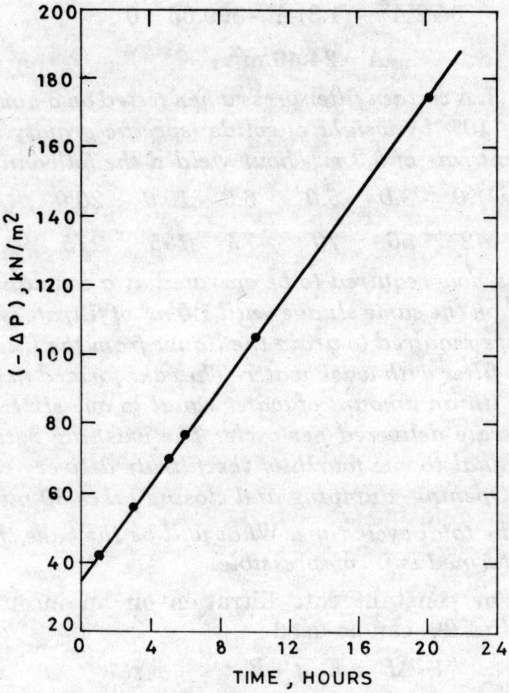

Fig. 5.3.1

When the filter is operated at constant pressure, we can use equation (5.1.21) :

$$\frac{dt}{dV} = K_p V + B$$

On integration, $t = K_P \dfrac{V^2}{2} + BV$

or, $$t = \frac{(\alpha v)\,\mu_f}{A^2\,(-\Delta P)}\,(V^2/2) + \frac{R_m\,\mu_f}{A\,(-\Delta P)}\,V \qquad ...(ii)$$

Substituting the values of $[(\alpha v)\,\mu_f/A^2]$ and $[R_m\,\mu_f/A]$ already determined and $(-\Delta P) = 70{,}000 \text{ N/m}^2$ we get

$$t = (2000)\,V^2 + (6000)\,V \qquad (iii)$$

$$\text{Time of washing, } t_{wash} = \frac{(1/16)\, V_f}{(1/4)\, (dV/dt)_f} = \frac{V_f}{4(\, dV/dt)_f}$$

where V_f = volume of filtrate collected per cycle

$$\left(\frac{dV}{dt}\right)_f = \text{ final rate of filtration} = 1/(K_P\, V_f + B)$$

$$K_P = \frac{(\alpha v)\, \mu_f}{A^2\, (-\Delta P)} = \frac{28 \times 10^7}{7 \times 10^4} = (4000)\text{ sm}^{-6}$$

$$B = \frac{R_m\, \mu_f}{A\, (-\Delta P)} = \frac{42 \times 10^7}{7 \times 10^4} = (6000)\text{ sm}^{-3}$$

$$\text{Therefore} \qquad t_{wash} = \frac{K_P\, V_f^2 + BV_f}{4} = 1000\, V_f^2 + 1500\, V_f$$

As we have stated at the beginning of this chapter, a full batch cycle includes the following steps :

Filtration
Drain
Fill
Wash
Drain
Opening, dumping and reassembling
Fill

The total cycle time therefore becomes,

$$t_{cycle} = t_f + 2\,(15 \times 60) + 2\,(10 \times 60) + t_{wash} + (30 \times 60)$$

$$= (2000\, V_f^2 + 6000\, V_f) + (1000\, V_f^2 + 1500\, V_f) + 4{,}800$$

$$= 3000\, V_f^2 + 7500\, V_f + 4800 \qquad \text{...}(iv)$$

The cycle time for collecting 1.0 m^3 of filtrate will be therefore,

$$t_{cycle} = 3000 + 7500 + 4800$$

$$= 15{,}300 \text{ seconds} = 4.25 \text{ hours}$$

Assuming the voidage of the cake formed is fairly small, we can compute v as,

$$v = \left(\frac{x}{1-x}\right)\frac{\rho_f}{\rho_s} = \frac{0.1}{0.9}\,\frac{(1.0)}{(2.33)} = 0.0477$$

$$\text{Thickness of cake,} \quad L_c = \frac{vV}{A} = \frac{(0.0477)\,(1.0)}{A}$$

$$= 4.77 \text{ cm per m}^2 \text{ of filtering surface.}$$

5.2. Continuous Filtration

Continuous filters employ some means for the continuous removal of the deposited cake. The cake thickness is thus not allowed to increase to large values and therefore the filtration process can be conducted at a constant rate employing a constant pressure difference. An excellent example for a popularly used continuous filter is the rotary drum filter. It is a vacuum filter consisting of a cylindrical drum partly submerged in the feed slurry (see Fig. 5.1). At any instant, a segment of the drum is in position (*ab*) and is thus in contact with the slurry. Due to the vacuum applied inside the drum, the filtrate is drawn in through the filter medium and the cake is deposited on the outer surface of the drum. This part of the cycle is indicated as "cake forming". As the drum rotates, this segment moves up to the position (*bc*) where it is subjected to dewatering by the simultaneous flow of air and filtrate. Then it moves to the position (*cd*) where the cake is washed by spraying wash water. At position (*de*) a second dewatering occurs and finally the cake is removed by the scraper or the "doctor knife" which may be assisted by introducing a slight positive air pressure that loosens the cake from the filter medium. At the end of the cycle, the segment comes back to the position (*ab*) where it again receives the slurry. Thus, it can be seen that a full rotation of the drum is equivalent to a complete batch cycle involving cake formation, dewatering, washing and cake removal. Therefore, the equations developed for batch filtration can be used for continuous filtration as well, keeping in mind that the equation stands for one full rotation of the drum only.

Thus

$$\frac{dt}{dV} = \frac{\mu_f}{A\,(-\Delta P)}\left[\frac{(\alpha v)}{A}V + R_m\right] \qquad ...(5.2.1)$$

or,

$$t = \frac{\mu_f}{A\,(-\Delta P)}\left[\frac{(\alpha v)}{A}\frac{V^2}{2} + R_m V\right] \qquad ...(5.2.2)$$

where t is the time for cake formation. If t_c is the time for one full rotation of the drum,

$$t = f\,t_c \qquad ...(5.2.3)$$

where f is the fraction of the cycle available for cake formation. For the rotary drum filter, f is equal to the fractional submergence of the drum in the slurry. It must not be forgotten that V in the above equations is the volume of filtrate collected during one rotation of the drum and (V/t_c) stands for the rate of filtration.

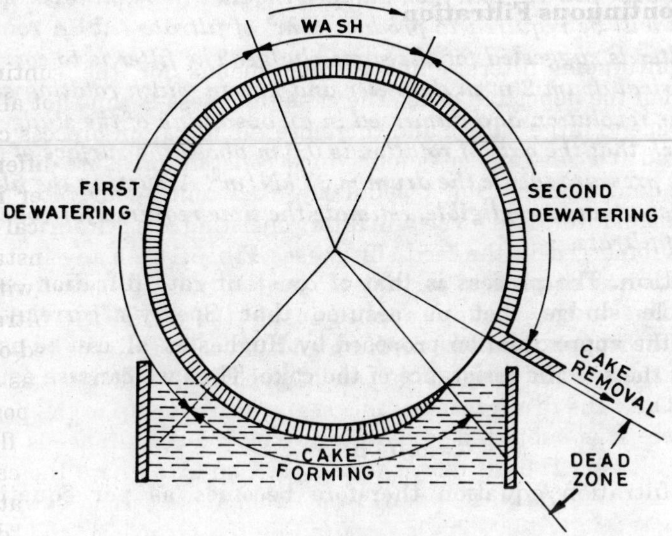

Fig. 5.1

If the cake formed is compressible so that $\alpha = \alpha_o\,(-\Delta P)^s$ then equation (5.2.2) modifies as,

$$(f\,t_c) = \left[\frac{(\alpha_o\,v)\,\mu_f}{2A^2\,(-\Delta P)^{1-s}}\right] V^2 + \left[\frac{R_m\,\mu_f}{A\,(-\Delta P)}\right] V \qquad \text{...(5.2.4)}$$

In many continuous vacuum filters, the filter medium resistance can be treated as negligible and in such case, the above equation reduces to,

$$(f\,t_c) = \left[\frac{(\alpha_o\,v)\,\mu_f}{2A^2\,(-\Delta P)^{1-s}}\right] V^2 \qquad \text{...(5.2.5)}$$

Example 5.4. *A Sweetland filter with a filter area of 0.2 m^2 handling a compressible sludge at a constant rate of 7.6×10^{-5} m^3/s yields the data given below :*

$(-\Delta P)$, kN/m^2	70.2	140.5	210.8	316.1	421.5	526.9	632.[illegible]	[illegible]72.8	969.5
Volume of filtrate, m^3	0.016	0.0318	0.045	0.0682	0.084	0.101	0.113	0.1[illegible]	0.132

(a) If this filter is operated on the sludge so that the filtration is at constant rate until the pressure difference becomes 455 kN/m^2, then at constant pressure until 0.5 m^3 filtrate is collected, then washed at 455 kN/m^2 with 0.1 m^3 of wash liquor (same physical and transport

properties as the filtrate) and then dumped the cake in 30 minutes, how much time will be required to produce 5 m³ of filtrate ? (b) A rotary vacuum filter is suggested for the same sludge. The filter is to consist of a cylindrical drum 2 m in diameter and 2 m in width rotating at 6 minutes per revolution and immersed in an open tank of the sludge to a depth such that the axis of rotation is 0.5 m above the surface of the liquid. The pressure inside the drum is 33 kN/m². Assuming the filter medium resistance is negligible, estimate the time required for collecting 5 m³ of filtrate.

Solution. The process is that of constant rate filtration on a compressible sludge. Let us assume that Sperry's correlation alongwith the approximation proposed by Hughes et. al. can be used to describe the specific resistance of the cake. Thus we can use equation (5.1.31) :

$$\alpha = \alpha_o\,(-\Delta P_c)^s \qquad ...(i)$$

The filtration equation therefore becomes as per equation (5.1.32) :

$$[(-\Delta P) - (-\Delta P_m)]^{1-s} = (-\Delta P_c)^{1-s} = K_r\,V \qquad ...(ii)$$

where $$K_r = \frac{(\alpha_o\,v)\,\mu_f}{A^2}\,(dV/dt)$$

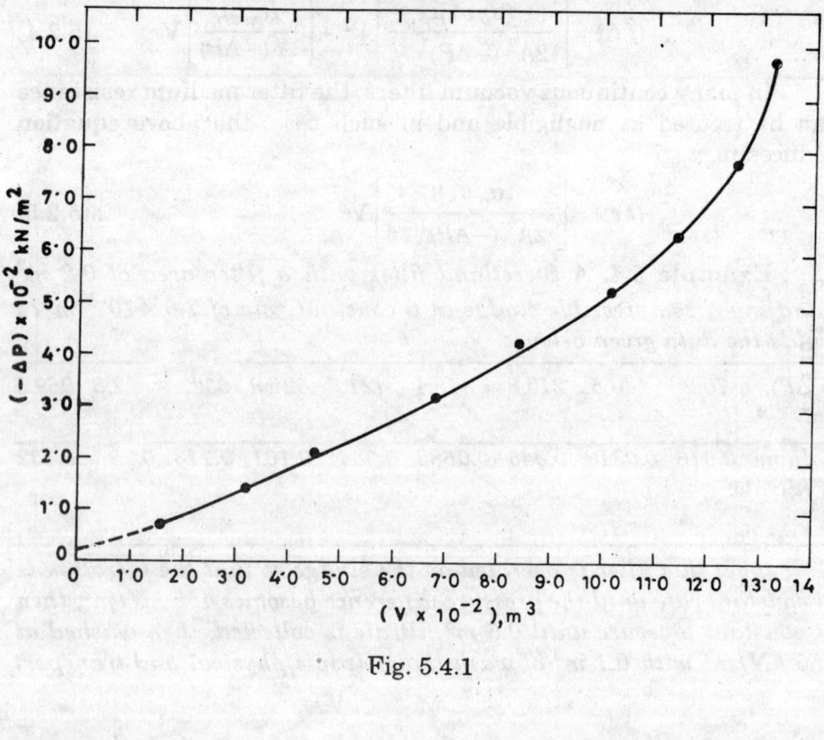

Fig. 5.4.1

We also assume that the cake voidage is fairly small so that v can be treated as a constant. To determine the value of $(-\Delta P_m)$, we plot a graph of $(-\Delta P)$ *versus* V and extrapolate the curve back to the pressure axis at $V = 0$, as shown in Figure (5.4.1). From the Figure $(-\Delta P_m)$ = [value of $(-\Delta P)$ at $V = 0$] = 20 kN/m^2. Taking logarithm, equation (*ii*) can be rewritten as,

$$\ln V = (1 - s) \ln (-\Delta P_c) - \ln K_r \quad \text{...}(iii)$$

We therefore make a plot of V *versus* $(-\Delta P_c)$ on log-log co-ordinates. Since the value of $(-\Delta P_m)$ has been determined, $(-\Delta P_c)$ can be computed as,

$$(-\Delta P_c) = (-\Delta P) - (-\Delta P_m)$$

The results are given below :

$(-\Delta P_c)$, kN/m^2	V, m^3
50.2	0.016
120.5	0.0318
190.8	0.045
296.1	0.0682
401.5	0.084
506.9	0.101
612.3	0.113
752.8	0.125
949.5	0.132

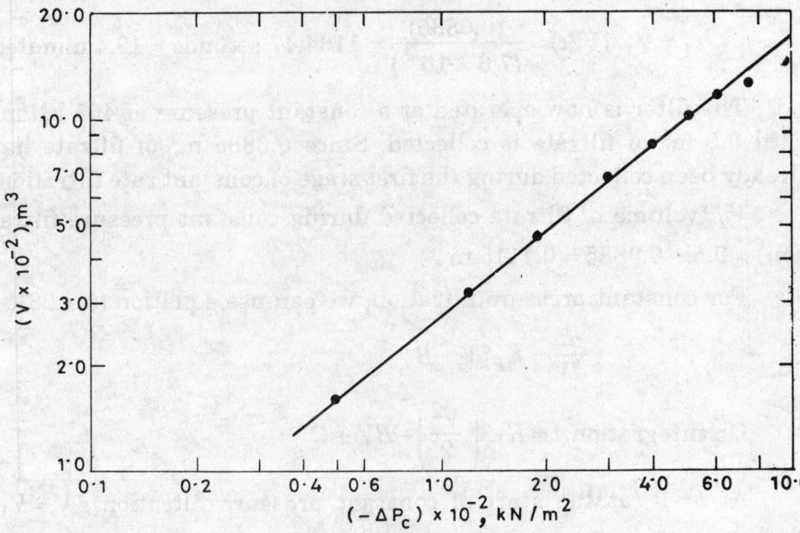

Fig. 5.4.2

The log-log plot of V *versus* $(-\Delta P_c)$ is given in Fig. (5.4.2). The plot is linear and therefore the value of $(-\Delta P_m)$ computed by the approximate method is correct. From the plot,

Slope of the straight line $= (1-s) = 0.8$

or,
$$s = 0.2$$

The value of K_r can be obtained by considering any convenient point on the straight line plot. For example, at $(-\Delta P_c) = 450$ kN/m^2, $V = 0.091$ m^3. Therefore from equation (*ii*),

$$K_r = \frac{(-\Delta P_c)^{1-s}}{V} = \frac{[450 \times 1000]^{0.8}}{(0.091)}$$

$$= 366.04 \times 10^3 \ (\text{Nm}^{-2})^{0.8} \ \text{m}^{-3}$$

(*a*) It is given that the filter is operated at the constant rate of 7.6×10^{-5} m^3/s until $(-\Delta P)$ reached 455 kN/m^2. Since $(-\Delta P_m) =$ 20 kN/m^2, $(-\Delta P_c)$ at the end of constant rate filtration = 435 kN/m^2.

Thus from equation (*ii*),

V_1 (volume of filtrate collected during constant rate filtration)

$$= \frac{(-\Delta P_c)^{1-s}}{K_r} = \frac{(435 \times 1000)^{0.8}}{(366.04 \times 10^3)}$$

$$= 0.0885 \ \text{m}^3$$

$$t_1 = V_1/(V/t) = \frac{(0.0885)}{(7.6 \times 10^{-5})} = 1164.47 \text{ seconds} = 19.4 \text{ minutes}$$

The filter is now operated at a constant pressure of 455 kN/m^2 until 0.5 m^3 of filtrate is collected. Since 0.0885 m^3 of filtrate has already been collected during the first stage of constant rate filtration,

V_2 (volume of filtrate collected during constant pressure filtration) $= 0.5 - 0.0885 = 0.4115$ m^3

For constant pressure filtration, we can use equation (5.1.28) :

$$\frac{dt}{dV} = K_P' V + B$$

On integration, $t = K_P' \left(\frac{V^2}{2}\right) + BV + C$

At $t = 0$ (at the start of constant pressure filtration), $V = V_1$. Therefore, $C = -K_P' (V_1^2/2) - BV_1$. Substituting for C, we get

$$t = \frac{K_P'}{2}(V^2 - V_1^2) + B(V - V_1) \quad \text{...(iv)}$$

where $$K_P' = \frac{(\alpha_o\, v)\,\mu_f}{A^2(-\Delta P)^{1-s}}$$

$$B = \frac{R_m\,\mu_f}{A(-\Delta P)}$$

Since $K_r = 366.04 \times 10^3$,

$$\left[\frac{(\alpha_o\, v)\,\mu_f}{A^2}\right] = K_r/(dV/dt) = \frac{(366.04 \times 10^3)}{(7.6 \times 10^{-5})} = 48.163 \times 10^8$$

Therefore, $$K_P' = \frac{(48.163 \times 10^8)}{(455{,}000)^{0.8}} = (1{,}43{,}319.2)\ \text{sm}^{-6}$$

Also, $$(-\Delta P_m) = \left(\frac{R_m\,\mu_f}{A}\right)\frac{dV}{dt} = 20\ \text{kN/m}^2$$

or, $$\left[\frac{R_m\,\mu_f}{A}\right] = \frac{(20{,}000)}{(7.6 \times 10^{-5})} = 263.16 \times 10^6\ \text{kg/(m}^4\ \text{s)}$$

Therefore, $$B = \frac{(263.16 \times 10^6)}{(455{,}000)} = (578.369)\ \text{sm}^{-3}$$

Thus, equation (*iv*) becomes,

$$t = 71{,}659.6\,(V^2 - 0.0885^2) + (578.369)\,(V - 0.0885)$$

When $V = V_2 = 0.4115\ \text{m}^3$,

$$t = t_2 = 11759.84\ \text{seconds} = 196\ \text{minutes}$$

Final rate of filtration

$$= \frac{1}{(K_P'\, V_2 + B)}$$

$$= [143.3192 \times 10^3 \times 0.4115 + 578.369]^{-1}$$

$$= (1.679 \times 10^{-5})\ \text{m}^3/\text{s}$$

Since washing is done at the same pressure of 455 kN/m^2 and since the wash liquor has the same physical and transport properties as the filtrate, rate of washing = final rate of filtration

Therefore, $$t_{wash} = \frac{(1.0)}{(1.679 \times 10^{-5})} = 5955.92\ \text{seconds}$$

$$= 99.25\ \text{minutes}$$

It is given that t_{etc} = 30 minutes = 1800 seconds.

Therefore, the total cycle time will be,

$$t_{cycle} = (t_1 + t_2) + t_{wash} + t_{etc}$$
$$= (19.4 + 196) + 99.25 + 30 = 344.65 \text{ minutes}$$

This is the time for collecting 0.5 m^3 of filtrate. Therefore, the time required for collecting 5 m^3 of filtrate will be 3446.5 minutes or 57.44 hours.

(*b*) Let us now consider the rotary drum filter used for the same slurry. Since the filter medium resistance is given to be negligible, $R_m = 0$. Also, since the sludge is the same, the values of α_o, s, v and μ_f will also be the same. We have already evaluated in (*a*)

$$\left[\frac{(\alpha_o\, v)\, \mu_f}{A^2}\right] = 48.163 \times 10^8 \;(\text{N/m}^2)^{0.8} \text{ sm}^{-6}$$

Since $A = 0.2$ m^2 for the Sweetland filter,

$$(\alpha_o\, v)\, \mu_f = 1.9265 \times 10^8 \;(\text{N/m}^2)^{0.8} \text{ sm}^{-2}$$

Let us thus use equation (5.2.5) :

$$ft_c = \frac{(\alpha_o\, v)\, \mu_f}{2A^2\, (-\Delta P)^{1-s}}\, V^2 \qquad \text{...}(v)$$

where t_c = 6 minutes = 360 seconds

$A = \pi DL = \pi\,(2.0)\,(2.0) = (4\pi)$ m^2

Assuming the atmospheric pressure to be 101 kN/m^2,

$$(-\Delta P) = (101 - 33) = 68 \text{ kN/m}^2$$
$$s = 0.2 \text{ [determined in } (a)]$$

To determine the fractional submergence f, consider Figure (5.4.3). If (2θ) is the angle subtended by the submerged surface at the centre, then from the figure,

$$\sin\,(90 - \theta) = \frac{OB}{OA} = \frac{0.5}{1.0} = 0.5$$

or, $$\theta = 60°$$

Therefore, $$f = \frac{(2\theta)}{360°} = \frac{120}{360} = 1/3$$

Substituting in equation (v), we get,

$$V = 1.202 \text{ m}^3$$

This is the volume of filtrate collected in one full revolution of the drum, that is in 6.0 minutes. The time required for collecting 5 m^3 of filtrate will be therefore,

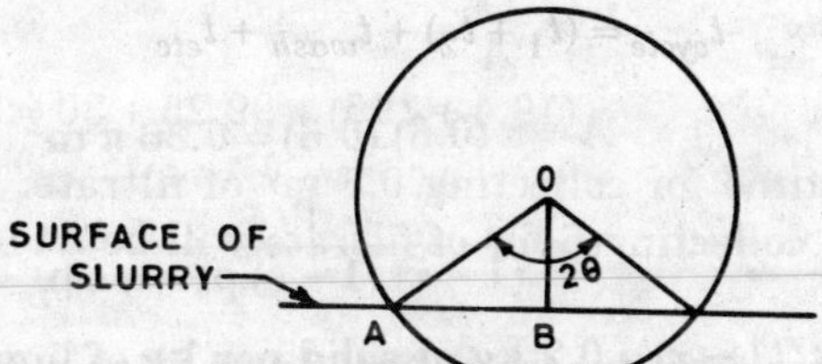

Fig. 5.4.3. Fractional Submergence of a Rotary Drum Filter.

$$= \frac{(5.0)\,(360)}{(1.202)} = 1497.5 \text{ seconds} \cong 25 \text{ minutes}$$

It can be seen that the total time required for collecting the same volume of filtrate is much less for the continuous filter as compared to the batch filter.

Example 5.5. *A slurry containing 0.2 kg of solid (specific gravity = 3.0) per kg of water is fed to a rotary drum filter 0.6 m long and 0.6 m in diameter. The drum rotates at one revolution in 6.0 minutes and 20% of the filtering surface is in contact with the slurry at any instant. If the filtrate is produced at 450 kg/hour and the cake has a voidage of 0.5, what thickness of cake will be produced when filtering with a vacuum of 59 cm of mercury ?*

The rotary filter breaks down and the operation has to be carried out temporarily in a plate and frame press with frames 0.3 m square. The press takes 2 minutes to dismantle and 2 minutes to reassemble and in addition 2 minutes are required to remove the cake from each frame. If filtration is to be carried out at the same overall rate as before with an operating pressure differential of 175 kN/m², what is the minimum number of frames that need to be used and what is the thickness of each ? Assume the cakes to be incompressible and neglect the resistances of filter media.

Solution. Since the overall rate of filtration for the rotary drum filter is 450 kg/hr,

$$\frac{V}{t_c} = \left[\frac{450}{1000 \times 3600}\right] \text{m}^3/\text{s}$$

Since t_c = 6 minutes = 360 seconds,

$$V = \frac{450 \times 360}{1000 \times 3600} = 0.045 \text{ m}^3$$

The thickness of cake formed can be computed from equation (5.1.15) :

$$L_c = \frac{Vv}{A}$$

where $\quad A = \pi\,(0.6)\,(0.6) = 0.36\,\pi\ \text{m}^2$

$$v = \frac{\rho_f x}{(1-x)(1-\varepsilon)\rho_s - x\,\varepsilon\,\rho_f}$$

Given that, $x/(1-x) = 0.2$ kg of solid per kg of liquid.

or, $\quad x = 1/6$

$$\varepsilon = 0.5$$

$$\rho_s = 3000\ \text{kg/m}^3$$

$$\rho_f = 1000\ \text{kg/m}^3$$

Therefore, $\quad v = 0.143$

$$L_c = \frac{(0.045)\,(0.143)}{(0.36)\,\pi} = 5.7 \times 10^{-3}\ \text{m} = 5.7\ \text{mm}$$

For the rotary drum filter, we can use equation (5.2.2) after putting $R_m = 0$ (since resistance of filter medium is negligible) :

$$t = ft_c = \frac{(\alpha\,v)\,\mu_f}{2A^2\,(-\Delta P)}\,V^2$$

where $\quad f = 0.20$

$$t_c = (6 \times 60) = 360\ \text{seconds}$$

$$A = 0.36\,\pi\ \text{m}^2$$

$$V = 0.045\ \text{m}^3$$

$$(-\Delta P) = (76 - 50) = 26\ \text{cm of mercury}$$

$$= 34.66\ \text{kN/m}^2$$

Substituting the values,

$$(\alpha v)\,\mu_f = 3.15 \times 10^9\ \text{kg/m}^3\text{s}$$

Now, let us consider the plate and frame press. From equation (5.1.21),

$$\frac{dt}{dV} = K_P\,V \quad (B = 0, \text{ since } R_m = 0)$$

or, $\quad t = K_P \dfrac{V^2}{2}, \quad \text{where, } K_P = \dfrac{(\alpha v)\,\mu_f}{A^2\,(-\Delta P)}$

In a plate and frame press (see section 5.3), the cake is deposited on both sides of the plate. Therefore, the filtration area will be,

$$A = 2\,(0.3 \times 0.3)\,n = 0.18\,n$$

where n = number of frames

Given that $(-\Delta P) = 175\ \text{kN/m}^2$

Therefore, $$t = \frac{K_P V^2}{2} = \frac{(\alpha\, v)\, \mu_f V^2}{2A^2\,(-\Delta P)}$$

$$= \frac{(3.15 \times 10^9)\, V^2}{2\,(0.18n)^2\,(175 \times 1000)} \quad ...(i)$$

Assuming each frame is completely filled with the cake, volume of cake = volume of frames

$$= (0.3 \times 0.3)\,(d/100)\,n = 9 \times 10^{-4}\,nd$$

where d = thickness of each frame in cm.

We know

$$v = \frac{(AL_c)}{V} = \frac{\text{Volume of cake}}{\text{Volume of filtrate}} = \frac{(9 \times 10^{-4})\,nd}{V}$$

or, $$V = \frac{(9 \times 10^{-4})\,nd}{v} = \frac{(9 \times 10^{-4})\,nd}{0.143} \quad ...(ii)$$

Substituting equation (*ii*) in (*i*) and simplifying we get,

$$t = 11.0\,d^2 \quad ...(iii)$$

Given that,

time for dismantling and reassembling = (2 + 2) = 4 minutes

= 240 seconds

Time for cake removal $= (2 \times 60)\,n = 120\,n$ seconds

Therefore, total cycle time $= 11d^2 + 240 + 120n$

Since the overall rate of filtration is to remain at 450 kg/hr,

$$\frac{450}{1000 \times 3600} = \frac{V}{11d^2 + 240 + 120n} = \frac{(9 \times 10^{-4})\,nd}{0.143\,(11d^2 + 240 + 120n)}$$

Simplifying and rearranging the above equation, we get,

$$n = \frac{11d^2 + 240}{50.35d - 120} \quad ...(iv)$$

To find the minimum number of frames required, we differentiate n with respect to d and put $(dn/dd) = 0$. Thus, $dn/dd = 0$ gives,

$$(50.35d - 120)\,(22d) - (11d^2 + 240)\,(50.35) = 0$$

or, $$(553.85)\,d^2 - (2640)\,d - 12{,}084 = 0$$

$$d = 7.6\ \text{cm}$$

Then, from equation (*iv*), $n = 3.33$

Thus, a minimum of 4 frames will be required. The value of d can be now recalculated by substituting $n = 4$ in equation (*iv*). Thus,

$$11d^2 - (201.4)d + 720 = 0$$

or, $$d = 13.438 \text{ or } 4.87 \text{ cm.}$$

Thus, 4 frames each of 5 cm thickness shall serve the purpose.

5.3. Industrial Filtration Equipment

We shall briefly discuss here the specifications of some of the popular filtration equipment used in chemical process industry. More detailed descriptions of these equipment are available in references (6) and (7).

Gravity-operated sand filters are one of the oldest types, still widely used in water purification. The tanks containing the beds of quartz sand are usually made of concrete. They have a perforated bottom covered with a layer of crushed rock or coarse gravel to retain the sand above. Instead of sand, crushed coke or crushed limestone beds are also used, the former, for example, for filtering sulfuric acid and the latter for alkaline liquors. Charcoal beds are used to clarify organic liquors and sugar solutions both by filtration and adsorption. For high capacity services, the filter beds may be placed in closed vessels and operated under pressure. Close uniform size of particles is a must for bed filters to provide maximum porosity and maximum rate of filtration.

Plate and frame filter presses are widely used particularly when the cake is valuable and relatively small in quantity. They are simple in construction and can be made from a wide range of materials starting from wood to cast iron, gun metal as well as stainless steel. Their maintenance and power costs are low and they can be operated at high pressures as much as 2.0 MN/m^2. However, they are intermittent in operation and due to high labour costs they are often limited to small scale applications. They consist of plates and frames (normally square) assembled alternately with filter cloths over each side of the plate. The assembly is held together as a unit by means of a hand screw or hydraulically. The feed slurry enters through the conduit formed by the holes in the upper right corner of both the plates and frames. Each frame carries an inlet or hole leading from this conduit through which the slurry enters the space between the plates. Due to the pressure with which the slurry is fed, the filtrate passes through the cloths on either side of the plates and thus cake is deposited on both sides of the plates. The filtrate enters the outlet from both sides of the plate.

Once the frames are essentially full with the cake, the feed is cut off and the cake is washed. Wash water enters the cake more or less from the centre of the frame and passes towards the plates on either side. If the wash liquor is fed through the same channel as the slurry and thus follows the same path as the filtrate, the process is called "simple washing". It is more preferable to use "through washing" in which the wash liquor enters through a separate channel behind the filter cloth on alternate plates known as the washing plates and flows through the entire thickness of the cake first in the reverse direction and then in the same direction as the filtrate. Since the area during washing is thus only half of that during filtration and since the wash liquor flows through twice the cake thickness, the rate of washing would be about one-quarter of the final rate of filtration. The filtrate and wash liquor can be discharged through separate outlets, the filtrate leaving through the lower left conduit and wash liquor through the lower right conduit on the alternate (washing) plate. The cake may be dewatered after washing by passing air. The press is then opened and the cake dumped off. It is usual practice to emboss small buttons for ease of identification such as one button on non-washing plates, two on frames and three on washing plates. Plate and frame filters provide large filtering area in small floor space. They also have the advantages that the filter cloths can be readily replaced and the capacity and cake thickness can be varied over wide ranges by changing the number and the size of the frames.

Leaf filters utilise a number of individual leaves each consisting of a grooved plate over which the filter cloth is wound. The leaves are immersed in the slurry which is either fed under pressure or sucked in by a vacuum pump. As in the plate and frame press, cake is deposited on both sides of the leaves. The Kelly filter uses rectangular leaves arranged longitudinally in a horizontal cylindrical shell whereas the Sweetland filter employs circular leaves of same size mounted transversely in the horizontal shell. In the latter case, the shell is divided into two halves with the lower portion hinged so as to provide easy access to the leaves. The cake can be therefore discharged without removing the leaves and corrosion becomes a less serious problem. Cakes of any desired thickness can be formed and the filter is therefore particularly suitable with cakes of high specific resistance. Sweetland filters are often fitted with a perforated pipe for spraying wash water onto the cake and very efficient washing of the cakes can be affected here. The main drawbacks of Sweetland filters are their high initial cost and the difficulty of clothing the circular leaves. Also, since they are usually made of cast iron, they cannot be operated at high pressures. In comparison, the rectangular leaves used in the

Kelly filter are easy to clothe and economical in the use of filter cloth. These filters are normally made of mild steel and can be operated at pressures upto 700 kN/m^2. However, corrosion problems are more acute here and since the leaves are of unequal size, they tend to form uneven cakes. The Vallez filter is a rotating leaf filter in which the circular leaves are mounted on a slow rotating hollow shaft and gives a more uniform cake. This type of filter also incorporates two screw conveyors for mechanical discharge of the cake without opening the press. However, due to the mechanical complications, its initial and maintenance costs are high.

The *rotary drum filter* is one of the most widely used continuous vacuum filters. It consists of a cast cylinder mounted horizontally and rotated at a very low rpm. The cylinder has a perforated surface over which the filter cloth is fixed. The cloth is sometimes separated from the drum by a coarse metal gauze so as to increase the effective area of filtration. The drum is immersed to the required depth in the slurry which is kept agitated to prevent settling of solids. Vacuum is applied to the segment that is submerged in the slurry and as a result the filtrate is drawn in through the filter medium depositing the suspended solids on the drum surface as the cake. The cake thickness depends on the speed of rotation of the drum. At higher speeds, thinner cake is formed resulting in higher rate of filtration. As the drum rotates, this segment alongwith the deposited cake that is now saturated with the filtrate is drawn outside the slurry and the cake is subjected to the first dewatering by the simultaneous flow of air and liquor. The cake is then washed by spraying with wash water through a series of nozzles mounted on wash headers. A cake compressor which is nothing but an endless canvas belt forced against the drum by two heavy rollers is sometimes used to consolidate the cake and decrease its moisture content. When washing is very difficult, the unwashed cake is discharged and mixed with wash liquor to form a fresh slurry that is fed back for refiltration.

After washing, the cake is subjected to a second dewatering, once again by the two-phase flow of air and the liquor. The filtrate and air pass through the ports and through the discharge head into a receiver where air is removed by a vacuum pump and filtrate by a liquid pump. The cake is then removed by means of a scrapper called the "doctor knife." The discharge is often facilitated by the application of compressed air or steam to the underside of the cloth which loosen the cake. A string discharge is sometimes used which employs a series of closely spaced strings passing round the drum. These strings remain embedded in the cake and thus carry the cake to the discharge end where they pass over rollers and the cake falls off. The cake may be discharged to a conveyor or a repulper for repulping with water or weak liquor. Rotary drum filters have very large capacity and operate continuously and automatically with least manpower requirements. However, it is a vacuum filter and therefore the maximum available pressure difference for filtration is limited. Therefore, it cannot be used for materials that form relatively impermeable cakes or cakes that are slimy and are difficult to remove from the cloth. It is difficult to handle hot liquids since they have a tendency to boil due to the vacuum maintained. Though the capital cost of the filter and the vacuum equipment are high, they are widely used in chemical process industries since they provide high filtration rates and excellent washing.

Another popularly used continuous filter is the *rotary disc filter*. It is similar to the drum filter in operation except that instead of a cylindrical drum it consists of a number of circular disks mounted on a horizontal tubular shaft and spaced by means of hubs. Different discs can be immersed in different slurries by dividing the slurry tank into a number of compartments each containing a separate slurry by using division plates. Thus, several slurries can be filtered simultaneously and separately on the same filter provided the filtrates may be mixed. Rotary disc filters provide much larger filtering area than the drum filter in the same floor space. However, they give poor washing and the discharge of the cake is more difficult.

Membrane filtration is the most recent advent in filtration technology. Membrane filters are widely used for bioseparation processes such as ultrafiltration, reverse osmosis and dialysis. The design and operation of artificial kidney or commonly called the haemo-dialyser is based on filtration through such semipermeable biomembranes. Filtration is also widely employed for, sterilising gases and liquids (removing undesirable viable cells and viruses) before feeding to bioreactors. For this purpose, polymeric microporous membranes are routinely used which remove trace particulates from air and liquid streams to render them sterile and free from pathogens. For more details, reference (8) may be consulted.

The most suitable filter for a given industrial practice is evidently the one that fulfils the requirements at the minimum overall cost. Since the cost of the equipment is closely related to the filtration area, it is always desirable to obtain a high overall rate of filtration with minimum filtration surface. This however involves use of high pressure for filtration but the maximum magnitude of pressure that can be employed is often limited by considerations of mechanical design. Though continuous filters provide higher rate of filtration for a given filtering surface, batch filters are often preferred particularly for handling materials that form cakes of high resistance. This is because, as discussed earlier, most continuous filters operate under a degree of vacuum and therefore the maximum pressure difference available for filtration is limited. Other factors that decide the selection of filters are the ease of discharge of the cake formed and the availability of a convenient method for observing the quality of the filtrate collected.

Filter aids are extensively used for handling sludges that form relatively impermeable cakes or slurries containing very fine solids or slimy and gelatinous materials that easily plug or clog the filter medium. Filter aids such as kieselguhr, diatomaceous earth, asbestos etc. are materials that pack to form beds of high voidages and therefore increase the porosity of the final filter cake if added to the feed slurry. The cake resistance is thus considerably reduced. However, this also increases the ultimate thickness of the cake and therefore filter aids must be used in optimised proportions. The filter aid can be subsequently separated from the cake by dissolving away the solids or by burning off the filter aid. If the cake is a waste material, then it can be dumped off as such alongwith the filter aid. Incidentally, filter cakes incorporating filter aids are often highly compressible and therefore care should be taken to see that the advantage of using filter aid is not destroyed by employing too high a filtration pressure. Filter aids can also be precoated on the filter medium prior to filtration. This prevents gelatinous solids from plugging or clogging the filter medium. Batch filters employ a thin precoat layer whereas thicker layers are used in rotary drum filters, commonly called precoat filters. The doctor knife continuously scraps off the top of the precoat layer for exposing fresh filtering surface.

5.4. Washing and Dewatering of Filter Cakes

When the filter cake is washed with a wash liquor that is miscible with the filtrate and has the same physical and transport properties as the filtrate, the rate of washing will be roughly equal to the final rate of filtration, provided washing is conducted at the same pressure. If the wash liquor has a lower viscosity (which helps in increasing the washing rate), the rate of filtration must be multiplied by the viscosity ratio of filtrate to wash liquor to obtain the actual washing rate. With highly compressible cakes washing may be conducted using a smaller pressure difference to prevent channeling and consequent incomplete washing of the cake.

The process of washing may be assumed to be taking place in three stages. During the first stage, the filtrate is displaced from the cake by the wash liquor without dilution. This is called "displacement washing" and during this stage about 90 per cent of the filtrate is removed from the cake if the wash liquor has approximately the same viscosity as the filtrate. During the second stage, the concentration of filtrate in the stream leaving the cake decreases continuously. The amount of filtrate that remains behind in the cake at the end of this stage depends primarily on the size of solids in the cake and this stage requires a volume of wash liquor that is approximately twice the volume of filtrate originally in the cake. During the third stage called the "diffusional washing", the filtrate diffuses into the wash liquor from the less accessible voids of the cake.

When a non-wetting fluid like air that is immiscible with the filtrate is used for dewatering and partially drying the cake, the process becomes that of a steady state, two phase flow of air and liquor through the packed bed of solids forming the cake. Two phase flow through packed beds is relatively complex to analyse. We shall present here a somewhat simplified method of analysis. The term "saturation" is often used in two-phase flow and its significance should be properly understood. Saturation (S) is usually defined with respect to the wetting fluid (say, the filtrate) and is therefore the fractional volume of voids occupied by the wetting fluid. Thus,

$$S = \frac{\text{Volume of voids filled with wetting fluid}}{\text{Total volume of voids}}$$

The residual saturation S_r is defined as,

$$S_r = \frac{\text{Maximum volume wetting fluid eliminated from flow}}{\text{Total volume of voids}}$$

The magnitude of S_r depends on the porosity (or voidage) of the bed, interfacial tension of the fluids and the pressure drop across the bed. One of the experimental correlations that can be used for computing S_r is given below[6] :

$$S_r = \frac{1}{K_1}\left[\frac{\varepsilon^3}{K(1-\varepsilon)^2}\frac{D_p^2(-\Delta P)}{36\,L\,\sigma\,(\cos\theta_c)}\right]^{-0.264} \qquad \text{...(5.4.1)}$$

where L = height or thickness of the bed,

K = Kozeny's constant (defined in section 5.1)

= (25/6)

σ = interfacial tension, N/m

θ_c = contact angle measured through the denser phase

D_p = volume-surface diameter of the particles in the bed

= $(\psi_s D_v)$ where ψ_s is the sphericity and D_v the volumetric diameter of the particles

K_1 = empirical constant

For thin beds upto 5 cm in thickness (as is normally encountered on rotary vacuum filters) $K_1 = 40.0$ and for relatively thick beds where the entrance and exit effects are negligible, $K_1 = 86.3$.

For defining the two phase system, it is the effective saturation S_e that is commonly used. S_e is defined as,

$$S_e = \frac{\text{Voids containing wetting fluid active in flow}}{\text{Voids containing both fluids in flow}}$$

S_e is related to S and S_r as[6],

$$S_e = \frac{S - S_r}{1 - 2S_r + SS_r} \qquad ...(5.4.2)$$

When air is passed through the cake, the saturation of the cake is reduced from the initial value to a desired limit. If V is the volume of filtrate removed from the cake, then we can write,

$$-dS = \frac{dV}{\varepsilon\,(AL_c)} \qquad ...(5.4.3)$$

where L_c = thickness of the cake (assumed constant during washing/dewatering)

Substituting for S from equation (5.4.2), the above equation becomes,

$$-\left[\frac{1 - S_r}{1 - S_r\,S_e}\right]^2 dS_e = \frac{dV}{\varepsilon\,(AL_c)} \qquad ...(5.4.4)$$

Since $v = (1/A)\,dV/dt$, where v is the superficial velocity of the filtrate through the cake during two phase flow,

$$dt = -\left[\frac{\varepsilon\,L_c}{v}\right]\left[\frac{1 - S_r}{1 - S_r\,S_e}\right]^2 dS_e \qquad ..(5.4.5)$$

If the flow of filtrate is laminar (as it usually is), v can be related to U_{sup} [superficial velocity of filtrate in single phase flow, given by equation (5.1.5)] as[6],

$$v = U_{sup}\,S_e^{\,y} \qquad ...(5.4.6)$$

where the value of y depends on the particle size D_p. However, the value of y varies from 2.4 for 0.8 mm particles to 2.8 for 0.15 mm particles and therefore an average value of 2.5 could be used for many of the computations. Substituting for U_{sup} from equation (5.1.5), we get

$$v = \left[\frac{(-\Delta P)}{K\,\mu_f\,L_c}\right]\left[\frac{\varepsilon^3}{s_p^2\,(1-\varepsilon)^2}\right]S_e^{\,y} \qquad \text{...(5.4.7)}$$

Thus, equation (5.4.5) becomes,

$$dt = -K_c\left[\frac{1-S_r}{1-S_r\,S_e}\right]^2\frac{dS_e}{S_e^y} \qquad \text{...(5.4.8)}$$

where
$$K_c = \frac{K\,\mu_f\,L_c^2}{(-\Delta P)}\,\frac{s_p^2\,(1-\varepsilon)^2}{\varepsilon^2}$$

or,
$$t = -K_c\int_1^{S_e}\left[\frac{1-S_r}{1-S_r\,S_e}\right]^2\frac{dS_e}{S_e^y} \qquad \text{...(5.4.9)}$$

The integral on the right hand side can be evaluated either graphically or numerically. Incidentally, it can be seen that when $S_e = 1$, $S' = [(1 - S_r)/(1 - S_r\,S_e)]^2$ becomes equal to 1 and when $S_e = 0$, it becomes equal to $(1 - S_r)^2$. Since the value of S' is normally close to unity, in many computations it will not cause any serious error if S' is taken as constant and equal to the arithmetic average of the two extreme values. Thus

$$S' \cong \frac{1 + (1 - S_r)^2}{2}$$

In that case, equation (5.4.9) reduces to,

$$t = -K_c\,S'\int_1^{S_e}\frac{dS_e}{S_e^y} \qquad \text{...(5.4.10)}$$

The above equation can be directly integrated as

$$t = \left[\frac{K_c\,S'}{y-1}\right][S_e^{1-y} - 1] \qquad \text{...(5.4.11)}$$

In a rotary vacuum filter for example, at the end of the cake forming step, the cake is almost completely saturated with filtrate so that $S_e = 1.0$ (thereby $S = 1.0$). The time required for reducing S_e from 1.0 to the required value during the dewatering step can be then computed from the above equation. The amount of air required for this purpose can also be computed by estimating the velocity of air through the cake. Since the flow of air is seldom in the laminar zone but will usually be in the transition zone (between laminar and turbulent flow), Ergun's equation[1] can be recommended for computing the air velocity :

$$\frac{(-\Delta P)\,D_p}{v_a^2\,\rho_a\,L_c}\left[\frac{\varepsilon^3}{1-\varepsilon}\right] = \left[\frac{150\,\mu_a\,(1-\varepsilon)}{D_p\,v_a\,\rho_a}\right] + 1.75 \qquad \text{...(5.4.12)}$$

$$\text{or,}\quad \left[\frac{1.75\,\rho_a\,(1-\varepsilon)}{D_p\,\varepsilon^3}\right]v_a^2 + \left[\frac{150\,\mu_a\,(1-\varepsilon)^2}{D_p^2\,\varepsilon^3}\right]v_a - \left[\frac{(-\Delta P)}{L_c}\right] = 0 \quad ...(5.4.13)$$

where v_a = superficial velocity of air through the cake

ρ_a = density air at the arithmetic average of end pressures

D_p = as used in earlier equations is the volume-surface diameter of particles in the cake

$= (\psi_s\, D_v)$

The above equation has been developed for single phase flow through a packed bed of solids. However, the same equations (5.4.12) and (5.4.13) can be used to estimate the velocity of air in two phase flow (v_a') as well, provided the porosity ε is replaced by the equivalent porosity ε' and the sphericity of the particles (used for computing D_p) is replaced by the wetted sphericity ψ_s'. These factors ε' and ψ_s' are defined as,

$$\varepsilon' = \frac{(1-S)}{(1-S_r)}\,\varepsilon \quad ...(5.4.14)$$

The wetted sphericity is a function of the effective saturation S_e and can be estimated from standard plots of ψ_s' versus S_e for different particles of different sizes available in literature.[6] A typical set of plots of this kind is given in Figure (5.2). These corrections are required since in two phase flow of air and filtrate, the wetting fluid (filtrate) on the surfaces of the particles changes the shape (and thereby the sphericity) of the particles exposed to the nonwetting fluid (air)

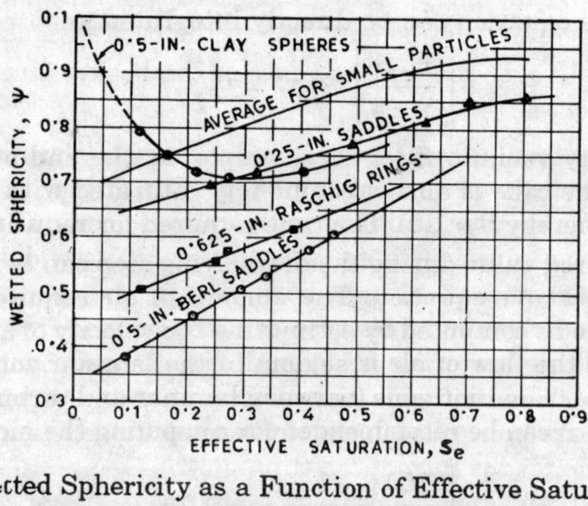

Fig. 5.2. Wetted Sphericity as a Function of Effective Saturation for Different Materials (from G.G. Brown and Associates, Unit Operations, Wiley, 1950, with permission).

and also occupies selectively the small pores and capillaries leaving only the large pores open to the nonwetting fluid.

The instantaneous values of air velocity v_a' at any time t [and corresponding values of S_e from equation (5.4.11)] can be thus computed using equation (5.4.13) after incorporating the above-said corrections. The total air flow per unit area is then obtained as,

$$V_a = \int_0^t v_a' \, dt \qquad \text{...(5.4.15)}$$

The integral may be evaluated graphically or numerically.

The quantity of air that must be drawn through the cake to reduce the filtrate content is an important consideration, particularly in continuous vacuum filters as it determines the required capacity of the vacuum pumps. The computation flow graph based on the procedure discussed in this section for estimating the air requirement for any dewatering operation is given in Section (5.6).

5.5. Centrifugal Filtration

As stated in section (4.2) of chapter (4), whenever centrifugal forces are employed to affect separation, the separation efficiency of the equipment is very much enhanced. Centrifugal filtration is therefore used for separating suspensions containing coarse, granular solids and also for drying crystals. Centrifugal filters, commonly called centrifugals, are larger diameter and relatively low speed machines than centrifugal sedimentors (centrifuges). They use perforated baskets, the mother liquid passing out through the perforations. A coarse gauze is often laid over the inner surface of the basket and the filter cloth rests on the gauze.

Batch centrifugals are either suspended basket (over-driven) vertical shaft or underdriven vertical shaft type. The former is more versatile, possessing greater stability with uneven loads and permits greater speed for a given diameter. The latter one is widely used in laundries and pharmaceutical industries because the open top allows easy charging and cleaning. This type can also be made vapour tight for handling volatile materials and requires less headroom than the former type. Batch centrifugals can also be operated automatically. The operations are controlled by a timing mechanism and are run continuously. The feed is introduced through the feed nozzle and once a cake of desired thickness has been built up, the feed is shut off automatically, wash water is introduced through sprays and after dewatering, the scraper knife is automatically raised to remove the cake through the discharge chute.

Continuous centrifugals incorporate a mechanism for the continuous removal of solids such as spiral scrapers or discharge plows. The cake can also be removed by a reciprocating pusher operated hydraulically that shoves the cake along the perforated surface of the basket.

Let us now analyse the process of centrifugal filtration. Consider a centrifugal of radius R and height b rotating at an angular speed ω as shown in Fig. (5.3.). Let us assume that the liquid surface inside the basket is vertical and the cake is also deposited parallel to the wall of the basket, as shown in the figure (if the liquid forms a parabolic vortex inside the basket, equation (4.2.2) given in Chapter 4 could be

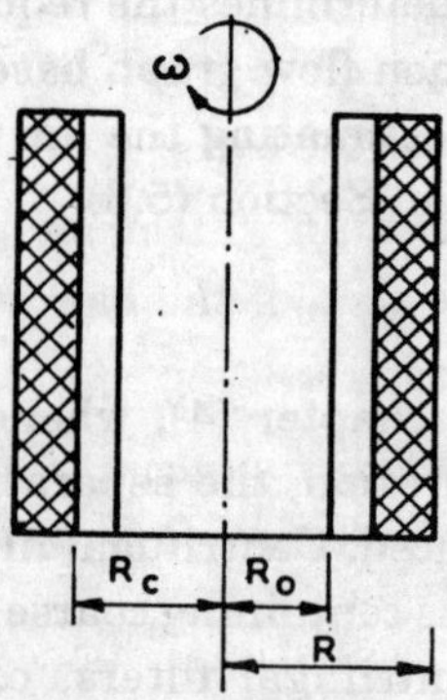

Fig. 5.3. Cake and Liquid Layers inside a Batch Centrifugal.

used to describe the shape of the liquid surface inside the basket). Since the centrifugal forces are many-fold larger in magnitude than the gravitational forces, the effective pressure difference driving force for filtration may be assumed to be due to centrifugal action only. Thus,

$$(-\Delta P) = \frac{1}{2}\rho_f\,\omega^2\,(R^2 - R_o^2) \qquad \text{...(5.5.1)}$$

We can therefore use an equation similar to the one developed for constant pressure filtration in section (5.1) here also, provided the inherent assumptions such as the flow of filtrate through the cake is laminar and the voids of the cake are completely filled with the filtrate (no channeling) are kept alive. Thus,

$$\frac{dt}{dV} = \frac{\mu_f}{(-\Delta P)}\left[\frac{(\alpha v)}{A_c^2}\,V + \frac{R_m}{A_m}\right] \qquad \text{...(5.5.2)}$$

where $(-\Delta P)$ is obtained from equation (5.5.1). It must be noted that the cross-sectional area of the cake A_c perpendicular to the direction of flow of filtrate changes as the thickness of the cake increases. A specific value of A_c cannot be therefore used in the above equation since A_c is a function of time. However, Grace[9] has shown that for many of the practical purposes, A_c^2 can be written as,

$$A_c^2 = [\bar{A}_a \bar{A}_L] \qquad \text{...(5.5.3)}$$

where $\bar{A}_a$ = arithmetic mean cake area

$$= 2\pi b \left[\frac{R_c + R}{2}\right] = \pi\, b\, (R_c + R)$$

$\bar{A}_L$ = logarithmic mean cake area

$$= 2\pi b \left[\frac{R - R_c}{\ln (R/R_c)}\right]$$

$(R - R_c)$ = final thickness of cake formed

A_m is the area of the filter medium which can be assumed to be roughly equal to the inside surface area of the basket. Thus,

$$A_m = 2\pi R b \qquad \text{...(5.5.4)}$$

Example 5.6. *A leaf filter filtering an incompressible sludge containing 70 kg of solids per m³ of liquid at 0.49 kg/(m² s) gave the following results :*

Pressure drop, kN/m² :	*30.8*	*56.0*	*71.4*	*84.0*	*96.0*
Time (seconds) :	*10*	*40*	*60*	*75*	*90*

If the above slurry is to be filtered in a centrifugal 0.75 m in diameter and 0.45 m in height rotating at 300 rpm forming a 2 cm liquid layer inside the basket, how much time will be required to wash the cake formed using 0.2 m³ of wash water ? Final thickness of cake = 15 cm. Assume that the filtrate and wash liquor have the same physical and transport properties. Specific gravity of solids = 2.0. The filter medium resistance may be assumed to be constant and to be the same for both the leaf filter and the centrifugal.

Solution. For constant rate filtration on an incompressible sludge, equation (5.1.26) can be used :

$$(-\Delta P) = K_r'\, t + B_r \qquad \text{...}(i)$$

where
$$K_r' = \frac{(\alpha w)\,\mu_f}{A^2}\,(dV/dt)^2$$

$$B_r = \frac{R_m \mu_f}{A} \frac{dV}{dt}$$

A plot of $(-\Delta P)$ *versus* time is thus made as shown in Fig. (5.6.1). From the figure,

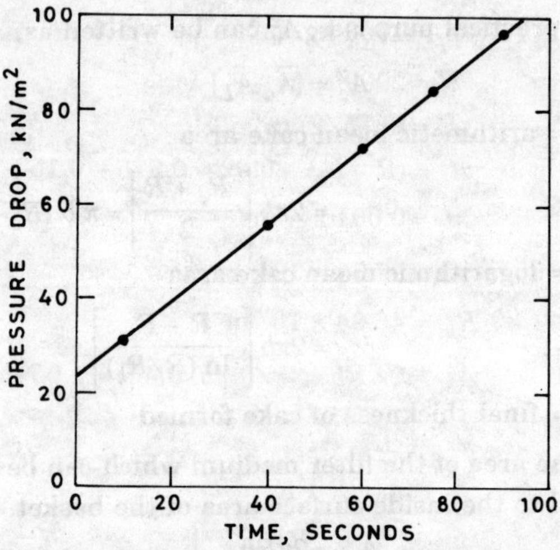

Fig. 5.6.1. Pressure Drop Versus Time Plot.

$$\text{Slope} = K_r' = 0.8214 \text{ kN/m}^2 \text{ s}$$

$$y\text{-intercept} = B_r = 23.0 \text{ kN/m}^2$$

Since $\left(\frac{1}{A}\frac{dV}{dt}\right) = \left(\frac{0.49}{1000}\right) \text{m}^3/\text{m}^2 \text{ s}$, and $v = \left(\frac{70}{2 \times 1000}\right) = 0.035$,

$$\alpha = \frac{K_r'}{v \mu_f \left(\frac{dV/dt}{A}\right)^2} = \frac{(0.8214 \times 1000)}{(0.035)(0.001)(0.49 \times 10^{-3})^2}$$

$$= 97.71 \times 10^{12} \text{ m}^{-2}$$

$$R_m = \frac{B_r}{\mu_f \left[\frac{dV/dt}{A}\right]} = \frac{(23 \times 1000)}{(0.001)(0.49 \times 10^{-3})}$$

$$= 46.94 \times 10^9 \text{ m}^{-1}$$

Now, for the centrifugal let us use equation (5.5.2) :

$$\frac{dt}{dV} = \frac{\mu_f}{(-\Delta P)} \left[\frac{(\alpha v)}{A_c^2} V + \frac{R_m}{A_m}\right]$$

This can be rewritten as,

$$\frac{dt}{dV} = \frac{\mu_f}{(-\Delta P)}\left[\frac{(\alpha L_c)}{A_c} + \frac{R_m}{A_m}\right] \quad ...(ii)$$

where $$(-\Delta P) = \frac{1}{2}\rho_f \omega^2 (R^2 - R_o^2) = \frac{1}{2}\rho_f (2\pi N/60)^2 (R^2 - R_o^2)$$

$$\rho_f = 1000 \text{ kg/m}^3$$

$$N = 2000 \text{ rpm}$$

$$R = (0.75/2) \text{ m}$$

$$R_o = (R - L_c) - 0.02 = 0.375 - 0.15 - 0.02 = 0.205 \text{ m}$$

$$\mu_f = 0.001 \text{ kg/ms}$$

$$\alpha = 97.71 \times 10^{12} \text{ m}^{-2}$$

$$R_m = 46.94 \times 10^9 \text{ m}^{-1}$$

$$A_m = 2\pi Rb = [\pi (0.75)\, 0.45] = 1.06 \text{ m}^2$$

$$A_c = \sqrt{\bar{A}_a \bar{A}_L}$$

$$\bar{A}_a = \pi b (R + R_c)$$

$$\bar{A}_L = 2\pi b\left[\frac{R - R_c}{\ln (R/R_c)}\right]$$

$$R_c = R - L_c = \left(\frac{0.75}{2}\right) - 0.15 = 0.225 \text{ m}$$

Substituting the values in equation (*ii*), we get,

$$\frac{dV}{dt} = 2.78 \times 10^{-4} \text{ m}^3/\text{s}$$

Since wash water and filtrate have same properties, we take rate of washing = 2.78×10^{-4} m^3/s. Therefore,

$$\text{Time of washing} = \frac{(0.2)}{(2.78 \times 10^{-4})(60)} \text{ minutes} = \textbf{12 minutes.}$$

5.6. Computer Aided Analysis[10]

Once a high speed computer is available at our disposal, filtration calculations can be made faster and easier. Let us first consider the procedure for dewatering the filter cake in a rotary drum vacuum filter. The methodology has been described in section (5.4). The computation flow graph is given in Fig. 5.4 (*a*) and 5.4(*b*). The total air flow V_a required in m^3/m^2/cycle has been computed assuming dewatering is conducted for t_w seconds. If θ_1 is the angle subtended at the

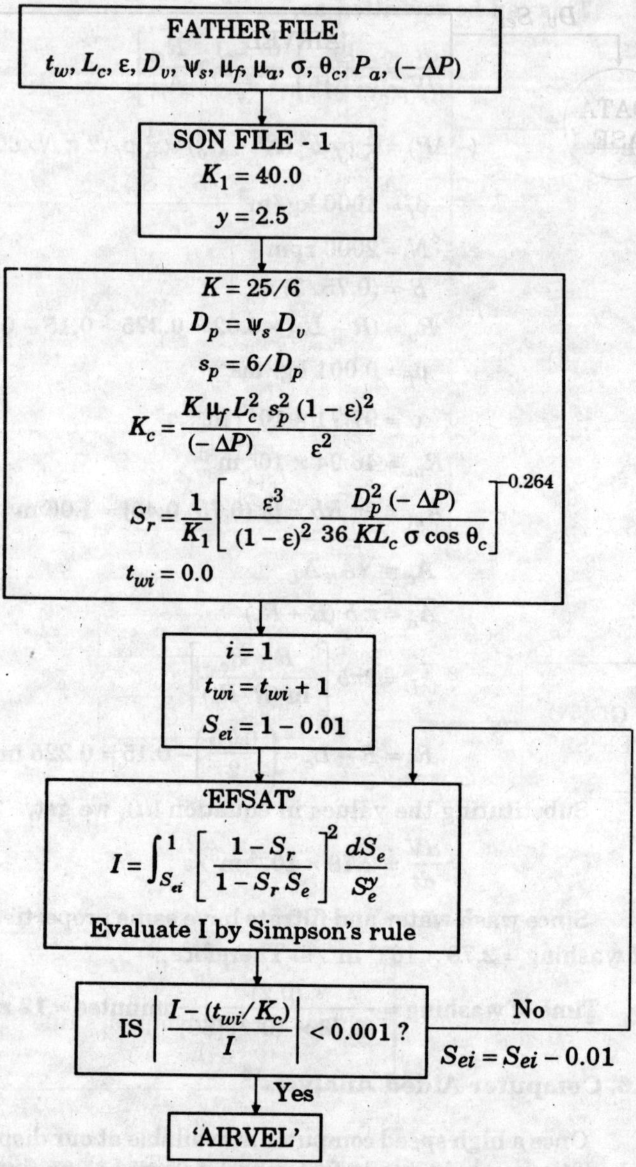

Fig. 5.4.(*a*) Computer-aided Analysis of Two Phase Flow Through Filter Cake.

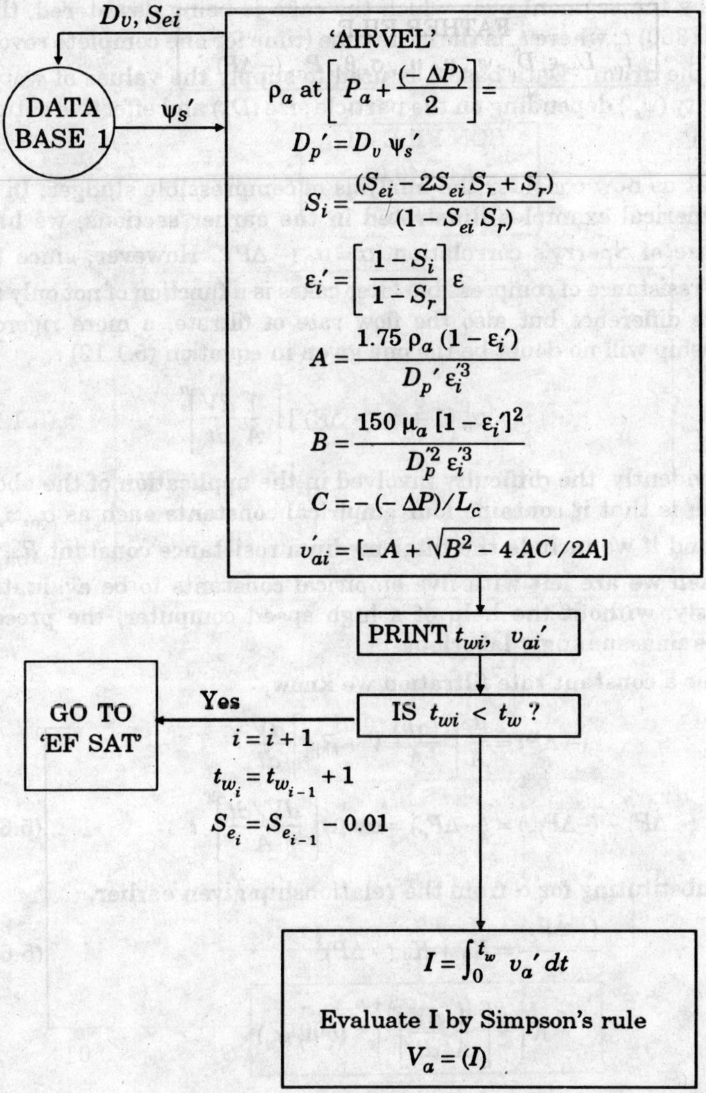

Fig. 5.4.(*b*) Computer-aided Analysis of Two Phase Flow Through Filter Cake.

center by the segment over which the cake is being dewatered, then $t_w = (\theta_1/360)\, t_c$ where t_c is the cycle time (time for one complete revolution of the drum). Data base-1 is used to supply the values of wetted sphericity (ψ_s') depending on the particle size (D_v) and effective saturation (S_e).

Let us now consider the analysis of compressible sludges. In all the numerical examples illustrated in the earlier sections, we have made use of Sperry's correlation, $\alpha = \alpha_0 (-\Delta P)^s$. However, since the specific resistance of compressible filter cakes is a function of not only the pressure difference but also the flow rate of filtrate, a more rigorous relationship will no doubt be the one given in equation (5.1.12) :

$$\alpha = \alpha_o\, [1 + m\, (-\Delta P)^s] \left[\frac{1}{A}\frac{dV}{dt}\right]^n \qquad \text{...(5.1.12)}$$

Evidently, the difficulty involved in the application of the above equation is that it contains four empirical constants such as α_o, s, m and n and if we include the filter medium resistance constant R_m as well, then we are left with five empirical constants to be evaluated. Obviously, without the help of a high speed computer, the process could be unassumingly laborious.

For a constant rate filtration we know,

$$(-\Delta P) = \frac{\mu_f}{A}\left[\frac{(\alpha v)}{A} V + R_m\right]\frac{dV}{dt}$$

or $$(-\Delta P) - (-\Delta P_m) = (-\Delta P_c) = \alpha v\, \mu_f \left[\frac{dV/dt}{A}\right]^2 t \qquad \text{...(5.6.1)}$$

Substituting for α from the relationship given earlier,

$$\frac{(-\Delta P_c)}{t} = K_1 + K_2\, (-\Delta P)^s \qquad \text{...(5.6.2)}$$

where $$K_1 = \left[\frac{1}{A}\frac{dV}{dt}\right]^{2+n} (v\, \mu_f\, \alpha_o)$$

$$K_2 = K_1\, m$$

Thus, first we determine $(-\Delta P_m)$ by extrapolating the plot of $(-\Delta P)$ *versus* time (t) to $t = 0$. Then assuming a value of s, a straight line fit using the method of least squares between $(-\Delta P_c)/t$ and $(-\Delta P)^s$ will give the values of K_1 and K_2. Then, $m = K_2/K_1$. If the values of m determined at different values of (dV/dt) do not agree with each other, the assumed value of s is to be manipulated.

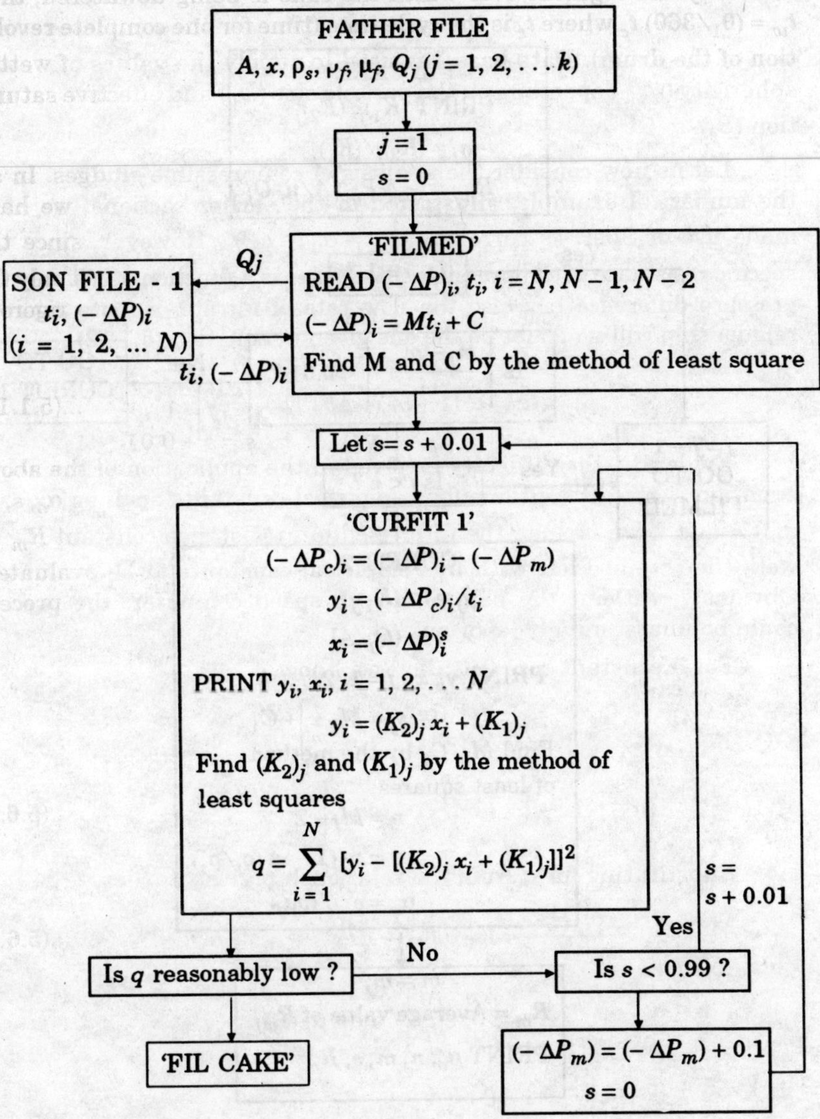

Fig. 5.5. (*a*) **Computer-aided Anlysis of Filtration on Compressible Sludges.**

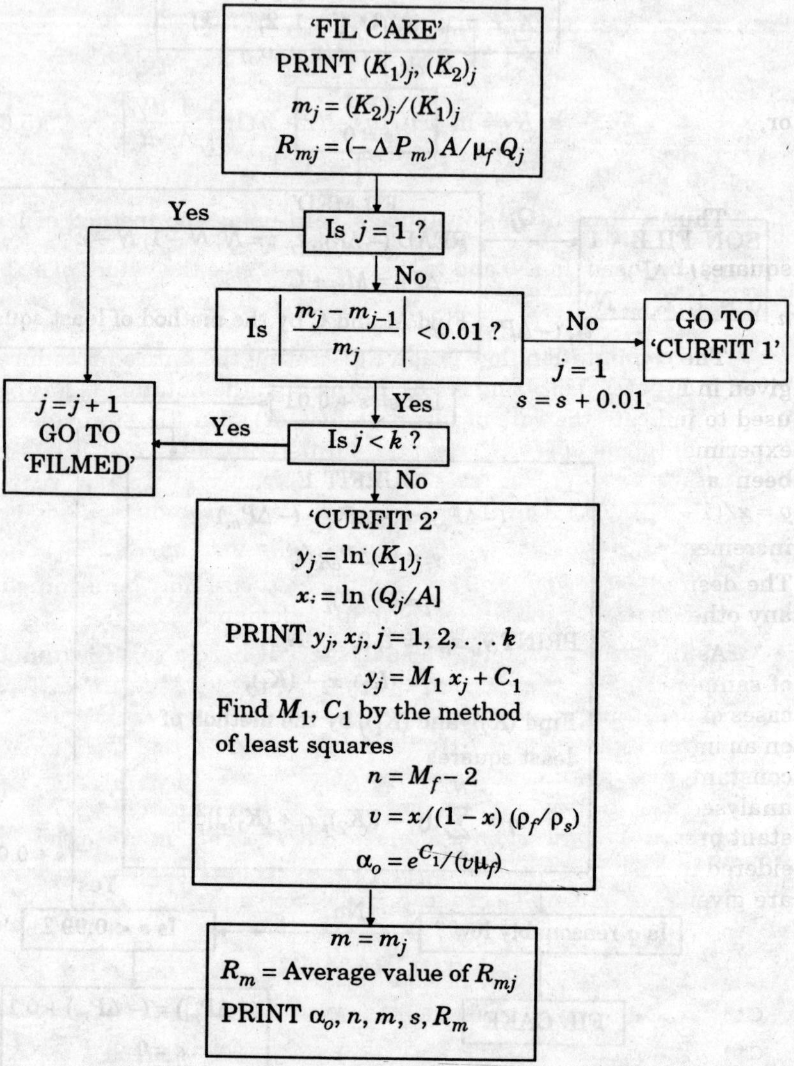

Fig. 5.5.(*b*) Computer-aided Analysis of Filtration on Compressible Sludges.

Now,

$$K_1 = \left[\frac{1}{A}\frac{dV}{dt}\right]^{2+n} (v\,\mu_f\,\alpha_o)$$

or,

$$\ln K_1 = \ln (v\,\mu_f\,\alpha_o) + (2+n)\ln\left[\frac{1}{A}\frac{dV}{dt}\right] \quad ...(5.6.3)$$

Thus a straight line fit (once a gain using the method of least squares) between ($\ln K_1$) and $\ln\left[\frac{dV/dt}{A}\right]$ will give the values of α_o and n.

The computation flow graph illustrating the entire procedure is given in Figures 5.5(*a*) and 5.5(*b*). In the Fig., the notation Q has been used to indicate the rate of filtration (dV/dt). Son file-1 provides the experimental data of ($-\Delta P$) *versus* t at different values of Q. It has also been assumed that the cake voidage remains fairly low so that $v = x/(1-x)\,(\rho_f/\rho_s)$. During the trial and error procedure, s has been incremented by 0.01 and ($-\Delta P_m$) increased in increments of 0.1 N/m^2. The desired degree of accuracy and the step size may be modified to any other specific values if the situation demands so.

As in earlier chapters, we shall present here also a few number of sample computer programs. Let us first consider the three typical cases of operation of a batch filter such as constant pressure filtration on an incompressible sludge (similar to that discussed in Example 5.1), constant pressure filtration on a compressible sludge (similar that analysed in Example 5.2) and constant rate filtration followed by constant pressure filtration on a compressible sludge (similar to that considered in Example 5.4). The computer programs for these three cases are given respectively in Program (5.1), (5.2) and (5.3).

PROGRAM 5.1

```
C**     CONSTANT PRESSURE FILTRATION ON AN
C**     INCOMPRESSIBLE SLUDGE IN A BATCH FILTER.
        REAL M, NUMR, KP, KPE, LC, MEUF
C**     IN THE DIMENSION STATEMENT THE INDEX
C**     IS TAKEN AS 10 AS AN EXAMPLE.
        DIMENSION V(10), T(10), DV(10), DT(10), DTV(10)
        VA(10)
        READ (*, *) A, SX, ROWS, ROWF, DPO
C**     FILTRATION DATA ON THE SAME SLUDGE
```

```
C**     AT A PRESSURE DIFFERENTIAL (DPE) IN AN
C**     EXPERIMENTAL FILTER OF AREA (AE) ARE
C**     AVAILABLE.
        READ (*, *) N
        READ (*, *)  (V(I), T(I), I = 1,N)
        DO 10 I = 1, N - 1
        DV(I) = V(I + 1) - V(I)
        DT(I) = T (I + 1) - T(I)
        DTV(I) = DT(I)/DV(I)
        VA(I) = [V(I) + V(I + 1)]/2.0
 10     CONTINUE
C**     FIT A STRAIGHT LINE BETWEEN DTV(I)
C**     AND VA(I) BY THE METHOD LEAST SQUARES.
        SUMX = 0.0
        SUMY = 0.0
        SUMXX = 0.0
        SUMXY = 0.0
        DO 15 I = 1, N - 1
        SUMX = SUMX + VA(I)
        SUMY = SUMY + DTV(I)
        SUMXY = SUMXY + VA(I) * DTV(I)
 15     SUMXX = SUMX + VA(I) * * 2
        AN = N - 1
        NUMR = AN * SUMXY - SUMX * SUMY
        DENR = AN * SUMXX - SUMX * * 2
        M = NUMR/DENR
        C = (SUMY - M * SUMX)/AN
        KPE = M
        BE = C
C**     EVALUATE THE FILTRATION CONSTANTS.
C**     THE FILTER MEDIUM RESISTANCE IS ASSUMED SAME FOR
        EXPERIMENTAL FILTER AND INDUSTRIAL FILTER.
        SV = SX * ROWF/[(1.0 - SX) * ROWS]
        ALFA = KPE * AE * AE * DPE/(SV * MEUF)
        RM = BE * AE * DPE/MEUF
C**     COMPUTE THE VOLUME OF FILTRATE COLLECTED
```

```
C**    WITHIN A FILTERING TIME TF.
       READ (*, *) TF
       KP = MEUF * ALFA * SV/(DPO * A * A)
       B = RM * MEUF/(A * DPO)
       VF = [- B + SQRT (B * * 2 + 2.0 * KP * TF)]/KP
C**    COMPUTE FINAL RATE OF FILTRATION.
       DVTF = 1.0/(KP * VF + B)
C**    COMPUTE FINAL CAKE THICKNESS.
       LC = VF * SV/A
C**    SPECIFY THE RATIO OF VOLUME OF WASH WATER
C**    USED TO FINAL VOLUME OF FILTRATE COLLECTED
C**    (RX) AND THE RATIO OF RATE OF WASHING TO
C**    FINAL RATE OF FILTRATION (RY)
       READ (*, *) RX, RY
C**    COMPUTE TIME OF WASHING.
       TWA = (RX * VF)/(RY * DVTF)
C**    COMPUTE THE CYCLE TIME AND OPTIMUM
C**    CYCLE TIME.
       READ (*, *) TETC
       A1 = KP/2.0 + (KP * RX/RY)
       A2 = (1.0 + RX/RY) * B
       TC = A1 * VF * * 2 + A2 * VF + TETC
       VOPT = SQRT (TETC/A1)
       TCOPT = A1 * VOPT * * 2 + A2 * VOPT + TETC
       WRITE (*, *) VF, DVTF, TWA, VOPT, TCOPT
       STOP
       END
```

PROGRAM 5.2

```
C**    CONSTANT PRESSURE FILTRATION ON A COM-
C**    PRESSIBLE SLUDGE IN A BATCH FILTER.
C**    SPERRY'S CORRELATION (EQUATION 5.1.9)
C**    IS ASSUMED VALID FOR THE COMPRESSIBLE CAKE
       REAL KPP(10)
       REAL NUMR, MM, MEUF
C**    IN THE DIMENSION STATEMENT BOTH INDICES
```

```
C**     ARE TAKEN AS 10 AS AN EXAMPLE.
        DIMENSION V(10), DP(10), T(10, 10), B(10), DV(10),
        DT(10), DTV(10), VA(10), RMC(10), X(10), Y(10)
C**     THE REQUIRED AREA OF FILTERING SURFACE
C**     FOR DELIVERING VF CUBIC METERS OF FILT-
C**     RATE IN TIME TF IS TO BE COMPUTED.
        READ (*, *) SX, ROWS, ROWF, MEUF, VF, TF, DPO
C**     FILTRATION DATA ON THE SAME SLUDGE IN AN
C**     EXPERIMENTAL FILTER OF AREA (AE) ARE AVAILABLE.
        READ (*, *) N, M, AE
        READ (*, *) [V(I), I = 1, N]
        READ (*, *) [DP (J), J = 1, M]
        READ (*, *) [(T(I, J), I = 1, N), J = 1, M]
        J = 1.0
10      DO 15 I = 1, N - 1
        DV(I) = V(I + 1) - V(I)
        DT(I) = T(I + 1, J) - T(I, J)
        DTV(I) = DT(I)/DV(I)
        VA(I) = [V(I) + V(I + 1)]/2.0
15      CONTINUE
C**     FIT A STRAIGHT LINE BETWEEN DTV(I)
C**     AND VA(I) BY THE METHOD LEAST SQUARES
        SUMX = 0.0
        SUMY = 0.0
        SUMXX = 0.0
        SUMXY = 0.0
        DO 20 I = 1, N - 1
        SUMX = SUMX + VA(I)
        SUMY = SUMY + DTV(I)
        SUMXY = SUMXY + VA(I) * DTV(I)
20      SUMXX = SUMXX + VA(I) * VA(I)
        AN = N - 1
        NUMR = AN * SUMXY - SUMX * SUMY
        DENR = AN * SUMXX - SUMX * * 2
        MM = NUMR/DENR
        C = (SUMY - MM * SUMX)/AN
```

```
      KPP(J) = MM
      B(J) = C
      RMC(J) = B(J) * AE * DP(J)/MEUF
      IF (J. EQ. M) GO TO 25
      J = J + 1
      GO TO 10
 25   SM = 0.0
      DO 30 J = 1, M
      SM = SM + RMC(J)
 30   CONTINUE
      RM = SM/M
C**   FIT A STRAIGHT LINE BETWEEN ALOG
C**   [KPP(J)] AND ALOG [DP(J)] BY THE
C**   METHOD OF LEAST SQUARES.
      SUMX = 0.0
      SUMY = 0.0
      SUMXX = 0.0
      SUMXY = 0.0
      DO 35 J = 1, M
      X(J) = ALOG [DP(J)]
      Y(J) = ALOG [KPP(J)]
      SUMX = SUMX + X(J)
      SUMY = SUMY + Y(J)
      SUMXY = SUMXY + X(J) * Y(J)
      SUMXX = SUMXX + X(J) * * 2
 35   CONTINUE
      AN = M
      NUMR = AN * SUMXY - SUMX * SUMY
      DENR = AN * SUMXX - SUMX * * 2
      MM = NUMR/DENR
      C = (SUMY - MM * SUMX)/AN
      S = 1.0 + MM
      SV = SX * ROWF/[(1.0 - SX) * ROWS]
      ALFO = [AE * AE/(MEUF * SV)] * EXP(C)
C**   COMPUTE THE REQUIRED AREA OF FILTERING
C**   SURFACE.
```

```
C**     THE FILTER MEDIUM RESISTANCE IS ASSUMED
C**     THE SAME FOR THE EXPERIMENTAL FILTER
C**     AND THE INDUSTRIAL FILTER.
        A0 = - (ALFO * SV * MEUF * VF * VF)/[2.0 * DPO * *
        (1.0 - S)]
        A1 = - RM * MEUF * VF/DPO
        A2 = TF
        A = [- A1 + SQRT (A1 * A1 - 4.0 * A2 * A0)]/(2.0 *
        A2)
        WRITE (*, *) ALFO, S, RM, A
        STOP
        END
```

PROGRAM 5.3

```
C**     CONSTANT RATE FILTRATION FOLLOWED BY
C**     CONSTANT PRESSURE FILTRATION ON A
C**     COMPRESSIBLE SLUDGE IN A BATCH FILTER.
C**     FILTER MEDIUM RESISTANCE IS ASSUMED NEGLIGIBLE.
        REAL M, NUMR, MEUF, KR, KRE, KPP
        DIMENSION V(10), DP(10), DPC(10), X(10), Y(10)
        READ (*, *) A, SX, ROWS, ROWF, MEUF, DPO, DVTO
        READ (*, *) VC, TETC
C**     THE TIME REQUIRED TO COLLECT A GIVEN
C**     VOLUME OF FILTRATE (VF) IS TO BE COMPUTED
        READ (*, *) VF
C**     CONSTANT RATE FILTRATION DATA ON THE
C**     SAME SLUDGE IN AN EXPERIMENTAL BATCH
C**     FILTER OF AREA AE ARE AVAILABLE.
        READ (*, *) AE, DVTE
        READ (*, *) N
        READ (*, *) [DP(I), V(I), I = 1, N]
        DPM = 0.0
        DO 10 I = 1, N
 10     DPC(I) = DP(I) - DPM
C**     SPERRY'S CORRELATION ALONGWITH AP-
C**     PROXIMATION PROPOSED BY HUGHES ET. AL.
C**     IS USED TO DESCRIBE THE SPECIFIC RESI-
```

```
C**     STANCE OF THE CAKE.
C**     FIT A STRAIGHT LINE BETWEEN ALOG
C**     [V(I)] AND ALOG [DPC(I)] BY THE
C**     METHOD OF LEAST SQUARES.
        SUMX = 0.0
        SUMY = 0.0
        SUMXX = 0.0
        SUMXY = 0.0
        DO 15 I = 1, N
        X(I) = ALOG [DPC(I)]
        Y(I) = ALOG [V(I)]
        SUMX = SUMX + X(I)
        SUMY = SUMY + Y(I)
        SUMXX = SUMXX + X(I) * X(I)
        SUMXY = SUMXY + X(I) * Y(I)
  15    CONTINUE
        AN = N
        NUMR = AN * SUMXY - SUMX * SUMY
        DENR = AN * SUMXX - SUMX * * 2
        M = NUMR/DENR
        C = (SUMY - M * SUMX)/AN
C**     EVALUATE THE FILTRATION CONSTANTS.
        S = 1.0 - M
        KRE = EXP (- C)
        SV = SX * ROWF/[(1.0 - SX) * ROWS]
        ALFO = KR * AE * AE/(SV * MEUF * DVTE)
        KR = ALFO * SV * MEUF * DVTO/(A * A)
C**     COMPUTE TIME OF CONSTANT RATE FILTRATION
        VR = [(DPO - DPM) * * (1.0 - S)]/KR
        TR = VR/DVTO
C**     COMPUTE THE TIME OF CONSTANT PRESSURE FILTRATION
        VP = VC - VR
        KPP = ALFO * SV * MEUF/[A * A * DPO * * (1.0 - S)
        RM = DPM * A/(MEUF * DVTO)
        B = RM * MEUF/(A * DPO)
C**     INCIDENTALLY, SINCE DPM IS ASSUMED
```

```
C**     ZERO, RM = 0.0 AND B = 0.0 IN THIS CASE.
        TP = (KPP/2.0) * (VP * * 2 - VR * * 2) + B * (VP -
        VR)
C**     SPECIFY THE RATIO OF VOLUME OF WASH
C**     WATER USED TO TOTAL VOLUME OF FILTRATE
C**     COLLECTED IN ONE CYCLE (RX) AND THE
C**     RATIO OF RATE OF WASHING TO FINAL RATE
C**     OF FILTRATION (RY)
        READ (*, *) RX, RY
        DVTF = 1.0/(KPP * VP + B)
        TWA = (RX * VC)/(RY * DVTF)
C**     COMPUTE TOTAL CYCLE TIME(TC).
        TC = TR + TP + TWA + TETC
C**     COMPUTE TIME REQUIRED TO COLLECT VF
C**     VOLUME OF FILTRATE.
        TF = TC * VF/VC
        WRITE (*, *) S, ALFO, RM, TF
        STOP
        END
```

We shall now consider filtration of a compressible sludge in a rotary drum filter (Program 5.4). This includes computation of total air flow required per cycle for dewatering the cake, the procedure of which is illustrated in the computation flow graph given in Figures (5.4*a*) and (5.4*b*). Incidentally, the plots of Figure (5.2) which constitute database — 1, may be fitted into an analytical correlation of the form

$$\psi_s' = a_0 + a_1 S_e + a_2 (S_e)^2 \quad ...(5.6.4)$$

The values of the correlation constants a_0, a_1 and a_2 are listed in Table (5.1).

Table 5.1

Values of Correlation Constants of Equation (5.6.4)

Material	a_0	a_1	a_2	*Range of* S_e
12.7 mm Berl saddles	0.3268	0.61594	0.0	≤ 0.7
6.35 mm saddles	0.61875	0.3125	0.0	≤ 0.5
6.35 mm saddles	0.60508	0.414885	–0.117775	> 0.5

Material	a_0	a_1	a_2	*Range of* S_e
15.875 mm Raschig rings	0.46	0.40	0.0	≤ 0.6
Average for small particles	0.6791	0.4167	0.0	≤ 0.3
Average for small particles	0.6221	0.7161	− 0.40475	> 0.3

In Program (5.4) however, we have considered the case of average small particles only.

PROGRAM 5.4

```
C**     FILTRATION OF A COMPRESSIBLE SLUDGE
C**     IN A CONTINUOUS FILTER (ROTARY DRUM
C**     FILTER)
C**     TO COMPUTE THE VOLUME OF FILTRATE
C**     DELIVERED PER REVOLUTION (VC) AND
C**     THE TOTAL AIR FLOW REQUIRED (SVAC) PER
C**     CYCLE FOR DEWATERING THE CAKE.
C**     FILTER MEDIUM RESISTANCE ASSUMED
C**     NEGLIGIBLE.
        REAL L, LC, MEUF, MEUA, K, K1, KC, LHS
        DIMENSION  TW(100),  SVA(100),  SE(100),  Y(101),
        PSIP(100), SN(100), ABSP(100), H1(100)
C**     THE FILTRATION CONSTANTS ALFO AND S
C**     ARE DETERMINED FROM THE FILTRATION
C**     DATA ON THE SAME SLUDGE IN AN EXPE-
C**     RIMENTAL BATCH FILTER AS SHOWN IN
C**     PROGRAM (5.2)
        READ (*, *) ALFO, S
        READ (*, *) SX, ROWS, ROWF, MEUF
        READ (*, *) D, L, TC, P, HS
        PI = 3.14
        A = PI * D * L
        ATM = 101. 3E 03
        DPO = ATM - P
        SV = SX * ROWF/[(1.0 - SX) * ROWS]
        TETA = ARC SIN (2.0 * HS/D)
```

```
      TETA = 90.0 - TETA
      F = 2.0 * TETA/360.0
      VC = SQRT [2.0 * F * TC * A * A * DPO * * (1.0 -
      S)/(ALFO * SV * MEUF)]
      LC = VC * SV/A
C**   COMPUTE THE AIR FLOW RATE REQUIRED
C**   TO DEWATER THE CAKE FORMED.
      READ (*, *) TWT, DV, PSIS, MEUA, PA, TA, ST, TETAC
      ALFA = ALFO * DPO * * S
      K = 25.0/6.0
      SP = 6.0/(PSIS * DV)
C**   COMPUTE THE VOIDAGE OF CAKE BY TRIAL.
      ABSN = 0.8
      LHS = ALFA/(K * SP * * 2)
 10   RHS = [(1.0 - ABSN) * * 2]/(ABSN * * 3)
      DIF = ABS (LHS - RHS)/LHS
      IF (DIF. LT. 0.001) GO TO 15
      ABSN = ABSN - 0.001
      GO TO 10
 15   K1 = 40.0
      SY = 2.5
      KC = ALFA * ABSN * MEUF * LC * LC/DPO
      DVS = PSIS * DV
      SR = [DVS * DVS * DPO * ABSN * * 3]/[36.0 * K * LC
      * ST * COSD (TETAC) * (1.0 - ABSN) * * 2]
      SR = SR/K1
      TW(1) = 0.0
      SVA(1) = 0.0
      SE(1) = 1.0
      I = 2
 20   SE(I) = SE(I - 1) - 0.01
C**   EVALUATE TW(I) BY NUMERICAL INTEGRA-
C**   TION OF EQUATION (5.4.9) BY SIMPSON'S RULE.
      N = 100
      H = [1.0 - SE(I)]/N
      DO 25 J = 1, N + 1
      X = (J - 1) * H + SE(I)
```

```
      Y(J) = [(1.0 - SR)/(1.0 - SR * X)] * * 2/(X * * SY)
 25   CONTINUE
      SUM = Y(1) + Y(N + 1)
      M = 4
      DO 30 J = 2, N
      SUM = SUM + M * Y(J)
      M = 6 - M
 30   CONTINUE
      SUM = SUM * H/3.0
      TW(I) = KC * SUM
C**   COMPUTE THE AIR VELOCITY SVA(I).
      PP = PA + DPO/2.0
      R = 0.082
      ROWA = (PP * 29.0)/(101.3 E 03 * R * TA)
C**   AMONG THE WETTED SPHERICITY VERSUS
C**   EFFECTIVE SATURATION PLOTS, THE AVERAGE
C**   CURVE FOR SMALL PARTICLES IS ONLY CONSIDERED.
 35   IF [SE(I). LE. 0.3) THEN
      A0 = 0.6791
      A1 = 0.4167
      A2 = 0.0
      ELSE
      A0 = 0.6221
      A1 = 0.7161
      A2 = - 0.40475
      END IF
      PSIP(I) = A0 + A1 * SE(I) + A2 * SE(I) * * 2
      IF [SE(I).GT.0.8] PSIP(I) = 0.933
      DVSP = DV * PSIP(I)
      SN(I) = [SE(I) - 2.0 * SE(I) * SR + SR]/(1.0 -
      SE(I) * SR)
      ABSP(I) = [1.0 - SN(I)] * ABSN/(1.0 - SR)
      AA = 1.75 * ROWA * [1.0 - ABSP(I)]/(DVSP * ABSP(I)
      * * 3)
      BB = 150.0 * MEUA * [1.0 - ABSP(I)] * * 2/(DVSP *
      DVSP * ABSP(I) * * 3) ABSP(I)
      CC = - DP/LC
```

```
      SVA(I) = [- AA + SQRT (BB * BB - 4.0 * AA * CC)]/(2.0
      * AA)
      IF [TW(I). EQ. TWT] GO TO 40
      IF [TW(I).LT.TWT] THEN
      I = I + 1
      GO TO 20
      ELSE
      TW(I) = TWT
      SAV = [1.0 + (1.0 - SR) * * 2]/2.0
      SE(I) = TW(I) * (SY - 1.0)/[KC * SAV * (SE * * (1.0
      - SY) - 1.0)]
      GO TO 35
 40   M = I
C**   COMPUTE THE AIR REQUIREMENT BY EVA-
C**   LUATING THE INTEGRAL OF EQUATION (5.4.15)
C**   NUMERICALLY USING TRAPEZOIDAL RULE.
C**   SIMPSON'S RULE CANNOT BE USED HERE
C**   SINCE TW(I) VALUES NEED NOT BE AT EQUAL
C**   INTERVALS.
      SUM = 0.0
      DO 45 I = 1, M
      IF (I. EQ. 1) THEN
      H1(I) = TW(I)
      ELSE
      H1(I) = TW(I) - TW(I - 1)
      SUM = SUM + 0.5 * H1 (I) * [SVA (I - 1) + SVA(I)]
      END IF
 45   CONTINUE
      SVAC = SUM
      WRITE (*, *) VC, SVAC
      STOP
      END
```

Let us now analyse centrifugal filtration of an incompressible sludge (see Example 5.6). Let it be that the centrifugal is operated at a constant speed until the rate of filtration dropped to a particular value and we have to compute the total volume of filtrate delivered

during this period of operation. The computer program (Program 5.5) is given below.

PROGRAM 5.5

```
C**     FILTRATION OF AN INCOMPRESSIBLE SLUDGE
C**     IN A CENTRIFUGAL FILTER.
        REAL NUMR, M, KRP, MEUF, LC
C**     IN DIMENSION STATEMENT AN INDEX OF
C**     10 IS USED AS AN EXAMPLE.
        DIMENSION DP(10), T(10), X(10), Y(10)
        READ (*, *) SX, ROWS, ROWF, MEUF
        READ (*, *) R, SB, RPM, RO
C**     FILTRATION DATA ON THE SAME SLUDGE AT
C**     CONSTANT RATE IN A BATCH EXPERIMENTAL
C**     PRESSURE FILTER OF AREA AE ARE AVAILABLE
        READ (*, *) AE, AVTE
        READ (*, *) N
        READ (*, *) (DP(I), T(I), I = 1, N)
C**     FIT A STRAIGHT LINE BETWEEN DP(I)
C**     AND T(I) BY THE METHOD OF LEAST SQUARES
        SUMX = 0.0
        SUMY = 0.0
        SUMXX = 0.0
        SUMXY = 0.0
        DO 10 I = 1, N
        X(I) = T(I)
        Y(I) = DP(I)
        SUMX = SUMX + X(I)
        SUMY = SUMY + Y(I)
        SUMXX = SUMXX + X(I) * X(I)
  10    SUMXY = SUMXY + X(I) * Y(I)
        AN = N
        NUMR = AN * SUMXY - SUMX * SUMY
        DENR = AN * SUMXX - SUMX * * 2
        M = NUMR/DENR
        C = (SUMY - M * SUMX)/AN
```

```
      KRP = M
      SV = SX * ROWF/[(1.0 - SX) * ROWS]
      ALFA = KRP * AE * AE/(MEUF * SV * DVTE * * 2)
      BR = C
      RM = BR * AE/(MEUF * DVTE)
C**   FILTER MEDIUM RESISTANCE IS ASSUMED
C**   TO BE THE SAME FOR THE EXPERIMENTAL
C**   PRESSURE FILTER AND THE CENTRIFUGAL FILTER.
C**   TO COMPUTE THE VOLUME OF FILTRATE DELIVERED
C**   (VF) AND THE TIME OF FILTRATION (TF), IF
C**   THE CENTRIFUGAL IS OPERATED UNTIL FILTRA-
C**   TION RATE DROPPED TO DVTF.
      READ (*, *) DVTF
C**   FIND FINAL CAKE THICKNESS BY TRIAL. FIRST
C**   ASSUME THAT LC IS 0.1 CM LESS THAN
C**   (R - RO).
      LC = (R - RO) - 0.001
 15   RC = R - LC
      PI = 3.14
      OMEGA = 2.0 * PI * RPM/60.0
      DPO = 0.5 * ROWF * (R * R - RO * RO) * OMEGA * * 2
      AM = 2.0 * PI * R * SB
      AA = PI * SB * (R + RC)
      AL = 2.0 * PI * SB * (R - RC)/ALOG (R/RC)
      AC = SQRT (AA * AL)
      DVTFC = (MEUF/DP) * (ALFA * LC/AC + RM/AM)
      DVTFC = 1.0/DVTFC
      DIF = ABS (DVTFC - DVTF)/DVTF
      IF (DIF. LE. 0.001) GO TO 20
      LC = LC - 0.001
      GO TO 15
 20   VF = AC * LC/SV
      TF = (MEUF/DP) * [0.5 * ALFA * SV * (VF/AC) * * 2
      + (RM/AM) * VF]
      WRITE (*, *) VF, TF
      STOP
      END
```

NOMENCLATURE

A	area of filtration, m^2
A_c	cross-sectional area of filter cake perpendicular to the direction of flow of filtrate in a centrifugal, m^2.
$\overline{A}_a, \overline{A}_L$	arithmetic mean and logarithmic mean cake area respectively, m^2.
A_m	area of filter medium (measured perpendicular to the direction of flow of filtrate), m^2.
d	thickness of each frame of plate and frame filter press, cm.
dV/dt (or, Q)	rate of filtration, m^3/s.
D_p	volume-surface diameter of particles in the filter cake, m.
D_v	volumetric diameter of particles in the filter cake, m.
f	fraction of filtration cycle available for cake formation in continuous filtration (fractional submergence of rotary drum filter).
K	Kozeny's constant, dimensionless.
K_1	empirical constant in equation (5.4.1).
L_c	cake thickness, m.
n	total number of frames of a plate and frame filter press.
R	radius of centrifugal, m.
R_c	final radius of the cake in a centrifugal filter, m.
R_H	hydraulic radius, m.
R_o	radius of inner surface of liquid layer in a centrifugal, m.
R_m	filter medium resistance constant, m^{-1}.
s	compressibility coefficient, dimensionless.
s_p	specific surface of particles forming the cake, m^2/m^3.
S, S_e, S_r	saturation, effective saturation and residual saturation of the filter cake respectively.
t_c	time for one full rotation of rotary drum filter, s.
t_{cycle}	total time of a full batch filtration cycle, s.
t_{etc}	time for opening the filter, cleaning and dumping the cake and reassembling the filter (or, time for which the filter is out of use), s.
t_f	time of filtration, s.

t_w time of dewatering the cake, s.

t_{wash} time of washing the cake, s.

U', U_{sup} actual and superficial velocity respectively of liquid (filtrate) through the filter cake, m/s.

v volume of cake deposited by passage of unit volume of filtrate (see equations 5.1.15 and 5.1.16), superficial velocity of filtrate through the cake during two-phase flow, m/s.

v_a, v_a' superficial velocity of air through the cake in single-phase flow and two-phase flow respectively, m/s.

V volume of filtrate collected, m^3.

V_{day} daily output of filtrate, m^3/day.

V_{wash} volume of wash water used, m^3.

x mass fraction of solids in the feed slurry.

Greek Letters

α specific cake resistance, m^{-2}.

α_o constant in Sperry's correlation (see equation 5.1.9).

α_o, m, s empirical constants in Ruth's correlation (equation 5.1.10).

α_o, m, s, n empirical constants in Donald and Hunneman's correlation (equation 5.1.12).

$(-\Delta P)$ pressure of filtration (pressure difference driving force), N/m^2.

$(-\Delta P_c)$ pressure drop across the filter cake, N/m^2.

$(-\Delta P_m)$ pressure drop across the filter medium, N/m^2.

θ_c contact angle, degrees.

ε voidage (void fraction) of filter cake, dimensionless

ε' equivalent porosity of filter cake (see equation 5.4.14). dimensionless.

μ_a viscosity of air, kg/(ms).

μ_f fluid (filtrate) viscosity, kg/(ms).

ρ_a density of air, $kg/(m)^3$.

ρ_f density of fluid (filtrate), kg/m^3.

ρ_s density of solids forming the cake, kg/m^3.

σ interfacial tension, N/m.

ψ_s sphericity, dimensionless.

ψ_s' wetted sphericity (see Fig. 5.2), dimensionless.
ω angular speed of centrifugal, radians/s.

Computer Notations

A area of filtration, m^2
AA arithmetic mean cake area ($\overline{A}_a$), m^2
ABSN cake voidage (ε), dimensionless
ABSP(I) equivalent porosity of filter cake (ε_i')
AC cake cross-sectional area in centrifugal (A_c), m^2
AE filtration area of experimental filter (test filter), m^2
AL logarithmic mean cake area ($\overline{A}_L$), m^2
ALFA specific cake resistance (α), m^{-2}
ALFO constant in Sperry's correlation (α_o)
AM area of filter medium (A_m), m^2
ATM atmospheric pressure, N/m^2
B parameter defined in Equation (5.1.21)
B(J) value of B when filtration pressure is DP(J)
BE value of *B* for experimental (test) filter
BR parameter defined in Equation (5.1.25)
C *y*-intercept of least square fit
D diameter of rotary drum filter, m
DP(J) values of pressure of filtration, ($-\Delta P$), N/m^2
DPC(I) values of pressure drop across the cake, ($-\Delta P_c$), N/m^2
DPE operating pressure (filtration pressure) of experimental (test) filter, N/m^2
DPM pressure drop across the filter medium, ($-\Delta P_m$), N/m^2
DPO operating pressure (filtration pressure) of industrial filter, N/m^2
DT(I) values of time difference (Δt), s
DTV(I) values of ($\Delta t/\Delta V$), s/m^3
DV volumetric diameter of particles in cake (D_v), m
DV(I) values of volume difference (ΔV), m^3
DVS volume-surface diameter of particles in the cake (D_{vs} or D_p), m

DVSP	volume-surface diameter of particles in the cake based on wetted sphericity (D_{vs}' or D_p'), m
DVTE	rate of filtration (dV/dt) in experimental (test) filter, m^3/s
DVTF	final rate of filtration, $(dV/dt)_f$, m^3/s
DVTFC	calculated value of DVTF, m^3/s
DVTO	operating rate of filtration in industrial filter, m^3/s
F	fractional submergence (f), dimensionless
HS	height of axis of rotation of rotary drum filter above slurry surface, m
K	Kozeny's constant, dimensionless
K1	empirical constant (K_1) in Equation (5.4.1)
KC	parameter (K_c) defined in Equation (5.4.8)
KP	parameter (K_p) defined in Equation (5.1.21)
KPE	value of KP for experimental (test) filter
KPP(J)	parameter (K_p') defined in Equation (5.1.28)
KR	parameter (K_r) defined in Equation (5.1.25)
KRE	value of KR for experimental (test) filter
KRP	parameter (K'_r) defined in Equations (5.1.26) and (5.1.34)
L	length of rotary drum filter, m
LC	cake thickness (L_c), m
OMEGA	angular speed of centrifugal (ω), radians/s
P	pressure inside rotary drum filter, N/m^2
PA	inlet pressure of air, N/m^2
PSIP(I)	values of wetted sphericity (ψ_s'), dimensionless
PSIS	sphericity of particles in the cake (ψ_s), dimensionless
R	radius of centrifugal, m
RC	radius of cake layer in centrifugal (R_c), m
RM	filter medium resistance constant (R_m), m^{-1}
RMC(J)	calculated values of RM, m^{-1}
RO	radius of liquid layer in centrifugal (R_o), m
ROWF	fluid density (ρ_f), kg/m^3
ROWS	solid density (ρ_s), kg/m^3
RPM	speed (in revolutions per minute) of centrifugal
RX	ratio of volume of wash water to final volume of filtrate

RY	ratio of rate of washing to final rate of filtration
S	compressibility coefficient (s)
SAV	average value of parameter S' (see equation 5.4.10)
SB	height of centrifugal (b), m
SE(I)	values of effective saturation (S_e)
SN(I)	values of saturation (S)
SP	specific surface (surface area per unit volume) of particles in the cake (s_p), m^2/m^3
SR	residual saturation (S_r)
ST	interfacial tension (σ), N/m
SV	volume of cake deposited by passage of unit volume of filtrate (v), m^3/m^3
SVA(I)	instantaneous values of air velocity (v_a'), m/s
SVAC	total air flow required per unit area (V_a), $m^3/(m^2.s)$
SX	mass fraction of solids in feed slurry (x)
SY	exponent (y) in Equation (5.4.6)
T (I) T (I, J)	time, seconds
TA	temperature of inlet air, K
TC	cycle time (or, time for one full revolution of rotary drum filter), s
TCOPT	optimum cycle time, s
TETC	time for which the filter is out of use in one cycle (t_{etc}), s
TETA	half of the angle subtended by submerged portion of the drum at the centre (θ), degrees
TETAC	contact angle (θ_c), degrees
TF	time of filtration (t_f), s
TP	time of constant pressure filtration, s
TR	time of constant rate filtration, s
TW(I)	value of dewatering time (t_{wi}), s
TWA	time of washing the cake (t_{wash}), s
TWT	total time of dewatering the cake, s
V(I)	values of volume of filtrate collected, m^3
VA(I)	values of V_{avg}, m^3
VC	volume of filtrate collected in one cycle (or, in one full revolution of rotary drum filter), m^3

VF final volume of filtrate collected (V_f), m^3

VOPT volume of filtrate collected in optimum cycle time (V_{opt}), m^3

VP volume of filtrate collected during constant pressure filtration, m^3

VR volume of filtrate collected during constant rate filtration, m^3

REFERENCES

1. Bird, R.B., Stewart, W.E. and Lightfoot, E.N., Transport Phenomena, Wiley, New York, 1960.
2. Sperry, D.R., Ind. Eng. Chem., **20**, 892, 1928.
3. Ruth, B.F., Ind. Eng. Chem., **27**, 708, 1935.
4. Donald, M.B. and Hunneman, R.D., Trans. Inst. Chem. Eng., **1**, 96, 1923.
5. Hughes, O.D., Ver Hoeve, R.W. and Luke, C.D., AIChE paper meeting, Columbus, Ohio, December, 1950.
6. Brown, G.G. and Associates, Unit Operations, Wiley, New York, 1950.
7. Perry, J.H., Chemical Engineers' Handbook, 5th Ed., McGraw Hill, New York, 1973.
8. Bailey, J.E. and Ollis, D.F., Biochemical Engineering Fundamentals, Second edition, McGraw Hill, New York, 1986.
9. Grace, H.P., Chem. Eng. Prog., **49**, 303, 367, 427, 1953.
10. Narayanan, C.M., Computer Aided Analysis of Filtration on Compressible Sludges and Two Phase Flow through Filter Cakes, Proc. Fourth National Convention of Chemical Engineers, Roorkee, 1988.

6

Gas-Solid Separations

Environmental pollution has been the talk of the day. Chemical industries have been blamed maximum for being primarily responsible for air, soil and water pollution. Whether such a step-motherly treatment to chemical process industries can be fully justified or not, it remains a fact that the exhaust gases from chemical plants do contain lot of suspended particles (dust) and entrained liquid droplets (mist) that could ultimately cause serious damage to the public health. A number of carbonaceous materials and finely powdered metals could also form explosive mixtures with air. Separation of dust and mist from gas streams finds its primary importance in this context. Besides, it also helps in preventing wastage of valuable minerals that could otherwise be carried away by the exhaust gases. During in-plant operation, the process gases are also subjected to such separation processes for separating different constituents from the process gas stream.

A variety of methods are available for gas purification depending on the size range of commercial aerosols. The choice of the equipment depends not only on the particle size but also on the quantity of gas to be handled, concentration of dust or mist, and the physical properties of the suspended particles.

6.1. Momentum Separators, Filters and Scrubbers

Momentum separators, commonly called *dust collectors* (when used to separate suspended dust) or *entrainment separators* (when used to separate liquid mist), are very similar in operation to the surface velocity classifiers discussed in Chapter 3. The dust laden gas is admitted to a chamber of large cross-sectional area and due to the sudden increase in flow area, the gas velocity drops and the dust particles tend to settle down to the bottom of the chamber. By using a number of chambers in series, dust particles of different sizes can be separated. However, though fairly cheap in construction, these equipment do not provide sharp separations and are best suitable for separating coarse aerosols having sizes above 100 microns.

Filtration through a porous medium is one of the widely used methods for the separation of suspended dust or mist. *Bag filters* that are widely used for separating process dusts fall essentially into two categories. The first and older type employs a relatively thin woven fabric as the filter medium whereas the second type uses felt as the medium and is therefore capable of permitting higher gas velocities. The separation process in fact is not that of a simple filtration, since the pores of the filter fabric are usually much larger than the size of the particles to be separated. When the dust laden gas first passes through the filter cloth, the efficiency of separation will be low until enough particles are removed to build up what corresponds to a precoat in the fabric pores. This initial deposition of dust takes place because of interception and impingement on cloth fibres and by gravity settling and Brownian movement in the pores. With dusts normally encountered in industrial processes, this precoat layer will form in a few minutes, usually only a matter of seconds. Once this layer has formed, then the process is that of filtration and the efficiency of separation will usually be well over 99 per cent.

Filter fabrics are made of a wide range of materials such as cotton, wool, nylon, teflon, saran, orlon, glass and polyester fibres. The bags may be round or oval, mounted in series on frames and shaken at intervals to discharge the accumulated solids to discharge hoppers. Filter cloth envelopes supported on screens are also sometimes used. These units may be shaken manually if in small sizes or by a motor. Complete automatic operation incorporating a timer apart from the shaker motor and pneumatically operated gas discharge valves is also possible. For ordinary mechanical filters, shaking is required every 15 minutes or 8 hours depending on the service. Fully automatic filters may be shaken every 2 minutes but usually a time interval of 15 to 20 minutes is used to reduce bag maintenance. The gas flow should be stopped during shaking. Since a number of bags are used in series, one of them can be cut out of service at a time and shaken to discharge the collected dust. For automatic units, this involves closing the dampers, shaking the bags either pneumatically or mechanically sometimes accompanied by a reverse flow of clean gas and finally reopening the dampers, the entire operation taking only 2 to 10 seconds in compressed air operated, automatic filters. It is also essential that the gas is kept above its dew point during operation to avoid plugging of the bag pores. These filters however have been successfully used under steam atmosphere (such as that encountered in vacuum dryers) and in such cases the filter housing is steam-chased.

Air filters are used to eliminate atmospheric dust and they are designed to handle low dust concentrations since atmospheric dust concentrations are normally much lower than process dust concentrations. Also, no attempt is usually made to recover the separated dust. The viscous filters use mats of asbestos, glass or metal wires wet with a non-volatile oil that helps in retaining the dust. The mats may be replaced by new ones once the maximum permissible dust load has accumulated or reused after washing or steaming and reoiling. The viscous filters can be operated automatically so that continuous gas cleaning can be achieved. Dry filters employ low air velocities since they possess relatively smaller passages for air flow than the viscous mediums. They are usually arranged in the form of pockets, since due to the low air velocity larger filter surface is required per unit volume of gas handled.

Impingement separators in general operate on the basic principle that whenever a dust-laden fluid impinges on a body, the fluid will be deflected around the body whereas the dust particles by virtue of their greater inertia will tend to be collected on the surface of the body. In the viscous air filters discussed above, dust collection is achieved by the impingement of particles on the filter surface, with the oil coating serving to prevent re-entrainment of the separated dust. In the bag filters also, we have already stated that the initial formation of cake on the filter medium is by impingement. Once this layer is formed, subsequent retention of solids is by filtration. In the momentum separators or dust collectors also, baffles are often incorporated against which the gas impinges, to facilitate separation.

Wet separators or scrubbers utilise a combination of impingement action and washing by a counter-current stream of liquid. The contacting may be conducted in packed towers, that is, towers containing a packed bed of inert solids. Alternately, a baffle-plate scrubber may be used which consists of a tower with cross plates set one above the other and with perforations staggered to force the gas stream to change direction during its upward flow. The scrubbing fluid, say water, flows down the tower and across the plates while the gas passes through successive sheets of water and impinge upon the wet plates. The solids are retained in the liquid and washed down to be discharged from the bottom of the tower. In the rotary spray scrubber, the liquid is admitted through a number of fine injection nozzles in the form of a rotating spray. This causes a dense fog across the tower through which the gas passes. It is used particularly when the gas is heavily laden with solids. Availability of a cheap scrubbing fluid that does not chemi-

cally react with the gas neither dissolve the gas is the primary requirement of a scrubbing process. If the particles are to be collected separately, then the liquid should not dissolve or chemically react with the solids as well. To improve economy, the scrubbing fluid should be easily recoverable from the solids so that it can be recycled back to the top of the tower for reuse.

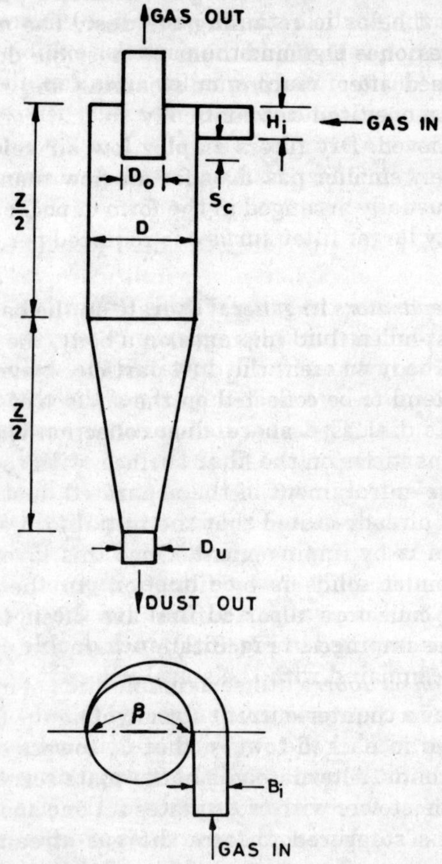

Fig. 6.1. Conventional Gas Cyclone. Standard Proportions : $Z = 4D$, $D_o = D/2$, $H_i = D/2$, $B_i = D/4$ ($H_i = B_i$ for square inlet), $S_c = D/8$, D_u = arbitrary, $\beta = 180°$

6.2. Centrifugal Separators (Cyclones)

Cyclone separators offer one of the least expensive means of dust collection from both operating as well as investment view points. The

attractive feature of such equipment is that separation is affected in centrifugal field but the separator does not have any moving or rotating parts. The centrifugal action is introduced by admitting the dust-laden or mist-laden gas tangentially at a high velocity. A typical cyclone separator is sketched in Fig. (6.1). Gas cyclones that are used to remove dust and mist from gases have been successfully operated at temperatures as high as 1000°C and pressure as high as 50 atm. Liquid-liquid separation is also possible in cyclones and then they are called hydrocyclones. We shall deal with them later. Gas cyclones are best suitable when the particle size is above 5-10 microns. However, if the dust concentration is high and the particles exhibit a high degree of flocculation, then dusts of much smaller sizes can also be removed efficiently. Separation efficiencies as high as 98 per cent have been reported on dusts having ultimate size of 0.1 to 2.0 microns, mainly due to the predominant effect of flocculation and inter-particle agglomeration.

As stated earlier, in a cyclone, the dust-laden gas is admitted tangentially at a high velocity into a cylindrical chamber having a conical bottom. As a result, the gas develops a spiral or helical motion inside the chamber and the particles experience very large centrifugal forces and are thus thrown outwards towards the wall. The gas then passes up along the inner core near the axis of the chamber and goes out through the top outlet. The separated particles are discharged from the bottom outlet. It is important that the top outlet projects below the gas inlet (as shown in Fig. 6.1) in order to prevent short-circuiting of the gas. The path of the gas in the separator in fact involves a double vortex with the gas spiralling downward at the outside and upward at the inside. A double eddy may be superimposed on this double spiral. However, it has been reported that for the popular types of cyclones like the one sketched in Fig. (6.1), such double eddy velocities are quite small as compared with the spiral velocity.

Every particle in the gas is thus subjected to two opposing forces inside the separator such as the outward centrifugal force that tends to throw the particle to the walls and the inward drag of the fluid on the particle. Both these forces are a function of the size of the particle as well as its radius of rotation so that particles of different sizes rotate at different radii. For an effective separation of the particles from the gas, the outward force on the particles should be as large as possible so that the particles are held against the wall of the chamber and the gas coming out will be clean and free from dust. If V_{gt} is the tangential velocity of the gas, then the outward force (centrifugal) on the particle

$$= m\, V_{gt}^2/r \qquad \text{...(6.2.1)}$$

where m = mass of the particle

r = radius of rotation of the particle

We have assumed that there is no slip between the gas and the particle in the tangential direction. Assuming the relative velocity between the gas and the particle is small, the fluid drag on the particle can be estimated by Stokes' Law (discussed in section 3.1 of chapter 3). Thus, the inward drag on the particle

$$= 3\,\pi\,\mu_g\,D_p\,V_r \qquad \text{...(6.2.2)}$$

where D_p = diameter of the particle

μ_g = viscosity of gas

For most computations, V_r can be taken as the radial component of the velocity of gas. At equilibrium, these two forces will balance with each other so that the particle will rotate at a specific radius. Thus,

$$m\,V_{gt}^2/r = 3\,\pi\,\mu_g\,D_p\,V_r$$

or,

$$V_{gt}^2/r = (3\,\pi\,\mu_g\,D_p\,V_r)/m \qquad \text{...(6.2.3)}$$

Assuming the particle is spherical, $m = (\pi D_p^3/6)\,\rho_s$. Equation (6.2.3) therefore becomes,

$$\frac{V_{gt}^2}{r} = \frac{18\,\mu_g}{D_p^2\,\rho_s}\,V_r \qquad \text{...(6.2.4)}$$

It will be convenient to express the right hand side of the above equation in terms of the laminar gravitational free settling velocity V_t of the particle, given by Stokes' equation [see equation (3.1.8) of chapter 3] :

$$V_t = (\rho_s - \rho_g)\,g\,D_p^2/18\,\mu_g \qquad \text{...(6.2.5)}$$

Since the density of the particle is much larger than that of the gas, $(\rho_s - \rho_g) \cong \rho_s$. Therefore,

$$V_t = \rho_s\,g\,D_p^2/18\,\mu_g$$

or,

$$\frac{18\,\mu_g}{D_p^2\,\rho_s} = \frac{g}{V_t} \qquad \text{...(6.2.6)}$$

Substituting equation (6.2.6) in (6.2.4) we get,

$$\frac{V_{gt}^2}{r} = \left[\frac{V_r}{V_t}\right] g \qquad \text{...(6.2.7)}$$

The tangential velocity V_{gt} has been found to vary inversely with the nth power of the radius of rotation[1]. Though experimental studies[2,3] have shown that the value of n could vary from 0.5 to 0.7, an average value of $n = 0.5$ will be satisfactory for many of the computations. Thus,

$$\frac{V_{gt}}{(V_{gt})_c} = \frac{(D/2)^{\frac{1}{2}}}{R^{\frac{1}{2}}}$$

or, $$V_{gt} = (V_{gt})_c \sqrt{\frac{D}{2r}} \qquad \text{...(6.2.8)}$$

where D = diameter of the separator

$(V_{gt})_c$ = tangential velocity at the circumference of the separator

Further, it has been found[4] that $(V_{gt})_c$ is very nearly equal to the inlet velocity of the gas, V_i. In other words, if G is the mass flow rate of gas and A_i the area of cross-section of gas inlet (usually square or rectangular),

$$(V_{gt})_c \cong \frac{G}{A_i \, \rho_g} \qquad \text{...(6.2.9)}$$

Therefore, equation (6.2.8) becomes,

$$V_{gt} = \left[\frac{G}{A_i \, \rho_g}\right] \sqrt{\frac{D}{2r}} \qquad \text{...(6.2.10)}$$

The radial velocity V_r is found to be approximately constant at a given radius and to be given by the volumetric flow rate of gas divided by the cylindrical area for flow at the radius r. Thus,

$$V_r = \frac{G}{(2\pi r Z) \, \rho_g} \qquad \text{...(6.2.11)}$$

where Z = depth of the separator

It is clear that if the particle rotates at a large radius, its probability of getting separated from gas is higher. If the radius of rotation of the particle is so small that the particle rotates within a central core of radius $0.2\, D_o$ (where D_o is the diameter of the top outlet), it will be carried away in the outgoing gas and will not be separated. This is why very fine dusts are difficult to be separated in commercial cyclones. Thus, if a particle is to be separated from the gas stream, its radius of rotation r must be at least equal to $0.2\, D_o$. Substituting $r = 0.2\, D_o$ and the expressions for V_{gt} and V_r from equations (6.2.10) and (6.2.11) in equation (6.2.7), we get

$$(V_t)_{\min} = \frac{0.2\, A_i^2 \, D_o \, \rho_g \, g}{\pi \, Z \, D \, G} \qquad \text{...(6.2.12)}$$

If the gravitational free settling velocity of the particle is equal to or more than $(V_t)_{min}$, it will be separated from the gas.

Since $(V_t)_{min} = \dfrac{\rho_s \, g \, (D_p)^2_{min}}{18 \, \mu_g}$, equation (6.2.12) can be rewritten as,

$$(D_p)_{min} = \left[\frac{3.6 \, A_i^2 \, D_o \, \rho_g \, \mu_g}{\pi \, Z \, D \, \rho_s \, G} \right]^{1/2} \quad ...(6.2.13)$$

The above equation specifies the minimum size of the particle of density ρ_s that can be separated from the gas. It can be seen that $(D_p)_{min}$ depends on the dimensions of the cyclone separator (A_i, D_o, Z, D) and the gas flow rate.

No general correlation of cyclone pressure drop data is available yet in literature. Although several attempts[1] have been made to estimate the friction losses in cyclones, most of them have neglected the effects of entrance compression, wall friction, exit contraction etc. all of which could have a significant influence on the overall pressure drop in the separator. One of the experimental correlations proposed by Shepherd and Lapple[2] for cyclones with rectangular inlet is given below:

$$(-\Delta P) = (0.7475) \, \rho_g \, V_i^2 \left[K \left(\frac{A_i}{D_o^2} \right) + \left(\frac{A_i}{A_o} \right)^2 - 1 \right] \quad ...(6.2.14)$$

where A_o = cross-sectional area of top gas outlet, m^2

$= (\pi D_o^2/4)$

V_i = average gas inlet velocity (m/s) = $G/(A_i \, \rho_g)$

$A_i = (B_i \, H_i)$, B_i being the breadth and H_i the height (or depth) of the gas inlet

$(-\Delta P)$ = pressure drop, N/m^2.

K is an empirical constant and its value is usually 16.0. However, if the inner side of the inlet duct is extended past the cyclone cylinder wall and into the annular space halfway to the opposite wall to form an inlet vane, the friction losses in the separator have been found to get reduced by over 50 per cent and in that case $K = 7.5$. Equation (6.2.14) is based on tests conducted on cyclones having the following proportions : $(B_i/D) = 1/12$ to $1/4$; $(H_i/D) = 0.25$ to 0.5 and $(D_o/D) = 0.25$ to 0.5. Re-expressing equation (6.2.14) in terms of G, A_i and D_o, we get,

$$(-\Delta P) = (0.7475) \, (G^2/\rho_g) \left[\frac{K}{D_o^2 \, A_i} + \frac{16}{\pi^2 \, D_o^4} - \frac{1}{A_i^2} \right] \quad ...(6.2.15)$$

From equation (6.2.13), it can be seen that to decrease $(D_p)_{\min}$ so that even smaller size particles could get separated from the gas, either A_i and D_o should be decreased or the height and diameter of the separator (Z and D) are to be increased. However, with decrease in A_i and D_o, the pressure drop $(-\Delta P)$ will also increase as evident from equation (6.2.15). Hence, a practical limit is required to be set at which the separation efficiency is satisfactorily high but at the same time the pressure drop penalty is also reasonably low. Increasing Z and D to very large values is also not a practical suggestion since such large size separators will be expensive to construct, instal and maintain. The value of $(D_p)_{\min}$ can be decreased by increasing the gas flow rate (G) as well. But increase in G causes increase in the pressure drop $(-\Delta P)$. Also, this makes the separator less versatile since in a chemical plant, process gases will be available at different rates and a good separator will be the one that can handle all those streams satisfactorily. Moreover, at large values of G, excessive turbulence is created inside the separator and as a result the collection efficiency goes down. Commercial cyclones therefore offer high collection efficiency when the average size of particles in the feed gas does not fall below 5-10 microns. However, as stated at the beginning of this section, if the dust particles have a large tendency to agglomerate forming flocs of large sizes, then high collection efficiency can be achieved even if the particle size is much lower. At the same time, it is also not desirable that the gas contains a large proportion of coarse particles and if so, they must preferably be removed in a preliminary separator before feeding the gas to the cyclone. This is because relatively large particles have a tendancy to bounce off the walls of the separator back into the central core of the fluid and thus get carried away by the gas.

The capacity of cyclone can be increased by using a number of cyclones in parallel keeping the load on each approximately the same or by using cyclones in series. Multicyclones employ two or more concentric cyclones one inside the other. The feed gas is introduced tangentially into the outermost separator where the coarsest particles are separated. The partially cleaned gas then passes into the inner separator through tangential openings and less coarser particles get removed here since the separating force in the inner separator is larger than that in the outer one. Thus, the finest sizes are separated in the innermost cyclone. Such units are highly flexible and they are particularly useful when particles of large size range are present in the gas stream.

The gas inlet to the separator is usually either square or rectangular. A square cross-section is preferred over cylindrical cross-section since it requires lower depth for the same cross-sectional area. Since the vertical component of the velocity in the cyclone is downwards everywhere outside the central core, the particles will rotate at a constant distance from the central axis and move continuously downwards until they settle on the conical base of the separator. Continuous removal of solids is desirable so that the particles do not get re-entrained in the gas stream and a deep conical base of small angle helps in minimising entrainment. In some cases, a stream of water is run down the walls of the separator to facilitate the discharge of solids which also helps in reducing the risk of particle re-entrainment in the gas. However, this will cause wetting of particles with the liquid. Though the cyclone can be mounted in any desired direction, it is usually mounted vertically except where there is a shortage of headroom since discharge of solids is more readily achieved in the vertical mount.

Hydrocyclones that are used for separating immiscible liquids of different densities operate on the same principle as the gas cyclones. However, it has been observed that the performance characteristics of hydrocyclones differ from those of gas cyclones in some respects. The volumetric flow rate of the heavy phase (normally the dispersed phase) as the underflow and that of the light phase (normally the continuous phase) as the overflow both affect the separation efficiency of a hydrocyclone significantly. The ratio of the volumetric rate of underflow Q_u (through the bottom outlet) and that of the overflow Q_o (through the top outlet) is designated as the volume split, S. An effective separation means the overflow contains the lighter phase only and the entire heavy phase (and only the heavy phase) is collected in the underflow. Let us define the separation efficiency E of the hydrocyclone as follows :

$$E = \left[\frac{Q_o}{Q_F}\right]\left[\frac{Y_o - Y_F}{Y_F\,(1 - Y_F)}\right] \qquad \text{...(6.2.16)}$$

where Y_o, Y_F = Volume fraction of lighter phase in the overflow and feed streams respectively

Mahajan and Pai[5] have reported that E increases with increase in volume split (S), reaching a maximum value at $S \simeq 1.0$ and thereafter decreases. This observation is not surprising. For example, consider $S > 1.0$. That is, $(Q_u/Q_o) > 1.0$ or $Q_u > Q_o$. Since the underflow rate is larger than the overflow rate, though the underflow will be containing the entire heavy phase, some light phase will also get collected in the underflow. In other words, though the overflow will be composed of the light phase only, the entire light phase is not separated since a part is lost in the underflow. Since the separation efficiency depends both on the quality as well as the yield of the product (say, the light phase), the overall efficiency will be lower in this case. Similarly, if S is less than 1.0, the overflow rate will be larger than the underflow and some heavy phase also will escape in the overflow. As a result, the quality goes down (though the yield could be 100 per cent) and E decreases. Thus, best results are obtained when $Q_u = Q_o$.

For gas cyclones, we have already discussed earlier that increase in the inlet Reynolds number (or, increase in the inlet velocity of gas) increases the collection efficiency of the separator, since the centrifugal forces on the particles get increased. However, the separation efficiency of hydrocyclone has been found to decrease with increase in inlet Reynolds number.[5] This can be explained as follows :

Firstly, the dispersed phase in a hydrocyclone is constituted by liquid droplets which are basically compressible media. As a result, when the inlet velocity is increased, the droplets will have a larger tendancy to deform and also to split or shred into smaller droplets. The effective size of the droplets thus decreases which ultimately reduces the radial velocity of the droplets. Secondly, when the inlet Reynolds number is increased, the residence time of the droplets in the separator also decreases. Consequently, the dispersed phase does not get sufficient time to coalesce with each other so as to form larger sizes and thus get clarified from the continuous phase. This problem of coalescence or splitting is not predominant for gas cyclones since the discrete phase is constituted by solid particles. Also, since the gas is much lighter than the solids, the possibility gas escaping alongwith solids through the bottom outlet shall not arise. Thus, the parameter S does not come into picture for gas cyclones and it is due to the same reason, the dimension of the bottom outlet is arbitrarily chosen in gas cyclones (see Fig. 6.1).

The use of hydrocyclones in process industries is on the increase not only as liquid-liquid separators but also as extractors, crystallisers as well as continuous reactors.

Example 6.1. *A cyclone separator 1.0 m in diameter and 3.0 m in depth has been used to handle 144,000 kg/day of dust-laden gas. The gas inlet is 0.3 m square and the gas outlet is 0.4 m in diameter. If the size distribution of the particles (specific gravity = 1.2) in the feed gas is as given below, estimate what per cent of particles will be separated from the gas stream :*

Particle size (microns)	*Mass fraction*
– 11.7 + 8.3	*0.098*
– 8.3 + 5.9	*0.234*
– 5.9 + 4.2	*0.277*
– 4.2 + 2.9	*0.149*
– 2.9 + 2.1	*0.101*
– 2.1	*0.141*

Viscosity of gas = 0.03 centipoises and its specific gravity = 0.001.

Solution. To estimate the size of the smallest particle that will be separated from the gas, we can use equation (6.2.13) :

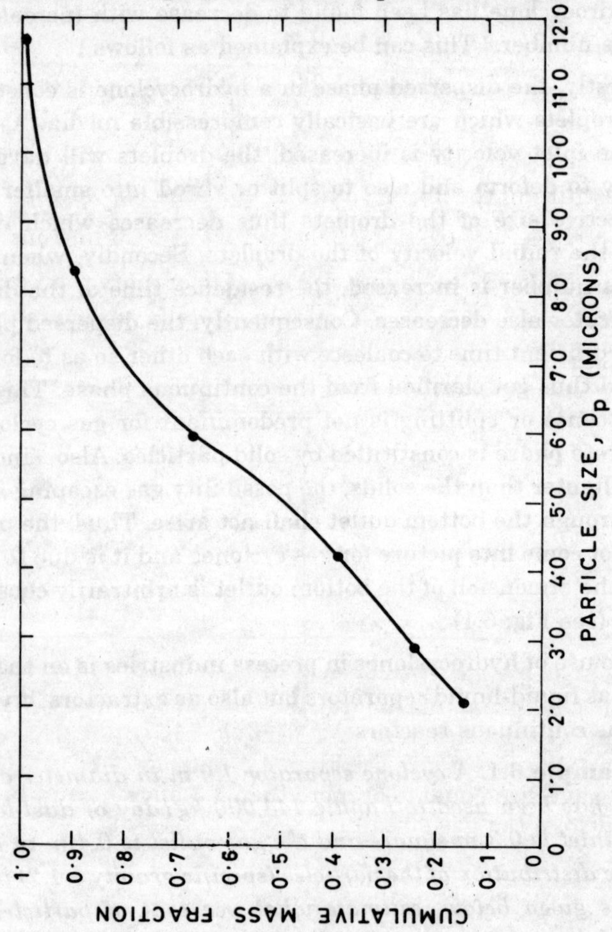

Fig. 6.1.1

$$(D_p)_{\min} = \left[\frac{3.6\, A_i^2\, D_o\, \rho_g\, \mu_g}{\pi\, Z\, D\, \rho_s\, G}\right]^{\frac{1}{2}} \qquad ...(i)$$

where $A_i = (0.3 \times 0.3) = 0.09 \text{ m}^2$

$D_o = 0.40$ m

$\rho_g = 1.0$ kg/m^3

$\mu_g = 3 \times 10^{-5}$ kg/m.s

$Z = 3.0$ m

$D = 1.0$ m

$\rho_s = 1200$ kg/m^3

$$G = \left[\frac{144{,}000}{24 \times 3600}\right] = 1.667 \text{ kg/s}$$

Substituting the above values in equation (*i*), we get,

$$(D_p)_{\min} = 0.043 \times 10^{-4} \text{ m} = 4.3 \text{ microns}$$

Thus, all particles having size equal to or more than 4.3 microns will get separated from the gas stream. From the given size distribution, we can construct a cumulative mass fraction table as follows :

Particle size (microns)	*Cumulative mass fraction*
11.7	1.0
8.3	0.902
5.9	0.668
4.2	0.391
2.9	0.242
2.1	0.141

The plot of cumulative mass fraction *versus* particle size is given in Fig. (6.1.1). From the figure, the cumulative mass fraction corresponding to a particle size of 4.3 microns is 0.403. Thus, 40.3 per cent of particles are of size less than 4.3 microns. Or, 59.7 per cent of particles have size equal to or more than 4.3 microns and thus will be separated from the gas stream.

6.3. Electrostatic Precipitation

This is used for removing very fine dust or mist from gases. The dust-laden gas is passed between two electrodes, one small in cross-section (discharge electrode or high tension electrode) and the other the collector electrode (which is earthed). When a high potential difference of the order of 30,000 to 100,000 volts is struck between the two electrodes, the gas gets ionised at the discharge electrode as the intensity of electric field will be very high at its surface due to its small cross-sectional area. The ions attach themselves to the particles and thereby charge them and the charged particles are then attracted towards the collector electrode and get deposited there.

Electrostatic precipitators offer very high collection efficiencies (99.0 to 99.9%) even with very fine particles. They can be used with moist or wet gases and have been successfully employed at temperatures as large as 600°C and pressures upto 10 atm. Their demerit lies in their high initial cost and high maintenance cost. Special care must be taken if the carrier gas contains combustible particles. Also, if some charged particles remain entrained in the outgoing gas due to low efficiency operation or an electrical breakdown, then this can cause serious harm to public health.

The precipitators may be operated in single stage or in two stages. Process gases are handled in single stage precipitators whereas the two stage precipitator (in which ionisation and collection take place in two separate stages) finds its application essentially in air-conditioning units. The single stage precipitators (most popular ones are the Cottrell precipitators) fall into two main classes such as the plate-type in which the collector electrodes are parallel plates or screens and the pipe-type in which the collecting electrodes consist of a nest of parallel pipes either square, round, hexagonal or of any other shape. The discharge or precipitating electrodes in each case are wires, barbed wires or rods (either round or edged) and are placed midway between the plates (in the plate-type or more commonly called the wire-plate type) or at the centre of the pipes (in the pipe-type or wire-in-cylinder type). Heavier gauge square or star sectioned wires with sharp edges are usually preferred since these provide a stable corona discharge. The wires are generally hung from an insulated frame and are individually weighted. They are loosely held near the bottom in a guide assembly thus allowing for individual wire expansion, preventing buckling of wires when there is an uneven temperature rise. In the plate-type precipitators, gas is passed parallel to the plate and sometimes through it whereas in pipe-type, the gas flow is normally vertically upwards through the pipe. Downward vertical flow is not preferred since this causes re-entrainment of particles in the outgoing gas. The pipe-type precipitator is usually used for the removal of liquid droplets and volatalised fumes whereas the plate-type is preferred for dust removal.

The mist droplets after getting deposited on the passive electrode coalesce with each other forming larger droplets which run down the plates or pipes and thus get discharged. Mist precipitators are often irrigated with streams of water to increase the rate of droplet removal. However, in such cases water consumption could often be fairly high and while handling hot gases, these gases can get cooled emitting a cold gas plume which settles in the immediate vicinity of the plant without dispersing and thus causes harmful effects particularly when toxic or poisonous constituents are present in the gas stream. When dust particles are deposited, they can also be washed down but most commonly they are dislodged by rapping with hammers or vibrators either continuously or intermittently. The timing of intermittent rapping is determined by the amount of dust being collected. Usually a 6-12 mm dust layer is allowed to develop on the collecting electrodes before rapping. When the dust layer is too thick, re-entrainment becomes large and problems with dust resistivity become more acute (this we shall be discussing later). If dust layer thickness is too low, the agglomerates will not be sufficiently large to fall into the hoppers. Rapping devices can be electromagnetic vibrators, cam operated drop hammers or spring-loaded hammers, or impulse rappers (magnetic or pneumatic) controlled by timing switches. If semiconductors such as concrete re-inforced with conducting rods are used as collecting electrodes, then the dust may be removed by dragging scraper chains across the concrete slab.

The basic functional mechanism of electrostatic precipitators thus involves the following : formation of corona or ionised zone around the high tension wire (discharge electrode), charging and migration of particles, particle deposition and discharge and possibilities of particle re-entrainment. When an electric voltage is applied between two parallel plates and if the field strength increases beyond a critical value (around 30,000 volts/cm in ambient air), electrical breakdown of the gas occurs and a spark flashes between the plates. On the other hand, if the electric field is non-uniform as in the case between a fine wire and an enclosing pipe or a plate, electrical breakdown occurs mainly near the curved surface that produces a glow discharge or corona without sparkover. While a D.C. corona produces a steady force that drives the particles towards the collector electrode, the A.C. corona causes oscillating motion of charged particles. Commercial precipitators therefore require a unipolar discharge. Since the negative corona is more stable than the positive corona, it is preferred for industrial applications. In air conditioning units however, positive corona is employed since it gives rise to low ozone concentrations in air.

The ultra-violet radiation from the corona glow produces more and more ionised gas molecules. The positive gas ions and photons formed in this way are accelerated towards the negative conductor (discharge electrode) and release electrons from the surface of the conductor. These electrons moving through the strong electric field near the conductor further generate newer electrons and positive ions by molecular impact. The electrons then swarm outside this region, slowing to a speed less than that required for ionisation by collision and attach themselves to the gas molecules forming gas-ions which move towards the passive electrode (collecting electrode) with a velocity that is proportional to the charge on the ions and the strength of the electric field. The space outside corona is thus filled with a dense cloud of unipolar ions (consisting of as much as 50×10^6 ions/cm^3) and it is in this zone that the majority of dust particles acquire their negative charge. Some dust particles may pass through the corona zone and may become positively charged and then they are precipitated on the discharge electrode. Also, if the dust or mist concentration is very large, then these particles or droplets can act as absorbers of ions and electrons and reduce the corona current. This is called corona quenching or corona suppresion and in such cases, it will be necessary to use precipitators with several stages in series.

The particles get charged by two mechanisms such as bombardment charging (in which gas ions moving across the gas stream collide against the particles and thus charge them) and diffusional charging (where the ions land on the particles due to their thermal movement). Particles having size more than 1 micron get charged essentially by bombardment charging while diffusional charging is predominant for sub-micron particles. The charge q (in coulombs) acquired by a particle of diameter d_p (assuming it to be essentially spherical) at any time t due to bombardment charging can be computed using Pauthenier's equation[6] as given below :

$$q = ne = \left[\frac{3\delta}{\delta + 2}\right]\left[\frac{d_p^2 E_i}{4}\right]\left[\frac{t}{t+\tau}\right] \qquad \text{...(6.3.1)}$$

where δ = dielectric constant of the particle

E_i = field strength or electrostatic potential gradient during ionisation and charging, Volts/cm

τ = time constant

= $1/(\pi N_i e U_i)$

N_i = ion concentration per unit volume (ion density)

U_i = ionic mobility, (cm/sec)/(volts/cm)

e = elementary electric charge (electronic charge)

= 1.602×10^{-19} coulomb

n = number of elementary charges

d_p = particle size, cm

It has been assumed that the gas ions move along the lines of force between the discharge electrode and collecting electrode and are intercepted by the particles when the charge gets deposited on them. The charged particles repel some of the gas ions thus reducing the rate of charging. After some time, the charge on the particle reaches the ultimate maximum value. In commercial precipitators, this limiting charge is attained within a fraction of a second. Its magnitude can be obtained from equation (6.3.1) by taking the limit as t tends to infinity. Thus,

$$q_e = \lim_{t \to \alpha} \left[\frac{3\,\delta\, d_p^2\, E_i}{(\delta + 2)\, 4\,(1 + \tau/t)} \right]$$

$$= \frac{3\,\delta\, E_i\, d_p^2}{4\,(\delta + 2)} \qquad ...(6.3.2)$$

Diffusion charging is controlled by the thermal movement of the gas ions. White[7] has given a correlation to estimate the total charge on the particle as,

$$q' = (ne) = \frac{kTd_p}{2e} \ln \left[1 + (\pi\, d_p\, N_i\, e^2) \sqrt{\frac{3N_o}{4MkT}}\; t \right] \qquad ...(6.3.3)$$

where k = Boltzmann constant

T = absolute temperature, °K

M = molecular weight of gas

N_o = Avagadro number

However, for charging times (t) usually encountered in commercial precipitators, the ultimate change q_e' acquired by spherical particles of size less than 1 micron can be approximated by the empirical expression[1],

$$q_e' = 3{,}400\, d_p\, eT \qquad ...(6.3.4)$$

where T is absolute temperature in °K and d_p the particle size in cm.

Once we have determined the charge on the particle, let us now proceed to determine the migration velocity of the particle towards the collecting electrode. An accurate estimation of migration or drift velocity is difficult due to the large number of parameters superimposed on it. We can however make a reasonable estimate of the migration velocity after making the following simplifying assumptions :

(*a*) The particle is moving at its terminal velocity normal to the gas stream and has acquired the ultimate charge on it. This is a reasonably good assumption since the ultimate charge is attained in practice within a fraction of a second.

(*b*) The fluid resistance to particle motion is in the viscous flow regime and therefore can be estimated by applying Stokes' law (see equation 3.1.7 of chapter 3). Thus,

$$F_R = \frac{3 \pi d_p \mu_g U_p}{K_m} \qquad ...(6.3.5)$$

where K_m = Stokes-Cunningham correction factor (see section 3.5 of chapter 3)

U_p = particle migration velocity (normal to the gas steam)

(*c*) The effect of electric wind or ionic wind is neglected. Electric or ionic wind means a gas circulation (of the order of 0.5-0.6 m/s) that is set up due to the transfer of momentum from gas ions moving in the electric field to the gas molecules. As a result of this, the pressure at the collecting electrode will be slightly higher than that at the discharge electrode.

(*d*) The particles do not interfere with each other's momentum and the repulsion effects between particles charged with same polarity are neglected. We also assume that there is sufficient turbulence inside the precipitator so as to provide a uniform distribution of particles across the cross-section of the precipitator. We have also neglected the possibility of hindered settling near the concentrated dust layer which alongwith residual charge on the deposited particles could resist rapid precipitation.

A force balance on the particle thus becomes,

$$F_e - F_R = 0 \qquad ...(6.3.6)$$

where F_e is the electrical force on the particle directed towards the collecting electrode which depends on the charge on the particle and the strength of electric field. Thus,

$$F_e = q_e E_c \qquad ...(6.3.7)$$

where E_c = field strength (electrostatic potential gradient) during collection or precipitation

For particles of size greater than 1 micron, the ultimate charge on them (q_e) can be obtained from equation (6.3.2). Substituting this and also for F_R from equation (6.3.5) in equation (6.3.6), we get,

$$U_p = \frac{\delta}{(\delta+2)}\left[\frac{E_i\, E_c\, d_p}{4\,\pi\,\mu_g} K_m\right] \qquad \text{...(6.3.8)}$$

For a single stage precipitator, $E_i \simeq E_c = E$.

Therefore, $$U_p = \frac{\delta}{(\delta+2)}\left[\frac{E^2\, d_p\, K_m}{4\pi\,\mu_g}\right] \qquad \text{...(6.3.9)}$$

For particles of size less than 1 micron, diffusion charging will be predominant and q_e is to be substituted from equation (6.3.4).

Accordingly, $$U_p = \frac{3400\, E_c\, e\, TK_m}{3\,\pi\,\mu_g} \qquad \text{...(6.3.10)}$$

Thus, the migration velocity of submicron particles can be seen to be virtually independent of the size of the particles and consequently the collection efficiency of the precipitator will also be essentially the same irrespective of particle size (provided there is no re-entrainment).

It is to be noted that to maintain dimensional consistency, in the above equations (6.3.9) and (6.3.10), E is to be expressed in statvolts (or e.s.u.)/cm, e in statcoulombs, μ_g in poise and d_p in cm so that U_p will be in cm/s. The same shall be followed in the subsequent equations as well. Incidentally, 1 statvolt = 299.8 volts and 1 coulomb or ampere = 299.8×10^7 statcoulombs or statampere.

For utilising the above equations, the field strength E is required to be known. In a pipe-type (wire-in-cylinder) precipitator, the field strength is not uniform and it varies with the radial distance r from the centre of the wire (discharge electrode). The magnitude of E at any point is affected by the presence of dust particles and gas ions. Thus,

$$\frac{1}{r}\frac{d}{dr}(r\,E) = [\text{charge on gas ions}] + (\text{Charge on particles}) \qquad \text{...(6.3.11)}$$

A relatively simplified solution of the above equation is given by Strauss[6] as,

$$E = \left[\frac{2I}{U_i}\left(1 + \frac{2\,\delta\,S_a}{(\delta+2)}\,r\right)\right]^{1/2} \qquad \text{...(6.3.12)}$$

where I = **corona current**

U_i = **ionic mobility**

S_a = **aggregate surface area of all particles per unit volume of gas**

However, in the space outside the immediate vicinity of corona discharge, the field strength is essentially constant and an average value of E can be computed as,

$$E = [2I/U_i]^{1/2} \quad \text{...(6.3.13)}$$

It is to be noted that for corona to set in, the field strength at the discharge electrode must exceed a critical value E_{cr} and the above equation is applicable only when the applied voltage has exceeded this critical value. A reasonably good estimate of corona current can be obtained using the correlation proposed by Ladenburg[8] (though this assumes a constant ion density) :

$$I = \frac{8\, U_i\, V\,(V - V_{cr})}{D_c^2 \ln (D_c/D_d)} \quad \text{...(6.3.14)}$$

where V = applied voltage

V_{cr} = critical voltage required for corona to commence

D_c = inside diameter of collecting electrode

D_d = outside diameter of discharge electrode

Substituting in equation (6.3.13) we get,

$$E = \left[\frac{16\, V\,(V - V_{cr})}{D_c^2 \ln (D_c/D_d)}\right]^{1/2} \quad \text{...(6.3.15)}$$

The magnitude of critical voltage V_{cr} or critical field strength E_{cr} depends evidently on the electrical breakdown strength of the gas. For the wire-in-cylinder type precipitator, V_{cr} is given by[1],

$$V_{cr} = \left[\frac{E_o\, \rho'\, D_d}{2}\right]\left[1 + \sqrt{\frac{k_o}{\rho'\, D_d}}\right] \ln (D_c/D_d)$$

or,

$$E_{cr} = E_o\, \rho' \left[1 + \sqrt{\frac{k_o}{\rho'\, D_d}}\right] \quad \text{...(6.3.16)}$$

where ρ' = Density of gas relative to its density at N.T.P. (0°C and 760 mm of mercury)

E_o = Electrical breakdown constant of the gas. For air, E_o = 110 statvolts/cm.

k_o = Energy distance constant.
For air, k_o = 0.18 cm.

It has also been observed that corona sets in only if $(D_c/D_d) > 2.718$. Otherwise, sparking will result.

The collection or precipitation efficiency of electrostatic precipitators is a function of the time for which the gas remains in the active field. Based on a constant effective migration velocity of the particles, Deutsch[9] has proposed the following correlation for estimating the collection efficiency of single stage precipitators :

$$\eta = 1 - \exp(-K_e U_p) \qquad ...(6.3.17)$$

where $K_e = 4L_c/(D_c V_{avg})$, for pipe-type (wire-in-cylinder) precipitator

$= 4 L_c/(B_c V_{avg})$, for plate-type (wire-plate) precipitator

L_c = length of collecting electrode in the direction of gas flow

V_{avg} = average velocity of gas through the precipitator

B_c = distance between wire and plate in wire-plate type precipitator

In general, $K_e = A/Q$ where A is the area of the collecting electrode and Q the volumetric gas flow rate. If an empirical average value of particle migration velocity determined experimentally is available, then it can be substituted in the above equation to obtain a more accurate estimation of collection efficiency. Deutsch has assumed uniform distribution of dust particles at the beginning as well as for the uncollected dust and strictly speaking, equation (6.3.17) is valid only for a specific particle size. However, if the size range of particles present is very close, the above equation can be applied satisfactorily without any serious error. Also, as stated earlier, for submicron particles the particle migration velocity U_p and thereby the collection efficiency will be essentially independent of particle size.

If the particles present follow a wide size distribution, then the correlation proposed by White[19] can be used :

$$(1 - \eta) = \exp(-k') + k' \int_{d_{p_1}}^{d_{p_2}} [X e^{-k' d_p/2}] \, dd_p \qquad ...(6.3.18)$$

where $$k' = \frac{K_e E_i E_c}{2 \pi \mu_g}$$

X = cumulative mass fraction corresponding to particle size d_p

Since X is a function of d_p, once the cumulative mass fraction table for the particle size distribution is available, the integral on the right hand side of above equation can be evaluated either graphically or numerically. It can be seen that the collection efficiency of the precipitator can be made to approach 100 per cent by increasing the length of the precipitator. But the size and cost of the equipment usually places an economic limit at about 90 to 99 per cent. Increased pressure in fact increases the precipitation efficiency since it lowers the ion mobility and thus increases the critical potential required for corona discharge. However, increased temperature lowers the efficiency since ion mobility is increased lowering the critical potential required and since the gas viscosity is increased, the particle migration velocity gets decreased.

It must not be forgotten that the above equations provide only an order-of-magnitude estimation of collection efficiency since in actual practice a number of secondary factors affect the precipitator performance. The most important of these factors is the particle resistivity. When dust particles or mist droplets arrive at the collecting electrode, they get partly discharged by the electrode and adhere to it by a combination of molecular, electrostatic and surface tensional (due to the moisture present) forces. The extent of electrostatic adhesion depends on the rate at which the charge leaks away from the particles to the earthed collector which obviously depends on the dust resistivity. Liquid droplets and most of metallic and carbon particles are good conductors while particles from industrial smelting plants and roasting furnaces consist of metallic oxides which are excellent insulators when dry. Industrial fumes always contain some moisture and when the temperature is sufficiently low, sufficient moisture will be there to form a conducting film. When particles have low resistivity as in the case of carbon black, they are rapidly discharged on meeting the earthed collector. However, since the molecular and surface tensional forces are inadequate to hold these particles on the collecting electrode, they get re-entrained in the gas stream. In the case of air cleaning precipitators, it is therefore usual practice to cover the collector plates with a sticky, soluble oil to prevent re-entrainment. The dust concentration in atmospheric air being small, the deposited dust barely covers the plates before the oil is washed off and replaced, usually at intervals of one to six weeks.

When the resistivity of the particles is very high (greater than 5×10^{10} ohm. cm), the rate at which they are discharged at the collecting electrode will be very small and as a result, a charge builds up on the collected particles until electrical break-down of the gas occurs first in the spaces between particles and then on the surface of the dust layer. This is called "back corona." As a result of this, some ions of opposite polarity to that of the charge on the particles are formed and these migrate back towards the discharge electrode. They reduce the charge in the charging zone and neutralise the charge on the charged particles. To overcome this problem, more time will have to be provided for the charge on the particles to leak away. This can be done by temporarily reducing the precipitator current and thereby the precipitator efficiency. Gases can be conditioned with water before feeding to the precipitator or during operation to bring down the resistivity of the deposited dust. Chemical conditioning agents such as sulfur dioxide, sulfur trioxide, ammonia etc. can also be used. Injection of sulfur trioxide has been used for difficult cement and fly ash problems and it has been observed that injection of ammonia into a gas stream containing powdered aluminium silicate catalyst from a petroleum cracking unit reduces the dust resistivity from 5×10^{11} to 10^{10} ohm. cm and thus improves the precipitator efficiency from 96 to 99 per cent.

The two stage precipitators commonly used for cleaning environmental air operate with positive corona. The corona discharge takes place in the first stage between two electrodes having a non-uniform electric field such as a fine wire discharge electrode and a large diameter collecting electrode. This is the ionisation stage and the applied potential must be above that required for corona discharge. The second stage, that is the precipitation stage, involves a relatively uniform electrostatic field consisting of either alternately charged parallel plates with close spacing or concentric cylinders with relatively close clearances compared with their diameters. The stage operates at a lower voltage. Since collection occurs in the absence of corona, there is no way of recharging re-entrained and discharged particles. Some means such as coating the collecting surface with a viscous oil must be therefore provided to prevent re-entrainment of the collected dust. The cost advantage of two stage precipitators lies in the smaller equipment size made possible by the close plate spacing employed and in the lower power consumption due to the two-stage operation. However, the close plate spacing is objectionable in process applications where large dust concentrations are involved and therefore these are restricted primarily to air-conditioning applications. The close plate spacing permits streamlined gas flow and absence of electric wind. Consequently, neglecting re-entrainment, the collection efficiency can be expressed as[11],

$$\eta = K_e U_p \qquad \text{...(6.3.19)}$$

As discussed earlier, the actual efficiency could be lower than that predicted by the above equation due to secondary factors like resistivity of dust particles.

Typical applications of electrostatic precipitators in chemical and allied industries include detarring of manufactured gas, removal of acid mist in contact sulfuric acid plants, recovery of phosphoric acid mists, removal of dusts in gases from roasters, calciners, cement and lime kilns, blast furnaces, carbon black furnaces, recovery furnaces in soda and sulfate pulp mills and also catalyst dust collection in fluid-catalyst units.

6.4. Sonic Agglomeration

One of the most efficient methods of rapidly agglomerating dust particles or mist droplets to larger sizes so that they can be conveniently collected in any of the conventional mechanical collectors such as cyclones is by subjecting the dust or mist laden gas to standing sound waves or high intensity acoustic vibrations. The sonic generator may be a static generator like the whistles or dynamic generator like the sirens. It is placed at one end of an agglomeration chamber through which the gas passes and the agglomerated particles are then collected by a cyclone or multicyclones. Gas velocities of the order of 100 cm/s have been suggested to be suitable.

The average sound intensity in the agglomeration chamber I_s can be found from the relation[12],

$$I_s = \beta I_o / A \qquad \text{...(6.4.1)}$$

where I_o = Intensity of sound produced by the siren or whistle (watts)

A = Cross-sectional area of the chamber

$= \pi D^2/4$, for cylindrical column of diameter D

β is a constant and its value varies such that $0.07 < (\beta\, \eta_a) < 0.16$, η_a being the acoustic efficiency of the generator. For most sonic agglomeration systems, $(\beta\, \eta_a)$ is close to 0.07.

The application of sound waves to aerosol collection depends on a number of factors such as the sound frequency and intensity, the aerosol concentration and turbulence and the exposure time of aerosols to sound waves. At low frequencies (upto about 50 kHz), co-vibration of particles with the vibrating gas called orthokinetic coagulation takes place. The particles also tend to migrate to the antinodal regions under the action of the sonic radiation pressure. At very high frequencies (of the order of several hundred kHz), orthokinetic flocculation becomes negligible and hydrodynamic forces become the major contributor to agglomeration.

At low frequencies when Stokes' law can be applied to the relative motion of the particle through the gas, the ratio of the amplitude of vibration of the particle A_p to that of the gas A_g can be expressed as[6],

$$(A_p/A_g) = \left[\left(\frac{\pi\, d_p^2\, \gamma\, \rho_s}{9\, \mu_g\, K_m}\right)^2 + 1\right]^{-1/2} \qquad \text{...(6.4.2)}$$

where γ is the frequency and K_m the Stokes-Cunningham correction factor. For particles smaller than 3 microns in air, the assumption of Stokes' law is reasonable at frequencies of 10 kHz or less. The above equation also neglects the buoyancy effect of gas on the particle. It has been shown that when the size of the aerosol particles is less than a particular value (critical size), they vibrate with the gas at that particular frequency. Similarly, there exists a critical frequency for a given particle size. For particles of density close to unity vibrating in air, this has been found to occur at (A_p/A_g) equal to around 80 per cent. Substituting $(A_p/A_g) = 0.8$ in equation (6.4.3) we get,

$$\left[\frac{d_{pc}^2\, \rho_s\, \gamma}{\mu_g\, K_m}\right] \cong 2.16 \qquad \text{...(6.4.4)}$$

Thus we can make a reasonable estimate of the critical frequency or critical particle size. Since a smoke or mist cloud usually contains a mixture of particles of different sizes, a wide range of frequencies greater than a few kHz are employed in practice. In industrial plants however, sound generators are normally operated between 1 to 4 kHz only since at high frequencies it becomes more difficult to produce the desired sound intensity.

The particle concentration should not be less than 1 to 2 gm/Nm^3 for particles of size between 1 to 10 microns while concentrations of 5 gm/Nm^3 have been found most suitable. When the particle concentration becomes very high (say 200 g/Nm^3), sonic energy gets lost due to increased attenuation of sound on the aerosols. Introduction of a water mist often improves collection particularly at low concentrations, as in the case of agglomeration of carbon black particles. It has also been shown that turbulent flow introduced by the acoustic field enhances agglomeration.

The degree of flocculation is significantly affected by the duration of exposure of aerosol to sound waves. If d_1 is the initial particle size and d_2 that of the final aggregate, then (d_2/d_1) is called the index of agglomeration I. This index is a function of the exposure time t and sound intensity I_s according as,

$$I = \exp \frac{t}{3} \sqrt{I_s} \qquad \text{...(6.4.5)}$$

Industrial practices employ contact times of about 4 seconds which may be reduced to 2 seconds when sound intensities greater than 165 decibels are used.

It is possible to calculate the volume in which a particle will collide with other particles and coagulate with them, that is the volume of the aggregation zone. The volume swept by a vibrating particle of diameter d_p so as to coagulate with another particle of diameter d_p' will be $[(\pi/4)(d_p + d_p')^2 A_p]$. But, as stated earlier, the particle also moves towards the antinode owing to the sonic radiation pressure and after a time t, having moved a distance L, it will have a new amplitude of vibration A_p'. The swept volume during this period will be,

$$V_a = (A_p + A_p')(d_p + d_p')[L + (\pi/4)(d_p + d_p')] \quad ...(6.4.6)$$

Once the values of A_p and A_p' are based on the critical particle size at the frequency of vibration, the ratio (V_a/V), where V is the total volume of the agglomeration chamber enclosing the cloud of particles, gives a measure of the efficiency of flocculation.

The velocity with which the particle moves towards the antinode can be estimated by equating the force F_r due to radiation pressure on the particle to the resistance offered by the gas F_R. For a spherical particle of diameter much smaller than the wave length λ, F_r is approximately given by[6],

$$F_r = \frac{5}{12}\left[\frac{\pi^2 d_p^3}{\lambda}\overline{E}\right]\sin(2\pi a/\lambda) \quad ...(6.4.7)$$

where $\overline{E}$ is the energy intensity (joules/m^3) and a is the distance from the node. Assuming the fluid resistance is in the Stokes' Law region, the velocity of particle towards the antinode will be,

$$\frac{dl}{dt} = \frac{F_r}{(3\pi \mu_g d_p/K_m)}$$

$$= \frac{5\pi d_p^2 \overline{E} K_m \sin(2\pi a/\lambda)}{36 \lambda \mu_g} \quad ...(6.4.8)$$

where l is the distance traversed towards the antinode. The time required for a particle to move to within a short distance of the antinode is obtained from the solution of the above equation[6] and this will indicate the desirable residence time for particles in the sonic field.

As stated earlier, at very high frequencies, the hydrodynamic forces contribute maximum to agglomeration. If two spherical particles of diameters d_p and d_p' are at a distance (centre to centre) l apart, the hydrodynamic attractive force F_h at right angles to the direction of vibration is given by[6] :

$$F_h = \left[\frac{3\pi\,\rho_g}{128}\right] d_p^3\, d_p'^{\,3} \left[\frac{(\Delta\,v)^2}{l^4}\right] \qquad \text{...(6.4.9)}$$

where (Δv) is the relative velocity amplitude of the particles. If both particles are of same size then the above equation reduces to,

$$F_h = \frac{3\pi\,\rho_g\,d_p^6\,(\Delta v)^2}{128\,l^4} \qquad \text{...(6.4.10)}$$

Once again, we can equate F_h to the fluid resistance F_R (estimated using Stokes' Law) to determine the velocity of particles towards one another. Thus,

$$3\,\pi\,\mu_g\,d_p\,\frac{dl}{dt} = \frac{3\pi\,\rho_g\,d_p^6\,(\Delta v)^2}{128\,l^4}$$

or

$$\frac{dl}{dt} = \frac{(\Delta v)^2\,\rho_g\,d_p^5}{128\,\mu_g\,l^4} \qquad \text{...(6.4.11)}$$

The time t required for the particles to come in contact with each other can be obtained by integrating the above equation from $l = l$ to $l = d_p$. Thus,

$$t = \frac{128\,\mu_g}{5\,(\Delta v)^2\,\rho_g}\,[1 - (l/d_p)^5] \qquad \text{...(6.4.12)}$$

For effective coagulation at high frequencies, the residence time of the particles in the acoustic field must be therefore equal to or higher than the value of t determined from the above equation.

Sonic agglomeration has been successfully employed on a number of difficult collection problems. It has been reported that sulfuric acid mist has been agglomerated successfully at efficiencies of 96 to 99.5 per cent depending on the mist residence time ranging from 0.6 to 3.0 seconds. Collection efficiency as high as 82 per cent is reported for agglomeration of carbon black with a particle concentration of 8-10 gm/Nm^3 and a residence time of 4.5 seconds in a sound field of 155 db. Sonic agglomeration has also been tried on fume collection for several metallurgical operations such as zinc oxide fumes from copper recovery furnaces (reported average efficiency = 78 per cent) and lead oxide fumes (95 to 98 per cent efficiency reported when a 15 kHz siren is used).

The operating and maintenance costs of sonic agglomeration cum collection systems are rather high, though the installation costs are reported to be around 15 per cent lower than for electrostatic precipitators of similar capacity. The efficiency of sonic agglomeration is virtually independent of temperature and therefore the technique could find application in high temperature precipitation. Since a sound whistle can be made very robust and the agglomeration chamber can be easily constructed from corrosion resistant materials, highly corrosive fumes can also be handled without difficulty. The acoustic power or sound intensity requirements of sonic agglomeration systems are invariably high. The threshold value for noticeable flocculation is around 130–140 db (around 10^{-3} watt/cm^2) while values over 150 db are necessary for large scale industrial units. Also, ultrasonic waves can cause harmful effects on personnel working in the vicinity.

6.5. Miscellaneous Methods

Alternate sundry mechanisms for particle collection from gases include thermal precipitation, separation in a magnetic field and collection by beds of fluidised solids[6]. Molecular impacts tend to repel dispersoids away from a heated body. This principle is utilised in thermal precipitation for removing suspended particles from gas streams by passing the dust-laden gas through or over a heated grid at low velocity[6,13]. This method is being experimented for industrial dust collection, but it has been very successful for atmospheric dust sampling.

NOMENCLATURE

A cross-sectional area of sonic agglomeration chamber, m^2.

A_i, A_o cross-sectional area of gas inlet and gas outlet respectively of cyclone separator, m^2.

A_p, A_g amplitude of vibration of particle and that of gas respectively, m.

a distance of the particle from the node, m.

B_c distance between wire and plate in wire-plate type ESP, m.

B_i, H_i breadth and height (or, depth) respectively of gas inlet of cyclone separator, m.

D diameter of cyclone separator, m.

D_p, d_p particle size, m (d_p is used in cm in section 6.3).

d_{pc} critical particle size (see equation 6.4.4), m.

D_c inside diameter of the collecting electrode of ESP, m.

D_d outside diameter of the discharge electrode of ESP, m.

D_o diameter of gas outlet of cyclone separator, m.

E electrostatic field strength, statvolts/cm ; separation efficiency of hydrocyclone, dimensionless.

E_i, E_c electrostatic potential gradient during ionisation and collection respectively, statvolts/cm.

E_{cr} critical field strength required for corona to commence, statvolts/cm.

E_o electrical breakdown constant of gas, statvolts/cm. (see equation 6.3.16).

$\overline{E}$ energy intensity (see equation 6.4.7), J/m^3.

e elementary electronic charge (= 1.602×10^{-19} coulomb).

F_e electrical force on the particle in an ESP, N.

F_R kinematic force, N.

F_r force on the particle due to radiation pressure, N.

F_h hydrodynamic attractive force, N.

G mass flow rate of gas, kg/s.

g gravitational acceleration, m/s^2.

I corona current, statamperes ; index of agglomeration, dimensionless.

I_s sound intensity, W/m^2 or db.

K empirical constant used in equation (6.2.14).

k Boltzmann constant, J/K.

K_e parameter defined in equation (6.3.17), s/cm.

K_m Stokes-Cunningham correction factor, dimensionless.

k_o energy distance constant, cm (see equation 6.3.16).

L_c length of collecting electrode in the direction of gas flow, m.

l distance traversed by the particle towards antinode, m ; centre-to-centre distance between two particles of sizes d_p and d_p' m.

m mass of the particle, m.

N_i ion density, cm^{-3}

N_o Avagadro number.

Q_F rate of inflow of feed mixture, m^3/s.

Q_o, Q_u volumetric rate of over-flow and underflow respectively, m^3/s.

q, q' charge on a particle at any time t by bombardment charging and diffusion charging respectively in an ESP, coulombs.

q_e, q_e' ultimate charge acquired by a particle due to bombardment charging and diffusion charging respectively, coulombs.

r radius of rotation of the particle inside a cyclone separator, m.

S volume split ($= Q_u/Q_o$), dimensionless.

T absolute temperature, °K.

U_i ionic mobility, (cm/s)/(volts/cm).

U_p particle migration velocity, cm/s.

V_{avg} average velocity of gas through the electrostatic precipitator, cm/s.

V, V_{cr} applied voltage and critical voltage required for corona to commence respectively, statvolts.

V_{gt} tangential velocity of gas, m/s.

$(V_{gt})_c$ tangential velocity at the circumference of the cyclone separator, m/s.

V_i inlet velocity of feed gas, m/s.

V_r radial velocity, m/s.

V_t gravitational free settling velocity of the particle, m/s.

X cumulative mass fraction.

Z depth of the cyclone separator, m.

Greek Letters

β constant used in equation (6.4.1).

γ sound frequency, s^{-1}.

δ dielectric constant of the particle.

$(-\Delta P)$ pressure drop through the separator, N/m^2.

(Δv) relative velocity amplitude of the particles, m/s.

η collection efficiency of ESP, dimensionless.

η_a acoustic efficiency of sound generator, dimensionless.

λ wave length of sound waves, m.

μ_g viscosity of gas, kg/(ms).
(μ_g is expressed in poise in section.6.3).

ρ_g, ρ_s density of gas and that of solid particles respectively, kg/m^3.

ρ' density of gas relative to its density at NTP (at 0°C and 760 mm of mercury), dimensionless.

τ time constant, s (see equation 6.3.1).

REFERENCES

1. Perry, J.H. (Ed.), Chemical Engineers' Handbook, 5th edition, McGraw-Hill, New York, 1973.
2. Shepherd, C.B. and Lapple, C.E., Ind. Eng. Chem., **31**, 972, 1939 ; **32**, 1246, 1940.
3. Ter Linden, A.J., Inst. Mech. Engrs. J., **160**, 233, 1949
4. Stairmand, C.J., Trans. Inst. Chem. Engrs., **29**, 356, 1951.
5. Mahajan, S.P. and Pai, V.J., Ind. Chem. Engr., **19**(3), 3-9, 1977.
6. Strauss, W., Industrial Gas Cleaning, Pergamon Press, Oxford, 1966.
7. White, H.J., Trans. AIEE, **70**, II, 1186, 1951.
8. Ladenburg, R., Ann. Physik, **4**(5), 863, 1930.
9. Deutsch, W., Ann. Phys. (Lpzg), **68**, 335, 1922.
10. White, H.J., Ind. Eng. Chem., **47**, 932, 1955.
11. Penny, H., Elec. Eng., **56**, 159, 1937.
12. Boucher, R.M.G., Chem. Eng., **68**(20), 83, 1961.
13. Blacktin, S.C., Trans. J. Soc. Chem. Ind., **58**, 334, 1939 ; **59**, 153, 1940.

7

Mixing and Agitation

Mixing and agitation are two unit operations that have become essentially synonymous. A hard and fast distinction between the two is difficult; however we may use the term agitation for an operation involving only a single phase such as agitation of a liquid to promote heat transfer whereas mixing involves inter-dispersion of two or more phases such as suspending particles in a liquid (solid-liquid mixing or slurry mixing), blending of two miscible liquids (homogenising), inter-dispersion of two immiscible liquids to form emulsions, gas-liquid dispersion, mixing of dry powders and granular solids (solid-solid mixing) and blending of pastes and plastic masses. Since agitation causes mixing, these two operations are commonly superimposed on each other. Most of the process equipment such as flotation cells, extractors, emulsifiers, creamers, homogenisers, reactors, crystallisers, dryers and so on employ agitation by one method or another, so much so that mixing and agitation have become practically omnipresent in chemical process industries.

Agitation can be accomplished using mechanical impellers or by pneumatic means (by injecting air under pressure). The so-called *jet mixing or injection mixing* is employed mainly for liquid-liquid systems or for mixing of combustible gases just before ignition. This involves impingement of one fluid stream on the other, say injecting one of the liquids through a fine nozzle or orifice into a flowing stream of the other. In case of gases, both gases may be fed through jets under pressure. Jet mixing can be used successfully only for liquids of low interfacial tension. In the so-called *static or motionless mixers*, the fluid streams are made to follow tortuous flow paths and as a result they get interdispersed. The flow geometry can be made tortuous by introducing a number of short helical elements in the fluid passage. Such mixers are useful in gas-liquid and liquid-liquid dispersions, but the overall pressure drop in such systems could be often 3-4 times that in an empty pipe of same length.

Mechanical impellers can be broadly classified as radial flow impellers and axial flow impellers. *Axial flow impellers* have their blades making an angle equal to or less than 90° with the drive shaft and therefore produce currents in the liquid essentially parallel to the impeller shaft. Propellers, fan turbines and pitched paddles (see Fig. 7.1)

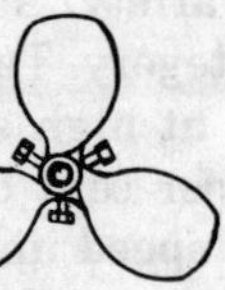

(*a*) three bladed marine propeller

(*b*) fan turbine

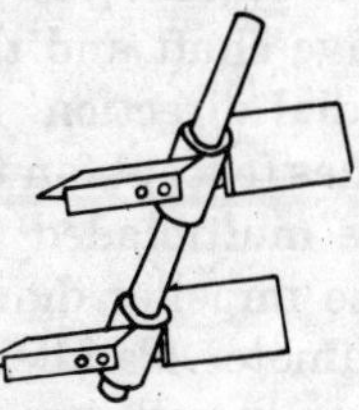

(*c*) pitched paddle

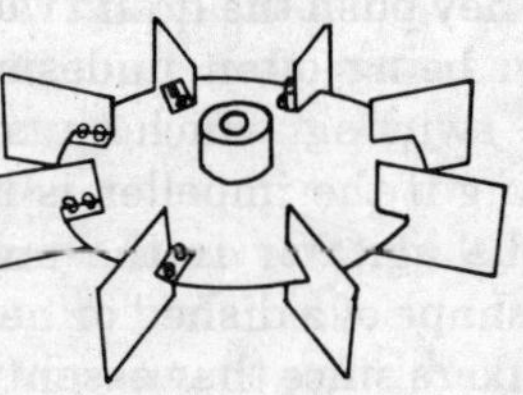

(*d*) flat bladed turbine

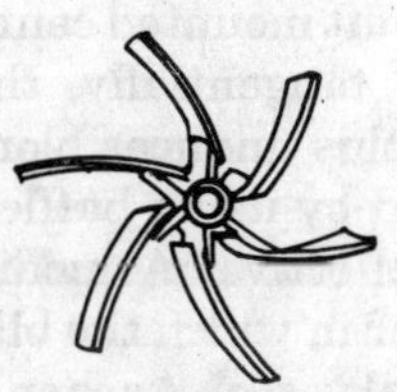

(*e*) spiral backswept turbine

(*f*) paddle

(*g*) shrouded curved blade turbine with diffuser ring.

Fig. 7.1. Types of impellers.

fall under this class. Among them, propellers are most popular particularly for agitating liquids of low viscosity and for solid-liquid mixing. They are quite effective in very large vessels. A revolving propeller traces out a helix in the fluid and if there were no slip between the liquid and the propeller, one full revolution would move the liquid longitudinally a fixed distance depending on the angle of inclination of the propeller blades. The ratio of this distance to the propeller diameter is called the pitch of the propeller. A propeller with a pitch of 1.0 is said to be of square pitch. Three bladed marine propellers with square pitch are most commonly employed in process industries. The speed of commercial propellers varies from 400 to 1750 rpm. They are usually used in the top-entering vertical mount and are positioned centrally along the axis of the mixing vessel. Off-center, inclined or side-entering mounts are used for special purposes.

Radial flow impellers have their blades parallel to the axis of the drive shaft and they create currents in the liquid in a tangential or radial direction. Paddles (except the pitched blade variety) and turbines (except fan turbines) generally fall under this category. Turbines are multibladed with short blades and are operated at high speeds. The impeller diameter is usually between 30 to 60 per cent of tank diameter. Paddles on the other hand are large, slower speed impellers usually with two or four blades. The total length of the impeller is 60 to 80 per cent of the tank diameter while the width of the blades is 10 to 15 per cent of the length. Paddles and turbines are normally run on a shaft mounted centrally in the vessel. They push the liquid radially and tangentially, the tangential motion being often undesirable since this induces vortex formation and swirling which must be stopped by using baffles or by a diffuser ring if the impeller is to be most effective. A modified design of paddle agitator is the anchor agitator in which the blades conform to the shape of a dished or hemispherical vessel. Anchor agitators are poor mixers since they essentially scrap the vessel walls and can be used for removing deposites from surfaces. They are usually operated in conjunction with another high speed impeller usually rotating in the opposite direction.

The flow pattern in an agitated vessel depends on the type of impeller used (whether radial flow or axial flow), the physical and transport properties of the fluid, the geometric dimensions of the tank, impeller and baffles (if used). Consider an impeller mounted on a vertical shaft and located centrally in the tank. The rotation of the impeller can cause longitudinal or axial flow in the liquid (in a direction parallel to the impeller shaft) or radial flow in a direction perpendicular to the drive shaft and these are advantageous since they provide the necessary flow for mixing action. However, there will always be a tangential flow that follows a circular path around the shaft which is generally undesirable since this creates a vortex at the surface of the liquid and tends to perpetuate stratification at various levels preventing longitudinal flow between levels (see Fig. 7.2). In solid-liquid mixing, these circulatory currents throw the particles outwards by centrifugal forces from where they settle down to the bottom of the tank. Thus, instead of mixing, separation will result. Also, since in a circulatory flow, the liquid flows with the direction of motion of the impeller blades, the relative velocity between the blades and the liquid is reduced and as a result, the power that can be absorbed by the liquid is also diminished. In an unbaffled tank, circulatory flow is induced by all types of impellers whether radial flow or axial flow. In fact, when the swirl is strong, the flow pattern in the vessel becomes virtually independent of the type of impeller used.

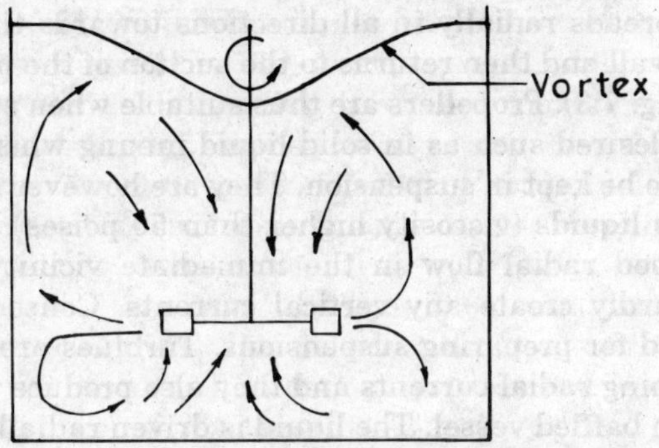

Fig. 7.2. Flow pattern in an unbaffled tank with a turbine agitator.

One of the best ways of avoiding swirling and vortex formation is to use baffles which impede rotational flow without affecting radial or longitudinal flow. Normally, four baffles shall serve the purpose unless the tank is very large. Longitudinal baffles which are nothing but vertical strips fixed perpendicular to the tank wall are most widely used (see Fig. 7.3). The baffle width is usually one twelfth of tank diameter for turbines and one-eighteenth of tank diameter when propellers are used. In small tanks, circulatory flow and swirling can be stopped by mounting the impeller off-center and slightly tilted. It is also possible to use side-entering propellers in comparatively larger tanks that avoids the use of baffles. Also, if shrouded turbines with diffuser rings (see Fig. 7.1) are used, then baffles can be avoided.

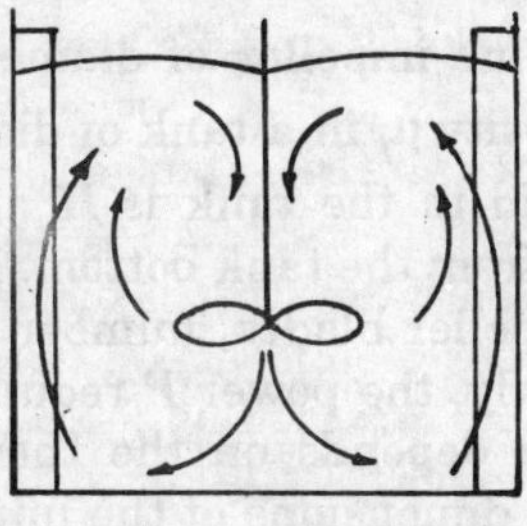

Fig. 7.3. Flow pattern in a baffled tank with a propeller agitator.

However, diffuser rings are difficult to instal and maintain and they have the additional drawback that they tend to prevent liquid currents from reaching the far corners of the tank.

As stated earlier, in presence of a strong swirling flow, the type of impeller does not matter. But if the swirling is stopped by any of the methods discussed above, then the flow pattern in the vessel is decided by the type of impeller used. Propellers, being axial flow impellers, drive the liquid straight down to the bottom of the tank where the stream spreads radially in all directions towards the wall, flows up along the wall and then returns to the suction of the propeller from the top (see Fig. 7.3). Propellers are thus suitable when strong vertical currents are desired such as in solid-liquid mixing when heavy solid particles are to be kept in suspension. They are however not used with highly viscous liquids (viscosity higher than 50 poises). Paddles give reasonably good radial flow in the immediate vicinity of impeller blades but hardly create any vertical currents. Consequently, they cannot be used for preparing suspensions. Turbines are highly effective in developing radial currents and they also produce vertical flows particularly in baffled vessel. The liquid is driven radially against the wall where the stream divides into two parts, one part flows downward to the tank bottom and then back to the center of the impeller from below and the other part flows upward towards the surface and then back to the impeller from above. Thus, two separate circulation currents are generated (see Fig. 7.2).

To affect uniform agitation, the height of liquid in the tank is normally maintained equal to the tank diameter. However, if the tank is too tall and a large liquid holdup is desired, then multiple impellers, that is two or more impellers mounted on the same shaft, may be used. Each impeller then acts as a separate mixing device. A clearance of about one impeller diameter is to be provided between the tank bottom and the bottom-most impeller.

7.1. Agitator Design

Let us consider a turbine impeller of diameter D_a agitating a liquid of density ρ_f and viscosity μ_f in a tank of diameter D_t (see Fig. 7.4). The height of the liquid in the tank is H and the impeller is positioned at an elevation E from the tank bottom. It is also necessary to specify the number of impeller blades, number of baffles (if used) and the baffle width J. Clearly, the power P required for driving the impeller at a given speed n depends on the these factors such as D_a, D_t, H, E, J, μ_f, ρ_f and the dimensions of the impeller blade W and

L. Also, if baffles are not used or no provision has been made to eliminate swirling, then a vortex will appear at the surface of the liquid and some of the liquid must have to be lifted above the average level of the liquid surface against the force of gravity. As a result, the gravitational acceleration g will also become an influencing factor. Thus, we can write,

$$P = f_n\,[n, D_a, D_t, E, L, W, J, H, \mu_f, \rho_f, g] \quad ...(7.1.1)$$

where f_n means "function of."

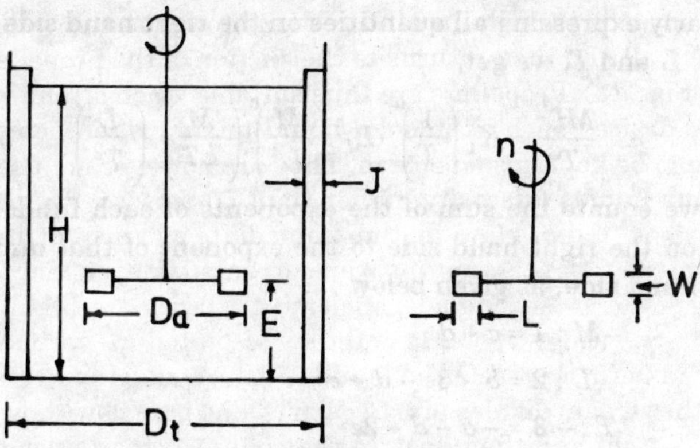

Fig. 7.4.

To rearrange the above equation in a more workable form, let us perform a dimensional analysis. Incidentally, the linear dimensions such as D_t, E, L, W, J and H can be made dimensionless by dividing each of them by a suitable chosen characteristic length. Normally, the impeller diameter D_a is used as the characteristic length. Thus,

$$S_1 = D_t/D_a, \quad S_2 = E/D_a, S_3 = L/D_a, S_4 = W/D_a$$
$$S_5 = J/D_t, \quad \text{and } S_6 = H/D_t \text{ or } H/(S_1\, D_a). \quad ...(7.1.1a)$$

These dimensionless factors S_1, S_2, S_3, S_4, S_5 and S_6 are called shape factors. If we temporarily exclude these shape factors, then equation (7.1.1) can be rewritten as,

$$P = f_n\,(n, D_a, \rho_f, \mu_f, g) \quad ...(7.1.2)$$

It is to be noted that we have assumed the liquid to be Newtonian. If the liquid is non-Newtonian, then its rheological parameters also will have to be included in the above equation. For the purpose of dimensional analysis, equation (7.1.2) can be expressed as,

$$P = K_1\, n^a\, D_a^b\, \rho_f^c\, \mu_f^d\, g^e \quad ...(7.1.3)$$

where K_1 is a dimensionless constant.

Let us now express all the quantities in the above equation in terms of the fundamental dimensions such as mass (M), length (L) and time (T). For example,

$$P = \text{Watts} = \text{Joules/sec} = \text{Nm/s}$$
$$= \text{kg (m/s}^2\text{) (m/s)}$$
$$= ML^2/T^3$$

Similarly expressing all quantities on the right hand side also in terms of M, L and T, we get,

$$\frac{ML^2}{T^3} = K_1 \left(\frac{1}{T}\right)^a (L)^b \left(\frac{M}{L^3}\right)^c \left(\frac{M}{LT}\right)^d \left(\frac{L}{T^2}\right)^e \quad ...(7.1.4)$$

Now we equate the sum of the exponents of each fundamental dimension on the right hand side to the exponent of that dimension on the left hand side, as given below :

For $\quad M : 1 = c + d$

For $\quad L : 2 = b - 3c - d + e$

For $\quad T : -3 = -a - d - 2e$

Solving for a, b and c in terms of d and e, we get,

$$a = 3 - d - 2e$$
$$b = 5 - 2d - e$$
$$c = 1 - d$$

Thus equation (7.1.3) becomes,

$$P = K_1\, n^{3-d-2e}\, D_a^{5-2d-e}\, \rho_f^{1-d}\, \mu_f^d\, g^e \quad ...(7.1.4)$$

Grouping variables having like exponents together we get,

$$P = K_1 \left[(n^3 D_a^5 \rho_f) \left(\frac{n D_a^2 \rho_f}{\mu_f}\right)^{-d} \left(\frac{n^2 D_a}{g}\right)^{-e} \right]$$

or, $$\left[\frac{P}{n^3 D_a^5 \rho_f}\right] = K_1 \left[\left(\frac{nD_a^2 \rho_f}{\mu_f}\right)^{-d} \left(\frac{n^2 D_a}{g}\right)^{-e} \right] \quad ...(7.1.5)$$

Incorporating the shape factors also, we can write,

$$\left[\frac{P}{n^3 D_a^5 \rho_f}\right] = f_n \left[\left(\frac{nD_a^2 \rho_f}{\mu_f}\right), \left(\frac{n^2 D_a}{g}\right), S_1, S_2, S_3, S_4, S_5, S_6 \right] \quad ...(7.1.6)$$

Table 7.1

Impeller type	S_1	S_2	S_3	S_6	a	b
1. Three bladed marine propeller, pitch = 2	3.3	0.75 — 1.3	—	1.0	1.7	18.0
2. Three bladed marine propeller, pitch = 1.04	4.5	0.75 — 1.3	—	0.6 — 0.9	0.0	18.0
3. Three bladed marine propeller, pitch = 1.05	2.7	0.75 — 1.3	—	1.0 — 1.45	2.3	18.0
4. Flat-bladed turbine, with six blades	3.0	0.75 — 1.3	0.25 (S_4 = 0.2)	0.9 — 1.3	1.0	40.0
5. Three bladed marine propeller, with square pitch	3.0	0.75 — 1.3	—	0.9 — 1.3	2.1	18.0

The dimensionless group on the left hand side of the above equation is called the power number, *Po*. It is analogous to the drag coefficient we discussed in chapter 3. It represents the characteristic ratio of the drag force acting on a unit area of the impeller to the inertial stress. The dimensionless groups on the right hand side are,

$$\left[\frac{nD_a^2\,\rho_f}{\mu_f}\right] = \text{Re}_m = \text{mixing or impeller Reynolds number}$$

$$\left[\frac{n^2\,D_a}{g}\right] = Fr_m = \text{mixing Froude number}$$

We know that Reynolds number represents the characteristic ratio of inertial stress to viscous stress whereas Froude number gives the relative magnitude of inertial stress to gravitational force acting on unit area of the fluid. Thus, we can rewrite equation (7.1.6) as,

$$Po = f_n\,[\text{Re}_m, Fr_m, S_1, S_2, S_3, S_4, S_5, S_6] \qquad \text{...(7.1.7)}$$

It must not be forgotten that though not included in the above equation, the power consumption *P* depends not only on the impeller diameter D_a and blade dimensior V and *L*, but also on the number of impeller blades and apart from the baffle width *J*, the number of baffles used as well. If a propeller is used, the pitch of the propeller should also be specified. Equation (7.1.7) is normally re-expressed in a more convenient form as,

$$\frac{Po}{Fr_m^m} = \phi = f_n\,[\text{Re}_m, S_1, S_2, S_3, S_4, S_5, S_6] \qquad \text{...(7.1.8)}$$

where ϕ is called the power function. The exponent *m* is defined as,

$$m = (a - \log \text{Re}_m)/b \qquad \text{...(7.1.9)}$$

where *a* and *b* are impeller constants. The magnitudes of *a* and *b* depend on the type of impeller and the shape factors S_1 to S_4 and S_6. Some typical values of *a* and *b* are given in Table (7.1).

Standard plots of ϕ *versus* Re_m on log-log coordinates are available in the literature.[1,2] One such family of plots is shown in Fig. (7.5). It is to be noted that each curve in the figure corresponds to a particular type of impeller and a given set of values of S_1 to S_6. Since many curves overlap on each other, the plots should be utilised with great care.

The effect of Froude number Fr_m becomes significant only when there is vortex formation and at large values of Reynolds number Re_m ($\text{Re}_m > 300$). At low Reynolds number ($\text{Re}_m < 300$) or when baffles are used or with off-center inclined and side-entering impellers (when vortex formation is eliminated), Fr_m will not be a factor and its effect can be neglected. In such cases,

$$\phi = Po$$

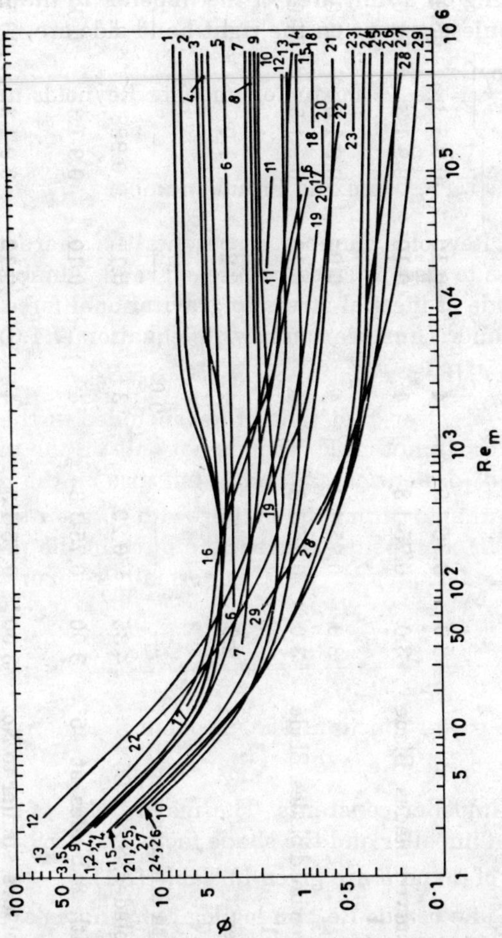

Fig. 7.5. Power Function *versus* Reynolds number plots. (Please See Table 7.2 for the Nomenclature of these plots). Reproduced from Brown, G.G. and Associates, Unit Operations, Wiley,1950, with permission.

Equation (7.1.8) then reduces to,

$$Po = f_n\ [\text{Re}_m, S_1, S_2, S_3, S_4, S_5, S_6] \qquad \text{...(7.1.10)}$$

It can be seen from Fig. (7.5) that the plot is essentially linear with a slope of -1 when Re_m is very low (less than 10). The impeller is then said to be operating in the laminar zone and in this zone,

Table 7.2

Nomenclature for Fig. 7.5

Curve No.	*Type of impeller*	S_1	S_2	*Number of baffles*	S_5	S_6	K_L	K_T
1.	Turbine with 6 flat blades, $S_3 = 0.25$, $S_4 = 0.20$	3.0	0.75-1.3	4	0.17	0.9-1.3	68.0	7.0
2.	Same as above	3.0	0.75-1.3	4	0.10	0.9-1.3	68.0	6.3
3.	Turbine with 6 curved blades. Blade sizes same as No. 1	3.0	0.75-1.3	4	0.10	0.9-1.3	71.0	4.8
4.	Same as No. 1	3.0	0.75-1.3	4	0.04	0.9-1.3	68.0	4.4
5.	Turbine with 6 arrowhead blades. Blade sizes same as No. 1	3.0	0.75-1.3	4	0.10	0.9-1.3	71.0	4.0
6.	Disk with 16 vanes. $S_3 = 0.35$, $S_4 = 0.10$	2.5	0.75	4	0.25	1.0	—	3.0
7.	Radial turbine with diffuser ring.	—	—	0.0	—	—	—	2.2
8.	Paddle with two blades. $S_4 = 0.25$	4.35	0.29	3	0.11	0.988	—	2.0
9.	Axial turbine with 8 blades at 45° angle	3.00	0.75-1.3	4	0.10	0.9-1.3	0.0	1.8
10.	Paddle with two blades, similar to No. 8	3.00	0.75-1.3	4	0.10	0.9-1.3	36.5	1.7
11.	Shrouded turbine with 6 blades, 20-blade deflector ring.	2.4	0.9	0.0	—	0.308	—	—

12.	Similar to No. 11	3.0	0.75-1.3	0.0	—	0.9-1.3	172.5	1.12
13	Same as No. 11, but no deflector ring.	3.0	0.75-1.3	4	0.10	0.9-1.3	97.5	1.08
14.	Same as No. 1	3.0	0.75-1.3	0.0	—	0.9-1.3	68.0	—
15.	Marine propeller with 3 blades. Pitch = 2.0	3.0	0.75-1.3	4	0.10	0.9-1.3	43.5	0.9
16.	Paddle with 4 blades. Blade size same as No. 8	3.0	0.5	0.0	—	1.0	—	—
17.	Axial turbine with 4 blades at 60° angle	3.0	0.5	0.0	—	1.0	—	—
18.	Same as No. 15 but pitch = 1.33	16	—	3	0.06	—	—	—
19.	Axial turbine with 4 blades at 45° angle	5.2	0.87	0.0	—	1.0	—	—
20.	Paddle with 2 blades, same as No. 8	3.0	0.33	0.0	—	1.066	—	—
21.	Same as No. 15	3.3	0.75-1.3	0.0	—	0.818-1.18	42.0	—
22.	Same as No. 19	2.4-3.0	0.4-0.5	0.0	—	1.0	—	—
23.	Same as No. 15, but pitch = 1.09	9.6	—	3	0.06	—	—	—
24.	Same as No. 15, but pitch = 1.0	3.0	0.75-1.3	4	0.10	0.9-1.3	41.0	0.32
25.	Same as No. 15, but pitch = 1.04	4.5	0.75-1.3	0.0	—	0.6-0.867	—	—
26.	Same as No. 15, but pitch = 1.0	3.0	0.75-1.3	0.0	—	0.9-1.3	—	—
27.	Same as No. 15, but pitch = 1.05	2.7	0.75-1.3	0.0	—	1.0-1.44	—	—
28.	Same as No. 15, but pitch = 1.0	3.8	1.0	0.0	—	0.92	—	—

$$\phi \, \mathrm{Re}_m = K_L = \text{constant} \quad ...(7.1.11)$$

Since Re_m is very low, Froude number will not be a factor and therefore we can write,

$$Po \, \mathrm{Re}_m = K_L \quad ...(7.1.12)$$

Substituting for Po and Re_m we get

$$\frac{P}{n^2 D_a^3 \mu_f} = K_L = f_n (S_1, S_2, S_3, S_4, S_5, S_6)$$

or,

$$P = K_L n^2 D_a^3 \mu_f \quad ...(7.1.13)$$

It can be seen that the power consumption in the laminar zone is independent of fluid density but varies with the square of the impeller speed. It is to be noted that the value of K_L depends on the impeller type and the magnitude of the shape factors. For example, for a vessel fitted with four baffles (baffle width = 0.1 D_t) K_L = 41.0 for a three bladed propeller with square pitch, whereas it is 68.0 for a six bladed (flat blades) turbine and for a shrouded turbine with diffuser ring operating in an unbaffled vessel, K_L is as high as 172.5.

If the Reynolds number Re_m is very large (> 10,000), then the impeller is said to be operating in a fully developed turbulent zone. In such a case, for baffled vessels, ϕ can be seen to be essentially constant and independent of Re_m. Thus,

$$\phi = K_T = \text{constant} \quad ...(7.1.14)$$

Since the vessel is baffled, $\phi = Po$. Therefore,

$$Po = \frac{P}{n^3 D_a^5 \rho_f} = K_T$$

or,

$$P = K_T n^3 D_a^5 \rho_f \quad ...(7.1.15)$$

Thus, the power consumption is independent of fluid viscosity in the fully developed turbulent zone. However, it is more dependent on the impeller speed as it varies with the cube of n. Once again, the value of K_T depends on the impeller type and the magnitude of shape factors. For a four-baffled vessel (baffle width = 0.1 D_t), K_T = 0.32 when a three bladed propeller with square pitch is used, but K_T = 0.9 if the pitch of the propeller is 2.0. For a six bladed (flat blades) turbine operating in the same tank, K_T = 6.30 while for a two bladed paddle, K_T is only 1.7.

The values of K_L and K_T can be deduced from the standard plots given in Fig. (7.5). For the convenience of the readers, a few typical values of K_L and K_T are given in table (7.2).

Once the impeller Reynolds number Re_m is specified, the value of power function or power number can be obtained from the standard plot and the power required for driving the impeller at the given speed can be computed therefrom. It the impeller speed for a given power consumption is to be computed, then a trial and error procedure becomes invariable since both power number and Re_m contain the term n. However, a graphical procedure similar to that discussed in chapter-3 for the estimation of particle settling velocity using Newton's law, can be used here also so that the trial and error procedure can be avoided. For example, let us consider baffled tank. Now,

$$\phi = Po = P/n^3 D_a^5 \rho_f$$

since $$Re_m = nD_a^2 \rho_f/\mu_f,\ n = Re_m \mu_f/\rho_f D_a^2.$$

Substituting for n in the expression for Po we get,

$$Po = P \rho_f^2/Re_m^3 \mu_f^3 \quad \text{...(7.1.16)}$$

Taking logarithm on both sides,

$$\ln (Po) = \ln \left[\frac{P \rho_f^2}{\mu_f^3}\right] - 3 \ln (Re_m) \quad \text{...(7.1.17)}$$

Thus, a plot of Po *versus* Re_m on log-log co-ordinates will yield a straight line of slope-3. The point of intersection of this straight line with the standard plot of Po versus Re_m (Fig. 7.5) gives the value of Re_m, from which the impeller speed n can be easily computed.

7.2. Solid-Liquid Mixing

Preparation of slurries or uniform suspensions of solids in liquids is one of the popular applications for which mechanical impellers, particularly propellers, are employed. Whether the particles can be easily kept in suspension in a liquid or not depends on the free settling velocity of the particles in the liquid, since the impeller is now working against the settling velocity of the particles and thus trying to prevent them from settling down. If the free settling velocity of the particles is very low (less than 0.3 m/min), then they can be easily kept in suspension using mechanical agitators. However, even if the particles are heavier or coarser but their settling velocity falls below 3m/min, a uniform suspension can be prepared though this will demand a high impeller speed and high power consumption. If the free settling velocity of the particles is greater than 3 m/min, they are fast-settling particles and a uniform suspension is difficult to be prepared using commercial impellers.

Only empirical correlations based on experimental results are available for estimating the power consumption in solid-liquid mixing. Weisman and Efferding[3] have proposed the following correlation for estimating the power P required for raising the particles from the vessel floor to a height Z_s using a turbine impeller :

$$\left[\frac{Z_s - E}{D_t}\right] = C_1 \ln \left[\frac{P\,(1-\varepsilon)^{-2/3}}{g\,\rho_m\,V_m\,V_t}\left(\frac{D_a}{D_t}\right)\right]^{1/2} + 0.1 \qquad ...(7.2.1)$$

where V_m, ρ_m = total volume and bulk density of solid-liquid suspension, considering the zone within Z_s from vessel floor only

ε = volume fraction of liquid in the suspension (for zone within Z_s)

V_t = terminal free settling velocity of particles computed from Stokes' law (see equation (3.1.8) of chapter-3)

E = elevation of impeller from vessel floor

C_1 is an empirical constant and its value varies from 0.23 (for $E/D_a > 0.5$) to 0.27 (for $E/D_a = 0.20$). The above correlation is valid for impeller operating in fully developed turbulent zone only and also for $D_a/D_t < 0.5$ and $(Z_s - E) > 0.5\,D_t$. Since the correlation is empirical, its limitations must be properly taken into consideration before applying the same.

The power required for just detaching the particles from the vessel floor so that they remain in suspension can also be calculated using another correlation proposed by the same authors, as given below :

$$\left[\frac{1.74\,P}{g\,(\rho_s - \rho_f)\,V_T\,V_t}\right] = 0.16\left(\frac{1-\varepsilon}{\varepsilon}\right)^{1/2}\left[\frac{D_t}{D_a}\right]e^{5.3\,E/D_t} \qquad ...(7.2.2)$$

where V_T is the volume of the tank. V_t is the relative velocity between particles and the fluid in the fully developed turbulent zone (see equation 3.1.6) of Chapter - 3). This correlation is valid for (D_a/D_t) ratios between 0.36 and 0.43, with other conditions as specified for equation (7.2.1).

Example 7.1. *A slurry containing 25 per cent (by weight) of solid particles (specific gravity = 2.0) in water is to be mixed in a vessel 2m in diameter and 3m deep, fitted with four baffles each of width 10 per cent of tank diameter. The tank is filled to a height of 2m with the slurry and a 0.6 m diameter, 100 rpm six-bladed turbine impeller is set at one impeller diameter above the vessel floor. Estimate the power consumption for lifting at least 80 per cent of particles to a height of*

1.8 m from the vessel floor, if the size distribution of particles present is as given below :

Particle size (mm)	*Mass fraction*
– 0.4 + 0.3	*0.09*
– 0.3 + 0.2	*0.08*
– 0.2 + 0.1	*0.03*
– 0.1 + 0.05	*0.25*
– 0.05 + 0.02	*0.35*
– 0.02 + 0.01	*0.20*

Solution. We can apply equation (7.2.1) here. But at the outset, we must make sure that all the restrictions of the correlation are properly met. Firstly, let us therefore find out whether the impeller is operating in the fully developed turbulent zone or not. Thus,

$$\text{Re}_m = \frac{nD_a^2\,\rho_f}{\mu_f} = \frac{(100/60)\,(0.6)^2\,(1000)}{0.001} = 600{,}000$$

Since Re_m is much above 10,000, the impeller is operating in fully developed turbulent zone. The other two conditions are (D_a/D_t) should be less than 0.5 and $\left(\frac{Z_s - E}{D_t}\right) > 0.5$. In the present case,

$$\frac{D_a}{D_t} = \frac{0.6}{2.0} = 0.3$$

$$\frac{(Z_s - E)}{D_t} = \frac{(1.8 - 0.6)}{2.0} = 0.6$$

Thus, the above conditions are also satisfied. We can therefore confidently use equation (7.2.1).

Let us assume that the particles are essentially spherical. To find the maximum size among 80 per cent of particles, let us construct a cumulative mass fraction table from the size distribution given :

Particle Size (mm)	*Cumulative mass fraction, X*
0.4	1.00
0.3	0.91
0.2	0.83
0.1	0.80
0.05	0.55
0.02	0.20
0.01	0.00

From the above table, particle size corresponding to $X = 0.8$ is 0.1 mm. That is, 80 per cent of particles have size less than 0.1 mm. Thus, if the particle of size 0.1 mm is lifted to the height of 1.8, all other particles having size less than this (that is, 80 per cent of particles) will also be lifted. Therefore,

$$V_t = (\rho_s - \rho_f)\, g d_p^2 / 18\, \mu_f \text{ (from equation 3.1.8)}$$

$$= \frac{(2.0 - 1.0)\,(1000)\,(9.8)\,(0.1 \times 10^{-3})^2}{18\,(0.001)}$$

$$= 5.4 \times 10^{-3} \text{ m/s}$$

$$V_m = \frac{\pi D_t^2}{4} Z_s = \frac{\pi}{4} (2.0)^2\,(1.8) = 5.65 \text{ m}^3$$

It is to be kept in mind that V_m is the volume of slurry within the height Z_s.

Total volume of slurry $= (\pi D_t^2/4)\, H$

$= (\pi/4)\,(2.0)^2\,(2.0) = 6.28 \text{ m}^3$

Since the above slurry contains 25 per cent by weight of solids, density of above slurry

$$= \frac{(100)}{(25/2000) + (75/1000)}$$

$$= 1142.857 \text{ kg/m}^3$$

The above value is not equal to ρ_m, since ρ_m is the density of slurry within the height Z_s only. We can compute ρ_m as follows :

Mass of total slurry $= (1142.857)\,(6.28) = 7177.14$ kg

Mass of solids in the total slurry

$= (7177.14)\,(0.25) = 1794.28$ kg

Since solids are lifted to a height Z_s, it will not be wrong to assume that there are no solids above this height. Therefore,

Mass of solids in the zone within Z_s

$= 1794.28$ kg

Volume of liquid within this zone

$= V_m - (1794.28/\rho_s)$

$= 5.65 - (1794.28/2000) = 4.7528 \text{ m}^3$

Mass of liquid within $Z_s = (4.7528)\,(1000) = 4752.8$ kg

Therefore, density of slurry within Z_s

$$\rho_m = \frac{(1794.28) + (4752.8)}{(5.65)}$$

$$= 1158.786 \text{ kg/m}^3$$

And, $\quad \varepsilon \text{ (within } Z_s) = \frac{(4.7528)}{(5.65)} = 0.8412$

Since $(E/D_a) = 1.0$, $C_1 = 0.23$.

Substituting all the values in equation (7.2.1), we get,

$$P = 1632.67 \text{ Watts} = 1.63 \text{ kW}.$$

7.3. Agitator Selection

The most suitable agitator for a given industrial operation is the one that produces the given degree of mixing within a reasonably low time and with a reasonably low power consumption. It is therefore convenient to define two additional dimensionless groups such as the *mixing number* N_t and the modified power number N_L, the former being a function of the blending time t_T but is independent of the power consumption P whereas the latter decides the power consumption but is independent of t_T. Thus,

$$N_t = (nt_T)/(\text{Re}_m\ S_1^2) \qquad \text{...(7.3.1)}$$

Since $\text{Re}_m = (nD_a^2\ \rho_f/\mu_f)$ and $S_1 = (D_t/D_a)$, the expression for N_t becomes,

$$N_t = \frac{t_T\ \mu_f}{D_t^2\ \rho_f} \qquad \text{...(7.3.2)}$$

It can be seen that N_t is proportional to the blending time t_T but is independent of P.

$$N_L = Po\ (\text{Re}_m)^3\ S_1 \qquad \text{...(7.3.3)}$$

Substituting for Po, Re_m and S_1, we get

$$N_L = \frac{P\ \rho_f^2\ D_t}{\mu_f^3} \qquad \text{...(7.3.4)}$$

Thus, N_L is proportional to P but is independent of t_T. It is possible to prepare plots of N_t *versus* N_L for the different impellers used in commercial practice. These plots will help us in choosing the agitator that is most satisfactory for a given industrial application. For example, consider the plots sketched in Fig. (7.6). Let the process criterion be that the blending time t_T should not exceed a value t_1. Let the value of N_t at $t_T = t_1$ be at (a) as shown in the Figure. It can be

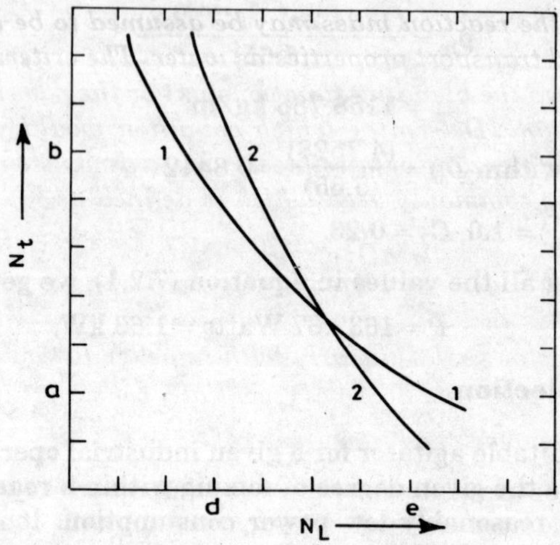

Fig. 7.6. Plots of Mixing Number *versus* Modified Power Number.

seen that the value of N_L (and thereby the power consumption P) is lower for impeller-2 than that for impeller-1, corresponding to $t_T = t_1$. Thus, impeller-2 will produce the same degree of mixing within the same time but consuming lesser power and therefore it must be preferred for the final application. If a larger blending time t_2 is available (may be for lowering the power consumption or for achieving a higher degree of mixing) and at $t_T = t_2$, N_t is at (b), then it can be seen that impeller-1 will produce the same effect with a lower power consumption and therefore it is to be preferred here. Conversely, we may fix the maximum permissible power consumption and thereby the value of N_L [say at (d) or (e)] and find out which of the impellers shall do the work within a lesser amount of time. If N_L is fixed at (d), then the value of N_t and thereby the blending time required for impeller-1 is lower and it is to be our final choice. However, if a larger power consumption is permissible so that N_L is fixed at (e), then impeller-2 is to be preferred since it will do the job within a lesser duration of time.

Example 7.2. *A pilot plant vessel using a 400 rpm (optimum speed determined experimentally) six-bladed turbine impeller and four longitudinal baffles (each of width 0.1 D_t) is of such size that 1 kg of a material charged to it is equivalent to 512 kg of same material charged to the production unit. The specifications of the production vessel are, diameter = height = 2m, impeller diameter = 0.3 D_t, baffle width = 0.1 D_t, number of baffles = 4. The process consists of blending of two mis-*

cible liquids and the reaction mass may be assumed to be having the same physical and transport properties as water. The criteria for scale up are either to keep the blending time constant or the power input per unit volume constant. Determine which condition would you recommend and why. For blending of miscible liquids, a dimensionless blending time factor f_t is commonly used which is defined as,

$$f_t = \frac{t_T\,(nD_a^2)^{2/3}\, g^{1/6}\, D_a^{1/2}}{H^{1/2}\, D_t^{3/2}}$$

The above factor varies linearly with impeller Reynolds number Re_m in the laminar zone and becomes essentially constant (independent of Re_m) in the fully developed turbulent zone.

Solution. For the scale up of process equipment, we utilise what is called the "similarity criteria". This can be broadly classified into three such as geometric similarity, kinematic similarity and dynamic similarity. Two process vessels are said to be geometrically similar when their like dimensions bear a constant ratio. Mixers and agitators are possibly the only equipment that obey geometric similarity almost precisely, though not always. If kinematic similarity exists between two systems, then the radii of curvature of the flow lines or flow paths at corresponding points in the two systems occur in a fixed ratio regardless of the path or point selected. At these corresponding points the velocity ratios will also be constant regardless of which particular point is selected. If the ratios of the accelerations (and thereby forces) at corresponding points are also fixed independent of the position of the points selected, then the systems are said to be dynamically similar. Geometric similarity is a prime requisite for dynamic similarity. Often, though geometric similarity may be obtained between laboratory and plant equipment, kinematic and dynamic similarities are hardly achieved and the designer has to depend on judgement based on experience.

For the present case, we assume the pilot plant vessel and the final production unit are geometrically similar. This means,

$$\left(\frac{D_{a1}}{D_{a2}}\right) = \left(\frac{D_{t1}}{D_{t2}}\right) = \left(\frac{H_1}{H_2}\right) \text{ and so on.}$$

or,
$$\frac{D_{t1}}{D_{a1}} = \frac{D_{t2}}{D_{a2}} = S_1 \text{ (shape factor)}$$

Similarly,
$$\frac{H_1}{D_{t1}} = \frac{H_2}{D_{t2}} = S_6$$

Suffixes "1" and "2" refer to pilot plant vessel and final production vessel respectively. We can therefore rewrite the expression for f_t in terms of D_a by substituting for D_t and H as $D_t = S_1 D_a$ and $H = S_6 D_t = S_6 S_1 D_a$:

$$f_t = \frac{t_T (nD_a^2)^{2/3} g^{1/6} D_a^{1/2}}{(S_1 D_a)^{1/2} (S_1 S_6 D_a)^{3/2}}$$

Since S_1 and S_6 are constants,

$$f_t = C_1 t_T n^{2/3} / D_a^{1/6} \qquad \text{...}(i)$$

where $$C_1 = \left(\frac{g^{1/6}}{S_1^2 S_6^{\ 3/2}} \right) = \text{constant}$$

Since it is given that 1 kg of a material charged to the pilot reactor is equivalent to 512 kg of same material charged to the production unit, we can write

$$\frac{(\pi D_{t1}^2/4) H_1}{(\pi D_{t2}^2/4) H_2} = \frac{1}{512}$$

or, $$\frac{(S_1 D_{a1})^2 (S_1 S_6 D_{a1})}{(S_1 D_{a2})^2 (S_1 S_6 D_{a2})} = \frac{D_{a1}^3}{D_{a2}^3} = \frac{1}{512}$$

Therefore, $$\frac{D_{a1}}{D_{a2}} = \left(\frac{1}{512} \right)^{1/3} = \frac{1}{8}$$

or, $$D_{a1} = D_{a2}/8 = 0.6/8 = 0.075 \text{ m}$$

Similarly, $$D_{t1} = D_{t2}/8 = 2/8 = 0.25 \text{ m}$$

$$H_1 = H_2/8 = 2/8 = 0.25 \text{ m}$$

The impeller Reynolds number for the pilot plant vessel can be now estimated as,

$$(\text{Re}_m)_1 = \frac{n_1 D_{a1}^2 \rho_f}{\mu_f} = \frac{\left(\frac{400}{60} \right) (0.075)^2 (1000)}{(0.001)} = 37{,}500$$

The value of Re_m for the production vessel will obviously be larger than this and since $\text{Re}_m > 10{,}000$, impellers in both vessels are operating in fully developed turbulent zone. Since f_t is constant and independent of Re_m in turbulent zone,

$$f_{t1} = f_{t2}$$

or, from equation (*i*), $\dfrac{C_1\, t_{T1}\, n_1^{2/3}}{D_{a1}^{1/6}} = \dfrac{C_1\, t_{T2}\, n_2^{2/3}}{D_{a2}^{1/6}}$

or, $$(t_{T1}/t_{T2}) = \left[\frac{D_{a1}}{D_{a2}}\right]^{1/6}\left[\frac{n_2}{n_1}\right]^{2/3} \qquad ...(ii)$$

Let us now consider the first criterion, that is the blending time is kept constant. Thus, $t_{T1} = t_{T2}$. Then, from equation (*ii*),

$$\left(\frac{n_2}{n_1}\right) = \left[\frac{D_{a2}}{D_{a1}}\right]^{1/4} = (8)^{1/4} = 1.68$$

So, $$n_2 = (1.68)\, n_1 = (1.68)\,(400) = 672 \text{ rpm}$$

The impeller speed in the production vessel is therefore not very large. However, to ascertain the suitability of the criterion, we must determine the power consumption per unit volume. Since the impeller is operating in fully developed turbulent zone,

$$P \text{ (from equation 7.1.15)} = K_T\, n^3\, D_a^5\, \rho_f$$

The power input per unit volume P' therefore becomes,

$$P' = \frac{P}{\frac{\pi}{4} D_t^2\, H} = \frac{K_T\, n^3\, D_a^5\, \rho_f}{(\pi/4)\, S_1^3\, S_6\, D_a^3}$$

$$= C_2\, n^3\, D_a^2 \qquad ...(iii)$$

where $$C_2 = (4K_T\, \rho_f/\pi\, S_1^3\, S_6) = \text{constant}$$

Thus, $$\frac{P_1'}{P_2'} = \left(\frac{n_1}{n_2}\right)^3\left(\frac{D_{a1}}{D_{a2}}\right)^2$$

Since $$(n_2/n_1) = (D_{a2}/D_{a1})^{1/4},$$

$$(P_1'/P_2') = \left(\frac{D_{a1}}{D_{a2}}\right)^{11/4} = (1/8)^{11/4}$$

or, $$P_2' = P_1'\,(8)^{11/4} = (304.44)\, P_1'$$

Thus, the power consumption per unit volume in the production unit will be more than 300 times that for the pilot plant vessel. This could turn out to be uneconomical and therefore the criterion of keeping blending time constant cannot be considered acceptable.

Let us now consider the second criterion. If power input per unit volume is kept constant,

$$P_1' = P_2'$$

$$C_2\, n_1^3\, D_{a1}^2 = C_2\, n_2^3\, D_{a2}^2$$

or, $$\frac{n_1}{n_2} = \left(\frac{D_{a2}}{D_{a1}}\right)^{2/3}$$

Substituting in (*ii*), we get, $$\frac{t_{T1}}{t_{T2}} = \left(\frac{D_{a1}}{D_{a2}}\right)^{11/18} = (1/8)^{11/18}$$

or, $$t_{T2} = t_{T1}\,(8)^{11/18} = (3.56)\, t_{T1}$$

Thus, the blending time required in the production vessel is only 3.56 times that required in the pilot plant vessel, with the same power consumption per unit volume. Therefore, this can be considered as an acceptable criterion.

7.4. Mixing of Pastes and Plastic Masses

When the viscosity of the mix is very large (greater than about 2 kilopoises), then conventional impellers such as turbines, paddles etc. become unsuitable for doing the job. Highly sturdy and rugged mixing devices are required for such viscous materials such as thick pastes and plastic masses. The operation demands high power consumption and due to the high viscosity of the mix, there could be large viscous dissipation of heat on the impeller. Mixing of heavy pastes and plastic masses is being practised more as an art rather than science. Most paste mixers have been designed based mainly on experience. However, once the mixer has been designed, its effectiveness for producing a uniform mix can be estimated using what is called the *tracer technique*, which we shall be discussing subsequently.

Stationary agitated tanks can be employed for paste mixing provided the agitators are specifically designed for the purpose. Because of the flow properties of pastes, high velocity impellers are not generally effective as they tend to bore holes in the mass without producing any circulation. Impact and shear forces must be developed adjacent to the mixer blades, not at a distance. This calls for impellers with intermeshing blades and small clearances to be maintained between the blades and the body. Some pastes cling very tightly to the working surfaces so that a very slow-speed shear, preferably coupled with a smearing or wiping action, will be required. Such slow speed will give the material sufficient time to work its way into the active zone. One of the popular types of impellers used successfully for mixing paints, starch pastes, coatings etc. is the gate impeller that consists of a flat rotating structure of horizontal and vertical bars that cuts the paste at different levels and at the tank wall where stationary bars are often fastened to give points of intensive shear. Slow mass mixing is produced by the mild centrifugal action of the rotating gate. The speed is kept low to avoid rotating of the entire mass of the tank. Anchor agitators, slightly modified to suit to the purpose, can also be used, particularly for handling adhesives, greases, cosmetics and pastes that require quick cooling or heating during mixing. In this case, two sets of intermeshing paddles are mounted on concentric counter-rotating shafts. The relative shearing speed (the sum of the two speeds of rotation) is applied with very little centrifugal action. The outer sweep assembly is often fitted with scraper blades to clean the container wall and improve heat transfer. The *rotating cone mixer* employs a pair of rotating hollow cones with their diverging ends facing each other. The hollow cones are also fitted with narrow vertical internal vanes extending from top to bottom of the cones or even beyond. Centrifugal force holds the material against the inside surface of the cone and the slope of the cone walls produces movement of the mass from the converging end to the diverging end of the cone. Shear is produced along the inner edge of the vanes and at the ends where the material enters or leaves the cones.

A *pug mill* consists of one or two shafts fitted with short, heavy paddles mounted in a cylinder or trough which holds the material being processed. The paddles may or not intermesh. The shafts are parallel and can be vertical or horizontal. Wide clearances are provided to achieve considerable mass mixing. The feed is introduced at one end and the paddles push the material forward as they cut through it, thus carrying the charge towards the discharge end as it is mixed. The product is discharged either through open ports or through extrusion nozzles. Pug mills are often built with jackets for heating or cooling and they find wide application in the ceramic industry for blending and homogenising clay products.

The *change can mixer* uses a removable can or container that forms a separate unit and can be easily placed or removed from the framework of the machine. The can containing the material to be processed is kept on a turntable and the agitator consists of a number of vertical, twisted blades or fingers suspended from a rotating head that can be raised or lowered. The agitator is mounted eccentrically with respect to the axis of the can so that the blades are close to the wall of the can. The turntable is driven in a direction opposite to that of the agitator. Once the mixing is complete, the blades are lifted out of the can and wiped clean and the can containing the mixed paste is removed. In some mixers, the can is dropped away from the mixing elements. Alternately, the can may be held stationary and the agitator is rotated with a planetary motion so that the rotating blades sweep the entire circumference of the can. Change can mixers are widely used for blending light pastes such as in food processing, manufacture of paint and ink.

Kneading involves squashing the material flat, folding it back on itself and then compressing it until the desired uniformity is obtained. Industrial kneading machines employ two specially shaped blades set on parallel, horizontal shafts mounted with close clearances inside a U-shaped trough. The bottom of the trough is usually curved upward to form a ridge between the blades. The mixing blades cover the entire bottom of the mixing chamber and either no top cover is used or the operating level is kept so low that the material does not come into contact with the domed cover. The blades are rotated towards each other at different speeds. Usually, a speed ratio of 1.5 : 1 is employed. As a result, the material is torn apart and sheared between the blades and the wall of the trough. Different forms of kneader blades are available such as the Z-blade (in the shape of the English latter Z), stigma blade (in the shape of the greek letter Σ) and the fishtail blade. All these are shaped so that their rotation draws the material down into the active zone. Relative positioning of the blades and suitable overlapping avoid build up of sticky material on the blades. The produce may be discharged by tilting or through side or bottom doors. Typical applications of kneaders include those in compounding lacquer bases from pigments and carriers and shredding cotton linters into the acetylating bath (containing acetic acid and acetic anhydride) in the manufacture of acetate rayon. A heavier construction called disperser is used to work additives and colouring agents into stiffy materials.

A different type of kneader is the *Banbury mixer* which is also called an intensive mixer or masticator. In this mixer, the top of the charge is confined by a cover that can be forced down on the charge by mechanical or hydraulic means. The clearance between the blades and the chamber walls is very small and it is here where the mixing action takes place and not between the blades. Banbury mixer draws large amount of power even at operating speeds of 40 rpm or lower. As a result, heavy, large diameter agitator shafts are required. This, in combination with stubby blades (usually in the form of interrupted spirals), close clearances and the confined charge, limits the application of Banbury mixer to small batches only. Also, since the friction in the confined space is quite large, with heat-sensitive materials, cooling could be a problem. The most important application of Banbury mixer is in the plastics and rubber industries such as for compounding rubber and plastic solids, devulcanising scrap rubber and masticating crude rubber.

Muller mixers can handle such diversified materials as clays, storage battery paste, welding rod coatings, chocolate coatings etc. They are especially effective for coating surfaces of particles with a small amount of liquid. In foundry industry, they find wide application in mixing small amounts of moisture and binder materials with sand particles for both core and moulding sand. Mulling means a smearing or rubbing action similar to that occurs in a mortar and pestle that is commonly used in households for making sandal paste. In industrial mixers, heavy muller wheels or mixing plows roll over a layer of material contained in a stationary pan. The rubbing or mulling action results from the slip between the wheels and the solids. Alternately, the wheels may be held stationary and the pan rotated or the wheels may be mounted off-center and both the pan and the wheels driven relative to each other. By using a number of pans in series, the operation can also be made continuous.

Mixer-extruders employ a continuous screw or screws that rotate in a closely fitting barrel. The pitch of the screw changes along its length. This helps in deaerating and compacting the material and generating enough pressure to force the material through the extrusion die. The material is subjected to shearing, rubbing and kneading inside the barrel. As the mixing zone is of small cross-section and the movement of the material is essentially one-directional, there is little volume blending. The ingradients should therefore be blended uniformly before feeding to the feed hopper. Mixer-extruders are used for extrusion of a large variety of materials starting from soft food and chemical mixes to large tonnages of hard plastics and resins.

The *double roll mixer* is analogous to the double roll crusher described in chapter-2, except that the rolls are rotated at different speeds. By repeated passes between such mixing rolls, solid additives can be thoroughly dispersed into pasty or stiff plastic materials. The double roll mixer operate batchwise whereas three roll mixers are continuous units. All the rolls are usually of same diameter but operate at different speeds, the receiving roll being the slowest and the discharge roll the fastest. The clearances between individual rolls can be adjusted independently. The roll diameters should be large enough to avoid bowing since the pressure developed between rolls is often very high. The chief application of mixing rolls is for preparing colour pastes for the ink, paint and surface coating industries.

As stated earlier, the effectiveness of a paste mixer in producing a uniformly mixed product can be analysed using the tracer technique. A given amount of a standard tracer material is added to the mix and the mixer is operated for a given duration of time. At the end of the period of batch mixing, the distribution of tracer in the mixed paste is determined by taking a number (say N) of spot samples and finding out the concentration of the tracer in each sample. Let x_i represents the mass fraction of tracer in sample i (i = 1, 2, ...N) and let $\bar{x}$ be the average value of the measured concentrations. If N is very large, then $\bar{x}$ will be equal to the overall fraction of tracer in the mix, y. Obviously, the larger the number of spot samples collected, the more will be the accuracy of the experimental analysis. If the mixed paste is perfectly uniform, then $x_i = \bar{x}$, for all values of i. This indicates a mixer with 100 per cent effectiveness. As a corollary, the extent to which x_i deviates from $\bar{x}$, that is the standard deviation σ_p, will give a measure of the quality of mixing. The standard deviation is defined as,

$$\sigma_p = \left[\frac{\sum_{i=1}^{N} (x_i - \bar{x})^2}{(N-1)} \right]^{1/2} \quad \text{...(7.4.1)}$$

It is to be noted that the value of σ_p is a relative measure of mixing, valid only for a given set of tests with a specific material in a specific mixer. It has been found that a more general measure of mixer effectiveness is given by the ratio of σ_p to standard deviation at zero mixing (σ_o). At $t = 0$, when the mixing operation has not yet begun, there will be two layers in the mixing vessel, one containing the tracer only and the other containing no tracer. Thus, the standard deviation at $t = 0$ will be,

$$\sigma_o = \sqrt{y\,(1-y)} \quad \text{...(7.4.2)}$$

The ratio (σ_p/σ_o) is called the *mixing index* I_p.

Thus

$$I_p = \left(\frac{\sigma_p}{\sigma_o}\right) = \left[\frac{\sum_{i=1}^{N} (x_i - \bar{x})^2}{(N-1)\,y\,(1-y)} \right]^{1/2} \quad \text{...(7.4.3)}$$

Evidently, at $t = 0$, $I_p = 1.0$. If a perfectly uniform product results, then $I_p = 0$ at the end of mixing. However, in actual practice, I_p starts decreasing starting from an initial value of 1.0 as mixing proceeds and approaches an ultimate value $I_{p,f}$ asymptotically as $t \to \infty$. The closer the magnitude of $I_{p,f}$ to zero, the better will be the uniformity of the final mix. It is also important that the value of $I_{p,f}$ is attained within a reasonably low duration of time. The rate at which I_p decreases with time, dI_p/dt, indicates the rate of mixing. It must be remembered that the magnitude and variation of I_p depend both on the type of mixer as well as the type of material handled.

7.5. Solid-Solid Mixing

Mixing of dry powders or granular solids is important in a large number of industrial operations such as in the manufacture of insecticides, fertilisers, packaged foods, cosmetics etc. Powder mixers commonly employ mechanical shuffling or tumbling action to affect random distribution of particles among each other. The *ribbon mixer* utilises two counteracting helical ribbons mounted on the same central shaft inside a horizontal trough. Since the ribbons are counteracting, one moves the solids slowly in one direction whereas the other moves them quickly in the other direction and mixing results from the turbulence induced by these counteracting agitators. The operation may be batchwise or continuous. The trough is closed (and made heavy-walled) when operation under pressure or vacuum is desired, otherwise the trough is kept open. Ribbon blenders are effective mixers for thin pastes and for powders that do not flow readily.

The *tumbling mixers* are exactly similar to the tumbling mills discussed in chapter-2, except that they do not use any grinding media. For example, the tumbling barrels resemble ball mills without balls and they effectively mix free-flowing dry powders. Tumbling mixers may also contain internal sprays for introducing small amounts of liquid into the mix or mechanically driven devices for breaking up agglomerates of solids.

There are several variations of *vertical screw mixers*. In general, an endless screw or helical conveyor is made to rotate about its own axis while also orbiting around the center axis of a conical tank. As a result, the solids get mixed while being transported upwards and discharged at the top. Free flowing grains and other light solids can be conveniently handled in these mixers.

Impact wheels resemble attrition mills and are widely used for blending fine, light powders such as insecticides. The feed mixture is introduced continuously near the center of a disk, either vertical or horizontal, spinning at a very high speed. As a result, the solids are thrown outwards into a stationary casing. The solids experience very large shearing forces as they travel along the disk surface and therefore they get blended thoroughly. To improve efficiency, the product may be repeatedly recycled back to the mixer or a number of units in series may be used. The capacity of impact wheels ranges from 1,000 to 25,000 kg/hour.

Gas fluidised beds are also used as solid-solid mixers. When the gas used is air, they can be roughly grouped under the category of "pneumatic mixers" we discussed at the beginning of this chapter. The principle behind the operation of fluidised beds is discussed in detail in Chapter-8.

In gas fluidised beds, aggregative fluidisation occurs. Here, instead of gentle oscillation of particles, the particles get splashed upwards as the gas "bubbles" through the bed. At high fluid velocity, this bubbling action of the gas becomes more violent and considerable amount of solids get ejected upwards over large distances before returning. It is therefore obvious that if the bed is composed of particles of different materials, they will get intermixed and get randomly distributed among each other during aggregative fluidisation.

Gas fluidised beds are efficient solid-solid mixers. However, often the pressure drop required to fluidise the bed of solids is so large that the operation may turn out to be uneconomical for large-scale use.

As in the case of paste mixing, for blending of dry solids also, the mixer effectiveness can be measured in terms of the mixing index, I_s. However, it must be noted that in the case of solid-solid mixing, even for a completely random, fully blended mixture there will exist a standard deviation (σ_e) between the measured concentrations of the tracer in the spot samples and the average concentration (The tracer concentrations are normally expressed as number fractions, that is the ratio of the number of tracer particles to the total number of particles in the sample). This is because a sample drawn from a random mixture, even if it has been completely and perfectly blended, could always contain a larger (or smaller) proportion of one kind of particle than the population from which it is drawn. It must be remembered that during mixing of dry solids, we are only distributing randomly one kind of particles among another and as a result, the mixed product does never form a continuous phase, it remains as a discrete phase. Thus, the standard deviation for a completely random mixture is given by,

$$\sigma_e = [y\,(1-y)/n_p]^{1/2} \qquad ...(7.5.1)$$

where n_p = number of particles in each spot sample

Now, mixing index I_s for dry powders is defined as the ratio (σ_e/σ_s) given by,

$$I_s = \left[\frac{\dfrac{y\,(1-y)\,(N-1)}{N}}{n_p \sum\limits_{i=1} (x_i - \bar{x})^2}\right]^{1/2} \qquad ...(7.5.2)$$

It is interesting to note that mixing index at zero mixing $I_{s,o}$ (which is 1.0 for pastes) will be,

$$I_{s,o} = \left[\frac{\sigma_e}{\sigma_o}\right] = \frac{1}{\sqrt{n_p}} \qquad \text{...(7.5.3)}$$

The values of I_s increases starting from the initial value of $(1/\sqrt{n_p})$ as mixing proceeds and the rate at which it increases with time (dI_s/dt) gives the rate of mixing. However, experimental observations indicate that the variation of I_s with time is often random and at very long blending time, it even decreases steadily. This is due to the presence of unblending forces (usually electrostatic) whose effects in many dry solid mixers are quite significant. Weidenbaum and Bonilla[4] report that for short mixing times, (dI_s/dt) can be correlated as follows :

$$\frac{dI_s}{dt} = k\,(1 - I_s) \qquad \text{...(7.5.4)}$$

where k is the rate constant whose value for any particular application is to be determined experimentally. Integrating the above equation from $t = 0$ (when $I_s = I_{s,o} = 1/\sqrt{n_p}$) to $t = t$, we get,

$$t = \frac{1}{k} \ln\left[\frac{1 - (1/\sqrt{n_p})}{1 - I_s}\right] \qquad \text{...(7.5.5)}$$

From the above equation, the time required to achieve any desired degree of mixing can be computed, provided the value of k is known and unblending forces are absent.

7.6. Liquid-Liquid and Gas-Liquid Dispersions by Mechanical Agitators

Mechanical impellers such as turbines, paddles and propellers have been successfully employed for inter-dispersion of immiscible liquids as well as for the dispersion of gases in liquids. However, published data on liquid-liquid mixing by mechanical agitators is very limited. One of the interesting studies is that of Laity and Treybal[5]. They report that for dispersion of immiscible liquids in baffled tanks, the same correlations as those developed for agitation of single liquids, represented graphically in Fig. (7.5), can be used provided the density ρ_f and viscosity μ_f of the medium are replaced by ρ_b and μ_b which are defined as follows :

$$\rho_b = \rho_c\,\varepsilon_c + \rho_d\,\varepsilon_d \qquad \text{...(7.6.1)}$$

$$\mu_b = \frac{\mu_c}{\varepsilon_c}\left[1 + \frac{1.5\,\mu_d\,\varepsilon_d}{\mu_d + \mu_c}\right] \qquad \text{...(7.6.2)}$$

where ρ_c, ρ_d = densities of liquids forming continuous phase and dispersed phase respectively

μ_c, μ_d = viscosities of liquids forming continuous and dispersed phases respectively

ε_c, ε_d = volume fraction of continuous phase and dispersed phase respectively

Though Laity and Treybal have reported data based on experiments using six-bladed flat-blade turbine impeller with $(D_t/D_a) = 3.0$ and D_t in the range of 0.3 to 0.45 m, the procedure suggested by them has been found to satisfy a good number of industrial systems.

If the vessel is unbaffled, the same authors report that Fig. (7.5) can still be used for batch agitation of immiscible liquids (mainly water and oil) provided ρ_f is replaced by ρ_b and μ_f by μ_b' which is defined as given below :

$$\mu_b' = \frac{\mu_w}{\varepsilon_w}\left[1 + \frac{6\,\varepsilon_o\,\mu_o}{\mu_o + \mu_w}\right] \quad \text{for } \varepsilon_w > 0.40$$

$$= \frac{\mu_o}{\varepsilon_o}\left[1 - \frac{1.5\,\varepsilon_w\,\mu_w}{\mu_o + \mu_w}\right] \quad \text{for } \varepsilon_w < 0.40 \qquad \text{...(7.6.3)}$$

where the suffixes "*w*" and "*o*" stand for water and oil respectively.

The question of which liquid shall form the continuous phase and which the dispersed phase could depend not only on the properties of the liquids but also on the impeller speed. It is difficult to disperse a liquid in a continuum of another if the dispersed phase occupies more than 75 per cent of the total volume. In batch operation of baffled vessels, the phase in which the impeller is immersed when at rest will normally be the continuous phase. For equal volumes of liquids and with the impeller at the interface when at rest, Laity and Treybal found water continuous when agitated with a motor oil but dispersed when agitated with kerosene. Under the same conditions, Rodger et. al.[6], report that water forms the continuous phase while organic liquids dispersed at low impeller speeds, but the reverse occurs when the impeller speed is high and particularly when the magnitude of $(\rho_d - \rho_c)/\rho_c$ is large. With water constituting the dispersed phase, dual emulsion (continuous phase found in small droplets within large droplets of dispersed phase) are frequently formed. If the dispersion operation is to be continuous, first the vessel is filled with the liquid to be the continuous phase, agitation started and then the liquid to be dispersed is introduced.

For the dispersion of gases in liquids, probably the most fundamental study is that of Calderbank et. al[7,8]. They have proposed the following correlations based on experiments using six-bladed flat-blade turbine impeller in tanks of 0.15 to 0.5 m in diameter at low superficial gas velocities upto 1 m/min (gas hold-up, $H_g < 0.15$) :

$$a_i = 1.44\,(P'/V)^{0.4}\,\rho_L^{0.2}\,(\sigma_i)^{-0.6}\,(V_g/V_t)^{0.5} \qquad ...(7.6.4)$$

$$H_g = [V_g H_g/V_t]^{0.5} + 0.015\,a_i \qquad ...(7.6.5)$$

where a_i = specific interfacial area between gas and liquid, cm^2/cm^3

P' = agitator shaft power during dispersion, ergs/s (1 erg = 10^{-7} joule)

V = total volume of agitated mass, cm^3

V_g = superficial gas velocity, cm/s

V_t = terminal velocity of rise of the gas bubble, cm/s

ρ_L = liquid density, gm/cm^3

σ_i = interfacial tension, dynes/cm (1 N/m = 10^3 dynes/cm)

H_g = fractional gas hold-up (volume fraction of gas in suspension).

It is important to note that the above two correlations are dimensional and while applying them the dimensions mentioned above must be followed. The value of V_t generally will not be known, but for all but the finest bubbles, a mean value of 26 cm/s can be used with allowable error. Correlations (7.6.4) and (7.6.5) are applicable for N_R < 20,000, where N_R is defined as,

$$N_R = Re_m^{0.7}\,[nD_a/V_g]^{0.3} \qquad ...(7.6.6)$$

Re_m being the impeller Reynolds number, $(nD_a^2\,\rho_L/\mu_L)$.

For $N_R > 20{,}000$,

$$H_g = \frac{a_i'}{a_i}\left[\frac{V_g H_g}{V_t}\right]^{1/2} + 0.015\,a_i' \qquad ...(7.6.7)$$

where the new interfacial area per unit volume a_i' can be obtained from

$$\log\left[\frac{2.3\,a_i'}{a_i}\right] = 1.95 \times 10^{-5}\,N_R \qquad ...(7.6.8)$$

Attempts have also been made to correlate P' with P, where P is the power consumption for agitating the ungassed liquid that can be determined from Fig. (7.5) as discussed in section (7.1). The ratio

(P'/P) has been found to be a function of the flow number N_Q given by,

$$N_Q = Q/nD_a^3 \qquad \text{...(7.6.9)}$$

where Q is the volumetric flow rate of the gas. One of the most interesting findings in this connection is that of Michel and Miller[9] who report that a log-log plot of P' *versus* $[P^2 nD_a^3/Q^{0.56}]$ yields a straight line (incidentally P and P' are in hp, D_a in feet, Q in ft³/min and n is the rpm of the impeller). This calls for a correlation of the form,

$$P' = 0.1\,[P^2\, nD_a^3/Q^{0.56}]^{0.45} \qquad \text{...(7.6.10)}$$

or, in terms of the flow number N_Q,

$$P' = 0.1\left[\frac{P^2\,(nD_a^3)^{0.44}}{N_Q^{0.56}}\right]^{0.45} \qquad \text{...(7.6.11)}$$

The fact that the above equation is a dimensional one should not be overlooked. Also, the correlation is not valid for $N_Q > 0.03$, since at $N_Q > 0.03$, the impeller tends to get flooded by the gas and then (P'/P) will become independent of the gas flow rate, Q.

Treybal[10] has given a simplified correlation based on Calderbank's data as given below :

$$(P'/P) = 1.0 - 12.2\,N_Q \qquad \text{...(7.6.12)}$$

$$\text{for } N_Q < 0.037$$

$$= 0.62 - 1.85\,N_Q \qquad \text{...(7.6.13)}$$

$$\text{for } N_Q > 0.037$$

The above equations are based on experimental data on water and aqueous solutions of non-electrolytes, using disk flat blade turbine impellers with $(D_a/D_t) = 0.25$ to 0.33.

The overall observation is that correlations that have been proposed in the literature for the estimation of P' lack consistency and many of them suffer from serious inadequacies. Recently, Luong and Volesky[11] have reported graphical data (a plot of (P'/P) *versus* N_Q) based on their experiments with water and aqueous solutions of alcohols. It has been reported that their data give fairly conservative estimates of P' for systems with $(P'/V) > 0.5$ kW/m³. However, for lower power inputs and for noncoalescing systems with small bubbles and large gas holdup, the data predict conspicuously higher values of P'.

7.7. Computer Aided Analysis

Most of the computations associated with the analysis of agitation of liquids are straight forward. Readers shall not find any difficulty in preparing sample computer programs if necessary, on problems dealing with this operation. Elaborate number of computer programs are, therefore, not presented in this chapter. As examples, the computer programs for the estimation of power consumption for suspending solid particles in a liquid (solid-liquid mixing) are given below (Programs 7.1 and 7.2).

PROGRAM 7.1

```
C**     TO COMPUTE THE POWER CONSUMPTION FOR
C**     LIFTING SOLID PARTICLES TO HEIGHT ZS
C**     FROM VESSEL FLOOR.
        REAL MEUF, MS, ML
        READ (*, *) SX, ROWS, ROWF, MEUF, DT, HL, DA, E
        READ (*, *) RPM
C**     DP IS THE DIAMETER OF THE LARGEST
C**     PARTICLE IN THE MIXTURE.
        READ (*, *) DP, ZS
C**     CHECK THE APPLICABILITY OF EQUATION (7.2.1)
        REM = (RPM/60.0) * DA * DA * ROWF/MEUF
        IF (REM. LT. 10000.0) GO TO 10
        IF (DA/DT. GT. 0.5) GO TO 10
        IF [(ZS - E). LT. 0.5 * DT] GO TO 10
        G = 9.80
        VT = (ROWS - ROWF) * G * DP * DP /(18.0 * MEUF)
        PI = 3.14
        VM = PI * DT * DT * ZS/4.0
        ROWB = 1.0/[(SX/ROWS) + (1.0 - SX)/ROWF]
        MS = (PI * DT * DT/4.0) * HL * ROWB * SX
        ML = (VM - MS/ROWS) * ROWF
        ROWM = (MS + ML)/VM
        ABSN = (ML/ROWF)/VM
        C1 = 0.25
        IF (E/DA. GT. 0.5) C1 = 0.23
        IF (E/DA. EQ. 0.2) C1 = 0.27
        ZZ = [(ZS - E)/DT - 0.1]/C1
```

```
      P = G * ROWM * VM * VT * (1.0 - ABSN) * * 0.6666
      P = P * [(DT/DA) * * 0.5] * EXP (ZZ)
      WRITE (*, *) P
      GO TO 20
10    WRITE (*, 15)
15    FORMAT (2X, 'NOT APPLICABLE')
20    STOP
      END
```

PROGRAM 7.2

```
C**   TO COMPUTE POWER CONSUMPTION FOR JUST
C**   DETACHING SOLID PARTICLES FROM VESSEL FLOOR.
      REAL KT(5)
      REAL MEUF, KTC
      DIMENSION PSI(5)
      READ (*, *) SX, ROWS, ROWF, MEUF, DT, HT, HL, DA
      READ (*, *) E, RPM
C**   DP IS THE VOLUMETRIC DIAMETER OF THE
C**   LARGEST PARTICLE IN THE MIXTURE.
      READ (*, *) DP, PSIS
C**   CHECK THE APPLICABILITY OF EQUATION (7.2.2)
      REM = (RPM/60.0) * DA * DA * ROWF/MEUF
      IF (REM. LT. 10000.0) GO TO 20
      IF (DA/DT. LT. 0.36) GO TO 20
      IF (DA/DT. GT. 0.43) GO TO 20
      PI = 3.14
      VTV = (PI * DT * DT/4.0) * HT
      VM = (PI * DT * DT/4.0) * HL
      ROWB = 1.0/[(SX/ROWS) + (1.0 - SX)/ROWF]
      ABSN = ROWB * (1.0 - SX)/ROWF
C**   COMPUTE THE TERMINAL FREE SETTLING
C**   VELOCITY OF THE LARGEST PARTICLE (OF
C**   DIAMETER DP) IN THE FULLY DEVELOPED
C**   TURBULENT ZONE AS SHOWN IN
C**   PROGRAM (3.1)
      READ (*, *) (PSI(J), KT(J), J = 1, 5)
      DO 10 J = 1, 5
```

```
      IF [PSIS. LE. PSI(J)] GO TO 15
10    CONTINUE
15    KTC = KT (J - 1) + [KT (J) - KT (J - 1)] * [PSIS -
      PSI (J - 1)]/[PSI(J) - PSI (J - 1)]
      FD = KTC
      G = 9.8
      VT = [(4.0/3.0) * (ROWS - ROWF) * G * DP/(ROWF *
      FD)] * * 0.5
      RH1 = (DT/DA) * SQRT [(1.0 - ABSN)/ABSN]
      RH2 = EXP (5.3 * E/DT)
      P = (0.16 * G * (ROWS - ROWF) * VTV * VT/1.74) *
      RH1 * RH2
      WRITE (*, *) P
      GO TO 30
20    WRITE (*, 25)
25    FORMAT (2X, 'NOT APPLICABLE')
30    STOP
      END
```

NOMENCLATURE

a, b impeller constants (see Table 7.1), dimensionless.

a_i specific interfacial area, m^{-1} or cm^{-1}.

a_i' modified interfacial area per unit volume (see equation 7.6.8), m^{-1} or cm^{-1}.

d_p particle size, m.

D_a impeller diameter, m.

D_t diameter of mixing tank, m.

E elevation of impeller above vessel floor, m.

f_t blending time factor, dimensionless.

Fr_m mixing Froude number, dimensionless.

g gravitational acceleration, m/s^2.

H height of liquid in the tank, m.

H_g fractional gas hold-up (volume fraction of gas in the dispersion), dimensionless.

I_p mixing index for pastes, dimensionless.

I_s mixing index for dry powders, dimensionless.

I_{so} value of I_s at zero time ($t = 0$), dimensionless.

J baffle width, m.

K_L, K_T laminar and turbulent constants respectively (see equations 7.1.11 and 7.1.14), dimensionless.

L, W dimensions of impeller blade (see Fig. 7.4), m.

m exponent defined in equation (7.1.9), dimensionless.

n speed of impeller, rps.

n_p number of particles in each spot sample (in tracer analysis).

N total number of spot samples taken in the tracer experiment.

N_L modified power number, dimensionless.

N_Q flow number, dimensionless.

N_R dimensionless group defined equation (7.6.6).

N_t mixing number, dimensionless.

P power consumption in agitation, W.

Po power number, dimensionless.

P' power input per unit volume, W/m^3, power consumption during gas-liquid dispersion, W or erg/s.

Q volumetric flow rate of gas, m^3/s.

Re_m mixing Reynolds number (or impeller Reynolds number), dimensionless.

S_1 to S_6 shape factors (see equation 7.1.1a), dimensionless.

t_T blending (or, mixing) time, s.

V_g superficial gas velocity, m/s or cm/s.

V_m volume of slurry, m^3.

V_T volume of tank, m^3.

V_t terminal free settling velocity of particle, terminal velocity of rise of gas bubble, m/s.

W, L dimensions of impeller blade (see Fig. 7.4), m.

x_i mass fraction of tracer in the ith spot sample.

$\bar{x}$ average value of all measured tracer concentrations in spot samples.

X cumulative mass fraction.

y overall fraction of tracer in the mix.

Z_s height to which particles are to be lifted in solid-liquid mixing, m.

Greek Letters

ε volume fraction of liquid in a solid-liquid suspension.

ε_c, ε_d volume fraction of continuous phase and dispersed phase respectively in a liquid-liquid dispersion.

μ_f fluid viscosity, kg/(ms).

μ_c, μ_d viscosity of continuous phase and that of dispersed phase respectively, kg/(ms).

ρ_c, ρ_d density of continuous phase and that of dispersed phase respectively, kg/m^3.

ρ_f, ρ_s density of fluid and that of solid particles respectively, kg/m^3.

ρ_m density of suspension, kg/m^3.

σ_i interfacial tension, N/m.

σ_p, σ_s standard deviation for paste mixing and powder mixing respectively.

σ_0 standard deviation at zero mixing (at $t = 0$).

σ_e standard deviation for a completely random mixture of particles.

ϕ power function, dimensionless.

Computer Notations

ABSN volume fraction of liquid in slurry (ε)

C1 empirical constant (C_1) of equation (7.2.1)

DA impeller diameter (D_a), m

DP diameter of largest particle in the mixture, m

DT tank diameter (D_t), m

E elevation of impeller above vessel floor (E), m

FD drag coefficient (f_D), dimensionless

HL height of liquid in the tank (H), m

HT height of tank, m

KT(J) values of turbulent constant (K_t), see table (3.1) of Chapter-3.

KTC calculated value of KT.

MEUF fluid viscosity (μ_f), kg/(m.s)

ML mass of liquid in slurry, kg

MS mass of solids in slurry, kg

P	power consumption, W
PSI(J)	values of particle sphericity (ψ_s), see table (3.1) of Chapter-3
PSIS	sphericity of particles in slurry, dimensionless
REM	mixing Reynolds number (Re_m), dimensionless
ROWB	bulk density of slurry, kg/m^3
ROWF	fluid density (ρ_f), kg/m^3
ROWM	density of slurry with in height Z_s (ρ_m), kg/m^3
ROWS	solid density (ρ_s), kg/m^3
SX	mass fraction of solids in slurry
VM	volume of slurry (V_m), m^3
VT	terminal free settling velocity of largest particle (V_t), m/s
VTV	volume of tank (V_T), m^3
ZS	height to which solid particles are to be lifted in solid-liquid mixing (Z_s), m

REFERENCES

1. Rushton, J.H., Costich, E.W. and Evereet, H.J., Chem. Eng. Prog., **46**, 470, 1950.
2. Perry, J.H. (ed.), Chemical Engineers' Handbook, 5th ed., McGraw- Hill, New York, 1973.
3. Weisman, J. and Efferding, L.E., AIChE J., **6**, 419, 1960.
4. Weidenbaum, S.S. and Bonilla, C.F., Chem. Eng. Prog., **51**, 27-J, 1955.
5. Laity, R. and Treybal, R.E., AIChE J., **3**, 176, 1957.
6. Rodger, Trice and Rushton. J.H., Chem. Eng. Prog., **52**, 515, 1956.
7. Calderbank, P.H., Trans. Inst. Chem. Eng., **36**, 443, 1958; Calderbank, P.H. and Moo-Young, M.B., **37**, 26, 1959.
8. Uhl, V.W. and Gray, J.B., Mixing-Theory and Practice, Vol. 2, Academic Press, New York, 1967.
9. Michel, B.J. and Miller, S.A., AIChE J., **8**, 262, 1962.
10. Treybal, R.E., Mass Transfer Operations, third ed., McGraw Hill, New York, 1981.
11. Luong and Volesky, AIChE J., **25**, 893, 1979.

8

Fluidisation

8.1 Flow through Packed Beds and Porous Media

The use of packed beds and porous media is frequently encountered in process industries. Packed beds are extensively used for gas-liquid absorption, for continuous distillation/fractionation of liquid mixtures, for liquid-liquid extraction and as catalytic/noncatalytic reactors. Packed bed adsorbers find large scale applications in water softening, waste water treatment, ion exchange and chromatographic separations.

We have already discussed in Chapter - 5 that for the filtration of slurries and suspensions, they are fed to a porous medium (which is called the filter medium) through which the liquid permeates and collected as the filtrate, while the solids are retained on the filter medium. The solid particles accumulate on the medium forming a packed bed of solids. Industrial filtration thus involves flow of liquid (filtrate) through the packed bed of solids (namely, the filter cake) and then through the porous medium (filter medium). Shallow beds of fine, granular particles such as crushed coke, sand etc. are directly employed as filters (for example, the sand filter is widely used for filtering corrosive sludges). Packed beds are also used as heat transfer and heat storage equipment. Examples are pebble bed heaters, cooling towers. Fluid dynamics in packed beds and porous media is thus of considerable interest to process engineers.

One of the simplest and earliest theories on fluid flow through packed beds is the *capillary bundle theory**. This theory assumes that the void space (interstitial space between particles) of a packed bed is equivalent to a bundle of tangled capillary tubes. If this is true and if the flow is laminar (at low Reynolds number), then the Hagen-Poiseuille equation derived for laminar flow through straight cylindri-

* This theory has already been outlined in Section (5.1) of Chapter - 5.

cal conduits may be used to describe the flow of a Newtonian fluid through a packed bed of solid particles as well. Thus

$$(-\Delta P) = 32\, L\, v\, \mu_f / D_e^2 \quad \text{...(8.1.1)}$$

It may be noted that we have replaced the pipe diameter D by the equivalent diameter D_e of the system. The fluid takes a tortuous path through the bed and the equivalent diameter of this flow path is D_e. In the above equation,

$(-\Delta P)$ = pressure drop across the packed bed

L = height (or length) of the bed

v = average velocity of fluid through the bed#

We know, by definition,

$$D_e = (4\, r_H)$$

$$= \frac{(4.0)\,(\text{Flow area or cross sectional area available for flow})}{(\text{Wetted perimeter})}$$

$$= \frac{(4.0)\,(\text{Volume available for flow})}{(\text{Wetted surface})} \quad \text{...(8.1.2)}$$

If we assume that all the voids of the packed bed are completely filled with the fluid and all the solid particles of the bed are uniformly wet by the fluid (in other words, *channeling* is assumed absent), then

$$D_e = \frac{(4.0)\,(\text{Void volume})}{(\text{Total surface area of solids})} \quad \text{...(8.1.3)}$$

If ε is the void fraction (also called *porosity*) of the packed bed, then

$$\text{Void volume} = \varepsilon\,(A_c L) \quad \text{...(8.1.4)}$$

$$\text{Total volume of solid particles} = (1-\varepsilon)\, A_c\, L \quad \text{...(8.1.5)}$$

where A_c is the cross sectional area of the packed bed/packed column. If all particles are of the same size and if s_p be the specific surface (surface area per unit volume) of each particle, then the specific surface of all solid particles constituting the bed will also be equal to s_p. In such a case,

$$D_e = \frac{4\varepsilon\, A_c L}{(1-\varepsilon)\, A_c L\, s_p}$$

$$= \frac{4\varepsilon}{s_p\,(1-\varepsilon)} \quad \text{...(8.1.6)}$$

Since $s_p = 6/D_{vs}$

In Chapter - 5, this velocity is denoted as U' and the superficial velocity (v_0) as U_{sup}.

where D_{vs} is volume-surface diameter (or Sauter diameter) of the particles,

$$D_e = \frac{2\varepsilon D_{vs}}{3(1-\varepsilon)} \quad \text{...(8.1.7)}$$

To note that the volume-surface diameter of the particles is related to the volumetric diameter D_v of the particles by the relation,

$$D_{vs} = \psi_s D_v \quad \text{...(8.1.8)}$$

where ψ_s is the sphericity of the particles. If we substitute equation (8.1.7) in equation (8.1.1), we get

$$v = \frac{(-\Delta P) D_{vs}^2 \varepsilon^2}{2(36) L \mu_f (1-\varepsilon)^2} \quad \text{...(8.1.9)}$$

Instead of the actual velocity of the fluid through the bed (which is difficult to record), the superficial fluid velocity v_o (which is equal to the volume flow rate of fluid divided by the empty cross sectional area A_c of the packed column) is of popular interest. These two are inter-related by $v_o = \varepsilon v$. Therefore,

$$v_o = \frac{(-\Delta P) D_{vs}^2 \varepsilon^3}{2(36) L \mu_f (1-\varepsilon)^2} \quad \text{...(8.1.10)}$$

The above developed relationship suffers from two serious limitations. First of all, the concept of hydraulic radius (and equivalent diameter) is precisely valid only for turbulent flow and its use in laminar flow could induce serious error. Secondly, the length of fluid path through the bed has been assumed equal to L, which is far from accurate. Since the fluid traverses a tortuous path through the bed, the actual length of fluid path will be much larger than L. Experimental studies of Kozeny[1] and Carman[2] showed that the above two discrepancies could be reasonably corrected by replacing the constant 2 in the denominator of the above equation by a constant K, the average value of which has been found to be (25/6). The experimental data of Blake[3] also substantiate this. Accordingly, equation (8.1.10) gets modified to

$$v_o = \frac{(-\Delta P) D_{vs}^2 \varepsilon^3}{150 L \mu_f (1-\varepsilon)^2} \quad \text{...(8.1.11)}$$

The above relation is called the *Blake-Kozeny* equation or *Carman-Kozeny* equation.* This equation is in consonance with *Darcy's*

\# Readers can easily notice that this equation (8.1.11) is nothing but equation (5.1.5) of Chapter - 5, except that this equation is written in terms of D_{vs} (and not specific surface) and we have substituted the numerical value of K.

law since it predicts that the average velocity (and thereby the volume flow rate) is directly proportional to the pressure drop.

If we define a friction factor (f_b) for the packed bed analogously to Fanning friction factor for pipe flow then

$$(-\Delta P)/\rho_f = 2\, f_b\, L\, v_o^2 / D_{vs} \quad \text{...(8.1.12)}$$

Substituting for $(-\Delta P)$ from equation (8.1.11), we get

$$f_b = \frac{(1-\varepsilon)}{\varepsilon^3} \frac{75}{Re_b} \quad \text{...(8.1.13)}$$

or

$$f_b' = 2 f_b\, [\varepsilon^3/(1-\varepsilon)] = 150/Re_b \quad \text{...(8.1.14)}$$

where Re_b = bed Reynolds number

$$= \frac{D_{vs}\, v_o\, \rho_f}{\mu_f (1-\varepsilon)} \quad \text{...(8.1.15)}$$

f_b' = modified bed friction factor

Thus, the bed friction factor (f_b') is inversely proportional to bed Reynolds number (Re_b) in the laminar zone (compare with $f = 16/Re$, for pipe flow). This result is illustrated in figure (8.1).

It can be seen that flow through the bed is laminar when $Re_b < 10$. Thus, Blake-Kozeny equation is valid only for $Re_b < 10$ and it predicts good results for void fractions less than 0.5.

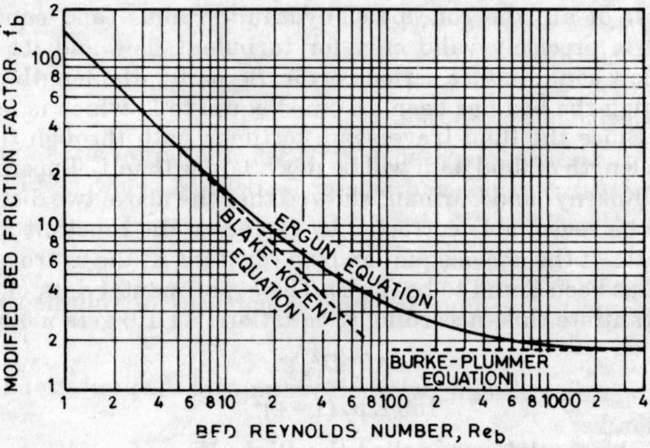

Fig. 8.1

Burke and Plummer[4] showed that at high Reynolds numbers ($Re_b > 1000$), the bed friction factor (f_b') is essentially constant and is independent of Reynolds number. Thus, at $Re_b > 1000$,

$$f_b' = 1.75 \quad \text{...(8.1.16)}$$

The above relationship is called the *Burke-Plummer equation*. This is valid when the flow through the bed is fully turbulent.

If Blake-Kozeny equation for laminar flow and Burke-Plummer equation for turbulent flow are added together, we get

$$f_b' = (150/Re_b) + 1.75 \qquad ..(8.1.17)$$

This is called *Ergun's equation*[5]. Substituting for f_b' from equations (8.1.14) and (8.1.12), we get

$$\left[\frac{(-\Delta P)\,\rho_f}{G_o^2}\right](D_{vs}/L)\left[\frac{\varepsilon^3}{1-\varepsilon}\right] = (150/Re_b) + 1.75 \qquad ...(8.1.18)$$

where $G_o = (v_o\,\rho_f)$. It can be easily seen that at low Reynolds numbers, the first term on the right hand side of above equation shall be too large and the second term will be relatively negligible and can be dropped. Accordingly, the above equation reduces to Blake-Kozeny equation (eq. 8.1.14). Similarly, at high Reynolds numbers, the first term on the right hand side becomes negligibly small and equation (8.1.18) reduces to Burke-Plummer equation. The general behaviour of these equations is sketched in figure (8.1).

All the above equations have been developed for the flow of Newtonian, incompressible liquids through the packed bed. However, if the pressure drop across the bed is not large, then these equations may be applied to flow of compressible fluids like gases as well. In such cases, ρ_f in equation (8.1.18) will be the density of gas at the arithmetic average of end pressures. At high pressure drops, equation (8.1.18) will have to be written in the differential form and then integrated between the end pressures.

If the bed is composed of particles of different sizes, then a mean value of volume surface diameter as defined below, is to be used in equation (8.1.18) :

$$D_{vs}\,(\text{mean}) = 1/\Sigma\, x_i/d_i \qquad ...(8.1.19)$$

where x_i is the volume fraction of particles of volume-surface diameter d_i.

Before concluding, we shall summarise the limitations of Ergun's equation here :

1. This equation is applicable to steady flow of Newtonian fluids only.

2. It has been assumed that channeling is absent. This is fairly true when the particles are of the same size and the bed porosity (ε) is uniform throughout the bed. In nonuniform beds, the fluid tends to bypass the tightly packed portions of the bed and preferentially

traverse through the loosely packed areas. As a result, some particles are completely wetted by the fluid, while others only partly. For such cases, the pressure drop predicted by Ergun's equation shall be inaccurate.

3. The particle size has been assumed to be less than at least one-eighth of the column diameter. This is once again to ensure that channeling is absent since in a random packed tower, the packing density (number of particles per unit volume) shall ordinarily be less in the immediate vicinity of the tower wall and as a result, the liquid will have a tendency to segregate towards the wall. This effect is much less pronounced when the particle size is much smaller than the tower diameter (preferably, less than one-fifteenth of tower diameter).

4. Over and above, Ergun's equation is based on the capillary bundle theory which has the inherent limitation that it does not effectively take into account the form drag. In a packed bed, the fluid flows not only through the voids, but also over the particles and we know that in flow over submerged objects, the frictional resistance is governed by the form drag. Alternate flow models, such as those proposed by Brinkman[6] and Ranz[7], assume that the packed tower is equivalent to a collection of submerged objects and the pressure drop is predicted by summing up the resistances of the submerged particles. Flow models which visualise the void space as an agglomeration of periodically constricted tubes are also available[8]

In commercial packed towers, the type of packing used could be granular solids, rings (Raschig rings, Pall rings), saddles (berl saddles, intalox saddles) etc.

Example 8.1 *A cylindrical tower 0.6m in diameter packed to a height of 3.0 m with activated alumina was used to refine naphtha flowing downward under the following operating conditions :*

$$\text{Temperature} = 27°\text{C}$$

$$\text{Density of naphtha} = 790 \text{ kg/m}^3$$

$$\text{Viscosity of naphtha} = 0.916 \text{ centipoise}$$

$$\text{Porosity of bed} = 0.40$$

$$\text{Flow rate of naphtha} = 7.0 \text{ m}^3/\text{hr}$$

$$\text{Pressure difference} = 2.38 \text{ atm}$$

(a) *It is desired to convert the tower into an air dryer, removing excess moisture from 28 m³ of air per hour (measured at 15°C and 1 atm) flowing upward. If the drier operates isothermally at 38°C and the air must leave the tower at 2.7 atm, what must be the inlet pressure ? Viscosity of air at 38°C = 0.000019 kg/(ms).*

(*b*) *If a 3m bed of 38 mm carbon raschig rings (specific packing surface = 125 m^2/m^3, bed porosity = 0.67) is used instead of alumina, what pressure difference is to be maintained across the bed to obtain the same flow rate of naphtha at 27°C ?*

Solution. Let us first compute the average diameter of the alumina particles. Since the flow zone is not known in advance, let us apply Ergun's equation (equation 8.1.18). Given that

$$(-\Delta P) = 2.38 \text{ atm}$$

$$= (2380 \times 101.3) \text{ N/m}^2$$

$$\rho_f = 790 \text{ kg/m}^3$$

$$L = 3.0 \text{ m}$$

Mass flow rate of naphtha

$$= (7.0)(790) = 5530 \text{ kg/hr}$$

$$G_o = \frac{(5530/3600)}{(\pi/4)(0.6)^2} = 5.433 \text{ kg/(m}^2 \text{. s)}$$

$$\varepsilon = 0.40$$

$$Re_b = \frac{D_{vs}(5.433)}{(0.000916)(1.0 - 0.4)} = 9885.156\, D_{vs}$$

Substituting these values in equation (8.1.18) and multiplying throughout by D_{vs}, we get

$$(229493.3734)\, D_{vs}^2 - 1.75\, D_{vs} - 0.015174 = 0$$

or $$D_{vs} = 0.261 \text{ mm}$$

(*a*) It is given that flow rate of air (measured at 15°C and 1 atm) is 28 m^3/hr. Assuming ideal gas behaviour, density of air at 15°C and 1 atm may be computed as

$$= PM/RT$$

$$= \frac{(1.0)(29.0)}{(0.082)(288)} = 1.227 \text{ kg/m}^3$$

Mass flow rate of air $= (28.0)(1.227)$

$$= 34.3583 \text{ kg/hr}$$

$$G_o = (34.3583/3600)/[\pi (0.6)^2/4]$$

$$= 0.03375 \text{ kg/(m}^2 \text{. s)}$$

$$Re_b = \frac{(0.000261)(0.03375)}{(0.000019)(1 - 0.4)} = 0.7727$$

Substituting in equation (8.1.18), we get

$$(-\Delta P)\,\rho_f = 24042.462\ (\text{N/m}^2)\ (\text{kg/m}^3)$$

Let P_1 atm be the inlet pressure of air. Then,

$$\rho_f = \frac{[(P_1 + 2.7)/2]\,(29.0)}{(0.082)\,(311)}$$

$$= 0.568\,(P_1 + 2.7)$$

$$(-\Delta P) = (P_1 - 2.7)\ \text{atm}$$

$$= (P_1 - 2.7)\,(101.3)\,(1000)\ \text{N/m}^2$$

Therefore, $(101300)\,(0.568)\,(P_1 + 2.7)\,(P_1 - 2.7) = 24042.462$

or $$P_1 = 2.7763\ \text{atm.}$$

Since $(-\Delta P)$ is quite small, the use of ρ_f at the arithmetic average of end pressures is justified. We have however neglected the change in the properties of air (mainly, change in its density) as a result of moisture removal.

(*b*) For carbon raschig rings, it is given that the specific packing surface (a_p) is 125 m²/m³. Specific packing surface is defined as,

$$a_p = \frac{(\text{Total surface area of rings})}{(\text{Volume of bed})}$$

Therefore, specific surface of rings

$$= \frac{a_p\,(\text{Volume of bed})}{(\text{Volume of rings})} = a_p/(1 - \varepsilon)$$

Thus, $$6/D_{vs} = a_p/(1 - \varepsilon)$$

or $$D_{vs} = 6\,(1 - \varepsilon)/a_p$$

$$= 6\,(1 - 0.67)/(125.0) = 0.01584\ \text{m}$$

$$Re_b = \frac{(0.01584)\,(5.433)}{(0.000916)\,(1 - 0.67)} = 284.7$$

$$L = 3.0\ \text{m}$$

$$\varepsilon = 0.67$$

Substituting these values in equation (8.1.18), we get

$$(-\Delta P) = 17.6785\ \text{N/m}^2$$

The pressure difference required is thus much smaller than that for the alumina bed. This is due to the fact that granular solids like activated alumina pack to form beds of fairly low porosity (around 0.4), while rings and saddles (raschig rings, berl saddles etc.) form beds of relatively high voidage (0.6 to 0.8).

8.2. Fluidisation

Fluidisation is a phenomenon that has been investigated for the last three decades or more. However, needless to comment, the theoretical information regarding the actual mechanism of fluidisation phenomenon and the behaviour of fluidised bed systems is still painfully incomplete.

What is a fluidised bed ? Consider a fluid (liquid or gas) flowing up through a packed bed of solids. The solid particles remain stationary and the fluid flows through the tortuous passages between the particles and also over the particles. As the fluid velocity is increased, the pressure drop across the bed also increases (as is evident from equation (8.1.18). Conversely, a larger pressure difference is essential to maintain a larger fluid flow rate through the bed. Now, if the fluid velocity is progressively increased, then at a particular stage, the pressure drop across the bed will just balance the weight of the bed per unit cross-sectional area of the packed column. At this point, the solids start moving. The particles remain suspended in the fluid and start oscillaitng (but are not carried out with the fluid). The bed is then said to be *fluidised.* The fluid velocity at which this motion of particles just starts is called the *minimum fluidisation velocity* or the *incipient* fluidisation velocity (v_{mf}).

The phenomenon may also be illustrated by plotting the pressure drop versus the superficial fluid velocity on log-log coordinates (see figure 8.2). The zone OA represents the static bed for which the plot is a straight line as per Ergun's equation (equation 8.1.18). Porosity or void fraction (ε) of this bed remains constant even if fluid velocity is increased. At the point *A*, the bed becomes unstable and a minor movement and readjustment of particles begin to take place to offer maximum cross-sectional area for fluid flow. Instability of the bed continues as the fluid velocity is increased, until at point *B* the loosest arrangement of particles is established. This point *B* is the point of minimum or incipient fluidisation and at this point, $v_o = v_{mf}$.

From the point *B*, the bed begins to expand with increasing fluid velocities, since the porosity or void fraction of the bed increases. At point *C* fluidisation is complete and all the particles are in motion. Beyond the point *C*, further increase in fluid velocity can be obtained by relatively slight increase in pressure drop, merely that required to overcome the increase in friction losses between the fluid and the suspended particles and that between the fluid and the walls of the column. Consequently, $(-\Delta P)$ remains essentially constant with increase in fluid velocity from point *C* to point *D* (see figure 8.2). At point

D, the fluid velocity is so large that it becomes equal to (or slightly more than) the terminal free settling velocity (V_t) of the particles. As a result, the particles get carried by the fluid to outside the column. This entrainment of solid particles in the outgoing fluid starts at *D* and gets completed at *E*, when all the particles are being carried off by the fluid and the porosity or void fraction of the bed becomes equal to unity (the bed, in fact, ceases to exist). The column now acts as a conveyor (pneumatic conveyor or hydraulic conveyor depending on whether air or water is used as the fluid).

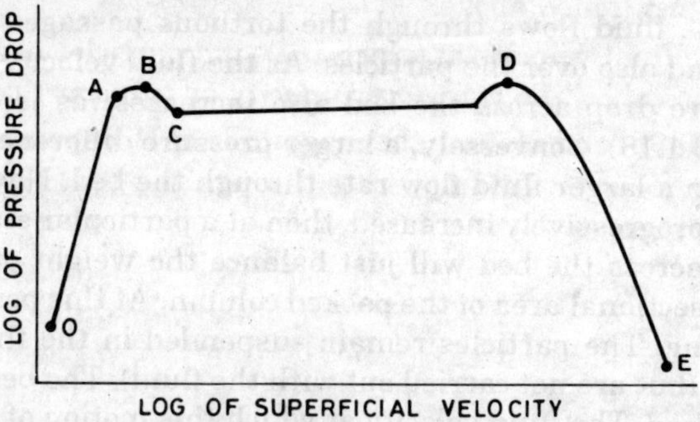

Fig. 8.2

It can be seen that from point *D* to *E*, ($-\Delta P$) decreases with increase in fluid velocity. This is mainly due to the fact that as more and more particles are carried off the column, the cross-sectional area available for fluid flow becomes larger and larger and the flow resistance becomes less and less.

Theoretically speaking, at the point *D* when the superficial fluid velocity becomes equal to the terminal free settling velocity of the particles, the porosity of the bed must become equal to unity. However, this seldom occurs in actual practice. The reasons are many fold :

Firstly, the bed is seldom composed of particles of exactly the same size. As a result, the fine particles get entrained off first and coarser particles subsequently.

Secondly, in fluidised beds composed of fine particles, even if the particle size is uniform, the particles have a tendency to flocculate. That is, small particles collect together and form large aggregates or flocs by adhering to each other. Each floc is larger in size than the individual particles and therefore, settles at a larger velocity. Consequently, these flocs are carried off the column only at larger fluid velocities.

Thirdly, in gas fluidised beds, aggregative fluidisation occurs (this is described in more detail in the subsequent paragraphs). Here, a significant amount of gas passes through the column in the form of bubbles carrying little or no particles with them. As a result, these beds can be operated without serious entrainment at fluid velocities much larger than the terminal free settling velocity of the particles.

No doubt, in certain liquid fluidised beds composed of coarse particles of uniform size, it has been observed that $\varepsilon_f = 1.0$ when the superficial liquid velocity equals the terminal free settling velocity of a single particle. However, this can not be generalised due to the reasons mentioned above.

The fluid velocity at which the solid particles are carried off the column is called the *carry-over velocity* or *transport velocity* (U_t). For a given fluid-solid system, the magnitude of U_t depends on the particle size, degree of flocculation and in a gas-fluidised bed, the extent of bubble formation.

It is necessary to distinguish between particulate fluidisation and aggregative fluidisation. *Particulate fluidisation* occurs mainly in liquid-fluidised beds where the fluid and solid densities are not too different and where the particles are small in size. In this case, the fluid velocity required to fluidise the bed is low. The beginning of fluidisation is marked by gentle oscillating motion of the particles. The bed fluidises evenly with each particle moving individually through a relatively uniform mean free path.

When the fluid and solid densities are greatly different (as in gas-solid systems) or when the particle size is large, the fluid velocity required to fluidise the bed will be relatively high. In such a case, fluidisation is uneven and the fluid passes through the bed mainly as large bubbles. These bubbles carry little or no particles with them. The fluid bubbles rise through the bed and break at the surface of the bed, splashing a few solid particles upwards. As the fluid velocity is increased, the bubbling action becomes more and more violent and streamers or ribbons of solids get ejected to considerable distances above the bed before returning. This is called *aggregative fluidisation*. The superficial velocity of fluid at which the fluid bubbles start getting formed is called the *minimum bubbling velocity* (v_{mb}). It may be assumed that the gas in excess of that required for minimum fluidisation manifests itself as bubbles. This is evidenced from the fact that in many gas-fluidised beds, the values of v_{mf} and v_{mb} are almost equal. In liquid-fluidised beds however, essentially particulate fluidisation occurs.

It is thus clear that between $v_o = v_{mf}$ and $v_o = v_{mb}$, particulate fluidisation occurs and at $v_o > v_{mb}$, aggregative fluidisation results. An approximate criterion is that when the Froude number at minimum fluidisation (Fr_{mf}) is less than 1.0, particulate fluidisation occurs and when $Fr_{mf} > 1.0$, aggregative fluidisation occurs. Here, Fr_{mf} is defined as

$$Fr_{mf} = v_{mf}^2/(D_{vs}\, g) \qquad .(8.2.1)$$

Rice et.al[9] and Remoero et.al[10] have proposed four dimensionless groups to characterise the quality of fluidisation. According to them,

$$N = Fr_{mf} Re'_{mf} \left(\frac{\rho_s - \rho_f}{\rho_f} \right) (L_{mf}/D) \qquad ...(8.2.1a)$$

If $N < 100$, particulate fluidisation occurs and when $N > 100$, aggregative fluidisation will occur. Re'_{mf} is defined in equation (8.2.8).

In many industrial applications, a highly bubbling fluidised bed is considered undesirable. This is due to the fact that since the gas bubbles carry little or no solid particles with them and thus practically bypass the solid phase, the basic purpose of fluidisation (namely, the intimate mixing between the two phases) is not met.

The operating fluid velocity (v_{of}) in a fluidiser is thus more than v_{mf} but less than the carry-over or transport velocity (U_t). In liquid-fluidised beds, the operating fluid velocity is commonly maintained at 3-4 times v_{mf}, while in gas-fluidised beds, superficial fluid velocities ranging from ($2\, v_{mf}$) to as large as ($200\, v_{mf}$) are not unusual. This is because due to reasons discussed earlier, gas-fluidised beds can be operated at superficial velocities several times the settling velocity of the particles without any serious entrainment of solids. Gas- fluidised beds operating with $v_{of} < 20\, v_{mf}$ are termed as *bubbling fluidised beds* and those operating with $20\, v_{mf} < v_{of} < 200\, v_{mf}$ are termed as *turbulent fluidised beds*. These systems generally operate batchwise with little or no entrainment of particles. A typical batch fluidisation system is shown in figure (8.3). It can be seen that sufficient free space (called *free board*) is provided above the fluidised bed to minimise entrainment of particles in the outgoing fluid (estimation of the required height of this free board or the *transport disengagement height* is discussed in one of the subsequent paragraphs). However, some amount of fines does get entrained in the outgoing fluid and therefore, a fluid-solid separator (such as a gas cyclone or a dust collector) is used at the top of the fluidiser to separate these entrained solids (see figure 8.3). Batch fluidisation without particle entrainment is often called *dense phase fluidisation*.

In continuous fluidisation (also called *lean-phase* or *disperse-phase* fluidisation), the superficial fluid velocity (v_{of}) employed is much larger (but still less than the transport velocity). No freeboard is used and the bed is allowed to expand to beyond the top of the column. As a result, the solids are carried off by the fluid, keeping them in suspension. In other words, the fluid passes upwards through the column keeping the particles in suspension in it. At the top of the column, the fluid-solid suspension is sent to a separator (a gas cyclone or a settling tank/centrifuge) to separate the solid particles which are returned to the bottom of the fluidiser or to the feed gas (or feed liquid) inlet. This is what is called a *circulating fluidised bed*. In gas-solid systems of this kind, the superficial velocity of gas often exceeds (200 v_{mf}). The contact time between the fluid and the solids is decided by the residence time of the solids in the column and this is controlled by the fluid flow rate. Circulating fluidised beds are quite popular in petroleum refineries for the fluidised bed catalytic cracking (FCC) of heavy gas oils and also for the fluidised bed catalytic reforming (FCR) of gasoline/naphtha.

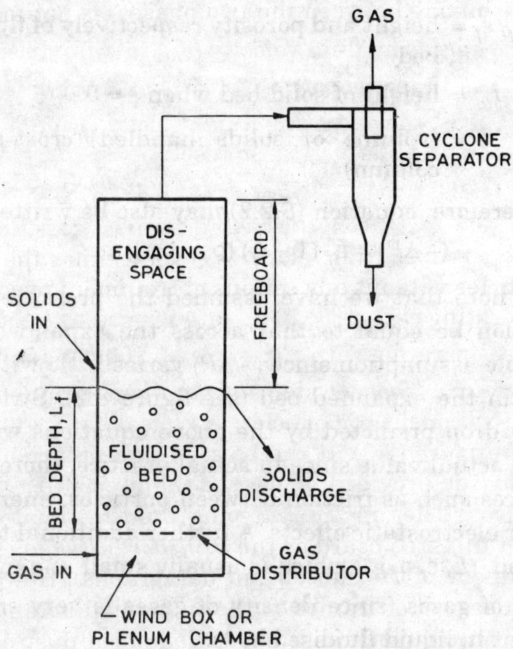

Fig. 8.3

The design variables of a fluidiser are, therefore,

(*a*) the minimum or incipient fluidisation velocity (v_{mf}), (*b*) **pressure drop across the fluidised bed $(-\Delta P)$,**

(*c*) **the height and porosity of fluidised (expanded) bed (L_f, ε_f),**

(*d*) **freeboard height or transport disengagement height (TDH),**

(*e*) **column diameter.**

We know that at incipient fluidisation, the pressure drop across the bed is equal to the weight of the solids minus the buoyant force (exerted by the displaced fluid) per unit cross-sectional area of the bed/column. Thus

$$(-\Delta P)\,A_c = A_c\,L_{mf}(1-\varepsilon_{mf})\,\rho_s\,g - A_c\,L_{mf}(1-\varepsilon_{mf})\,\rho_f\,g$$

or
$$(-\Delta P) = L_{mf}(1-\varepsilon_{mf})\,(\rho_s-\rho_f)\,g \qquad \text{...(8.2.2)}$$

where L_{mf}, ε_{mf} = height and porosity respectively of bed at incipient fluidisation

Now, a simple solids balance yields

$$L\,(1-\varepsilon) = L_{mf}(1-\varepsilon_{mf}) = L_f(1-\varepsilon_f) = L_o \qquad \text{...(8.2.3)}$$

where L, ε = height and porosity respectively of static bed

L_f, ε_f = height and porosity respectively of fluidised (expanded) bed

L_o = height of solid bed when $\varepsilon = 0$

= (volume of solids handled)/(cross-sectional area of column)

Therefore, equation (8.2.2) may also be written as

$$(-\Delta P) = L_f(1-\varepsilon_f)\,(\rho_s-\rho_f)\,g \qquad \text{..(8.2.4)}$$

To note that we have assumed the pressure drop at incipient fluidisation be equal to that across the expanded bed, which is a reasonable assumption since $(-\Delta P)$ varies little with increase in fluid velocity in the expanded bed (see figure 8.2). Strictly speaking, the pressure drop predicted by the above equations will be slightly less than the actual value since in actual practice, there will be additional resistances such as friction between particles, energy loss due to collisions or electrostatic effects. A further additional term is the vertical fluid head, $(L_f\,\varepsilon_f\,\rho_f\,g)$, which is usually small and may be neglected in the case of gases (since density of gases is very small) but could be important in liquid fluidised beds.

The minimum fluidisation velocity may be determined experimentally by plotting measured values of pressure drop against superficial fluid velocity as shown in figure (8.2). To compute the same analytically, Kunii and Levenspiel[11] suggest that Ergun's equation

(equation 8.1.18) may be extrapolated to the point of minimum fluidisation with allowable error. Thus,

$$\left[\frac{(-\Delta P)\,D_{vs}}{L_{mf}\,v_{mf}^2\,\rho_f}\right]\frac{\varepsilon_{mf}^3}{(1-\varepsilon_{mf})} = (150/Re_{mf}) + 1.75 \qquad \text{...(8.2.5)}$$

where $Re_{mf} = D_{vs}\,v_{mf}\,\rho_f/\mu_f\,(1-\varepsilon_{mf})$. Substituting for $(-\Delta P)$ from equation (8.21) and putting $D_{vs} = (\psi_s\,D_v)$, we get on rearrangement,

$$1.75\,(Re_{mf})^2 + 150\,Re_{mf} - Ar_m\,(\psi_s\,\varepsilon_{mf})^3/(1-\varepsilon_{mf})^2 = 0 \qquad \text{...(8.2.6)}$$

where Ar_m = modified Archimedes number (also called Galileo number)

$$= D_v^3\,(\rho_s-\rho_f)\,g\,\rho_f/\mu_f^2 \qquad \text{...(8.2.7)}$$

The above equation is more commonly rewritten in terms of a modified Reynolds number, Re'_{mf}, which is defined as

$$Re_{mf} = D_{vs}\,v_{mf}\,\rho_f/\mu_f\,(1-\varepsilon_{mf})$$

$$= \frac{\psi_s}{(1-\varepsilon_{mf})}\,\frac{D_v\,v_{mf}\,\rho_f}{\mu_f}$$

$$= \frac{\psi_s}{(1-\varepsilon_{mf})}\,Re'_{mf} \qquad \text{...(8.2.8)}$$

Thus, equation (8.2.6) may be re-expressed as

$$1.75\,(Re'_{mf})^2 + 150\,Re'_{mf}\,(1-\varepsilon_{mf})/\psi_s - \psi_s\,\varepsilon_{mf}^3\,Ar_m = 0 \qquad \text{...(8.2.9)}$$

Once the bed voidage at incipient fluidisation (namely, ε_{mf}) is known, the above equation can be solved for Re'_{mf}, from which the value of v_{mf} could be obtained. Experimental values of ε_{mf} for some selected materials are given graphically in figure (8.4). It can be seen that different plots are given for different materials of different sphericities. It is thus clear that the value of ε_{mf} depends not only on particle size but also on particle shape. For those particles for which no data is available, an approximate estimate of ε_{mf} can be obtained from the *dimensional* correlation given by Leva[12] :

$$\varepsilon_{mf} = 1.356 - 0.356\,\log_{10} D_v \qquad \text{...(8.2.10)}$$

where D_v is to be expressed in microns. This correlation has been developed for gas-fluidised beds and it has the inherent limitation that it does not consider the dependence of ε_{mf} on particle sphericity.

Wen and Yu[13] have proposed a simpler form of equation (8.2.9). They showed that for many materials, the value of $(\psi_s\,\varepsilon_{mf}^3)$ is

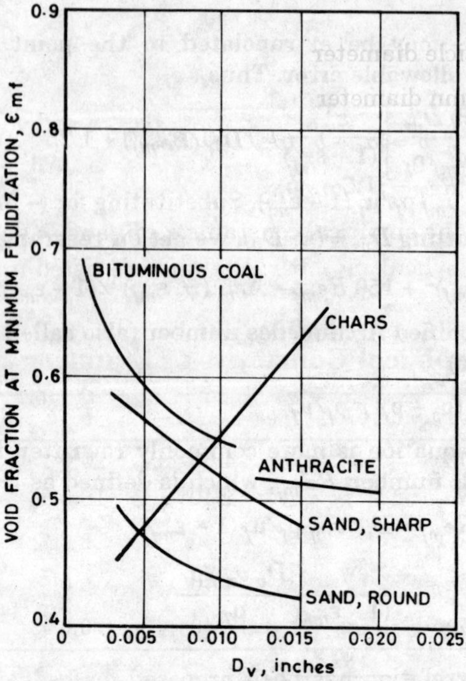

Fig. 8.4

approximately (1/14) and that of $(1 - \varepsilon_{mf})/\psi_s$ is (11/14). Substituting these values in equation (8.2.9) and solving for Re'_{mf}, we get

$$Re'_{mf} = \sqrt{(33.67)^2 + 0.0408\,Ar_m} - 33.67 \qquad \text{...(8.30)}$$

The above equations (8.2.9) and (8.2.11) are applicable to both gas fluidised beds and liquid fluidised beds.

As stated earlier, an operating superficial fluid velocity (v_{of}) of 3 to 4 times v_{mf} is common in liquid-fluidised beds, while in gas-fluidised beds, operating fluid velocities as large as 20 to 200 v_{mf} are not unusual.

The porosity of the expanded bed (ε_f) is a parameter that is difficult to estimate analytically. For particulate fluidisation, the value of ε_f may be estimated with reasonable accuracy from the experimental correlation proposed by Richardson and Zaki[14] :

$$\varepsilon_f^n = v_{of}/U_i \qquad \text{...(8.2.12)}$$

$$\log_{10} U_i = \log_{10} V_t - d_p/D \qquad \text{...(8.2.13)}$$

where V_t = terminal free settling velocity of particles

d_p = particle diameter

D = column diameter

$$n = [a_o + b_o (d_p/D)] (Re_T)^m \qquad ...(8.2.14)$$

$$Re_T = DV_t \rho_f/\mu_f \qquad ...(8.2.15)$$

The values of the empirical constants a_o, b_o and m depend on the magnitude of the Reynolds number, Re_T and are listed in table (8.1).

Table 8.1
Values of Empirical Constants of Equation (8.2.14)

Reynolds number, Re_T	a_o	b_o	m
< 0.2	4.65	20.0	0.0
$0.2 < Re_T < 1.0$	4.40	18.0	– 0.03
$1.0 < Re_T < 200$	4.40	18.0	– 0.01
$200 < Re_T < 500$	4.40	0.0	– 0.1
> 500	2.40	0.0	0.0

The above correlation has been proposed for beds composed of spherical particles. However, with allowable error, the same may be used for non-spherical particles after replacing d_p by D_v.

For aggregative fluidisation (common in gas fluidised beds), reliable correlations for the estimation of ε_f are scarce. A straight forward method (though approximate) is to extrapolate Ergun's equation to the expanded bed and then solve it for ε_f. In other words, we may rewrite equation (8.2.6) in terms of Re_f and ε_f and then solve it for ε_f. Here, Re_f is defined as

$$Re_f = \frac{D_{vs}\, v_{of}\, \rho_f}{\mu_f (1 - \varepsilon_f)} \qquad ...(8.2.16)$$

Leva[12] reports that even for gas-fluidised beds, a plot of ε_f versus v_{of} on log-log coordinates is essentially linear. If this is so, then we can write

$$\varepsilon_f = A\, (v_{of})^n \qquad ...(8.2.17)$$

where A and n are constants. To plot this straight line or to evaluate the constants A and n, we require two points. One point is already available since we know that at $v_{of} = v_{mf}$, $\varepsilon_f = \varepsilon_{mf}$. Therefore, if we know the value of ε_f (say, ε_1) at a particular value of v_{of} (say, v_1), then the above straight line can be plotted or the empirical constants A and n

could be evaluated. Thereafter, the value of ε_f at any desired value of operating fluid velocity can be obtained from this plot/correlation.

Once ε_f is known, the height of expanded bed (L_f) can be computed from equation (8.2.3).

It is to be kept in mind that since the upper surface of a fluidised bed is usually uneven and more or less oscillating (especially in gas-fluidised systems), the bed height (L_f) and the bed voidage (ε_f) are, in fact, time-averaged values. For an accurate estimation of bed voidage in aggregative fluidisation, the nature and dynamics of the fluid bubbles in the bed are to be known.

We have already stated earlier that a free board or free space is provided between the top of the fluidised bed and the top fluid outlet in order to minimise entrainemnt of fines in the outgoing fluid (see figure 8.3). Most fluidised beds are composed of certain amount of fines and additional fines could also form due to mutual attrition between particles. Apart from entrainment of fines, solids are also carried into the freeboard by the erupting bubbles. However, particles ascending the free board space gradually lose their kinetic energy and some of them (the coarser and denser ones) return to the bed. The particle concentration in the freeboard gas thus decreases, until it reaches a constant value at which the terminal free settling velocity of the accompanying particles is close to or less than the velocity of the outgoing fluid. The free board height corresponding to this constant entrainment rate is called the transport disengagement height (TDH) and this determines the optimum distance for fluid exit ports above a fluidised bed.

One of the *dimensional* correlations that illustrates the relationship between fractional entrainment (E) and the transport disengagement height (Z_d) is given below[15] (all variables are expressed in S.I. units).

$$E = 0.154\,(v_{of}^2/Z_d\,g)^{1.53}\,(D)^{0.75}\,(\mu_f/\mu_o)^{1.78}\,(1000/\rho_s)^{2.5}\,(1/v_{mf})^{1.5} \quad \text{...(8.2.18)}$$

where E = fractional entrainemnt, (kg solids/kg gas)

Z_d = transport disengagement height (TDH)

μ_o = viscosity of gas at 25°C

The diameter of the column (D) obviously depends on the fluid flow rate and the operating superficial fluid velocity (v_{of}) employed. The (L/D) ratio of the column does influence the fluidiser performance as is seen from equations described above. Tall, narrow beds cause an additional problem of what is called *slugging*. We know gas bubbles are formed at the gas distributor and these bubbles grow in size due to coalescence as they rise through the bed. In narrow columns, it may so happen that at one stage, the bubble diameter becomes equal to the column diameter. Solids on top of such a large bubble are pushed up by the bubble as a slug and the phenomenon is called slugging. This disturbs the operation of the fluidiser. Slugging can be avoided by choosing proper particle size (bubble growth is slow in beds composed of small and light particles) and by using shallow beds. It has been observed that when $L/D \leq 1$, no slugging occurs.

Commercial fluidised beds are generally composed of fine particles of less than 800 microns in size. In gas-fluidised beds, particle sizes ranging from 10 microns to 150 microns are preferred. Such particles provide smooth fluidisation with least formation of large bubbles. Coarser particles cause instability and slugging, while finer particles have a tendency to flocculate forming agglomerates and fissures in the bed. Bed depths upto 10 m are not unusual. Coarser particles (larger than 250 microns) are fluidised in so called *teeter beds* which use shallow beds (around 1m in height). These are primarily used for roasting ores and sometimes for the gasification of coal.

Still coarser particles (that are too coarse to be handled in commercial fluidised bed systems) may be handled in the so called *spouted beds*. In spouted beds, the method of gas-solid contacting is quite different from that in a conventional fluidised bed. A schematic view of a typical spouted bed is shown in figure (8.5). Gas-solid contacting first takes place in the fluid *spout* flowing upward through the center of a loosely packed bed of solids. The solids get entrained in the fluid and are thus conveyed to the top of the bed. From there, they move down under gravity in the surrounding annulus countercurrently to gas flow. The gas flow in a spouted bed is thus partly through the spout and partly through the annulus. About 30 per cent of gas entering the system immediately diffuses into the downward-flowing annulus. As the fluid spout rises in the bed, it entrains more and more particles losing velocity and gas into the annulus. The volume of solids displaced by the spout is roughly 6 per cent of the total bed. The minimum superficial fluid velocity required for spouting (v_{ms}) may be computed from the experimental correlation of Mathur and Gishler[16] :

$$v_{ms} = (D_v/D)\,(D_o/D)^{0.33}\,\sqrt{2gL\,(\rho_s - \rho_f)/\rho_f} \qquad ...(8.2.19)$$

where D_o = fluid inlet orifice diameter. The above correlation is based on experiments in columns of 7.5 cm to 30 cm in diameter. It is clear from the above correlation that increasing bed diameter increases spoutable depth. In other words, deeper beds can be spouted in larger diameter columns. Also, for a given column diameter, decrease in fluid inlet orifice size increases the spoutable depth. It has been observed that size reduction of solids due to mutual attrition is significantly large in a spouted bed, which could form one of its limitations.

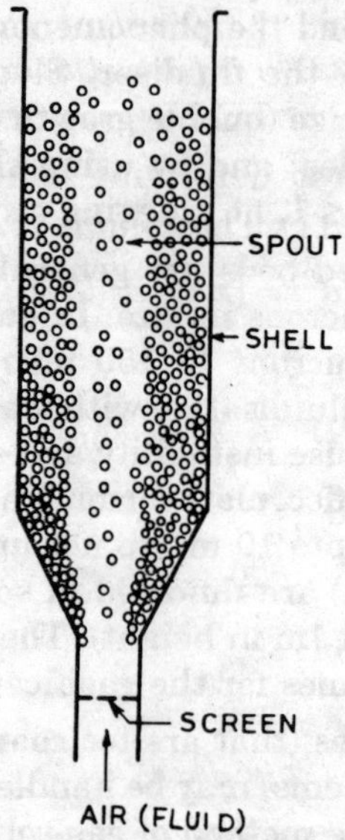

Fig. 8.5

Fluidised bed systems have found extensive applications in process industries. They are used as catalytic/noncatalytic reactors, as batch/continuous dryers, as heat transfer media and for fluidised bed combustion of coal, for roasting/calcination of minerals, as adsorption-desorption equipment, as solid-solid mixers and as classifiers. Continuous operation with few moving parts, the ease of adding and removing solids and above all, effective contact between fluid and the solids are the chief advantages of fluidised bed systems. The high degree of turbulence, the high heat capacity of solids relative to the fluid and the high heat transfer rates between the fluid and the solids associated with large interfacial area result in a remarkably uniform temperature throughout the fluidised bed. However, these systems are not without disadvantages. This technique may not be useful with solids that tend to agglomerate and with those which do not flow freely. Size reduction of solids due to mutual attrition and consequent loss of fines, the additional provision required for dust retrieval equipment and the higher operating cost are the drawbacks of fluidisation. Over and above, from the design engineer's view point, the greatest hurdle could be the very complex nature of contacting that causes uncertainties in scale up.

Example 8.2. *It is desired to fluidise 2.5 tonnes of catalyst particles that are in the form of cylindrical pellets 165 microns in diameter (length = half the diameter) with 565 m^3/hr of a gas having a density of 2.292 kg/m^3 and a viscosity of 0.011 centipoise at the process conditions. The catalyst density is 1370 kg/m^3. Design the fluidiser, if an operating gas velocity that is three times the minimum is being recommended.*

Solution. Let us first determine the minimum fluidisation velocity from equation (8.2.11). The volume of each catalyst particle is

$$V_p = (\pi/4)\, d^2 l = (\pi/4)\, d^2\, (d/2), \text{ since } l = d/2$$

$$= \pi\, d^3/8$$

We know that $V_p = \pi\, D_v^3/6$. Therefore,

$$\pi\, D_v^3/6 = \pi\, d^3/8$$

or $$D_v = 0.90856\, d = (0.90856)\,(165)$$

$$= 150 \text{ microns.}$$

Surface area of each particle

$$= (\pi\, dl) + 2\,(\pi\, d^2/4)$$

$$= \pi d\,(d/2) + \pi d^2/2 = \pi d^2$$

Therefore, the sphericity of catalyst particles is

$$\psi_s = \pi D_v^2/\pi d^2 = (0.90856\, d)^2/d^2$$

$$= 0.82548$$

Now, from equation (8.2.7) :

$$Ar_m = \frac{(150 \times 10^{-6})^3\,(1370 - 2.292)\,(2.292)\,(9.8)}{(0.011 \times 10^{-3})^2}$$

$$= 856.885$$

Therefore, from equation (8.2.11),

$$Re'_{mf} = 0.51523$$

or $$v_{mf} = \frac{(0.51523)\,(0.011 \times 10^{-3})}{(2.292)\,(0.15 \times 10^{-3})} = 0.016485 \text{ m/s}$$

The operating fluid velocity is, therefore,

$$v_{of} = (3.0)\,(0.016485) = 0.04945 \text{ m/s}$$

$$= 178.038 \text{ m/hr}$$

Since volume flow rate of gas is 565 m^3/hr,

$$A_c = 565/178.038 = 3.1735 \text{ m}^2$$

$$D = \sqrt{(4.0)\ (3.1735)/\pi} = 2.01 \text{ m}$$

This is the required column diameter. However, we must ensure that the chosen operating velocity does not exceed the terminal free settling velocity of the particles (V_t). To estimate V_t, since the settling zone is not known in advance, we shall apply equation (3.1.6) of Chapter - 3, which is to be solved by trial. Thus, let $V_t = 0.34$ m/s.

Now, from equation (3.2.1),

$$Re_p = (150 \times 10^{-6})\ (0.34)\ (2.292)/(0.011 \times 10^{-3})$$
$$= 10.626$$

From figure (3.1), corresponding to this value of particle Reynolds number and $\psi_s = 0.82548$, $f_D = 10.0$. Therefore, from equation (3.1.6),

$$V_t = \left[\frac{(4.0)\ (1370 - 2.292)\ (9.8)\ (150 \times 10^{-6})}{(3.0)\ (2.292)\ (10.0)}\right]^{0.5}$$

$$= 0.342 \text{ m/s}$$

Since this value of V_t agrees closely with that assumed at the outset, no further trials are required. The operating superficial gas velocity (v_{of}) chosen is thus satisfactory since it is much below the terminal free settling velocity of the particles.

We may now determine the bed porosity at incipient fluidisation by solving equation (8.2.9). Thus, substituting the known values of Re'_{mf}, ψ_s and Ar_m in equation (8.2.9) and simplifying, we get

$$7.555\ \varepsilon_{mf}^3 + \varepsilon_{mf} = 1.004962$$

Solving by trial,

$$\varepsilon_{mf} = 0.425$$

Since the mass of solids handled is 2.5 tonnes or 2500 kg,

$$L_o = \frac{\text{(Volume of solids)}}{\text{(Cross sectional area of column)}}$$

$$= \frac{(2500/1370)}{(3.1735)} = 0.575 \text{ m}$$

Therefore, from equation (8.2.3),

$$L_{mf}\,(1 - 0.425) = 0.575$$

or $$L_{mf} = 1.0 \text{ m}$$

We can now check the type of fluidisation prevailing. Since $D_{vs} = \psi_s D_v = (0.82548)(150) = 123.822$ microns,

$$Fr_m = \frac{(0.016485)^2}{(123.822 \times 10^{-6})(9.8)} = 0.224$$

Since Fr_m is much less than unity, particulate fluidisation must be expected. We may further verify this from equation (8.2.1*a*). Thus,

$$N = (0.224)(0.51523)(1367.708/2.292)(1.0/2.01) = 34.258$$

Since N is much less than 100, particulate fluidisation occurs. We can therefore use Richardson and Zaki's correlation (equation 8.2.12) for computing the porosity of the expanded bed. Thus,

$$Re_T = \frac{(2.01)(0.34)(2.292)}{(0.011 \times 10^{-3})} = 142395.709$$

Since $Re_T > 500$, $n = 2.4$. Also, from equation (8.2.13),

$$\log U_i = \log (0.34) - (150 \times 10^{-6})/(2.01)$$

or $$U_i = 0.33994 \text{ m/s}$$

Therefore, from equation (8.2.12),

$$\varepsilon_f = (0.04945/0.33994)^{1/2.4} = 0.4479$$

Now, from equation (8.2.3),

$$L_f(1 - 0.4479) = 0.575$$

or $$L_f = 1.0414 \text{ m}$$

The pressure drop across the bed can be now obtained from equation (8.2.4) :

$$(-\Delta P) = (1.0414)(1 - 0.4479)(1370 - 2.292)(9.8)$$

$$= 7707.034 \text{ N/m}^2 = 7.707 \text{ kN/m}^2$$

The freeboard height required or the transport disengagement height (Z_d) depends on the degree of entrainment that can be tolerated. For example, let us take $E = 0.001$. Then, from equation (8.2.18), neglecting viscosity correction,

$$0.001 = (0.154)\left[\frac{(0.04945)^2}{9.8\, Z_d}\right]^{1.53} (2.01)^{0.75} (1000/1370)^{2.5} (1/0.016485)^{1.5}$$

or $$Z_d = 0.3163 \text{ m}$$

The total column height required (above the gas distributor) is, therefore,

$$= 1.0414 + 0.3163$$

$$= 1.3577 \text{ m} \simeq 1.36 \text{ m}$$

The results are summarised below :

Column diameter = 2.01 m

Column height (above gas distributor) = 1.36 m

Pressure drop = 7.707 kN/m^2

Gas flow rate = 565 m^3/hr.

8.3. Semifluidisation

A good compromise between a fixed bed and a fluidised bed is the semifluidised bed. It may be viewed as a combination of a batch fluidised bed at the bottom and a packed bed at the top. This is achieved by restricting the expansion of the fluidised bed by providing a restraint (say, a porous plate) at the top of the bed. This restraint prevents the escape of particles, but permits the fluid to go out. As a result, the particles collect below the restraint forming a packed bed there.

A semifluidised bed eliminates many of the inherent disadvantages of fluidised bed systems and packed bed systems. For example, problems of entrainment of particles and unstable bed expansion (that are common in fluidised bed units) are avoided. The semifluidised bed also reduces or eliminates plugging of the bed by fine solids, a problem experienced in fixed bed operations. Consequently, semifluidised beds have found wide applications as deep bed filters, ion exchangers and also as chemical and biological reactors. When used as reactors, the fluidised bed section acts as a completely backmixed reactor or continuous stirred tank reactor (CSTR) and the top packed bed section as a plug flow reactor (PFR). Such a reactor combination has been found to be quite advantageous, particularly for conducting exothermic adiabatic reactions.

In spite of its many-sided advantages, there is hardly any theoretical model available for predicting the performance characteristics of a semifluidised bed system analytically. Most of the process/design variables are required to be determined experimentally. Though a very large number of experimental correlations have been reported in literature for the estimation of some of the design variables, all of them are highly empirical in nature and possess very restricted applicability. Each correlation can be used with confidence only for the particular fluid-solid system studied and only for the specific range of operating/system variables (fluid velocity; particle size, column diameter) employed in the experiments. Also, reliable correlations are scarce for the successful estimation of many of the key variables.

The chief design parameters of a semifluidised bed are the pressure drop, minimum semifluidisation velocity (v_{osf} or G_{osf}), the maximum semifluidisation velocity (v_{msf} or G_{msf}) and the height of the semifluidised bed (L_{sf}). The minimum semifluidisation velocity is defined as the fluid velocity at which the top of the fluidised bed just touches the top restraint, while the maximum semifluidisation velocity is the fluid velocity at which all the solid particles are supported by the fluid in the packed portion of the bed (in other words, at $G = G_{msf}$, the voidage of the fluidised section of the bed = $\varepsilon_f = 1.0$). Experimental correlations are available[17] for the estimation of (G_{osf}/G_{msf}) ratio, which are of the form

$$G_{osf}/G_{msf} = C_1\,(D/d_p)^a\,(\rho_s/\rho_f)^b\,(L_{sf}/L_{pa})^c \qquad \text{...(8.3.1)}$$

where d_p = average particle size

L_{pa} = height of packed section of semifluidised bed.

The values of empirical constants C_1, a, b and c differ for different gas-solid and liquid-solid systems. They also differ for different particle shapes, for different particle size ranges and for different ranges of column diameter[17]. The particle size (d_p) has also been defined in different ways by different authors (some have used volumetric diameter and some volume-surface diameter).

Similarly, the maximum semifluidisation velocity (G_{msf}) may be empirically computed from correlations of the form

$$G_{msf} = C_2\,(d_p)^e\,[\rho_f\,(\rho_s - \rho_f)]^f\,(\mu_f)^g \qquad \text{...(8.3.2)}$$

The operating semifluidisation velocity (G_{sf}) has also been empirically correlated with the height of the semifluidised bed (L_{sf}), height of the packed section (L_{pa}) and other system variables in the following form[17] :

$$G_{sf}/G_{msf} = C_3\,(D/d_p)^m\,(L/D)^n\,(\rho_s/\rho_f)^p\,(L_{pa}/L)^q\,(L_{sf}/L_{pa})^s \qquad \text{...(8.3.3)}$$

where L = height of static bed (prior to fluidisation). The above two classes of correlations are also as empirical as equation (8.3.1).

Though we have three sets of correlations such as equations (8.3.1) to (8.3.3), there are four unknowns in them such as L_{pa}, L_{sf}, G_{osf} and G_{msf}. Consequently, they can be solved simultaneously only if one of these design variables is experimentally determined. Often, for some systems, an additional correlation is also available which is of the form[17]

$$(L_{sf} - L)/(L_{sf} - L_{pa}) = [(G_{sf} - G_{osf})/(G_{msf} - G_{osf})]^j \quad ...(8.3.4)$$

where j is another empirical constant. In such a case, the above four correlations could be solved for the four design variables L_{sf}, L_{pa}, G_{osf} and G_{msf}. To note that the operating semifluidisation velocity (G_{sf}) is chosen more than G_{osf} but less than G_{msf} and to start with, it may be chosen equal to the arithmetic average of G_{osf} and G_{msf}. The height of the fluidised section (L_f) can be now obtained as

$$L_f = L_{sf} - L_{pa} \quad ...(8.3.5)$$

To compute the bed voidage, we may make a solid balance for the semifluidised bed, which gives

$$L_f(1 - \varepsilon_f) + L_{pa}(1 - \varepsilon_{pa}) = L_o \quad ...(8.3.6)$$

where L_o = (volume of solids handled)/(cross-sectional area of column). Thus, if the porosity of the packed section, ε_{pa}. is known experimentally, then ε_f could be computed from the above equation. Since granular solids usually pack to form beds of average porosity 0.40, an approach (though approximate) is to take $\varepsilon_{pa} = 0.40$ and then solve the above equation for ε_f.

The pressure drop in the semifluidised bed may be assumed equal to the algebraic sum of the pressure drop across the packed section and that across the fluidised section. Thus

$$(-\Delta P) = (-\Delta P)_{pa} + (-\Delta P)_{fb} \quad ...(8.3.7)$$

The pressure drop across the packed section may be computed from Ergun's equation (equation 8.1.18) and that across the fluidised section from equation (8.2.4). However, it has been observed that values of pressure drop computed from the above equation are often lower than those experimentally measured. This may be attributed to several reasons such as particle agglomeration, possible occurrence of channeling and other supplementary effects.

Readers are encouraged to consult reference (17) that provides an elaborate survey of the experimental correlations available for the design of semifluidisation systems. A few sample correlations are listed here in table (8.2). Since these correlations are highly empirical in nature, readers are cautioned not to apply them without properly verifying their ranges of applicability.

Table 8.2. Correlations for Semifluidised Bed Systems

S.No.	*Correlation**	*Ref. No.*
1.	$G_{osf}/G_{msf} = 1.625\,(D/d_p)^{0.266}\,(\rho_f/\rho_s)^{0.228}\,(L_{sf}/L_{pa})^{0.585}$	18
2.	$G_{msf} = (18500.0)\,d_p^{0.65}\,[\rho_f\,(\rho_s - \rho_f)]^{0.55}/\mu_f^{0.1}$	17
3.	$G_{sf}/G_{msf} = 0.945\,(D/d_p)^{-0.15}\,(L/D)^{-0.1}\,(\rho_s/\rho_f))^{-0.11}\,(L_{pa}/L)^{0.66}\,(L_{sf}/L_{pa})^{0.57}$	18
4.	$(L_{sf} - L)/(L_{sf} - L_{pa}) = [(G_{sf} - G_{osf})/(G_{msf} - G_{osf})]^{0.2}$	17

* For the range of applicability of each correlation, consult the coresponding reference.

8.4. Three Phase Fluidisation

A bed of solids may be fluidised instead of by a single fluid, simultaneously by two fluids (a gas and a liquid). Such a process is known as three phase fluidisation or gas-liquid-solid fluidisation. The gas and the liquid may flow cocurrently (in the same direction) or countercurrently (in the opposite directions). Either the gas or the liquid could form the continuous phase. Accordingly, there can be four modes of operation such as cocurrent upflow with liquid as the continuous phase, cocurrent upflow with gas as the continuous phase, countercurrent operation with liquid as continuous phase and countercurrent operation with gas as continuous phase. Among these four modes, the first and the last (namely, cocurrent upflow with liquid as continuous phase and countercurrent operation with gas as the continuous phase) are the ones that have been widely investigated.

In cocurrent operation with liquid as the continuous phase, the particles are supported by the liquid with the gas forming discrete bubbles. Both the gas and the liquid are admitted from the bottom of the column. This mode of operation is generally referred to as *gas-liquid fluidisation.* The system thus resembles a gas-sparged slurry column (or a three phase slurry reactor), but there are some distinct differences. In a slurry column, the size of solids handled is usually less than 100 microns, the volume fraction of solids in the slurry less than 0.1 and the particles are maintained in the suspended state by bubble agitation. In three-phase fluidisation on the other hand, the particle size is relatively large, normally greater than 200 microns, the volume fraction of solids in the bed varying from 0.2 to 0.6. In both systems, solids may be continuously added or removed. But, in the slurry column, the solid particles are usually carried in or out by the liquid stream, while in the fluidised bed, the solids are supplied or withdrawn independent of the liquid stream.

If the gas flow rate is progressively increased, then a stage will be reached when the gas becomes the continuous phase and the liquid becomes the dispersed phase in the form of liquid films or droplets. Relatively little work has been conducted on this mode of operation and reported data on systems of this kind are scarce.

Countercurrent three phase fluidisation with liquid as the continuous phase is known as *inverse three-phase fluidisation*. Here, the bed is composed of particles with density lower than that of liquid and are fluidised by a downward liquid flow, opposite to the net buoyant force on the particles. The gas is introduced from the bottom and it moves up in the form of discrete bubbles copuntercurrently to the liquid. No much studies have been conducted on this mode of operation as well and relatively little data are available on the performance characteristics of systems operating in this mode.

Countercurrent operation with gas as the continuous phase has attracted a lot of attention. Systems operating in this mode have been given a variety of names such as fluidised bed scrubber, turbulent contact absorber (TCA), mobile bed contactor and fluidised packing contactor. Among these, the term *turbulent contact absorber* (TCA) is, by far, the most popular designation. In this mode of operation, an irrigated bed of low density particles is fluidised by the upward flow of gas as a continuous phase. The liquid is sprayed from the top. When the bed is in a fully fluidised state, the vigorous movement of wetted particles gives rise to excellent gas-liquid contacting. The gas and liquid flow rates in a TCA are much higher than those possible in conventional countercurrent packed beds since the bed can easily expand to reduce the hydrodynamic resistances.

As stated earlier, cocurrent operation with liquid as continuous phase and the turbulent contact absorber are the ones most widely investigated. We shall therefore discuss here design equations for these two. Let us first consider the cocurrent operation. The expression for pressure drop in a system like this can be written in the same way as for conventional fluidisation (see equation (8.2.4). Thus,

$$(-\Delta P) = L_f\,[(1-\varepsilon_f)\,\rho_s + \varepsilon_l\,\rho_L + \varepsilon_g\,\rho_g]\,g \qquad \text{...(8.4.1)}$$

where ε_l = liquid holdup in the bed (volume fraction of liquid in the bed)

ε_g = gas holdup in the bed

$$\varepsilon_f = (\varepsilon_l + \varepsilon_g) \qquad ...(8.4.2)$$

= total fluid holdup in the bed (may be called the bed voidage)

We also know that a solids-balance (see equation 8.2.3) gives

$$L_f(1 - \varepsilon_f) = L_o \qquad ...(8.4.3)$$

Thus, once the bed voidage (ε_f) and the fractional liquid holdup (ε_l) are known, the pressure drop can be evaluated from the above three equations. A very large number of experimental correlations have been reported in literature for the estimation of ε_f and ε_l. An extensive survey of these correlations has been presented by Muroyama and Fan[19]. Based on the survey, they have recommended the correlation of Dakshinamurthy et.al.[20] for the computation of bed voidage (ε_f) since this correlation is reportedly based on a large number of data obtained with various properties of particles. For liquid holdup (ε_l) estimation, the correlation of Kato et.al.[21] is recommended because of the wide coverage of particle size and liquid viscosity and the unified expression they have developed in terms of dimensionless parameters. These two correlations are listed in Table (8.3).

Table 8.3
Bed Voidage and Liquid Holdup in Three Phase Fluidiser

S.No.	*Correlation*	*Ref. No.*	*Remarks*
1.	$\varepsilon_f = k\,(v_{ol}/V_t)^m\,[v_{og}\,\mu_L/\sigma]^{0.08}$ $k = 2.12,\ m = 0.41$ for $Re_p < 500$ $k = 2.65,\ m = 0.60$ for $Re_p > 500$ $Re_p = d_p\,V_t\,\rho_L/\mu_L$	20	periments with spherical particles. v_{og}, v_{ol} = superficial velocity of gas and that of liquid respectively.
2.	$(v_{ol}/V_t) = (\varepsilon_l/\varepsilon^*)^n$ $\varepsilon^* = 1 - 9.7\,(N^{0.092})/[350 + Re_p^{1.1}]^{0.5}$ $\left[\dfrac{5.1 + 86.2\,(N)^{0.285} - n}{(n - 2.7)}\right] = [0.1 + 0.443\,N^{0.165}]\,(Re_p)^{0.9}$ $N = [v_{og}^4\,\rho_L/g\,\sigma]$	21	

A few theoretical models have also been proposed in the literature for the prediction of phase holdup and pressure drop in fluidisers of this kind. An example is the generalised wake model proposed by El-Temtamy and Epstein[22]. However, this model is based on measured values of gas holdup (ε_g). As a result, for making calculations using this model, experimental values of ε_g are required to be known.

Let us now consider the turbulent contact absorber (TCA). Typically, a TCA consists of a mass of particles confined between two retaining grids (or porous plates). The particles are popularly molded spheres of polyethene, polypropylene or foam polystyrene with a density between 100 and 400 kg/m^3 and diameters between 10 and 38 microns. The open area of the lower retaining grid in industrial units is normally greater than 70 per cent. This large open area also allows the liquid to be drained by gravity. The distance between the lower and upper retaining grids is usually set at about three times the static bed height. The gas flows upwards as a continuous phase, while the liquid is sprayed over the top of the fluidised bed and flows downward by gravity.

Equations (8.4.1) to (8.4.3) may be used for computing the pressure drop in a TCA as well, once the liquid holdup (ε_l) and gas holdup (ε_g) are obtained from reliable experimental correlations. All the correlation equations available for the estimation of (ε_l) and (ε_g) in a TCA have also been summarised by Muroyama and Fan[19]. It is a observed that the liquid holdup in a TCA depends, apart from the other system variables, on the static bed height (L) also. The height of the static bed (prior to fluidisation) and its porosity (ε) are therefore assumed available. To note that once L is known, the value of ε could be computed since we know (from equation 8.2.3) that $L(1 - \varepsilon) = L_0$. Also, for the design of TCA, it will be convenient to re-express equation (8.4.3) in the following form :

$$L_f(1 - \varepsilon_g) - L_f \varepsilon_l = L_o \qquad \text{...(8.4.4)}$$

Among the available experimental correlations, those proposed by Vunjak-Novakovic et. al[23] are fairly popular and are listed in Table (8.4). It can be seen from Table (8.4) that the gas holdup (ε_g) can be computed straightaway since the correlation is a simple one. Thereafter, the correlation for ε_l and equation (8.4.4) can be solved simultaneously for L_f and ε_l.

Expressions for the computation of minimum fluidisation velocity, v_{gmf}, are also proposed by the same authors and these are also tabulated in Table (8.4). In TCA columns composed of relatively lighter particles (with density less than 300 kg/m^3), the onset of fluidisation occurs much below the point of flooding in the equivalent countercurrent packed bed. However, in TCA columns containing high density packings ($\rho_s > 300$ kg/m^3), the onset of fluidisation occurs practically at the flooding point itself. Flooding is a phenomenon that could occur in all countercurrent packed towers (that is, packed towers operating with countercurrent flow of gas and liquid). The flooding gas velocity, G_f (that is, the superficial mass velocity of gas at the onset of flooding) may be estimated from the graphical data of Eckert[24, 25] or from Chen's analytical correlation.[25, 26] Then, for the second type of TCA columns (handling solids of density more than 300 kg/m^3), $G_f \simeq$ minimum fluidisation mass velocity of gas. In such columns, when the gas flow rate is further increased, the particles are pushed up to the upper retaining grid where they form a packed bed. In such a bed, the pressure drop sharply increases with increasing gas velocity and the liquid is entrained in the exhaust gas stream. Due to the intense liquid turbulence and high mass transfer effects, TCA columns of this kind are preferred for chemical reaction applications, unless the pressure drop is too high to be acceptable.

Table 8.4. Phase Holdups and Minimum Fluidisation Velocity in TCA Columns

S.No.	*Correlation*	*Ref. No.*	*Remarks*
1.	$\varepsilon_g = 0.628\,(v_{og})^{0.237}$ $(L_f\varepsilon_l/L) = k(Re_L)^m(Fr_L)^n(L/D)^p(\rho_s/\rho_L)^q + 0.02$ $k = 6.4848, m = -0.1387, n = 0.4287, p = -0.5672, q = 0$ (if $\rho_s < 300$ kg/m^3) $k = 7.326, m = -0.0591, n = 0.4354, p = 0.4328, q = 0.0904$ (if $\rho_s > 300$ kg/m^3) $Re_L = d_p\,G_L/\mu_L$ $Fr_L = G_L^2/(\rho_L^2\,d_p\,g)$	23	All variables in S.I. units. Particles assumed spherical. log = $\log_{10}$ G_L = superficial mass velocity of liquid v_{og} = superficial velocity of gas.
2.	$\log(v_{gmf}) = 1.2\log(d_p) + 0.5\log N - 0.0133\,G_L + 1.0531$ $N = (1-\varepsilon)(\rho_s - \rho_g) + 1.1\,G_L^{0.6}/d_p^{0.5}$ (for $\rho_s < 300$ kg/m^3 only)	23	

In three phase fluidised beds, plug flow can often be assumed for the gas phase. Appreciable backmixing, however, may occur in the liquid phase especially for beds of fine particles in cocurrent three-phase fluidisation. The backmixing of the liquid and the solid particles in such a bed is primarily caused by the rising motion of coalesced large gas bubbles.

Gas-liquid-solid fluidised beds have found wide applications in chemical, petrochemical and biochemical processing. Most notably, they are being used as three phase reactors in many industrial processes such as in hydrogenation and hydro desulfurisation of petroleum oils, in coal hydrogenation (production of liquid fuels from coal), for the desulfurisation of flue gases (TCAs) and in the biooxidation process of waste water treatment. For many gas-liquid absorption processes, the turbulent contact absorber has been found to be superior to the conventional packed column.

NOMENCLATURE

A_c cross-sectional area of column/bed, m^2
Ar_m modified Archimedes number, dimensionless
D column diameter, m
D_2 equivalent diameter, m
D_o diameter of fluid inlet orifice, m
D_v volumetric diameter of particles, m
D_{vs} volume-surface diameter (or Sauter diameter) of particles, m
E fractional entrainment, (kg solids)/(kg gas)
f_b bed friction factor, dimensionless
f'_b modified bed friction factor (see equation 8.1.14) dimensionless
Fr_{mf} Froude number at incipient fluidisation, dimensionless
g gravitational acceleration, m/s^2
G_f flooding mass velocity of gas, $kg/(m^2.s)$
G_{msf} maximum semifluidisation mass velocity, $kg/(m^2.s)$
G_o superficial mass velocity of fluid through packed bed, $kg/(m^2.s)$
G_{osf} minimum semifluidisation mass velocity, $kg/(m^2.s)$
G_{sf} operating semifluidisation mass velocity, $kg/(m^2.s)$
L height (or length) of packed bed/static bed, m
L_f height of fluidised bed, m
L_{mf} height of bed at incipient fluidisation, m
L_o volume of solids handled per unit cross-sectional area of tower, m
L_{pa} height of packed section of semifluidised bed, m
L_{sf} height of semifluidised bed, m
r_H hydraulic radius, m
Re_b bed Reynolds number, dimensionless

Re_f operating Reynolds number of fluidised bed (see equation 8.2.16), dimensionless

Re_{mf} Reynolds number at incipient fluidisation, dimensionless

Re'_{mf} modified Reynolds number (see equation 8.2.8), dimensionless

Re_T modified Reynolds number defined in equation (8.2.15), dimensionless

s_p specific surface of particles, m^2/m^3

U_i parameter defined in equation (8.2.13), m/s

U_t carry-over velocity or transport velocity, m/s

v average velocity of fluid through packed bed (denoted as U' in Chapter - 5), m/s

v_{gmf} minimum fluidisation velocity in turbulent contact absorber (TCA), m/s

v_{mb} minimum bubbling velocity, m/s

v_{mf} minimum fluidisation velocity, m/s

v_{ms} minimum spouting velocity, m/s

v_{msf} maximum semifluidisation velocity, m/s

v_o superficial velocity of fluid through packed bed (denoted as U_{sup} in Chapter - 5), m/s

v_{of} operating fluid velocity in fluidiser, m/s

v_{osf} minimum semifluidisation velocity, m/s

V_t terminal free settling velocity of particles, m/s

Z_d transport disengagement height (TDH), m

Greek Letters

$(-\Delta P)$ pressure drop across packed bed/fluidised bed, N/m^2

ε void fraction (porosity) of packed bed, dimensionless

ε_f void fraction of fluidised bed, dimensionless

$\varepsilon_g, \varepsilon_l$ gas holdup and liquid holdup respectively in three phase fluidised bed, dimensionless

ε_{mf} void fraction of bed at incipient fluidisation, dimensionless

ε_{pa} void fraction of packed section of semifluidised bed, dimensionless

ψ_s sphericity of particles, dimensionless

μ_f fluid viscosity, kg/(m.s)

μ_L liquid viscosity, kg/(m.s)

ρ_f fluid density, kg/m^3

ρ_g, ρ_L gas density and liquid density respectively, kg/m^3

ρ_s density of solids, kg/m^3

σ interfacial tension, N/m

REFERENCES

1. Kozeny, J., Sitzber. Akad. Wiss. Wien, Math-Naturv. Kl. Abt. IIa, **136**, 271, 1927.
2. Carman, P.C., J.Soc. Chem. Ind., London, **57**, 225 T, 1938.
3. Blake, F.C., Trans. Am. Inst. Chem. Engrs., **14**, 415, 1921-22.
4. Burke, S.P. and Plummer, W.B., Ind. Eng. Chem., **20**, 1196, 1928.
5. Ergun, S., Chem. Eng. Progr., **48**, 89, 1952.
6. Brinkman, H.C. Appl. Sci. Research, **A1**, 27-34, 81-86, 333-346, 1949.
7. Ranz, W.E., Chem. Eng. Progr., **48**, 247, 1952.
8. Payatakes, A.C. et.al, AIChE J., **19** (1), 58, 1973.
9. Rice, W.J. and Wilhelm, R.H., AIChE J., **4**, 423, 1958.
10. Romeo, J.B. and Johanson, L.N., Chem. Eng. Progr. Symp. Series, **58** (38), 28, 1962.
11. Kunii, D. and Levenspiel, O., Fluidisation Engineering, Wiley, New york, 1969.
12. Leva, M., Fluidisation, McGraw Hill, New York, 1959.
13. Wen, C.Y. and Yu, Y.H., AICHE J., **12**, 610, 1966.
14. Richardson, J.F. and Zaki, W.N., Trans. Inst. Chem. Eng., **32**, 35, 1954.
15. Perry, R.H. and Associates, Chemical Engineer's Handbook, 6th edition, McGraw Hill, New York, 1984.
16. Mathur, K.B. and Epstein, N., Spouted Beds, Academic Press, New York, 1974.
17. Murthy, J.S.N. and Roy G.K., Ind. Chem. Engr., **29**, No. 2, 9, 1986.
18. Roy, G.K. and Sarma, K.J.R., Chem. Engg. J., No. 4, 1972 ; Ind. J. Tech., **11**, 237, 1973.
19. Muroyama, K. and Fan, L.S., Fundamentals of Gas-Liquid-Solid Fluidisation, AIChE J., **31** (1), 1-34, 1985.
20. Dakshinamurthy, P., Subramanyam, V. and Rao, J.N., Ind. Eng. Chem. Process Des. Dev., **10**, 322, 1971.
21. Kato, Y. et.al, Powder Technol., **28**, 173, 1981.
22. El-Temtamy, S.A. and Epstein, N., Int. J. Multiphase Flow, **4**, 19, 1978.
23. Vunjak-Novakovic, G.V. and Vukovic, D.V., in *Fluidisation* by Grace, G.R. and Matsen, G.M. (eds.), Plenum Press, New York, 1980.
24. Treybal, R.E., Mass Transfer Operations, Third edition, McGraw Hill, New York, 1981.
25. Narayanan, C.M. and Bhattacharya, B.C., computer Aided Design of Chemical Process Equipment, pp. 185-186 New Central Book Agency, Calcutta, 1992.
26. Chen, N.H., Ind. Eng. Chem., **53**, No. 6, 1961.

9

Flotation

Flotation represents the unit operation in which solids are separated from one another depending on their difference in surface characteristics. Formally confined essentially to ore dressing and mineral beneficiation processes, today flotation is employed in a large number of industrial practices such as separating potassium chloride from sodium chloride, printing ink from reclaimed newspaper pulp as well as separating wheat hulls from kernels. Consider the mixture of two solid materials A and B that is fed to a flotation medium (normally water) and agitated vigorously. The surface properties of A are such that it adsorbs water on its surface and therefore gets surrounded by a thin film of water. Since the surface characteristics of B are different, it selectively adsorbs air on its surface and thus gets either partially or fully covered with air bubbles. Since the density of air is much lower than that of water, the solid-air aggregate (aggregate of B and air) will be much lighter than the solid-water aggregate (aggregate of A and water) and as a result, the former rises to the surface in the form of a froth that can be continuously skimmed off as an overflow, whereas the latter sinks down and is collected as the bottom product or *tailings*. The overflow material is often called the *concentrate* (this terminology originated from ore dressing where in most cases, the ore is floated off in the overflow). Since flotation separates materials by virtue of their difference in surface characteristics, separation can be affected regardless of their densities. Flotation agents are employed to modify the surface properties of materials and for selectively enhancing their flotability.

Flotation thus depends on the relative adsorption or wetting of the solid by the fluid. This, in turn, is controlled by the surface or interfacial energy or interfacial tension, σ. If the solid is easily and completely wetted by the liquid (water), the liquid will exist as a skin between the solid and air and there is no point of contact of the three phases (see Figure 9.1*a*). The contact angle θ is then equal to zero and the solid will not float. If the surface of the solid is not completely wetted, the liquid is forced to recede to an equilibrium position where the surface tensional forces at the three interfaces are in balance (see Figure 9.1*b*). The tangent to the gas-liquid interface at this point forms the contact angle, θ. Thus,

$$\sigma_{SG} = \sigma_{SL} + \sigma_{GL} \cos\theta \qquad \text{...(9.1)}$$

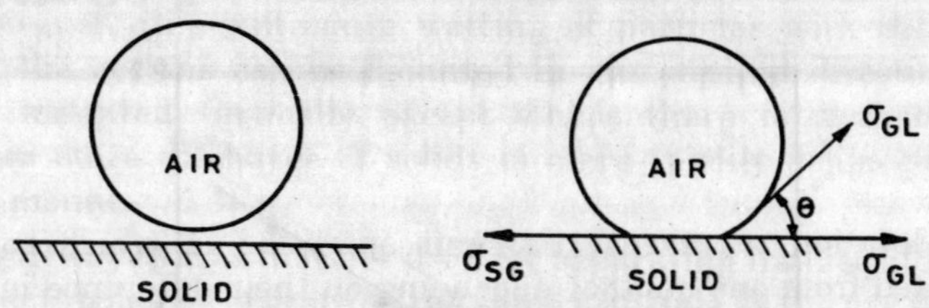

Fig. 9.1 (*a*), (*b*)

The force of gravity and the vigorous agitation provided tend to dislodge the solid particle from the bubble. If the contact angle is small, the liquid will advance over the surface of the solid since the surface forces holding the bubble and solid together will be weak. A large contact angle therefore indicates easy flotability. Also, when a solid particle attaches itself to a bubble, there will be a loss in surface energy ($-\Delta E$) per unit surface area, equal to the loss in surface tension. This loss in energy ($-\Delta E$) is a measure of the wettability of the solid by air and therefore an indication of the flotability. It represents the work required to separate air from a unit surface of solid and is equal to the work of adhesion W_a in magnitude. If the magnitude of this work is large, it means a lot of work is to be expended for detaching the air bubble from the solid surface or for decreasing the air-solid interface. In other words, the air-solid contact is quite strong and therefore the flotability of the solid is large. Mathematically,

$$(-\Delta E) \text{ per unit surface} = \sigma_{SL} + \sigma_{GL} - \sigma_{SG}$$

$$= \sigma_{GL}(1 - \cos\theta), \text{ by incorporating equation (9.1)} \qquad \text{...(9.2)}$$

It can be seen from the above equation that a large value of contact angle θ means cos θ is small and the magnitude of ($-\Delta E$) will be large which indicates, as discussed earlier, a high flotability.

9.1. Flotation Agents

The primary flotation agents are the *collectors and promoters.* These are adsorbed on the solid surface, forming a thin film on the surface of the solid. The solid surface is thus made hydrophobic (water repellant) and therefore will be little wetted by water. The contact angle is increased and so is the flotability. A sharp distinction between a collector and a promoter is difficult. However, promoters generally form a monomolecular layer on the solid surface, whereas collectors form films that are several molecules thick. Petroleum is an example of a true collector. Other collectors are pine oil and cresylic acid.

The most commonly used promoters are Xanthates, aerofloats and thiocarbanilide. The mechanism of the action of promoter is not fully understood. For example, in sodium xanthate, Na SCS OR, the R-group (commonly alkyl or amyl group) is called the water repellant group, the xanthate radical (–SCS–) is called the solidophilic group which causes adhesion to the mineral surface and the –ONa group is the nonwater-repellant group. It is understood that when the compound gets adsorbed on the solid surface, the R-group remains at the outer edge in contact with water. As a result, the entire solid surface tends to be hydrophobic and the flotability of the mineral gets enhanced. It has also been observed that the larger the chain length of the hydrocarbon group (nonpolar group), the larger will be the contact angle and thereby the flotability. The anionic agent may be sodium or potassium and since all xanthates are ionised, it is a matter of cost whether sodium or potassium salts are to be used. The latter, though dearer, is used widely as it is more soluble. For the beneficiation of sulphide ores, xanthates are most popular. However, xanthates are dissociated by strong acids and therefore they are not usually used when the p_H of the medium is less than 7.0. The exception is the flotation of pyrites which is done in a slightly acidic medium. Aerofloats or dithiophosphates are weaker promoters than xanthates and are reaction products of phosphorus pentasulphide with a phenol, cresol, mercaptane, thioalcohol or an amine. The general structure is

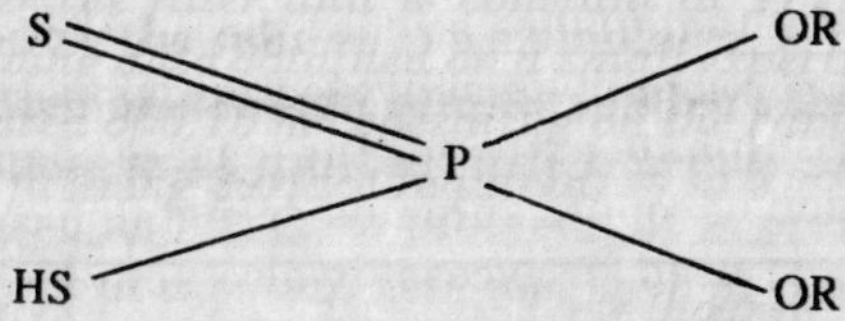

For example, A-239 which is diamyl dithiophosphoric acid neutralised with ammonia and thinned with 10 per cent ethyl or isopropyl alcohol, is used for floating copper. Aerofloats are both promoters as well as frothing agents. This could be disadvantageous on occasions particularly when a close control over the action of both reagents is separately desired. Thiocarbanilide, HSC (NC_6H_5) (NHC_6H_5), is a non-ionic collector or promoter. It is only slightly soluble in water but disperses well. The aerophillic quality is imparted to the solids by smearing action rather than ionisation. Fatty acids and soaps are also used as collectors particularly for the flotation of non-sulphidic ores such as oxides, halides, silicates etc. The basic collecting action seems to be abstraction (reaction and extraction) of the carboxylic group (– COOH) by the nonsulphide mineral. However, since the reaction is very slow, very long conditioning time (as much as 24 hours) is often required. The quantity of collectors or promoters used varies from 0.01 to 0.1 kg/ton of solids treated.

Once the solid surface has been rendered water repellant by the collector or promoter, the stability of bubble attachment to the particle will depend on the efficiency of the frother or frothing agent used. *Frothing agents* are used to prevent coalescence of air bubbles when they reach the surface of water and thereby help maintain a persistent froth. They must be sparingly soluble in water without ionisation and they get adsorbed on the air-water interface, thereby reducing the surface tension of water. Higher alcohols such as hexyl and octyl alcohols are good frothers. But alcohols above octyl are too insoluble in water and those below amyl are too soluble to make good frothing agents. Pine oil and eucalyptus oil are widely used as good frothing agents. Cresylic acid, though a good frother, produces an unsatisfactory brittle froth unless used with a trace of petroleum. About 0.025 to 0.15 kg of frothing agent is used per ton of solids treated. After the removal of froth, it must be broken as completely as possible to recover the mineral present in it. This can be done by a strong jet of water or by passing through a thickener or centrifuge or by subjecting the froth to high frequency sound waves. An excessively stable froth will be difficult to break and is generally undesirable.

Modifying agents are used in selective flotation when more than one material is to be floated off. They are reagents that react with the surface of the solid either by chemical action or by adsorption, thus alter the surface characteristics so that the adsorption of the filming agent (collector or promoter) is activated or depressed. For example, addition of copper sulphate activates the surface of sphalerite, may be due to the formation of copper sulphide or metallic copper itself on its surface. If $CuSO_4$ is used in excess, it also activates pyrite. Sodium cyanide is a depressant to pyrite when it is present with galena and zinc sulfate is depressant to sphalerite. Dichromates in general are depressants to galena. Sodium sulphide or sulfuric acid is used to activate pyrite that has been depressed in a previous flotation. Another popular types of modifying agents are the *p_H controllers.* There exists a critical p_H of the medium corresponding to any given mineral below which only the mineral will float when a specific amount of a collector or promoter is used. Typical values of critical p_H for different materials with different promoters are given below :

Table 9.1

Collector / promoter and concentration	*Critical p_H*		
	Sphalerite	*Galena*	*Pyrite*
Potassium ethyl xanthate (25 mg/litre)	—	10.4	10.5
Sodium diethyl dithiocarbonate (26.7 mg/litre)	6.2	13.0	10.5
Potassium isoamyl xanthate (31.6 mg/litre)	5.5	12.1	12.3
Potassium diamyl dithiocarbonate (42.3 mg/litre)	10.4	13.0	12.8

Alkalies like soda ash, caustic soda and hydrated lime are used for raising the p_H of the medium. If the p_H of the medium is maintained in between the critical p_H values of two materials, then one of them will float and the other will not. Thus the separation can be affected.

Dispersing agents such as sodium silicate, sodium metaphosphate, citric acid and soluble starches are used to break up agglomerations of mineral and gangue. In such cases, the mineral gets coated with a slime of silicates and thus becomes unfloatable.

9.2. Flotation Equipment

Flotation cells are tanks, normally rectangular or cylindrical in cross-section, provided with a feed inlet at one end, an overflow for froth removal and a discharge for tailings at the opposite end. They should also have a provision for introducing air for froth formation and agitation. They can be broadly classified as pneumatic cells and mechanical cells. Pneumatic cells (Callow-MacIntosh cells, "air-lift" cells etc.) use compressed air for agitation. They provide relatively mild agitation and produce a clean froth essentially free from gangue. However, they require around 50 per cent more contact time than mechanical cells and the feed should be fully conditioned with flotation agents before charging to the cells. Mechanical cells (Denver cells, Fagergren flotation machine etc.) incorporate a mechanical agitator that draws in air and beats into the pulp. Since violent agitation is provided in such cells, more thorough flotation is obtained, but some gangue also could escape in the froth. The quality of the floated material will be therefore poorer (though the yield will be almost 100 per cent) than that obtained from pneumatic cells. Occasionally, auxiliary air is supplied to mechanical cells under moderate pressure to facilitate the flotation process. Mechanical cells have greater capacity per unit volume and part of the conditioning of the pulp is achieved in the cells themselves. As many as six flotation machines may be combined into a single unit having a common tank separated by suitable partition plates and a discharge box is provided at the end of the string. The froth is removed from each unit by a rotating skimmer.

The feed to a flotation unit is finely ground in advance in a ball mill or any other fine grinding equipment. This is to increase the surface area per unit volume of the particles. Also, coarse particles are difficult to be kept in suspension in the flotation medium. Usually, a ball mill operating in closed circuit with a classifying screen or a hydraulic classifier is used. The finely ground material is then coated with the properly chosen flotation agents in the conditioning tank. Some conditioning may be done in the ball mill itself and as stated earlier, if mechanical cells are used, they help condition the pulp and thereby provide greater capacity to the conditioner. The well-conditioned feed is then given to the first set of flotation cells called the *rougher*. If the rougher concentrate (the floated material) contains a good amount of the undesired constituent (the constituent expected in the tailings), then it is further fed to another set of flotation cells called the *cleaner*. The cleaner concentrate is usually collected as the final concentrate. The tailings from cleaner are fed back to the rougher. If the rougher tailings contain a considerable proportion of the desired constituent (that is being floated off), then it is further processed in the *scavenger*. The scavenger tailings are usually collected as the final tailings and the concentrate from the scavenger is recycled back to the rougher. A complete flotation unit therefore consists of a closed circuit grinding unit, the conditioner, rougher, cleaner and the scavenger. If the feed mixture contains a large number of constituents, then a number of such units can be used in series so that in each unit one particular constituent is floated off. This is called *selective flotation* or *preferential flotation*. The selective flotation of galena, pyrite and sphalerite from silica is illustrated in Figure (9.2). The flotation agents used are xanthate (promoter), pine oil (frother and collector), copper sulphate (activator to sphalerite and if in excess to pyrite also), sodium cyanide (depressant to pyrite), zinc sulphate (depressant to sphalerite), lime (p_H controller). The critical p_H for pyrite is taken as 10.5 and that for sphalerite 14.0. The feed to the first flotation unit is conditioned with sodium cyanide and zinc sulphate apart from the promoter (xanthate) and the frother (pine oil) to depress pyrite and sphalerite so that only galena is floated off in this unit. In the second flotation unit, copper sulphate is added to activate sphalerite that has been depressed in the previous flotation and also lime to raise the p_H to about 12.0. Since this value of p_H is less than the critical p_H of

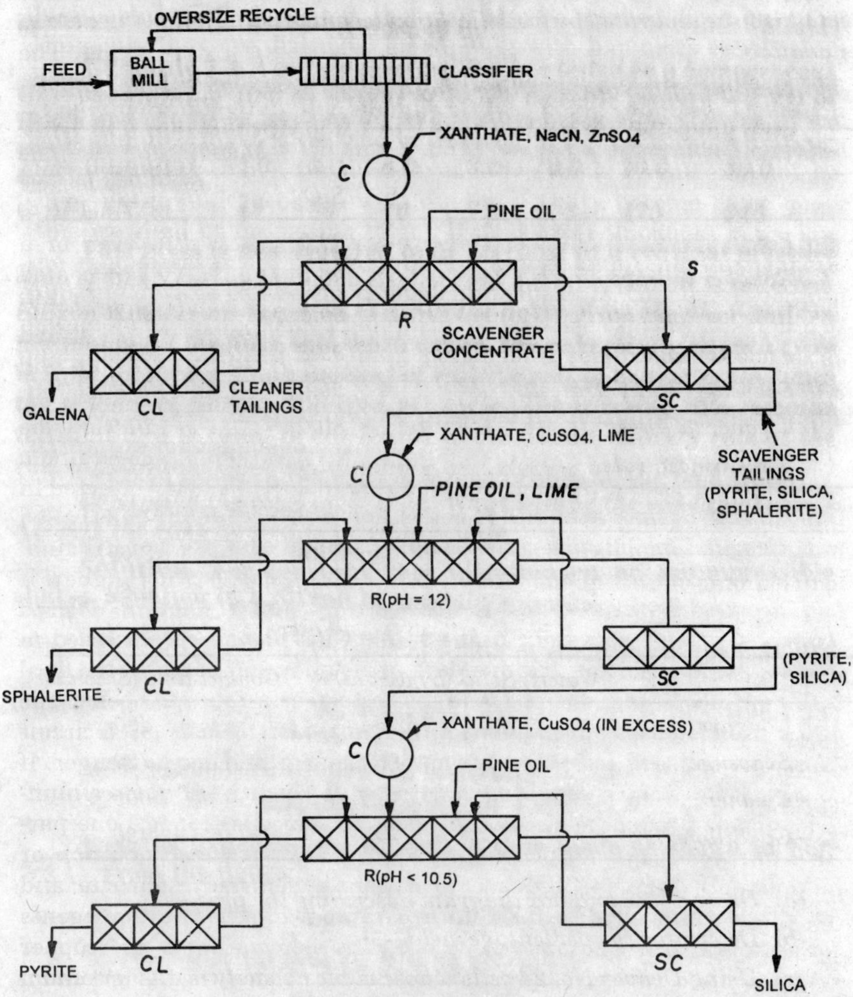

Fig. 9.2
Selective flotation of galena, sphalerite and pyrite from silica. C = conditioner, R = rougher, CL = cleaner, SC = Scavenger.

sphalerite but more than that of pyrite, only sphalerite gets floated off. Thus, the scavenger tailings from this unit will contain only pyrite and silica. This is now conditioned with excess of copper sulphate to activate pyrite and the p_H is lowered to a value less than 10.5. As a result, pyrite gets floated off in the third unit and silica is collected as the final tailings.

Example 9.1. *A mixture of copper sulphide (CuS) and silica (SiO_2) is to be separated by froth flotation technique. The following data is available :*

Net feed of the ore = 10^6 kg / day

	Mass%	
	SiO_2	*CuS*
Feed	*98.0*	*2.0*
Rougher tailings	*99.0*	*1.0*
Rougher concentrate	*60.0*	*40.0*
Final tailings	*99.6*	*0.40*
Scavenger concentrate	*50.0*	*50.0*
Cleaner tailings	*80.0*	*20.0*
Final concentrate	*1.0*	*99.0*

	Specific gravity
SiO_2	*2.65*
CuS	*4.60*
Water	*1.00*

	Water : Solid (by weight)	*Contact time (Seconds)*
Rougher	*2 : 1*	*480*
Scavenger	*4 : 1*	*720*
Cleaner	*6 : 1*	*600*
Conditioner	*—*	*480*

(a) *Draw a line and box diagram describing the process.*

(b) *Determine the percentage yield.*

(c) *Using Denver No. 24 cells whose cubic capacity is 1.45 m^3 and whose power consumption is 3.13 kW per cell, compute the capacity (tank volume) and number of flotation cells in each unit (rougher, scavenger, cleaner) and the power consumption. What should be the capacity of the conditioner ?*

Solution. The process is sketched in Figure (9.1.1). Let us now compute the different mass streams by material balance. An overall material balance for the entire system gives,

$$a = e + g \qquad ...(i)$$

A CuS balance for the entire system yields,

$$ax_a = ex_e + gx_g \qquad ...(ii)$$

where x stands for the mass fraction of CuS in any individual stream.

Since it is given that $a = 10^6$ kg/day and $x_a = 0.02$, $x_e = 0.99$ and $x_g = 0.004$, equations (i) and (ii) can be solved for e and g.

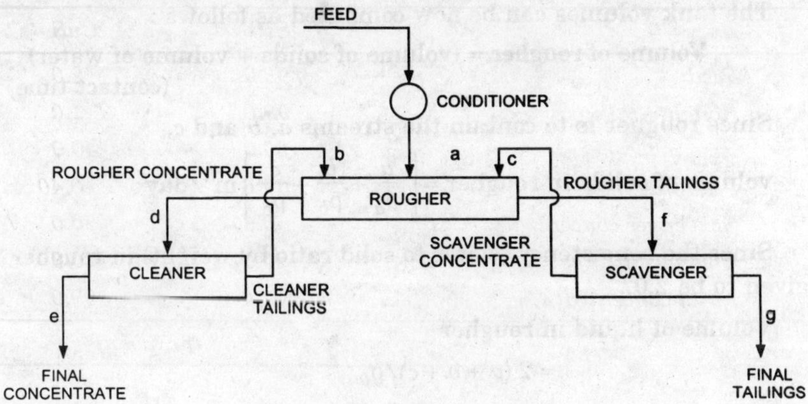

Fig. 9.1.1

Thus, $$e = 16{,}227.2 \text{ kg/day}$$

$$g = 9{,}83{,}772.8 \text{ kg/day}$$

Now, making a mass balance for scavenger alone we get,

overall balance : $f = c + g$ ...(iii)

CuS balance : $fx_f = cx_c + gx_g$ ...(iv)

Since $g = 9{,}83{,}772.8$ kg/day and $x_f = 0.01$, $x_c = 0.50$, $x_g = 0.004$, we can solve the above two equations for c and f. Thus,

$$c = 12{,}046.2 \text{ kg/day}$$

$$f = 9{,}95{,}819.0 \text{ kg/day}$$

Similarly, a mass balance for cleaner alone gives,

$$d = e + b \qquad ...(v)$$

$$dx_d = ex_e + bx_b \qquad ...(vi)$$

We know $e = 16{,}227.2$ kg/day, $x_d = 0.40$, $x_e = 0.99$, $x_b = 0.20$.

Therefore,

$$d = 64{,}097.4 \text{ kg/day}$$

$$b = 47{,}870.2 \text{ kg/day}$$

The percentage yield is given by,

$$= \frac{ex_e}{ax_a} \times 100$$

$$= \frac{16{,}227.2\ (0.99)}{10^6\ (0.02)}\ (100)$$

$$= 80.33\%$$

The tank volumes can be now computed as follows :

Volume of rougher = (volume of solids + volume of water) (contact time)

Since rougher is to contain the streams a, b and c,

$$\text{volume of solids in rougher} = \left[\frac{a}{\rho_a} + \frac{b}{\rho_b} + \frac{c}{\rho_c}\right] \text{m}^3\text{/day}$$

Since the consistency (water to solid ratio by weight) in rougher is given to be 2.0,

Volume of liquid in rougher

$$= 2\ (a + b + c)/\rho_w,$$

where ρ_w = density of water, kg/m³.

Therefore, volume of rougher

$$= \left[\frac{a}{\rho_a} + \frac{b}{\rho_b} + \frac{c}{\rho_c} + \frac{2\ (a + b + c)}{\rho_w}\right] \frac{(480)}{(3600)\ (24)}$$

$$= \left[\frac{10^6}{\rho_a} + \frac{47{,}870.2}{\rho_b} + \frac{12{,}046.2}{\rho_c} + \frac{21{,}19{,}832.8}{1000}\right] \times \left[\frac{(480)}{(3600)\ (24)}\right] \text{m}^3 \quad ...(vii)$$

The bulk densities of streams a, b, c can be computed as follows :

Since densities of CuS and SiO_2 are 4600 and 2650 kg/m³ respectively,

$$\rho_a = \frac{a}{\left(\dfrac{ax_a}{4600}\right) + \dfrac{a\ (1 - x_a)}{(2650)}} = \frac{1}{\dfrac{x_a}{4600} + \dfrac{(1 - x_a)}{2650}}$$

$$= \frac{1}{\frac{0.02}{4600} + \frac{0.98}{2650}} = 2672.66 \text{ kg/m}^3$$

Similarly, $\rho_b = \dfrac{1}{(x_b/4600) + (1 - x_b)/2650}$

$= 2895.49 \text{ kg/m}^3$

and $\rho_c = 3362.76 \text{ kg/m}^3$

Substituting these values of ρ_a, ρ_b, ρ_c in equation (*vii*), we get,

Volume of rougher = 14.0 m^3

Since the cubic capacity of each Denver cell is 1.45 m^3,

Number of cells for rougher = $(14.0/1.45) \cong 10$

Therefore, 10 cells are required in rougher.

Similarly, since scavenger is to contain only the stream f and since the consistency is 4.0 and contact time 720 seconds in scavenger,

Volume of scavenger

$$= [(f/\rho_f) + (4f/\rho_w)] \frac{(720)}{(3600)(24)}$$

where f = 9,95,819.0 kg/day, ρ_w = 1000 kg/m^3. The bulk density ρ_f is calculated in the same way as ρ_a, ρ_b and ρ_c :

$$\rho_f = \frac{1}{(x_f/4600) + (1 - x_f)/2650} = 2661.28 \text{ kg/m}^3$$

Thus, volume of scavenger = 36.3 m^3

Number of cells = $(36.3/1.45) \cong 25$

In the same way,

$$\text{Volume of cleaner} = [(d/\rho_d) + (6d/\rho_w)] \frac{(600)}{(3600)(24)} \text{ m}^3$$

where $\rho_d = \dfrac{1}{(x_d/4600) + (1 - x_d)/2650} = 3191.10 \text{ kg/m}^3$

d = 64,097.4 kg/day

ρ_w = 1000 kg/m^3

Thus, volume of cleaner = 2.8 m^3

Number of cells required = $(2.8/1.45) \cong 2$.

Thus, total number Denver cells to be used = (10 + 25 + 2) = 37

Total power consumption = (37 × 3.13) = **115.8 kW**

Since the contact time in conditioner is 480 seconds,

Capacity of conditioner

$$= (a/\rho_a)\left(\frac{480}{3600 \times 24}\right) \text{m}^3$$

$$= \frac{10^6\,(480)}{(2672.66)\,(3600)\,(24)} = 2.08 \text{ m}^3$$

NOMENCLATURE

x	mass fraction
W_a	work of adhesion, J
θ	contact angle, degrees
ρ_a to ρ_f	bulk density of solid fractions, kg/m^3
ρ_w	density of water (flotation medium), kg/m^3
σ_{SL}, σ_{SG}, σ_{GL}	interfacial tension at solid-liquid, gas-solid and gas-liquid interface respectively, N/m.

REFERENCES

1. Gaudin, A.M., Flotation, McGraw-Hill, New York, 1932.
2. Brown, G.G. and Associates, Unit Operations, Wiley, New York, 1950.
3. Perry, J.H. (ed.), Chemical Engineers' Handbook, 5th ed., 21-71, McGraw-Hill, New York, 1973.

10

Handling and Transport of Solids

10.1. Storage of Solids

Solids like coal, sulphur, sand and gravel are usually stored outdoors in open piles. The maximum height at which the solids can be piled depends on the angle of repose α_r, of the material. It is the maximum slope measured from the horizontal at which a heap of loose solids will stand without sliding. If the solid mass were truly homogeneous, then α_r will be equal to the angle of internal friction, α. In practice however, $\alpha_r < \alpha$. The value of α_r is about 27° for anthracite coal, 31° for fine sand, 35° for bituminous coal, 17° for wet clay and 39 to 48 degrees for gravel. Outdoor storage in open piles is usually restricted to coarse, water-insoluble materials. Rock salt however is often stored outdoor in shallow basins that collect the rainwater. A part of the salt gets dissolved in this water and the resultant brine is pumped frequently to the neighbouring process units.

Solids are also stored indoors in storage bins or silos or bunkers. They are usually made of metal, reinforced concrete or wood. Bins for abrasive materials are lined with replaceable steel plates or special wear-resistant glass. Heat-insulated or heated bins are employed in cases when the delivered materials are wet or frozen. Every storage bin usually has two sections such as a rectangular, prismatic or cylindrical upper section and a pyramidal or conical lower section (narrowing to the discharge opening). Bins are charged through the open top or charging holes in the top cover and discharged usually through openings in the bottom or bottom portion of side walls. The shape of a storage bin should be such that it ensures almost complete loading and unloading without the formation of what are called the dead zones.

These are zones where the material is retained and cannot flow by gravity to the discharge opening. This is mostly due to an insufficient slope of the side walls along which the material is directed to the discharge. Also, the bin shape should be such that it prevents bridging of the material inside the bin which otherwise disturbs or even blocks the discharge.

It will be therefore interesting to estimate the total pressure exerted by a given amount of stored solids on the floor of a storage bin. There will be normally friction between the bin wall and the solids and due to the interlocking of the particles, the effect of this friction will be felt throughout the stored mass. This frictional force at the wall tends to offset the weight of the solids and as a result, the pressure exerted by the mass on the bin floor is reduced. In the extreme case however, this force can cause the material to arch or bridge so that it will not discharge even if the material below is removed. Let us consider a cylindrical bin of diameter D which is filled upto a height H with solids of bulk density ρ_s. Any differential layer dh of solids inside the bin is acted upon by two forces such as the force of gravity dF_g and the vertical component of the force of friction dF_f. Thus, a force balance on the differential layer yields,

$$dF_v = dF_g - dF_f \qquad \text{...(10.1.1)}$$

But $\quad dF_f = \mu' (p_L \pi D dh)$

where p_L is the lateral pressure and μ' is the coefficient of friction at the bin wall. We can therefore rewrite equation (10.1.1) as,

$$\left(\frac{\pi D^2}{4}\right) dp_v = \left(\frac{\pi D^2}{4}\right) dh\, \rho_s g - \mu' p_L \pi D\, dh \qquad \text{...(10.1.2)}$$

The ratio (p_L/p_v) is designated as K' which is a constant (sometimes called the coefficient of flowability of the material) that depends on the shape and interlocking tendencies of the particles, the degree of packing and the stickiness of particle surface. For cohesive materials like wet clay, it is almost equal to zero. For free flowing materials, its value varies from 0.3 to 0.6 K' is related to the angle of internal friction α of the material as

$$K' = (1 - \sin \alpha)/(1 + \sin \alpha) \qquad \text{...(10.1.3)}$$

Equation (10.1.2) can be therefore rearranged as,

$$\int_0^H dh = \int_0^{p_b} \frac{D\, dp_v}{(D \rho_s g - 4 \mu' K' p_v)} \qquad \text{...(10.1.4)}$$

where p_b is the vertical pressure on the bin floor.

On integration and rearrangement, we get,

$$p_b = (\rho_s\, g/K_b)\,(1 - e^{-K_b H}) \qquad ...(10.1.5)$$

where $K_b = (4K'\,\mu'/D)$.

The above equation is called the *Janssen equation.* Clearly, when (H/D) is very large, $p_b \cong (\rho_s\, g/K_b)$. This means, once the holdup of solids is very large (H more than around $3D$), further addition of solids to the bin will not materially change the total pressure on the bin floor. This is in contrast with what occurs when a liquid of same density (that is, $\rho_L = \rho_s$) is stored, in which case the pressure on the bin floor will increase proportionally with the liquid height since,

$$(p_b)_{liquid} = H\,\rho_L g = H\,\rho_s\, g \qquad ...(10.1.6)$$

The above two equations (10.1.5) and (10.1.6) also show that for a given holdup H, the solids will exert less pressure on the bin floor than a liquid of same density.

Since $(p_L/p_v) = K'$ and K' is less than 1.0, the lateral pressure on the bin wall will be less than the vertical pressure at the same cross-section. Therefore, a bottom discharge of solids is always preferred over discharge through a side outlet. As the bottom discharge gate is opened, only the vertical column of solids just above the discharge opening comes into motion and as a result, a cone or a conical depression gets formed on the surface of the material and as the material flows out, the particles pour down along the sides of this cone. If the discharge opening is arranged near a vertical wall of the bin, then the material will slide along that wall and the cone will be unsymmetrical. A typical discharge pattern of solids through a central discharge opening is sketched in Figure (10.1). First the portion (a) that has the shape of a cone or wedge flows out, after that solids in the elliptical portion (b) above (a) fall out and finally the portions (c) and (d) come into motion so that at the end of discharge, solids in areas (e_1) and (e_2) remain behind in the bin forming a conical "dead zone". Since the material slides laterally into the central column at an angle approximately equal to the angle of internal friction α of the solids, the slope of the bottom section of the bin must be at least equal to α so that formation of such dead zones could be avoided. Moreover, as stated earlier, as the material pours out from the discharge opening, the remaining material in the bin may often form a bridge in the form of a dome or arch. This effect is common with materials containing large lumps but can also occur with small-size, lumpy materials having a high moisture content. The bridge is compressed transversely by the weight of the material above it and is supported at the ends by the bin walls. As a result, it does not fall even when the material below has been discharged. Bridging in bins can be eliminated by hand tools such as pokers or by mechanical means such as by attaching vibrators to the bin walls for activating the outflow of solids. Alternately, compressed air may be blown in intermittently through air tuyeres arranged slightly below the level of probable bridging. This is particularly suitable with pulverised materials.

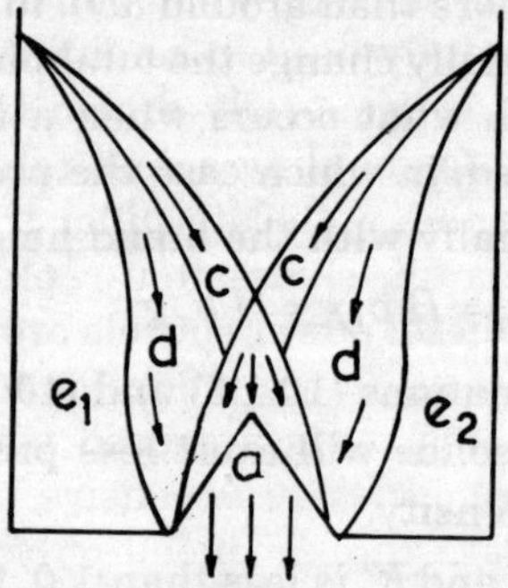

Fig. 10.1. Solid discharge from the central bottom outlet of a storage bin.

The size of the discharge opening should be so chosen that it is sufficient to ensure the required throughput capacity. If it is too small, it gets clogged quickly. On the other hand, the opening should not be excessively large since then the discharge rate will be difficult to control. Also, discharge openings will require heavy gates which might be difficult to operate. For lumpy, bulk materials, the size of a rectangular discharge opening should not necessarily be less than 4.0 to 5.5 times the average size of the lump.

10.2. Transport of Solids (In-plant Transport)

For in-plant transport of solids (transport within the chemical plant), the simplest method shall be to utilise unassisted manpower, that is to carry the load on one's own shoulders. However, this is applicable only to where manpower is cheap and easily available and also to short distance transport. Assisted manpower utilising hand trucks, trolleys or carts is recommended when the radius of transport is larger (say, 40 to 70 m). This can be applied for lifting loads weighing more than 50 to 75 kg as well, where mechanical devices like chain falls, pulley blocks, hand-power hoists and jacks (all of them operating on the lever principle) could be employed to supplement the manual labour. Portable power driven machines can be employed for longer distances and larger capacities. Electric trucks, either the general purpose truck with fixed platform or the lift-platform truck with a platform that can be elevated by power (used mainly for handling material on skids) or the special types such as the crane truck, dump body truck, tiering or high-lift trucks etc. are examples. They are operated by storage batteries and can run continuously without recharging or battery substitution for periods ranging from 8 to 24 hours. They carry solids in batches of 2,000 to 3,000 kg and have speeds of 8 to 15 km/hr. For longer hauls outdoors, gasoline-powered industrial trucks are preferred over electric trucks since they can run at speeds of 25 to 30 km/hour. Trailers are frequently used in conjunction with industrial trucks. The larger trailers are generally drawn by tractors. Rubber tired tractors are employed for hauling across relatively smooth and paved surfaces whereas tractors with caterpillar treads are used over rough terrain. In rough terrain, skids often replace trailers. Power shovels such as gasoline or diesel power shovels are widely used either in conjunction with commercial dump trucks or for loading railroad cars directly. Electric power shovels are used where cheap electric power is available. Power shovels are expensive and require skilled operators. They are therefore recommended only when large quantities of bulk materials are being handled at changing locations. They operate on a turntable and have a boom which may be raised or lowered. The material to be handled is picked up by a thrust or drag motion, elevated with the boom, and rotated to the point of discharge by the turntable. Discharge is by gravity and occurs when the scoop is inverted or a gate at the back of the scoop is opened. Often, these shovels are provided with capterpillar treads and can be moved from place to place under their own power. Gantry or bridge cranes driven electrically are used for loading and unloading railroad cars or ships. They consist of two supporting towers with a bridge in between. A trolley with a grab bucket or lift moves back and forth across the bridge. The entire crane is on wheels and can be moved along a track. The operator rides in a cab that is situated on one of the towers or in the trolley itself. Gravity feed through vertical chutes can be used economically, particularly when the material has to pass through a series of operations. In such cases, the material is first brought to the top of the building or structure by a conveyor or elevator and then fed downwards by gravity, operation by operation, until removed as product at the bottom. The only power requirement will be that for lifting the solids to the required elevation. The chutes may be straight or spiral. The inclination of the chute or slide with horizontal must be sufficient to overcome the frictional resistance. The coefficient of friction varies with different materials but is about 0.3 to 0.6 for most dry solids on steel slides. Material often becomes wedged between the sides of the chute creating additional resistance and therefore a slope of 45° or steeper is usually recommended for the slide. Electromagnetic vibrators that give the slide vibrations in the direction of flow of solids may be incorporated to facilitate free discharge.

10.3. Transport of Solids by Mechanical Conveyors

For long distance transport of large tonnages of solids, bulk transport by rail, road or by ships (if the locations are conveniently connected by waterways) is used. However, when the distance covered is very large (more than 600 to 1,000 km), rail or road transport often becomes uneconomical. In such cases, a continuous mode of transport such as hydraulic or pneumatic transport or more commonly called the slurry transportation, is required to be employed. We shall discuss this later.

Mechanical conveyors are used both for short distance as well as long distance transport of solids. For transporting solids at the rates of 12,500 to 60,000 kg/hour within 10-20 km distances, mechanical conveyors have been found to be more economical than transport by rail or road vehicles. The popular types of conveyors are screw conveyors, flight conveyors, belt conveyors, apron conveyors and bucket conveyors and elevators. Among them, the screw and flight conveyors are often called scrapers since they push the material along an endless trough or tube whereas belt, apron and bucket conveyors are called carriers since the load is carried on belts, aprons, or in buckets.

10.3.1. Screw Conveyors

Screw conveyors are widely used for transporting pulverised and granular solids such as grain, asphalt, crushed coal, ashes, gravel and sand to relatively short distances (usually upto 40 m horizontally and 30 m vertically). They are less recommended for handling sticky, slumping and abrasive materials. Screw conveyors are normally horizontal or slightly inclined (upto around 20°). Vertical screw conveyors and screw pipes are used for special purposes. The advantages of screw conveyors lie in the simple design, easy maintenance, compactness requiring little headroom, convenient intermediate unloading and tightness of conveying space which is of special value when dusty, hot or odourous materials are handled. Their drawbacks are high unit power consumption, substantial rubbing and crushing of the conveyed material, high wear on the screw and the trough and a high sensitivity to overloads which can lead to load accumulation in the trough, especially at the bearings.

The horizontal or slightly inclined screw conveyor consists of an screw arranged on a shaft supported on bearings, a trough with a semicylindrical bottom arranged coaxially with the screw and a drive (electric motor and reducer gear) to rotate the shaft with the screw. The material to be conveyed is fed into the trough and as the screw rotates, the material gets propelled along the shaft in the same way as a nut would move on a threaded rod if it is prevented from rotating together with the rod. Rotation of the material together with the screw is prevented by its own weight as well as the friction on the trough walls. The material is unloaded at the discharge end through openings provided with gates.

The conveyor screw may be right handed or left handed with one or more leads. The screw surface may be continuous, band-like or bladed (see Figure 10.2). Continuous screws are used for conveying dry, granular and pulverised solids whereas discontinuous screws are effective with slumping materials. Also, the band-like and bladed screws are particularly suitable when thorough intermixing of the material during conveying is preferred. The screw shaft, either solid or tubular, is supported by end bearings. Intermediate bearings can also be used, but since they can interrupt the helix, their diameter and length should be chosen as small as possible. The throughput capacity Q (kg/s) of an screw conveyor depends on the screw diameter d, the lead of the screw t and the speed of rotation n (rpm). Thus,

$$Q = C_\beta\,(\pi d^2/4)\,t\,(n/60)\,\rho_s\,C_{fs} \qquad ...(10.3.1)$$

where ρ_s = density of the material conveyed, kg/m^3

C_β is a correction factor [may be called angle factor or inclination factor] that depends on the angle of inclination β of the conveyor as given below :

β (degrees) :	0	5	10	15	20
C_β :	1.0	0.9	0.8	0.7	0.6

The coefficient C_{fs} is called the filling coefficient (or the coefficient of filling of screw cross-section) and its value depends on the type of material conveyed (see Table 10.1).

It can be seen that the correction factor C_β decreases with increase in the value of β. That is, the throughput capacity decreases with increase in the angle of inclination of the conveyor. This is particularly true when the screw shaft is supported by intermediate bearings. If the material is free flowing and easily movable, then the lead of the screw t is taken equal to its diameter d. However, for poorly moving materials, a smaller screw lead ($t = 0.8\,d$) is chosen or an screw with two or three leads is employed. The speed of rotation n of the screw employed depends on the type of conveyed material and the screw diameter. Its maximum permissible value n_{max} (in rpm) can be determined from the empirical relation,

$$n_{max} = C'/\sqrt{d} \qquad ...(10.3.2)$$

where the coefficient C' depends on the type of material conveyed (see Table 10.1). It can be seen from Table (10.1) that the magnitude of C' is lower for heavier and more abrasive materials. The operating speed of the screw should be chosen in such a way that it ensures smooth flow of the material without overflowing over the shaft. The screw diameter d should be fixed such that it satisfies equation (10.3.1) as well as (10.3.2). It should also be rounded off to any of the standard screw sizes available such as 0.1, 0.125, 0.16, 0.2, 0.25, 0.32, 0.4, 0.5, 0.63 or 0.8 m. For conveying of lumpy loads, if the lumps are of uniform size, the screw diameter should not be less than 10-12 times the average size of the lump. If the material is ungraded, then d should not be chosen less than 4-6 times the size of the largest lump present.

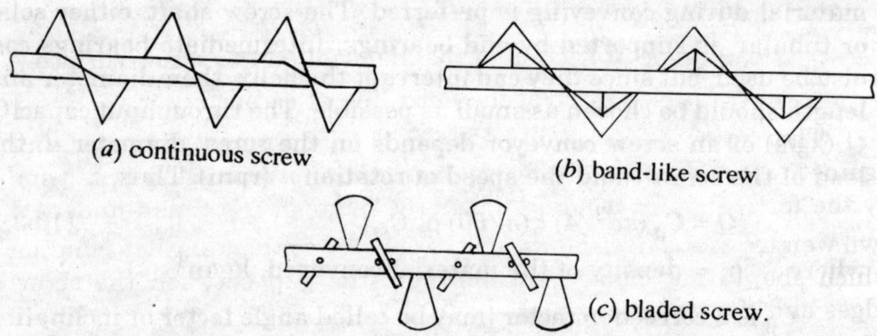

(*a*) continuous screw (*b*) band-like screw (*c*) bladed screw.

Fig. 10.2. Types of screws for screw conveyors :

The total resistance to the motion of the material in a screw conveyor is chiefly made up of the friction of the load on the trough and the screw surface, resistances in the intermediate and end bearings (including the thrust bearing) and the resistance to the ascending motion. These resistances can be more or less readily calculated, once the coefficients of friction are known. However, there are some additional resistances that can hardly be calculated such as the resistance due to accumulation of material in the intermediate bearings, due to friction of the screw edges on the material drawn into the gap between them and the trough and due to intermixing of the material. Therefore, for estimating the power consumption of the conveyor motor, a total coefficient of resistance K_{ts} (that is experimentally determined) is employed, which depends mainly on the properties of the conveyed material (see Table 10.1). Thus, the power consumption P (in watts) is given by,

$$P = Q\,(H + LK_{ts})\,g \qquad ...(10.3.3)$$

where L = horizontal length over which the material is conveyed, m

H = vertical displacement of the material, m

Q = throughput capacity of the conveyor, kg/s (from equation 10.3.1)

The torque on the screw shaft will be therefore,

$$M = P\eta/(2\pi n/60) \quad ...(10.3.4)$$

where η = mechanical efficiency of the drive.

The maximum longitudinal force acting on the screw will be,

$$F_m = \frac{M}{r \tan(\theta + \alpha)} \quad ...(10.3.5)$$

where r = radius of application of the force, m

$\cong$ (0.7 to 0.8) times $(d/2)$

α = angle of friction of the material on the screw surface

θ = angle of rise of the helix line at radius r

The screw shaft should therefore be designed for resistance against torsion by the torque M, longitudinal compression or tension by the force F_m and bending under the moment $(F_m r)$ and under its own weight. The screw should also be checked for bending deformation which should not change substantially the gap between the screw edges and the trough.

Table 10.1

Type of material, handled	C_{fs}	C'	K_{ts}
Light, non-abrasive material (grains, flour, saw dust etc.)	0.4	65.0	1.2
Light, slightly abrasive materials (pulverised coal, peat, chalk, soda, asbestos)	0.32	50.0	1.6
Heavy, less abrasive materials (lumpy coal, dry clay, salt)	0.25	45.0	2.5
Heavy, abrasive material (Ash, cement, sand, wet clay, crushed ore, slag)	0.125	30.0	4.0

Vertical screw conveyors that are used for special purposes have a limited throughput capacity and are hardly used for elevating materials to a height more than 15 *m*. As compared with bucket elevators, they have smaller dimensions and permit more convenient unloading in any direction, but they require an appreciably higher power of the drive. The conveyor consists of a vertical shaft with a continuous helix that is suspended from a thrust bearing and rotates inside a cylindrical casing. The bottom portion of the vertical screw which receives the feed material, is made with a varying diameter (decreasing upwards) or with a smaller screw lead. The material is fed by a short horizontal screw feeder to the vertical screw. The centrifugal forces developed press the solids to the cylindrical wall of the conveyor casing. However, the particles lag somewhat behind the motion of the helix and rotate at a lower angular velocity and as a result, they are moved upwards along the screw axis. Thus, in contrast to a horizontal screw conveyor whose speed of rotation is limited by the maximum value n_{max}, the speed of a vertical screw must always be larger than the critical speed which is the minimum speed required to move the material upwards along the screw. An expression for this critical speed can be derived by making a force balance. If θ is the helix angle of the screw, component of force of gravity acting downwards along the helix surface = $mg \sin \theta$.

Force of friction of the particle on the helix surface = $(mg \cos \theta)\mu'$, where μ' is the coefficient of friction and m is the mass of the particle.

Centrifugal force on the particle $= mv^2/R$

$$= (2mv^2/d)$$

where d is the screw diameter.

Force of friction of the particle on the wall of the cylindrical casing

$$= (2mv^2/d)\,\mu_c'$$

where μ_c' is the coefficient of friction of the particle on the wall of the casing. The component of the above force that acts on the helix surface is $(2mv^2/d)\,\mu_c' \cos \theta$ and the corresponding force of friction on the helix surface is $\mu'\,(2mv^2/d)\,\mu_c' \sin \theta$. When $v = v_c$ (critical velocity), the particle has no axial motion but rotates together with the screw. Therefore, making a force balance we get,

$$mg \sin \theta + (mg \cos \theta)\mu' + (2mv_c^2/d)\mu'\,\mu_c' \sin \theta - (2mv_c^2/d)\mu_c' \cos \theta = 0$$

or

$$v_c = \left[\frac{gd\,(\sin \theta + \mu' \cos \theta)}{2\mu_c'\,(\cos \theta - \mu' \sin \theta)}\right]^{1/2}$$

$$= \left[\frac{gd}{2\mu_c'} \tan(\theta + \alpha)\right]^{1/2} \quad \text{...(10.3.6)}$$

where $\alpha = \tan^{-1} \mu'$ = angle of friction of the particle on the helix surface.

Since $v_c = (\pi d n_c/60)$, the critical rpm will be,

$$n_c = \frac{60}{\pi}\left[\frac{g \tan(\theta + \alpha)}{2\mu_c' d}\right]^{1/2} \quad ...(10.3.7)$$

At rotational speeds $n > n_c$, the solid particles will be conveyed upwards along the helix surface.

Example 10.1. *The following data are given for a horizontal screw conveyor for handling moulding sand in a foundry :*

Bulk density of material	*= 1600 kg/m³*
Diameter of screw	*= 0.4 m*
Screw pitch	*= 0.32 m*
Conveying length	*= 15 m*
Filling coefficient	*= 0.125*
Speed of screw shaft	*= 40 rpm*
Reducer efficiency	*= 0.77*
Total coefficient of resistance	*= 4.0*

Determine (a) the rate of conveying of the material in kg/hour and (b) the motor power.

Solution. The rate of conveying of the material can be computed from equation (10.3.1) :

$$Q = C_\beta (\pi d^2/4)\, t\, (n/60)\, \rho_s\, C_{fs} \quad ...(i)$$

Given that,

d = screw diameter = 0.4 m

t = 0.32 m

n = 40 rpm

ρ_s = 1600 kg/m^3

C_{fs} = 0.125

Since the conveyor is horizontal, $C_\beta = 1.0$.

Substituting these values in (*i*), we get,

$$Q = 5.361 \text{ kg/s} = 19{,}300 \text{ kg/hr}$$

The power consumption P is now computed from equation (10.3.3) :

$$P = Q\,(H + LK_{ts})\, g \quad ...(ii)$$

Since the material is conveyed horizontally, $H = 0$.

$$L = 15 \text{ m},\ K_{ts} = 4.0 \text{ and } g = 9.8 \text{ m/s}^2$$

Therefore, $P = 3.15$ kW

Since the reducer efficiency is given to be 0.77,

Actual power to be supplied = (3.15/0.77) = **4.09 kW**.

10.3.2. Belt Conveyors

Belt conveyors may be called the most versatile among the mechanical conveying equipment. They have found wide application in all branches of industry and are the principal means of mechanical transport in foundry shops (for the supply and distribution of moulding sands and removal of wastes), in fuel supply systems of power stations, for underground as well as surface transport of coal and for the delivery of ores, coke and fluxes in metal making industries. They also transport building materials, fossil minerals, grain, sand and gravel. These conveyors are often used as principal components of some complex machines such as wheel excavators, transfer trestles, conveyor bridges etc. Belt conveyors have large load carrying capacity (upto 30 million kg/hour) over long distances (upto 3-4 km in a single conveyor and upto 100 km in systems comprising of a number of conveyors). Simple design, easy maintenance and high reliability of operation are their additional features.

The principal components of a belt conveyor are a supporting structure or frame with two pulleys at its ends such as the drive pulley at the head and the take-up pulley at the rear end and a vertically closed belt that runs around these pulleys and supported along its length by roller supports or idlers which are fastened to the frame. The width of the belt varies from 0.3 m to 3.0 m and the number of idlers varies accordingly. The idlers must be so spaced that there will be no sagging of the belt between them. This spacing varies from about 1.5 m for narrow belts down to 1.0 m for the widest belts. The return idlers are normally cylindrical rollers and are spaced at greater intervals than those carrying the loaded belt. The idlers may be equipped with antifriction (ball or roller) bearings or ordinary bush bearings. Power requirements are considerably lower for antifriction bearings, but initial costs are higher. In some cases, idle rollers may be replaced by a continuous flooring on which the belt can slide. The drive pulley is rotated by a drive and thus moves the belt along the path of the conveyor. Usually, a single pulley drive with one or two motors or a double pulley drive with two closely spaced driving pulleys is employed. The material to be transported is fed onto the belt through one or more filling funnels or hoppers. The material is carried on the upper run (carrying run) of the belt, while the return run is usually empty. It is also possible to convey materials simultaneously on both runs of the belt in opposite directions. At the discharge point (at the head pulley), the material is unloaded from the belt through an unloading funnel or hopper or by means of plough-type or pulley-type unloaders. Cleaning devices are mounted at the terminal or head pulley from which the material is unloaded. The external (load carrying) surface of belts is cleaned from stuck-on dry or moist particles by means of scraper plates whereas wet and sticky materials are removed using a rotating brush. Hydraulic cleaning in which a powerful jet of water is used to remove the deposits, is also employed ; however in that case, the belt must be dried up properly after the cleaning operation.

Belt conveyors may have a rubberised, all-steel rolled or wire belt. Rubberised belts are used most extensively. In the general purpose conveyors, the belt serves both as the load-carrying and the tractive element, whereas in the chain-belt and cable-belt conveyors, the belt functions only as the load carrying element while a chain or two cables serve as the tractive element. Belt conveyors may be horizontal, inclined or the mixed type such as inclined-horizontal, horizontal-inclined with one or more bends or those having an intricate path. It is always preferable to design the conveyors in such a way that their path be as much as possible simple and straight. Long conveyors, however, have a complicated path according to the profile of the terrain. The angle of inclination of the conveyor with the horizontal (β) depends on the type of material handled, the nature of belt surface whether smooth or ribbed, the angle of repose of the bulk load, the method of loading and the speed of the belt. A material can remain on the belt without sliding down longitudinally if the angle of inclination of the conveyor (β) is roughly 10-15° less than the angle of friction of the material at rest on the belt. Such a large margin is needed because the belt sags between the supports so that its angle of inclination at a roller support could be substantially larger than the average geometrical angle of conveyor incline. Besides, the moving belt gets shaken on the roller supports which promotes downward sliding of the material. This effect is more predominant at high belt speeds and with less accurately manufactured rollers. A continuous uniform loading of the conveyor is always preferred since this allows a higher angle of inclination β than a periodic loading with interruptions in the load flow.

Modern belt conveyors are provided with automatic control and safety devices with sensors for measuring or detecting the belt speed, transverse shift of the belt, longitudinal belt breakage, breakage of cables in rubber-cable belts, the functioning of the lubricating system of the drive etc. At any deviation from the normal operation, the sensors automatically stop the conveyor and send warning signals.

The cross-sectional profile of a bulk material on the conveyor belt depends on whether the belt is supported on straight rollers (see Figure 10.3*a*) or on troughing rollers (see Figure 10.3*b*). On a belt supported on straight rollers, the cross-sectional area of the bulk load which takes a triangular shape on the belt, will be

$$A_b = \frac{1}{2} bh\, C_\beta$$

$$= \frac{1}{2} b\, (b/2 \tan \alpha_r')\, C_\beta \qquad \text{...(10.3.8)}$$

where b is the carrying width of the belt (that is, that portion of the width which carries the load) and h is the height of the load layer on the belt. The value of b is usually taken to be,

$$b = 0.9B - 0.05 \qquad \text{...(10.3.9)}$$

where B is the total width of the belt. It can be seen that b is taken to be less than B. This is to avoid spilling of the material from the belt. The angle α_r' is the angle of repose of the bulk load across the moving belt, which is slightly less than its angle of repose at rest α_r. Normally, $\alpha_r' = 0.35\ \alpha_r$. The coefficient C_β depends on the angle of inclination of the conveyor (β) and the flowability of the material. For smooth rubber belts, some typical values of C_β are given in Table (10.2). Equation (10.3.8) is sometimes written in terms of an additional coefficient K_a as,

$$A_b = [0.25 \tan \alpha_r']\, C_\beta\, b^2$$

$$= K_a\, C_\beta\, b^2 \qquad \text{...(10.3.10)}$$

On a belt supported by troughing rollers (Figure 10.3*b*), the total cross-sectional area of the load will be the sum of the area of the upper triangle and that of the lower trapezium whose sides are formed by the side roller supports. The maximum rated capacity of the conveyor will thus be,

$$Q_m = A_b\, v\rho_s = K_a\, C_\beta\, b^2\, v\rho_s \qquad \text{...(10.3.11)}$$

where v is the linear speed of the belt (m/s) and ρ_s is the bulk density of the materials conveyed (kg/m^3). Typical values of K_a for different types of materials and for different types of roller supports are given in Table (10.3).

Table 10.2

Flowability of material	α'_r	C_β				
		$\beta = 1 - 5°$	$\beta = 6 - 10°$	$\beta = 11 - 15°$	$\beta = 16 - 20°$	$\beta = 20 - 24°$
High	10°	0.95	0.95	0.85	0.80	—
Medium	15°	1.0	0.97	0.95	0.90	0.85
Low	20°	1.0	0.98	0.97	0.95	0.90

Materials of high flowability are free-flowing materials like cement, dry coke, dry sand, coal dust etc. which have a low angle of repose α_r (30 to 35°). Solids of moderate or medium flowability have a higher angle of repose (40 to 45°) and include coal, crushed stone, wet sand, peat and slag. Materials like wet clay, wet lime etc. possess low flowability and high angle of repose (50-56°).

The required width of the belt can be now obtained from equation (10.3.9)

$$B = (1.1)b + 0.056$$

$$= (1.1)\,[Q_m / K_a\, C_\beta\, v \rho_s]^{1/2} + 0.056 \qquad ...(10.3.12)$$

The values of K_a and C_β can be obtained from Tables (10.2) and (10.3).

Table 10.3. Values of Coefficient K_a

Type of idler	*Angle of inclination of side rollers, θ_r*	*Flowability of material transported*		
		High	*Medium*	*Low*
Straight	—	0.044	0.067	0.091
Troughing	20°	0.109	0.1306	0.1528
	30°	0.133	0.1528	0.1736
	45°	0.161	0.1758	0.1922
	60°	0.1617	0.1722	0.1839

If the conveyor is intended to transport lumpy materials, then the belt width determined from equation (10.3.12) should be checked for the lumpiness of the material by the condition,

$$B \geq C_a\,(a) + 0.2 \qquad ...(10.3.13)$$

where a is the maximum lump size (maximum linear dimension) for ungraded material and the average lump size for graded material. The coefficient C_a may be taken to be 3.5 for graded materials and 2.5 for ungraded ones. The final belt width is then rounded off to any one among the standard series such as 0.3, 0.4, 0.5, 0.65, 0.8, 1.0, 1.2, 1.4, 1.6, 2.0, 2.5 and 3.0 m.

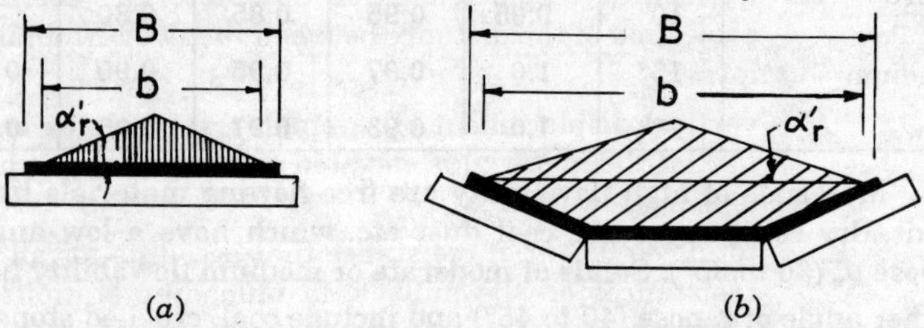

Fig. 10.3. Cross-sectional profile of bulk load on conveyor belt supported on (*a*) straight rollers, (*b*) troughing rollers.

The speed of the conveyor belt is selected depending on the characteristics of the conveyed material, belt width, provisions for intermediate unloading and the location as well as final application of the conveyor. For conveyors provided with pulley-type intermediate unloaders, the speed of the belt should not be more than 2.0 m/s and for those with the plough-type unloaders 1.0 to 1.6 m/s. Recommended speeds of conveyor belts under different conditions are specified in manufacturers' catalogues.[1, 2] The most frequently employed conveyor speeds are 0.8, 1.0, 1.25, 1.6, 2.0, 2.5, 3.15, 4.0, 5.0, 6.3, 8.0 and 10.0 m/s. Wider belts moving in more steady and centred position lose little material to the floor. As a result, they can be operated at larger speeds than narrow belts. Similarly, steeply inclined conveyors should be operated at lower speed than horizontal conveyors and outdoor conveyors can be run at higher speeds than those operating in closed buildings.

If the conveyor is being employed for transporting unit loads (boxes, bags etc.), then the belt width is selected depending on the dimensions of the boxes or bags and the method of their loading onto the belt. The loading device must place the load units symmetrically on the belt (with the longest side along the belt and not transversely) so that a clearance of at least 0.05 to 0.1 m is maintained between the edge of the load unit and the edge of the belt on both sides. The belt speed is usually 0.5 to 1.0 m/s and varies with the conveyor capacity and the type of goods handled.

Let us now proceed to compute the power consumption or the power required for the drive motor. The total resistance W to the motion of the belt over the entire conveyor path, which is equal to the tractive force of the drive, will obviously be due to the weight of the load, weight of empty belt and rotating elements of idlers. It will also depend on the total displacement of the load (the distance over which it has been conveyed) both horizontally as well as vertically. Thus,

$$W = K_{tb} L [(q_l + q_{us} + q_b) C_u + (q_b + q_{1s}) C_l] \pm q_l H \quad ...(10.3.14)$$

where L = horizontal displacement of the material (horizontal projection of the distance between the two terminal pulleys)

H = vertical displacement of the material (the plus sign is used if the material is elevated and minus sign when it is being lowered)

K_{tb} = total coefficient of resistance that accounts for all local resistances on the pulleys, in unloading stations and other places.

Typical values of K_{tb} as a function of the conveyor length are given below :

Table 10.4

Conveyor length, m :	10	20	30	40	50	100	200	300	500	1,000 and more
K_{tb} :	4.5	3.2	2.8	2.6	2.4	1.7	1.5	1.4	1.3	1.1

q_l is the weight of the load conveyed per unit length or more commonly called the linear gravity force of the load. If Q_a is the average rated capacity of the conveyor (kg/s) and v linear speed (m/s), then

$$q_l = (Q_a g/v) \quad ...(10.3.15)$$

For unit loads, if m_l is the mass of the heaviest piece of load and l_o is the spacing between the adjacent pieces,

$$q_l = (m_l g/l_o) \quad ...(10.3.16)$$

Similarly, the linear gravity force of the belt q_b will be,

$$q_b = m_b gB \quad ...(10.3.17)$$

where m_b = mass per unit area (kg/m^2) of the belt (available from manufacturers' catalogues)

The linear gravity forces of the rotating elements of the roller supports on the upper and lower runs of the belt q_{us} and q_{ls} can also be obtained in similar way :

$$q_{us} = m_{us}\, g / l_{us} \quad ...(10.3.18)$$

$$q_{ls} = m_{ls}\, g / l_{ls} \quad ...(10.3.19)$$

when m_{us} and m_{ls} are the masses of the rotating elements of upper and lower roller supports respectively (available from manufacturers' catalogues) and l_{us} and l_{ls} are the spacings between the roller supports in the upper and lower run of the belt respectively. The value of l_{us} is chosen on the basis of the density of the material conveyed (ρ_s) and the belt width (B) and it varies from 1.1 m to 1.5 m. A lower spacing is employed for wide belts and when the material handled is heavy. For the return run, the spacing between roller supports is usually taken to be 2.0 to 2.5 times that for the carrying run, but not more than 3.5 m.

The coefficients C_u and C_l take care of the resistance to the motion of the upper run and lower run of the belt respectively. If the belt runs on a flat steel or wooden floor, C_u = 0.35 to 0.60, depending on the operating conditions of the conveyor. If the belt is moving on troughing three roller supports, the value of C_u will depend on the conveyor length as well as given below :

Table 10.5

Conditions of conveyor operation	C_u	
	Conveyor length ≤ 100 m	*Conveyor length > 100 m*
Good	0.02	0.018
Moderate	0.025	0.022
Heavy (summer season)	0.035	0.032
Heavy (winter season)	0.045	0.042

For belt running on straight single roller supports, typical values of C_l are given below :

Table 10.6

Conditions of conveyor operation:	Good	Moderate	Heavy in summer	Heavy in winter
C_l	0.018	0.022	0.03	0.04

The conveyor is said to be operating under "good" conditions when it is operating in clean, closed, heated or cooled, ventilated rooms where there is little abrasive dust in air (less than 5 mg/m^3) and the relative humidity of air is rather low ($\leq$ 40%). Also, harmful gases and vapours are to be practically absent in the atmosphere. Such conditions can occur in radio and television making shops, machine and assembly shops or in printing houses or libraries, but hardly in chemical plants. Moderate operating conditions exist in closed, heated rooms but without temperature and humidity control. As a result, the humidity of air will be higher ($\leq$ 65%) and abrasive dust upto 10 mg/m^3 and small amounts of gases and vapours could be present in the atmosphere. Examples are fuel supply sections of thermal power plants and sand-making and moulding sections of foundry shops. Outdoor conveyors subjected to atmospheric influence (such as wind and dust) throughout the year are operating under "hard" conditions. This also applies to rooms and sheds in which variations in air temperature and humidity differ only slightly from those outdoor and where access of outdoor air is practically unobstructed and also to closed rooms with a high concentration of abrasive dust (more than 10 mg/m^3), harmful gases and moisture (relative humidity of air > 80%). Chemical process plants, open cast collieries and mines, mineral beneficiation units etc. fall under this category.

Once we have estimated W, the power consumption or power of the drive motor can be computed as,

$$P = \left[\frac{Wv}{\eta}\right] K_{ma} \qquad \text{...(10.3.20)}$$

where η is called the mechanical efficiency of the drive mechanism (usually between 80 and 90 per cent) and K_{ma} is called the margin of adhesion between the belt and the drive pulley. Its value varies from 1.1 to 1.2 and an average value of 1.15 can be used for most of the computations.

To determine the required strength of the belt, we have to estimate the rated tension in the belt. If T_o is the tension in the belt section running on a pulley and T_f in that running off that pulley, then,

$$(T_o/T_f) \leq e^{\mu' \alpha_w} \qquad \text{...(10.3.21)}$$

where μ' is the coefficient of friction between the belt and the pulley and α_w is the wrapping angle of the belt on the pulley in radians (π radians = 180°). The tractive force W will then be equal to the difference between T_o and T_f as,

$$W = (T_o - T_f)/K_{ma}$$

$$= T_f(e^{\mu' \alpha_w} - 1)/K_{ma} \quad ...(10.3.22)$$

The coefficient K_{ma} has been introduced as stated earlier to ensure the required margin of frictional force on the drive pulley. Equation (10.3.22) can be rewritten as,

$$T_f = K_{ma} \; W/(e^{\mu' \alpha_w} - 1)$$

Therefore, $T_o = K_{ma} \; We^{\mu' \alpha_w}/(e^{\mu' \alpha_w} - 1)$ ...(10.3.23)

Some of the rated values of μ' for rubber-covered belt are given below :

Table 10.7

Surface of drive	*State of contacting surfaces of pulley and belt*	*Atmospheric conditions*	*Conditions of operation*	μ'
Steel or cast iron, without lining	Clean	dry	good	0.35
	Dusty	dry	moderate	0.30
	Contaminated by unsticky materials (sand, coal etc.)	humid	heavy	0.20
	Contaminated by sticky materials like clay	humid	heavy	0.10
Rubber-lined	Clean	dry	good	0.50
	Dusty	dry	moderate	0.40
	Contaiminated by unsticky materials	humid	heavy	0.25
	Contaminated by sticky material	humid	heavy	0.15
Lined with rubberised tape without coating	Clean	dry	good	0.45
	Dusty	dry	moderate	0.35
	Contaminated by unsticky material	humid	heavy	0.25
	Contaminated by sticky material	humid	heavy	0.10

For a double pulley drive, equation (10.3.23) can be modified to determine the rated tension in the belt as,

$$T_{o1} = K_{ma}\ We^{\mu'(\alpha_{w1}+\alpha_{w2})}/[e^{\mu'(\alpha_{w1}+\alpha_{w2})} - 1] \qquad ...(10.3.24)$$

where T_{o1} is the tension in the belt section running on the first pulley along the path of the belt and α_{w1} and α_{w2} are the wrapping angle on the first and second pulleys respectively. It has been assumed that the coefficient of friction (μ') of the belt on both pulleys is the same, which is usually so.

For single pulley drives, the wrapping angle α_w is limited by not more than 240° , whereas a larger wrapping angle (upto 400°) can be employed with double pulley drives.

The safety margin of the belt strength is determined as,

$$K = 7.0/(K_{pl}\, K_j\, K_{cp}\, K_{op}), \text{ for rubber-fabric belts}$$

$$= 7.0/(K_j\, K_{cp}\, K_{op}), \text{ for rubber-cable belts} \qquad ...(10.3.25)$$

In rubber-fabric belts, the tractive carcass is made up of a number of fabric plies arranged layerwise and separated by rubber interlayers. K_{pl} is thus the coefficient to take care of non-uniform stressing of plies and its value depends on the number of plies used (N) as given below :

Table 10.8

N	:	3	4	5	6	7	8
K_{pl}	:	0.95	0.90	0.88	0.85	0.82	0.80

The coefficient K_j is to take care of the strength of the belt joint. For vulcanised joints, $K_j = 0.9 - 0.85$; for belt ends connected by staples or hinges, $K_j = 0.5$ and for lapped riveted joints, $K_j = 0.4 - 0.3$. Incidentally, the ends of rubble-cable belts are connected only by vulcanisation and therefore for them $K_j = 0.9 - 0.85$. The coefficient K_{cp} depends on the configuration of the conveyor path. For horizontal conveyors, $K_{cp} = 1.0$; for inclined straight conveyors, $K_{cp} =$ 0.9 and for inclined conveyors with an intricate path profile, $K_{cp} = 0.85$. K_{op} is the coefficient that depends on the operating conditions of the conveyor such as good ($K_{op} = 1.1$), moderate ($K_{op} = 1.0$), heavy ($K_{op} = 0.95$) and sometimes very heavy ($K_{op} = 0.85$).

Once we have evaluated K, the required strength of the carcass of a rubber-cable belt (S_{rc}) is obtained as,

$$S_{rc} \geq (T_o \text{ or } T_{o1})\, K/B \qquad \text{...(10.3.26)}$$

Similarly, the number of belt plies required (N_r) for a rubber-fabric belt is obtained as,

$$N_r \geq (T_o \text{ or } T_{o1})\, K/(S_{pl}\, B) \qquad \text{...(10.3.27)}$$

where S_{pl} is the strength of the ply fabric, in N/m of belt width. Polyamide fabrics have strengths ranging from 100 to 400 N/mm of ply width, while blends of polyester and cotton have strengths in the range of 65 to 150 N/mm of ply width. It is also important to see that $[(T_o \text{ or } T_{01})/B]$ does not exceed the maximum allowable tension per unit width prescribed in the manufacturers' catalogue.

It may be noted that the term ($e^{\mu' \alpha_w}$) in equation (10.3.21) is often called the pull factor F_p since it determines the tractive capacity of a driving pulley. For a double pulley drive, F_p will be expressed as $e^{\mu' (\alpha_{w1} + \alpha_{w2})}$. The factor $(F_p - 1)/F_p$ is called the coefficient of utilisation of belt strength, K_{ut}. This coefficient has a special significance particularly when a double pulley drive is employed. The total power P required for the motors of a double pulley drive can be distributed between the pulleys as given below :

$$P_1 = (C_m/C_m + 1)\, P$$

and
$$P_2 = P/(C_m + 1) \qquad \text{...(10.3.28)}$$

Obviously, $\quad P = P_1 + P_2$

Similarly, the tractive forces W_1 and W_2 developed by the first and second pulley respectively will be,

$$W_1 = (C_m/C_m + 1)\, W$$

$$W_2 = W/(C_m + 1) \qquad \text{...(10.3.29)}$$

In the above equations, C_m is the distribution coefficient or the coefficient of load distribution. Its value varies from 1.0 to 3.0 and depends on the magnitude of K_{ut} and the coefficient of friction μ' between the belt and the pulley (see Table 10.9). The design tension of the belt section running off the second pulley can be now independently determined as,

$$T_{f2} = K_{ma}\, W_2/[e^{\mu' \alpha_{w2}} - 1] \qquad \text{...(10.3.30)}$$

Similarly, the tension in the section that runs on the second pulley and runs off the first pulley can be obtained as,

$$T_{o2} = T_{f1} = T_{f2}\, e^{\mu' \alpha_{w2}} \qquad \text{...(10.3.31)}$$

Table 10.9
Values of K_{ut} for double pulley drive

C_m	K_{ut}				
	$\mu' = 0.1$	$\mu' = 0.2$	$\mu' = 0.3$	$\mu' = 0.4$	$\mu' = 0.5$
1.0	0.51	0.73	0.84	0.94	0.94
1.5	0.57	0.77	0.87	0.93	0.94
2.0	0.50	0.82	0.89	0.91	0.95
3.0	0.45	0.76	0.92	0.90	0.96

The diameter of the pulleys for rubber-fabric belts can be selected using the following relation,

$$d = C_p\,(N\,C_{pl}) \qquad \text{...(10.3.32)}$$

where N is the number of fabric plies and C_p is a coefficient that depends on the type of pulley. For pulleys in single pulley drives, $C_p = 1.0$; for those in double pulley drives $C_p = 1.1$; for terminal, reverse and take-up pulleys $C_p = 0.8 - 0.85$ if the belt tension is less than 60 per cent of the allowable value and $C_p = 0.9$, if it is above 60 percent; for deflector pulleys $C_p = 0.5$. The coefficient C_{pl} depends on the strength of the ply fabric as given below :

Table 10.10

Ply fabric Strength, N/mm :	55	100	150	200	300	400
C_{pl}	125-140	141-160	161-170	171-180	181-190	191-200

For rubber-cable belts, the recommended diameter of the drive pulley d_d is prescribed in the manufacturers' catalogue. The diameters of other pulleys can be then selected based on the expression,

$$d = d_d\,C_p \qquad \text{...(10.3.33)}$$

The coefficient C_p has been defined earlier.

The selected diameter of the drive pulley d_d should be checked for the belt pressure P_b acting on the pulley surface, which should not exceed the maximum permissible value P_{ba} :

$$P_b = [2T_o/\alpha_w\,d_d\,B]\left[\frac{e^{\mu'\alpha_w}+1}{e^{\mu'\alpha_w}}\right] \qquad \text{...(10.3.34)}$$

where α_w is the wrapping angle of the belt on the pulley, in radians. The value of P_{ba} for rubber-fabric belts is 0.2-0.3 MN/m^2 (0.2×10^6 to 0.3×10^6 N/m^2) and that for rubber-cable belts is 0.35 - 0.55 MN/m^2. The estimated diameters of the pulleys must be ultimately rounded off to the nearest standard values such as 0.16, 0.2, 0.25, 0.315, 0.4, 0.5, 0.63, 0.8, 1.0, 1.25, 1.4, 1.6, 2.0 and 2.5 m.

Example 10.2. *A belt conveyor inclined at 0.6° with the horizontal is to be used for transporting iron ore (size = 10–30 mm, density = 2500 kg/m^3 and moisture content = upto 10 per cent) from the quarry to a wharf store. The material is to be conveyed horizontally by 800 m while elevated by 7.5 m. The conveyor is installed outdoors and it operates in two shifts for 14 hours per day and the season is summer. The highest humidity of air is 75% and the air may contain upto 20 mg/m^3 of abrasive dust. The planned average capacity of the conveyor is 66 × 10^6 kg/day and the highest capacity as allowed by the loading device is 10^8 kg/day. The availability factor C_Y (that decides the durability and reliability of the machine during its service life) is 0.96. The coefficient of utilisation of operating time C_t and the coefficient of non-uniform loading C_n may be taken as 0.85 and 0.92 respectively. The conveyor is to be provided with heavy-type troughing roller supports with a troughing angle of 30°. From manufacturers' catalogue, the masses of rotating elements of the upper and lower roller supports are 108 kg and 53 kg respectively and the mechanical efficiency of the drive mechanism may be taken to be 80 per cent. Two types of rubber-cable belts whose standard specifications are given below, are available :*

Rated mass per unit area, kg/m^2	*Belt strength, kN/m of belt width*	*Maximum allowable tension, kN/m of belt width*	*Recommended diameter of drive pulley, m*
I 43	3150	380	1.25
II 28	1500	180	0.8

Design the belt conveyor and specify which of the above two belts shall suit best to the purpose.

Solution. At the outset, let us determine the rated capacity of the conveyor (on which the design will be based) which is obtained by dividing the given planned capacity by the total operating coefficient (or total coefficient of utilisation of the machine) C_{op}.

Thus, rated average capacity, $Q_a = \dfrac{66 \times 10^6}{(14)\, C_{op}}$ kg/hr

C_{op} is the product of C_Y, C_t and C_n and therefore,

$$C_{op} = (0.96)\,(0.85)\,(0.92) = 0.75$$

$$\text{Therefore}\quad Q_a = \frac{66 \times 10^6}{14\,(0.75)\,(3600)} = 1746 \text{ kg/s}$$

Similarly, the rated maximum capacity

$$Q_m = \frac{10^8}{14\,(0.75)\,(3600)} = 2645.5 \text{ kg/s}$$

Since the ore that is to be transported is heavy, lumpy and of large size, let us choose a belt speed of 2.5 m/s. The ore can be assumed to be of moderate flowability. Therefore, from Table (10.2), $C_\beta = 1.0$ and from Table (10.3), $K_a = 0.1528$ (since θ_r is given to be 30°). Now, the required belt width can be determined from equation (10.3.12) :

$$B = 1.1\left[\frac{2645.5}{(0.1528)\,(1.0)\,2.5\,(2500)}\right]^{1/2} + 0.056$$

$$= 1.8868 \text{ m}$$

This can be rounded off to the nearest standard width, 2.0 m. The selected belt width is now checked for the lumpiness of the material using equation (10.3.13). Since the material is ungraded, $C_a = 2.5$. The maximum lump size is 0.3 m. Therefore,

$$C_a\,(a) + 0.2 = 0.95 \text{ m}$$

Since the chosen value of B is more than this, no correction is required.

To compute the tractive force W, we require to know q_l, q_b, q_{us} and q_{ls}. From equation (10.3.15),

$$q_l = \frac{Q_a\,g}{v} = \frac{(1746)\,(9.8)}{(2.5)} = 6844.32 \text{ N/m}$$

Similarly, from equation (10.3.17),

$$q_b = m_b\,gB$$

$$= (43)\,(9.8)\,(2.0), \text{ considering belt–I}$$

$$= 842.8 \text{ N/m}$$

If we consider belt-II, then

$$q_b = 28(9.8)\,2.0$$

$$= 548.8 \text{ N/m}$$

Since the belt is quite wide and the load is fairly heavy or dense, a spacing of $l_{us} = 1$ m will be sufficient for the upper run of the belt.

Accordingly, let us take $l_{ls} = (2.0)\,(1.0) = 2.0$ m. Now the values of q_{ls} and q_{us} can be computed from equations (10.3.18) and (10.3.19) :

$$q_{us} = \frac{m_{us}\,g}{l_{us}} = \frac{(108)\,(9.8)}{(1.0)} = 1058.4 \text{ N/m}$$

$$q_{ls} = \frac{m_{ls}\,g}{l_{ls}} = \frac{(53)\,(9.8)}{(2.0)} = 259.7 \text{ N/m}$$

Given that $L = 800$ m and $H = 7.5$ m.

$$\text{Conveyor length} = \frac{800}{\cos\beta} = \frac{800}{\cos(0.6)} = 800.0439 \text{ m}$$

Thus, from Table (10.4), $K_{tb} = 1.2$.

Since the operating conditions of the conveyor are "heavy" and the season is summer, from Table (10.5), $C_u = 0.032$ and from Table (10.6), $C_l = 0.03$. Now, we can substitute these values in equation (10.3.14) to compute W as,

$$W = 351.747 \text{ kN, when belt–I is used}$$

$$= 334.25 \text{ kN, when belt–II is used}$$

Now, from equation (10.3.20), taking $K_{ma} = 1.15$,

$$P = \frac{(351.747)\,(2.5)\,(1.15)}{(0.8)} = 1264 \text{ kW, for belt–I}$$

$$= \frac{(334.25)\,(2.5)\,(1.15)}{(0.8)} = 1201.21 \text{ kW, for belt–II}$$

Let us select a double pulley drive for the conveyor. From Table (10.7), for a rubber-lined pulley for "heavy" operating conditions of the conveyor in a humid atmosphere, $\mu' = 0.25$. Since double pulley drives can employ a wrapping angle as large as 400°, let us assume $(\alpha_{w1} + \alpha_{w2}) = 400°$ or 6.98 radians. Now, the rated tension in the belt T_{o1} can be obtained from equation (10.3.24) :

$$T_{o1} = \frac{K_{ma}\,WF_p}{F_p - 1}$$

where $K_{ma} = 1.15$

$$F_p = \text{pull factor} = e^{\mu'(\alpha_{w1} + \alpha_{w2})}$$

$$= e^{0.25\,(6.98)} = 5.7259$$

Therefore, $T_{o1} = 490.1$ kN, for belt–I

$$= 465.724 \text{ kN, for belt–II}$$

From equation (10.3.25),

$$K = 7.0/(K_j\, K_{cp}\, K_{op})$$

Since rubber-cable belt ends are joined only by vulcanising, $K_j = 0.9$. Since the conveyor is inclined, $K_{cp} = 0.9$ and since the operating conditions are heavy, $K_{op} = 0.95$. Thus,

$$K = 7.0/(0.9)\,(0.9)\,(0.95) = 9.0968$$

The required strength of the belt is now obtained from equation (10.3.26) as,

$$S_{rc} = T_{01}\, K/B$$

$$= \frac{490.1\ (9.0968)}{(2.0)} = 2229.17 \text{ kN/m (for belt–I)}$$

$$= \frac{(465.724)\ (9.0968)}{(2.0)} = 2118.3 \text{ kN/m (for belt–II)}$$

It can be seen that belt-II is unsuitable for the given application since its strength is only 1500 kN/m which is less than the required strength computed above. We therefore choose belt-I whose strength is well above the required value. Also, for belt-I, $(T_{o1}/B) = 245.05$ kN/m which is less than the maximum allowable tension.

Let us select the diameter of the drive pulley as recommended, $d_d = 1.25$ m. This is to be checked by determining the pressure on the surface of the drive pulley. Now, $K_{ut} = (F_p - 1)/F_p = 0.8253$. Then, from Table (10.9), $C_m = 2.0$. From equation (10.3.28),

$$P_1 = (2/3)\, P = 842.67 \text{ kW}$$

$$P_2 = P/3 = 421.33 \text{ kW}$$

Similarly,

$$W_1 = (2/3)\, W = 234.498 \text{ kN}$$

$$W_2 = (W/3) = 117.249 \text{ kN}$$

Let us assume that

$$\alpha_{w2} = (400/2) = 200° \text{ or } 3.46 \text{ radians.}$$

Then from equation (10.3.30),

$$T_{f2} = K_{ma}\, W_2/[e^{\mu'\, \alpha_{w2}} - 1]$$

$$= (1.15)\,(117.249)/(1.393) = 96.795 \text{ kN}$$

And from equation (10.3.31),

$$T_{f1} = T_{f2}\, e^{\mu'\, \alpha_{w2}} = 231.63 \text{ kN}$$

Therefore, $e^{\mu' \alpha_{w1}} = T_{o1}/T_{f1} = (490.1/231.63) = 2.16$

or $\alpha_{w1} = 3.0$ radians

Since $(\alpha_{w1} + \alpha_{w2}) = (3.49 + 3.0) = 6.49$ radians is very close to the value we had taken initially, we avoid further trial. The pressure on the surface of the first drive pulley is now determined using equation (10.3.34) :

$$P_b = \left[\frac{2T_{o1}}{\alpha_{w1} B d_d}\right]\left[\frac{e^{\mu' \alpha_{w1}} + 1}{e^{\mu' \alpha_{w1}}}\right]$$

$$= \frac{(2.0)\,(490.1)}{(3.0)\,(2.0)\,(1.25)}\left[\frac{3.16}{2.16}\right]$$

$$= 191.2 \text{ kN/m}^2$$

$$= 0.1912 \text{ MN/m}^2$$

This is quite permissible since the maximum permissible value P_{ba} for rubber-cable belts is 0.35–0.55 MN/m². Therefore, no further correction is required. The speed of rotation of the drive pulley is,

$$n_d = \left(\frac{60v}{\pi d_d}\right) = \frac{60\,(2.5)}{\pi\,(1.25)} = \mathbf{38\ rpm.}$$

10.3.3. Apron Conveyors

Apron conveyors are similar to belt conveyors except that the solids are carried in a moving trough (called apron, by virtue of its shape) that is formed of articulating sections of wood or metal (steel) instead of a continuous flexible belt. The apron moves on a guide track. The tractive element of apron conveyors is usually formed by two laminated wheel chains with a standard pitch of 0.08, 0.1, 0.125, 0.16, 0.2, 0.25, 0.315, 0.4, 0.5, 0.63 or 0.8 m. Other types of chains such as the sleeve-type, roller-type or round-link type are also used for special purposes. Light conveyors with apron width less than 0.4 m may have a single chain only. In wheel chains, the wheels serve as supporting elements which transmit the gravity force of the apron and the load onto the guide tracks of the conveyor. Flanged as well as flangeless wheels are in use, on sliding or roll bearings, the latter being employed for heavy duty conveyors. In light conveyors that are used for transporting light unit loads such as bottles, small machine parts etc., the functions of the tractive and load carrying elements are often combined in an articulated flat apron having a width of 0.08 to 0.2 m and sliding on metallic or plastic guide tracks.

The apron is the load carrying element of the apron conveyor. It may be made in different configurations such as flat open, flat closed or corrugated with or without side walls. Aprons with flat side walls are employed for conveying unit loads. Fall-off of the load is sometimes prevented by arranging wooden board or steel strip protections, called skirt boards, along the apron especially at the loading stations. Walled flat and corrugated aprons with skirt boards are widely used for both bulk and unit loads (for example, for conveying hot castings). The box-cell walled aprons, a special design, are used exclusively for bulk loads at high angles of inclination (upto 45-60°) and high throughput capacities. Standard width of aprons varies from 0.4 to 1.6 m and the wall height (for walled aprons) from 0.08 to 0.5 m. The angle of inclination β of the conveyor depends on the characteristics of the transported material and the type of apron used. In any case, β should be less than $(\alpha_r' - 5°)$, where α_r' is the angle of repose of the material while in motion on the conveyor. For bulk materials on box-cell aprons, β may be as high as 45-60°, but at angles above 35°, the conveyor throughput capacity decreases considerably since the material tends to flow back along the transverse walls of the cells. While transporting unit loads, the value of β used may be increased upto 60° by providing transverse cleats on the apron. Apron conveyors may be actuated by a corner or straight (caterpillar) drive. The drive consists of drive sprockets, a transmission mechanism (reducer gear) and an electric motor. Drive sprockets in a corner drive usually have five to eight teeth. The two sprockets must be mounted on the drive shaft such that their teeth strictly coincide, to obtain the same tension in the chains and also to avoid skewing of the apron. A speed controller may be provided between the electric motor and the reducer gear when it is required to vary the conveyor speed continuously. Long and heavily loaded conveyors are sometimes provided with a number of intermediate drives, for example nine caterpillar drives within a conveyor length of 2 km. The take-up device may be of the screw or spring-screw type and is mounted with the terminal sprockets.

Apron conveyors (horizontal and inclined) are widely employed in chemical, coal processing and metal making industries and also in thermal power plants. They can also be employed for the transfer of materials or articles within production flowlines. While being conveyed, the material may be subjected to operations like hardening, tempering, cooling, washing, painting, assembling etc., which is an additional advantage. Unlike belt conveyors, apron conveyors can handle heavier, lumpy and abrasive materials (ores, stones etc.) as well as hot materials like forgings, castings etc. The length of a single conveyor can be as large as 2 km and they provide large throughput capacities (more than 2000 m^3/hr) due to the high strength of hauling chains and the use of intermediate drives. They have a smooth and noiseless run and can be loaded directly from hoppers without using feeders. Apron conveyors are capable of moving loads on more intricate and steeper paths than belt conveyors, with slopes upto 35-60° and smaller radii of curved sections. Among the drawbacks of apron conveyors are the appreciable weight of apron and chains and consequently their higher cost and more careful maintenance required for the numerous joints of the chains.

The bulk load on a flat apron without side walls forms a triangle in cross-section like on a belt conveyor with straight roller supports. However, due to the higher rigidity and lower speed of the apron, the base length b of the triangle and the base angle α_r' will be larger than those for the belt conveyor. For the apron conveyor, $b = 0.85\ B$ and $\alpha_r' = 0.4\ \alpha_r$ where α_r is the angle of repose of the material (static) and B is the width of the apron. The cross-sectional area of the load will be therefore,

$$A_b = (1/2)\ bh\ C_\beta = 0.25\ C_\beta\ b^2 \tan \alpha_r' \qquad \text{...(10.3.35)}$$

where h is the altitude of the triangle and C_β is a correction coefficient (sometimes called the angle factor) to account for the reduction in the cross-sectional area on an inclined conveyor. Some typical values of C_β are given below :

Table 10.11

β, *degrees*	C_β	
	Apron without side walls	*Apron with side walls*
≤ 10	1.0	1.0
11 to 20	0.9	0.95
> 20	0.85	0.90

The throughput capacity of the conveyor can be then obtained as,

$$\begin{aligned} Q &= A_b\ \rho_s\ v = [0.25\ C_\beta\ b^2 \tan \alpha_r']\ \rho_s\ v \\ &= 0.25\ C_\beta\ (0.85B)^2\ (\tan \alpha_r')\ \rho_s v \\ &= 0.18\ C_\beta\ B^2\ \rho_s\ v \tan \alpha_r' \qquad \text{...(10.3.36)} \end{aligned}$$

where ρ_s is the bulk density of the material handled (kg/m^3) and v is the speed of the conveyor (m/s).

On an apron with side walls or with fixed skirt boards, the cross-sectional area of the bulk load will be equal to the sum of the areas of the upper triangle and lower rectangle (see Fig. 10.4).

Thus,

$$A_b = (1/2)\, Bh_1\, C_\beta + (Bh_2)$$

$$= [0.25\, C_\beta\, B^2 \tan \alpha_r'] + (C_{fa}\, h)\, B \qquad ...(10.3.37)$$

where B = width of the apron or distance between the skirt boards (Fig. 10.4).

h = height of the walls or skirt boards

C_{fa} = coefficient of filling of the apron cross-section along the height h = 0.65 – 0.80.

The throughput capacity Q can be obtained once again using the relation $Q = A_b\, v\, \rho_s$. With large-size lumpy materials when the apron is loaded all over its width, the load may be considered to form a rectangular layer on the apron and in that case, $A_b = B\,(C_{fa}\, h)$, with $C_{fa} = 0.8 - 0.9$.

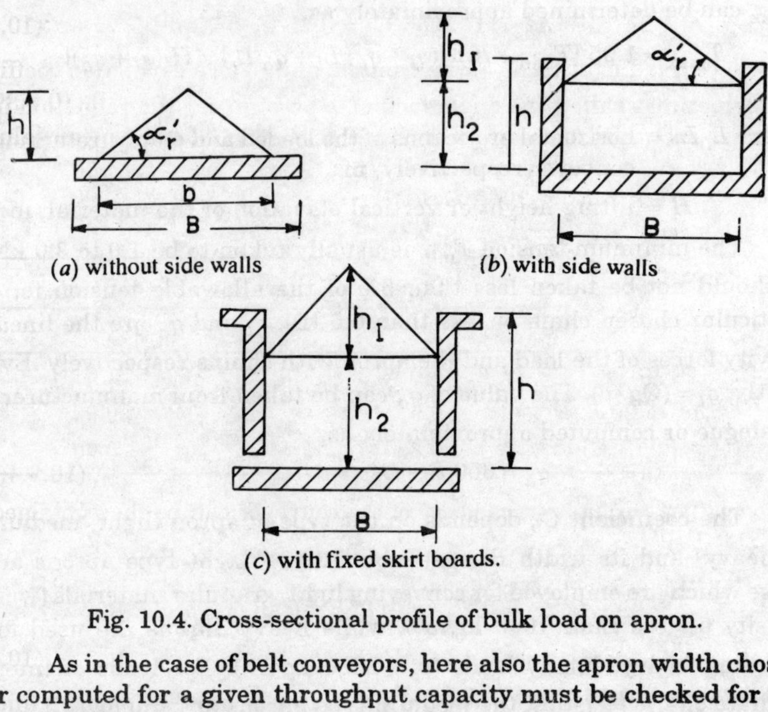

(*a*) without side walls (*b*) with side walls

(*c*) with fixed skirt boards.

Fig. 10.4. Cross-sectional profile of bulk load on apron.

As in the case of belt conveyors, here also the apron width chosen or computed for a given throughput capacity must be checked for the lumpiness of the material :

$$B \geq C_a\,(a) + 0.2 \qquad ...(10.3.38)$$

where a is the average lump size for the graded material ($C_a = 2.7$) and the maximum lump size (provided such lumps occupy more than 10 per cent of the total mass) for ungraded material ($C_a = 1.7$). The finally selected width of the apron and the height of its walls must be then rounded off to the nearest standard sizes. For unit loads, the apron width is chosen in the same manner as for belt conveyors, such as depending on the size of the units, their number and the method of placing on the conveyor. The spacing between adjacent pieces of unit goods should not be kept less than 0.1 to 0.3 m.

Apron conveyors are normally run at low speeds of 0.05 to 0.65 m/s with a view to minimising the dynamic loads on the chains that might be caused by the non-uniform motion of the chains. The conveyor speed may be raised to as much as 1.25 m/s on special occasions, by using all-welded, round-link chains of small pitch.

The maximum static tension of the chains (or a single chain) T_{max} can be determined approximately as,

$$T_{max} = 1.05\,[T_{min} + K_{ta}\,[(q_l + q_a)\,L_l + q_a\,L_r] \pm H\,(q_l + q_a)] \qquad ...(10.3.39)$$

where L_l, L_r = horizontal projections of the loaded and empty (returning) conveyor respectively, m

H = lifting height or vertical elevation of the material, m

The minimum tension T_{min} is usually taken to be 1.0 to 3.0 kN. It should not be taken less than 5% of the allowable tension for a particular chosen chain or less than 0.5 kN. q_l and q_a are the linear gravity forces of the load and the apron with chains respectively. Evidently, $q_l = (Qg/v)$. The value of q_a can be taken from manufacturer's catalogue or computed approximately as,

$$q_a = 600\,B + C_b \qquad ...(10.3.40)$$

The coefficient C_b depends on the type of apron (light, medium or heavy) and its width B (see Table 10.12). Light type aprons are those which are employed for conveying light, granular materials (with density ρ_s less than 1000 kg/m^3), while heavy aprons are used for handling heavy, lumpy loads ($\rho_s \geq 2000$ kg/m^3). For loads of intermediate characteristics, the medium-type aprons are employed.

Table 10.12

Type of apron	C_b *(for corrugated steel aprons with side walls)*		
	$B = 0.4$ *to* 0.5 *m*	$B = 0.6$ *to* 0.8 *m*	$B > 0.8$ *m*
Light	400	500	700
Medium	600	700	1000
Heavy	800	1100	1500

For aprons without side walls, the values of C_b obtained from the above table must be diminished by 10–15%.

The coefficient K_{ta} in equation (10.3.39) is the coefficient of total resistance to the motion of the apron in the straight sections of the conveyor. It can be computed as,

$$K_{ta} = C\,[\mu_b'\,d + 2k]/D \quad \text{...(10.3}$$

where C = coefficient of resistance due to friction of wheel flanges on the rails

= 1.1 – 1.2

d = diameter of wheel shaft, m

D = diameter of the wheel, m

The values of the coefficient of friction μ_b' (in bearings) and the coefficient of rolling friction of the wheels k are given in Table (10.13).

Table 10.13

Conditions of conveyor operation	μ'_b *for plain bearings*		μ'_b *for roll bearings*	*k, m*
	With continuous liquid lubrication	*With periodic greasing*		
Good	0.10	0.15	0.01	0.06×10^{-2}
Moderate	0.15	0.20	0.025	0.08×10^{-2}
Heavy	0.20	0.25	0.045	0.10×10^{-2}

The classification of operating condition of the conveyor has already been discussed under belt conveyors.

For conveyors with fixed skirt boards, an additional resistance W_s due to the friction of the load on the skirt boards should be considered :

$$W_s = \mu_s' (h_s^2 L_s) \rho_s g n_s \qquad ...(10.3.42)$$

where h_s, L_s = height and length of skirt boards respectively, m. (h_s must be the working height, that is the height in contact with the load).

μ_s' = coefficient of friction of the bulk load on the skirt-boards

n_s = coefficient of side pressure = 0.6 – 0.9

For design calculations, equation (10.3.39) gives reasonably good results for selecting the chain and the drive motor. The tractive force W can be taken as,

$$W = (T_{max} - T_{min}) \qquad ...(10.3.43)$$

And the power of the drive motor will be,

$$P = Wv/\eta \qquad ...(10.3.44)$$

A safety margin may also be incorporated in the above equation. However, if computations have been done for the maximum throughput capacity, the safety margin may be taken as 1.0.

More accurate estimation of the tractive force (particularly when the conveyor path consists of a number of sections) can be made by performing detailed point to point computations of the pull and thus determining the tensions in individual sections of the conveyor[2].

When the tractive element consists of two chains, the rated force on a single chain can be estimated as,

$$S_{r1} = T_{max}/C_{nu} \qquad ...(10.3.45)$$

where C_{nu} is the coefficient of nonuniform distribution of the load between the hauling chains. For single chain conveyors, C_{nu} = 1.0 and for those having two chains, C_{nu} = 1.6 – 1.8 depending on the accuracy of chain manufacture and assembly of the conveyor. The rupture strength of the chain S_{rs} is found as,

$$S_{rs} = S_{r1} (n_{sm}) \qquad ...(10.3.46)$$

where n_{sm} is the safety margin of the chain. For horizontal conveyors n_{sm} = 6 – 7 and for conveyors having inclined sections of the path n_{sm} = 8 – 10. Thus, a standard hauling chain whose rupture strength is more than the value of S_{rs} computed from above may be selected.

Example 10.3. *An inclined apron conveyor is used to carry crushed dolomite to a discharge point at a horizontal distance and a vertical height of 20 m and 4.0 m respectively from the tail end. Find the width of the apron if the capacity of the conveyor is 85,000 kg/hour at a conveying speed of 0.2 m/s. The height of the side walls is one-fourth of the apron width. The bulk density of the material is 1350 kg/m*^{3} *and its angle of repose (static) is 35°. Take the inclination factor* C_β *to be 0.95.*

The tractive element for the conveyor is in the form of two laminated wheel chains, with wheels running on plain (sliding) bearings. The wheel diameter is 0.05 m and that of wheel shaft is 0.02 m. Assume the operating conditions of the conveyor are moderate and take the flange friction factor to be 1.2. Determine the maximum chain tension if the minimum tension is to be 1.5 kN. If three standard hauling wheel chains with rated rupture (breaking) strengths of 56.80 and 112 kN are available, determine which one will suit best to the purpose.

Solution. The apron width can be determined using the relation,

$$Q = A_b\, v \rho_s \qquad \text{...}(i)$$

where A_b from equation (10.3.37) is,

$$A_b = (0.25 C_\beta B^2 \tan \alpha_r') + C_{fa}\, hB$$

Given that, $C_\beta = 0.95$

$$\alpha_r' = 0.4\alpha_r = 0.4\,(35) = 14°$$

$$h = (B/4) = 0.25B$$

Since C_{fa} varies from 0.65 to 0.80, let us take an average value of 0.75.

$$v = 0.2 \text{ m/s}$$

$$\rho_s = 1350 \text{ kg/m}^3$$

$$Q = 85{,}000/3600 = 23.61 \text{ kg/s}$$

Substituting these values in equation (*i*), we get,

$$23.61 = (66.609)\, B^2$$

or $$B = 0.595 \text{ m}$$

Rounding off to the nearest standard size, $B = 0.65$ m

The maximum chain tension can be estimated from equation (10.3.39):

$$T_{max} = 1.05\,[T_{min} + K_{ta}\,[(q_a + q_l)\,L_l + q_a\,L_r] + H\,(q_l + q_a)] \qquad \text{...}(ii)$$

Given that $T_{min} = 1500\, N$

$$L_l = L_r = 20 \text{ m}$$

$$H = 4.0 \text{ m}$$

$$q_l = Qg/v = \frac{(23.61)\ (9.8)}{(0.2)} = 1156.89 \text{ N/m}$$

From equation (10.3.40),

$$q_a = 600\ B + C_b$$

From Table (10.12),

$C_b = 700$ (since $1000 < \rho_s < 2000$ kg/m^3, the load is of intermediate characteristics and therefore a medium type apron can be used).

Therefore, $q_a = 600\ (0.65) + 700 = 1090$ N/m

The value of K_{ta} can be computed from equation (10.3.41) :

$$K_{ta} = C\ (\mu_b'\ d + 2k)/D$$

Given that, $D = 0.05$ m

$$d = 0.02 \text{ m}$$

$$C = 1.2$$

Since the conveyor is operating under moderate conditions, $k = 0.08 \times 10^{-2}$ m (from Table 10.13). Also, μ_b' in plain bearings (assuming continuous lubrication) = 0.15. Thus, $K_{ta} = 0.1104$. Substituting these values in equation (*ii*), we get,

$$T_{\max} = 18.72 \text{ kN}$$

The hauling chains are selected as follows. From equation (10.3.45), the rated force on a single chain will be,

$$S_{r1} = T_{\max}/C_{nu}$$

Taking

$$C_{nu} = 1.8, \quad S_{r1} = (18.72/1.8) = 10.4 \text{ kN}$$

Now from equation (10.3.46), the required rupture strength of the chain will be,

$$S_{rs} = S_{r1}\ (n_{sm})$$

Since the conveyor is inclined, let us take $n_{sm} = 9.0$.

Thus, $S_{rs} = (10.4)\ (9.0) = 93.6$ kN

Therefore, the third standard chain that has rupture strength of 112 kN is to be selected.

10.3.4. Flight Conveyors

Flight conveyors constitute a separate group of conveying machines of diverse design in which the load is pushed along a trough (or tube) by means of moving scrappers or flights. The shape and height of the flights are the principal features by which the flight conveyors are categorised. The general purpose flight conveyors employ solid flights whose height is roughly equal to the depth of the trough (also called high fight conveyors). If the height of the flight is only one third or one sixth of the depth of the trough, then they are called low flight conveyors. The flights may be rectangular, semicircular or trapezoidal in shape. Doubled rectangular flights are used in conveyors with two working runs (material transported both in the lower as well as the upper runs in opposite directions). According to the shape of the flights, the trough can also be rectangular, trapezoidal or semicircular. They are usually made of steel with a wear-resistant cladding inside. Wooden troughs are sometimes employed for conveying light materials such as saw dust, grain etc. and also those materials that cause corrosion of the metal (such as rock salt). High flight conveyors are manufactured in the open and closed versions. In the latter version, the metal structure of the conveyor is closed with steel sheets. The tractive element is usually in the form of one or two laminated wheel chains with a standard pitch of 0.16, 0.2, 0.25, 0.315 or 0.4 m. Conveyors employing flights having width less than 0.4 m are hauled by a single chain and those using wider flights by two chains.

The pitch of flights (interspacing between adjacent flights) is selected depending on the lump size and the angle of repose of the material to be conveyed. It also depends on the height of the flights and the pitch of the chain. The flight pitch a_f is usually taken equal to twice the chain pitch (0.32 to 0.8 m) or two to four times the height of the flights. The selected flight pitch should ensure the highest possible filling of the spaces between flights. It should not be less than the size of the largest lump for lumpy loads. Flight conveyors may be used in the horizontal, inclined or in the mixed modes. The angle of inclination is seldom more than 30–40° since at higher slopes, the capacity of the conveyor diminishes considerably. The take-up device is usually of the screw or spring-screw type and the conveyor drive is of the reducer type mounted at the terminal sprocket.

Flight conveyors are employed for the transport of various pulverised, granular and lumpy materials of a high flowability, such as grain, food waste, garbage and coal. They are not suitable for handling brittle, moist and sticky materials. Friable abrasive materials like clinkers, gravel and crushed ore are also not handled by them. Brittle materials get crushed by the flights while sticky and moist ones adhere to flights and cause difficulties in unloading, diminish the capacity of the conveyor and can clog the return run. Conveyors with low flights are being employed for underground transportation of coal in collieries. Flight conveyors are of simple design and they can be loaded or unloaded at any intermediate point in the conveyor path. The load can be sealed tightly during conveying which could be an advantage when dusty, gas-evolving and hot goods and handled. Their main drawbacks are large wear on the moving elements and troughs particularly while handling abrasive materials, higher power consumption due to increased friction of the load and moving parts on the trough. Crushing of lumps of load during conveying could be unwanted and often objectionable (such as while transporting coke). With hard lumps, the wedging of lumps between flights and the trough can increase the chain tension substantially, leading to damage of the conveyor. Flight conveyors are therefore operated at low speeds of 0.16 to 0.4 m/s. Only in rare cases such as in coal conveyors, speed of 0.5 to 1.0 m/s are employed. The length of the conveyor is seldom more than 100 m and the throughput capacity varies from 50 to 700 tonnes per hour.

Special types of flight conveyors are Redler conveyors which use contoured flights of different shapes for different specific applications. Another special version is represented by tubular flight conveyors with round (or rectangular) solid flights. They can move loads along paths of very diverse configurations. Push-bar flight conveyors employ solid, high flights hinged to a rigid bar or rigidly fixed tenon-shaped flights. The former are often called pendulam-flight conveyors and are employed for the transportation of hot moulding sand in foundry shops. The latter are effective for conveying curled metal chips. Another variety of flight conveyors are the cable-disc conveyors used for hauling wood logs and similar goods in open troughs. A still alternate variety consists of an overhead tramway with a hauling chain and carriages that has a trough suspended beneath, with flights fastened to the carriages pushing the load along the trough.

Unlike the conveyors discussed earlier, different materials acquire different cross-sectional shapes in a flight conveyor and this can be determined only by experimental tests. For example, free-flowing, granular materials collect in heaps before the flights, each heap having the shape of an unsymmetric trapezium in its longitudinal section, whereas poorly flowing, lumpy materials like coal move on the conveyor in a rather smooth layer, almost filling up the entire space between adjacent flights. As a result, the rated cross-sectional area of the load in a trough is usually expressed by the generalised expression,

$$A_b = C_\beta \, (B_t \, h_t) \, C_f \qquad \text{...(10.3.47)}$$

where B_t, h_t = working width and depth of the trough (width and depth occupied by the load) respectively.

Normally, a (B_t/h_t) ratio of 2.5 to 4.0 is used. C_f is called the filling coefficient which indicates the fraction of the volume occupied by the load between the flights. For free flowing materials (angle of repose, $\alpha_r < 30 - 35°$), $C_f = 0.5 - 0.6$ and for poorly flowing lumpy materials, $C_f = 0.7 - 0.8$. The inclination factor C_β depends on the angle of inclination of the conveyor and the flowability of the material as given in Table (10.14). The throughput capacity of the conveyor will then be,

$$Q = A_b \, v \rho_s \qquad \text{...(10.3.48)}$$

Table 10.14

β, *degrees*	C_β	
	Free flowing materials	*Poorly flowing, lumpy materials*
0	1.0	1.0
10	0.85	1.0
20	0.65	1.0
30	0.50	0.75
35	—	0.60
40	—	0.50

Depending on the method of fastening of flights to chains, the structural height of flights should be 0.025 to 0.05 m more than the depth of the trough. The width of the flights can be upto 0.65 m and is usually taken to be 2-3 times their height. As stated earlier, the pitch of the flights a_f is chosen to be twice the chain pitch or 2–4 times the height of the flights. The width of the trough and flight pitch chosen should be checked for the lump size as given below :

$$B_t \geq C_a \, (a)$$

$$a_f \geq 1.5 \, (a) \qquad \text{...(10.3.49)}$$

where a is the average lump size for graded material and the size of the largest lump (provided such lumps occupy more than 10% of the total mass) for ungraded material. For double chain conveyors, $C_a = 3 - 4$ for ungraded materials and 2.0 – 2.5 for graded ones. For single chain conveyors, $C_a = 5.0 - 7.0$ and $3.0 - 3.5$ for ungraded and graded materials respectively.

If the conveyor path consists of only one section (horizontal or inclined), then the total resistance to the motion of the conveyor W will be given by,

$$W = [q_o C_{ch} + q_l C_{lt}] L \pm (q_0 + q_l) H \qquad ...(10.3.50)$$

where L = horizontal projection of that section of the conveyor path (when there is only one section, the total horizontal displacement of the load), m

H = vertical projection of that section (or total vertical displacement (elevation) of the load), m

q_l = linear gravity force of the load, N/m = (Qg/v)

q_o = linear gravity force of the moving parts (chains and flights) of the conveyor (both runs), N/m

The value of q_o is available from manufacturers' catalogue. The coefficient C_{lt} considers the friction of the load on the bottom and walls of the trough. For a steel trough, $C_{lt} = 0.7$ to 1.0 for coarse coal, 0.6 to 0.7 for coal fines and coal dust. For other materials, $C_{lt} = (1.1)\,\mu'$, where μ' is the coefficient of friction of the material on the trough. The coefficient C_{ch} takes care of the resistance to the motion of the chain with support wheels and may be taken to be 0.1 – 0.13, depending upon the operating conditions. For wheel-less chains sliding on the trough, $C_{ch} = 0.25 - 0.4$. The power of the drive motor will then be, $P = (Wv/\eta)$.

If the conveyor path consists of a number of sections, then the pull in each section must be determined separately through detailed computations[2]. In such case, the general formula that can be used for the carrying run of the conveyor is,

$$T_n = T_{n-1} + W \qquad ...(10.3.51)$$

where T_n and T_{n-1} are the chain tensions at the end and beginning of a straight section respectively. W can be determined from equation (10.3.50), taking q_o for the carrying run only.

10.3.5. Bucket Elevators

Elevators are conveying machines employed for lifting solids vertically upwards or over a steeply inclined path (inclined at 60 – 80° with the horizontal). Bucket elevators are most popular for handling bulk materials in process industries. The alternate types such as cradle and shelf (flight) elevators are employed mainly for lifting unit loads such as bags, boxes, barrels etc.

Bucket elevators may be vertical or inclined. In the latter version, the return run may either sag freely or may be supported. Buckets are usually made of steel (though fibre glass or plastic is also occasionally used) and they may be deep or shallow with cylindrical bottoms. Such buckets are used in elevators that employ widely spaced buckets. V-shaped buckets with guiding side walls are employed in low speed, chain elevators whereas trapezoidal buckets are common with inclined elevators. The tractive element may be made up of a belt (rubber-fabric or rubber-cable belt as in the case of belt conveyors) or one or two chains (either laminated chains or welded round-link chains). The width of the belt should be 0.025 to 0.15 m greater than that of buckets. With narrow buckets having width less than 0.25 m, a single hauling chain will be sufficient which is fastened in the middle of the back wall of the buckets. Wider buckets with width more than 0.32 m require two chains and are fastened to them by the back or side walls. Abrasive materials are transported wherever possible by belt elevators since the chains get worn off quickly. Rubber-cable belts are particularly suitable for elevators of large height and with wide buckets. Chains are preferred in elevators of large throughput capacity and for elevating heavy lumps and hot materials to substantially large heights, which cannot be handled by rubber belt conveyors.

The buckets are filled or loaded by scooping the material at the bottom of the elevator or by pouring the material directly into the buckets. Scooping can be employed only with dry, free-flowing and low size materials and also when high speed elevators (v = 0.8 to 4 m/s) having widely spaced buckets are used. Pulverised coal, cement, sand, grain and saw dust are loaded by this way. Large size, lumpy and abrasive materials like ore, gravel etc. are difficult to scoop by buckets since they offer high resistance and can cause breakage of buckets or even the tractive element. Such materials are poured directly into the buckets. In such case, the elevator must employ closely placed buckets and should run at low speeds (less than 1 m/s) since at higher speeds the buckets are filled poorly and may throw off the material.

The buckets may be unloaded by centrifugal discharge, free gravity discharge or by directed gravity discharge. *Centrifugal discharge* is due to centrifugal forces that develop when the buckets revolve over the head pulley or sprocket. The buckets are bolted through the back onto a single strand of chain or belt. The load is thrown out of the buckets by centrifugal forces as they pass over the head or upper wheel and the material falls directly into the unloading spout of the elevator casing. For effective centrifugal discharge and in order to avoid fall-off of the material, the speed of rotation of the pulley or sprocket and the relative position of the unloading spout should be carefully chosen. The speed of the buckets is usually 1.0 to 4.0 m/s. The spacing between buckets should be selected in such a way that the jet of discharged material does not strike the preceding bucket. Centrifugal discharge is employed in high speed belt (and less frequently chain) elevators handling free-flowing, granular and pulverised materials. In *free gravity discharge or "positive discharge"* elevators, the buckets are carried on two strands of chain which are snubbed under the head wheels and afford a more positive discharge. The buckets are "end-hung" between the two strands of chain and are inverted as they pass over the head sprockets and behind the idler wheels, thereby effectively discharging the materials that are not well handled by centrifugal discharge elevators. Therefore, this type of discharge can be used with poorly flowing, moist or flaky materials such as chalk, wet ash, saw dust and various chemicals. In single chain conveyors, such deflection or snubbing is possible only if the centrally arranged chain carries the buckets at its sides while its internal and external surfaces are free to engage the snubbing sprockets. In inclined elevators, free gravity discharge is ensured by the inclined position of the elevator. *Directed gravity discharge* is typical of vertical and inclined elevators (either belt or chain type) with buckets mounted very close to one another and thus forming a continuous row of buckets. During revolving over the top pulley or sprocket, the material pours out by gravity from each bucket onto the back surface of the previous bucket and is then directed by the bucket walls to the unloading spout. This method is employed in low speed elevators (bucket speed = 0.4 to 0.8 m/s) for handling heavy, lumpy and brittle materials such as gravel, ores, slag, peat, charcoal, coke etc. High capacity is obtained by the large number of buckets and not by the speed.

Bucket elevators have relatively small cross-sectional dimensions and they are capable of lifting loads to large heights (upto 60 – 75 m). They also possess a wide range of throughput capacities, from 5.0 m^3/hr to as large as 500 m^3/hr and more. Their main limitation is that the material must be supplied in a uniform flow since on overloading, the buckets may break off from the belt or chains. The speed of buckets usually ranges from 0.4 to 2.5 m/s.

The throughput capacity of bucket elevators depends on the volume of the buckets, the pitch of the buckets and the bucket speed. It can be therefore computed as,

$$Q = (V_b/a_b)\, v \rho_s\, C_{fb} \qquad \text{...(10.3.52)}$$

where V_b = useful geometrical volume of each bucket, m^3 (available from manufacturers' catalogue)

a_b = pitch of buckets, m

v = speed of belt of chain, m/s

For widely spaced deep or shallow buckets, $a_b = (2.5 - 3.0)\ H_b$ and for closely spaced buckets with guiding side walls, $a_b \cong H_b$, where H_b is the height (depth) of the bucket. For chain elevators, the bucket pitch is taken as a multiple of one or two chain pitches. C_{fb} is the coefficient of bucket filling and its typical values are given in Table (10.15). For lumpy loads, the length of the bucket chosen (L_b) must be checked for the largest lump size (a) as given below :

$$L_b \geq C_a\ (a) \qquad ...(10.3.53)$$

where the coefficient $C_a = 2.0 - 2.5$ for ungraded loads and $4.0 - 5.0$ for graded ones.

The pull of the elevator is to be computed by the successive summation of the resistances in the elevator path. In this connection, the scooping resistance W_{sc} should also be considered which is the resistance offered by the material during loading to the buckets at the elevator boot. This can be determined experimentally or roughly calculated by the relation,

$$W_{sc} = K_{sc}\ q_l \qquad ...(10.3.54)$$

where K_{sc} = scooping coefficient or the unit work expended for scooping, Nm/N

q_l = linear gravity force of the load, N/m

= (Qg/v)

With the bucket speed of 1.0 to 1.25 m/s, it may be recommended to take $K_{sc} = 1.25 - 2.5$ Nm/N for pulverised and fine size lumpy loads and $K_{sc} = 2.0 - 4.0$ Nm/N for medium size lumps.

Table 10.15

Type of discharge	*Type of load*	C_{fb}
High speed centrifugal discharge	Dry, pulverised (e.g. : cement, flour, pulverised coal)	0.8
	Pulverised, granular, wet, poorly flowing (soil, sand, chalk, chemicals etc.)	0.6
	Granular, fine lumps, less abrasive (Food grains, saw dust, wood chips, milled peat, dry clay in lumps)	0.75-0.80

	Medium size, lumpy ($a \cong$ 60 mm), less abrasive (e.g. : dug peat)	0.65
Low speed free gravity discharge	Dry, pulverised (e.g. : pulverised coal)	0.85
	Granular, fine lumps, less abrasive (Lime, soot etc.)	0.8
Low speed directed gravity discharge	Granular, small lump, highly abrasive (Gravel, ore, slags etc.)	0.8
	Medium size, lumpy $y(a \cong$ 60 mm), less abrasive (e.g. : coal)	0.7
	Medium size, lumpy, highly abrasive (stone, ore, slag etc.)	0.7
	Lumpy, brittle (e.g. : charcoal)	0.6

For belt elevators, the diameter of the drive pulley d_d is selected depending on the method of bucket unloading employed. Since, as discussed earlier, the discharge can be either by gravity or centrifugal means, the ratio of gravity force to centrifugal force on the load C_g becomes the deciding factor :

$$C_g = \frac{g}{(2v^2/d_d)} = \frac{d_d\, g}{2v^2} \qquad ...(10.3.55)$$

Thus, the recommended criteria is as follows[2] :

For high speed elevators employing centrifugal di‹charge, $C_g \leq 1$ and therefore $d_d \leq (2v^2/g)$. If the elevator is emplc‸ ıg combined (centrifugal and gravity) discharge, then $C_g = 1.0 - 1.4$ or $d_d = (2.0 \text{ to } 2.8) \times (v^2/g)$. For low speed elevators employing gravity discharge, C_g should be greater than 3.0 and therefore $d_d \geq (6v^2/g)$. If a rubber-fabric belt is used, d_d = (0.125 to 0.15) N, where N is the number of fabric plies. The diameter of the take-up pulley (or sprocket) is usually the same as that of the drive pulley.

Example 10.4. *A vertical bucket elevator is to be used for lifting moulding sand to a height of 22 m at 30,000 kg/hr. The bulk density of sand = 1500 kg/m^3. The bucket speed is 1.6 m/s and the recommended bucket spacing is 0.4 m. Standard deep buckets with volumes 1.3, 2.0 and 4.0 litres (corresponding bucket width and belt width being 0.2, 0.25, 0.32 m and 0.25, 0.3, 0.37 m respectively) are available. Determine which specifications shall suit best to the purpose. Estimate also the power of the drive motor if the efficiency of the drive mechanism* *is 85%. The conveyor is operating outdoors and take the coefficient of pulley resistance (for both take-up and drive pulleys) to be 1.08 and the scooping coefficient 2.0 Nm/N.*

Solution. Let us first decide the type of discharge to be employed. We select a four-ply rubber-fabric belt (this we shall verify later) having a strength of 55 kN/m. Then, diameter of drive pulley $d_d = (0.125)\,(4) = 0.5$ m

Now, from equation (10.3.55),

$$C_g = \frac{d_d g}{2v^2} = \frac{(0.5)\,(9.8)}{(2.0)\,(1.6)^2} = 0.957$$

Since $C_g < 1.0$, the buckets can be unloaded centrifugally. The used moulding sand can be considered to be a granular, small-lump and less abrasive material. Therefore, from Table (10.15), $C_{fb} = 0.8$. The required volume of each bucket from equation (10.3.52) will be,

$$V_b = \left[\frac{Q}{v\rho_s\, C_{fb}}\right] a_b$$

$$= \frac{(30{,}000)\,(0.4)}{(1.6)\,(1500)\,(0.8)\,(3600)}$$

$$= 1.736 \times 10^{-3}\ \text{m}^3 = 1.736\ \text{litre}$$

We can therefore select the 2 litre buckets. Correspondingly, bucket width (B_b) = 0.25 m and belt width (B) = 0.3 m.

To compute the power of the drive motor, let us first estimate the linear gravity forces of the load (q_l) and the buckets and belt (q_o). From manufacturer's catalogue,

mass of four-ply rubber-fabric belt = 2.55 kg/m

and, mass of the standard deep bucket selected = 3.38 kg

Therefore, $q_o = (2.55)\,(9.8) + (3.38)\,(9.8)/0.4$

$$= 24.99 + 82.81 = 107.8\ \text{N/m}$$

$$q_l = (Qg/v) = \frac{(30{,}000)\,(9.8)}{(3600)\,(1.6)} = 51.04\ \text{N/m}$$

Thus, the total gravity force in the carrying run,

$$q = (q_o + q_l) = 158.84\ \text{N/m}$$

Referring to Figure (10.4.1), it is reasonable to expect the lowest tension of the belt at point (1). Let us assume that $T_1 = T_i$ (initial tension in the belt). Then,

$$T_2 = C_{pu}\,T_1 + W_{sc} = C_{pu}\,T_i + K_{sc}\,q_l$$

Given that $C_{pu} = 1.08$

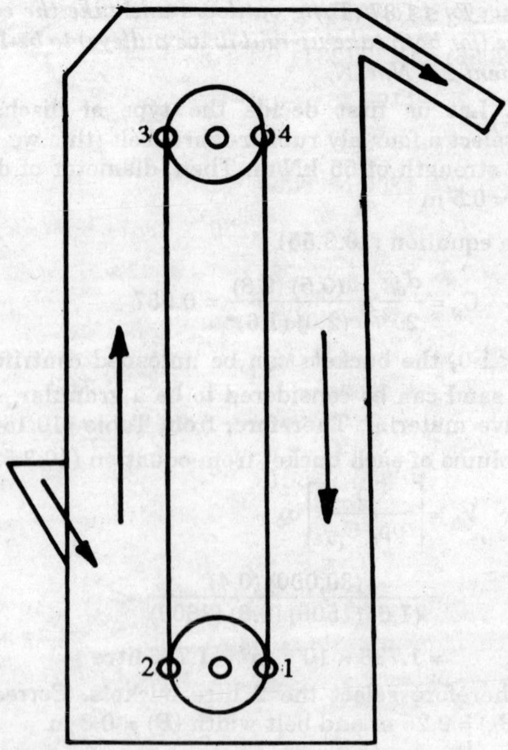

Fig. 10.4.1

$$K_{sc} = 2.0 \text{ Nm/N}$$

Therefore, $$T_2 = (1.08)\, T_i + 2.0\, (51.04)$$

$$= 102.08 + 1.08\, T_i$$

$$T_3 = T_o = T_2 + qH = (102.08 + 1.08\, T_i) + (158.84)\,(22)$$

$$= 3596.56 + 1.08\, T_i$$

$$T_4 = T_f = T_1 + q_o H = T_i + (107.8)\,(22)$$

$$= 2371.6 + T_i$$

According to the theory of frictional drives (equation 10.3.21),

$$(T_o / T_f) \le e^{\mu' \alpha_w}$$

or, $$T_3 \le T_4\, e^{\mu' \alpha_w}$$

From Table (10.7), for a steel pulley for heavy operating conditions under humid atmosphere (since the elevator is operating outdoors), $\mu' = 0.1$. At $\alpha_w = 180° = \pi$ radians, $e^{\mu' \alpha_w} = e^{0.1\pi} = 1.37$

Therefore, $T_3 \le 1.37\,(T_4)$

or, $(1.08T_i + 3596.56) \le [1.37\,(2371.6 + T_i)]$

or $T_i \ge 1198.16$

Let us therefore take

$T_i = 1200$ N. Thus,

$$T_4 = T_f = (2371.6 + 1200) = 3571.6 \text{ N}$$

$$T_3 = T_o = 1.37\,(3571.6) = 4893.1 \text{ N}$$

The required number of belt plies can be now computed from equation (10.3.27) :

$$N_r = KT_o/S_{pl}\,B$$

where S_{pl} = Strength of ply fabric = 55 kN/m

$B = 0.3$ m

$T_o = 4893.1$ N

$K = 7.0/(K_{pl}\,K_j\,K_{cp}\,K_{op})$

Since we had initially selected four plies, let us take $K_{pl} = 0.9$ (Table 10.8). Since vulcanised joints are most efficient, $K_j = 0.85$. Since operating conditions of the elevator is heavy, $K_{op} = 0.95$ and $K_{cp} = 1.0$.

Thus, $K = 7.0/[(0.9)\,(0.85)\,(1.0)\,(0.95)] = 9.63$

Therefore, $N_r = (9.63)\,(4893.1)/(55{,}000)\,(0.3) = 2.86 \cong 3$

Noting that the belt is weakened by bolts and firm fastening of buckets is to be ensured, the original choice of four plies is justified. The circumferential force on the drive pulley will be,

$$W = C_{pu}\,(T_o - T_f) = C_{pu}\,(T_3 - T_4)$$

$$= 1.08\,(4893.1 - 3571.6) = 1427.22 \text{ N}$$

Since $\eta = 0.85$ and taking a safety margin of 1.25,

$$P = \text{motor power} = \frac{(1427.22)\,(1.6)\,(1.25)}{(0.85)}$$

$$= 3.36 \text{ kW}$$

10.4. Hydraulic and Pneumatic Transport

As stated earlier, long distance transport of solids by rail or road often becomes uneconomical. In a country like India where the coal fields are highly localised, it has been observed that the cost of transportation of coal over long distances (600 – 1000 km) by railways often exceeds the cost of the transported coal itself. It is in such situations, a continuous mode of transport such as slurry transportation becomes highly desirable. Solids can be conveniently conveyed through pipe lines in the form a slurry or suspension in a fluid. If the carrier fluid is water, then it is called *hydraulic transport* and if air is used as the carrier fluid, then it is called *pneumatic transport.* Hydraulic transport through underground pipelines can be employed for transport over long distances. Even for inplant transport of solids such as lifting of solid particles to the top of a tall column for continuous feeding, pneumatic or hydraulic transport can be efficiently utilised. Particularly for long distance applications, slurry transportation through underground pipe lines has the distinct advantages such as continuous operation, practically immune to adverse weather conditions, less manpower requirement and the possibility of following a relatively shorter route. Various studies on transportation of coal-water slurries over long distances have shown that the pipe line transport offers higher specific transportation capacity and lower power consumption than those for transport by rail or road. Some typical figures are given below[3] :

Table 10.16

Mode of transport	*Specific transportation capacity, kg/kW*	*Power consumption, W/(kg.km)*
Automobiles	65 — 200	0.149
Railways	270 — 800	0.037
Waterways	2,700 — 6,700	0.011
Airways	1.5 — 4.0	0.746
Pipeline transport	5,400 — 40,000	0.011

10.4.1. Hydraulic Transport

Let us first consider hydraulic transport through horizontal pipes. Suspensions of solids in water may be classified as settling slurries and non-settling slurries. When the particle size is very small (less than 50 microns) and the volume fraction of solids in the slurry is large (more than 0.50), the settling velocity of the particles will be so small that they hardly settle and remain practically in suspension. Such non-settling slurries may be treated as a single non-Newtonian fluid and the two-phase character of the slurry can be neglected. The rheological equation obeyed by aqueous suspensions is either that of Bingham plastic fluids or that of psuedoplastic (power-law) fluids. The rheological equation can be broadly represented as,

$$\tau = -\eta\Delta \quad ...(10.4.1)$$

where τ is the shear stress or momentum flux and Δ is the rate of deformation tensor. For unidimensional flow in rectangular co-ordinates, the above equation reduces to,

$$\tau_{yx} = -\mu\left(\frac{dV_x}{dy}\right), \text{ for Newtonian fluids} \quad ...(10.4.2)$$

where τ_{yx} is the x-component of the momentum flux acting in y-direction and μ is the viscosity of the fluid.

For power law fluids, the equivalent equation (also called Ostwald-de-Waele equation) is,

$$\tau_{yx} = -m\,(dV_x/dy)^n \quad ...(10.4.3)$$

where m is called the consistency index and n is called the flow behaviour index. The values of m and n are empirical and are to be experimentally determined. If $n < 1$, the fluid is called psuedo-plastic and if $n > 1$, it is called dilatant fluid. For Bingham plastic fluids,

$$\tau_{yx} = \tau_o \pm \mu_o\left(\frac{dV_x}{dy}\right) \quad ...(10.4.4)$$

where τ_o is called the threshold shear stress.

Once the suspension has bee ı considered to be a single non-Newtonian fluid, the power requirement for transporting it through pipelines can be determined using the classical Bernoulli equation, after modifying it for non-Newtonian flow. For steady state flow through a horizontal conduit of diameter D, the shaft work done by the pump $(-W_s)$ will be essentially equal to the frictional resistance in the pipe. Thus, from Fanning's equation,

$$(-W_s) = \frac{2f_n L V_{avg}^2}{D\eta} \text{ J/kg} \quad ...(10.4.5)$$

where η = mechanical efficiency of the pump

V_{avg} = average velocity of the fluid through the pipe, m/s

f_n = friction factor for non-Newtonian flow.

For psuedo-plastic fluids, f_n is defined as,

$$f_n = \frac{2^{n+1} m}{D^n \rho_f V_{avg}^{2-n}}\left[3 + \frac{1}{n}\right]^n \quad ...(10.4.6)$$

As in the case of Newtonian fluids, f_n depends on the Reynolds number Re_n and standard plots are available in literature[4,5] showing the dependence of f_n on Re_n. The Reynolds number Re_n for psuedo-plastic fluids is defined as given below :

$$Re_n = 2^{3-n}\left[\frac{n}{3n+1}\right]^n\left[\frac{D^n V_{avg}^{2-n}\rho_f}{m}\right] \qquad ...(10.4.7)$$

The critical Reynolds number $Re_{n,c}$ at which the transition to turbulent flow begins (which is 2,100 for Newtonian fluids) is given by,

$$Re_{n,c} = (2100)\left[\frac{(4n+2)(5n+3)}{3(3n+1)^2}\right] \qquad ...(10.4.8)$$

In the laminar zone ($Re_n < Re_{n,c}$),

$$f_n = 16/Re_n \qquad ...(10.4.9)$$

For $Re_n > Re_{n,c}$, Dodge and Metzner[6] have proposed the following correlation :

$$f_n^{-0.5} = (4.0/n^{0.75})\,[\log Re_n f_n^{1-0.5n}] - [0.4/n^{1.2}] \qquad ...(10.4.10)$$

Once the value of f_n has been determined either by using any of the above correlations or from the standard plots, the pump work $(-W_s)$ can be computed from equation (10.4.5). If $\dot{m}$ is the mass flow rate of the fluid, then the total power consumption will be,

$$P = (-W_s)\,\dot{m} \text{ watts} \qquad ...(10.4.11)$$

We have not included additional resistance offered by pipe fittings in the above equations, which may occasionally amount to as much as 15 to 20 per cent.

In the case of settling slurries, the two-phase character of the slurry cannot be neglected. In such cases, for horizontal transport, the minimum conveying velocity required (V_{min}) can be determined from the correlation proposed by Spells[7] :

$$\left[\frac{V_{min}^2}{D_p g}\right]\left[\frac{\rho_L}{\rho_s - \rho_L}\right] = 0.0251\left[\frac{D V_{min}\,\rho_b}{\mu_L}\right]^{0.775} \qquad ...(10.4.12)$$

It has been assumed that 85 per cent (by weight) of particles have a size less than D_p. ρ_b is the bulk density of the slurry and can be estimated from the solid density ρ_s and density of water ρ_L as,

$$\rho_b = (1-\varepsilon)\,\rho_s + \varepsilon\rho_L \qquad ...(10.4.13)$$

where $\quad \varepsilon$ = volume fraction of liquid (water) in the slurry

The above equation (10.4.12) is based on experiments performed using slurries containing particles of size less than 1 mm and pipe diameters in the range of 0.025 to 0.3 m.

It will be of interest to find out the transport velocity V_2 at which the pressure gradient for slurry becomes equal to that for a pure liquid of same density as the slurry and of viscosity same as water. As reported by Spells,

$$\left[\frac{V_2^2}{gD_p}\right]\left(\frac{\rho_L}{\rho_s - \rho_L}\right) = 0.074\left[\frac{DV_2\,\rho_b}{\mu_L}\right]^{0.775} \quad ...(10.4.14)$$

Thus, it can be seen that with finely divided solids, the pressure gradient at high velocities may be less for the slurry than that for the liquid alone because the solids tend to damp the turbulence.

Although there are considerable data on pressure drop for the flow of water suspensions of sand, gravel, coal and the like in horizontal pipes, no single correlation has been found to be entirely satisfactory for all particle sizes, particle densities, concentrations and pipe sizes. The modified Durand equation[8] is fairly acceptable for a good number of practical purposes :

$$\alpha_p = \frac{(-\Delta P_m)}{(-\Delta P_L)} = 1 + 150\,(1-\varepsilon)\left[\frac{Dg\,(\rho_s - \rho_L)}{V_{avg}^2\,\sqrt{f_D}\,\rho_L}\right]^{3/2} \quad ...(10.4.15)$$

where V_{avg} = average velocity of slurry through the pipe, m/s

V_t = free settling velocity of particles in water, m/s

$(-\Delta P_m)$ = pressure drop for transporting slurry, N/m^2

$(-\Delta P_L)$ = pressure drop for transporting water at the same velocity through the same pipe, N/m^2

α_p = relative pressure drop

f_D = drag coefficient, the value of which can be obtained from the standard f_D versus Re_p plot (see Fig. 3.1 of chapter 3)

The above equation is based on the flow of water suspensions containing particles of size 0.025 to 2.5 cm with particle concentrations upto 30 per cent ($\varepsilon = 0.7$) in pipes of diameter 0.04 to 0.6 m. The equation is applicable for closely sized particles and for liquid velocities greater than 1.0 m/s.

For hydraulic transport of solids vertically upwards, the principal condition is that the conveying velocity must be significantly higher than the free settling velocity of the particles. For slurry velocities more than 4–5 times the free settling velocity of particles, the pressure drop can be estimated as,

$$(-\Delta P_m) = (-\Delta P_L) + \rho_b\,Lg \quad ..(10.4.16)$$

Once the pressure drop ($-\Delta P_m$) has been estimated, the power consumption can be computed as,

$$P = \frac{(-\Delta P_m)}{\rho_b}\dot{m} \qquad ...(10.4.17)$$

where $\dot{m}$ is the mass flow rate of slurry, kg/s

Example 10.5. *Bituminous coal (specific gravity = 1.3) from a coal processing unit has the following size distribution. If the entire coal is to be transported hydraulically through a 0.25 m horizontal pipe to a distance of 10 km in the form of a homogeneous slurry containing 20% by weight of solids, estimate the minimum conveying velocity that is to be maintained.*

Particle size (mm)	*Mass fraction*
– 1.6 + 1.4	0.03
– 1.4 + 0.8	0.06
– 0.8 + 0.6	0.09
– 0.6 + 0.4	0.35
– 0.4 + 0.3	0.30
– 0.3	0.17

Solution. The minimum conveying velocity V_{min} can be estimated from equation (10.4.12) :

$$\left[\frac{V_{min}^2}{gD_p}\right]\left(\frac{\rho_L}{\rho_s - \rho_L}\right) = 0.0251\left[\frac{DV_{min}\,\rho_b}{\mu_L}\right]^{0.775}$$

where
$$\rho_L = 1000 \text{ kg/m}^3$$
$$\rho_s = 1300 \text{ kg/m}^3$$
$$D = 0.25 \text{ m}$$
$$\mu_L = 0.001 \text{ kg/ms}$$

Since the suspension contains 20 per cent by weight of solids,

$$\rho_b = \frac{100}{(20/1300) + (80/1000)}$$
$$= 1048.387 \text{ kg/m}^3$$

To find D_p, let us construct the cumulative mass fraction table from the size distribution data given :

Particle size (mm)	*Cumulative mass fraction*
1.6	1.0
1.4	0.97
0.8	0.91
0.6	0.82
0.4	0.47
0.3	0.17

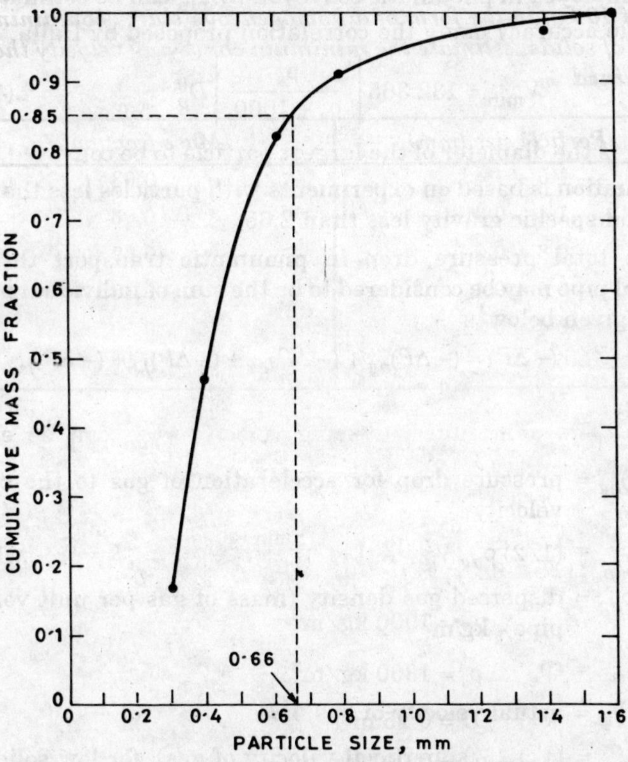

Fig. 10.5.1. Cumulative mass fraction versus particle size plot.

The plot of cumulative mass fraction (X) versus particle size is given in Figure (10.5.1). From the figure, at X = 0.85, particle size = 0.66 mm or 6.6×10^{-4} m. Thus, 85% of particles have a size less than 0.66 mm or D_p in the above equation is 6.6×10^{-4} m. Substituting all the values and solving for V_{min}, we get,

$$V_{min} = 0.809 \text{ m/s}$$

10.4.2. Pneumatic Transport

In pneumatic transport through horizontal pipes, the air velocity should be adjusted in such a way that the particles remain uniformly distributed in the fluid. With low-density solids or low solid to gas ratios and high gas velocities, the solids normally remain fully suspended and fairly uniformly dispersed over the pipe cross-section. No single correlation is available for the accurate prediction of minimum carrying velocity (V_{min}) for all solid to gas ratios in horizontal pipes. However, at low solid to gas ratios (less than 10.0 by weight) as usually employed in pneumatic conveyors, V_{min} can be estimated with reasonable accuracy using the correlation proposed by Dalla Valle[9] :

$$V_{min} = 132.365 \left[\frac{\rho_s}{\rho_s + 1000} \right] D_p^{0.4} \quad ...(10.4.18)$$

where D_p is the diameter of the largest particle to be conveyed, m. The above equation is based on experiments with particles less than 8 mm in size and specific gravity less than 2.65.

The total pressure drop in pneumatic transport through a horizontal pipe may be considered to be the sum of individual pressure drops as given below[4] :

$$(-\Delta P) = (-\Delta P)_{ag} + (-\Delta P)_{as} + (-\Delta P)_{fg} + (-\Delta P)_{fs} \quad ...(10.4.19)$$

where

$(-\Delta P)_{ag}$ = pressure drop for acceleration of gas to the carrying velocity

$= (1/2)\, \rho_{dg} V_g^2$ ...(10.4.20)

ρ_{dg} = dispersed gas density (mass of gas per unit volume of pipe), kg/m^3

$= \varepsilon \rho_g$

V_g = actual velocity of gas, m/s

$= (V_g)_{sup}$ (superficial velocity of gas), for low solid to gas ratios commonly employed in pneumatic transport.

$(-\Delta P)_{as}$ = pressure drop for acceleration of solid particles

$= \rho_{ds} V_s^2$ ...(10.4.21)

ρ_{ds} = dispersed solid density, kg/m^3

$= (1 - \varepsilon)\, \rho_s$

V_s = actual velocity of solids, m/s (see equation 10.4.29)

$$(-\Delta P)_{fg} = [2fL\,\rho_{dg}\,V_g^2/D] \quad ...(10.4.22)$$

f = Fanning friction factor (available from standard plots[1,4] of f versus Re where $Re = DV_g\,\rho_g/\mu_g$)

The above relation (10.4.22) is to account for the friction between gas and the pipe wall. For friction between gas and particles, between particles and between particles and pipe wall, we can write a similar expression,

$$(-\Delta P)_{fs} = (2f_s\,L\rho_{ds}\,V_s^2/D] \quad ...(10.4.23)$$

However, the friction factor f_s is required to be defined. This can be done by making a force balance on a particle in the pipe. Assuming the particle to be essentially spherical, the total drag force on the particle F_R can be written as,

$$F_R = AKf \text{ (see equation 3.1.4 of chapter 3)}$$

$$= (\pi\,D_p^2/4)\,[\,(1/2)\,\rho_g\,(V_g - V_s)^2]\,f_D \quad ...(10.4.24)$$

where f_D is the drag coeffcient, the value of which is available from standard plot of f_D versus Re_p (see Figure 3.1 of chapter 3) . For the present case, Re_p should be defined as,

$$Re_p = D_p\,(V_g - V_s)\,\rho_g/\mu_g \quad ...(10.4.25)$$

Thus, the force balance equation will be,

$$F_R = (-\Delta P)_{fs}\,(\pi D^2/4) \quad ...(10.4.26)$$

Also, $$\rho_{ds} = \frac{\text{mass of solid}}{\text{volume of pipe}} = \frac{(\pi D_p^3/6)\,\rho_s}{(\pi D^2/4)\,L} \quad ...(10.4.27)$$

Substituting for F_R, $(-\Delta P)_{fs}$ and ρ_{ds} from equations (10.4.23), (10.4.24) and (10.4.27) respectively in equation, (10.4.26) and rearranging, we get,

$$f_s = \left(\frac{3}{8}\right)\left[\frac{\rho_g\,f_D\,D}{D_p\,\rho_s}\right]\left[\frac{V_g - V_s}{V_s}\right]^2 \quad ...(10.4.28)$$

At the low solid to air ratios usually employed in pneumatic conveyors, the solid velocity V_s can be reliably estimated using the correlation developed by Hinkel[4] :

$$[V_s/(V_g)_{sup}] = [1 - 0.06368 D_p^{0.3}\,\rho_s^{0.5}] \quad ...(10.4.29)$$

The total pressure drop $(-\Delta P)$ for vertical transport can be computed in the same way as horizontal transport, except that two additional terms such as the pressure drop for supporting the column of gas of height L, $(-\Delta P)_{hg}$ and that for supporting solids, $(-\Delta P)_{hs}$ are also to be included. Thus,

$$(-\Delta P) = (-\Delta P)_{ag} + (-\Delta P)_{as} + (-\Delta P)_{fg} + (-\Delta P)_{fs} + (-\Delta P)_{hg} + (-\Delta P)_{hs} \quad ...(10.4.30)$$

where $(-\Delta P)_{hg} = L\,\rho_{dg}\,g$

$$(-\Delta P)_{hs} = L\,\rho_{ds}\,g$$

For vertical transport, at the low solid to air ratios (less than 5 to 10 by weight) normally employed in pneumatic conveying, it may be assumed that

$$V_g \cong (V_g)_{sup}$$

and $(V_g - V_s) \cong V_t$

(terminal free settling velocity of particles in air)

Example 10.6. *Estimate the power consumption for lifting ore particles (specific gravity = 1.2) pneumatically at the rate of 30 kg/minute to a height of 50 m from the following data :*

Air : solid ratio (by weight) maintained = 1 : 5

Diameter of pipe (G.I.) = 0.07 m

Particle size = – 0.45 + 0.4 mm

Viscosity of air = 0.018 centi poises

Specific gravity of air = 0.0013

The roughness parameter ε_r *for the G.I. pipe may be taken to be 0.0112 cm.*

Solution. The total pressure drop $(-\Delta P)$ can be computed from equation (10.4.30). Let us therefore estimate each factor separately. Given that the mass ratio of air to solids is 1 : 5.

Thus, $(m_a/m_s) = 1/5$

Since $m_s = 30$ kg/min, $m_a = (30/5) = 6$ kg/min

Now, ε = volume fraction air in the mixture

$$= \frac{(m_a/\rho_a)}{(m_a/\rho_a) + (m_s/\rho_s)} = \frac{1}{1 + (5\rho_a/\rho_s)}$$

$$= \frac{1}{1 + [5\,(1.3)/1200]} = 0.9946$$

Therefore $\rho_{dg} = \varepsilon\rho_g = 0.9946\,(1.3) = 1.293 \text{ kg/m}^3$

$$\rho_{ds} = (1 - 0.9946)\,1200 = 6.465 \text{ kg/m}^3$$

Since the solid to air ratio is very low, we can take

$$V_g = (V_g)_{sup} = \frac{m_a}{\rho_a\,(\pi D^2/4)} = \frac{6.0\,(4.0)}{60\,(1.3)\,\pi\,(0.07)^2} = 20 \text{ m/s}$$

Therefore,

$$(-\Delta P)_{ag} = \frac{(1.293)\,(20.0)^2}{2} = 258.6 \text{ N/m}^2 \qquad ...(i)$$

Let us assume that the particles are essentially spherical. Since the flow zone is not always likely to be laminar, let us utilise Newton's law to estimate the free settling velocity of particles. This involves a trial and error procedure. Thus, let $f_D = 1.5$. Now, from Newton's law,

$$V_t = \left[\frac{4}{3}\left(\frac{\rho_s - \rho_g}{\rho_g}\right)\frac{gD_p}{f_D}\right]^{1/2}$$

Since $(\rho_s - \rho_g) \cong \rho_s = 1200$ kg/m^3 and considering the largest particle to be conveyed ($D_p = 0.45$ mm),

$$V_t = \left[\frac{(4)}{(3)}\,\frac{(1200)}{(1.3)}\,\frac{(9.8)\,(0.45\times10^{-3})}{(1.5)}\right]^{1/2} = 1.902 \text{ m/s}$$

$$Re_p = \frac{(0.45\times10^{-3})\,(1.902)\,(1.3)}{(0.018\times10^{-3})} = 61.815$$

Corresponding to this Re_p the value of f_D from the standard plot (Fig. 3.1 of chapter 3) is 1.45. Since this value is very close to our initial assumption, we avoid further trial.

Thus, $\quad V_t = 1.9$ m/s

$$V_s \cong (V_g - V_t) = (20 - 1.9) = 18.1 \text{ m/s}$$

$$(-\Delta P)_{as} = \rho_{ds}\,V_s^2 = (6.465)\,(18.1)^2 = 2118.0 \text{ N/m}^2 \qquad ...(ii)$$

$$Re = \frac{DV_g\,\rho_g}{\mu_g} = \frac{(0.07)\,(20.0)\,(1.3)}{(0.018\times10^{-3})} = 10.11\times10^4$$

Since it is given that

$$\varepsilon_r = 1.12\times10^{-4} \text{ m},$$

$$(\varepsilon_r/D) = \left[\frac{1.12\times10^{-4}}{0.07}\right] = 0.0016$$

For turbulent flow ($Re > 10^4$), the Moody chart that gives the standard plots of f versus Re at different values of (ε_r/D) can be roughly correlated as[10]

$$\frac{1}{\sqrt{f}} = -4 \log_{10}\left[\frac{1.255}{Re\sqrt{f}} + \frac{(\varepsilon_r/D)}{3.7}\right]$$

Substituting for Re and (ε_r/D) as $Re = 10.11 \times 10^4$ and $(\varepsilon_r/D) = 0.0016$, we get by trial and error, $f = 0.006$.

Therefore, $$(-\Delta P)_{fg} = \frac{2fL\,\rho_{dg}\,V_g^2}{D}$$

$$= \frac{2.0\,(0.006)\,(50.0)\,(1.293)\,(20)^2}{(0.07)}$$

$$= 3694.3 \text{ N/m}^2 \qquad \ldots(iii)$$

Now, $$f_s = \frac{3}{8}\left[\frac{\rho_g f_D D}{D_p \rho_s}\right]\left[\frac{V_t}{V_s}\right]^2$$

$$= \frac{3.0\,(1.3)\,(1.5)\,(0.07)}{8.0\,(0.45 \times 10^{-3})\,(1200)}\left[\frac{1.9}{18.1}\right]^2$$

$$= 1.0445 \times 10^{-3}$$

$$(-\Delta P)_{fs} = \frac{2f_s\,L\rho_{ds}\,V_s^2}{D}$$

$$= \frac{(2.0)\,(1.0445 \times 10^{-3})\,(50)\,(6.465)\,(18.1)^2}{(0.07)}$$

$$= 3160.356 \text{ N/m}^2 \qquad \ldots(iv)$$

$$(-\Delta P)_{hg} = L\,\rho_{dg}\,g = (50)\,(1.293)\,(9.8) = 633.57 \text{ N/m}^2 \qquad \ldots(v)$$

$$(-\Delta P)_{hs} = L\,\rho_{ds}\,g = (50)\,(6.465)\,(9.8) = 3167.85 \text{ N/m}^2 \qquad \ldots(vi)$$

Adding up (*i*), (*ii*), (*iii*), (*iv*), (*v*) and (*vi*), we get

$$(-\Delta P) = 13032.67 \text{ N/m}^2$$

$\dot{m}$ = mass flow rate of slurry = (30 + 6) = 36 kg/min

ρ_b = bulk density of slurry = (6.465 + 1.293)

$= 7.758 \text{ kg/m}^3$

Therefore, P = power consumption

$$= \frac{(13032.67)}{(7.758)}\left(\frac{36}{60}\right) = 1.0079 \text{ kW}$$

The actual power consumption will be the above value divided by the mechanical efficiency of the pump or blower used.

10.5. Computer Aided Analysis of Pneumatic Conveying System

Since the computational procedure for pneumatic conveyors is rather lengthy, the use of high speed computers shall be desirable. A consolidated computation flow-graph for the design of a pneumatic conveyor for vertical transport of solids is given in Figure (10.5). In the figure, $\dot{m}_s$ is the amount of solids handled (kg/s) and (S/G) is the solid to air ratio maintained (normally less than 5 to 10). D_{pm} is the screen size of the largest particle to be conveyed and ψ_s is the average sphericity of particles. Data base-1 stores the standard plot of n (specific surface ratio) versus screen size (D_{avg}) so that once the screen size D_{pm} is supplied to it, the corresponding value of n can be retrieved (the standard plot is given in Figure 1.1 of chapter 1). Data base-2 stores the standard plots of f_D versus Re_p (see Figure 3.1 of chapter-3) for different values of particle sphericity, ψ_s and data base-3 stores the Moody chart that gives values of Fanning friction factor f at specified values of Reynolds number Re and the ratio (ε_r/D). The theoretically computed power consumption P may be divided by the pump or blower efficiency to obtain the magnitude of the actual power requirement.

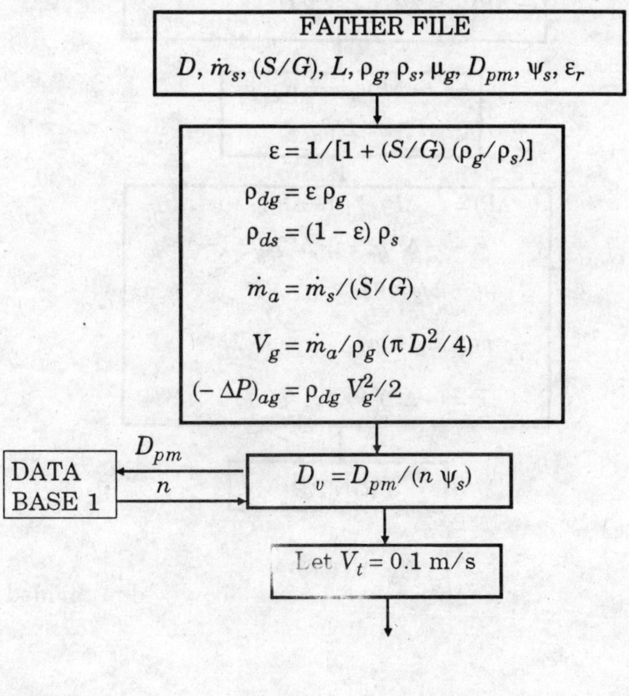

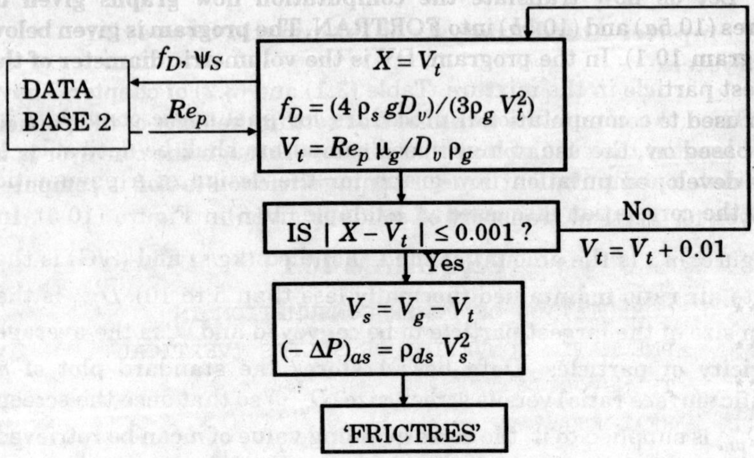

Fig. 10.5(*a*)

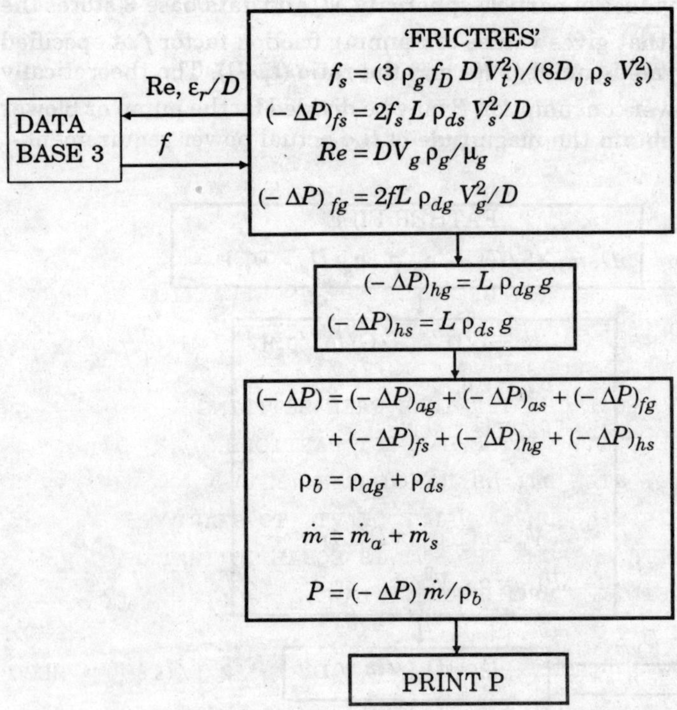

Fig. 10.5 (*b*)

Let us now translate the computation flow graphs given in figures (10.5*a*) and (10.5*b*) into FORTRAN. The program is given below (Program 10.1). In the program, DV is the volumetric diameter of the largest particle in the mixture. Table (3.1) and (3.2) of chapter-3 have been used to compute the terminal free settling velocity of the particle and based on the assumption that air flow through the conveyor is in fully developed turbulent zone, Fanning's friction factor is computed from the correlation discussed in Example (10.6).

PROGRAM 10.1

```
C**    COMPUTATION OF POWER CONSUMPTION IN
C**    PNEUMATIC CONVEYING OF SOLIDS (VERTICAL
C**    TRANSPORT).
       REAL KT(5)
       REAL L, MS, MA, MEUG, KTC, KR, MT, LHS
       DIMENSION PSI(5), C1(5), FD(13, 5), REP(13)
       READ (*, *) D, MS, RSG, L, DV, PSIS, ROWS, ROWG
       READ (*, *) MEVG, ABSR
       ABSN = 1.0/(1.0 + RSG * ROWG/ROWS)
       RODG = ABSN * ROWG
       RODS = (1.0 - ABSN) * ROWS
       MA = MS/RSC
       PI = 3.14
       VG = 4.0 * MA/(PI * D * D * ROWG)
C**    COMPUTE PRESSURE DROP FOR ACCELERATION
C**    OF GAS TO THE CARRYING VELOCITY.
       DPAG = RODG * VG * VG/2.0
C**    COMPUTE THE TERMINAL FREE SETTLING
C**    VELOCITY OF THE LARGEST PARTICLE
C**    (OF SIZE DV) AS IN PROGRAM (3.1).
C**    FIRST ASSUME A VALUE OF VT. TO START
C**    WITH, ASSUME THAT VT IS EQUAL TO THAT
C**    OBTAINED FROM STOKES' LAW.
       G = 9.8
       VT = [(ROWS - ROWG) * G * DV * * 2 ]/(18.0 * MEUG)
 10    X = VT
       REPC = DV * VT * ROWG/MEUG
C**    COMPUTE THE DRAG COEFFICIENT AT REP = REPC.
```

```
      IF (REPC. LE. 0.1) GO TO 15
      IF (REPC. GE. 1000.0) GO TO 20
      IF (PSIS. EQ. 1.0) THEN
      FDC = (24.0/REPC) * (1.0 + 0.15 * REPC * * 0.687)
      GO TO 65
      ELSE
      READ (*, *) (PSI (J), J = 1, 5)
      READ (*, *) (REP (I), I = 1, 13)
      READ (*, *) [(FD (I, J), I = 1, 13), J = 1, 5]
      END IF
      DO 25 I = 1, 13
      IF [REPC. LE. REP(I)] GO TO 30
 25   CONTINUE
 30   DO 35 J = 1, 5
      IF [PSIS. LE. PSI (J)] GO TO 40
 35   CONTINUE
 40   FD1 = FD (I - 1, J) + [FD (I, J) - FD (I - 1, J)]
      * [REPC - REP (I - 1)]/[REP (I) - REP (I - 1)]
      FD2 = FD (I - 1, J - 1) + [FD (I, J -1) - FD (I -
      1, J - 1)] * [REPC - REP (I - 1)]/[REP (I) - REP
      (I - 1)]
      FDC = FD2 + [FD1 - FD2) * [PSIS - PSI (J - 1)]/[PSI
      (J) - PSI (J - 1)]
      GO TO 65
 15   READ (*, *) (PSI (J), C1 (J), J = 1,5)
      DO 45 J = 1,5
      IF [PSIS LE. PSI (J)] GO TO 50
 45   CONTINUE
 50   C1C = C1 (J - 1) + [C1 (J) - C1 (J - 1)] * [PSIS -
      PSI (J - 1)]/[PSI (J) - PSI (J - 1)]
      FDC = C1C/REPC
      GO TO 65
 20   READ (*, *) [PSI (J), KT (J), J = 1, 5]
      DO 55 J = 1, 5
      IF [PSIS. LE. PSI (J)] GO TO 60
 55   CONTINUE
 60   KTC = KT (J - 1) + [KT (J) - KT (J - 1)] * [PSIS -
```

```
        PSI (J - 1)]/[PSI (J) - PSI (J - 1)]
        FDC = KTC
C**     COMPUTE THE TERMINAL FREE SETTLING VELOCITY
 65     VT = [(4.0/3.0) * (ROWS - ROWG) * G * DV/(ROWG *
        FDC)] * * 0.5
C**     CHECK FOR CONVERGENCE.
        DIF = ABS (VT - X)/X
        IF (DIF. LT. 0.001) GO TO 70
        VT = (VT + X)/2.0
        GO TO 10
C**     COMPUTE PRESSURE DROP FOR ACCELERATION OF
C**     SOLID PARTICLES.
 70     VS = VG - VT
        DPAS = RODS * VS * * 2
C**     COMPUTE PRESSURE DROP DUE TO FRICTION
C**     BETWEEN GAS AND PARTICLES, BETWEEN
C**     PARTICLES AND BETWEEN PARTICLES AND
C**     PIPE WALL.
        FS = (3.0 * ROWG * FDC * D * VT * VT)/(8.0 * DV *
        ROWS * VS * * 2)
        DPFS = 2.0 * FS * L * RODS * VS * VS/D
C**     COMPUTE PRESSURE DROP DUE TO FRICTION
C**     BETWEEN GAS AND PIPE WALL.
        RE = D * VG * ROWG/MEUG
C**     IT IS ASSUMED THAT GAS FLOW THROUGH
C**     THE COLUMN IS IN FULLY DEVELOPED TURBULENT ZONE.
C**     THE VALUE OF FANNING FRICTION FACTOR
C**     (F) IS FIRST ASSUMED.
        F = 0.02
 75     LHS = 1.0/SQRT (F)
        KR = RE * SQRT (F)
        RHS = - 4.0 * ALOG 10 [1.255/KR + ABSR/(3.7 * D)]
C**     CHECK FOR CONVERGENCE.
        DIF = ABS (LHS - RHS)/LHS
        IF (DIF. LT. 0.001) GO TO 80
        F = F - 0.001
```

```
      GO TO 75
 80   DPFG = 2.0 * F * L * RODG * VG * VG/D
C**   COMPUTE THE PRESSURE DROP FOR SUPPORTING
C**   THE COLUMN OF GAS AND THAT FOR
C**   SUPPORTING THE SOLIDS.
      G = 9.8
      DPHG = L * RODG * G
      DPHS = L * RODS * G
C**   COMPUTE THE TOTAL PRESSURE DROP.
      DP = DPAG + DPAS + DPFS + DPFG + DPHG + DPHS
      ROWB = RODG + RODS
      MT = MA + MS
      P = DP * MT/ROWB
      WRITE (*, *) P
      STOP
      END
```

NOMENCLATURE

- a lump size of conveyed material (average size for graded material and maximum size for ungraded ones), m.
- a_b pitch of buckets, m.
- a_f pitch of flights, m.
- A_b cross-sectional area of load on the conveyor, m^2.
- b carrying width of belt (that portion of the width that carries the load), m.
- B width of belt or apron, m.
- B_b width of bucket, m.
- B_t, h_t working width and depth respectively (width and depth occupied by the load) of the trough of the flight conveyor, m.
- C coefficient of resistance due to friction of wheel flanges on the rails (see under apron conveyors), dimensionless.
- C' coefficient used in equation (10.3.2) that depends on the type of material conveyed, dimensionless.
- C_a coefficient that depends on whether the conveyed material is graded or ungraded, dimensionless.
- C_b coefficient that depends on the type of apron (see Table 10.12), dimensionless.

C_{ch} coefficient to take care of the resistance to the motion of the chain with support wheels (see equation 10.3.50), dimensionless.

C_f filling coefficient for flight conveyors, dimensionless.

C_{fa} coefficient of filling of the apron cross-section, dimensionless.

C_{fb} coefficient of bucket filling, dimensionless.

C_{fs} coefficient of filling of screw cross-section, dimensionless.

C_g ratio of gravity force to centrifugal force.

C_l see C_u

C_{lt} coefficient that accounts for the friction of the load on the bottom and the walls of the trough (see equation 10.3.50), dimensionless.

C_m coefficient of load distribution, dimensionless (see Table 10.9).

C_n coefficient of non-uniform loading, dimensionless.

C_{nu} coefficient of non-uniform distribution of load between the hauling chains (see equation 10.3.45), dimensionless.

C_{op} total operating coefficient (or, total coefficient of utilisation of the machine), dimensionless.

C_p coefficient that depends on the type of pulley (see equation 10.3.32), dimensionless.

C_{pl} coefficient that depends on the strength of the ply fabric of rubber-fabric belts (see Table 10.10), dimensionless.

C_{pu} coefficient of pulley resistance, dimensionless.

C_t coefficient of utilisation of operating time, dimensionless.

C_u, C_l coefficients that take care of the resistance to the motion of the upper run and lower run of the belt respectively, dimensionless.

C_y availability factor, dimensionless.

C_β angle factor or inclination factor, dimensionless.

d screw diameter, m ; pulley diameter, m ; diameter of wheel shaft, m.

d_d diameter of drive pulley, m.

D diameter of storage bin, m ; diameter of wheel, m ; pipe diameter, m.

D_p particle size, m.

$D_{p,m}$ screen size of largest particle to be conveyed, m.

f fanning friction factor, dimensionless.

f_D drag coefficient, dimensionless.

f_n fraction factor for non-Newtonian flow, dimensionless.

f_s friction factor defined in equation (10.4.28), dimensionless.

F_p pull factor.

F_R kinematic force, N.

g gravitational acceleration, m/s^2.

h height of load layer on the belt, m ; height of side walls or skirt hoards of apron conveyor, m.

h_s working height (height in contact with the load) of skirt boards of apron conveyor, m.

h_t, B_t working depth and width respectively (depth and width occupied by the load) of the trough of the flight conveyor, m.

H holdup of solid in the bin, m ; vertical displacement of conveyed material, m.

H_b height (depth) of bucket, m.

k coefficient of rolling friction, m (see Table 10.13).

K safety margin of belt strength, dimensionless.

K' coefficient of flowability of the material, dimensionless.

K_a coefficient (dimensionless) used in equations (10.3.10) and (10.3.11) (See Table 10.3).

K_{cp} coefficient that depends on the configuration of conveyor path (see equation 10.3.25), dimensionless.

K_j coefficient that takes care of the strength of the belt joint (see equation 10.3.25), dimensionless.

K_{ma} margin of adhesion between the belt and the drive pulley, dimensionless.

K_{op} coefficient that depends on the operating conditions of the conveyor (see equation 10.3.25), dimensionless.

K_{pl} coefficient that takes care of non-uniform stressing of plies of rubber fabric belts (see Table 10.8), dimensionless.

K_{sc} scooping coefficient, m.

K_{ta} coefficient of total resistance to the motion of apron in the straight sections of the conveyor (see equation 10.3.41), dimensionless.

K_{tb} total coefficient of resistance for belt conveyors (see Table 10.4), dimensionless.

K_{ts} total coefficient of resistance for screw conveyors (see Table 10.1), dimensionless.

K_{ut} coefficient of utilisation of belt strength (see Table 10.9), dimensionless.

l_{us}, l_{ls} spacing between roller supports in the upper run and lower run of the belt respectively, *m*.

L horizontal displacement of conveyed material, *m* ; height or length of pipe/column, *m*.

L_b length of the bucket, *m*.

L_l, L_r horizontal projections of the loaded and empty (returning) conveyor respectively, *m*.

L_s, h_s length and working height (height in contact with the load) respectively of skirt boards of apron conveyor, *m*.

m, n rheological constants of power law fluid.

$\dot{m}$ mass flow rate of fluid (or, slurry), kg/s.

m_b mass of belt per unit area, kg/m^2.

m_1 mass of the heaviest piece of unit load conveyed, kg.

m_{ls}, m_{us} mass of the rotating elements of lower roller supports and upper roller supports of belt conveyor respectively, kg.

M torque on the screw shaft, *Nm*.

n speed of rotation of screw, rpm ; specific surface ratio, dimensionless.

n_c critical rpm of vertical screw conveyor.

n_d speed of rotation of drive pulley, rpm.

n_s coefficient of side pressure, dimensionless.

n_{sm} safety margin of hauling chain (see equation 10.3.46), dimensionless.

N number of fabric plies.

N_r minimum number of fabric plies required.

p_b vertical pressure on the bin floor, N/m^2.

p_L lateral pressure on bin walls, N/m^2.

p_v vertical pressure at any section of the bin, N/m^2.

P power consumption, *W*.

P_b belt pressure acting on the pully surface, N/m^2.

P_{ba} value of maximum permissible pressure (stress) for the belt, N/m^2.

q_a linear gravity force of apron with chains, N/m.

q_b linear gravity force of belt, N/m.

q_l linear gravity force of the load conveyed, N/m.

q_{ls} see q_{us}.

q_o linear gravity force of chains and flights, N/m.

q_{us}, q_{ls} linear gravity force of rotating elements of roller supports on the upper run and lower run respectively of the belt, N/m.

Q throughput capacity of the conveyor, kg/s.

Q_a, Q_m average rated capacity and the maximum rated capacity respectively of the conveyor, kg/s.

Re Reynolds number (for flow through pipes), dimensionless.

Re_n Reynolds number of non-Newtonian flow, dimensionless.

Re_p particle Reynolds number, dimensionless.

(S/G) mass ratio of solids to air.

S_{pl} strength of ply fabric, N/m of belt width.

S_{rc} required strength of carcass of rubber-cable belt, N/m.

S_{rs} rupture strength of hauling chain, N.

S_{r1} rated force on a single chain (when the tractive element consists of two chains), N.

t lead of the screw, m.

T_f tension in a belt section that is running off a pulley, N.

T_{f1}, T_{f2} tension in a belt section running off the first pulley and the second pulley respectively of a double pulley drive, N (note that, $T_{f1} = T_{o2}$).

T_{max}, T_{min} maximum and minimum static tension respectively of the hauling chain (see equation 10.3.39), N.

T_o tension in the belt section that is running on a pulley, N.

T_{o1}, T_{o2} tension in the belt section running on the first pulley and running on the second pulley respectively of a double pulley drive, N.

v linear speed of the conveyor, m/s.

v_c critical linear velocity of vertical screw conveyor, m/s.

V_{avg} average velocity of fluid (or slurry) through the pipe, m/s.

V_b useful geometrical volume of bucket, m^3

V_g actual velocity of gas in the pneumatic conveyor, m/s.

$(V_g)_{sup}$ superficial velocity of gas in the pneumatic conveyor, m/s.

V_{min} minimum carrying velocity, m/s.

V_s actual velocity of solids in the pneumatic conveyor, m/s.

V_t terminal free settling velocity of particle, m/s.

W tractive force, N.

W_s additional resistance due to friction of the load on the skirt boards, N.

$(-W_s)$ shaft work done by the pump, J/kg.

W_{sc} scooping resistance, N.

Greek Letters

α angle of internal friction, degrees

α_p relative pressure drop, dimensionless

α_r angle of repose of the material while at rest, degrees

α_r' angle of repose of the material while in motion on the conveyor, degrees

α_w wrapping angle, radians

β angle of inclination of the conveyor, degrees

Δ rate of deformation tensor

$(-\Delta P)$ total pressure drop, N/m^2

$(-\Delta P_m)$ pressure drop for transporting slurry, N/m^2.

$(-\Delta P_L)$ pressure drop for transporting water at the same velocity as the slurry through the same pipe, N/m^2.

$(-\Delta P)_{ag}$ pressure drop for acceleration of gas (air) to the carrying velocity, N/m^2.

$(-\Delta P)_{as}$ pressure drop for acceleration of solid particles, N/m^2.

$(-\Delta P)_{fg}$ pressure drop due to friction between gas and pipe wall, N/m^2.

$(-\Delta P)_{fs}$ pressure drop due to friction between gas and the particles, between particles and between particles and the pipe wall, N/m^2.

ε volume fraction of fluid (air or water) in the suspension.

ε_r roughness parameter for commercial pipes, m [relative roughness = ε_r/D]

τ momentum flux, N/m^2

τ_{yx} x-component of momentum flux acting in the y-direction, N/m^2

τ_o threshold shear stress, N/m^2

ψ_s average sphericity of particles, dimensionless.

η mechanical efficiency of the drive mechanism or the pump, dimensionless.

θ helix angle of the screw, degrees.

θ_r troughing angle (angle of inclination of the side rollers of the troughing roller support), degrees.

μ' coefficient of internal friction at the bin wall, between the belt and the pulley, dimensionless.

μ_b' coefficient of friction in bearings (see Table 10.13), dimensionless.

μ_c' coefficient of friction of the particle on the casing wall of vertical screw conveyor, dimensionless.

μ_s' coefficient of friction of the bulk load on the skirt boards, dimensionless.

μ_g, μ_L viscosity of gas (air) and liquid (water) respectively, kg/(ms).

μ_o, τ_o rheological constants of Bingham plastic fluid.

ρ_b bulk density of slurry or suspension, kg/m^3.

ρ_{dg} dispersed gas density kg/m^3.

ρ_{ds} dispersed solid density, kg/m^3.

ρ_g density of gas (air), kg/m^3.

ρ_L density of liquid (water), kg/m^3.

ρ_s density of solids, kg/m^3.

Computer Notations

ABSN volume fraction of air in the suspension (ε)

ABSR roughness parameter (ε_r), m

C1(J) values of parameter C_1 (see Table 3.1 of Chapter - 3)

C1C calculated value of parameter C_1

D column (or pipe) diameter, m

DP	total pressure drop, $(-\Delta P)$, N/m^2
DPAG	pressure drop for acceleration of gas to the carrying velocity, $(-\Delta P)_{ag}$, N/m^2
DPAS	pressure drop for acceleration of solid particles, $(-\Delta P)_{as}$, N/m^2
DPFG	pressure drop due to friction between gas and pipe wall, $(-\Delta P)_{fg}$, N/m^2
DPFS	pressure drop due to friction between gas and particles, between particles and between particles and pipe wall, $(-\Delta P)_{fs}$, N/m^2
DPHG	pressure drop for supporting the column of gas of height L, $(-\Delta P)_{hg}$, N/m^2
DPHS	pressure drop for supporting solids, $(-\Delta P)_{hs}$, N/m^2
DV	volumetric diameter of largest particle, m
F	Fanning friction factor (f), dimensionless
FD (I, J)	values of drag coefficient (see Table 3.2 of chapter - 3)
FDC	calculated value of drag coefficient
FS	friction factor (f_s) defined in equation (10.4.28)
KR	Karman number, dimensionless
KT(J)	values of turbulent constant (K_t), see Table (3.1) of Chapter 3.
KTC	calculated value of KT.
L	column height, m
MA	mass flow rate of air (m_a), kg/s
MEUG	viscosity of gas (air), kg/(ms)
MS	mass flow rate of solids (m_s), kg/s
MT	total mass flow rate of slurry, kg/s
P	power consumption, W
PSI(J)	values of particle sphericity (ψ_s, see Table 3.1 of chapter 3)
PSIS	sphericity of particles being conveyed, dimensionless
RE	Reynolds number (Re), dimensionless
REP(I)	values of particle Reynolds number (Re_p, see Table 3.2 of chapter-3)
REPC	calculated value of Re_p
RODG	dispersed gas density (ρ_{dg}), kg/m^3

RODS	dispersed solid density (ρ_{ds}), kg/m^3
ROWB	bulk density of slurry (ρ_b), kg/m^3
ROWG	density of gas (ρ_g), kg/m^3
ROWS	density of solids (ρ_s), kg/m^3
RSG	mass ratio of solids to air (S/G), kg/kg
VG	actual velocity of gas (V_g) through conveyor, m/s
VS	actual velocity of solids through conveyor (V_s), m/s
VT	terminal free settling velocity (V_t) of largest particle, m/s

REFERENCES

1. Brown, G.G. and Associates, Unit Operations, Wiley, New York, 1950.
2. Spivakovsky, A. and Dyachkov, V., Conveying Machines, Vol. 1 and 2, Mir Publishers, Moscow, 1985.
3. Sarkar, S., "Hydraulic Transport of Coal", Chemical Age of India, **33**, No. 12, 715, 1982.
4. Perry, J.H., Chemical Engineers' Handbook, 5th ed., Chapter 5, McGraw Hill, New York, 1973.
5. Skelland, A.H.P., Non-Newtonian Flow and Heat Transfer, Wiley, New York, 1962.
6. Dodge, D.W. and Metzner, A.B., AIChE J., **5**, 189, 1959.
7. Spells, H., Trans. Inst. Chem. Engrs., **33**, 79, 1955.
8. Anon, A., The Transportation of Solids in Steel Pipelines, Colorado School of Mines Research Foundation, Goldin, Colo., 1963.
9. Dalla Valle, Heating, Piping Air Conditioning, **4**, 639, 1932.
10. Baumeister, T. et. al (ed.), Mark's Standard Handbook for Mechanical Engineers, 8th ed., pp. 3-54, McGraw-Hill, New York, 1978.

Appendix-A

1. Simpson's rule. Simpson's rule is one of the most popular methods used for numerical integration. Let the following integral is to be evaluated :

$$I = \int_a^b f(x)\, dx$$

where $f(x)$ is any function in x and a and b are numerical figures. We take the step size h as,

$$h = (b - a)/n$$

where n should be an even integer so that we get an even number of sub-intervals. Now, let $x_0 = a, x_1 = a + h, x_2 = a + 2h,$ ... and so on. Finally, $x_n = a + nh = b$. Then, the rule states,

$$I \cong \frac{h}{3} [f(x_0) + 4 [f(x_1) + f(x_3) + \,.\,.\, f(x_{n-1})] + 2 [f(x_2) + f(x_4) + \,.\,.\,.\, f(x_{n-2})] + f(x_n)]$$

A computer program in Fortran-IV for the above scheme is given below. Let $f(x) = 1/x$, $a = A = 1$, $b = B = 2$, $n = N = 6$.

```
C**     NUMERICAL INTEGRATION BY SIMPSONS RULE
        IMPLICIT REAL * 8 (A-H, O-Z)
        READ (*, 1) A, B, N
  1     FORMAT (2F10.0, I4)
        WRITE (*, 2) A, B, N
  2     FORMAT (2X, 2E15.7, I5)
        CALL DSIM (A, B, N, S)
C**     SUBROUTINE DSIM OBTAINS THE INTEGRATION VALUE
C**     OF F(X)
```

```
C**     ON RETURN S CONTAINS THE INTEGRATION VALUE
        WRITE (*, 3) S
  3     FORMAT (2X, F10.6)
        STOP
        END
        SUBROUTINE DSIM (A, B, N, S)
        IMPLICIT REAL *8 (A-H, O-Z)
        F(X) = 1/X
        X = A
        H = (B - A)/N
        IP = 4
        S = F(X) + F(X + N * H)
        I = 1
 20     IF (I.EQ.N) GO TO 30
        S = S + IP * F (X + I * H)
        I = I + 1
        IP = 6 - IP
        GO TO 20
 30     S = S * H/3
        RETURN
        END
```

We shall give one more example. Let $f(x) = 1/(x^2 + 1)$, $a = A = 2, b = B = 5$, $n = N = 20$. We denote $f(x_0) = y_1$ $f(x_1) = y_2$, $\ldots f(x_n) = y_{n+1}$. The computer program for the above integration in BASIC is given below :

```
 10   PROGRAM FOR SIMPSONS RULE
 20   DIM Y (21)
 30   INPUT A, B, N
 40   LET H = (B - A)/N
 60   FOR J = 1 TO N + 1
 70   LET X = (J - 1) * H + A
 80   LET Y(J) = 1/(X * X + 1.0)
 90   NEXT J
100   LET S = Y(1) + Y(N + 1)
110   LET I = 4
120   FOR M = 2 TO N
```

```
130     LET S = S + I * Y(M)
140     LET I = 6 - I
150     NEXT M
160     LET S = (H * S/3.0)
170     WRITE (*, *) S
180     END
```

2. Method of Least Squares. This is one of the most widely used methods for curve fitting. Let there be n number of points such as $(x_1, y_1), (x_2, y_2) \ldots (x_n, y_n)$ and we want to fit a smooth, continuous curve through them. In other words, we want to find out how does y vary with x. For instance, let y be varying linearly with x, so that

$$y = mx + C$$

Thus, we have to fit a straight line through the points $(x_1, y_1), (x_2, y_2), \ldots (x_n, y_n)$ and find out its slope m and y-intercept C. Based on the method of least squares, the error (sometimes called truncation error) involved in such a process is indicated as,

$$q = \sum_{i=1}^{n} (y_i - mx_i - C)^2$$

A necessary condition for q to be minimum is,

$$\frac{\partial q}{\partial C} = -2 \sum_{i=1}^{n} (y_i - mx_i - C) = 0$$

$$\frac{\partial q}{\partial m} = -2 \sum_{i=1}^{n} x_i (y_i - mx_i - C) = 0$$

Solving the above two equations simultaneously we get

$$m = \frac{n \sum x_i y_i - \sum x_i \sum y_i}{n \sum x_i^2 - (\sum x_i)^2}$$

$$C = \left[\sum y_i - m \sum x_i \right] / n$$

A computer program in FORTRAN-IV for the above scheme is given below :

```
C**     FITTING STRAIGHT LINE
        REAL M, NUMR
        DIMENSION X(100), Y(100)
        READ (*, *) N
```

```
      SUMX = 0.0
      SUMY = 0.0
      SUMXY = 0.0
      SUMXX = 0.0
      READ, (X(I), Y(I), I = 1, N)
      DO 10 I = 1, N
      SUMX = SUMX + X(I)
      SUMY = SUMY + Y(I)
      SUMXY = SUMXY + X(I) * Y(I)
   10 SUMXX = SUMXX + X(I) * X(I)
      AN = N
      NUMR = AN * SUMXY - SUMX * SUMY
      DENR = AN * SUMXX - SUMX ** 2
      M = NUMR/DENR
      C = (SUMY - M * SUMX)/AN
      WRIRE (*, *) M, C, N
      STOP
      END
```

The above scheme can be generalised for any function $f(x)$. For example, let $f(x)$ be a polynomial of degree m. Thus,

$$y = f(x) = a_0 + a_1 x + a_2 x^2 + \ldots + a_m x^m$$

The truncation error q then takes the form

$$q = \sum_{i=1}^{n} [y_i - f(x_i)]^2$$

where n is the number of points (x, y) available. Our conditions for minimising q will be therefore,

$$\frac{\partial q}{\partial a_0} = 0$$

$$\frac{\partial q}{\partial a_1} = 0 \quad \ldots \text{ and so on.}$$

Finally, $$\frac{\partial q}{\partial a_m} = 0$$

Thus, we have $(m + 1)$ equations and they can be solved simultaneously for the $(m + 1)$ unknowns such as $a_0, a_1, a_2, \ldots a_m$.

If in the straight line fit, given above, the magnitude of the ultimate truncation error q is also to be printed, then the program can be extended as follows :

```
      Q = 0.0
      DO 20 I = 1, N
      Q = Q + (Y(I) - M * X(I) - C) * * 2
20    CONTINUE
      WRITE (*, *) Q
      STOP
      END
```

Appendix-B

Objective Type Questions and Problems

1. Comment on the following statements giving reasons.

   You may agree with or contradict against any of the statements, but do justify your answers. Give examples and/or brief sketches wherever necessary.

   (*a*) The volumetric diameter of a cubical particle is less than its Sauter diameter,

   (*b*) For a cylindrical particle of length equal to its diameter, $d_v < d_{vs} < d_s$,

   (*c*) Sphericity of +100 mesh galena will always be larger than that of –100 mesh,

   (*d*) A trommel should always be operated above its critical speed,

   (*e*) A low Rittinger's number indicates easy crushability,

   (*f*) Maximum crushing takes place in a ball mill at its critical speed of rotation,

   (*g*) Size ratio will always be less than the settling ratio,

   (*h*) Hindered settling velocity is more than the free settling velocity,

   (*i*) Dense medium separation and jigging differ from each other in the sense that the former separates particles on the basis of size as well as density, whereas the latter separates on the basis of density only,

   (*j*) A batch filter is first operated at constant pressure and then at constant rate,

   (*k*) The rate of batch filtration increases with increase in filtration pressure if the sludge is incompressible, but not so if it is compressible, (*l*) A spare cross-section is preferred for the gas inlet in a gas cyclone,

(*m*) Separation is maximum in a hydrocyclone when flow rates of light and heavy phases are equal,

(*n*) Electrostatic precipitators are best suitable for separating submicron particles from gases and their collection efficiency is highly dependent on particle size,

(*o*) Increase in inlet Reynolds number increases the separation efficiency of a hydrocyclone, but not that of a gas cyclone,

(*p*) Work of adhesion in flotation is independent of particle size, but depends very much on the p_H of the medium,

(*q*) Solids exert more pressure on the vessel floor in a storage bin than a liquid of same density.

2. Distinguish between :

(*a*) Classification and jigging,

(*b*) Open-circuit and closed-circuit grinding units,

(*c*) Jaw crusher and a Gyratory crusher,

(*d*) Sphericity and wetted sphericity,

(*e*) Vibrating screen and trommel,

(*f*) Shape factor and specific surface ratio,

(*g*) Rittinger's law and Bond's law,

(*h*) Screening efficiency and screen effectiveness,

(*i*) Mixing index and mixing number,

(*j*) Compressible and incompressible sludges,

(*k*) Hindered settling and free settling,

(*l*) Power number and power function,

(*m*) Hydrocyclone and gas cyclone,

(*n*) Centrifuge and centrifugal,

(*o*) Radial flow and axial flow impellers,

(*p*) Belt conveyor and screw conveyor,

(*q*) Gravity sedimentation and centrifugal sedimentation,

(*r*) Particulate and aggregative fluidisation.

3. Discuss what happens when,

(*a*) near-mesh particles are fed to a screen,

(*b*) the speed of a ball mill is gradually increased,

(*c*) the inlet Reynolds number is increased in (*i*) a gas cyclone, (*ii*) a hydrocyclone.

4. Answer briefly :
   (*a*) You are familiar with Newton's law and Stokes law that are used for computing the terminal velocity of spherical particles settling in a liquid. Discuss how would you modify these laws for applying to, (*i*) gas bubbles rising in a quiescent liquid, (*ii*) liquid drops falling in a gas, (*iii*) fine dust particles (having size less than a micron) settling in a gas.
   (*b*) Discuss how would you use a fluidiser as, (*i*) an elutriator (*ii*) a pneumatic conveyor.
5. Outline the significance and applications of the following equations/laws :
   (*a*) Gaudin-Schumann distribution law,
   (*b*) Kynch's theory,
   (*c*) Janssen's equation,
   (*d*) Kick's law.
6. Discuss on the following :
   (*a*) Washing and dewatering of filter cakes in a rotary drum filter,
   (*b*) Charging and migration of dust particles in a electrostatic precipitator,
   (*c*) Effect of particle size on the collection efficiency of a gas cyclone,
   (*d*) The significance of Σ factor in the design of centrifugal sedimentors.
   (*e*) Flooding in a packed bed.
7. Name the type of separation technique (and outline its principle) you would recommend for separating.
   (*a*) Particles of same size but having densities wide apart,
   (*b*) Particles equally falling but of different densities and sizes,
   (*c*) Particles of same density and size,
   (*d*) Particles of the same material having different sizes,
   (*e*) Two immiscible liquids of different densities.
8. Explain how would you proceed to compute,
   (*a*) Free settling velocity (at any instant) of a spherical particle in water,
   (*b*) Air requirement of a rotary drum filter,
   (*c*) Pressure drop in a pneumatic conveyor,
   (*d*) Effectiveness of a classifying screen.

9. Recommend a suitable equipment for each of the following operations and outline its working principle :
   (a) Breaking of run-of-mine coal,
   (b) Fine grinding of explosives,
   (c) Separation of a kerosene-water emulsion,
   (d) Drying of ammonium sulphate crystals in a fertiliser plant,
   (e) Removal of precipitated wax from a heavy gas oil in a petroleum refinery,
   (f) Mixing of dry salt and sand,
   (g) Washing of extraneous mineral matter associated with coal meant for a carbonisation unit,
   (h) Conveying of catalyst particles to the top of a tall column,
   (i) Crushing of wood and asbestos,
   (j) Transporting hot molasses from a sugar plant to a distillery that is around 5 km away,
   (k) Mixing of a rubber compound,
   (l) Separation of fine dust of fly ash from an exhaust gas stream,
   (m) Transporting coal from the mine to a thermal power plant situated at more than 100 km away,
   (n) Separation of coarse and fines from a slurry.

10. Determine the surface mean diameter and harmonic mean diameter of an ore sample that has the following size distribution :

ISS mesh	*Percentage retained*
– 480 + 340	3.4
– 340 + 240	6.3
– 240 + 160	8.1
– 160 + 120	10.2
– 120 + 85	16.5
– 85 + 60	13.1
– 60 + 40	10.1
– 40 + 30	9.5
– 30 + 20	7.0
– 20 + 15	4.7
– 15 + 10	3.1
– 10 + 8	2.0
– 8	6.0

Tests show that the specific surface ratios of the ore are identical with those of calcite.

11. The following data were collected when a crushed ore was screened using a 3.0 mm screen to separate the undercrushed material so that it can be returned to the crusher for further processing. Compute the effectiveness of the screen.

ISS mesh	*Feed*	*Mass fraction*	
		Oversize from screen	*Undersize from screen*
+ 480	0.548	0.596	0.00
– 480 + 340	0.146	0.168	0.113
– 340 + 120	0.109	0.096	0.147
– 120 + 60	0.045	0.039	0.086
– 60 + 30	0.034	0.029	0.033
– 30	0.118	0.072	0.621

12. Quartz is fed at the rate of 25,000 kg/hr to a ball mill that is operating in closed circuit with a hydraulic classifier. The screen analyses of known streams are given below :

ISS mesh	*Mass fraction*		
	Raw feed to mill	*Overflow material from classifier*	*Underflow material from classifier*
– 480 + 340	0.548	0.0	0.0
– 340 + 240	0.086	0.0	0.308
– 240 + 160	0.055	0.0	0.030
– 160 + 120	0.047	0.0	0.154
– 120 + 85	0.027	0.0	0.169
– 85 + 60	0.035	0.0	0.207
– 60 + 40	0.029	0.042	0.034
– 40 + 30	0.019	0.127	0.028
– 30 + 20	0.020	0.193	0.014
– 20 + 15	0.097	0.137	0.022
– 15 + 10	0.022	0.117	0.018
– 10 + 8	0.015	0.098	0.016
– 8	0.0	0.286	0.0

The mill is being operated with a recycle of 75,000 kg/hr. If the total power supplied to drive the mill is 75 kW, determine the energy efficiency of the mill,

(a) from Rittinger's law,

(b) from Bond's law.

13. Estimate the power consumption of comminuting 20,000 kg/hr of a hard rock (specific gravity = 3.8, Rittinger's number = 0.0175 m^2/J) in a hammer mill of efficiency 18%, operating in closed circuit with a 100 micron screen from the following data :

Average size, mm	*Mass fraction*		
	Raw feed to mill	*Oversize from screen*	*Undersize from screen*
0.25	0.818	0.730	0.0
0.18	0.104	0.207	0.123
0.1296	0.065	0.043	0.142
0.0933	0.013	0.020	0.135
below 0.0933	0.0	0.0	0.60

Tests have shown that the average ratio of undersize to oversize from screen is 1.0 and the specific surface ratios are identical with those of sphalerite. What will be the Sauter diameter of the product ? What will be the classifying screen effectiveness ?

14. Determine the time required for ore particles each weighing 4 gm (specific gravity = 7.5) to settle in water from an initial velocity of 0.2 m/s until a velocity of 0.7 m/s is attained relative to the fluid. Assume that the particles are isometric (sphericity = 0.8) and free settling prevails.

15. For the beneficiation of tungsten oxide that is contaminated with silica, it is first elutriated in a rising stream of water at 30°C. The feed mixture has the size distribution given below :

Size, cm	*Mass fraction*
– 0.068 + 0.045	0.25
– 0.045 + 0.027	0.33
– 0.027 + 0.013	0.22
– 0.013 + 0.0078	0.20

Determine the upward velocity of water that is to be maintained in the elutriator so as to obtain an uncontaminated tungsten oxide as the product. What will be the size range of this product ? Specific gravity of pure tungsten oxide = 7.2.

16. A sample of coal weighing 18 gm was tested in the laboratory by feeding it separately to different solutions, collecting the

floated material and checking its ash content. The following data were collected :

When fed to a solution of	*Amount floated, gm*	*Its ash content, gm*
Specific gravity = 1.43	14.5	1.343
1.40	11.0	0.835
1.30	4.44	0.120
1.35	7.36	0.363
1.25	0.99	0.009

If the above coal is to be cleaned in a coal washery until its ash content reduces to 4.5%, specify what specific gravity of dense medium is to be employed. What shall be the percentage yield of clean coal ?

17. A limestone-water slurry is to be thickened to 50% solids (by weight) within 3.4 hours in a Dorr thickener of cross-sectional area 1000 m^2. The slurry is fed to the thickener at the rate of 200 m^3/hr. Estimate the depth of the thickener you shall recommend for final industrial design from the following batch sedimentation test data :

Time, (hr)	*Height of interface, (cm)*
0.0	36.0
0.25	32.4
0.50	28.6
1.00	21.0
1.75	14.7
3.00	12.3
4.75	11.55
12.00	9.80
20.00	8.80
∞	7.70

Specific gravity of limestone = 2.1.

18. A coal-water suspension is to be clarified at the rate of 5000 kg/hr to provide an underflow sludge that contains 85% solids in a 1050 m^2 continuous thickener. However, the thickener broke down and the job has to be done in a centrifuge 600 mm in diameter and 400 mm in height. Estimate the speed of the centrifuge if it is to have the same sedimentation character-

istics as the above thickener. The thickness of liquid layer inside the centrifuge basket may be taken to be extremely small.

State and explain any assumptions made.

19. The causticizing of soda ash follows the reaction

$$Na_2CO_3 + Ca(OH)_2 \longrightarrow 2\,NaOH + CaCO_3 \downarrow$$

After the reaction is complete, the product liquor containing 2 kg of calcium carbonate per kg of NaOH-free water is fed continuously at the rate of 1000 kg/hr to a series of thickeners in which it is washed countercurrently with neutral water. It is desired to recover 95 per cent of NaOH and the final solution obtained from the system is to contain 0.128 mass fraction NaOH.

(*a*) Compute the amount of neutral water required and the number of thickeners if the thickened sludge from each thickener contains 40 per cent solids. It is observed that the leach solution (overflow) from each stage (thickener) is clear. Equilibrium is attained at each stage and the compositions of the overflow solution and the solution leaving with the underflow are the same.

(*b*) How many thickeners would be required if the underflow sludge from each thickener contains 1 kg of solids per 1.5 kg of water ?

20. A plate and frame press of 1.2 m² filtering area handling a homogeneous slurry containing 10 per cent (by weight) of solids (specific gravity = 2.33) in water gave the following results :

Time (min):	10	30	60	110
Volume of filtrate (m^3):	80	115	152	200

Tests show that the following relation is valid for the present case (for $t_f > 0$) :

$$V_f^2 = K_1 t_f + K_2$$

where, V_f is the volume of filtrate (m^3) delivered in filtering time t_f hours and K_1 and K_2 are constants.

The cake is washed with water at a constant rate of one-third of final rate of filtration. The volume of wash water used is equal to one-twelveth of the volume of filtrate delivered per cycle. Opening, closing and reassembling take 45 minutes. Determine the optimum cycle time that will produce maximum daily output of filtrate.

21. A leaf filter handling a compressible sludge at 0.5 kg/(m^2s) gave the following results :

Time (seconds) :	10	40	60	90
Pressure drop (kPa) :	2.8	24.5	43.4	78.4

If the filter is operated at constant rate until the pressure difference becomes 70 kN/m^2, then at constant pressure until the filtrate collected is 2000 lit./m^2, estimate the total cycle time. Assume the filter medium resistance is negligible and the time for washing, cleaning and dumping is 60 minutes.

22. A 2000 rpm centrifugal filter 0.75 m in diameter and 0.45 m in height used to filter an incompressible sludge gave the following results. The final thickness of cake and liquid layer inside the bowl were 0.15 m and 0.025 m respectively.

Filtrate volume (litres) :	1.0	1.5	2.0	2.5	3.0
Time (seconds) :	40	70	105	150	200

If the same sludge is to be filtered in a filter press at a constant rate of 0.49 litres/(m^2s), estimate the pressure difference that should be maintained across the filter at the end of 60 seconds. Assume the filter medium resistance is constant and is the same for both the centrifugal filter and the filter press.

23. A rotary drum filter 2 m in diameter and 4 m long is used to filter a slurry containing 10 mass per cent solids. The particles are 0.075 mm cubes (sphericity = 0.81, specific gravity = 1.85). Compute what volume of filtrate will be delivered in one hour of operation from the following data :

Submergence = 40 per cent

Cake voidage = 0.35

Pressure inside the drum = 60 kN/m^2

Rotational speed = 0.33 rpm

Specific gravity of filtrate = 1.0

Viscosity of filtrate = 12.5 centipoises.

24. A flotation unit concentrates 1000 kg/min of an ore containing 20% pyrite (specific gravity = 4.9) and balance silica (specific gravity = 2.65) to 95% pyrite. The rougher, scavenger and cleaner contain four, three and two Denver cells respectively, each cell (L/D = 1.5) being fitted with four baffles (width = 0.1 D_t) and a 300 rpm six-bladed turbine impeller (diameter = 0.33 D_t). Rougher concentrate has 60% silica and tailings from rougher, scavenger and cleaner contain 95%, 99.5% and 80%

silica respectively. If pulp consistency is 4.0 in scavenger and 6.0 in cleaner and contact time 10 minutes in scavenger and 8.0 minutes in cleaner, estimate the hourly power consumption. State and explain any assumptions made.

25. A three-bladed marine propeller (pitch = 2.0) is used to agitate a solution of specific gravity 1.3 and viscosity 12.5 centipoises in an unbaffled tank of 1.0 m diameter and 1.5 m deep. The tank is filled to a depth of 1.0 m with the solution and the impeller (diameter = 0.3 D_t) is set at one impeller diameter above the vessel floor. Estimate the speed of the impeller if the power consumed to drive it is 0.34 kW. What will be the impeller speed if the tank is fitted with four longitudinal baffles each having a width equal to 10 per cent of tank diameter ?

26. Estimate the collection efficiency of a two-stage electrostatic precipitator having plates 2.2 m high and 1.0 m wide and spaced 0.14 m apart, if air containing dust particles (average size = 12 microns) is admitted at 10 m/s and the applied electrostatic potential gradient is 3000 volts/cm.

Viscosity of air = 0.01 centipoises

Dielectric constant of particles = 4.0

27. A kerosene-water dispersion containing 20 per cent (by volume) of kerosene is fed into a hydrocyclone. When a volume split of 0.85 was maintained, the overflow stream was found to contain 83 per cent (by volume) of kerosene while the underflow stream contained 48% (by volume) of kerosene.

Estimate the separation efficiency of the hydrocyclone.

28. A sample of bituminous coal (average size = 100 mm, bulk density = 1300 kg/m^3) is to be transported at the rate of 1,000 tonnes per hour (1 tonne = 1000 kg) horizontally over a distance of 100 m while being elevated by 5 m. Determine which among the following conveyors you shall recommend for the purpose and why :

(*a*) A screw conveyor that uses a 0.8 m diameter screw.

(*b*) A belt conveyor that uses a rubber-fabric belt (mass of belt = 2.55 kg/m) running at 1.25 m/s on straight roller supports. The masses of the rotating elements of upper and lower supports respectively are 12.0 kg and 7.5 kg. A roller spacing of 1.5 m is used for the upper run while a spacing of 3.0 m is employed for the lower run.

(*c*) An apron conveyor running at 0.5 m/s, hauled by two laminated wheel chains with wheels running on roll bearings (wheel diameter = 0.06 m and diameter of wheel shaft = 0.015 m).

Assume the sample coal to be a material of medium flowability and the conveyors are working under moderate operating conditions.

29. Determine the power consumption for transporting coal particles of average size 1.0 mm (specific gravity = 1.5) in the form of a coal-water slurry through a commercial steel pipe of 0.5 m in diameter. In all, 2700 tonnes of coal are to be transported per hour over a distance of 20 km. The solid concentration in the slurry is maintained at 25 per cent (by weight).

30. In a chemical plant, dry catalyst particles (specific gravity = 2.35) are to be delivered to the top of a tower 15 m high at the rate of 3000 kg/hour. The following two options are available. Determine which would you recommend and why.

    (*a*) A bucket elevator employing 2 litre buckets (mass of each = 3.38 kg) running at an average bucket speed of 1.0 m/s (coefficient of pulley resistance = 1.075),

    (*b*) A pneumatic conveyor employing a commercial steel pipe of 10 cm in diameter and an air to solid ratio of 1 : 3.

    Assume that the catalyst particles are essentially spherical and of average size 0.8 mm.

    State and explain your assumptions, if any.

Index

A

B

C

I

J

L

M

N

P

R

W